W9-BKB-087

The
Direct
Marketing
Handbook

The Direct Marketing Handbook

Edward L. Nash
Editor in Chief

Second Edition

McGraw-Hill, Inc.
New York   St. Louis   San Francisco   Auckland   Bogotá
Caracas   Lisbon   London   Madrid   Mexico   Milan
Montreal   New Delhi   Paris   San Juan   São Paulo
Singapore   Sydney   Tokyo   Toronto

Library of Congress Cataloging-in-Publication Data

The Direct marketing handbook / Edward L. Nash, editor in chief.—
2nd ed.
     p.   cm.
  Includes index.
  ISBN 0-07-046027-2
  1. Direct selling. 2. Direct marketing. I. Nash, Edward L.
HF5438.25.D555 1992
658.8′4—dc20   91-25694
                                      CIP

Copyright © 1992, 1984 by McGraw-Hill, Inc. All rights reserved. Printed
in the United States of America. Except as permitted under the United
States Copyright Act of 1976, no part of this publication may be
reproduced or distributed in any form or by any means, or stored in a
data base or retrieval system, without the prior written permission of the
publisher.

1 2 3 4 5 6 7 8 9 0   DOC/DOC   9 7 6 5 4 3 2 1

ISBN 0-07-046027-2

The sponsoring editor for this book was James H. Bessent, Jr., the
editing supervisor was Ann Armstrong Craig, and the production
supervisor was Donald Francis Schmidt. It was set in Baskerville
by McGraw-Hill's Professional Book Group composition unit.

Printed and bound by R. R. Donnelley & Sons Company.

To my wife, Diana, who through the years has helped me "meet with triumph and disaster, and treat those two imposters just the same."

Contents

Part 8. Applications

Foreword

Since 1984, when Ed Nash's *Direct Marketing Handbook* was first published, direct marketing has seen enormous growth and acceptance. Today, fueled by social change and technological advances, direct marketing occupies a secure place in the mainstream, satisfying the needs and wants of the American consumer. Conventional marketing wisdom has been displaced as markets have fragmented, communications vehicles have proliferated, and the cost of computer technology has plummeted.

Recent research (by Simmons Media and Markets) has shown that while the U.S. population grew 14.3 percent from 1983 to 1989, the number of American adults who shopped by mail or phone rose by 71.8 percent. In 1990, in fact, 98.6 million Americans filled their needs and wants through direct channels. Those numbers represent significant changes in American marketing history.

From the relative obscurity of their early days in the 1800s to their widespread acceptance today, direct marketing methods have come a long way. They are ideally suited to contemporary realities.

Lifestyles are much more complex than at any time in the past. Women today are securely in the work force, not only as a matter of choice, but of necessity. The target nuclear family of the 1950s, 1960s, and 1970s no longer predominates. Fifty-three percent of all U.S. households have only one or two members. Between 1980 and 1988, half the 10.4 million new households were formed by singles. For the first time in our history, time is a currency. Its scarcity dominates all our lives. Thirty million Americans are now over 65, and the baby boomers, formerly an important, well-defined target market, have matured. Discretionary income has shifted to older population segments.

The 1980s saw mass marketing lose its efficiency as the mass market splintered into hundreds of smaller markets. Traditional marketers were forced to take hard looks at just how affordable and cost-effective their methods were, and to compare those results against the accountability and effectiveness of direct marketing.

Technology has played an important role in transforming our lives. Time saving has become a passion for consumers and has led to the widespread acceptance of a broad range of convenience technologies, from the automatic teller machine to the microwave. The videocassette allows us to shift time. The advent of toll-free 800 numbers and credit cards allows shopping by phone at any hour of the day or night.

Advances in computer and information technology have allowed direct marketers to respond to consumer needs individually. We now have cost-effective means to identify prospective customers to a greater extent than ever before. We can compare extensive data, append and overlay endless amounts of information. Today, the computer cost for storage and access to a single name costs well under 1 cent, down from $7.14 in 1973. It is reported that more than 50 percent of the nation's package-goods advertisers are now building databases.

These advertisers' goal is similar, although not identical, to the traditional direct marketers' goal: to market to the individual; to know the customers' needs and wants; to build personal relationships and nurture them by providing goods and services, often through discounts, rebates, and other offers. For them, direct marketing is a channel of advertising, not distribution.

Mass marketers today can also reach special niches with targeted messages that seek out the prospects for whom the product or service was created. Marketers can no longer afford to speak to mass markets to locate the niche. Computer technology has enabled marketers to identify the niches and to reach them through cost-effective direct marketing methods.

But direct marketing is exacting and demanding in its methodology. It is a highly specialized art and craft that is constantly growing and changing in response to societal change and technological opportunity. We have seen enormous change and many new opportunities since the first edition of this valuable handbook was published, and I am pleased to commend this outstanding resource to your attention.

Side by side with the first edition, it effectively reflects the growth and change of a vibrant marketing methodology. It is written by many of the best-respected names in direct marketing. I believe that, whether you are a seasoned practitioner or are new to our field, you will find the handbook a resource to keep close at hand.

Jonah Gitlitz
PRESIDENT AND CEO
THE DIRECT MARKETING ASSOCIATION, INC.

Preface

As the field of direct marketing has grown more sophisticated, more complex, and more important, so has this handbook. When the first edition of *The Direct Marketing Handbook* came out in 1984, direct marketers were heralding the acceptance of our field by general advertisers and pointing out the lessons we in turn could learn from their experience. We proclaimed the beginning of a new marketing age in which direct marketing would finally come into its own. But no one guessed then just how important direct marketing would become.

Today, eight years later, there is no need to argue that we are more than just mail order, and that our method of communicating is more than direct mail. It would be difficult to find an advocate of an opposing view. Indeed, the agency I founded, Nash Direct, built its reputation in two areas unknown when the first edition was written: applications to package goods (now often referred to as database marketing) and broadcast direct response. Neither of these was a major factor in 1984.

The literature also reflects this change. My own basic teaching book, *Direct Marketing: Strategy/Planning/Execution*, once one of only a half-dozen books on the subject, is now in its second edition, with many translations. It is now one of dozens of other books on the subject, some highly useful or very specialized. Among these are: David Shepard's *The New Direct Marketing*, which offers valuable technical information; Rose Harper's *Mailing List Strategies* and Ed Burnett's *The Complete Direct Mail List Handbook*, both valuable introductions to the selection and management of mailing lists; Al Eicoff's *Eicoff on Broadcast Direct Marketing*; Stan Fenvessy's *Fenvessy on Fulfillment*; and the pioneering book on how direct marketing can be integrated with general marketing, *MaxiMarketing*, by Stan Rapp and Tom Collins. Julian Simon's *How to Start and Operate a Mail-Order Business* is still the essential book for the small-scale start-up business. I recommend them all.

Each of these specialties has expanded and improved its technologies, necessitating not just whole books on some subjects but a major revision of *The Direct Marketing Handbook*.

To compile the first book, I asked over 400 industry leaders to nominate the most knowledgeable people in each facet of direct marketing. Virtually all of them replied. Eventually, 60 writers—heads of businesses, ad agency executives, lecturers, consultants, marketing directors, and others—found time in the midst of their other responsibilities to research and write that first book. Most of the articles are still valuable today, and those who are fortunate enough to own or be able to find the first edition of that handbook should keep it in their library. Fifty-seven of the chapters are still valuable, and have not been duplicated in this edition.

This handbook started with an editorial review by McGraw-Hill's editors and consultants. They came to me with a list of new subjects not covered in the first edition and areas that had progressed dramatically. They wanted a new edition that was more advanced and more technical, one that placed greater emphasis on methodology than on application. The book you hold in your hands is the result.

Less than 10 percent of the book repeats the first edition. Ninety percent is brand-new, with some chapters by experts who contributed to the first edition, but many more by new experts and authorities who have emerged in the last several years or who were simply overlooked or not available when the first edition was prepared.

It is a maxim in all creative fields that the artist or writer always likes his latest work best. That is not the case here. I am equally proud of both editions of this handbook and of my other book. I actually feel some regret that the emergence of this new edition will result in the retirement of the first one.

Of course I am grateful to all the contributors. But I must also thank one other whose contribution was enormous: Stacy Shulman, the public relations director of Nash Direct, who took on the arduous job of associate editor. She did much of the work, and she should get much of the credit for the result. I selected the writers, reviewed the outlines, and read the manuscripts (yes, all of them). But Stacy sent out the letters, made the phone calls, worked with the editors, passed along revision requests, reminded contributors of their deadlines—and all with such tact and competence that all the writers are still talking to me. She left me free to do what I do best: developing marketing and creative strategies for my clients.

THE WHY OF THIS HANDBOOK

Why did all these people put in such a major effort? It wasn't for money. All the contributors are doing quite well in their careers. None received any royalty or other compensation for their efforts.

It wasn't for publicity. Virtually all the contributors were well known in their own right before this book was conceived. Many have lectured to direct marketing clubs and at Direct Marketing Association (DMA) conventions. Others write for industry publications, and some have written or are writing books of their own, spelling out in entire volumes what they can only introduce in the chapters they have contributed here.

The reason for the contributors' willing commitment of so much time and energy lies in the nature of the direct marketing field and its recent origins. For the most part, we have been an "oppressed minority" within the larger world of advertising and marketing. For many years we were the stepchild of the advertising world, the black sheep of the world of marketing, the "hucksters" who groped for coupons and phone calls in a crass struggle for immediate sales while others dealt with imagery and impressions on a far larger and "higher" scale.

Like any oppressed minority, we learned to stick together. The handful of direct marketing agencies always referred business we couldn't handle ourselves to our friendly competitors. The marketing executives of competing companies attended one another's lectures, discussed new methods, and congratulated one another on breakthroughs in technology or creativity. The DMA is a model of an industry working together for self-advancement and mutual self-education. It is in this spirit that these writers share their experiences, theories, facts, and wishes for success with every entrant to this exciting field.

Direct marketing is a much larger field today, and we are no longer oppressed or a minority. In fact, we have become not only respectable but downright fashionable on Madison and Michigan Avenues. Yet the tradition persists. By helping each other, we help direct marketing. By helping our industry, we create new and better opportunities for all marketers.

WHAT IS A HANDBOOK?

First of all, the name is a contradiction in terms. It seems a good handbook is one that can't possibly fit in your hand, one whose bulk is so great that it must rest on a desk when being read. Better terms might be "encyclopedia" or "desk reference," but those terms are confining in other ways. This volume combines all three concepts. In other words, this handbook is a one-volume encyclopedic desk reference.

The Direct Marketing Handbook is a reference work that belongs wherever direct marketing is dealt with: in companies, in agencies, at printers and list brokers, and probably most important, in advertising agencies and departments that are beginning to be exposed to direct marketing but don't really have a full working knowledge of it.

Everyone has experienced the phenomenon of reading a chapter or attending a lecture prematurely, of listening to information that has no relevance to one's life or work, and therefore, of not comprehending it. Later, the need for the knowledge occurs, and we wish that we had paid attention to the earlier input or that the knowledge was available right now, when and where we needed it.

A handbook composed of 52 chapters is too much to comprehend at one sitting. However, it is comforting to know that, like an instant memory, it is there at your fingertips any time the need for more information in a given area comes up. Each chapter stands alone, and each is designed to be read when and if the need arises, or when and if you wish to browse through the world of direct marketing and discover new facets of its interlocking expertise.

It is not a primer on direct marketing. If you need a primer, an example would be my own *Direct Marketing: Strategy/Planning/Execution* also published by McGraw-Hill. That book was written to be a "how-to" book; this one has been edited to be a reference work. Their purposes, and thus their content, are very different.

THE GROWTH OF DIRECT
MARKETING

According to the DMA *Fact Book*, 51.4 percent of all U.S. adults order some item by mail in any 12-month period. Other figures show that almost $22 billion is spent on direct marketing in the United States, producing $184 billion in sales. Around the world, other countries have similarly impressive marketing expenditures and sales figures.

More significant is the range of companies that are numbered among direct marketing practitioners. Currently, about half the corporations on the *Fortune* 500 list are engaged in some type of direct marketing activity, either by acquisition of a company that distributes primarily in this manner or by application of direct marketing techniques to the selling of products or services previously promoted only through general advertising methods.

Again, my company's experience serves as a good example. Nash Direct was engaged in applications of direct marketing for companies one would never think of as being users of this discipline: Procter & Gamble, Seagram's, Mattel, Avon, and Kellogg's. This is in addition to the expected applications in such fields as banking, insurance, fund-raising, catalog marketing, and collectibles.

Today, more than ever, the copywriter's "instinct" and the marketer's "intuition" are not adequate. Practitioners in this field may find themselves working for or competing with highly sophisticated, well-financed companies that are combining a variety of general advertising methods with those of direct marketing and that require a logical, strategy-based plan to justify every action and every investment. This requirement has forced our industry to get its act together. We have learned to use research in ways never before imagined. We have applied computer technology and mathematics to find new ways to plan, perfect, and analyze every step of the direct marketing process, from selecting lists and publications (and segmenting them in new and daring ways) to evaluating the dollars-and-cents effectiveness of alternative creative positioning.

THE EMERGENCE OF
DATABASE MARKETING

In this edition, we have tried to give special attention to the most advanced application of the direct marketing field. It is sometimes called database marketing, or one-on-one marketing, or relationship marketing. By any name, it is the key to the most powerful form of marketing ever imagined. The key difference between this new form of marketing and the original concept is that direct marketing deals with groups, while database marketing deals with individuals.

We have always been proud of the efficiency with which direct marketers could concentrate advertising or promotion budgets in campaigns aimed at groups of likely prospects. Such prospects identified themselves in three ways: geographically (by where they live, or their distance from a food or retail outlet), demographically, by their income, education, age, etc., as indicated by the average characteristics of the publications they read, the TV programs they watch, or the lifestyles of the neighborhoods they live in), and psychographically (by what we know about their hobbies, sports, book-buying or video-renting preferences—even by the imagery of other brands they choose to buy).

Database marketing goes further, in that we pursue the same characteristics, but do so by individual, rather than by groups. In its most obvious form, a mail-order catalog can work with its own customer lists. Individuals who have bought a certain type of product in a certain price range reveal much about their likelihood of buying similar products at similar prices. And package-goods companies can target their promotions at people who buy their product category but not their brand. Called "conquest advertising," such promotions eliminate the waste circulation of mass media and the knowledge that 80 percent of store coupons are redeemed by people who already use the brand. They can also target their own customers revealed with in-pack and other offers that identify their frequent users and offer incentives for customer loyalty, for cross-selling, and for recommending the product to others.

A perfect example of conquest advertising—a result of the merger of Time and Warner Brothers—was the mailing to promote the World War II movie *Memphis Belle*, sent to buyers of Time's World War II and aviation book series. Another was Dove's litmus paper mailing, sent to Ivory Soap users. Still another was our own agency's Barbie Pink Stamp Club, designed to motivate buyers of doll clothing and accessories to choose the authentic Mattel Barbie fashions instead of imitators. Jock Bickert's chapter in this handbook offers a score of other creative examples.

The pioneers of database marketing have been the cigarette companies. Motivated by impending restrictions on traditional advertising media, they have been leaders in identifying smokers and the brands they use, and in developing promotions to stimulate brand loyalty or to induce trial of an alternate brand. Cigarette databases have become so sophisticated that some even ask questions indicating subtle personality and character data that can be matched with cigarette imagery.

Today's ad agencies and list brokers have access to an infinite variety of information sources that can provide information by brand and category usage, by family configuration, by recency and frequency of purchasing activity, and by every conventional attribute of age, income, education, home ownership, creditworthiness, etc. Lists and data can be customized for any product and for any purpose.

TOMORROW'S CHALLENGES

Now, with the emergence of database, or one-on-one, marketing, we have the opportunity—and the responsibility—to deal with our customers as individuals. "Junk mail" is simply mail that is not relevant to the recipient. Our ability to refine lists and address the needs and desires of individuals reduces junk or irrelevant mail, and brings greater value to both sender and recipient. Those who blindly chant concerns for privacy do not seem to realize that limiting our ability to refine lists leads to more unwanted mail—and to more junk advertisements and commercials in the mass media.

Businessmen know that the ability to disseminate news of product improvements motivates even more improvements. The ability to announce more responsive customer service motivates better and faster service. Direct marketing allows us to bring the price/value benefits of mass national marketing to individual customer relationships. Perhaps if there were more businessmen and fewer lawyers in congress and the state legislatures, there would be fewer attempts to cripple our business in the name of "privacy."

The greatest threat to our industry today is the abuse of the telemarketing option, specifically the use of "cold calls" to residences or business addresses. Where a call from the agent of a preexisting relationship is perceived as a service, these other calls are always intrusions. Yes, tell me if my subscription is expiring, or if my clothing store is having a sale, or if a charity I have donated to before is having a special drive, or if my stockbroker has a specific recommendation. But don't call me if you don't know me. That is what direct mail is for. My fear is that telemarketing abuses will lead to an overreaction by legislators that will cover the whole mailing-list field and not just telephone abuses.

SYNERGETIC® MARKETING

The expanding world of direct marketing has never stopped changing. It is still entering what is probably its most profound period of change: a growing integration with the sophisticated technology of the world of general advertising.

The acquisition or start-up of direct marketing agencies by general agencies has led to a growing exchange of information and a deepening reservoir of shared experiences on behalf of shared clients. Research is no longer a discipline given lip service by direct marketers. It is a practical, powerful preamble to the development of concepts and the testing of alternative approaches by conventional split-run and other methods. Marketing planning is no longer a quickie proposal for a mailing, some ads, or a direct-response television test. It involves a methodically developed strategic plan that takes into account every aspect of the product, medium, offer, and creative alternatives.

Product benefits today are perceived not only on the superficial level of product benefits but with a deep insight into the emotional needs and desires that relate to a product and its attributes. "User self-image" is a new term frequently brought into play when a product is being positioned in the marketplace. It is becoming as important a concept in the world of direct marketing as it has been in general advertising.

We are more and more concerned with what I call the awareness by-product of our advertising, recognizing that each advertisement does not necessarily stand alone but is perceived in the context of its media environment and other consumer impressions. More important, each communication benefits by and contributes to the consumer's impression of the product, the company, and direct marketing overall.

Our field's understanding of psychology and emotion has advanced enormously. It gives us the power not to manipulate people's feelings, but to serve them. It permits us to answer deep, often unverbalized emotional questions. It allows us to avoid unintentional offenses to sensitive issues that relate to gender, race, age, and personal lifestyle.

It is ironic that much of the growth of direct marketing has resulted from the insensitivity of retailing and of mass media. Where retailers used to know their customers by name and their personal recommendations were respected, today's anonymous minimum-wage clerks barely know whether an item is in the store. No one even asks them how it works or if they recommend it. More information is available in any catalog.

Newspapers and magazines suffer from the same dilution of identity. Once special magazines served special needs, or local newspapers served the unicultural tastes of a community. The presence of an advertisement in such a medium indicated that it was intended for the needs of its readers. Today, with few exceptions, the media has become homogenized, attempting to serve larger, multicultural communities, attempting to be all things to all people.

Direct marketing is the last frontier of personal marketing. It serves the consumer without intrusion. It treats each prospect as an individual. It motivates the development of new products and services that meet real needs. Direct marketing is an established profession. We should find ways to rid ourselves of the bad apples who work on the theory that "a sucker is born every minute." We should demand to be treated as professionals in our relationships with clients, with government, and with the press. We will be regarded by others as we regard ourselves.

This book has been written at a time when these disciplines and their interaction are just beginning to be utilized. The initiate to the world of direct marketing should use this reference work and other books to understand the principles of direct marketing as they have evolved and as they have been applied traditionally. However, to get to and stay in this field, one must search for connections with other disciplines.

This handbook isn't enough, nor is a whole shelf of direct marketing books. The direct marketer today must understand and use the essentials of strategic planning, scientific decision making, interpersonal relations, computer sciences, statistical analysis, and qualitative and quantitative research. More and more, the field of psychology is being brought to bear on both the research and creative disciplines in direct marketing.

The direct marketer today must know more and work harder than in the recent past. On the other hand, the direct marketer has more varied and powerful tools available to meet the challenges of the marketing arena. In direct marketing today, nothing is easy. Yet as a result, nothing is impossible.

If this handbook makes your job easier and makes your business a little more successful, it will have accomplished its purpose and repaid your investment. I have tried to make it that kind of book. Please let me know if I have succeeded.

Edward L. Nash
CHAIRMAN
NASH/WAKEMAN/DEFORREST

Editor in Chief

Edward L. Nash is chairman of Nash/Wakeman/deForrest. He was formerly founder and president of Nash Direct, Inc., one of the largest independent direct marketing agencies in the United States, whose client list included some of the best-known corporations in America, including American Express, Citibank, Mattel Toys, Procter & Gamble, and Remy Martin. In 1990, his agency won the prestigious Henry Hoke Award for excellence in direct marketing.

Ed Nash began his career over 25 years ago as a copywriter and went on to serve as marketing vice president for Lasalle Extension University, president of Capitol Record Club, executive vice president of Rapp & Collins, and CEO of BBDO Direct, which he founded and ran for five years.

Mr. Nash has been called the "master strategist" of direct marketing in recognition of his work as chairman of the Direct Marketing Association's Marketing Council and its Awards Committee. Recently he has also been referred to as its "master psychologist" because of his utilization of emotional appeals in direct mail and direct-response television commercials. He has been chairman of Direct Marketing Day in New York and keynote speaker at DMA annual conferences, as well as at similar events in Australia, Belgium, Brazil, Canada, The Netherlands, Sweden, South Africa, Switzerland, and throughout the United States. He is also the author of *Direct Marketing: Strategy/Planning/Execution*, published by McGraw-Hill.

Foreword by

Jonah Gitlitz was named president and CEO of the Direct Marketing Association, the oldest and largest of the industry's trade associations, in 1985. Under his presidency, the DMA has taken the lead in addressing the industry's most crucial public issues. Mr. Gitlitz's leadership has supported the revisions of the DMA's ethical guideline series, encouraged cooperative liaison with all branches of the federal government, and instituted a twice-yearly dialogue series with state and local regulatory officials. Supporting close cooperation with the U.S.P.S., he has also encouraged competition through development of Alternate Delivery for third class mail.

During Mr. Gitlitz's tenure, DMA membership has increased by nearly 45 percent, with representation from more than 45 countries. During the same period, the DMA's annual conference schedule has expanded to more than 20, and its annual educational seminars nationwide to more than 15. He has been instrumental in establishing blue-ribbon task forces on privacy, delivery strategies, business-to-business, list practices information, consumer acceptance, and the environment. In 1989, the DMA launched its first certificate program to help insurance marketers achieve basic direct marketing expertise, and under his guidance, the DMA has published dozens of publications, pamphlets, and research reports.

Mr. Gitlitz joined the DMA in 1981 as senior vice president for public affairs, responsible for enhancing the association's stature and visibility with government and regulatory agencies through extensive government relations programs and public affairs activities. Mr. Gitlitz instituted the monthly *Washington Report* and *Washington Alerts*, as well as Capitol Hill seminars for congressmen.

Contributors

John Banslaben, a statistical marketing consultant, is founder and president of Applied Regression Technology (ARTECH), Inc., a New York–based company that creates state-of-the-art customer purchasing-affinity models and name-selection models for house files and rental list files. Formerly with *Reader's Digest*, Publishers Clearing House, and *Consumer Reports* magazine, he has been a speaker at conventions of both the DMA and the National Center for Database Marketing. Mr. Banslaben serves on the editorial review board of the *Journal of Direct Marketing*. He holds master's degrees in both mathematics and applied statistics from Columbia University and is a member of the American Statistical Association. (*Chapter 41*)

Richard A. Barton is the Direct Marketing Association's senior vice president for government affairs in charge of their Washington office. He also has responsibility for the association's ethics programs. Mr. Barton has spent most of his career in Washington. He started as staff director of the Subcommittee on Postal Rates of the U.S. House of Representatives Post Office and Civil Service Committee and was personal assistant to the vice chairman of the committee. Mr. Barton was then appointed to the professional staff of the full committee and subsequently served as staff director of three subcommittees. From 1973 to 1978, he was staff director of the Postal Operations and Services Subcommittee, the principal postal legislative committee of the House. Mr. Barton has testified on numerous occasions on direct marketing privacy issues. He holds a bachelor's degree from Louisiana State University and a master's degree from the University of North Carolina at Chapel Hill. (*Chapter 7*)

Jock Bickert is cofounder, president, and CEO of National Demographics & Lifestyles, which specializes in providing direct marketing and marketing research services utilizing database marketing systems. He serves on the board of directors of NDL International, Ltd., a London-based company providing database services in the United Kingdom, and is also a member of the DMA's board of directors, its Executive Committee, and its Privacy Committee. In August 1988, the DMA's List Council named Mr. Bickert List Leader of the Year for revolutionizing the concept of using lifestyle characteristics in target marketing. He received his degree from Princeton University and holds an M.A. degree in psychology from the State University of Iowa. He is a regular visiting lecturer on entrepreneurship at Harvard Business School, Stanford Business School, and Northwestern University. (*Chapter 8*)

Brent John Bissell, senior vice president and manager of the direct marketing division, McCann-Erickson Direct, is a veteran of over 20 years in the advertising business, 15 of them in direct marketing. Working for some of the world's largest corporations, he has had a wide range of experience, from designing retail traffic-building tactical direct-mail programs, mail order and catalogs, and direct-selling space advertising, to direct-response broadcast, international lead-generation campaigns, and sophisticated database construction and manipulation programs. A featured speaker for the DMA and a well-known educator on direct marketing methods, Mr. Bissell has advised a number of colleges and universities on forming postgraduate direct marketing curriculums. He is a published author on direct marketing and is recognized as one of the top direct marketers in the country. (*Chapter 16*)

Richard Bloch is associate creative director of the Seattle-based Manus Direct Response Marketing company, developers and implementers of business-to-business and consumer direct marketing programs for clients in travel, high technology, and retailing. Before joining Manus in 1991, Mr. Bloch was a principal of Bloch & McCarthy Direct Marketing, a direct-response consulting firm in the Boston area with clients in high technology and financial services. Mr. Bloch has taught graduate and undergraduate courses in marketing communications and direct marketing at Simmons College in Boston and in the direct marketing program at Bentley College in Waltham, Massachusetts. He is a graduate of the Boston University College of Communication and is a contributing editor to *The Business-to-Business Direct Marketer* and *The Direct Marketer*, newsletters published by Maxwell Sroge Publishing, Inc. (*Chapter 50*)

Arthur Blumenfield is president of Blumenfield Marketing Inc., of Stamford, Connecticut. He began his career at Standard Oil and has since worked or consulted for many leading companies and nonprofit organizations in the United States, Europe, and Australia. He is regarded within the direct marketing industry as an authority on the use of computers and database design, and is credited with creating the "mathematical equivalent analysis" method of identifying duplicate names on mailing lists and with the invention of the personalized children's book (Me-Books). He is the author of numerous articles on the use of computers in direct marketing, and of the DMA's "Standards for Computerized Mailing Lists." Mr. Blumenfield is a frequent speaker at industry seminars in the United States and abroad, most notably at the International Direct Marketing Symposium held each year in Switzerland and at the Pan-Pacific Direct Marketing Symposium in Australia. He serves as a director of Direct Marketing Day in New York, Inc., a nonprofit foundation dedicated to providing scholarship funds and seminars for professors and students of marketing. (*Chapter 15*)

George T. Bradbury is founder and president of Bradbury & Associates, Inc., a direct marketing consultancy serving both business-to-business and business-to-consumer clients in North America. Previously, Mr. Bradbury was president of Response Communications, Inc., the telemarketing division of the Direct Marketing Group of companies that operates state-of-the-art telemarketing centers and specializes in the financial-services, retail, fundraising, and package-goods industries. Prior to joining RCI, Mr. Bradbury had 20 years' experience with Pitney Bowes, where he held a variety of executive positions, including that of vice president of marketing planning for business systems in the U.S. (*Chapter 20*)

Ed Burnett is president of Ed Burnett Consultants, a Database America company. A 36-year veteran in direct mail, he is the creator of List Management and the originator of 5-digit (now 8-digit) SIC classification. Mr. Burnett is a major compiler of Business Consumer and New Moves files. He has served as a representative on the Technical Advisory Committee to the Postmaster General, and has been named Mail Advertising Services Association's Man of the Year. He was the first recipient of the Direct Marketing Association's List Leader award. Mr. Burnett is a prolific writer and a frequent keynote speaker at industry functions across this country and in Europe. He also conducts seminars on the art of mailing-list selection and use. His clients include such prestigious companies as Xerox, IBM, and AT&T. (*Chapter 12*)

James J. Carey is president of The Carey Group, a national network of senior direct
marketers based in Chicago. He specializes in helping clients build profitable relationships
with their customers. Before founding The Cary Group in 1988, Mr. Carey was a veteran
of leading direct-response advertising agencies in New York and Boston. Most recently he
was with Ogilvy & Mather Direct in Chicago, where he was director of client services. He
is active in the direct marketing community as a speaker, teacher, and author, and has
won several Direct Marketing Association Gold Echoes, as well as other local, national,
and international awards. (*Chapter 42*)

Jeffrey A. Coopersmith is president of DIRECTEL, Inc., a Columbus, Ohio–based company offering full-service product fulfillment to the catalog and direct-response industries. Mr. Coopersmith was formerly president of Distek, Inc., the parent company of
Directel. His affiliations include the DMA, the Council of Logistics Management, the
Warehouse Education and Research Council, and the Young Presidents Association. He is
a frequent lecturer on the subjects of product fulfillment, physical distribution, and finance at colleges, national conferences, and trade association meetings, and has authored
numerous articles on the management of the fulfillment function. (*Chapter 33*)

Lee Epstein is president of MAILMEN Inc., a volume mailing service located in Long
Island, New York. His credentials in the direct marketing field are impeccable. He has
served as chairman of the Third Class Mail Association, president of Mail Advertising
Service Association (MASA) International, president of the Direct Marketing Club of
New York, and industry chairman of the Postmaster General's Mailers Technical Advisory Committee (MTAC). A member of the DMA Government Affairs Committee,
Mr. Epstein has represented the industry before Congress and the Postal Rate Commission on postal matters. He is a frequent speaker on postal affairs around the country, and has received numerous service awards from both the Postal Service and the
industry. (*Chapter 30*)

Jeffrey Feinman is president of Feinman/Marlow/Carter, Inc., an organization involved
in the design and administration of sweepstakes and prize promotions. Mr. Feinman is
also the founder of another sweepstakes organization that he sold to a New York Stock
Exchange company in 1986. He is the author of a book on prize offers for Dow Jones. His
hobby is writing and he is the author of a dozen nonfiction books. Currently, he is a
consultant on a syndicated college marketing course. In addition, he is developing a TV
game show for a Los Angeles production company. Mr. Feinman lives in New York City.
(*Chapter 4*)

Stanley J. Fenvessy is an attorney and certified management consultant, and is the principal of Fenvessy Consulting, a New York–based management consulting firm that has
served over 200 direct marketing companies, publishers, and fund-raisers over the past 26
years. He is author of the widely used texts *Fenvessy on Fulfillment* and *Keep Your Customers and Keep Them Happy*, and writes a monthly column on fulfillment for *DM News*.
A member of the Fulfillment Hall of Fame, Mr. Fenvessy is also chairman of the Professional Conduct Committee of the Institute of Management Consultants. In addition, he
serves as a director of the Lighthouse for the Blind and of the Sharper Image, a retail and
catalog company. He is a past officer and director of the Direct Marketing Association and
of the Association of Consulting Management Engineers. He has conducted seminars and
lectured on fulfillment throughout North America, Europe, and Australia. (*Chapter 31*)

Robert Graham started his career in consumer credit and collections knocking on doors
in the South Bronx to collect $20 installment payments. He has a better job now as na-
tional sales manager for Retrieval Masters Creditors Bureau, a direct marketing credit
agency headquartered in New York. He has also held credit and financial management
positions with General Foods and Avco Financial Services. His clients include publishers,
magazines, continuity programs, and catalogers. (*Chapter 42*)

Behram J. Hansotia, senior consulting manager at Kestnbaum & Company, has had
over 20 years' experience in the fields of statistics and management science, spanning

academia, industry, and consulting. He holds a Ph.D. in management science from the University of Illinois at Urbana-Champaign and has been an associate professor of management at Bradley University, a fellow of the University of Illinois, and a visiting scholar at Stanford University. He has consulted for Caterpillar, Inc., and served as research manager and assistant vice president of list services at the Signature Group. A member of the Institute of Management Science, Dr. Hansotia has published extensively in the fields of operations research, marketing, and direct marketing in leading journals, and also serves on the editorial review board of the *Journal of Direct Marketing*. (*Chapter 38*)

Richard D. Haugan is president of Richard D. Haugan & Associates, a Seattle-based consulting firm specializing in database marketing and high-tech lettershops. Previously, he was general manager and division head at Pitney Bowes Direct, where he pioneered sophisticated computerized lettershop equipment and established a services business. He is the founder of Manus Direct, which he built into a $35-million full-service direct-mail agency and production shop. Mr. Haugan is a member of the DMA's computer, Business-to-Business, and Marketing councils, and of the Operating Committee of its International Council. He is also chairman of the DMA's Echo Committee. He founded the Seattle DMA and is a member of the National DMA, New York DMA, TCMA, NEDMA, and MASA. He holds a bachelor of science degree from Bradley University and an M.B.A. degree from Seattle University. (*Chapter 29*)

Barry Hauser is principal of Barry Hauser & Associates, which provides a wide range of services to the publishing and direct marketing industries, including development of advanced computer systems for applications in the areas of marketing strategy, database development and segmentation, catalog and circulation analysis, mailing and fulfillment operations, research and intelligence, and credit and collections. Mr. Hauser is a veteran of 20 years in the direct marketing industry, with stints at McCalls as a marketing research analyst and Publishers Clearing House, where he later became director of house marketing. In 1985 he started National Marketing Intelligence Service, Inc., an information services firm which publishes the Catalog Report, a monthly service covering everything from fulfillment performance to list rental activity of major catalogers. Mr. Hauser has been published in various sources and is a frequent speaker at DMA functions, Direct Marketing Day in New York, and FMA/Folio among others. He is a member of the DMA and the Direct Marketing Club of New York, and is on the board of the Long Island Direct Marketing Association. (*Chapter 14*)

Mark J. Heller is president of Marketing Alternatives, Inc., a consulting practice that specializes in helping all types of companies improve sales results through the innovative use of direct marketing techniques. He is an expert in telemarketing, database marketing, direct response, and new media, and has worked with both consumer and business-to-business marketers. His client list includes such giants as AT&T, Citicorp, British Telecom, MCI, and Time Warner, as well as companies just beginning to explore how best to use direct marketing. He was vice president of marketing services at Comp-U-Card (CUC) International. In other roles, he has managed product development and marketing for a $100-million consumer-services business and helped Fortune 500 companies plan and launch new businesses. Mr. Heller is a regular speaker at DMA and other industry events. (*Chapter 51*)

Leon Henry, Jr., is chairman and CEO of Leon Henry, Inc., a Scarsdale, New York, insert and mailing-list brokerage and management firm. He is a pioneer in the package-insert business. Since receiving an undergraduate degree from the Wharton School and a master's degree from Columbia School of Business, Mr. Henry has pursued the path of the entrepreneur. His firm now represents over 1500 mail-order distribution programs, from Ambassador leather goods to Zoysia grass plugs, as well as leading retail stores that accept inserts in their circulars and customer statements and banks that enclose inserts in their Mastercard and Visa statements. He is the author of *The Home Office Guide* and *How to Earn Twice as Much in Half the Time*. Mr. Henry is a member of the DMA, the XYZ Club, the Hudson Valley Direct Mail Club (of which he is president), and the Chicago Direct Mail Club. (*Chapter 19*)

Karen Hochman is president of Jordan, McGrath, Case & Taylor/Direct. Her beginning years in marketing were spent on the client side, first as a product manager and marketing director at American Home Products and International Playtex Company, then at Citicorp, where she developed a large national business through direct marketing. She subsequently cofounded Ad Hoc Marketing Resources, a direct-response advertising agency that was acquired by JMCT in 1991. Ms. Hochman is a frequent writer and speaker on both direct-response and financial marketing, and is on the board of directors of the Direct Marketing Creative Guild. (*Chapter 52*)

Jane Imber is vice president, marketing, for Neodata Services, Inc. She is author of Barron's *Dictionary of Advertising and Direct Mail Terms* and coauthor of the *Dictionary of General Business Terms*. Ms. Imber has served on the Operating Committee of the DMA's Circulation Council and as a board member of the Fulfillment Management Association. She holds an M.B.A. degree in marketing management from the Wharton School and earned her B.A. degree from Temple University. (*Chapter 34*)

Robert H. Jurick is chairman of Fala Direct Marketing, Inc., one of direct marketing's first companies (1916). At Fala for over 35 years, he is a recognized expert in every phase of direct-mail marketing. Mr. Jurick graduated from Syracuse University and is a frequent lecturer at Syracuse's Newhouse School of Communications. He is also actively involved in New York University's Management Decision Laboratory for masters degrees and serves on the faculty of Hofstra University. Mr. Jurick is a former vice president of the Mail Advertising Service Association (MASA) International, and past president of MASA's New York chapter. (*Chapter 28*)

Dee Kendall is vice president of Marketry, Inc., an international list brokerage, list management, list compiler, and direct marketing consulting firm. A 15-year direct marketing veteran, Ms. Kendall developed her career expertise in management positions at *Boardroom Reports*, where she started *Boardroom*'s list management division, at the publishing firm of Warren, Gorham, & Lamont, and at Auerbach Publishing. She received a Desi Award for Graphics for List Management Promotional Kit, and has been named one of *Target Marketing* magazine's 200 Industry Luminaries. She speaks at direct marketing functions and has authored articles in a number of U.S. and Canadian trade publications, including *DM News, Target Marketing, Circulation Management* magazine, and *Canadian Direct Marketing News*. As an active DMA participant, Ms. Kendall has served as a judge for the Echo award, and on the Circulation and List committees. She has also served on the board of directors for the National Mail Order Association, and is active in the Canadian Direct Marketing Association, Direct Marketing Association of Toronto, and Direct Marketing Creative Guild. (*Chapter 10*)

Robert D. Kestnbaum, CMC, is president of Kestnbaum & Company, management consultants offering strategic and technical direction for the introduction and improvement of consumer and business-to-business direct marketing and database marketing enterprises. Mr Kestnbaum is a recognized authority on business strategy, long-range planning, direct marketing strategy development, and the launching of new direct marketing ventures. As a consultant, and in his prior associations as cofounder of Robert Maxwell Company, (the original direct marketing division of Bell & Howell) and as direct marketing manager of Montgomery Ward, he has guided many of the landmark developments in the direct marketing field. Mr. Kestnbaum is a frequent speaker at direct marketing conferences and has authored portions of four major books and numerous articles in the field. He was the recipient in 1988 of the Charles Downs Direct Marketer of the Year award given by the Chicago Association of Direct Marketing. He holds degrees from the University of Chicago, Harvard, and Harvard Business School. (*Chapter 39*)

Mary Ann Kleinfelter is director of database marketing international for MISCO, Inc., a New Jersey–based computer-supplies cataloger. Former director of customer acquisition at Day-Timers, she has over 15 years' direct marketing experience with such firms as the Drawing Board, the American Management Association, *New York* magazine, and *Financial World* magazine. Her particular area of expertise is list selection, segmentation, and processing, and she is equally at home with consumer and business-to-business lists. Ms. Kleinfelter holds a master's degree from Columbia University and speaks and writes frequently for industry events and publications. (*Chapter 11*)

James B. Kobak, CPA, is founder and president of the consulting firm James B. Kobak & Company, which markets financial models and systems to publishers. Mr. Kobak has a worldwide clientele, including the Magazine Publishers of America, American Business Press, the Direct Marketing Association, and the Association of American Publishers. Prior to starting his consulting company, Mr. Kobak headed Lasser, Harmood-Banner, & Dunwoody, a public accounting firm with offices in 39 countries. He cofounded, and later sold, Kobak Business Models (now called Media Services Group), a business providing computer models and systems for the magazine and direct marketing fields. Mr. Kobak is the owner of *Kirkus Reviews*, a well-known service that reviews books prior to publication. (*Chapter 40*)

Eugene B. Kordahl, president of National Telemarketing, Inc., is one of the nation's foremost authorities on telemarketing. In telephone sales and marketing since 1956, he cofounded the American Telemarketing Association and served as its first president. Mr. Kordahl is the author of three telemarketing books, as well as articles and columns in over 300 trade and professional publications. He is coauthor and researcher of the *Annual Guide to Telemarketing*, and a contributing author to the *Handbook of Small Business Management* and the *Encyclopedia of Telemarketing*. He has served as consultant to more than 700 corporations in over 36 countries, and was adjunct professor of the first American postgraduate course in telemarketing at the university level. His affiliations include the Direct Marketing Club of New York, the President's Council of the American Telemarketing Association, and the American Marketing Association. (*Chapter 21*)

Marge Landrau is founder and president of Landrau's Hispanic Concepts, a direct marketing consulting agency specializing in the Hispanic market in the United States. Actively involved in direct marketing for over 28 years, she is considered the industry's foremost expert on the Hispanic market. Her experience spans direct marketing, merchandising, and financial services. In the course of her career, she has served on the boards of the Direct Marketing Club of New York, the Women's Direct Response Group, the Direct Marketing Minority Opportunities Association, and on the Executive Committee of the DMA's Marketing Council. In 1989, Ms. Landrau was honored with the coveted Silver Apple award for lifetime achievement. The same year, she was selected by *Target Marketing* as an Industry Luminary, and by *Minorities' and Women's Business* magazine as one of its "15 Women Who Make a Difference." She is a former editor of *ML/USA Journal*, a newsletter of the Mailing List Users and Suppliers Association, and is currently editor of *Proof*, the Direct Marketing Club of New York's monthly newsletter. (*Chapter 48*)

Barry R. Mark, currently senior consultant for David Shepard Associates, Inc., has over 20 years' management experience in direct marketing and publishing. His prior experience includes a vice presidency at Dell Publishing Company. He also served as vice president and director of marketing in the book club division of Doubleday, where he held responsibility for the Literary Guild, the Doubleday Book Club, continuity sets, mechandise catalogs, and specialty book clubs. Mr. Mark earned his B.A. degree from Brooklyn College and his M.S. degree from Polytechnic University. He is currently on the faculty of the New York University Management Institute and has spoken at many Direct Marketing Association programs. (*Chapter 3*)

Bruce R. McBrearty is cofounder and president of TransAmerica Marketing Services, Inc., a Washington, D.C.–based direct-response agency specializing in the creative application of telemarketing and direct mail. Well-known as a writer, speaker, and seminar leader on the subject of telemarketing, Mr. McBrearty has had the honor of addressing such prestigious organizations as the Direct Marketing Association, the American Management Association, and the American Society of Association Executives, among others. He has been featured in articles in *Fortune* and *USA Today*, and his own articles have appeared in numerous magazines, including *Ad Age, DM News, Telemarketing, Target Marketing* magazine, and *Barron's*. He writes a bimonthly column for *Fund-Raising Management* magazine. (*Chapter 47*)

Ed McLean was recently elected to the Hall of Fame of the Association of Direct Mail Writers. His annual seminars on the basics of direct marketing at Direct Marketing Day in New York and elsewhere have helped an entire generation of newcomers master the fundamentals of this highly effective marketing method. As a longtime member of the Education Committee of Direct Marketing Day in New York, he gives frequent talks on direct marketing careers to students at colleges and universities in New York, New Jersey, and Connecticut. He founded and was first president of the Direct Marketing Creative Guild, was a founder and vice president of the Association of Direct Marketing Agencies (ADMA), and taught the first college course in the United States on direct marketing copy at New York University in 1967. The author of four books on direct marketing, Mr. McLean has conducted seminars on the subject in 21 countries. He has received many awards for copy excellence, including the DMA's Gold Mailbox and the Creative Guild's William Baring-Gould award. In 1990 he received the Silver Apple award of the Direct Marketing Club of New York. (*Chapter 25*)

Richard Miller is founder and managing partner of Market Response International, Chatham, Massachusetts, a direct marketing consultancy specializing in worldwide markets. He has also held a senior vice president's post at Commercial Travelers Mutual, the nation's oldest direct-mail insurance company (founded in 1883). He is a cofounder and former chairman of the DMA's Direct Marketing Insurance Council and a past chairman of its International Council. Mr. Miller has 30 years' experience in advertising and marketing, with 20 years experience in the direct-response field. He has handled dozens of consumer and business-to-business accounts, both domestic and international. His international work has led to speaking engagements throughout the world. He was the guest lecturer on the European Community at the 1989 London Direct Marketing Fair and has addressed the IBIS International Conference in New York. His articles have appeared in *Money* magazine, *Massachusetts Business Review, Industry* magazine, *Direct Marketing, Target Marketing,* and *Catalog Business*. (*Chapter 6*)

Joshua Moritz is currently a vice president/group account director at Lowe Direct, Inc., a subsidiary of Interpublic. His career background includes stints at HDM Muldoon, where he was vice president of business development and client services, at Wunderman Worldwide, and at Young & Rubicam. Mr. Moritz has covered a broad spectrum of assignments, both direct and general, including IBM Direct, the U.S. Army, the U.S. Postal Service, Johnson & Johnson, Dr. Pepper, Chadwicks of Boston, and Colgate. A graduate of New York University's Direct Marketing program, Mr. Moritz is currently an instructor at that university, a regular contributor to several trade publications, and a frequent speaker at direct marketing events. (*Chapter 51*)

Eric Nussbaum is director of marketing services at Nash/Wakeman/deForrest. As such, he is concerned with strategic planning and account supervision for a variety of clients, as well as with new business development. Before joining Nash Direct, he worked on new-member acquisition efforts for Book-of-the-Month Club. These efforts were across all media, including direct mail, space advertising, and broadcast. Prior to BOMC, he managed Bantam Books' consumer catalog and direct marketing efforts and served as assistant marketing manager on Doubleday's special-interest book clubs. He holds an M.B.A. degree in marketing from New York University. (*Chapter 44*)

Robert Posch, Jr., is vice president of legal affairs at Doubleday Book & Music Clubs, Inc., with responsibility for all legal and postal functions, as well as liaison to regulatory agencies. He serves on the board of directors of the American Corporate Counsel Association's Metropolitan New York area chapter and edits their newsletter, *Directions*. He also serves on the board of the Third Class Mailers Association. Mr. Posch has authored four books on marketing law and writes a monthly column, "Legal Outlook," for *Direct Marketing* magazine. He has been published in *The Journal of Direct Marketing, Fund-Raising*

Management magazine, *The Market Place*, *The Better Business Bureau's Do's & Don'ts in Advertising Copy*, and *Postal Life*. Mr. Posch received his M.B.A. degree in marketing from Hofstra. He is a frequent speaker at colleges and at local and national trade groups on a variety of topics relating to the field of business and commercial law. (*Chapter 5*)

Suti Prakash is executive vice president at The Direct Marketing Group. During his 20-year career in the industry, Mr. Prakash has been involved in all facets of direct marketing, including business-to-business, high technology, financial services, and package-goods accounts. Among other industry honors, his teams have won Gold Echo and Best-in-Catalog awards. Mr. Prakash holds B.S. and M.B.A. degrees from MIT, and is a frequent speaker at industry forums and seminars. (*Chapter 32*)

Steve Roberts is president of Edith Roman Associates, Inc., a New York City–based firm that serves as a mailing-list consultant, compiler, broker, and full-service direct marketing agency for thousands of clients nationwide, including publishers, mail-order firms, and direct marketers in a wide variety of industries. Mr. Roberts's articles on mailing-list selection and testing have appeared in such publications as *Direct Marketing* and *Circulation Management* (*Chapter 9*)

James R. Rosenfield is chairman of Rosenfield & Associates, Inc., one of America's leading direct marketing firms. Among the world's most respected marketing and direct marketing authorities, he specializes in direct marketing for financial institutions, a subject on which he writes frequently and lectures internationally. Mr. Rosenfield is past chairman of the Direct Marketing Association's Financial Services Council and founder of its annual Financial Services Conference. His "Direct Response Marketing for Financial Institutions" seminar has been one of the DMA's best-attended and most highly acclaimed. He also leads a seminar entitled "Direct Response Marketing for Package-Goods and Other Consumer Products." Mr. Rosenfield provides in-house training as well, having conducted sessions for such companies as Citicorp, Charles Schwab, J. C. Penny, Fidelity, Bank of America, American Express, Australia New Zealand Bank, and National Australia Bank. He serves on the editorial review board of Northwestern University's *Journal of Direct Marketing* and has taught at the Bank Marketing School (University of Colorado) and at the Financial Institutions Marketing Association School (FIMA) at Ohio State University. He is a graduate of Columbia University. (*Chapter 46*)

Alan Rosenspan is vice president/group creative director at Bronner Slosberg Humphrey in Boston. He spent much of his career at Ogilvy & Mather in New York, where, in 1982, he moved over to Ogilvy & Mather Direct and began applying his general advertising skills to direct marketing. Mr. Rosenspan and his teams have won over 50 regional, national, and international awards, including seven Gold Echoes and a Gold Effie. His current client list includes AT&T, American Express, and Quaker. He gives regular presentations at national conferences and has been the instructor for the direct marketing course given by the Boston Ad Club. (*Chapter 23*)

David G. Rosenthal is senior vice president of sales and marketing at Webcraft Technologies, Inc. His involvement in print has included the production, manufacture, sale, and marketing of direct mail, commercial, outdoor printing, and packaging. Mr. Rosenthal has several articles and printing trade association addresses to his credit, including appearances at the Direct Marketing Association Fall Conference and Direct Mail Day in New York. A graduate of the Rochester Institute of Technology, he is a board member of the Association of the Graphic Arts and is an active participant in the formation, development, and implementation of the New York Metro Area Graphic Arts Campaign (MAGAC). (*Chapter 27*)

John L. Rosenthal is divisional sales manager for Queens Group New Jersey, Inc., a major commercial/direct mail sheet-fed and web printer located in New Jersey. He started his graphic arts career with Lee Associates, with responsibility for sales, estimating, production, scheduling, and materials purchasing. He also has sales experience with Lehigh Press, Tech Web, and Eagle Lithography. (*Chapter 26*)

Maxwell C. Ross is a former member of the Board of Governors of the Direct Marketing Association in New York and past president of the Kansas City Direct Marketing Association. One of the founders of the Direct Marketing Educational Foundation, he is currently one of its board of trustees. Mr. Ross speaks at direct marketing functions throughout the United States and Europe, and is the author of the *Manual of Successful Business Letter Writing*, *How to Work with Mailing Lists*, *NRB Public Speaking Manual*, and the DMA's *How to Write Successful Direct Mail Copy*. He has received KCDMA's Direct Marketer of the Year Award, is a three-time winner of the DMA's Best of Industry Award, and a ten-time winner of the Des Moines Ad Club's Award of Excellence. Mr. Ross's experience includes 16 years with *LOOK* magazine and 14 years with Old American Insurance Company before he started his own consulting company in 1967. (*Chapter 17*)

Henry W. Rossi's experience spans 30 years in operations, customer service, and credit and collections. He founded Eastern Credit Corporation (ECC) in 1983 to provide consulting and collection services for the industry. Mr. Rossi has produced many articles and presentations, including the DMA's Fulfillment and Customer Service seminars. (*Chapter 35*)

Robert Santangelo is vice president and creative supervisor at Nash/Wakeman/deForrest, where he has managed many of the agency's accounts, including Mattel, Unicover Collectibles, and Seagram's. He has over 10 years' experience with general advertising art direction and has won a number of awards for outstanding work. As a group supervisor at Saatchi & Saatchi, he worked on Proctor & Gamble, General Mills, Nabisco, Lifesavers, Leukemia Society of America, and Bank of New York accounts. He was a supervisor at Griffin Bacal, where he worked with Commodore computers and Milton Bradley, and spent some time at Foote Cone & Belding, where the Bermuda Board of Tourism, Western Electric, Citicorp, and British Airways were among his clients. (*Chapter 24*)

Eliot DeY. Schein is founder and president of Schein/Blattstein Advertising, Inc., a full-service Madison Avenue direct-response advertising agency. He has participated in the circulation promotion efforts of more than 400 magazines, newsletters, and books and is the author of the book *Renewals*. A past president of the Direct Marketing Club of New York, he was honored with the club's annual Direct Marketing Leadership Award in 1989. Mr. Schein has served as a professor in the Communications Arts Department of Iona College in New Rochelle, New York, and is currently a graduate professor at Pace University. He has lectured at Columbia University and New York University, and has delivered hundreds of seminar addresses and speeches in the United States, Canada, Switzerland, The Netherlands, Finland, and England. (*Chapter 45*)

Judy Shapiro is vice president/mid-Atlantic regional sales director for Response Communications, Inc., a unit of the Direct Marketing Companies. She spent a year in account management at Devon Direct Marketing and several years with Hunt Manufacturing Company in Philadelphia, responsible for consumer continuity for office and art products. She has a B.A. from Pennsylvania State University. (*Chapter 20*)

Dick Shaver, principal of Shaver Direct, Inc., specializes in strategic planning, creative concept and copy, training, and consulting for direct-mail and database marketing. He has been in sales, marketing, and management for 29 years and has 17 years' specialized experience in response marketing in consumer and business markets in the United States, Europe, Asia, and South America. His clients range from such Fortune 500 giants as American Express, AT&T, and General Motors, to such other organizations as Bird 'n' Hand, the Commonwealth of Massachusetts, Michigan National Bank, Oakland Technology Park, and Toys to Grow On. Formerly a vice president of marketing at McGraw-Hill, his background also includes positions as publisher of *The Architectural Forum*, executive vice president of Agawam Associates, and chairman of the DMA Marketing Council. Mr. Shaver is much in demand as an author, corporate strategic-planning facilitator, seminar leader, consultant, and convention speaker. (*Chapter 1*)

David D. Shepard is president of David Shepard Associates, Inc., a management consulting firm serving the mail-order and cable television industries. Prior to forming his own company in 1976, Mr. Shepard held vice presidential positions at Doubleday & Company, the Maxwell Sroge Company, and Throckmorton Satin Associates. He is a graduate of City College of New York and of the Columbia Graduate School of Business. (*Chapter 36*)

Eugene D. Sollo is president of Cariyle Marketing Corporation in Chicago, a full-service telemarketing agency. Formerly executive vice president of *Encyclopedia Britannica*, Mr. Sollo has distinguished himself in all phases of business and consumer lead development, and has received special recognition from the DMA as a pioneer in the use of the telephone as a lead medium. Mr. Sollo's career in direct marketing encompasses service as the president of the Chicago Association of Direct Marketing, membership of the board of directors and Executive Committee of the Direct Selling Association, and head of the Midwest Chapter of the Direct Marketing Association's Telephone Council Operating Committee. A graduate of Northwestern University, he is a frequent presenter, speaker, writer, and seminar leader on direct marketing and telemarketing topics. (*Chapter 43*)

Joan Throckmorton is president of Joan Throckmorton, Inc., a direct marketing consultancy. She has over 30 years' experience in direct mail and mail order. Before going on her own in 1970, she was associated with such major companies as Time, Inc., Doubleday & Company, and American Heritage. She has worked on significant direct marketing projects for a broad range of clients in consumer publishing, merchandising, and services, and in education and manufacturing. Ms. Throckmorton is a former member of the board of directors of the Direct Marketing Association. Under the sponsorship of the DMA, she currently conducts her renowned "Winning Direct Mail" seminar. In 1976, *Business Week* selected her as one of the top 100 Corporate Women in America. In 1986, the Women's Direct Response Group named her the Direct Marketing Woman of the Year, and in 1987 she received the Silver Apple award from the Direct Marketing Club of New York. She is the author of *Winning Direct Response Advertising*. (*Chapter 22*)

Jo-Von Tucker is direct marketing's foremost specialist in catalog marketing. She heads up JVT Direct Marketing, a catalog consultancy in Cape Cod, Massachusetts, and is owner and chairperson of Clambake Celebrations. She has 20 years' experience in producing upscale catalogs for such firms as the Horchow Collection, American Express, Sakowitz, Gucci, Williams-Sonoma, Bachrach's, C&P Telephone, Bon Appetit, G. Willikers, Neiman-Marcus, Fingerhut Corporation, and I. Magnin. She serves as a consultant to firms across the United States, Europe, and Asia and has won over 200 national and international awards for design, including the Silver Echo award for catalogs. Ms. Tucker is a member of the board of directors and the Executive Committee of the Direct Marketing Association. She is a sponsor and visiting executive for the Direct Marketing Educational Foundation and was the recipient in 1978 of the Matrix award for Advertising Woman of the Year, presented by Women in Communications. She has conducted seminars and given talks on catalog marketing all over the world. (*Chapter 49*)

Dana Vogel is vice president and director of broadcasting at Nash/Wakeman/deForrest, managing broadcast accounts and all aspects of marketing strategy, television production, media buying, telemarketing, and all other areas of client services and production. She is also vice president of Media Plus, Nash Direct's media-buying subsidiary. Before joining Nash in 1988, Ms. Vogel worked as direct-response manager for the Arts & Entertainment Network, where she handled both direct response and general advertisers. Some of her clients included AT&T, CBS, Inc., Time, Inc., Richardson-Vicks, and Proctor & Gamble. She has also worked as an advertising sales representative for *New York Magazine*, where she was in charge of the direct-mail category. Ms Vogel graduated from George Washington University with a degree in television production and broadcasting. (*Chapter 18*)

John T. White is vice president and general manager of the World of Beauty Division of GRI, one of the oldest continuity clubs in existence. His specialty is new-product development. Prior to joining GRI, Mr. White was vice president of general marketing for Unicover Corporation and general manager of its Fleetwood Division, where he conceptualized and launched dozens of new products and continuity clubs, including stamps, porcelain, commemorative coins, art prints, and other collectibles. He is an active member of the Direct Marketing Association and the Chicago Association of Direct Marketing. (*Chapter 37*)

Tom Zukas is president of Namebank of America, Inc. Formerly CEO of Magi Direct, he is an authority on computerized business and consumer database applications. Mr. Zukas is a prolific contributor to a variety of industry publications and speaks frequently at industry conferences and seminars. (*Chapter 13*)

PART 1
Strategy and Planning

1

Strategic Planning: An Overview

Dick Shaver

Shaver Direct, Inc.
Boston, Mass.

By definition, strategic planning is the managerial process by which a company manages change and develops the most profitable fit between its direct marketing operations and its changing marketing opportunities. Since the degree of change during the 1990s will dwarf that of the 1970s and 1980s, strategic planning and those direct marketers who master it will dominate the near-term future as well as generate the customer bases and needed skills for continued real growth beyond the year 2000.

Properly understood and employed, strategic planning is a tool of discovery and control that can be applied to two essential endeavors: long-range planning (LRP) and next year's marketing operations (SMP, or strategic marketing planning). While this essay is concerned with using strategic planning to optimize next year's growth, it is important to understand the similarities and differences between SMP and LRP. LRP steers your entire business toward growth opportunities beyond next year's operations. While LRP had some impact on growth in the 1980s, most direct marketing organizations had not truly mastered this discipline. As they approach the mature and aging stages of their base businesses in the 1990s, a command of LRP will be imperative.

THE DIFFERENCE BETWEEN
LRP AND SMP

On hearing the term *strategic planning,* most people tend to think of LRP and simultaneously position next year's operational planning as tactical. This confusion can be extremely costly in that next year's opportunities then are approached tactically, piece by piece, rather than strategically as a whole. Surprisingly to some, LRP and SMP are more alike than different. All the things a strategic planning group must have a command of—the process itself, the phases and sequence involved, the steps to be taken, the tools that can be used, and the skills required—are exactly the same. What differs is the people involved, their subject matter, the resulting document, and the kinds of work generated by the decisions made during the processes.

In the LRP process, presidents and senior executives (probably staff) analyze issues in the light of corporate strengths and weaknesses to develop a mission statement. Then macrogoals are set, and strategies are developed to achieve them. This process results in business plans that call for things such as research projects, acquisitions, new corporate structures, changed personnel requirements, and capital needs for the base business and new businesses over the next 2 to 5 (and sometimes 10) years.

While SMP takes its cue from the goals established during the LRP process, it usually involves line managers who make target market selections, establish next year's objectives, develop strategies, and then correlate tactical plans and a budget that will direct and control next year's marketing activities.

Since nearly all direct marketing companies, other than the most entrepreneurial firms in their startup years, attempt to plan operations 6 to 9 months in advance (simply because direct-response creative development and production require such lead times), there are two fundamental reasons why such planning should be strategic in nature. First, the operational planning must be done anyway. Second, operational plans that are rooted in effective strategic thinking not only catapult profit levels but also point out otherwise unseen disaster areas. It does not matter what size a direct marketer is. SMP is an imperative for realizing the profit potentials that are inherent in the degree of change expected for the 1990s—a degree of change that Alvin Toffler calls "the third wave"—which will make that of the 1970s and 1980s seem small in retrospect.

THE DIRECT MARKETING
PLAN: WHAT IT IS AND IS NOT

Before addressing how you should structure and manage the planning process itself, let's examine what a strategic marketing plan is and is not. It is not summary notes from a series of meetings, a proposal, a set of recommendations, an agency program, or a project outline. It is not a suggested course of action, a list of creative ideas or tactics, media or lists to be tested, or projects that may prove interesting to do.

Your direct-response marketing plan should be the written, comprehensive product of direct marketing professionals, resulting from their creative analysis and problem solving, decision making, and specification of all the direct-response operations that will be implemented in the next marketing year. It includes what will be done, who will do each project, when the projects will be started and completed, how they will be done, what they will cost, and the priority of each project. It also states clearly how each project relates to all others and how much revenue and profit, both acquisition year and life cycle, is expected from them.

It spells out the underlying strategies selected to overcome each obstacle identified as having the power to block the specifically stated objectives of the plan. Finally, it provides the essential substructure for everything that follows, the underlying strength for attaining objectives, and the key to maximum profit and growth.

OPERATIONAL BENEFITS OF STRATEGIC PLANNING

Once you have created a plan like the one described above, it has significant and various uses. Top management can use it to gain a more thorough understanding of why requested funding should be approved and how next year's operations relate to their long-range planning, and they can assess line performance more accurately. Line managers, departmental personnel, and vendors can use it to develop superior tactical work as well as to control implementation of project timing and costs and improve quality.

In sum, SMP delivers nine major benefits to a company, because it

1. Forces three-dimensional thinking
2. Allows specialists to perceive interfunction relationships otherwise missed
3. Generates an extraordinary enthusiasm that improves tactical creativity
4. Allocates resources to have an impact on the most profitable potentials
5. Creates benchmarks in advance for future decisions
6. Improves staff quality control and deadline performance
7. Elicits improved vendor performance
8. Enables faster rollouts of successful programs and faster shutoff of failures
9. Saves substantial top and middle management time and stress during the implementation stages

HOW TO STRUCTURE AND MANAGE THE STRATEGIC PLANNING PROCESS

Traditionally, many strategic marketing plans have been produced by a planning department staffed with specialists trained to work with senior and line management inside the traditional corporate structure. Usually these staff personnel begin as honeybees gathering input from line managers and then massage the data into hypothetical possibilities that are presented to and discussed with management. The advantages of this approach are twofold. There is a constant overview perspective that sees the whole and relates each part to bottom-line impact, and the planners are experienced in using the tools available for incisive strategic decision making.

The major disadvantage is that too often the planners, even though intelligent, dedicated to success, and thoroughly professional, are so far removed from the real world that the sometimes illogical but crucial human factors that can determine success or failure are lost in a quagmire of percentages, statistics, and scientific probabilities. Thinking tends to be linear and mathematical to the detriment of innovation and substance. While the planning specialist approach clearly has been effective in many instances, particularly in LRP, over the past 15 years I have found it deficient when applied to creating strategy and marketing plans for next year's direct-response operations.

What is really needed and wanted is a marriage of logical and quantitative factors with psychological and qualitative thinking that is three-dimensional as well as linear: perception that goes outside the lines without violating the principles of geometry. Just as art does not contradict science, marketing strategy need not violate the fundamental principles that govern direct marketing success.

> Genius, in truth, means little more than the faculty of perceiving in an unhabitual way.   — *William James*

> Creative thinkers continually waver between unimaginable fantasies and systematic attack.   — *Harry Hepner*

> Originality is simply a fresh pair of eyes.   — *Woodrow Wilson*

> When I examined myself, and my methods of thought, I came to the conclusion that the gift of fantasy has meant more to me than my talent for absorbing positive knowledge.   — *Albert Einstein*

These four quotations, all taken from the 1979–1980 Chevron exhibit Creativity: The Human Resource, apply to marketing just as much as they do to science, literature, or government. In analyzing 100 years of American creativity in all fields of endeavor, Chevron made an attempt to discover what truly creative people have in common with one another. They concluded that creative people from Socrates through Einstein shared seven basic characteristics. They

Construct networks by forming associations between people for the exchange of ideas, perceptions, and encouragement

Challenge assumptions and question what most automatically accept as true

Use chance to take advantage of the unexpected and are ready at all times to recognize accidents

See in new ways by transforming the familiar into the strange and seeing the commonplace with new perceptions

Recognize patterns by focusing on significant samenesses or differences in physical phenomena, events, or ideas

Make connections and bring together seemingly unrelated events, objects, or ideas

Take risks by daring to try new ways with no guarantee of the outcome

If you set up a strategic planning coregroup in such a way that it effectively forms a network capable of challenging assumptions and using chance, you will find individual members seeing in new ways, recognizing patterns, and making connections that enable the group as a whole to generate innovative and powerful strategic decisions.

As a first step, select your coregroup members from those line personnel who currently are producing your direct-response programs. They can be in house, from your agency, freelancers, or consultants. Make sure that each function needed to engage in direct marketing is represented: marketing, creative, media, financial, production, data processing, manufacturing or merchandising, and fulfillment (including customer service). If you're a smaller company in which single individuals wear many hats, that is fine. A coregroup can function with as few as three members as long as the various essential perspectives are represented.

Properly directed and interactive, the "composite eyes" of this group of direct marketing specialists can bring obstacles to the surface and create strategies that the best of planning experts by themselves generally could not. Here is what to look for when selecting each coregroup member who will become part of your creative network.

- The plan manager should be a direct marketing generalist who knows how to listen and has superior oral and written communications skills. Experience in planning techniques and strategic development is very helpful but not absolutely necessary. The plan manager will function as the group's job captain, responsible for scheduling meetings, start-and-stop tracking during meetings, recording and distributing coregroup decisions, and assigning between-meeting work projects to individual coregroup specialists.

- The marketing member should be a direct-response generalist with the deepest possible background in customer acquisition and life-cycle marketing, a creative strategist rather than a tactical specialist.

- The creative director should provide imaginative idea sparks, in contrast to the dimension of logical analysis provided by other group members. Experience in telephone and broadcast as well as direct mail and print space is desirable.

- The media specialist cannot be wedded to lists or publications only but also must bring an informed perspective on the relative strengths and weaknesses of all major response media: mail, magazine, newspaper, telephone, TV, radio, co-ops, syndication, and multimedia.

- The production manager must be conversant with all forms of direct-response production and costs, a tactical generalist whose major contribution will be to keep you in the world of the possible using state-of-the-art technology.

- The data processing specialist is needed for two primary reasons: realistic knowledge of what your marketing database can process and track, and information regarding what can and cannot be done in the expanding world of word processing.

- Manufacturing or merchandising and fulfillment members are needed to ensure that your response programs do not outrun or short-circuit your fulfillment and customer service resources. This all-too-common eventuality will destroy the future profits from customers converted in next year's operations unless expert and well-informed representation expresses itself during strategic planning meetings.

If you do not have sufficient know-how on research, testing, yield analysis, or specialized industry knowledge as a part of your coregroup members' experience and skills, these resources should be brought in on an ad hoc basis.

Whoever said that the whole is greater than the sum of its parts was right, and your coregroup may well prove that observation. There is a danger in this kind of group approach, however. You must ensure that the coregroup will develop and maintain the overview that is absolutely necessary for successful strategic planning and that the group will not get bogged down in detail by addressing pieces of your overall opportunity that are in actuality low-priority items in terms of bottom-line impact and significant growth.

These pitfalls can be avoided if you use proven planning techniques and tools that eliminate tunnel vision and vested interests. You also must make certain that each coregroup member understands the basic planning ground rules and how the tools are supposed to be used, and you must allocate sufficient time for individuals in the planning network to accomplish their normal line functions while participating fully in the strategic planning process. The basic coregroup operating ground rules are simple to state but require a greater than average effort to make them work because they contradict much of what we have been taught as well as the conventional wisdom.

1. **Hierarchy.**   During coregroup meetings, there is no pecking order whatsoever. Normal lines of authority and reportability do not obtain, and no individual has the authority to overrule any group decision.

2. **Perspective.**   The predominant perspective is that of the group as a whole. While each member can and should contribute from his or her area of expertise or specialization, each must strive to approach decisions and value judgments from the standpoint of a direct marketing generalist assessing the relationship of any part to the whole.

3. **Subject matter.**   While all subjects are to be addressed and stressed on an informal, free-form basis, the phases of the planning process cannot be taken out of sequence. Tactics cannot be worked on until all strategy has been fully developed; objectives must be established before obstacles and advantages develop; and objectives cannot be created till all background material has been dissected and organized.

4. **Decision making.**   Decision making is on a consensus basis only. Ideas, observations, opinions, and individual judgments should flow freely, with dissent encouraged. All coregroup members must realize, however, that their ideas must be presented in such a way as to obtain agreement of all other

members before positions can be adopted and decisions to be made can be considered. Given the divergent perspective of each coregroup member, a great deal of heat will be generated on occasion (if not, you probably are not doing it right). That is fine as long as the heat is transmuted into light by the group as a whole.

TOOLS THAT ENERGIZE
STRATEGIC PLANNING

I have found four tools to be particularly effective for developing direct-response strategy and plans. Two of these—the task method and fast-tracking—help maintain the needed overview. The other two—adversary analysis and brainstorming—help members of your network use chance, recognize patterns, and make connections.

The task method is in essence zero-base marketing. It requires that each individual block out preconceptions about what is "always best" or what "cannot be done." After relevant marketing information has been isolated from all the data assembled, coregroup members mentally block out all constraints and start to develop objectives, move on to identify and prioritize all obstacles and advantages, create strategy, and only then analyze available resources (total direct marketing resources: people skills, time, and money) to apply constraints to the task decisions that have been made. After modifications or an approved increase in resources that can be made available, tactics are developed, and then the entire plan is subjected to risk-gain analysis.

Fast-tracking is an ideal process for strategic market planning in that it is complementary to the task method, forces overview thinking and decision making, and speeds up the entire planning process by a substantial margin. Developed in the construction industry during the 1960s in order to reduce design and building cost and lapse times, the technique was radical. But it was a successful departure from the traditional step-by-step architectural design process. Instead of architects working virtually alone to interpret the building owner's needs from initial concept to finished specifications, coordinating at various stages with the engineering firms involved, and finally turning completed plans and final specifications over to the general contractor, who then would develop bids from many subcontractor specialists, all major disciplines worked together from the beginning of the design process. Architect, engineers (mechanical, electrical, and sanitary), contractor, and key subcontractors were directed by a construction manager charged with keeping this interdisciplinary group on track. Ideas, observations, and judgments flowed freely, with disagreement encouraged in order to apply maximum feasibility stress to any proposition under evaluation. No detail was allowed because major decisions were made in needed sequence (overall building performance requirements, site location, building size and shape, major systems, basic materials, etc.). Parameter specifications were created and then checked for viability between meetings. They were reviewed at the next group meeting and then modified or finalized before the next set of needed decisions was addressed. Final details were implemented just before actual project work commenced.

The results were significant and a bit startling. Costs were reduced substantially, building performance improved, and costly re-dos were eliminated.

The same process can be used to improve the design and reduce the costs of direct-response marketing programs. The basic criteria governing the process are exactly the same:

1. All major disciplines are involved throughout.

2. Discussions are informal and intensely interactive.

3. Major decisions only; no detail is allowed.

4. Fatigue-stress all proposals surfaced.

5. Develop parameter specifications that allow final detail to be created later.

6. No skipping ahead; subject matter is addressed in rigid sequence.

The adversary system is essentially a series of freewheeling rap sessions rooted in conversational debate by the members of the planning network. Unlike brainstorming, in which negatives are not allowed as ideas surface, all ideas are attacked in the open as they evolve. While coregroup specialists should speak from the standpoint of personal expertise, ideas can and should come from anywhere on any topic. (One of the best creative approaches I've witnessed over the past 6 years came from a dialogue between a plan manager and a media supervisor.)

Spontaneity and "top of the mind" reactions are essential, and network members must have the courage and maturity to see some of their ideas dismantled by the group as a whole. All decisions must be reached by a consensus of the entire group, and so it is necessary that votes for and against be taken on the basis of each member's overview rather than that member's specialty. While this ground rule may seem time-consuming on occasion, its importance cannot be overemphasized.

Brainstorming is a creative technique that is useful when a network gets blocked or when an impasse in conversational debate is reached. This fantasy approach is simple, and the ground rules are few; it does not require extensive training or experience with the process to make it work.

First, you select one coregroup member as your brainstorming leader, who will be the only one in the group to maintain contact with reality. All others think outside the lines and free-associate within the following guidelines.

No critical judgments on any ideas are expressed.

Group members let go and simply react to ideas as they evolve (except the leader).

The leader simplifies the meaning of each idea as it comes.

Each idea is developed till the leader stops discussion.

The more free-form and fun, the better.

This kind of brainstorming is a three-step process: preparation, brainstorming, and analysis. Define the problems to be addressed in writing at the outset.

Set quotas for the number of ideas to be developed and then set a time limit. Since you will not be analyzing the ideas as they evolve, you will find that you are able to bring many to the surface in a relatively short time period. Make certain that each participant understands the ground rules before you begin. As soon as all are prepared, have at it. After the brainstorming session, use the adversary system to place a comparative value on each idea in terms of logic, reality, and usable resources.

PHASE 1: TURNING DATA INTO DIRECT-RESPONSE MARKETING INFORMATION

Once you have chosen your method of planning and have assigned responsibility for strategic development, you are ready to begin work on the first of six phases that constitute the total planning process. In the first phase, coregroup members will turn raw data about potential markets into information that enables them to identify target markets on a qualitative and then a quantitative basis as well as evaluate the resources available to reach those markets.

If the data available are not reduced to direct marketing essentials, coregroup members will be swamped by unrelated facts and almost certainly will miss relationships that are crucial for strategic decision making.

It is not an exaggeration to state that as much direct-response profit is lost in phase 1 as in any other phase of your work or for any other reason: mispositioned creative strategy, weak media analysis, anemic strategy development, inferior tactical development, deficient capabilities for response tracking, etc.

Recognize the difference between data and information. At the end of each trading day, stock exchange floors are strewn with pieces of paper recording the day's transactions. Imagine the most skilled investment analyst trying to make decisions based on the information buried in all those data. It would be impossible.

But the next morning, when the transaction data have been converted to information in newspaper financial sections, judgment can be applied toward making informed decisions. Turning marketing data into marketing information for your strategic planning coregroup's use is just as critical a process. Too often the assumption that everyone comprehends "enough" leads to too little time and thought being dedicated to organizing and boiling down data so that residual information can be seen in its true significance.

The first step is for the plan manager to gather and format all relevant information. Two resources must be made available for the plan manager to accomplish this: in-depth knowledge of direct marketing principles and librarian skills. If the manager has only the organizing component, the significant will not be separated from the incidental; if he or she has only the direct marketing insight, information will be assembled in formats that confuse rather than enlighten. Available data must be turned into relevant information in each of the following areas:

- Preliminary situation statement
- Industry maturity and business phase

- Competition
- Direct marketing margins
- Product features
- Needs and wants
- Benefits
- Customer profiles
- The buying process
- Perception of need
- Profile summaries
- Marketing segments
- Current resource levels

Each area should be addressed individually and in this order.

The Preliminary Situation Statement

This should be written before any major effort is devoted to converting data into information. The purpose is to tell you and each coregroup member what you do not know as well as what you do know and what you think you know. The statement addresses each subject listed above in order and is comprehensive but not deep in detail; it is a précis rather than a fully documented narrative. Once completed, the written statement is distributed to each coregroup member as well as any other personnel who might be a source of marketing input. Each recipient should study this opening statement from two standpoints: to suggest any important ingredients that have not been included, and to determine what each recipient can input for amplification.

The following checklist is helpful as a stimulator for coregroup members and as a control reference for the plan manager to ensure that all potential sources of critical information have been probed.

- Your house list (recency, frequency, monetary, and variety)
- Right-hand drawers of company veterans
- Previous research and analytical reports
- Competitive data
- Complementary product information
- Customers
- Ex-customers
- Previous inquirers
- List brokers
- Media vendors
- Production vendors

- Award case histories
- Government reports (federal, state, and municipal)
- Foundation research
- Association reports and statistics
- Industry consultants
- Media libraries

As you all do your homework and scan your memories, contacts, and references, you often will be astonished at how much significant information surfaces from the most mundane and unlikely places.

Once relevant data have been collected by the plan manager, the data must be boiled down and organized into essential facts and relationships. Summary statements should be developed in each subject area in a sequence of most important to least important, and documentation should be included in the background appendix, classified and indexed for ready access. Insofar as possible, express all statistical data incrementally and comparatively as well as absolutely.

Do not spend undue time at this stage initiating research or indulging in work projects to extend the information in hand. When key elements are missing, simply note them as critical yet "missing." You will address them in depth when you reach the phases dealing with objectives and obstacles. When this in-depth revision of the original preliminary situation statement is completed, it should be distributed to each coregroup member for study before the first network session. If the documentation is too bulky for distribution, simply include the classification and index for the supporting materials and distribute them to individual members on request. All documentation should be available, however, at all coregroup meetings.

Finally, do not be surprised if this phase of your work consumes as much as 50 percent of the time needed for the whole process. Louis Nizer, the attorney, attributed his consistent courtroom brilliance to his three P's and commented that 95 percent of his success was due to preparation and perspiration and 5 percent to performance.

At the first meeting, the coregroup members should move on an adversary-and-evaluation basis through each of the background areas to satisfy themselves that the information at hand has been developed as much as possible before beginning the remaining phases of the planning process.

Do not short-circuit this effort in your anxiety to move on to the next phase. Key elements that are overlooked or not perceived here will have a disproportionately negative impact on strategic development and profits.

Where Are You Starting From? Industry Maturity and Business Phase

The second part of your background organization identifies whether the industry in which you are going to compete is embryonic, growing, mature, or aging. Where your industry is will have a great deal to do with the kinds of objectives you develop and the types of obstacles and advantages you have. Table 1-1 will

Table 1-1. Industry Maturity Guide

Descriptors	Development Stage			
	Embryonic	Growth	Mature	Aging
Growth rate	Accelerating; meaningful rate cannot be calculated because the base is too small	Faster than GNP but constant or decelerating	Equal to or slower than GNP; cyclical	Industry volume cycles but declines over long term
Industry potential	Usually difficult to determine	Substantially exceeds the industry volume but is subject to unforeseen developments	Well known; primary markets approach saturation industry volume	Saturation is reached; no potential remains
Product lines	Basic product line established	Rapid proliferation as product lines are extended	Product turnover but little or no change in breadth	Shrinking
Number of participants	Increasing rapidly	Increasing to peak; followed by shakeout and consolidation	Stable	Declines, but business may break up into many small regional suppliers
Share distribution	Volatile	A few firms have major shares; rankings can change, but those with minor shares are unlikely to gain major shares	Firms with major shares are entrenched	Concentration increases as marginal firms drop out; or shares are dispersed among small local firms
Customer loyalty	Little or none	Some; buyers are aggressive	Suppliers are well known; buying patterns are established	Strong; number of alternatives decreases
Entry	Usually easy, but opportunity may not be apparent	Usually easy; the presence of competitors is offset by vigorous growth	Difficult; competitors are entrenched, and growth is slowing	Difficult; little incentive
Technology	Concept development and product engineering	Product line refinement and extension	Process and materials refinement; new product-line development to renew growth	Role is minimal

help you assess this, but you also should define your industry in terms of total dollar sales per year and number of units sold and then in terms of competition by annual sales dollar volume, size of customer base, and market share. Do not at this stage spend much time on in-depth analysis of each competitor and be careful not to include sales figures that include products or services that are not competitive with you.

It is equally important to know the stage your business is in, as shown in Figure 1-1, as well as your own sales statistics in terms of customer base growth, attrition, average dollar sales per year per customer, cost per inquiry, cost per order, etc.

Competition: Curse or Cornucopia?

Usually only one business is "firstest with the mostest" in any given marketplace. If you are not that business, view your competitors as a strategic source of crucial information not otherwise available to you and then leverage that information to the maximum.

As competitors communicate in direct-response form, they are telling you continually what is and what is not working in your marketplace. Accurately analyzed, their offers, creative platforms, and media selections can focus customer profiles, needs, and wants related to benefits, price points, and size of markets. But you must work at organizing the signals they are sending you. Determine their media usage in terms of frequency and total expenditures, identifying pri-

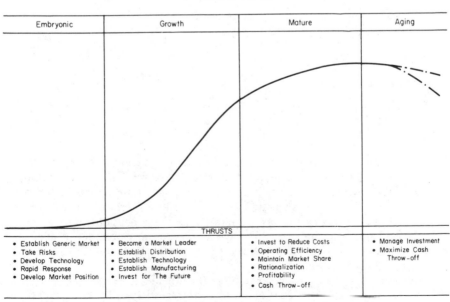

Business Life Cycle

Embryonic	Growth	Mature	Aging
THRUSTS			
• Establish Generic Market • Take Risks • Develop Technology • Rapid Response • Develop Market Position	• Become a Market Leader • Establish Distribution • Establish Technology • Establish Manufacturing • Invest for The Future	• Invest to Reduce Costs • Operating Efficiency • Maintain Market Share • Rationalization • Profitability • Cash Throw-off	• Manage Investment • Maximize Cash Throw-off

Figure 1-1. Stages in the business life cycle.

mary and secondary media. Assemble complete "swipe files" that display their controls, tests, and rollout solicitations: mailing packages, magazine and newspaper ads, TV and radio spots, and telephone work. Watch for test efforts that are not repeated. Knowing what did not work can be as valuable as knowing what did.

Once you have each competitor's solicitation activity in focus and prioritized, write summaries of their relative strengths and weaknesses. Then, when your coregroup members reach this part of their meeting, evaluate all the competitors qualitatively, defining the strategies that have provided them with whatever dominance in the marketplace they currently enjoy.

Direct Marketing Margins: Are They Worth the Effort?

Before you go any further, stop to calculate and reexamine the mathematics direct marketers live by: customer acquisition cost and breakeven, attrition curves, and life-cycle sales and profit potentials.

This is particularly important if you are entering a new market or marketing new products. But it also should be done for your base business in order to track precisely cost and price point trends that may be affecting your traditional markets and products.

For new products or new markets, be certain to apply all manufacturing or merchandise supplier costs and all fulfillment costs (including conservatively estimated sales costs if your program is lead-getting or traffic-building) to establish marketing margin ranges. Then use general media costs per thousand, as shown in the following table.

Media	Average CPM in, $
Telephone (outgoing)	1,800
Direct mail	400
Newspaper inserts	30
Magazines	15
Newspaper ROP	10
Television	5

In addition to CPM, you must use conservatively estimated response rates based on your own previous experience (if applicable) or general industry response ranges. (You will be surprised how much response information in terms of ranges is available if you work at: award case histories, companies with similar but noncompetitive products, consultants, etc.). Now allocate overhead costs, and your coregroup members will have a working measurement of allowable cost per order (CPO), cost per inquiry (CPI), and range of contribution to promotion and profit (CPP).

Be certain that these parameter statistics include life-cycle values for each customer acquired unless there is absolutely no potential for back-end sales and profits. To sum up, there are five steps involved in preplanning mathematics:

1. Identify conservatively estimated response rates.
2. Compute CPP.
3. Develop pro forma profit and loss statements (P&Ls).
4. Factor customer life-cycle values into your analysis.
5. Make a halt decision if your numbers don't make direct marketing sense in terms of risk-gain potential.

Your Product: Features and Descriptions

Here you simply want to define what each product is and what it does. Written descriptions by each coregroup member should be lean and skeletal yet comprehensive. No special effort should be made at this stage to translate product features into customer benefits, although any natural "top of the mind" benefits statements need not be removed. Costs of manufacturing and fulfillment as well as the percentage of overhead to be applied should be included in the written descriptions. There should be no attempt at creative copy since the thrust now is toward clarity, brevity, and inclusiveness.

Needs and Wants: The First Step in Isolating Markets

Although the phrase "Needs and Wants analysis" sounds dull, it often induces dynamic coregroup sessions and is the springboard to benefits evaluation, customer profile identification, market segmentation, and strong creative platforms.

No matter how self-evident needs or wants seem to be, the strategic planning coregroup should put them under a marketing microscope for closer inspection. They should be analyzed at two different stages in phase 1: from the standpoint of common sense, logic, and general knowledge, and again after each potential customer profile's perception of need has been established.

In consumer programs, it is useful for coregroup members to individually apply the basic 8 before discussing needs and wants. These are:

1. Making money
2. Saving money
3. Winning praise
4. Self-improvement
5. Saving time or effort
6. Impressing others
7. Helping children and family
8. Having fun

Then distinguish between a need and a want and decide which of these your product or service will be satisfying. The owner of an outdoor swimming pool may want a solar sun blanket to keep her pool water warm at less cost, but she needs a basic pool covering for winterizing if she lives in the Snowbelt. Similar real distinctions exist in business and industrial markets. When the EPA mandated a large leap in minimum gas mileage per gallon, Detroit needed to find a way to lighten their product by nearly 1000 pounds per car. Before that, product designers and management might have wanted to lighten cars by using lighter metals, but they did not need to.

As the coregroup raps about needs versus wants and the type of satisfaction delivered, inevitably customer characteristics will be mentioned: age, income, sex, education, occupation, and marital status. Lifestyle characteristics such as athletics, politics, intellectual, and hobbies also will be discussed. Capture these demographic and psychographic data as they evolve but do not at this point try to develop complete pictures of various customer potentials. Instead, coregroup members should start to be more specific in their descriptions of the kinds of needs or wants satisfied. How will the customer make more money? Or save it? Or impress others?

As you refine the satisfactions, more profile characteristics will emerge. Capture these and start connecting the characteristics. When you've connected as many as possible, prioritize the satisfactions you've identified from most important to least important by coregroup vote. Stay at it till the network reaches consensus. Then apply the six basic drives to your priority list:

1. Self-preservation
2. Love
3. Gain
4. Duty
5. Pride
6. Self-indulgence

After you have done this, repeat the whole process. Once this is completed, you will have a clear picture of which needs and wants can be satisfied by your products or services and some idea about the types of customers you should seek. These same criteria apply in business and industrial markets, but there you must overlay one pervasive motivation: recognition by business peers and management.

Focusing Benefits

Benefits are what prospects think about and evaluate before buying and what suspects give little or no serious consideration to. Consequently, your product's benefits not only govern creative strategy and tactics but also are a prime tool in determining who the best potential customers actually are. Benefits prioritization is a critical tool in certain marketing situations, and it is always an important one.

Here the coregroup starts by listing every possible benefit anyone can think of. Translate all the product features described in step 2 into clear, tight benefits statements. Take each need and want satisfaction developed in the previous session and state it in terms of benefits. Review the benefits statements in your competitors' solicitations.

Now have the coregroup vote on the most important benefit and rap till consensus is reached. Do the same until all benefits have been prioritized. Do you have a unique selling proposition, the USP all direct marketers covet? Be brutally honest with yourselves about this, for the marketplace will be. If you truly have the competitive advantage of a USP, your ultimate strategy will be vastly different.

As you are ranking benefits in terms of their sales-closing power, more customer characteristics will be mentioned and discussed. Add these to the profile pictures that emerged during the needs-and-wants session. If the coregroup cannot reach consensus after sufficient interaction and analysis, write tight descriptions of the disagreements and the reasons why agreement cannot be reached. These will be of key importance when you reach the objectives and obstacles phases of the planning process.

Customer Profiles

Customer profile analysis is crucial in direct-response marketing. A direct marketer's most important resource is not the order but the orderer, not the response but the responder. Discovery, accumulation, retention, maintenance, and retrievability of profiles and response history are the cornerstone of profit in direct marketing. Maximum profit is generated by defining customer profiles accurately, searching out segments of the total potential customer base with similar characteristics, and then soliciting and resoliciting them effectively to maximize sales during responder life cycles. When only a one-time sale is possible, identifying customer profiles in terms of best CPO through to breakeven profiles enables you to spend your direct-response dollars most cost-effectively.

In short, the more precisely you define and rank your profiles, the less you will spend to obtain initial orders and the higher will be your response rates, average order dollars, and dollars per customer per year. Direct mail, the parent of direct-response marketing, has proved this time and again. This is why your best zip codes will pull 300 percent better than your worst: there are more similar profiles within the best zips. (As soon as census tract geocoding becomes more widespread, even greater response swings will be obtained, because census tracts have been constructed on the basis of cluster homogeneity while zips have been constructed primarily for the convenience of the branch post office, therefore capturing only some of the clustering effect.) Profile similarity makes it possible for the various forms of regression analysis to identify markets on the basis of profitability.

Consequently, the strategic planning coregroup should spend whatever time and effort are necessary at this stage to categorize and rank profiles as precisely and accurately as possible.

Five major tools can be used to isolate the profiles you must find: response graphics, demographics, psychographics, geographics, and special graphics. While sufficient information from only one of these can be enough for profitable direct marketing, the more relevant information you have from each area, the sooner you will reach maximum profits, both acquisition and life cycle. Therefore, each source must be examined in depth.

Response graphics are simply the historical actions taken by customers in response to specific types of products. The basic formula employed by the mail-order industry since the 1930s has been recency, frequency, and monetary value (RFM), but it is helpful to isolate variety (V) also. Run this analysis against your house file first if applicable. It is axiomatic in direct-response marketing that previous responders will respond better than nonresponders. Most research supports the contention that roughly one-third of wage-earning Americans are not responders yet and may never be but that the remaining two-thirds are responders, with half of them responding on a regular basis and half on a sporadic basis. Some posit that 50 percent of adults in the United States are mail-order buyers and that the remainder are "see, touch, and feel" buyers at retail. Whatever the actual split, the difference between the two is critical in your profile analysis.

Keep in mind, however, that large numbers of previous nonresponders have been converted to responders over the past 10 years and that magazine subscription responders are not mail-order buyers until it is proved that they are. (TV and some telephone responders are not yet proven mail-order buyers in the traditional sense. Initial findings indicate that they respond to repeated solicitations at lower rates than mail- or print-generated responders.)

When you are entering a new market or selling a new product unlike those you have marketed before, your house file response information will not help much. Always test the house file, but explore to identify responder lists and publications for similar or complementary products, preferably products with comparable price points.

Demographics refer to characteristics that identify individuals by who they are — sex, age, marital and family status, occupation — and what they have — education, income, car, home, etc. In the United States today, nearly all the major database lists offer demographic selections on an *individual household* basis for virtually all households in the country. (Where selections are not available on an individual household basis, cluster information by census sub-tract of 300 households usually is.) You can rent these lists or use them to merge-purge with any other lists you want to mail to. The identification of potential customers by their key demographic characteristics had become, by 1990, an essential and extremely powerful tool. Demographics help you find out how to get an offer to those people who have a very high probability of wanting your product. At the same time, they help you avoid wasted mail to those who probably will not be interested in what you're offering.

In business and industrial markets, demographics relate to business entities rather than individual consumers, but are no less useful or important. SICs (Standard Industrial Classifications) isolate businesses by industry and type of business within an industry, and various list compilers further segment by annual dollar volume, number of employees, etc.

Psychographics identify individuals by what they like and how they live instead of who they are and what they have. For example, your income is a demographic but how you spend it is a psychographic. Everything from stamp collecting, book reading, and wine drinking to fishing, flying, and tennis is grist for marketing analysis to get the right buyers together with the right sellers. At the end of the 1980s, The Lifestyle Selector and Behavior Bank were leading the database builders in this area, each offering psychographic selections on more than 20 million people.

Geographics tells one where the current customers reside and in certain instances where the best prospects are likely to be. For example, salt-polluted areas adjacent to the U.S. coastline are clearly targets for the sale of home water distillers, whereas municipal wells invaded by toxic chemicals are not necessarily adjacent to bodies of salt water. In the United States, isolation of target markets by geographic location is nearly unlimited in flexibility and reach.

Country	1
Census regions	9
States	52
ADIs	200
SMAs	265
Sectional centers	970
Counties	3,150
School districts	12,500
Census tracts	34,600
Zips	36,000
Census blocks	287,000
Individual households	85,000,000+

Special graphics are any characteristics not included among the four first sources. For example, pool ownership could conceivably indicate a lifestyle characteristic, but it does not necessarily do so. Individuals with high blood pressure, who are prime targets for the sale of a water distiller, do not necessarily have any demographic, psychographic, geographic, or responder characteristics in common.

Once the coregroup has gathered and organized characteristics and preliminarily combined them into discrete profiles, here is a process that can be used to further verify or refine customer profiles:

1. Coregroup members study individually each profile established thus far.

2. Each member jots down "top of mind" characteristics that relate to specific product purchase potentials.

3. Each member then compares the prime benefit with each profile. Is it the same? If not, match benefits to appropriate profiles or describe a profile that would relate to the prime benefit.

4. Do the same for each benefit on the benefits list.

5. The coregroup adversary analyzes each member's benefits and profiles list, raps, and ranks agreed-on profile and benefit combinations from best to least.

6. Depending on the consensus and confidence level of the coregroup as a whole, profiles then are identified as viable or as needing further verification in the objectives, obstacles, or strategy phases of the planning process.

Diagraming the Buying Process

No matter what your market—consumer, business, or industrial—there are always steps before the buy–no buy decision is made. There are always buying actions and sometimes buying influences.

There are five steps, or buying actions:

1. Recognition of need (or want)

2. Evaluation of solutions

3. Recommendation of product types

4. Selection of brand

5. Approval of purchase decision

In consumer markets, very often one individual takes all the actions, sometimes in a matter of minutes in a very informal way. He or she recognizes the need (stimulated by the seller or self-recognized), mentally or actually compares and evaluates types of products that could satisfy the need, makes a mental recommendation about brand, and then mentally approves the expenditures needed to acquire the product.

In other instances, usually with more expensive products or products that will be used by more than the individual in question, there can be buying influences that have an impact on the buying decision. The sale of water distillers is a case in point. Any family member may recognize the need for pure drinking water, but the person who is most in charge of the house probably will want to compare makes, features, and benefits of various types of this kitchen appliance, and the person earning the income will have a voice in an expenditure of $250.

However, this type of multi-influence buying process is a prime characteristic of business and industrial markets, in which many individuals, often specialists, control the buying actions before a purchase decision can evolve. Professional analysis, specifications and requisitions, budgets, and approvals are par for the course. Be aware that the buying process is a gauntlet and that any one of the buying influences has the power to negate the sale.

Consequently, your creative strategy, the amount of versioning you do, the number of solicitations you make, and your entire marketing strategy may well depend on exactly what the buying process is: how many influences there are and the steps each influence must take in the process itself.

Once you have discovered the process as it relates to your products, revisit your list of profiles and link any buying influences that exist to the related profile. Assess whether any identified buying influence may be strong enough to constitute a discrete profile.

Perception of Need: Creative Quicksilver or Gold?

Never assume that actual needs are perceived needs. Often they are not the same, and your response will misfire to whatever degree your assumed perception of need was off target. Examples abound, but one of the best is Monex International's direct marketing program to sell Krugerrands shortly after Americans once again could buy and own gold. It was 1979, and Monex assumed that investors knew why they should invest in gold and understood the mechanics of making the purchase. They headlined their response ads in the financial press "Get 20 for the money and one for the show" and concentrated on convincing potential investors that gold coins were the best way to invest in gold as compared with bullion or gold stocks. The program was not a bomb, but someone challenged the assumption that most investors knew much about gold at all, since 40 years had passed since Americans could legally own it. After research, their new ad approach was headlined

GOLD—HOW TO BUY IT, WHERE TO BUY IT...
AND WHY YOU SHOULD

The ad went on to give the history of gold's reemergence into America's financial investment opportunities and how simple it was to buy and sell gold. The results? The cost for an inquiry was reduced by an increment of 56 percent, and the average order size grew by an increment of 20 percent. The reason for this was a more accurate assessment of perception of need combined with creative execution as professional as on the first attempt.

Take our home water-distilling appliance. In areas where municipal aquifers have been salt-polluted, perception of need is acute, as evidenced by the fact that these areas consume 56 percent of all bottled water in the United States, and in 1979 bottled water sales exceeded $550 million. Yet the actual need of residents in those areas was comparatively lower than that of residents in areas where the municipal wells had been invaded by toxic chemicals carried by groundwater movement. Until local people became seriously ill and water supplies were checked, actual need never would have helped you market a water distiller.

Your coregroup now should evaluate each customer profile identified in terms of perception of need and then rerank profile priorities according to the perception factor.

Building Profiles into Direct-Response Market Segments

While it is true in one sense that the medium is the market in direct response, do not limit your strategic analysis of target markets in terms of the existing media reach. Instead, start by identifying the quantity of customer potentials that exist within each one of the profile segments your coregroup has isolated and then start to work on where they are located and how to reach them cost-effectively. Do not start with any specific medium and explore laterally.

Here is a sequence of steps that can be used to examine the total U.S. marketplace to ferret out those market segments that represent profitable marketing potentials for direct-response operations. Not all the steps apply to each product or marketing situation. Your coregroup members may find themselves moving through any given step simply by deciding that it is not applicable to this specific situation.

1. Start with your number-one profile, complete your analysis of it, and then move on to the next profile until you have analyzed each profile on your list of potential customers.
2. Develop profiles of the customers you have already, from your best customers to new customers you don't know much about yet. Use database information to overlay demographic, psychographic, and other special characteristics against your customer file based on their RFM&V response history (the recency, frequency, monetary value, and variety of products they have purchased.) Then use regression analysis to learn which specific characteristics identify each different kind of customer you have. Compare these profiles to the prioritized profiles you developed in step one. Then integrate these two lists of customer profiles.
3. Define each profile segment geographically on the basis of any relevant distribution limits.
   a. For retail traffic building, apply store location parameters.
   b. For lead-getting programs for localized salespeople, apply sales office parameters. Keep in mind that all consumer segments are reachable by mail.
4. Reduce any geographic "wholes" by special graphics that are applicable: Snowbelt for pool covers, salt-polluted areas for water distillers, entire country for new mothers, etc.
5. Use national database lists to "locate" the different household densities of each of your customer profiles within regions, states, cities, SMAs (standard metropolitan statistical areas), ADIs (areas of dominant influence), zip codes, and census tracts, tracts, or sub-tracts.
6. Evaluate each medium in terms of response potential versus cost efficiency. Keep in mind that at this point, your coregroup is not specifying precise media to be employed (that will come later, in the strategy or tactics phase) but rather applying the relative strengths and weaknesses of each major response medium to the market segments you have isolated and ranked in order of response profitability potential.

Now that the coregroup has determined target markets by size and by the types of customers within them as well as product benefits and media available to reach each segment, you are ready to analyze the resources you have at your disposal to address these market opportunities.

Resource Analysis: Key to Future Profit

If the strategies and plans you create produce sales that outrun your organization's fulfillment capabilities, consider your program a failure rather than a success. One of the fundamental differences between selling and marketing is that the prime function of selling is to create an order, whereas the prime function of marketing is to create the most profitable customer. By definition, marketing must go beyond selling to produce satisfied, enthusiastic customers who will want to buy again and recommend your products and company to others.

Table 1-2. Capabilities of Major Direct-Response Media

Medium	Advantages	Disadvantages
Direct mail	Reaches all households Selectivity and personalization Most suitable for testing Most flexible Maximizes customer list dollars Second highest response rates Contains all action elements	Second most expensive Long startup time Profile analysis Potential limited
Telephone	Powerful "one-on-one" capability Fastest response time Selectivity Flexibility Excellent for research and pro- file analysis Can increase average order size substantially Highest response rates Powerful cross- and upgrade-sell	Dangerous with prospects No visual appeal Most expensive CPM 55% household reachability
Magazines	Reach mass or class Good color reproduction Long ad life Low CPM Test inexpensively Moderate lead time	Less space to tell story Less personal Slower response Less selectivity than mail or phone
Newspapers	Shortest startup time Fast response Wide variety of formats Broad local coverage Inexpensive to test	Poor color Poor ROP production Poor selectivity No personalization Rates vary Sometimes affected by local conditions
Television	Powerful demonstration capa- bility Fast response Wide choice of time buys Can reach all U.S. households Strong support medium Watch for strong selectivity as cable grows	Limited copy time No permanent response device Difficult to split-test Network time scarce Limited time available in second and fourth quarters
Radio	High-frequency, inexpensive Many profiles can be isolated by choice of show and time Short startup times Powerful support medium	No response device Limited copy time No visual appeal

This principle of marketing applies to all businesses but especially to mail-order and direct-response marketing because there is no person-to-person contact between buyer and seller. Consequently, the strategic planning coregroup must be as diligent and creative in providing for your order fulfillment and customer service performance as they are in providing for customer solicitation and order generation. A few years ago, an industry veteran claimed, "If we could deliver the product in three days, we'd own the world," and there is reason to believe he was right. Research clearly shows that repeat purchase and the lifetime value of a customer are directly related to the speed and accuracy with which initial orders are handled.

Starting in the late 1980s, American mail-order companies finally began to make substantial improvements in the time it took customers to receive what they'd ordered and in customer service. Previously, American mail-order firms had lagged behind European performance in the two areas, both of which have a different impact on the lifetime value of the customer.

As an integral part of the planning process, the following ten capabilities must be assessed in terms of handling current order levels and any growth that the strategic plan may call for:

1. Ordering forms and instructions
2. Receiving mail and telephone calls
3. Checking credit
4. Processing orders
5. Addressing and list maintenance
6. Controlling inventory
7. Billing
8. Reporting and controlling
9. Order filling and shipping
10. Handling complaints and adjustments

You cannot achieve 100 percent effectiveness in any of the ten areas because of three factors that are not under your complete control: customers, vendors, and carriers. But it is critical that you identify deficiencies in all operations that are under your complete control. Any that are discovered not to be controllable should be precisely identified for consideration in the objectives phase.

While all these areas are important, reporting and controlling bears further investigation, for it is this "feed" to your marketing database that enables you to track response, sales, and profits in terms of customer profiles (market segments). Any deficiency in this area of tracking and measuring response should be considered a major obstacle that must be corrected in the strategic planning process and the allocation of resources that the plan will call for.

The strength, weakness, and extent of your front-end resources also must be determined accurately in the planning process. Be as brutally honest with yourselves on this point as you were in assessing your USP. Do you really have state-of-the-art knowledge and hands-on skills in all the recently developed areas of direct-response marketing? If your creative people are great in print, are they as effective in telephone, film, or multimedia? Are your list personnel skilled in the other response media that have emerged or are emerging rapidly?

Of course, you must consider the financial resources available for use. This does not preclude the task method approach. It merely lets the coregroup know when additional financial resources must be requested if they are justified by risk-gain analysis in phase 6.

Comprehensive Situation Statement

After each of the foregoing areas has been addressed and evaluated by the coregroup, the plan manager is ready to put together the final preplanning situation statement, which should be written in the same sequence in which subjects were addressed during the background analysis process. Now all relevant information in order of importance under each information category will definitively identify what is known and that which is not yet known or in hand.

The completed document should be distributed to all coregroup members for in-depth study before the first coregroup meeting to establish objectives. Each coregroup member should bring his or her situation document to each meeting, and the plan manager should have all documentation available at each meeting.

PHASE 2: STRATEGIC OBJECTIVES— PRIORITIZING THE TARGETS

Developing objectives that permit effective strategic decision making is as much an art as a science, but it is not magic. Your planning group's command of this skill will determine whether you aim the organization's time, money, and talent at operations that in reality have a low priority or aim them into channels of substantial growth that are somewhat self-renewing. Objectives that are conceived or expressed too broadly spread your resources across too great a number of targets, many of which are incidental rather than essential. Objectives that are conceived too narrowly apply an enormously wasteful amount of direct marketing activity to profit potentials that represent only a small portion of the growth that is realizable.

Recognize that objectives are rudders that pull your direct-response strategies toward the most important marketing opportunities. Realize that a 10-degree error here can turn into a 1000-mile "miss" of the major ports you are headed for, leaving you at sea rather than unloading cargo. Here is a step-by-step method that can help you create objectives that are reachable and worth reaching.

1. Have your coregroup free-associate a list of possible objectives for next year's operations, never losing sight of life-cycle implications.

2. Adversary-analyze each potential objective on the list in terms of the following criteria:
   a. Does it *focus on results?*
   b. Is it *measurable? If yes, how?*

      Rate of return
      Ratio to sales
      Percentage of market
      Number of units
      Dollars to accomplish
      Time to accomplish
      Other

   c. Does it contain a *single theme?*
   d. Is it *challenging?* A strategic objective should stretch your existing capabilities but not break any corporate bones. Setting comfortable objectives is as damaging to profit production as tilting at windmills is to morale.
   e. Is it *realistic?* Do you have, or can you obtain, the resources needed in time?
   f. Does it contribute to *higher goals,* such as long-range goals, department-to-division goals, division-to-corporate goals, or corporate-to-parent goals?

      If any objective evaluated cannot be developed to the point where it satisfies the first five criteria of adversary analysis (coregroup consensus), remove it from your list of possible objectives. Only without meeting objective *f.* can you proceed without damage to your strategic plan. As a matter of business courtesy and practical judgment, it is best when ranking objectives to state why any objective has the priority assigned it even though it does not contribute to a higher goal.

3. Place any objectives that are totally financial in nature in a category separate from those that are not totally financial in nature. (Remember that many will contain some financial criteria, since all must be measurable in some way.)

4. Now prioritize all listed objectives on the basis of two criteria only: the lifetime value of your customer base and the net growth of your customer base.

5. Examine the kinds of objectives you have developed and prioritized in the light of the industry's phase and the phase your own business is in.

   Objectives will and should vary depending on the condition of your markets (emerging, growing, mature, or aging) and the stage your company is in (entry level, rollout and second-stage testing, growing, mature, or saturated). If either your markets or your company is moving from one stage to another and your objectives remain the same, something is wrong, and you should review the objectives in depth.

6. Bring in a fresh set of eyes, either a direct marketing generalist or a group that has not been part of the planning process thus far. This devil's advocate can be from within your company or the outside. Background should be provided prior to the attempt to find any weakness or omissions in your statement of objectives. Finalization of the objectives phase occurs only after your coregroup has analyzed objectives in light of the input from the devil's advocates.

PHASE 3: OBSTACLES AND
ADVANTAGES—THE BRIDGES FROM
OBJECTIVES TO STRATEGY

Most treatments of strategic planning move directly from developing objectives to the creation of strategy. While that sequence obviously has produced a great deal of profitable strategy, the introduction of a step between objectives and strategy can yield uncommon results. It is a step that illuminates the mind and vitalizes the judgment. It simply involves addressing, evaluating, and "connecting" obstacles and advantages to the objectives you just completed working on. Of the two, obstacles are the most misunderstood and underutilized.

Obstacles that are clearly seen and assessed can lead to profits. When discovered, evaluated accurately, and linked to objectives, they can galvanize the coregroup's innovative insights unlike any other tool available. To consider the point from another angle, if only one major obstacle is overlooked or badly underestimated during the planning process, it can turn a profitable marketing program into a total loser.

Two examples will clarify this point. For our manufacturer of pool covers, product quality was as good as but no better than that of two larger competitors, price was the same, and delivery was comparable. There was no realistic way to change those three factors. There was no competitive advantage. Clearly, a powerful strategy would have to be discovered and implemented if any significant gains were to be realized. For our manufacturer of water distillers, residents were drinking toxic chemicals in their tap water but had no knowledge of the danger, in contrast to residents in salt polluted areas. This was a major obstacle that steered the strategy for marketing to them.

Turning obstacles into profits during the planning process can be managed in much the same way that objectives were addressed, using the same basic planning tools.

1. Free-associate any and all obstacles of whatever type that come to mind. (Remember that obstacles can be internal as well as external and that a production problem can be as important as a marketing problem.)

2. Link each obstacle that surfaces to the specific objectives it impacts. Do not be concerned if a single obstacle blocks multiple objectives. List it under each one that is relevant, since it is likely that a different strategy may be needed to overcome it.

3. Rank the obstacles to each objective on the basis of the resources needed (time, money, people skills) to overcome each one. (The overall priority of any given obstacle is established by the objective to which it is related.)

Throughout this process, significant clues as to how to allocate resources and also some hints as to definitive strategies will evolve. Do not pursue strategy development at this point. Simply capture the ideas and bring them up for work in phase 4.

Once you have developed and assessed the obstacles to next year's direct marketing efforts, you are ready to work on competitive advantages. Use the same
process and the same tools to discover and evaluate your objectives and link
your advantages to them.

PHASE 4: STRATEGY—FINDING
THE LEVERAGE

Trying to answer the question "How do you actually develop strategy?" is like
trying to answer the question "How do you actually get an idea?" While both
questions are rooted in logic and understanding, both go beyond mere logical
analysis and linear thinking. Effective strategies, like creative ideas, emerge
from "outside-the-lines" thinking that does not violate fundamental principles.

"Eureka" moments—those moments of illumination and insight when you
know you have it—cannot be produced on demand or in a production-line atmosphere. Harry Hepner's comment, quoted earlier in the chapter, "Creative
thinkers continually waver between unimaginable fantasies and systematic attack," is relevant here. So it is of the utmost importance to establish an atmosphere in which the free play of the mind, and the free interplay of minds, can
readily occur. (While much strategic planning takes place away from the office,
this is not essentially a corporate reward of nontaxable income. The changed
environment and the intangible perception that this whole process is unusual
and fun are important to the success of the process itself.)

Let's define strategy before going any further. It is an elusive concept and too
often is confused with tactics. There is good reason for this confusion, as can be
seen when one consults the dictionary for clarification. The standard dictionary
defines strategy and tactics as follows:

Strategy: the art of devising a plan toward a goal

Tactics: a device for accomplishing an end

Since these definitions do not shed much light on the distinction, our working
definitions will be as follows:

Strategy is the advantageous employment of various resources as an integrated whole to cause a planned effect.

Tactics involve actions of lesser magnitude than strategy and are carried out
with a limited end in view.

With that distinction in mind, here are some guidelines for your strategy-
creating sessions.

1. Work on the strategy to achieve one objective at a time.
2. Review each objective and its associated obstacles and advantages before development activity begins.

3. Maximize the interaction between coregroup members during the strategy sessions.

4. Start with your highest-priority objective and work your way through to the last.

5. Assess the viability of your strategies between working sessions.

6. Prioritize the strategies agreed on within each objective the strategies impact.

7. Give your devil's advocate maximum latitude when he or she attempts to destroy the rationale for your strategies.

Keep in mind throughout the process that strategy can and does obtain in any activity related to direct-response marketing: production and fulfillment as well as creative and media, research and testing as well as financial and customer service, morale and administration as well as marketing and sales.

For the swimming-pool cover manufacturer with no unique selling proposition for its dealers in Snowbelt areas, three strategies were developed, and they resulted in an increase in sales volume of over 40 percent with no decrease in profit level on sales. They were:

1. A dealer push-pull program.   A customer information booklet comes from Century Products and the dealer who stocks Century pool covers. Pool owners will be offered the booklet "free from their dealer" through an ad in *Pool News,* which has a biennial circulation to 700,000 pool owners. Dealers are preinformed of this offer to their potential customers (see Figure 1-2). Those who stock Century covers receive an inventory of the booklets free of charge.

2. An offer that adds a customer information value to the basic commodity being sold.   The dealers said that it takes pool owners three days to winterize the pool properly and that they often make mistakes that cause their pools to deteriorate, or cost them money for repair. So the cornerstone of the October-to-April direct-response program is a small booklet entitled *How to Winterize Your Pool* (see Figure 1-3). It gives complete and truly useful step-by-step information to pool owners.

3. Use of integrated multimedia to dramatize the first two items.   Direct mail, print ads, and trade shows (see Figure 1-4).

PHASE 5: TACTICS—
DESIGNING THE LEVERS

Tactics are as natural and integral to a marketing plan as children are to a family. No strategic marketing plan can be considered complete without them, since no true assessment of the resources called for by the plan can be made without them.

Plan tactics are the written parameter specifications that define the work projects needed to implement strategic plans and guide the people who actually

Figure 1-2. The dealer push-pull strategy: A full-page advertisement in *Pool News*, a trade magazine.

Figure 1-3. The offer strategy: A full-page advertisement in *Poolife,* a consumer magazine. While this format is not typical of a direct-response ad, it *is* response advertising in that it contains the two *essentials* that distinguish direct marketing from general advertising: a specific-benefits offer and a call to action.

The marketing plan covered eight areas: Background; Objectives; Obstacles; Strategy;
Tactics; Implementation Schedules; Sales and Profit Projections; and Program Charges.

What Media and or Lists Were Used?

Direct mail was sent to a house list composed of Dealer/Distributor customers and prospects.
Advertisements appeared in POOL NEWS, a trade magazine, and POOLIFE, a consumer publication.

What were the demographics and/or psychographics of your market?

Many of the pool product dealers are not in the pool business on a year-round basis.

What were dates of mailings, print ads, broadcast, etc.? Indicate quantities mailed,
frequency of ads, estimated and/or actual audience reached.

Direct Mail, Print Ads, and Trade Show Handouts	Dates	Quantities Mailed or Handed Out	Frequency	Reach
1. Dealer/Distributor mailing prior to trade show	Oct.16,1978	3042	–	–
2. Full page ad in POOL NEWS prior to trade show	Nov.6, 1978	–	1	10,217
3. Trade show handouts	Nov.15-18,1978	3600	–	–
4. Follow-up telegraf to Dealer/Distributors	Dec. 1978	3042	–	–
5. Direct Mail Package	March 1979	3042	–	–
6. Direct Mail Package	April 1979	3042	–	–
7. Last chance telegraf mailing	June 1979	3042	–	–
8. Full page ad in POOLIFE	June 1979	–	1	700,000
9. Ad mats to Dealers/ Distributors	July 1979	240	–	–

Figure 1-4. The multimedia blitz strategy.

will do the tactics during the upcoming marketing year. It is important that
these parameter specifications control the work to be done without restricting
the creativity of those who actually will perform the work.

	Plan Tactics	Operational Tactics
Timing	During planning process	During marketing year
What is produced	Written document specify- ing project parameters	The "actual" direct-mail package, ad, telephone call, TV spot, focus group re- search, computer software, etc. Orders, dollars, and customers
Results	Line projects	

This part of your written plan spells out exactly what projects will be worked on
in the coming year, when they will start and finish, who will do each, approximately what they will cost, and how each project relates to all others called for
by the plan. Tactics include but are not necessarily limited to the following:

Solicitation packaging for all media: Direct-mail, magazine and newspaper
ROP and insert ads, telephone scripts, TV and radio ads, collateral, and mul-
timedia combination
 - Concept and themes

- Copy platforms or story boards
- Graphic approach
- Component specifications

Table 1-3 shows how specific this effort can be.

Media selections for all programs, both test and controls, in all media to be utilized
- Lists and specifications
- Magazines and newspapers
- Telephone, incoming and outgoing
- TV and radio
- Collateral outlets
- Support media such as co-ops, stuffers, and syndication

Research projects and test structures
- Focus group
- Intercept personal
- Direct mail and telephone
- Test cell specifications
- Timing and rollout parameters

Fulfillment, customer service, and response tracking specifications

Schedules, quality-control procedures, and costs for all projects

Remember, the planning process must go far enough into detail that there is absolutely no doubt in the minds of those who will implement the projects as to what is to be done and what results are expected from their efforts.

PHASE 6: FREEZING THE DESIGN

Now that you have completed the tactical elements of the marketing plan, six more steps are required before you "freeze" the plan for presentation to management for approval and funding:

1. Predictive yield analysis
2. Writing the plan
3. Devil's advocacy
4. Final coregroup consensus
5. implementation criteria
6. Formatting the presentation

Predictive Yield Analysis

This is the moment of truth in the planning process, the point at which you pull together all your cost factors, compare them with reasonable forecasts of re-

Table 1-3. Tactics: Parameter Specifications for Direct-Mail-Series Traffic Building

Category number	Category	Basic appeal category	Mailing 1			Mailing 2			Timing
			Format	Copy approach	Pieces included	Format	Copy approach	Pieces included	
1	Homeowners in right geographic area, segmented by income; Estimated recipients—3000	Have advantage of city life and easy-care apartment while staying in the North Shore area where your friends and ties are	Superelegant invitation, engraved, sealing wax commemorative stamp, etc.	1. Elegance of building 2. Location of building in their preferred area	1. Envelope 2. 1-page letter 3. Invitation 4. RSVP card 5. RSVP envelope 6. Comm. stamp (2) 7. Sealing wax	Testimonial from present resident of building	"These are the reasons I like living at Ferncroft Tower"	1. Envelope 2. Brief small note from Ferncroft manager 3. Letter from resident 4. Reply card 5. BRE 6. Comm. stamp (2)	2 weeks after mailing 1 to this category
2	Country club members in right area; Estimated recipients—1000	A golf course right at your door plus all the appeals for category 1	Same as category 1	1 and 2; same for category 1 plus 3; golf course at your door	Same as for category 1 but with different letter	Same as for category 1	Same as for category 1	Same as for category 1	Same as for category 1
3	Residents of expensive Boston apartments or condominiums; Estimated recipients—5000	Fears about city living versus security of Ferncroft Tower	Very nice; high quality, but not as elegant and formal as for categories 1 and 2	1. Play on fears of city living 2. Ferncroft security 3. Proximity to city with advantages of country of category 1 4. Lower car insurance 5. Desirability of building itself	1. Envelope 2. 3-page letter 3. Appointment reservation card 4. Small card with map and directions 5. BRE 6. Comm. stamp (2)	Very nice, high quality, similar to first mailing to this category	Position Ferncroft geographically, not so far from city, near to beaches, resort areas, etc.; use time-frame comparisons	1. Envelope 2. 2-page letter 3. Small flyer with driving times and map and directions 4. Appointment reservation card 5. BRE 6. Comm. stamp (2)	2 weeks after mailing 1 to this category

sponse, and then relate those to your calculations on Breakeven, CTOP, and life-cycle value. Use your own previous-response rates, recision data, and attrition curves if they are applicable. If they are not, search out industry statistics and apply them conservatively.

It is possible these calculations will send you back to the drawing board if the coregroup judges the amount of resources called for to be prohibitive in terms of risk-gain probabilities. As agonizing as this is when it occurs, it is less agonizing than failure after implementation, and much less costly.

Two examples of predictive yield analysis follow. Table 1-4 details acquisition-year exposure and gain levels, and Table 1-5 displays life-cycle gain potentials.

Writing the Plan

The entire plan, including documentation, must be committed to written form. The sequence of information is exactly the sequence in which the planning process took place:

Background summary	Tactics
Objectives	Yield analysis
Obstacles and advantages	Implementation criteria
Strategy	

Table 1-4. Dealer-Distributor Prospect Breakeven and Acquisition-Year Profit Potentials*

	Response Rate			
	0.5%	1%	1.5%	2.0%
Number of new customers	21	41	62	82
Gross dollars	$ 136,500	$266,500	$403,000	$533,000
25% margin	34,125	66,625	100,750	133,250
Promotion cost	47,932	47,932	47,932	47,932
Booklet cost	1,386	2,706	4,092	5,412
Net profit	15,193	15,987	48,726	79,906

Assumptions	
Cost of solicitation	$11.69
Average annual order	$6500.00
Margin per customer	$1625.00
Cost of winterizing booklets per prospect buyer (500 per buyer at 13¢ per booklet)	$66.00
Net profit	$1559.00
Breakeven response rate	0.74%
Number of customers acquired based on universe of 4100 prospects	30

*At four different rates of response.

Table 1-5. Potential Sales Dollars to be Generated from New Customers* over 6 Years

	Year 1	Year 2	Year 3	Year 4	Year 5	Year 6	Six-Year Total
Percentage of new customers retained	100%	75%	67.5%	61%	55%	50%	
Number of new customers retained	41	31	28	25	23	21	
Average annual gross revenue for customer	$10,000	$10,000	$10,000	$10,000	$10,000	$10,000	
Gross sales dollars	$410,000	$310,000	$280,000	$250,000	$230,000	$210,000	$1,690,000
Gross contribution	$102,500	$77,500	$70,000	$62,500	$57,500	$52,500	$422,500

Assumptions

1. New customer quantity based on a 1 percent response rate at a $10,000 annual revenue level from prospect program
2. Annual revenue for customer life cycle set at $10,000, with no upgrading considered
3. 25/10 attrition curve applied
4. Six-year life cycle (per client input)
5. Cost of additional solicitations not included
6. Gross profit based on prototype 25 percent gross margin

*Acquired from prospect program.

While all coregroup specialists should provide factual and rationale input at the plan manager's request, they also may be asked to contribute copy. If so, it is still the plan manager's responsibility for final editing that ensures that the written plan will reflect the decisions made by the coregroup consensus during the plan development process.

Devil's Advocacy

When the written plan is distributed to coregroup members before the final adversary review meeting, give it also to a devil's advocate who previously has not been part of the planning process in any way and include that person or group in the final coregroup review meeting.

Final Coregroup Consensus

The ground rules for adversary analysis and consensus approval also apply to this last meeting before presentation to management. The "we already decided that" mentality must not be allowed to govern this session, and so it is important that the devil's advocate participate as a forceful critic.

Implementation Criteria

Clearly, the line personnel who actually will implement the plan's projects must have some flexibility when addressing real-world problems that cannot be foreseen in any planning process. However, the plan's essential specifications cannot be changed arbitrarily without sacrificing the value and probably the intended performance of the projects undertaken. I recommend that you use the adversary system throughout implementation during your operational year. Any line personnel who interpret plan specifications differently—creative, graphics, and data processing, for example—must attempt to reach consensus on the best way to proceed. If they cannot reach consensus after a reasonable amount of time has been spent in discussion, the matter is taken to the next logical superior with oversight responsibility. All sides of the question at hand are presented with pros and cons, and then a decision is made. If the manager hearing the case is unable to decide, it goes up the line; in certain instances, the coregroup itself may have to be reconvened. Generally speaking,

Essential changes such as offer, creative platform, media, price, product, etc., require coregroup analysis and approval.

Important changes such as list substitutes, test structures, etc., require marketing director approval.

Incidental changes such as paper stock, copywriter switches, etc., require only approval by the appropriate department head.

The criteria and guidelines you use should be spelled out in writing as part of the written plan itself, because after the plan has been approved, all departments will use their copy of the plan's rationale and specifications in much the same way that a building contractor uses architectural plans and specifications to erect a building.

Formatting the Presentation

The plan in final written form should be distributed to top managers for review and study at least one week before the formal presentation for approval. But the sequence of the plan summary presented at that meeting should be different from the sequence in which the plan was written.

Financial analysis summary

Objectives

Obstacles and advantages

Strategy

Summary of tactics

As these summary areas are presented and discussed, the coregroup's knowledge and the written plan itself (plus all documentation, which should be available at the approval meeting sessions) can and should be used to respond to specific questions that arise, clarify positions taken, and explain decisions.

STRATEGIC MANAGEMENT: AN ESSENTIAL

There are, after all is said and done, only three types of direct marketing companies: those that really don't plan at all, those that plan and don't act, and those that plan and then turn the plan into action. You can tell which is which after observing any company for a few days. The first type is always wondering what happened, the second watches what is happening, and the third is making things happen.

Working with the third kind of company is electrifying. The shared belief that the company can largely create its own future is almost tangible. In fact, that attitude is one of the four characteristics this type of direct marketing enterprise almost always exhibits. Employees from top to bottom exude an entrepreneurial drive that does make things happen. Communications between peers is open at all times (there is no closet mentality), and the recognition of the value of teamwork as the major force in successfully completing preplanned tasks predominates.

How does this kind of direct marketing company come into being? Not surprisingly, it must start at the top with the chief executive officer (CEO) and the layer of management reporting directly to the CEO. They set the tone and then involve operating management in the strategic decision-making process. This in turn increases middle management's understanding and enthusiasm, which in turn transmits itself to those working for the middle managers. When people realize why they are doing what they are doing, the "what" begins to gain substantial ground. Soon business touchdowns occur, and the satisfaction of knowing that you have helped achieve the score develops a life of its own within the organization. Recognition of "planning the game and playing the plan" takes hold quickly, and the momentum soon becomes beautiful to behold. In companies in which incentive compensation and additional responsibility are linked to plan performance, strategic management becomes the norm rather than the exception. And with strategic management comes stable yet extraordinary growth.

2
Testing and Analysis

Edward L. Nash
Nash/Wakeman/deForrest
New York, N.Y.

The measurability of direct marketing is such an integral part of this business that the word *testing* is used very lightly. Direct marketers talk of testing media, testing copy, and testing an offer. We run test campaigns, dry tests, split-run tests, element tests, and concept tests.

In its simplest form the word can be used as a synonym for *try,* as in running an advertisement in a publication or using a mailing list for the first time and then seeing if the results are satisfactory. In its most complex form, it can mean two- and three-dimensional grid tests constructed to read media, offer, and copy variables simultaneously on a new business proposition.

If a mailing list has 1 million names and you mail to the entire list the first time you try it, you aren't testing, you're gambling. The pragmatic defining characteristic of "testing" in direct mail is the desire to minimize downside financial risk.

How many pieces of mail do you have to send out in order to rely on the test results? Because direct mail is believed to be subject to the rules of statistical projectability, you should be able to mail as few as 3000 or 5000 pieces and determine a range of response rates that might be expected from the entire list. Most books on direct marketing, including the previous edition of this work, included statistical validity tables to help determine the answer to this question. These tables are all based on formulas derived from game theory, the laws of chance, algebraic interpretations of sampling practice, and established formulas of statistical probability. Unfortunately, most of them have been difficult to put to practical use and have required many pages of explanation.

This chapter is adapted from Edward L. Nash, *Direct Marketing: Strategy, Planning, Execution* (New York: McGraw-Hill, 1986).

For this chapter, I have enlisted the aid of Lloyd Kieran, a prominent West Coast consultant who was formerly a senior vice president and management supervisor at BBDO Direct, to help solve this problem for our readers and for our own staff. The result is a completely new set of probability tables, never before published in any form. Instead of telling you what quantity you need at various response rates and error margins, the tables have been reconstituted into a more usable form.

PROBABILITY TABLES

One of the great advantages of the direct-mail medium is its predictability. If one has information about past direct-mail efforts, then it is not only possible but highly desirable to forecast the results of planned mailings. This is possible if some simple rules are followed:

When projecting the results of a planned mailing, one must keep in mind the basic rule of comparing apples to apples. For example, it is essential to roll out a new mailing with the same package as used in the test. If you were to change the offer, the rollout would really be a new package, and the results would not be projectable based on the previous effort.

The laws of statistical probability will apply only if you minimize the variables and measure like to like. There are some variables, however, that cannot be controlled. Time is a good example of such a condition. Even though you may mail the exact same package a second time to the exact same lists, you cannot overcome the time differential. You can minimize the variable to be sure—by mailing at the same time of year—but it is impossible to change the fact that you will have mailed in two different years. So there is always some difference, however small. (And if market conditions have changed dramatically, then time is a major differential.)

Probability Table Description

The probability tables (Tables 2-1 to 2-9) are based on a standard statistical formula for predicting a future outcome based on sample results. In all, there are three tables—one each for a 95 percent confidence level, a 99 percent confidence level, and a 90 percent confidence level. Each table shows the following:

- Sample sizes, ranging from 1000 pieces to 100,000 pieces, expressed in thousands
- Response rates, expressed as percentages, ranging from 0.5 percent to 10 percent in 0.5 percent increments
- Percent variation—that is, margin of error expressed as a percentage of the response rate
- Low projection—that is, the test response rate less the margin of error
- High projection—that is, the response rate plus the margin of error

Table 2-1. Statistical Variation: Margin of Error at 95 Percent Confidence Level*

Sample size (000)	0.50% % Var. +/-	Low	High	1.00% % Var. +/-	Low	High	1.50% % Var. +/-	Low	High	2.00% % Var. +/-	Low	High	2.50% % Var. +/-	Low	High	3.00% % Var. +/-	Low	High	3.50% % Var. +/-	Low	High
1.0	87.4	0.06	0.94	61.7	0.38	1.62	50.2	0.75	2.25	43.4	1.13	2.87	38.7	1.53	3.47	35.2	1.94	4.06	32.5	2.36	4.64
2.5	55.3	0.22	0.78	39.0	0.61	1.39	31.8	1.02	1.98	27.4	1.45	2.55	24.5	1.89	3.11	22.3	2.33	3.67	20.6	2.78	4.22
5.0	39.1	0.30	0.70	27.6	0.72	1.28	22.5	1.16	1.84	19.4	1.61	2.39	17.3	2.07	2.93	15.8	2.53	3.47	14.6	2.99	4.01
7.5	31.9	0.34	0.66	22.5	0.77	1.23	18.3	1.22	1.78	15.8	1.68	2.32	14.1	2.15	2.85	12.9	2.61	3.39	11.9	3.08	3.92
10.0	27.6	0.36	0.64	19.5	0.80	1.20	15.9	1.26	1.74	13.7	1.73	2.27	12.2	2.19	2.81	11.1	2.67	3.33	10.3	3.14	3.86
12.5	24.7	0.38	0.62	17.4	0.83	1.17	14.2	1.29	1.71	12.3	1.75	2.25	10.9	2.23	2.77	10.0	2.70	3.30	9.2	3.18	3.82
15.0	22.6	0.39	0.61	15.9	0.84	1.16	13.0	1.31	1.69	11.2	1.78	2.22	10.0	2.25	2.75	9.1	2.73	3.27	8.4	3.21	3.79
17.5	20.9	0.40	0.60	14.7	0.85	1.15	12.0	1.32	1.68	10.4	1.79	2.21	9.3	2.27	2.73	8.4	2.75	3.25	7.8	3.23	3.77
20.0	19.6	0.40	0.60	13.8	0.86	1.14	11.2	1.33	1.67	9.7	1.81	2.19	8.7	2.28	2.72	7.9	2.76	3.24	7.3	3.25	3.75
25.0	17.5	0.41	0.59	12.3	0.88	1.12	10.0	1.35	1.65	8.7	1.83	2.17	7.7	2.31	2.69	7.0	2.79	3.21	6.5	3.27	3.73
30.0	16.0	0.42	0.58	11.3	0.89	1.11	9.2	1.36	1.64	7.9	1.84	2.16	7.1	2.32	2.68	6.4	2.81	3.19	5.9	3.29	3.71
35.0	14.8	0.43	0.57	10.4	0.90	1.10	8.5	1.37	1.63	7.3	1.85	2.15	6.5	2.34	2.66	6.0	2.82	3.18	5.5	3.31	3.69
40.0	13.8	0.43	0.57	9.8	0.90	1.10	7.9	1.38	1.62	6.9	1.86	2.14	6.1	2.35	2.65	5.6	2.83	3.17	5.1	3.32	3.68
45.0	13.0	0.43	0.57	9.2	0.91	1.09	7.5	1.39	1.61	6.5	1.87	2.13	5.8	2.36	2.64	5.3	2.84	3.16	4.9	3.33	3.67
50.0	12.4	0.44	0.56	8.7	0.91	1.09	7.1	1.39	1.61	6.1	1.88	2.12	5.5	2.36	2.64	5.0	2.85	3.15	4.6	3.34	3.66
60.0	11.3	0.44	0.56	8.0	0.92	1.08	6.5	1.40	1.60	5.6	1.89	2.11	5.0	2.38	2.62	4.5	2.86	3.14	4.2	3.35	3.65
70.0	10.5	0.45	0.55	7.4	0.93	1.07	6.0	1.41	1.59	5.2	1.90	2.10	4.6	2.38	2.62	4.2	2.87	3.13	3.9	3.36	3.64
80.0	9.8	0.45	0.55	6.9	0.93	1.07	5.6	1.42	1.58	4.9	1.90	2.10	4.3	2.39	2.61	3.9	2.88	3.12	3.6	3.37	3.63
90.0	9.2	0.45	0.55	6.5	0.93	1.07	5.3	1.42	1.58	4.6	1.91	2.09	4.1	2.40	2.60	3.7	2.89	3.11	3.4	3.38	3.62
100.0	8.7	0.46	0.54	6.2	0.94	1.06	5.0	1.42	1.58	4.3	1.91	2.09	3.9	2.40	2.60	3.5	2.89	3.11	3.3	3.39	3.61

*Response rates expressed in percentages, with percentage variation (+ or −), low projection (−), and high projection (+).

Table 2-2. Statistical Variation: Margin of Error at 95 Percent Confidence Level*

Sample size (000)	4.00% % Var. +/-	Low	High	4.50% % Var. +/-	Low	High	5.00% % Var. +/-	Low	High	5.50% % Var. +/-	Low	High	6.00% % Var. +/-	Low	High	6.50% % Var. +/-	Low	High	7.00% % Var. +/-	Low	High
1.0	30.4	2.79	5.21	28.6	3.22	5.78	27.0	3.65	6.35	25.7	4.09	6.91	24.5	4.53	7.47	23.5	4.97	8.03	22.6	5.42	8.58
2.5	19.2	3.23	4.77	18.1	3.69	5.31	17.1	4.15	5.85	16.2	4.61	6.39	15.5	5.07	6.93	14.9	5.53	7.47	14.3	6.00	8.00
5.0	13.6	3.46	4.54	12.8	3.93	5.07	12.1	4.40	5.60	11.5	4.87	6.13	11.0	5.34	6.66	10.5	5.82	7.18	10.1	6.29	7.71
7.5	11.1	3.56	4.44	10.4	4.03	4.97	9.9	4.51	5.49	9.4	4.98	6.02	9.0	5.46	6.54	8.6	5.94	7.06	8.2	6.42	7.58
10.0	9.6	3.62	4.38	9.0	4.09	4.91	8.5	4.57	5.43	8.1	5.05	5.95	7.8	5.53	6.47	7.4	6.02	6.98	7.1	6.50	7.50
12.5	8.6	3.66	4.34	8.1	4.14	4.86	7.6	4.62	5.38	7.3	5.10	5.90	6.9	5.58	6.42	6.6	6.07	6.93	6.4	6.55	7.45
15.0	7.8	3.69	4.31	7.4	4.17	4.83	7.0	4.65	5.35	6.6	5.14	5.86	6.3	5.62	6.38	6.1	6.11	6.89	5.8	6.59	7.41
17.5	7.3	3.71	4.29	6.8	4.19	4.81	6.5	4.68	5.32	6.1	5.16	5.84	5.9	5.65	6.35	5.6	6.13	6.87	5.4	6.62	7.38
20.0	6.8	3.73	4.27	6.4	4.21	4.79	6.0	4.70	5.30	5.7	5.18	5.82	5.5	5.67	6.33	5.3	6.16	6.84	5.1	6.65	7.35
25.0	6.1	3.76	4.24	5.7	4.24	4.76	5.4	4.73	5.27	5.1	5.22	5.78	4.9	5.71	6.29	4.7	6.19	6.81	4.5	6.68	7.32
30.0	5.5	3.78	4.22	5.2	4.27	4.73	4.9	4.75	5.25	4.7	5.24	5.76	4.5	5.73	6.27	4.3	6.22	6.78	4.1	6.71	7.29
35.0	5.1	3.79	4.21	4.8	4.28	4.72	4.6	4.77	5.23	4.3	5.26	5.74	4.1	5.75	6.25	4.0	6.24	6.76	3.8	6.73	7.27
40.0	4.8	3.81	4.19	4.5	4.30	4.70	4.3	4.79	5.21	4.1	5.28	5.72	3.9	5.77	6.23	3.7	6.26	6.74	3.6	6.75	7.25
45.0	4.5	3.82	4.18	4.3	4.31	4.69	4.0	4.80	5.20	3.8	5.29	5.71	3.7	5.78	6.22	3.5	6.27	6.73	3.4	6.76	7.24
50.0	4.3	3.83	4.17	4.0	4.32	4.68	3.8	4.81	5.19	3.6	5.30	5.70	3.5	5.79	6.21	3.3	6.28	6.72	3.2	6.78	7.22
60.0	3.9	3.84	4.16	3.7	4.33	4.67	3.5	4.83	5.17	3.3	5.32	5.68	3.2	5.81	6.19	3.0	6.30	6.70	2.9	6.80	7.20
70.0	3.6	3.85	4.15	3.4	4.35	4.65	3.2	4.84	5.16	3.1	5.33	5.67	2.9	5.82	6.18	2.8	6.32	6.68	2.7	6.81	7.19
80.0	3.4	3.86	4.14	3.2	4.36	4.64	3.0	4.85	5.15	2.9	5.34	5.66	2.7	5.84	6.16	2.6	6.33	6.67	2.5	6.82	7.18
90.0	3.2	3.87	4.13	3.0	4.36	4.64	2.8	4.86	5.14	2.7	5.35	5.65	2.6	5.84	6.16	2.5	6.34	6.66	2.4	6.83	7.17
100.0	3.0	3.88	4.12	2.9	4.37	4.63	2.7	4.86	5.14	2.6	5.36	5.64	2.5	5.85	6.15	2.4	6.35	6.65	2.3	6.84	7.16

*Response rates expressed in percentages, with percentage variation (+ or −), low projection (−), and high projection (+).

Table 2-3. Statistical Variation: Margin of Error at 95 Percent Confidence Level*

Sample size (000)	7.50% % Var +/-	Low	High	8.00% % Var +/-	Low	High	8.50% % Var +/-	Low	High	9.00% % Var +/-	Low	High	9.50% % Var +/-	Low	High	10.00% % Var +/-	Low	High
1.0	21.8	5.87	9.13	21.0	6.32	9.68	20.3	6.77	10.23	19.7	7.23	10.77	19.1	7.68	11.32	18.6	8.14	11.86
2.5	13.8	6.47	8.53	13.3	6.94	9.06	12.9	7.41	9.59	12.5	7.88	10.12	12.1	8.35	10.65	11.8	8.82	11.18
5.0	9.7	6.77	8.23	9.4	7.25	8.75	9.1	7.73	9.27	8.8	8.21	9.79	8.6	8.69	10.31	8.3	9.17	10.83
7.5	7.9	6.90	8.10	7.7	7.39	8.61	7.4	7.87	9.13	7.2	8.35	9.65	7.0	8.84	10.16	6.8	9.32	10.68
10.0	6.9	6.98	8.02	6.6	7.47	8.53	6.4	7.95	9.05	6.2	8.44	9.56	6.0	8.93	10.07	5.9	9.41	10.59
12.5	6.2	7.04	7.96	5.9	7.52	8.48	5.8	8.01	8.99	5.6	8.50	9.50	5.4	8.99	10.01	5.3	9.47	10.53
15.0	5.6	7.08	7.92	5.4	7.57	8.43	5.3	8.05	8.95	5.1	8.54	9.46	4.9	9.03	9.97	4.8	9.52	10.48
17.5	5.2	7.11	7.89	5.0	7.60	8.40	4.9	8.09	8.91	4.7	8.58	9.42	4.6	9.07	9.93	4.4	9.56	10.44
20.0	4.9	7.13	7.87	4.7	7.62	8.38	4.5	8.11	8.89	4.4	8.60	9.40	4.3	9.09	9.91	4.2	9.58	10.42
25.0	4.4	7.17	7.83	4.2	7.66	8.34	4.1	8.15	8.85	3.9	8.65	9.35	3.8	9.14	9.86	3.7	9.63	10.37
30.0	4.0	7.20	7.80	3.8	7.69	8.31	3.7	8.18	8.82	3.6	8.68	9.32	3.5	9.17	9.83	3.4	9.66	10.34
35.0	3.7	7.22	7.78	3.6	7.72	8.28	3.4	8.21	8.79	3.3	8.70	9.30	3.2	9.19	9.81	3.1	9.69	10.31
40.0	3.4	7.24	7.76	3.3	7.73	8.27	3.2	8.23	8.77	3.1	8.72	9.28	3.0	9.21	9.79	2.9	9.71	10.29
45.0	3.2	7.26	7.74	3.1	7.75	8.25	3.0	8.24	8.76	2.9	8.74	9.26	2.9	9.23	9.77	2.8	9.72	10.28
50.0	3.1	7.27	7.73	3.0	7.76	8.24	2.9	8.26	8.74	2.8	8.75	9.25	2.7	9.24	9.76	2.6	9.74	10.26
60.0	2.8	7.29	7.71	2.7	7.78	8.22	2.6	8.28	8.72	2.5	8.77	9.23	2.5	9.27	9.73	2.4	9.76	10.24
70.0	2.6	7.30	7.70	2.5	7.80	8.20	2.4	8.29	8.71	2.4	8.79	9.21	2.3	9.28	9.72	2.2	9.78	10.22
80.0	2.4	7.32	7.68	2.3	7.81	8.19	2.3	8.31	8.69	2.2	8.80	9.20	2.1	9.30	9.70	2.1	9.79	10.21
90.0	2.3	7.33	7.67	2.2	7.82	8.18	2.1	8.32	8.68	2.1	8.81	9.19	2.0	9.31	9.69	2.0	9.80	10.20
100.0	2.2	7.34	7.66	2.1	7.83	8.17	2.0	8.33	8.67	2.0	8.82	9.18	1.9	9.32	9.68	1.9	9.81	10.19

*Response rates expressed in percentages, with percentage variation (+ or −), low projection (−), and high projection (+).

Table 2-4. Statistical Variation: Margin of Error at 99 Percent Confidence Level*

Sample size (000)	0.50% % Var. +/-	Low	High	1.00% % Var. +/-	Low	High	1.50% % Var. +/-	Low	High	2.00% % Var. +/-	Low	High	2.50% % Var. +/-	Low	High	3.00% % Var. +/-	Low	High	3.50% % Var. +/-	Low	High
1.0	99.7	.00	1.00	70.4	0.30	1.70	57.3	0.64	2.36	49.5	1.01	2.99	44.2	1.40	3.60	40.2	1.79	4.21	37.1	2.20	4.80
2.5	63.1	0.18	0.82	44.5	0.56	1.44	36.2	0.96	2.04	31.3	1.37	2.63	27.9	1.80	3.20	25.4	2.24	3.76	23.5	2.68	4.32
5.0	44.6	0.28	0.72	31.5	0.69	1.31	25.6	1.12	1.88	22.1	1.56	2.44	19.7	2.01	2.99	18.0	2.46	3.54	16.6	2.92	4.08
7.5	36.4	0.32	0.68	25.7	0.74	1.26	20.9	1.19	1.81	18.1	1.64	2.36	16.1	2.10	2.90	14.7	2.56	3.44	13.6	3.03	3.97
10.0	31.5	0.34	0.66	22.2	0.78	1.22	18.1	1.23	1.77	15.7	1.69	2.31	14.0	2.15	2.85	12.7	2.62	3.38	11.7	3.09	3.91
12.5	28.2	0.36	0.64	19.9	0.80	1.20	16.2	1.26	1.74	14.0	1.72	2.28	12.5	2.19	2.81	11.4	2.66	3.34	10.5	3.13	3.87
15.0	25.8	0.37	0.63	18.2	0.82	1.18	14.8	1.28	1.72	12.8	1.74	2.26	11.4	2.21	2.79	10.4	2.69	3.31	9.6	3.16	3.84
17.5	23.8	0.38	0.62	16.8	0.83	1.17	13.7	1.29	1.71	11.8	1.76	2.24	10.6	2.24	2.76	9.6	2.71	3.29	8.9	3.19	3.81
20.0	22.3	0.39	0.61	15.7	0.84	1.16	12.8	1.31	1.69	11.1	1.78	2.22	9.9	2.25	2.75	9.0	2.73	3.27	8.3	3.21	3.79
25.0	19.9	0.40	0.60	14.1	0.86	1.14	11.5	1.33	1.67	9.9	1.80	2.20	8.8	2.28	2.72	8.0	2.76	3.24	7.4	3.24	3.76
30.0	18.2	0.41	0.59	12.8	0.87	1.13	10.5	1.34	1.66	9.0	1.82	2.18	8.1	2.30	2.70	7.3	2.78	3.22	6.8	3.26	3.74
35.0	16.9	0.42	0.58	11.9	0.88	1.12	9.7	1.35	1.65	8.4	1.83	2.17	7.5	2.31	2.69	6.8	2.80	3.20	6.3	3.28	3.72
40.0	15.8	0.42	0.58	11.1	0.89	1.11	9.1	1.36	1.64	7.8	1.84	2.16	7.0	2.33	2.67	6.4	2.81	3.19	5.9	3.29	3.71
45.0	14.9	0.43	0.57	10.5	0.90	1.10	8.5	1.37	1.63	7.4	1.85	2.15	6.6	2.34	2.66	6.0	2.82	3.18	5.5	3.31	3.69
50.0	14.1	0.43	0.57	9.9	0.90	1.10	8.1	1.38	1.62	7.0	1.86	2.14	6.2	2.34	2.66	5.7	2.83	3.17	5.3	3.32	3.68
60.0	12.9	0.44	0.56	9.1	0.91	1.09	7.4	1.39	1.61	6.4	1.87	2.13	5.7	2.36	2.64	5.2	2.84	3.16	4.8	3.33	3.67
70.0	11.9	0.44	0.56	8.4	0.92	1.08	6.8	1.40	1.60	5.9	1.88	2.12	5.3	2.37	2.63	4.8	2.86	3.14	4.4	3.34	3.66
80.0	11.2	0.44	0.56	7.9	0.92	1.08	6.4	1.40	1.60	5.5	1.89	2.11	4.9	2.38	2.62	4.5	2.87	3.13	4.2	3.35	3.65
90.0	10.5	0.45	0.55	7.4	0.93	1.07	6.0	1.41	1.59	5.2	1.90	2.10	4.7	2.38	2.62	4.2	2.87	3.13	3.9	3.36	3.64
100.0	10.0	0.45	0.55	7.0	0.93	1.07	5.7	1.41	1.59	4.9	1.90	2.10	4.4	2.39	2.61	4.0	2.88	3.12	3.7	3.37	3.63

*Response rates expressed in percentages, with percentage variation (+ or −), low projection (−), and high projection (+).

47

Table 2-5. Statistical Variation: Margin of Error at 99 Percent Confidence Level*

Sample size (000)	4.00% % Var. +/-	Low	High	4.50% % Var. +/-	Low	High	5.00% % Var. +/-	Low	High	5.50% % Var. +/-	Low	High	6.00% % Var. +/-	Low	High	6.50% % Var. +/-	Low	High	7.00% % Var. +/-	Low	High
1.0	34.6	2.61	5.39	32.6	3.03	5.97	30.8	3.46	6.54	29.3	3.89	7.11	28.0	4.32	7.68	26.8	4.76	8.24	25.8	5.20	8.80
2.5	21.9	3.12	4.88	20.6	3.57	5.43	19.5	4.03	5.97	18.5	4.48	6.52	17.7	4.94	7.06	17.0	5.40	7.60	16.3	5.86	8.14
5.0	15.5	3.38	4.62	14.6	3.84	5.16	13.8	4.31	5.69	13.1	4.78	6.22	12.5	5.25	6.75	12.0	5.72	7.28	11.5	6.19	7.81
7.5	12.6	3.49	4.51	11.9	3.96	5.04	11.3	4.44	5.56	10.7	4.91	6.09	10.2	5.39	6.61	9.8	5.86	7.14	9.4	6.34	7.66
10.0	11.0	3.56	4.44	10.3	4.04	4.96	9.7	4.51	5.49	9.3	4.99	6.01	8.9	5.47	6.53	8.5	5.95	7.05	8.2	6.43	7.57
12.5	9.8	3.61	4.39	9.2	4.09	4.91	8.7	4.56	5.44	8.3	5.04	5.96	7.9	5.53	6.47	7.6	6.01	6.99	7.3	6.49	7.51
15.0	8.9	3.64	4.36	8.4	4.12	4.88	8.0	4.60	5.40	7.6	5.08	5.92	7.2	5.57	6.43	6.9	6.05	6.95	6.7	6.53	7.47
17.5	8.3	3.67	4.33	7.8	4.15	4.85	7.4	4.63	5.37	7.0	5.11	5.89	6.7	5.60	6.40	6.4	6.08	6.92	6.2	6.57	7.43
20.0	7.7	3.69	4.31	7.3	4.17	4.83	6.9	4.66	5.34	6.6	5.14	5.86	6.3	5.62	6.38	6.0	6.11	6.89	5.8	6.60	7.40
25.0	6.9	3.72	4.28	6.5	4.21	4.79	6.2	4.69	5.31	5.9	5.18	5.82	5.6	5.66	6.34	5.4	6.15	6.85	5.2	6.64	7.36
30.0	6.3	3.75	4.25	5.9	4.23	4.77	5.6	4.72	5.28	5.4	5.21	5.79	5.1	5.69	6.31	4.9	6.18	6.82	4.7	6.67	7.33
35.0	5.9	3.77	4.23	5.5	4.25	4.75	5.2	4.74	5.26	5.0	5.23	5.77	4.7	5.72	6.28	4.5	6.21	6.79	4.4	6.70	7.30
40.0	5.5	3.78	4.22	5.2	4.27	4.73	4.9	4.76	5.24	4.6	5.25	5.75	4.4	5.73	6.27	4.2	6.22	6.78	4.1	6.71	7.29
45.0	5.2	3.79	4.21	4.9	4.28	4.72	4.6	4.77	5.23	4.4	5.26	5.74	4.2	5.75	6.25	4.0	6.24	6.76	3.8	6.73	7.27
50.0	4.9	3.80	4.20	4.6	4.29	4.71	4.4	4.78	5.22	4.1	5.27	5.73	4.0	5.76	6.24	3.8	6.25	6.75	3.6	6.74	7.26
60.0	4.5	3.82	4.18	4.2	4.31	4.69	4.0	4.80	5.20	3.8	5.29	5.71	3.6	5.78	6.22	3.5	6.27	6.73	3.3	6.77	7.23
70.0	4.1	3.83	4.17	3.9	4.32	4.68	3.7	4.82	5.18	3.5	5.31	5.69	3.3	5.80	6.20	3.2	6.29	6.71	3.1	6.78	7.22
80.0	3.9	3.85	4.15	3.6	4.34	4.66	3.4	4.83	5.17	3.3	5.32	5.68	3.1	5.81	6.19	3.0	6.31	6.69	2.9	6.80	7.20
90.0	3.7	3.85	4.15	3.4	4.35	4.65	3.2	4.84	5.16	3.1	5.33	5.67	3.0	5.82	6.18	2.8	6.32	6.68	2.7	6.81	7.19
100.0	3.5	3.86	4.14	3.3	4.35	4.65	3.1	4.85	5.15	2.9	5.34	5.66	2.8	5.83	6.17	2.7	6.33	6.67	2.6	6.82	7.18

*Response rates expressed in percentages, with percentage variation (+ or −), low projection (−), and high projection (+).

Table 2-6. Statistical Variation: Margin of Error at 99 Percent Confidence Level*

Sample size (000)	7.50%			8.00%			8.50%			9.00%			9.50%			10.00%		
	% Var. +/-	Low	High	% Var. +/-	Low	High	% Var. +/-	Low	High	% Var. +/-	Low	High	% Var. +/-	Low	High	% Var. +/-	Low	High
1.0	24.8	5.64	9.36	24.0	6.08	9.92	23.2	6.53	10.47	22.5	6.98	11.02	21.8	7.43	11.57	21.2	7.88	12.12
2.5	15.7	6.32	8.68	15.2	6.79	9.21	14.7	7.25	9.75	14.2	7.72	10.28	13.8	8.19	10.81	13.4	8.66	11.34
5.0	11.1	6.67	8.33	10.7	7.14	8.86	10.4	7.62	9.38	10.1	8.10	9.90	9.8	8.57	10.43	9.5	9.05	10.95
7.5	9.1	6.82	8.18	8.8	7.30	8.70	8.5	7.78	9.22	8.2	8.26	9.74	8.0	8.74	10.26	7.7	9.23	10.77
10.0	7.9	6.91	8.09	7.6	7.39	8.61	7.3	7.88	9.12	7.1	8.36	9.64	6.9	8.84	10.16	6.7	9.33	10.67
12.5	7.0	6.97	8.03	6.8	7.46	8.54	6.6	7.94	9.06	6.4	8.43	9.57	6.2	8.91	10.09	6.0	9.40	10.60
15.0	6.4	7.02	7.98	6.2	7.50	8.50	6.0	7.99	9.01	5.8	8.48	9.52	5.6	8.96	10.04	5.5	9.45	10.55
17.5	5.9	7.05	7.95	5.7	7.54	8.46	5.5	8.03	8.97	5.4	8.52	9.48	5.2	9.00	10.00	5.1	9.49	10.51
20.0	5.6	7.08	7.92	5.4	7.57	8.43	5.2	8.06	8.94	5.0	8.55	9.45	4.9	9.04	9.96	4.7	9.53	10.47
25.0	5.0	7.13	7.87	4.8	7.62	8.38	4.6	8.11	8.89	4.5	8.60	9.40	4.4	9.09	9.91	4.2	9.58	10.42
30.0	4.5	7.16	7.84	4.4	7.65	8.35	4.2	8.14	8.86	4.1	8.63	9.37	4.0	9.12	9.88	3.9	9.61	10.39
35.0	4.2	7.19	7.81	4.1	7.68	8.32	3.9	8.17	8.83	3.8	8.66	9.34	3.7	9.15	9.85	3.6	9.64	10.36
40.0	3.9	7.21	7.79	3.8	7.70	8.30	3.7	8.19	8.81	3.6	8.68	9.32	3.5	9.17	9.83	3.4	9.66	10.34
45.0	3.7	7.22	7.78	3.6	7.71	8.29	3.5	8.21	8.79	3.4	8.70	9.30	3.3	9.19	9.81	3.2	9.68	10.32
50.0	3.5	7.24	7.76	3.4	7.73	8.27	3.3	8.22	8.78	3.2	8.71	9.29	3.1	9.21	9.79	3.0	9.70	10.30
60.0	3.2	7.26	7.74	3.1	7.75	8.25	3.0	8.25	8.75	2.9	8.74	9.26	2.8	9.23	9.77	2.7	9.73	10.27
70.0	3.0	7.28	7.72	2.9	7.77	8.23	2.8	8.26	8.74	2.7	8.76	9.24	2.6	9.25	9.75	2.5	9.75	10.25
80.0	2.8	7.29	7.71	2.7	7.79	8.21	2.6	8.28	8.72	2.5	8.77	9.23	2.4	9.27	9.73	2.4	9.76	10.24
90.0	2.6	7.30	7.70	2.5	7.80	8.20	2.4	8.29	8.71	2.4	8.79	9.21	2.3	9.28	9.72	2.2	9.78	10.22
100.0	2.5	7.31	7.69	2.4	7.81	8.19	2.3	8.30	8.70	2.2	8.80	9.20	2.2	9.29	9.71	2.1	9.79	10.21

*Response rates expressed in percentages, with percentage variation (+ or −), low projection (−), and high projection (+).

Table 2-7. Statistical Variation: Margin of Error at 90 Percent Confidence Level*

Sample size (000)	0.50% % Var. +/-	Low	High	1.00% % Var. +/-	Low	High	1.50% % Var. +/-	Low	High	2.00% % Var. +/-	Low	High	2.50% % Var. +/-	Low	High	3.00% % Var. +/-	Low	High	3.50% % Var. +/-	Low	High
1.0	73.4	0.13	0.87	51.8	0.48	1.52	42.2	0.87	2.13	36.4	1.27	2.73	32.5	1.69	3.31	29.6	2.11	3.89	27.3	2.54	4.46
2.5	46.4	0.27	0.73	32.7	0.67	1.33	26.7	1.10	1.90	23.0	1.54	2.46	20.5	1.99	3.01	18.7	2.44	3.56	17.3	2.90	4.10
5.0	32.8	0.34	0.66	23.1	0.77	1.23	18.9	1.22	1.78	16.3	1.67	2.33	14.5	2.14	2.86	13.2	2.60	3.40	12.2	3.07	3.93
7.5	26.8	0.37	0.63	18.9	0.81	1.19	15.4	1.27	1.73	13.3	1.73	2.27	11.9	2.20	2.80	10.8	2.68	3.32	10.0	3.15	3.85
10.0	23.2	0.38	0.62	16.4	0.84	1.16	13.3	1.30	1.70	11.5	1.77	2.23	10.3	2.24	2.76	9.4	2.72	3.28	8.6	3.20	3.80
12.5	20.8	0.40	0.60	14.6	0.85	1.15	11.9	1.32	1.68	10.3	1.79	2.21	9.2	2.27	2.73	8.4	2.75	3.25	7.7	3.23	3.77
15.0	18.9	0.41	0.59	13.4	0.87	1.13	10.9	1.34	1.66	9.4	1.81	2.19	8.4	2.29	2.71	7.6	2.77	3.23	7.1	3.25	3.75
17.5	17.5	0.41	0.59	12.4	0.88	1.12	10.1	1.35	1.65	8.7	1.83	2.17	7.8	2.31	2.69	7.1	2.79	3.21	6.5	3.27	3.73
20.0	16.4	0.42	0.58	11.6	0.88	1.12	9.4	1.36	1.64	8.1	1.84	2.16	7.3	2.32	2.68	6.6	2.80	3.20	6.1	3.29	3.71
25.0	14.7	0.43	0.57	10.4	0.90	1.10	8.4	1.37	1.63	7.3	1.85	2.15	6.5	2.34	2.66	5.9	2.82	3.18	5.5	3.31	3.69
30.0	13.4	0.43	0.57	9.4	0.91	1.09	7.7	1.38	1.62	6.6	1.87	2.13	5.9	2.35	2.65	5.4	2.84	3.16	5.0	3.33	3.67
35.0	12.4	0.44	0.56	8.7	0.91	1.09	7.1	1.39	1.61	6.2	1.88	2.12	5.5	2.36	2.64	5.0	2.85	3.15	4.6	3.34	3.66
40.0	11.6	0.44	0.56	8.2	0.92	1.08	6.7	1.40	1.60	5.8	1.88	2.12	5.1	2.37	2.63	4.7	2.86	3.14	4.3	3.35	3.65
45.0	10.9	0.45	0.55	7.7	0.92	1.08	6.3	1.41	1.59	5.4	1.89	2.11	4.8	2.38	2.62	4.4	2.87	3.13	4.1	3.36	3.64
50.0	10.4	0.45	0.55	7.3	0.93	1.07	6.0	1.41	1.59	5.1	1.90	2.10	4.6	2.39	2.61	4.2	2.87	3.13	3.9	3.36	3.64
60.0	9.5	0.45	0.55	6.7	0.93	1.07	5.4	1.42	1.58	4.7	1.91	2.09	4.2	2.40	2.60	3.8	2.89	3.11	3.5	3.38	3.62
70.0	8.8	0.46	0.54	6.2	0.94	1.06	5.0	1.42	1.58	4.4	1.91	2.09	3.9	2.40	2.60	3.5	2.89	3.11	3.3	3.39	3.61
80.0	8.2	0.46	0.54	5.8	0.94	1.06	4.7	1.43	1.57	4.1	1.92	2.08	3.6	2.41	2.59	3.3	2.90	3.10	3.1	3.39	3.61
90.0	7.7	0.46	0.54	5.5	0.95	1.05	4.4	1.43	1.57	3.8	1.92	2.08	3.4	2.41	2.59	3.1	2.91	3.09	2.9	3.40	3.60
100.0	7.3	0.46	0.54	5.2	0.95	1.05	4.2	1.44	1.56	3.6	1.93	2.07	3.2	2.42	2.58	3.0	2.91	3.09	2.7	3.40	3.60

*Response rates expressed in percentages, with percentage variation (+ or −), low projection (−), and high projection (+).

Table 2-8. Statistical Variation: Margin of Error at 90 Percent Confidence Level*

Sample size (000)	4.00% % Var +/-	Low	High	4.50% % Var +/-	Low	High	5.00% % Var +/-	Low	High	5.50% % Var +/-	Low	High	6.00% % Var +/-	Low	High	6.50% % Var +/-	Low	High	7.00% % Var +/-	Low	High
1.0	25.5	2.98	5.02	24.0	3.42	5.58	22.7	3.87	6.13	21.6	4.31	6.69	20.6	4.76	7.24	19.7	5.22	7.78	19.0	5.67	8.33
2.5	16.1	3.36	4.64	15.2	3.82	5.18	14.3	4.28	5.72	13.6	4.75	6.25	13.0	5.22	6.78	12.5	5.69	7.31	12.0	6.16	7.84
5.0	11.4	3.54	4.46	10.7	4.02	4.98	10.1	4.49	5.51	9.6	4.97	6.03	9.2	5.45	6.55	8.8	5.93	7.07	8.5	6.41	7.59
7.5	9.3	3.63	4.37	8.8	4.11	4.89	8.3	4.59	5.41	7.9	5.07	5.93	7.5	5.55	6.45	7.2	6.03	6.97	6.9	6.52	7.48
10.0	8.1	3.68	4.32	7.6	4.16	4.84	7.2	4.64	5.36	6.8	5.12	5.88	6.5	5.61	6.39	6.2	6.09	6.91	6.0	6.58	7.42
12.5	7.2	3.71	4.29	6.8	4.19	4.81	6.4	4.68	5.32	6.1	5.16	5.84	5.8	5.65	6.35	5.6	6.14	6.86	5.4	6.62	7.38
15.0	6.6	3.74	4.26	6.2	4.22	4.78	5.9	4.71	5.29	5.6	5.19	5.81	5.3	5.68	6.32	5.1	6.17	6.83	4.9	6.66	7.34
17.5	6.1	3.76	4.24	5.7	4.24	4.76	5.4	4.73	5.27	5.2	5.22	5.78	4.9	5.70	6.30	4.7	6.19	6.81	4.5	6.68	7.32
20.0	5.7	3.77	4.23	5.4	4.26	4.74	5.1	4.75	5.25	4.8	5.23	5.77	4.6	5.72	6.28	4.4	6.21	6.79	4.2	6.70	7.30
25.0	5.1	3.80	4.20	4.8	4.28	4.72	4.5	4.77	5.23	4.3	5.26	5.74	4.1	5.75	6.25	3.9	6.24	6.76	3.8	6.73	7.27
30.0	4.7	3.81	4.19	4.4	4.30	4.70	4.1	4.79	5.21	3.9	5.28	5.72	3.8	5.77	6.23	3.6	6.27	6.73	3.5	6.76	7.24
35.0	4.3	3.83	4.17	4.1	4.32	4.68	3.8	4.81	5.19	3.6	5.30	5.70	3.5	5.79	6.21	3.3	6.28	6.72	3.2	6.78	7.22
40.0	4.0	3.84	4.16	3.8	4.33	4.67	3.6	4.82	5.18	3.4	5.31	5.69	3.3	5.80	6.20	3.1	6.30	6.70	3.0	6.79	7.21
45.0	3.8	3.85	4.15	3.6	4.34	4.66	3.4	4.83	5.17	3.2	5.32	5.68	3.1	5.82	6.18	2.9	6.31	6.69	2.8	6.80	7.20
50.0	3.6	3.86	4.14	3.4	4.35	4.65	3.2	4.84	5.16	3.0	5.33	5.67	2.9	5.83	6.17	2.8	6.32	6.68	2.7	6.81	7.19
60.0	3.3	3.87	4.13	3.1	4.36	4.64	2.9	4.85	5.15	2.8	5.35	5.65	2.7	5.84	6.16	2.5	6.33	6.67	2.4	6.83	7.17
70.0	3.0	3.88	4.12	2.9	4.37	4.63	2.7	4.86	5.14	2.6	5.36	5.64	2.5	5.85	6.15	2.4	6.35	6.65	2.3	6.84	7.16
80.0	2.8	3.89	4.11	2.7	4.38	4.62	2.5	4.87	5.13	2.4	5.37	5.63	2.3	5.86	6.14	2.2	6.36	6.64	2.1	6.85	7.15
90.0	2.7	3.89	4.11	2.5	4.39	4.61	2.4	4.88	5.12	2.3	5.37	5.63	2.2	5.87	6.13	2.1	6.36	6.64	2.0	6.86	7.14
100.0	2.5	3.90	4.10	2.4	4.39	4.61	2.3	4.89	5.11	2.2	5.38	5.62	2.1	5.88	6.12	2.0	6.37	6.63	1.9	6.87	7.13

*Response rates expressed in percentages, with percentage variation (+ or −), low projection (−), and high projection (+).

Table 2-9. Statistical Variation: Margin of Error at 90 Percent Confidence Level*

Sample size (000)	7.50% % Var. +/-	7.50% Low	7.50% High	8.00% % Var. +/-	8.00% Low	8.00% High	8.50% % Var. +/-	8.50% Low	8.50% High	9.00% % Var. +/-	9.00% Low	9.00% High	9.50% % Var. +/-	9.50% Low	9.50% High	10.00% % Var. +/-	10.00% Low	10.00% High
1.0	18.3	6.13	8.87	17.6	6.59	9.41	17.1	7.05	9.95	16.5	7.51	10.49	16.1	7.97	11.03	15.6	8.44	11.56
2.5	11.6	6.63	8.37	11.2	7.11	8.89	10.8	7.58	9.42	10.5	8.06	9.94	10.2	8.54	10.46	9.9	9.01	10.99
5.0	8.2	6.89	8.11	7.9	7.37	8.63	7.6	7.85	9.15	7.4	8.33	9.67	7.2	8.82	10.18	7.0	9.30	10.70
7.5	6.7	7.00	8.00	6.4	7.48	8.52	6.2	7.97	9.03	6.0	8.46	9.54	5.9	8.94	10.06	5.7	9.43	10.57
10.0	5.8	7.07	7.93	5.6	7.55	8.45	5.4	8.04	8.96	5.2	8.53	9.47	5.1	9.02	9.98	4.9	9.51	10.49
12.5	5.2	7.11	7.89	5.0	7.60	8.40	4.8	8.09	8.91	4.7	8.58	9.42	4.5	9.07	9.93	4.4	9.56	10.44
15.0	4.7	7.15	7.85	4.6	7.64	8.36	4.4	8.13	8.87	4.3	8.62	9.38	4.1	9.11	9.89	4.0	9.60	10.40
17.5	4.4	7.17	7.83	4.2	7.66	8.34	4.1	8.15	8.85	4.0	8.64	9.36	3.8	9.14	9.86	3.7	9.63	10.37
20.0	4.1	7.19	7.81	3.9	7.68	8.32	3.8	8.18	8.82	3.7	8.67	9.33	3.6	9.16	9.84	3.5	9.65	10.35
25.0	3.7	7.23	7.77	3.5	7.72	8.28	3.4	8.21	8.79	3.3	8.70	9.30	3.2	9.19	9.81	3.1	9.69	10.31
30.0	3.3	7.25	7.75	3.2	7.74	8.26	3.1	8.24	8.76	3.0	8.73	9.27	2.9	9.22	9.78	2.8	9.72	10.28
35.0	3.1	7.27	7.73	3.0	7.76	8.24	2.9	8.25	8.75	2.8	8.75	9.25	2.7	9.24	9.76	2.6	9.74	10.26
40.0	2.9	7.28	7.72	2.8	7.78	8.22	2.7	8.27	8.73	2.6	8.76	9.24	2.5	9.26	9.74	2.5	9.75	10.25
45.0	2.7	7.30	7.70	2.6	7.79	8.21	2.5	8.28	8.72	2.5	8.78	9.22	2.4	9.27	9.73	2.3	9.77	10.23
50.0	2.6	7.31	7.69	2.5	7.80	8.20	2.4	8.29	8.71	2.3	8.79	9.21	2.3	9.28	9.72	2.2	9.78	10.22
60.0	2.4	7.32	7.68	2.3	7.82	8.18	2.2	8.31	8.69	2.1	8.81	9.19	2.1	9.30	9.70	2.0	9.80	10.20
70.0	2.2	7.34	7.66	2.1	7.83	8.17	2.0	8.33	8.67	2.0	8.82	9.18	1.9	9.32	9.68	1.9	9.81	10.19
80.0	2.0	7.35	7.65	2.0	7.84	8.16	1.9	8.34	8.66	1.8	8.83	9.17	1.8	9.33	9.67	1.7	9.83	10.17
90.0	1.9	7.36	7.64	1.9	7.85	8.15	1.8	8.35	8.65	1.7	8.84	9.16	1.7	9.34	9.66	1.6	9.84	10.16
100.0	1.8	7.36	7.64	1.8	7.86	8.14	1.7	8.35	8.65	1.7	8.85	9.15	1.6	9.35	9.65	1.6	9.84	10.16

*Response rates expressed in percentages, with percentage variation (+ or −), low projection (−), and high projection (+).

How Probability Tables Work

For example, if you mailed 5000 pieces and achieved a 2 percent response rate, you can predict a future response rate if you replicate the test *exactly*. Now refer to Table 2-1, which has a 95 percent confidence level. In the column for the 2 percent response rate on the line for a 5000 sample you will see a percentage variation of 19.4 percent in the "% Var." column. That means if you replicate the test exactly, you can expect to achieve a 2 percent response rate, plus or minus 19.4 percent, 95 times out of 100 replications. (There is the statistical probability that 5 times out of 100 replications you will *not* achieve that response rate plus or minus 19.4 percent. However, 95 times out of 100 are pretty good odds.) Then, looking in the "Low" column, you will see 1.61 percent. That projection is the low end of the range, or 2 percent less 19.4 percent. Looking in the "High" column, you will see 2.39 percent, which represents 2 percent plus 19.4 percent, the high end of the range. In other words, if your test mailing was one of 5000 pieces and it achieved a 2 percent response, you can expect to achieve a rollout response as low as 1.61 percent and as high as 2.39 percent, or somewhere in between. Your confidence (or odds) of attaining that result is 95 times out of 100.

Now, for the moment assume that a 95 percent confidence level isn't good enough. Refer to Table 2-4, which has a 99 percent confidence level, and you will see that the margin of error has changed to 22.1 percent. The response rate can now be projected in a range from 1.56 percent to 2.44 percent, 99 times out of 100, if the test is replicated exactly. While the differences in the two response rate ranges may seem small at first glance, it is important to note the difference between the margins of error for a 95 percent confidence level and for a 99 percent confidence level. Note that the former is 19.4 percent and the latter is 22.1 percent. There is a 14 percent differential between the two, which can be significant in some cases.

Let's complete our example now with a look at the 90 percent confidence level using the same example of a 5000-piece mailing and a 2 percent response rate (Table 2-7). In this case, the margin of error is 16.3 percent, and the range of the response rate will fall between 1.67 percent and 2.33 percent. While the projected response rate range is tighter, the confidence is not as great, for that response rate range can be expected only 90 times out of 100 — not quite as good as a 95 percent confidence level and certainly not as good as a 99 percent confidence level.

After examining the tables in some detail, you will see a pattern emerge that helps to clarify the concepts of margin of error and confidence in the projections. Simply stated, the pattern is that confidence decreases as sample sizes and response rates decrease. Conversely, confidence will increase as response rates increase and as sample sizes increase. Putting it another way, if you expect a relatively low response rate, be sure to use a sampling large enough to enable you to have confidence in the results. Otherwise, you may have a test that cannot be projected to a satisfactory degree of acceptance.

Using Probability Tables in Planning a Mailing

Let's assume you are planning a test mailing that will ultimately lead to a large-scale rollout. You wish to have results that will give you a response rate plus or minus 10 percent, and you decide that you wish to have a confidence level of 95 percent. Finally, you anticipate a response of 3 percent. (Either your product P&L [profit and loss] requires a 3 percent response rate or you may have some prior experience that leads you to that conclusion.) Now refer to the 3 percent column in Table 2-1. By scanning down the column, you will see that a 10 percent margin error is possible with a mailing of 12,500 pieces, and a replication of that test projects a yield of between 2.7 percent and 3.3 percent. So a 12,500 mailing will be a "safe" test within the parameters you have set. A "safer" test would be 15,000 pieces, which has a 9.1 percent margin of error.

After reviewing the 95 percent tables further, you will see that you can use a smaller test sample if your anticipated response rate is higher—for example, a 4 percent response rate would require a mailing of only 10,000 pieces to fall within the ±10 percent margin of error parameter (Table 2-2). However, a lower anticipated response rate—for example, 1 percent—would require a much higher test-mailing quantity (40,000 pieces for a 1 percent response rate) to have validity within your parameters (Table 2-1).

The decisions you make before your test mailing are quite important because all your rollout efforts can be predicted on a test. Therefore, it's a good idea to err on the conservative side when constructing a test. Once you have conducted a test, it's impossible to go back and change vital factors.

Using Probability Tables in Evaluating a Mailing

Having accomplished a test mailing, you can then evaluate the results in terms of a projection. Let's assume in this case that you mailed 10,000 pieces and achieved a response rate of 2.5 percent. Table 2-10 shows what you can read out of Tables 2-7, 2-1, and 2-4, in that order.

As discussed previously, the margin of error is less for a lower confidence level and greater for a higher confidence level. In this example, if you are satisfied with a confidence level of 90% (that is, 9 times out of 10), then you can plan on a rollout response of between 2.24 percent and 2.76 percent. But if you want to be more certain, look at the 99% confidence level (99 times out of 100), and you will see that you can then expect a wider range in your rollout response. How do these different possibilities work with other factors in your plans? If your product P&L is very tightly constructed, it may be advisable to try the more conservative projected response rate just to be sure in the balance of your planning. If you have some latitude, however, then a less conservative approach may be appropriate.

Table 2-10. Differences in Confidence Levels

	Confidence level, %	Margin of error, %	Projected low response, %	Projected high response, %
Table 2-7	90	10.3	2.24	2.76
Table 2-1	95	12.2	2.19	2.81
Table 2-4	99	14.0	2.15	2.85

Construction of Probability Tables

For those who are interested, the probability tables use a standard statistical formula for large samples. Using certain factors, we can determine the margin of error as follows:

Let E = Margin of error (expressed as a decimal variable—plus or minus—to be added or subtracted from the response rate)

r = response rate (expressed as a decimal)

n = sample size

S = standard deviation

The formula for margin of error is as follows:

$$E = \sqrt{\frac{(r)(1 - r)}{n}} \quad (S)$$

Here is an example of the formula in use to determine the margin of error for a mailing that has been accomplished, using a 95 percent confidence level:

Let r = 5% (response rate)

n = 10,000 (quantity mailed)

S = 1.96 (the standard deviation for a 95% confidence level)

Then:

$$E = \sqrt{\frac{(0.05)(1 - 0.05)}{10,000}} \quad (1.96)$$

$$E = \sqrt{\frac{(0.05)(0.95)}{10,000}} \quad (1.96)$$

$$E = \sqrt{\frac{0.475}{10,000}} \quad (1.96)$$

$$E = \sqrt{0.0000048} \quad (1.96)$$

$$E = 0.0021794 \quad (1.96)$$

$$E = 0.0042717$$

The margin of error, as shown above, is then applied to the response rate, plus or minus. Thus, in decimal form:

$$0.05 + 0.0042717 = 0.0542717, \text{ or } 5.43\% \text{ (rounded)}$$

$$0.05 - 0.0042717 = 0.0457283, \text{ or } 4.57\% \text{ (rounded)}$$

When expressed as a percentage variation, the margin of error is divided by the response rate. Using the above example:

0.0042717/.05 = 0.085434, or 8.5% (rounded)

The probability tables that have been constructed are intended to eliminate the intermediate steps, as demonstrated above, and show the results in immediately usable form. The important points are the margin of error relative to the response rate (percentage variation) and the result of that variation (response rate range, from low to high).

To determine the sample size for a given margin of error, the above formula is converted to the following:

$$n = \frac{(r)(1 - r)(S)^2}{E^2}$$

Using factors similar to our example above—a 5 percent anticipated response rate and a desired margin of error of 10 percent—the following is the solution:

$$n = \frac{(0.05)(1 - 0.05)(1.96)^2}{0.005^2}$$

$$n = \frac{(0.05)(0.95)(3.8416)}{0.000025}$$

$$n = \frac{0.182476}{0.000025}$$

$$n = 7299$$

A mailing quantity of 7299 pieces with a response rate of 5 percent will be projectable plus or minus 10 percent.

For those interested, the tables were constructed on a personal computer, using Lotus 1-2-3. The Lotus formula for determining the margin of error, expressed as a percentage, is as follows:

{@SQRT[E$66*(1 − E$66)/($B7*1000)]}*196/E$66

(E$66 and $B7 are cell addresses with constants.)

TESTING CAUTIONS

Theoretically, statistical probability tables are absolutely reliable, and after testing the proper sample and getting acceptable results, a company should be able to roll out any number of pieces it wishes. In practice, a favorable test result is usually followed by a test extension—a cautious remailing to a larger quantity—before committing a company's entire program to a new mailing package, offer, or audience. There are several theories about this.

Walter Marshall, who is an accomplished mathematician as well as a prominent direct marketing consultant, has pointed out that direct marketing is not a matter of chance but a business that involves a series of separate factors virtually impossible to quantify. If you send out 1000 pieces, how many will be addressed correctly, how many may get lost in the post office, how many will be opened, how many will be seen? How many people will be interested, how many will want to respond affirmatively or negatively, and how many will overcome inertia and respond at all? Each step may involve its own random, and unquantifiable, element of chance.

Also, in theory, if a 5 percent response to a sample would not produce a valid sample, but a 95 percent response would, then wouldn't it be fair to say that the fact that 95 percent of the sample ignored your offer is as significant as the fact that 5 percent accepted it? Yet direct marketers always base their decisions on the probability factors relating to the affirmative decision.

Marshall's most telling argument is the empirical one relating to actual business practice. If you test 20,000 pieces and get what is supposed to be a statistically valid answer, would you then risk your money to send out a mailing of 10 million pieces using the same package? I know of no direct marketers who would answer in the affirmative. We would schedule test extensions: first 250,000 names, then a few million, and finally the balance of the names. Yet testing theory should give us the confidence to go right to the 10 million.

I received a letter from a California marketer who suggested that the reason for this lack of confidence is that we, as an industry, "lack faith in the competence or honesty of the list broker or list source...that everyone has at least one horror story of salted lists or computer foul-ups." The same writer suggests that mailers should make it a practice always to physically inspect a mailing list in its Cheshire or other printed format. "That way, when they think they are mailing 10,000 needlepoint catalogs to sewing hobbyists they will learn before, not after, the mail is dropped that what they really had was 10,000 car dealers." This writer may or may not be correct. More probably, the root of the dilemma lies in the fact that we are dealing in a fluid environment. A mailing sent out even a few months after a test might encounter changed attitudes, economic circumstances, or competitive activity, not to mention weather, news events, and other influences on direct marketing results.

Grid Testing

The quantity used for each test being conducted, whether of copy or lists, is called a "test cell," and each test cell is assigned its own key number. If five new lists were being tested, you would have five test cells. If other mail were being sent to previously tested groups of names, each separately keyed group would be called a "rollout cell" or an "extension cell."

Often a variety of tests are being conducted simultaneously—perhaps new concepts, offer variations, and new lists. If the combination of anticipated response rate and required error limit produces large mailing samples, and if there are many variables to be tested, the test quantities can be enormous. In the interest of minimizing downside risk, an alternative method is needed, and that alternative is grid testing.

Under the grid method, each test cell is still the minimum quantity indicated in the discussion of sample size earlier in this chapter. The difference is that each cell may represent more than one variable, as long as the total number of cells for each variable meets the minimum sample-size test.

Let's say we have three copy tests and three list tests, and that a sample size of 60,000 was indicated. That would ordinarily require a mailing quantity of 540,000 pieces—nine cells of 60,000 names each. But if you structure the test as shown in Table 2-11, you can cut the total mailing quantity, and therefore the total test investment, by two-thirds.

Note that the total mailing required is only 180,000, yet there is a 60,000 quantity against each variable being tested. The results are read against the totals for each variable, not against each cell. Any observation of results against each individual cell would be futile because of the wide error limit for the smaller quantity; only the totals can be read.

For more substantial testing programs, greater economies can be achieved by not testing every variable in every list. If every variable is tested on one list and every variable is tested against a control somewhere in the grid, results can be interpolated.

Economies in Direct-Mail Testing

The grid test is one way to lower the investment in testing. There are others which depend on what is being tested.

List tests require only changes in the key number. Offer tests should require changes only in those areas where the offer appears. Substantial production economies can be effected by omitting the offer, if it isn't absolutely necessary, from the four-color brochure or other printed elements. A premium versus no-premium test can be accomplished by keeping the entire package the same and only adding a buck slip (a slip of paper stating the offer), changing the reply device, and adding a paragraph to the letter. It isn't necessary to do an entire new package for every variation.

When CBS Publishing introduced a new gardening magazine, there were several fundamental approaches that had to be tried: a conventional announcement package, a how-to positioning for beginners, and an "exotic-plants" positioning for advanced gardeners. This was accomplished very inexpensively by designing an envelope with a full-back cellophane window and a circular in which each appeal was centered on a different section. The brochure was designed so it could be folded with a different appeal facing out, visible through the window. Only one press run of the brochure was required, effecting substantial economies; only the folding had to be varied.

Table 2-11. An Example of Grid Testing

Lists copy	A	B	C	Total
X	20,000	20,000	20,000	60,000
Y	20,000	20,000	20,000	60,000
Z	20,000	20,000	20,000	60,000
Total	60,000	60,000	60,000	180,000

For Weight Watchers, I developed a package that varied only in the response card, part of which showed through a window of the outer envelope face, and in one insert. Everything else remained the same, except for the opening paragraph of the letter. A minimal production budget permitted two very different appeals to be tested—one dramatizing the social aspect of weight-reduction groups, the other the eating pleasure of the varied menus.

List Sampling

In testing a mailing list, it is essential that the names tested be representative of the entire list. Nth-name samples are the most accurate way of doing this. This system will provide a true cross section of the entire list, if it is supplied correctly by the list owner. Any short cuts, such as taking a single geographic area or a fifth zip-code digit, add a considerable measure of risk.

PRINT-MEDIA TESTING

Where direct-mail testing opportunities are limited only by imagination and economics, newspaper and magazine testing is limited by the production capabilities of the publications themselves.

There are two principal objectives of testing in magazine space: One is to test a magazine as a medium; the other is to test alternative copy, offers, or products.

Testing a New Magazine

Often downside risk can be minimized further by using only one portion of a magazine instead of the entire publication. Some magazines permit you to buy one-half of the circulation, across the board on a national basis. Many magazines will permit you to buy one or more sections of the country. Either plan will enable you to run an advertisement and discover a magazine's response rate without having to buy the entire circulation. Adjustments must be made, in such tests, for seasonal or position variations. Often regional insertions are placed in the back of a magazine, where response would be materially less than the same ad placed nationally.

As little as $5000 can test full-page ads in the largest magazines, such as *Time* and *TV Guide,* in small regional or city editions. As little as a few hundred dollars can test small-space advertisements in any of hundreds of magazines.

The small-budget advertiser can start with a fractional unit and work up, little by little, to larger sizes and even spectacular units. Some of the largest firms in the direct marketing business started in just this way. The only difference between them and advertisers with more substantial budgets and wider-reaching test programs is the element of time. The larger firms compress the testing experience and step-by-step building of smaller advertisers into one season, enabling them to establish a multimillion-dollar business quickly instead of building it slowly.

A-B Split-Run Testing

There is no more accurate way to determine which magazine advertisement is the best than split-run testing. Whether you are testing an offer, a copy approach, or one product or business against another, this testing approach will always give you a clear and meaningful basis for decision making.

SRDS defines split run this way: "A technique to measure the relative strength of different copy approaches...for example, by means of coupon returns from equally divided portions of a specific edition or issue of a publication's circulation, each identical except for the varying copy approaches." There are more than fifty magazines that offer split-run testing. Some require that a full page be purchased for the test; others offer A-B split runs on fractional units. The SRDS listing of U.S. and international consumer magazines with split-run advertising is as follows:

Allstate Motor Club RV Park & Campground Directory
American Legion Magazine
Athlon Sports Communications Inc.

Baby Talk
Bicycling
Bon Appétit
Bride's
Business Women Leadership Media

Capper's
Car Craft
Condé Nast Traveler

Down East

Elks Magazine, The
Esquire
Expecting

Family
Family Circle
Family Handyman
Fishing World
Fortune
4 Wheel & Off-Road
Four Wheeler

Gentlemen's Quarterly
Glamour
Good Housekeeping
Grit
Guide
Guns & Ammo

Harrowsmith Country Life
Health
Hot Rod

Ladies' Home Journal

Manhattan, Inc.
McCall's
Men's Health
Metropolitan Home
Modern Maturity
Money
Mother Earth News
Motor Trend

National Enquirer
National Lampoon
National Speed Sport News
New Woman
New Yorker, The
Newsweek
New York Woman

Off Duty
Omni
1,001 Home Ideas
Organic Gardening
Our Sunday Visitor

Parents
Penthouse
People Weekly
Petersen Magazine Network
Petersen's Photographic Magazine
Playboy
Practical Homeowner
Prevention

Reader's Digest
Redbook Magazine

Savvy Woman
Self

Ski

Sport

Sports Illustrated

Superman Group

Teen

TV Guide

U.S. News & World Report

USAir Magazine

Vermont Magazine

Vista

Weight Watchers Magazine

Woman's Day

Workbasket

Yankee

YM

Young American

Your Prom

To run a test, you simply prepare two different versions of your advertisement, each with a different key number, and place both of them in the publication as a split insertion on the same date. Usually some small extra fee is charged.

The publication is probably printed "two-up" on one or more enormous web or rotogravure presses. Either the magazines are bound separately and the streams of finished magazines merged, or a double magazine comes off the press and is sheared in half after binding.

In either case, every second magazine has a different advertisement. Usually, looking through a pile of magazines on a newsstand, you can see ad A in one magazine, B in the next, A in the next, and so forth. As these magazines are distributed throughout the country to magazine distributors or mailed out to subscribers in this same fashion, there is an absolutely perfect sampling of the whole—50 percent for one, 50 percent for the other. The validity of this type of test is virtually unchallenged, provided the difference between test results is large enough.

What result size is "large enough" to be meaningful is a controversial question. One commonly used guide for determining statistical significance in split-run print advertising involves "significance factors"—the percentage difference between two alternatives at varying total number of responses. Although at least one very well known company relies on this type of table, many statisticians appear to be at a loss to identify the underlying mathematical formula.

The chart in Table 2-12 is widely used and simple to understand. Just combine the total response to the two versions of your ad, usually the control and the variation, and you'll have the total response figure. Then divide the numbers for each split to produce the percentage of the total response (not the response rate). Look up the total response figure in the left-hand column, and refer to the significance figure in the right-hand column.

If your test result, expressed as a percentage of total response, is greater than the figure listed, then you have a significant improvement. The test ad should become your control ad in the future. If the test result is less, and if the control figure is also not greater than the significance figure, then you have a tie, and you can use the new advertisement or not based on nonstatistical considerations, such as its effect on the long-term image of your product and company. Some companies with extensive schedules will elect to use such tie ads to alternate with other ads and thus avoid the "fatigue" factor.

Table 2-12. Significance Factor in
Split-Run Advertising (95 Percent
Confidence Level)

Total (both sides)	Factor
50	64.24
100	60.00
200	57.07
300	55.77
400	55.00
500	54.47
1,000	53.16
1,500	52.56
2,000	52.23
3,000	51.83
4,000	51.58
5,000	51.41
10,000	51.00
20,000	50.71
30,000	50.58
40,000	50.50
50,000	50.45
100,000	50.31

Multiple Split-Run Testing

The A-B split provides a reliable comparison of one advertisement against another in a given publication. But what happens when there are a half-dozen valid concepts to be tested in magazines?

Multiple split-run testing, sometimes called "telescopic testing," is designed to solve this problem. It combines the A-B split, just described, with the availability of regional editions of magazines. If a magazine has four regional editions, as *House & Garden* does, you can test four different ads against your control ad. For example, see Table 2-13.

The results of such a test might be as shown in Table 2-14. The helter-skelter of result figures can be quickly made meaningful by either (1) calculating the "lift factor" for each insertion, independently of the results of the control ad A; or (2) by adjusting the ad A results to a national average, calculating the adjustment against all the other numbers, and restating the figures accordingly.

Either of these techniques compensates for geographic or distribution variations and enables you to read the results correctly. Similarly, the various adver-

Table 2-13. *House & Garden* Geographic Editions

West	Ad A versus ad B
South	Ad A versus ad C
Northeast corridor	Ad A versus ad D
Midwest	Ad A versus ad E

Table 2-14. *House & Garden* Test Results

Edition	Control	Response	Variation	Response
West	Ad A	351	Ad B	416
South	Ad A	297	Ad C	376
Northeast corridor	Ad A	328	Ad D	302
Midwest	Ad A	345	Ad E	420

Table 2-15. Hypothetical *House & Garden* Split-Run Test

Edition	Adjusted cost*	Control	Number	CPR	Test	Number	CPR	Lift %
West	$1,836	A	351	$2.62	B	416	$2.21	18
South	2,856	A	297	4.81	C	376	3.80	26
Northeast corridor	3,060	A	328	4.66	D	302	5.07	(7)
Midwest	2,448	A	345	3.55	E	420	2.91	21
Total	$10,228		1,321	$3.86		1,514	$3.37	

*Excluding $1800 split-run charge.

tisements can be indexed, with the control ad designated 100. Table 2-15 shows an example of an adjusted result report including all the preceding factors and with the figures adjusted against the control. Note that the greatest lift resulted from ad C, although ads B and E had lower CPR figures because of regional variation.

Referring to the significance chart in Table 2-12, we see that at this level of total response we need only a 54 percent factor for the new ad to be declared a valid winner. Ads B, C, and E all are valid winners. Statistically, ad D is also equivalent to ad A, though it did not beat it.

Some magazines have so many editions—*TV Guide* with 107 local editions or *Time* with 34 metropolitan editions, for instance—that it is possible for the sample sizes to get too small to be meaningful. In such cases the practice has been to cluster the editions by regional demographics, with each cluster containing a mix of urban, rural, eastern, and western areas of the country.

Flip-Flop Testing

Unfortunately, many magazines don't have split-run testing facilities, particularly those whose circulation is not large enough to enable them to be printed two-up. Very few newspapers offer this service, although most magazine sections of Sunday papers do.

The best available technique is "flip-flop testing," and even this requires geographic editions. *The Wall Street Journal* is sold in four editions but offers seventeen different plants, and each plant can carry separate copy. A local newspaper might have a city and a suburban edition.

In this kind of testing you run ad A in one edition and ad B in the other, on the same day. Then, a week or two later, you reverse the ads, running B where A ran and vice versa. By running two ads and reading the combined total response rates instead of individual ones, you cause the distortion factors to offset each other. One edition or region might be stronger than another. The ad that runs the first time will probably do better than the second ad in each section because it has "creamed" the market somewhat. This qualification applies to both ads and both editions, however. The total response rate of ad A compared with ad B should be valid.

Full-Page Bind-Ins

There are times when the best testing medium may be full-page bind-in cards, although they are too costly for most advertisers. These are preprinted by the advertiser and supplied to the publication for insertion in the magazine. Usually they are "perfect-bound" rather than saddle-stitched. The unit can include a perforated reply card, gummed areas for tokens or stamps, numbers for sweepstakes, pop-ups, or a variety of other techniques not possible with a conventional soft-space unit.

As the cards are preprinted and premixed by your own printer, virtually any number of variations can be tested simultaneously. This is an excellent technique for major advertisers whose potential investments are so large that six, eight, or twelve concepts must be tested before a major campaign is launched.

The unit is atypical in that the ad must be designed to utilize both sides of the bound-in card. Some advertisers have gotten around this requirement by placing a separate advertisement for a different product on the reverse side of the page. When this is done, one side of the reply card for one ad appears on the other side. This could be confusing, but my experience indicates that the format is successful.

If you are selecting a publication for this type of testing, you'll want to pick one that is sold mostly by subscription rather than newsstand. Though your space rates are based on actual circulation, you still have to print enough card units for the magazine's total press run, including unsold newsstand copies. Newsstand-sold magazines have a much greater waste factor than those sold mostly by subscription.

Bound-in Reply Cards

A more common format for major advertisers is the combination of a single- or double-page advertisement with a bound-in reply card, usually called an "insert card." While this is a very successful unit, producing four times the result of a page alone at an average cost increase only two or three times higher, it does have limitations as a test vehicle.

With few exceptions, there is no way to match cards to an alternative A-B split. If the card is to match the page, it is impossible to be sure that the cards are inserted in synchronization with the page. One error and the entire test can be ruined.

One solution is to confine the test to the card alone, without changing the advertisement for the page. This is really only suitable for testing offers or minor proposition variations. If it does not appear on the page, several different offers can be featured on the card itself. For instance it is easy to test one card with a premium featured and another with no premium at all, to determine the lift factor of the premium. Or you can try coupon wording modifications on the reply card, simplified commitment copy, postage and handling costs included in the price, the availability of a trade-up option, or quality-improvement tests such as requiring respondents to an inquiry ad to provide their own stamp as opposed to a business reply card paid by the advertiser.

Another way to do split testing when insert cards are involved is to use a transfer code. This is a useful device when several basic concepts are being tested for a proposition, which is usually only successful when an insert card is used. In this case, the insert card is constant and the ads change, with as many variations as A-B splitting and regional editions permit.

One version of the transfer code is to offer a choice of book bindings or other options, asking respondents to use a designated letter for one color and a different letter for the other. The letters change not only for the color but also for the different advertisement. In one ad, the customer is asked to select A for a black binding and B for a brown one. In the other, C represents black while D represents brown. The customer is asked to place the letter in a designated space on the insert card to indicate the choice. Better still, if you have product order numbers, put an A after each number on ad A, a B after those in ad B, and so on. These letters are later translated into key numbers, and the results are analyzed as with any other split run.

Where a choice is not available, a premium can be used instead. The respondent can be asked to place a designated letter on the card for a free poster, for example.

The most direct and straightforward approach of all seems to work as well as the others, but it might depend on the type of product being offered. This is a simple statement on the printed page which says "To help us evaluate our advertising, please put this letter in the space indicated on the reply card."

Deliberate Underspacing

If a proposition usually works in a page but as a half page doesn't do well, we say it is "underspaced." The same consideration applies to a format as well as space size. If a proposition works best with an insert card or a bound-in multipage unit, and we run a simple black-and-white page instead, we have also "underspaced" the ad.

Deliberate underspacing is one way that an advertiser with a modest budget can enjoy the benefits of multiple testing. All that is needed is to use regional editions and A-B splits for a smaller unit than would otherwise be profitable, knowing in advance that the overall results will be disappointing. If the primary objective is to test various copy appeals, for instance, and the basic proposition has already been proved, it may be less expensive to use soft-space black-and-white pages than to make the space, printing, and production investment of card testing. The reduced responses may be less of a price to pay than the multiple testing costs, but the relative pulling power of the different appeals will still be meaningful. One caution, though: Don't expect black-and-white ads to demonstrate the relative effectiveness of advertising appeals where the visual element is critical and must be in color. This approach will only work where the concept is not dependent on color.

One example of this technique is to use the listing pages of *TV Guide* in clusters of local editions to reduce regional distortion. This approach is far less costly than testing in preprinted full-page units.

Another technique is the use of half-page black-and-white ads in Sunday supplements of newspapers in a few regions before investing in a full-page, full-run, full-color advertisement. The trick with all of these underspacing approaches is to keep your focus on the original objective and the original expectations.

NEWSPAPER PREPRINTS

The possibilities for copy testing in preprints are infinite. You can arrange with your own printer to produce as many different versions of your advertisement as cost and statistical validity permit, and to deliver them, premixed, to newspapers for insertion in their Sunday editions. The only limitation would involve trying to mix formats, as the insertion equipment can only be set to handle one size and thickness of your preprint and they can't be interspersed.

The problems with preprint copy testing don't come at the publication; they come at your printer. It is essential that someone visually check the shipment of inserts after they are mixed and before they are sent out to the newspapers.

Some printers don't have the presses to "stream" the different versions together on press automatically, and they rely on something they call "hand spanning." This means that they pack the inserts from different stacks or skids, one handful from this stack, another from that stack, and so on. This is adequate for a test, if it's really done. Unfortunately, there are too many temptations for the individual supervisor to take shortcuts and invalidate your test. For instance, in a four-way split, if the press is only doing two versions at a time, the printer has to store the entire run of the first two versions before packing anything to wait for the beginning of the production of the second two versions. Unless the printer has adequate floor space, this may not happen—and no one is going to tell you. There are many scrupulous and careful printers who would never permit this to happen, but caution still requires that your own inspector check the skids before they are shipped.

Another caution might be to include a pure key test if possible, with no changes other than the code number itself. The results should be identical, within statistical error limits. If they're not, you'll know that something is wrong, but it will be too late to do anything about it other than change printers in the future. The on-site inspection is still the preferred choice.

Statistical validity is always a consideration, as with any other test factor. Use the same statistical validity chart as with direct mail, except that the response rates may be too low for the chart. It is reasonably accurate, as a rule of thumb, to adjust decimal points; that is, if you expect a 0.05 percent response, use the quantity indicated for 0.5 percent and multiply it by 10. For instance, at a 0.1 percent error limit you would need a circulation of 191,000 for each split.

Picking Test Markets

With the exception of a few large cities with more than one newspaper, print media provide a very broad range of demographics—rich and poor, educated and uneducated, mail-order buyer and retail buyer—representing the entire scope of the area covered by the newspaper.

Geographic characteristics, such as median income and buying power, are the key variables, and so they are the prime consideration in selecting which newspapers to use in conducting a preprint test. Size of market is generally the most influential characteristic. For a test, pick a variety of papers in different-sized markets: one or two large cities, several medium ones, and a handful of smaller towns.

In all cases the newspapers should be those where the sales representatives can demonstrate a large number of repeat insertions by other mail-order advertisers, with rate structures that are not punitive.

Within these broad parameters, availability will be the prime consideration. On key dates you may find that your competition has already reserved space, or there may be too many other advertisers scheduling preprints on the dates you want. You will have to check availabilities and weigh the trade-offs of preferred dates versus preferred markets in making your selections.

FORMAT TESTS

One of the old maxims of testing was that it was possible to split only within a given format—one preprint versus another, one full page versus another. Few magazines would permit tests of small-space units.

But just as rate cards are not always indicative of the rates available to direct-response advertisers, so are they not always the best guide to what kind of splits are available.

If your own budget or your agency has enough buying power and influence, and if your media specialist is respected by the media and a good negotiator as well, virtually anything is possible.

I have been able to provide clients with tests that I previously thought were impossible, thanks to the efforts of Lois Seiden, a media professional whose results have demonstrated the power of an optimistic outlook. Some of these tests follow:

- Black-and-white versus color
- Large space versus small
- Card versus no card
- Vertical third page versus horizontal
- Multiple splits in publications that supposedly offered none

- One position versus another in the same publication
- Custom-tailored geographic segmentation

While such tests are not generally available, and if available, usually only on a limited and confidential basis, they can provide definitive answers very quickly to media strategy questions that might otherwise take years of trial-and-error approaches to resolve.

BROADCAST

There are two very different kinds of broadcast—support and direct response. They are very different in their purposes and methodologies, and just as different with regard to the ways of testing their usefulness or refining scheduling.

Direct-Response Testing

This is the place to use the "best-foot-forward" approach. The place to test is not the stations expected to be most typical of the broadcast media at large. Testing should begin on those stations most likely to succeed, where experience shows that your own propositions or those of other direct marketers have been successful.

There can be substantial differences in response by type of market, and so a variety of stations should be included in a test schedule: urban, rural, East, West, South, Midwest, independent stations, network affiliates, and cable stations. Often there are patterns showing that one type of station works better than others. More often the key variable is the willingness of stations, regardless of type of market or programming, to establish a rate structure and make available time slots that will be cost-efficient.

Day Parts.   The time of day is usually the most constant and controllable variable other than the station itself. The time of day is the most effective selector of audience segments. Weekend mornings reach parents whose children are watching children's shows. Afternoons reach women at home, enjoying the never-ending stream of soap operas. News programs and adventure shows reach a higher number of men. Late-night programming seems to find older people, or at least restless ones. Programming adjacencies, to the extent they are available for direct response, offer even finer selection, for certain shows seem to attract audiences of predictable affinities.

Other Testing.   Other than the stations or type and time of programming, there are often times when it is necessary to test other factors, such as frequency, length of commercial, or the content of the commercial itself.

The technique most used is a variation of flip-flop testing discussed earlier in this chapter in the section on print media. A different phone number is assigned to the new campaign and it is run in alternate weeks on several stations, beginning with the new campaign on half the stations and the old one on the other half. Half the stations are running A-B-A-B-A while the others are playing B-A-B-A-B. This tends to offset differences by station and by whether a commercial is played earlier or later in a flight.

This test method is generally used to test entirely new commercials or frequency. It would not be possible to test prices or other offer variations this way. Such testing requires a "paired-market" test.

Audience Valuation

The newest testing technique attempts to evaluate specific audience segments in order to predict the success of possible television schedules. The result is a specific allowable media cost for audiences targeted by different stations.

To initiate such testing, spots are arranged for various times during a particular week, and then the actual audiences reached by the spots must be subjected to computerized analysis. This type of analysis requires access to all the audience evaluation tools used by general advertising. The analysis is difficult and complex but produces an analytical tool that reaches far beyond the old standard of pure cost per response. By being able to target future buys, it has been possible to make upscale, narrow-audience, regional, business-to-business, and cultural propositions work that might not have worked with past test methods.

Support Broadcast

The choice of markets in support broadcast is dictated by the media to be supported. Within each market, however, there are usually several stations to choose from, and within each station theris a choice of day parts and frequency.

Often it is necessary to use every station in a market in order to reach the 300 or so gross rating points most direct marketers feel is a minimum for effective media support. As support spots must be aired in a precise pattern during three or four days adjoining the appearance of the ad or mailing being supported, it may be difficult to line up enough good availabilities.

The first objective is usually to test the effectiveness of support broadcast itself. The usual technique is to select between six and ten similar markets, supporting some of them at one frequency level, others at a higher level, and some without any support at all.

The costs of the broadcast are added to the costs of the preprints or direct mail being supported. The total advertising cost is divided by the number of responses received and—voila!—we have cost-per-response figures for each market and a conclusion about whether support costs are justified and at which GRP level.

Similarly, an ongoing campaign can test various day-part concentrations, commercial lengths, or even different creative appeals.

I suggest that readers considering any type of broadcast testing keep in mind the objective of a broadcast support test. Support advertising cannot be expected to lower CPR, although it sometimes does. A more reasonable expectation is to extend the media being supported—a higher level of orders at the same CPR, or a CPR that is higher than unsupported preprints or direct mail but still less costly than other media alternatives.

TESTING STRATEGY

Now that we've covered how to test in each media, let's look at the basic philosophy that applies to any and all kinds of testing. The first consideration is what to test—how many tests to run, what kinds are the most important, and how to use the information you get from testing. And the approach to this depends on the personality of your company.

General Patton and Field Marshall Montgomery became archetypal examples of two different military strategies. Patton was aggressive—a man who seized every opportunity, took risks, bent the rules of warfare, and swept across miles of enemy terrain without bothering to mop up pockets of resistance. Montgomery was cautious. He planned carefully, regrouped slowly, and moved his forces ahead step by step, with due care to logistics and supply lines.

While I regard myself as a Patton fan, I know the Montgomery approach is right for some companies. One of my banking clients is a Patton-type company. They will test one or two fundamental approaches and, if successful, roll out a major national campaign so fast the competition is unable to copy the concept. Another corporation is a Montgomery-type company, with each direct-mail program studied and planned and poked at for such a long time that by the time the smallest test gets in the mail, the competition may have already tested, rolled out, and reaped the profits from similar programs.

What to Test

What you can test depends on your budget, mailing size, objectives, and willingness to assume risk. It is easy to test a wide variety of mailing lists, or a simple direct-mail variation. Each split costs very little to execute. It is more costly to test different TV commercials, color magazine ads, and total mailing concepts. The cost of testing should be in relation to the size of the expected benefits.

The greatest difference in results can be expected from changes that affect the product being offered or the way the product is positioned. Offer changes run a close second, with very dramatic changes resulting from changes in price, premium, commitment, term, etc.

Creative changes are next, with very broad differences sometimes created by a change in headline or illustration, or in print and direct-mail formats. Layout revisions or different copy treatments of the same theme usually show very little difference, assuming they were professionally executed in the first place.

The big differences—200 and 300 percent lift factors—almost always come from product positioning, offer changes, or the selection of different lists or publications.

You can't afford to test everything, so the selection of what to test has to be done methodically. First, list test opportunities within your basic mailing or media schedule—publications you are using anyway that make testing feasible. Then list the things you would like to test, in the order of expected result improvement.

In a recent mail-order product introduction I still had twelve possible ad variations even after focus panel reviews and predictive research. There were eight testing opportunities, between direct mail and a Sunday supplement regional—

A-B split. When the opportunities were reviewed, all the copy alternatives were set aside in favor of testing product and offer variations.

Evolutionists Versus Fundamentalists

Another issue is how boldly to test. One school, which I'll call the evolutionists, advocates strictly "readable" testing, with all elements in an ad or mailing piece identical except the single factor being tested. If you are testing a headline, they will tell you, don't change the layout anywhere and leave every element of type size and color exactly the same. The question to ask in this approach is "When the results come in, what conclusions will I be able to reach?" If more than one element changes, the ability to make a final pronouncement on what works or doesn't work is muddied. Barry Mark is a brilliant advocate of this approach, which he perfected for the Doubleday Book Clubs.

The fundamentalists, on the other hand, are looking for the big break-through, the dramatic result, regardless of whether or not they ever know why one approach works and another one doesn't. Publishing consultant Dick Benson has long advocated supplier versus supplier testing—a Bill Jayme direct-mail package versus a Linda Wells package, a Sol Blumenfeld package versus an Ed Nash package. His advice is not to try to work out an overall testing plan that leads to definitive knowledge, but to pit one supplier against another and see which approach does the best.

I personally lean to the evolution approach, as I find that even the best freelancers are pressured by the fundamentalist system into looking for creative gimmicks and major departures, sometimes overlooking the creatively less exciting but more profitable breakthroughs that often occur with a simple coupon revision or offer change.

I think the best approach depends on what you have to lose. If you are running a successful business, then changes should be evolutionary, building upon existing success in a manner that identifies principles that can be used in other mailings and for other products. On the other hand, if you're in trouble, go for broke with completely fresh, way-out approaches.

Which Medium to Test In

Each medium has its unique advantages. Direct mail offers great flexibility if you are testing a wide variety of offers and great economy if the basic color circular can remain the same with only the letter and reply card changing. It also offers a very low profile, in case you don't want your testing activity to be spotted by your competition.

Print media, on the other hand, let you test broad creative concepts very dramatically and inexpensively in black-and-white magazine or supplement splits. Such basic design differences cost less to execute in art, type, and platemaking for print media than for direct mail.

Broadcast is expensive to test, with each commercial variation costing thousands of dollars. If you are working under Screen Actors Guild (SAG) and American Federation of Television and Radio Artists (AFTRA) regulations,

then even the slightest variation requires payment of added session fees and re-
siduals.

It is possible to do broad testing in media units other than those that will
eventually be the most profitable. Larger units like bind-in cards, or smaller
ones like black-and-white fractional units, may give a reading that will project
accurately to color pages with bind-ins or other units that will be the mainstay of
the basic campaign. The added CPR, because of the less efficient unit, is a cost
to be charged against your testing budget.

In direct mail, for instance, tests are sometimes sent out as first-class mail,
with a small panel of bulk mail sent at the same time. The faster-arriving first-
class mail gets responses to you fast and gives a quick reading of which mailing
approach does best. The bulk-mail panel determines which class of postage to
pay in the subsequent rollout—a decision that can be made after everything is
printed. This permits a much faster turnaround than would be possible if testing were done by bulk mail.

An interesting advantage of print advertising is its virtually certain transfer-
ability into other media, including direct mail. A print-tested concept almost always proves out in direct mail and broadcast. A direct-mail concept, on the
other hand, hardly ever translates into a successful print ad.

When to Break Out the Champagne

In the introduction of a new product, or the challenge of bettering an established control, there is necessarily an element of impatience in awaiting the results. Part of the impatience is due to the desire to make use of the knowledge
as soon as possible; more is due to just plain curiosity.

"Doubling" is a convenient way to read results, as earlier returns are usually
not reliable indicators of eventual results. The doubling date is sometimes called
the "half-life" point, a concept borrowed from the world of nuclear physics.

Direct-mail results start dribbling in immediately. Even the machine operator
at the mailing house can send in an order or inquiry before the official mailing
date. Nothing is significant, however, until the first Monday after a first-class
mailing or the third Monday after a bulk-rate mailing. With first-class, half the
results are usually in two weeks after the first large Monday mail. With third
class, this point comes three weeks later. Usually first-class mail will have a doubling point three weeks after mailing, bulk mail in the sixth week. After that,
results dribble in for years.

Now that I've set forth the rule, let me warn you against counting on it. Mail
delivery is nothing less than erratic. It varies at different times of the year and
in different post offices. Carrier-presorted mail travels fast. Mail with business
reply envelopes may linger a few days at your local post office on the way back
to you. And so on.

Print Results

Direct mail uses a doubling date, and responses will arrive in a pattern sugges-
tive of the way the mail is delivered and read. The same is true for magazines
and newspapers. Daily papers are read immediately or never, and so the half-

life point is less than a week away. In a local Sunday paper, you can usually double the results that are in as of the following Thursday. (If the ad is part of a national schedule, you have to allow more time for the mail to arrive from across the country.)

Most monthly magazines have a doubling point three weeks after the first heavy Monday, or about four weeks after the magazine's on-sale date. An earlier, less reliable, 20 to 25 percent point may be reached after two weeks, for those who insist on making early forecasts.

Weekly magazines like *TV Guide* have a similar pattern. Once the returns start arriving, the halfway point is reached about twelve days later, or about two weeks after the publication is read.

"Hard space" such as business reply insert cards will come in faster than soft space, which requires the respondent to hunt for an envelope and stamp. Inquiries or responses to free offers will come in faster than those that require writing a check or filling in a credit card number.

Magazines with mostly subscription readers are usually received throughout the country at about the same time. The responses will come in as much as a week faster than responses from a newsstand-sold magazine, which is picked up by readers over a month's time.

Magazine response curves also vary by the editorial content. A magazine with a long, particularly interesting article may be saved for weeks, keeping the responses coming in for a longer time. A shelter book may be kept and referred to, while a news magazine is usually read the day it arrives. All these factors affect response curves.

To develop experience in the publications you use, I recommend tracking the results of your ads in each magazine on a daily basis, logging in the results, and drawing curves on graph paper until you discover what seems to be right for your ads with coupons sent to your geographic area.

Broadcast and Telephone

There is no curve in broadcast media or in telephone selling. Most responses come within hours or they don't come in at all. On telephone orders received in response to a radio or television offer, at least 90 percent will arrive in the first three or four hours. When a mail-in offer is used on broadcast, the response curve is the same as with a daily newspaper.

In telephone selling the responses are, of course, instantaneous. Each day's tallies can be obtained by phone to give you an immediate indication of the success of the techniques used that day.

Rollout Strategies

Once the results are in, there is usually little time to analyze the results and make decisions. New publication closing dates demand decisions on whether to place orders and run more ads or print more mail. Competitors are already speculating about the effect of your test program on their campaigns. Good mail-order seasons must be exploited or the opportunity is forever passed.

Some cautions should be observed. A new approach may work because it is fresh and new, not because it is better. It might work the first time it is run or mailed, but not again. Some ads tire more quickly than others. An approach may not work because of some unusual coincidence. Whenever results seem illogical, always check the medium in which the ad ran. Perhaps a competitive ad ran in the same issue, diluting your responses. Maybe a major news event kept readers from getting into the ads, or a weather aberration kept them from reading the paper or watching television at all.

Whether to act on half-life figures or wait until final results are in and back-end experience is gained is another decision that will depend on corporate personality.

Usually the best decision is somewhere in between. Unrepeatable opportunities—a key season, a difficult-to-get insert card or back-cover position—should be reserved at an early date, because the opportunity is perishable. Lists can be reused with increased quantities but not yet with the whole list. With broadcast you can drop the weak stations and add a larger number of new stations in order to gradually build up the schedule.

My own observations are that the risk takers do better in the long run and that a winning proposition should complete its rollout within a year. Taking longer to complete the rollout means marketing circumstances might change, mitigating the success of the early results. Remember, timing is a factor in the original test results as well, and next year may not be as good as this year. The maxim about making hay while the sun shines is very applicable to the field of direct marketing.

3

Research

Barry R. Mark

David Shepard Associates, Inc.
Dix Hills, N.Y.

General advertising has traditionally utilized market research to a greater extent than the direct marketing industry has. Direct marketers have tended to take the position that "it is easier and cheaper to test and get a definitive answer rather than go to all the time, trouble, and expense of market research study."

This attitude has been changing, however, and will continue to change, as more and more direct marketers understand the advantages of research and learn how to maximize the effectiveness of the data obtained. Direct marketers now recognize the need to know more about customers rather than treating them as merely "responses to the advertising."

It really does not come down to a choice between testing or research—both activities are critical in making decisions in direct marketing. In fact, the best approach is not to view research as an alternative to testing but to view testing as just one of many research methods available. The decision about whether to use testing or some other research method is a function of the objective you wish to accomplish and which method will be most effective.

This chapter will give you a general explanation of the type of problems that lend themselves to market research and the various research methods that can be used. In addition, it will suggest how you can best initiate and implement research projects so that the maximum amount of information is obtained. It will give you the tools to initiate appropriate research projects, manage research projects, and review research projects performed by others. The assumption is that the actual research will be done by specialists in research procedures.

OVERVIEW

It is important to understand that the purpose of research is very simply to gain information that will help you in making marketing decisions. The more information you have, the less uncertain you will be when making decisions and the greater the likelihood that you will make the correct one.

Of course, the gathering of information helps but does not replace the basic decision-making process. It is clearly the manager's responsibility to utilize the available information together with his or her own experience in order to make the appropriate marketing decision. Information can be misinterpreted, key factors can change, and many other factors can lead to decisions that don't work despite the best efforts of the manager. But information gained from research can go a long way in minimizing the chances of errors.

WHEN TO USE RESEARCH

General Problem Solving

You should think of utilizing research whenever you are faced with a situation in which having additional information would help you make the right decision. When it is clear that how customers think or how they are likely to act or what characteristics they have are important to your decision making, then you should think of research. For example, if some change is likely to make your product more attractive to older people but less attractive to younger people, then you should know the age of your customers before taking that action. And if you don't have the data, you should go and get them.

If you think that this type of information will help you to avoid problems or make better decisions, you should think of research as an ongoing part of your marketing effort.

WHAT RESEARCH SHOULD INCLUDE

Baseline Research

Baseline research is an ongoing research project designed to better understand your customers on a continuing basis. It will make you aware of changes as soon as possible and in general keep you from being surprised by events that you could have foreseen. You first establish procedures to monitor your customers. For example, you may want to include a written questionnaire in your new customer material. This questionnaire could include basic demographics, expectations about your products, or any other item that you think is important. As you get periodic data, you can see if the basic profile of your customer has changed and how that is likely to affect your business. This change can be a function of actions you are purposely taking or it can be a function of changes in the marketplace. In either case, the research allows you to know about the changes quickly so that you can take action or do further research to understand the causes of the change.

The same type of research could be done when customers no longer purchase or resign from your mail-order program, or at any other point in the relationship. At any chosen point you send out questionnaires that will help you understand why the customer took such actions. The questionnaire will also give you a way to compare past data from customers at the same stage.

This type of research establishes a "baseline," which allows you to determine if key characteristics of your market are changing. These changes may explain differences in marketing results that otherwise would not be clear.

New Product Introduction

When you are considering the testing of a new product, you should consider undertaking research to determine the possible reaction of a target market to the product. The resulting reactions of potential customers may:

1. Increase your confidence in the success of the new product.
2. Suggest changes in the product that would make it more acceptable.
3. Suggest that your product is viable but that a different market should be considered.
4. Indicate that the product should be dropped.

In any case a comparatively small amount of money spent in research may save a significant amount of marketing or manufacturing dollars.

New Advertising Approaches

New advertising approaches for a product should be exposed to the views of potential customers in the same way that a new product idea would be. No matter how creative a new approach is, you cannot be certain that the potential audience will respond as you want it to. This is particularly true when you are considering a large number of alternative advertising approaches. The best method may be to reduce the number of possibilities through market research and then test those that appear most likely to be successful.

Product or Company Image

One of the areas that general advertising has always been very concerned about is the image of a product. It is important that the image of a product as seen by the customer be known and understood so that products be positioned to maximize the attributes that are important to the customers. The automobile manufacturers have for many years attempted to establish a clear image for different models so that the sales can be maximized and the products be differentiated in the mind of the consumer.

HOW TO INITIATE RESEARCH

Problem Definition

The basic purpose of research is to obtain information. When you have a problem or a question that can be solved with information that is available through research, the critical point is to establish the problem very specifically before any research is initiated. If this is not done, you may find that the research has produced valid data but it is not the data needed to solve the problem.

Therefore, the critical first step in any research project is to define the problem very specifically. For example, if response rates to a particular advertising approach have declined, you may view the problem as finding a new creative approach—or more specifically, which of several advertising approaches are likely to be successful and what factors are significant. If some groups of customers are not purchasing as much as other comparable groups, you may want to define the problem as understanding why the sales are lower in order to take appropriate measures.

Information Required

Once the problem has been defined, then you can decide what information is needed to solve the problem. Again your choice must be very specific. In the case of new advertising approaches, the information required is how people will respond to the advertising. One approach is to test several of the ads and see which has the highest response rate. This is a very common approach and gives you a definitive answer in terms of response rate.

It does not, however, give you any hypothesis about what factors in the ad were significant. Therefore, the information required may be which ads are most likely to increase response and what factors are likely to be significant.

Source of Information

The next step is to determine where the information exists—that is, who holds the data and in what form? In the case of response to an ad, you would want to speak to the actual customers or potential customers. They would be the ones who know what they think of the ads. They might not "know" whether they will respond or not, however. Very few people are able to say how they will behave in a specific situation at some time in the future.

RESEARCH TECHNIQUES

Once you know the information needed and where it is located, then you can decide what research techniques are appropriate for obtaining the information. This is the heart of any research problem. It is critical that you think out the problems before you automatically seize on a specific research technique.

Research methods vary greatly and generally are not interchangeable; techniques that work well for a particular problem will not work for other problems. Therefore it is necessary to understand what research techniques are available and under what circumstances they should be utilized.

Before we review specific research techniques we should discuss some research principles.

Qualitative Versus Quantitative Research

In general, you can classify research techniques into two broad groups: qualitative research and quantitative research. Qualitative research, by definition, cannot be projected to larger groups. The intent is to obtain information that may be useful for aiding your understanding of a particular situation. Quantitative research, on the other hand, can be used to predict the responses of a larger group, with a measurable margin of error.

All research techniques can be described in terms of their projectability. These range from large-scale political telephone surveys, which are highly projectable, to an informal review of customer correspondence, which may be helpful in understanding your customers but which is *not* projectable. Quantitative research is dependent on the concept of *sampling from a universe*. This is simply the act of examining a small amount from a large quantity. For example, if a cook tastes a teaspoon of soup to determine if it has enough salt, she is taking a sample. The tablespoon that she removes from the pot is the sample from a universe that consists of all the soup in the pot.

She is also making some assumptions. She assumes that the sample, the contents of the tablespoon, will contain the same proportion of salt as the universe, the total contents of the pot. This assumption is valid in most cases because she has stirred the pot to ensure that it is completely mixed and that any sample will therefore be representative of the universe. Based on the taste of the sample tablespoon, she will decide whether or not to add salt to the universe of soup in the pot.

This procedure is in essence what quantitative research projects do. They define a universe they wish to examine. It doesn't really matter whether it is a pot of soup or everybody who has purchased a product from a catalog. Once the universe has been defined, a sample is obtained that is representative of that universe. The sample is then examined or measured to determine the factor in which we are interested. It is this principle that allows you to make statements about a large group of people based on a small sample. This is called *projectability*. Once the sample has been examined or measured, we then determine how certain we can be that the sample actually is representative of the universe and therefore how much risk we are taking in making decisions based on this sample. Projectability is generally dependent on how the sample was chosen, the size of the sample, and the research method used to obtain the information.

A significant amount of mathematical work has been done in this area and tables are available to allow you to determine how confident you can be of specific results given the sample size and nature of the population.

Bias

The classic case of bias in drawing a sample is probably the research project performed by the *Literary Digest* in 1936. Attempting to draw a representative sample of the voters, it relied on lists of telephone owners and magazine subscribers. Based on the answers of these people, they predicted that Alf Landon would receive more votes than Franklin Roosevelt. Their bias was assuming that their sample represented the population of voters when it was actually biased toward higher-income voters. The result of the election was of course that Roosevelt won in a landslide.

It is critical that all research be objective in order to be useful. You must be certain that the results you obtain are based on reality, unaffected by factors that might distort the results. This bias can come from many sources, including how you pick the sample, how you ask the questions, and how you interpret the data. For example, questions should be phrased in a neutral manner so that they don't suggest that you expect a certain answer. The question "Do you usually read the tabloids like *National Enquirer* or more intellectual newspapers like the *New York Times?*" is clearly biased by the use of the words "tabloid" and "intellectual." There would be a tendency to answer "*New York Times*" because of the implication that a "tabloid" is nonintellectual and most people would want to appear intellectual. This is a clear-cut example, but frequently the bias is more subtle. There is evidence from recent elections that some voters will say that they are going to vote for a black candidate and then actually vote for a white candidate. It would appear that they tended to want to appear to be unprejudiced people by giving what they thought would be the unprejudiced answer.

One research technique is not "better" than the other. Each is appropriate and efficient for particular projects but inappropriate for others. It is therefore extremely important that you understand the various techniques and how to determine which to use.

Primary Versus Secondary Research

Another important way to classify research is in terms of *primary research* or *secondary research*. Primary research indicates that you are going directly to the source of the information—that is, your customers, potential customers, or any other original source. Secondary research is based on review of research that has already been conducted and published in some form. This may have to be done by private or public organizations for any one of a number of reasons. For example, if you wanted to know the demographic characteristics of a specific state, you could do your own door-to-door questioning. But that isn't necessary, because that primary research has already been done by the U.S. Census Bureau and you need only examine the available data. This would be secondary research. In the same manner if you wanted information about readership of magazines you would be able to contact the magazine for the information or several other research companies that supply these data.

SPECIFIC RESEARCH METHODS

Focus Groups

A common example of a research method that is qualitative and therefore not projectable is a focus group. A focus group consists of a group of people invited to discuss a specific topic under the guidance of a group leader. The leader has a topic guide to direct the discussion so that you can learn their views. Two advantages of a focus group over other research techniques are that the group environment tends to encourage more open discussion and that the interaction of the people will frequently produce information that would not normally surface. Although the discussion is guided by the leader, it is not restricted. That is, the discussion may produce ideas that were not thought of when the research was initiated. Under these circumstances the leader will make certain that these new topics are fully explored—in fact, these new ideas frequently lead to whole new products or advertising approaches.

Another advantage of a focus group is that it allows you to see the individuals in person. You normally sit behind a mirror or view the groups on videotape. The focus group allows you to understand the people involved in a way that is not possible through reading and analyzing data. You can see how they actually describe their actions and explain the reasons for them. If the focus group is run by a psychologist or someone who understands psychology, he or she will be able to follow up these discussions with questions that frequently raise the issue of the underlying drives or desires that lead to the visible action.

Focus groups also present some limitations and dangers. There can be a tendency for one or two people to dominate the group if the leader is not careful. This will result in data that show only what the more dominant people in the group think. The same thing can occur if the leader is not objective and tends to lead the discussion in the direction that is biased toward his or her views.

Another key limitation is the fact that the results are *not* projectable. The people are not selected in a manner that makes them representative, and usually the actual number of people is too small to project the results adequately. In addition, the results themselves are qualitative and not in a form that lends itself to definitive conclusions.

Because of these factors, focus groups are primarily useful for *generating ideas or hypotheses* to be tested or examined. These ideas can be crucial in understanding the group you are dealing with, but before you take any significant action it is important that these ideas or hypotheses be tested to determine that they are worthy to be acted upon and really representative of the larger group.

Individual Interviews

There are many ways that individual interviews can be conducted. For example, they can be held at individuals' homes, at central locations, or at various geographic locations such as malls or supermarkets. They can be qualitative or quantitative, depending on how they are conducted. If the interviewer utilizes a general guide to the areas to be covered, as in a focus group, uses open-ended questions, and is trained to follow up in areas that may not have been covered in the guide, then the interview will tend to be qualitative and not projectable, although it may be very helpful in generating ideas and getting a sense of how the interviewee thinks. If the questions are fixed and the interviewer is trained only to record the answers and not follow up new areas, then the interview is essentially quantitative.

One advantage of individual interviews is the ability to utilize various types of material. The interviewee can be shown actual ads, products, or other materials. In addition, he or she can be asked to utilize products, manipulate materials, and otherwise duplicate real-life situations. These types of interviews also tend to have a high response rate.

There are disadvantages, too. Interviews are more expensive than other types of research, more difficult to control, and more susceptible to bias on the part of the interviewer.

Telephone Interviews

Telephone interviews are usually conducted from a central location. The interviewer is usually trained to read from a script that has been prepared to elicit the data needed. The advantages of telephone interviewing include the fact that they can be completed fairly quickly, can be monitored, and are less expensive than individual interviews.

The disadvantages include the fact that you may not be able to obtain some phone numbers or contact people with unlisted numbers. In addition, some people may hesitate to answer some questions over the telephone that they might answer in an individual interview or focus group situation.

Mail Interviews

Mailing questionnaires to people is advantageous primarily because it is comparatively inexpensive and does not require any personnel to speak to the responders. Response rates tend to be very low, however, and it may take a long amount of time to collect the data.

FURTHER CONSIDERATIONS

Cost and Time Restraints

What limitations exist in terms of availability of funds and decision points that will affect how you will conduct the research project? The research will only be useful if the research results are available in time to make the decision.

Action

What action will you take after you have the results of the research? The time to decide this in almost all cases is before the research is conducted, not after. This is to ensure that the research is worth doing.

4

Contests and Sweepstakes

Jeffrey Feinman

Feinman/Marlow/Carter, Inc.
New York, N.Y.

Sweepstakes have been proved historically to be the most successful method of dramatically increasing response to direct-mail offers. They are used for single-product offers, subscription mailings, catalogs of general merchandise, service firms, industrial mailers, and most recently, fund raisers. In fact, there is hardly a mail-order seller that has not used the device effectively.

The chance to win a valuable prize entices readers to open the mail and become involved with the product offered. It is not at all unusual to register sales increases of 40 to 100 percent over a control. As the cost is fixed (prizes, sweepstakes brochure, and administration), the incremental cost is minimal. That is, a typical sweepstakes may add less than 1 percent to the mailing cost, with a gain of 100 percent in response.

HISTORY

There are examples of prize promotions as early as 1900 in advertising mail. Sweepstakes in the form we know them, however, began in the early 1950s. By 1952, the states had liberalized legislation to permit widespread use of chance promotions. The real heyday was in the late 1950s and early 1960s.

By 1960, almost any piece of direct mail could be seen carrying the familiar words "you may have already won." The real difference was that prizes were awarded only to the degree to which they were claimed. That is, only winning prize numbers which actually were returned were given awards. Since mailers seldom receive a response of over 10 percent, they could be safe in knowing that not more than 10 percent of the "available" prizes would be awarded. A $50,000 sweepstakes seldom cost the advertiser more than $5000.

In April 1966, the Federal Trade Commission began its famous "Investigation of Pre-selected Winner Sweepstakes." There followed congressional hearings with a seemingly endless line of marketers that had awarded few if any of the promised prizes. Most marketers were convinced that sweepstakes were doomed. What emerged instead was an informed public and an industry that was stronger than ever. Through a series of agreements and self-policing, almost every marketer began to make the statement "All prizes guaranteed to be awarded." This return to sanity and honesty helped create the current billion-dollar prize promotion industry.

Today more firms use sweepstakes than ever before. Currently, they are conducted under safeguards that assure the awarding of all prizes and compliance with a host of regulatory actions.

TYPES OF PRIZE PROMOTIONS

Prize offers frequently are considered under the general heading of sweepstakes. However, there are a number of distinct types.

A lucky number is the most common type of direct-mail promotion. A number is preselected, and all returns are compared against this number. If offers the advantage of being able to say, "You may have already won," which is a powerful copy platform. It offers the disadvantage that all returns must be "screened" or checked for winning numbers. Screening is a costly process in large mailings.

With a random draw, all returns (buyers and nonbuyers) participate in a drawing from all returns for prizes.

In a contest of skill, the entrant must take a skill test. Typically, a request is made to complete a twenty-five-word statement. These traditionally have proved unsuccessful in the mail as response is slowed down while consumers work on their entries.

LEGALITY

All fifty states and the federal government have legislation governing prize promotions. Traditionally, this legislation changes to fit the climate of the country and the views of the current governing authorities. During periods of strong consumerism, the number of regulations and their enforcement tend to increase. The independent judging organization that administers a sweepstakes must be familiar with the latest laws. More important than the law is the practical application of this legislation, which is open to considerable interpretation. Currently, sweepstakes are legal in all fifty states.

It is important to understand that lotteries are illegal in all fifty states, except when conducted by the state. A lottery has the elements of prize, chance, and consideration present simultaneously. What transforms a lottery to a sweepstakes is the deletion of one of those elements, usually the element of consideration. That is, consumers are told that they do not have to buy to enter. In a contest of skill, the element of chance is eliminated. Skill rather than chance determines the winner.

Although various other laws are applicable, the lottery law is the most important. Violation carries both criminal and civil penalties. It is a serious matter. Disregard of the law can result in mail not being distributed by the post office or return mail not being delivered.

Consumers are further protected by New York State, Rhode Island, and Florida regulations that require the posting of a surety bond or an escrow account for each sweepstakes. This law assures residents of those states that should the sponsor fail to have funds for prize awards, the insurance company will meet the obligation.

The overall guideline is simply that rules must clearly, and in detail, disclose the mechanics of the offer. Figure 4-1 shows a typical one for *New York* magazine.

PSYCHOLOGY

On one level, it is unimportant why sweepstakes work. The mere fact that they are so successful should be enough. The power of the device, however, generates academic interest in the motivational forces.

To understand sweepstakes one need only look to Las Vegas, Atlantic City, or any state lottery. Rich and poor alike stream there for the opportunity to win a dream. In many western European countries—e.g., Spain—the lottery has become an institution.

In direct mail, sweepstakes recipients are offered an opportunity to play with no financial risk. In the process, they must at least open the envelope and become involved in the offer. As one widely touted study indicates, upwards of 60 percent of all third-class mail is thrown away unopened. Herein may lie one answer. It's hard to toss out an envelope that says, "You may have already won $25,000."

Once inside, the consumer must complete the order form even to reply no. Beyond this hurdle the sale is much easier.

The sweepstakes package itself, with cars and boats and TVs, is often more exciting than the direct-mail package with a straight offer.

Finally, there is one school of thought that still believes consumers buy because they believe it increases their chance to win. Smart mailers pander to this psychology by providing the recipient with a package that looks "lucky." Headlines that scream out about big dollar numbers and show customers' names on simulated passbooks, airline tickets, and bank vaults all contribute to the sweepstakes fantasy. Successful sweepstakes packages leave each consumer with a strong sense that he or she could easily be the winner.

"NO" NAMES

Even nonbuyers must be given a chance to enter. This legal requirement is actually a positive regulation. In fact, even if the law were changed, many would still emblazon their envelopes with the words "no purchase required." The

AMERICAN PRINTERS BESTSELLER AWARDS OFFICIAL RULES

The More Share Draft Books You Sell,
The More Chances to Win. No Purchase Necessary.

1. The Share Draft "Bestseller Awards" is an incentive sweepstakes for full- or part-time employees of a Credit Union whose responsibilities include opening new Share Draft Accounts.

2. Each time you open a new Share Draft Account, complete an Official Entry (and Bonus Entry, if applicable). Enclose with Share Draft order sent to American Printers, 1452 Main Street, Sioux Falls, SD 92071, February 15, 1991, through November 30, 1991.

3. Each time you open a new Share Draft Account, during the promotion period, is another opportunity to win. Enclose your entry with your order—there is no limit to winning opportunities.

4. There will be 30 periodic drawings throughout the promotion; each award will be a Collection of Cosmetics and Fragrances plus a "how-to" Beauty Book ($150 value). These drawings will be held on or about the following dates: 2/26, 3/5, 3/12, 3/19, 3/26, 4/2, 4/9, 4/16, 5/7, 5/14, 5/21, 5/28, 6/4, 6/11, 6/15, 6/25, 7/2. Again on 9/10, 9/17, 9/24, 10/1, 10/8, 10/15, 10/22, 10/29, 11/5, 11/12, 11/19, 11/26, 12/3. Each drawing will be from all Valid Entries and/or Bonus Entries submitted during the interval of the previous award.

5. On or about December 15, 1991, there will be one Grand Prize Award drawn from all Valid Entries and Bonus Entries submitted throughout the incentive period (2/15/91 to 11/30/91). The prize, a trip to Disney World, Orlando, FL, for four people, includes round-trip airfare from winner's nearest commercial airport, hotel accommodations (2 double-occupancy rooms), breakfast and dinner each day, plus passes to Disney World and Epcot and 10 major attractions. 4 nights/5 days. (Approximate retail value, $10,000). All arrangements made by sweepstakes administrator, and trip must be made before July 15, 1992. Travel dates subject to availability.

6. Winners will be selected by random drawings from among all timely received entries. Drawings will be conducted by Feinman/Marlow/Carter, Inc., an independent judging organization whose decisions are final. Odds of winning are determined by the number of Valid Entries and Bonus Entries received. All prizes will be awarded.

Figure 4-1. Sample sweepstakes rules.

7. Winners will be notified by mail no later than 14 days after prize drawings and will be required to send affidavits of eligibility and a liability release; these must be returned within 14 days of notification or prize will be forfeited. Winners agree to the use of their names and likenesses for publicity and promotion without additional compensation. No substitution or transfer of prizes is permitted. All taxes are the sole responsibility of the winner.

8. The sponsor reserves the right to offer special incentive entry opportunities to all participants from time to time within the promotion period.

9. Only full- or part-time employees of any Credit Union, 18 years or older, residing in the continental U.S. may participate. Employees and their families of CUNA, American Printers; Feinman/Marlow/Carter, Inc. and their respective subsidiaries, advertising/promotion agencies are not eligible. Sweepstakes is void where prohibited and restricted by law.

10. For a list of prize winners, send a stamped self-addressed envelope by 12/30/91 to FMC, Award Winners List, 866 United Nations Plaza, Dept. 4050, New York, New York 10017.

©1991 Feinman/Marlow/Carter, Inc., New York, NY 10017

"free" entry gets readers involved with the package. Having filled in the order blank, it's a short step to making a nonbuyer into a buyer.

Furthermore, a "no" name is not without merit. Many mailers remail to all those who reply no. They simply send a repeat of the offer with a cover letter that says, "We've forwarded your entry to the judging organization, but we did want to give you one last opportunity to take advantage of our special offer."

"No" names are also a good revenue source. List managers will usually put up "no" names on a special list. For some offers, they are better than buyers. What we know about "no" names is that they are interested in something for nothing, read their direct mail, and are willing to spend money on a stamp for a chance to win. The result is an excellent list for certain types of insurance offers, opportunity-seeker plans, good luck jewelry, and of course, puzzle and contest clubs. Many mailers earn significant revenue from rental of "no" names.

MYTHS

Probably no part of direct mail has as many myths as the sweepstakes industry. We'll seek to examine some of the frequently made statements and compare them with the facts.

Myth 1.	Sweepstakes work only on downscale offers.
Fact 1.	Sweepstakes have been successful for such upscale mailers as Revlon, American Express, Public Broadcasting, British Airways, and *Newsweek*. There is a psychographic aspect to sweepstakes respondents, not a demographic one. Sweepstakes transcend age, income, height, and other artificial, nonapplicable barriers to their use. The success rate applies equally to Adam & Eve (marital aids), Hanover House (general catalog), *Catholic Digest* (religious magazine), McGraw-Hill (business publications), and hundreds of other aggressive marketers.
Myth 2.	Sweepstakes are not good with complicated offers.
Fact 2.	Sweepstakes have worked with clubs, continuity plans, and almost every item that has been sold by mail. Vitamins, which require detailed product communication, find sweepstakes a key sales element. Vitamin companies that use sweepstakes include SturDee, BioOrganic, U.S. Health Club, Hudson Vitamin, RVP, and General Nutrition. In fact, it is almost impossible to find an aggressive mailer in this category that does not use sweepstakes.
Myth 3.	Bad pays make sweepstakes unaffordable.
Fact 3.	Sweepstakes people perform almost identically to nonsweepstakes people. This includes bad pays, bad checks, renewals, and mail list income.
Myth 4.	Sweepstakes have worn out.
Fact 4.	We've been hearing that for 20 years. This week's results:

Product	Sweeps Pkg., %*	Nonsweeps Pkg., %
X	8.2	5.1
Y	10.1	5.7
Z	4.2	1.9

*For purpose of sweepstakes reporting, we count only those who order, not those who do not buy but want to enter the sweepstakes.

Myth 5.	Most of the big prizes go to customers. Alternate myth: They go to noncustomers.
Fact 5.	As a practical matter, the marketer shouldn't care who gets the prize. The worth of a sweepstakes is decided long before the prize is awarded. In fact, prizes go to both buyers and nonbuyers, and show a fairly accurate ratio of buyer to nonbuyer entrants.
Myth 6.	Sweepstakes cannot be done within our image.
Fact 6.	Usually sweepstakes require a "look" to be effective. They need not always be "bells and whistles," however, and company image can be maintained.

PRIZES

Consumers enter for the chance to win a dream. To the degree that you can push that "dream button," you'll gain response. Traditionally, the most successful offers have a large first prize and lots of prizes at the bottom. The strong copy lines are "Win $25,000" and "Over 1000 chances to win." Consumers are attracted by big prizes. Pyramid prize structures tend to work best. And you don't have to spend millions to play in the sweepstakes game. Fully half of all successful sweepstakes have prize budgets under $25,000 in total.

Relating prizes to your audience is important. Trips to play golf in Bermuda will outpull cars for a golfing list. By the same token, be careful that you know enough about your audience to make the offer appealing. Spending a lot of money is seldom enough. An affluent, liberal, upscale audience doesn't want to win mink stoles. Downscale folks in rural Wyoming don't want to win boats or Louis XV furniture. The prize should reflect the audience.

Don't fall into the trap of substituting your personal taste for that of your buyer. For example, as a businessperson you probably would enjoy a vacation trip to Europe. Yet in a recent sweepstakes offering "twenty-five trips anywhere in the world," more than half chose domestic travel. In fact, several selected a location less than 500 miles from home.

Focus groups and the advice of judging agencies will help provide this answer. At one focus group, we searched for the best way to portray the excitement of winning $100,000. The client's ad agency opted for picturing vacation homes, boats, and gold. Interestingly, this blue-collar audience responded best to an offer of "$100,000 toward starting your own business." The idea came up at a focus group when someone said, "I'd sure like to have my own bait-and-tackle shop someday."

Equally important to prize selection is prize presentation. The same skill that goes into illustrating products should be used to arouse reader interest in prizes. There are stock photo houses that have shots of the most commonly used photos. The cost is minimal (less than $100 each). Frequently, these transparencies are better in subject matter and reproduction quality than manufacturer photos.

Choices can make a prize structure look bigger. If the grand prize is a car or a truck or $10,000 in cash or $10,000 in gold or a 1-carat diamond or a trip to Europe, you can show many prizes and still award only one prize.

Prizes are the fuel that make the promotion happen. Pay careful attention to their selection and presentation.

SWEEPSTAKES OBJECTIVES

Of course, the main objective served by sweepstakes is simply increasing response to direct mail, but there are some special objectives that can be served by use of sweepstakes.

Information gathering can be accomplished. A requirement of entry can be the answering of questions. In the early days of Mastercharge, the goal was to obtain completed applications. A requirement of entry in a Mastercharge sweepstakes was to "complete the application." Whereas it was difficult to get people to spend 20 minutes filling out an application, the offer of a compelling prize increased response. A current example is list development projects in which what is wanted is smokers' names and addresses and current brand preference. To obtain the information, the client simply made brand preference a requirement of entry.

Sweepstakes also work as a collection device. A number of mailers have increased the pay-up rate by adding a sweepstakes to their collection series.

Retention can be heightened through prize promotions. At least one book club and one major cable network find that subscribers who are offered monthly sweepstakes tend to stay as members longer. This usually can be accomplished even with a very small prize budget.

Traffic building is dramatically increased through the use of sweepstakes. This includes fast-food traffic, land-development-site traffic, and most recently, movie traffic.

Finally, sweepstakes can increase total readership of your marketing message. The excitement of sweeps offers gets consumers involved with direct-mail offers.

SWEEPSTAKES CREATIVE ELEMENTS

Sweepstakes creative elements are a response to the classical marketing task of attracting attention, creating interest, arousing desire, and forcing action. This is done through a series of hard-hitting words and visuals that leave readers with a belief that a dream prize is well within their grasp.

The creative tends to be more formularized, with eagles, fancy borders, special certificates, and a sense of genuine value. Coupled with this are devices to make the simplest prizes exciting and compelling. All the direct-mail devices (e.g., tokens, pull tabs, and computer letters) are doubly important as applied to direct mail.

SWEEPSTAKES RESEARCH

Focus groups are very helpful in eliciting consumer opinions about prize promotions. Specifically, ideas as to prizes, graphics, and type of offer frequently can be elicited from a well-run group. However, all the caveats about research are even more prevalent in this area. Even the most avid sweepstakes player usually associates the offer with gambling. The consumers' public image psychology must be regarded. Any researcher will tell you that consumers all say they read *Newsweek* and never the *National Enquirer*. Much of the same protective information exists here. In focus groups compiled from sweepstakes entrants only, the interviewer often is told, "I never enter sweepstakes."

In short, do research but be careful. You may be touted off sweepstakes by potential customers who would say no in a research home but would respond in the privacy of their own homes.

SWEEPSTAKES ECONOMICS

Sweepstakes tend to have a fixed cost. That is, the basic elements are prizes, administration, and creative actions. These costs are essentially the same whether amortized over 200,000 pieces mailed or 20 million. The successful approach is to amortize one's sweepstakes over the greatest number of pieces. This can be accomplished by keeping the sweepstakes open 12 months or longer in order to use over several mailings and using it as an overlay to all products mailed.

Here are some sample costs.

Table 4-1. Fixed and Variable Costs for a Sample
Sweepstakes

Fixed Costs	
Prizes	$30,000
Administration	5,000
Creative, art, copy, mechanicals	15,000
Total fixed cost	$50,000
Variable Costs	
Additional brochure (4C/4C) to promote sweepstakes prizes	$20,000
Additional buckslip	10,000
Total variable cost	$30,000

Table 4-2. Economic Comparison of Sweepstakes and Nonsweepstakes Packages

	Sweepstakes		Nonsweepstakes	
Control direct-mail package	$300,000	$275,000	$300,000	$275,000
Fixed costs ($50,000)	50,000	5,000	–	–
Variable costs	30,000	30,000	–	–
Package cost	$380,000	$310,000	$300,000	$275,000
Orders per thousand	80	80	50	50
Cost per order	$4.70	$4.00	$6.00	$5.50

CO-OP SWEEPSTAKES

So that a marketer can test the sweepstakes idea, a number of judging agencies have begun offering co-op sweepstakes. Essentially, they put together a number of marketers to share the cost of prizes, creative elements, and administration. Usually the cost is under $10,000 in total. Obviously, the benefit of tailoring an offer to your exact market is lost. Furthermore, the sweepstakes brochure is generic and therefore loses the benefit of developing a piece to your specification. But this is a method of testing the waters without making a major commitment of money or labor power.

THE FUTURE OF SWEEPSTAKES

At least one economic authority indicates that gambling (legal and illegal) is a $150 billion industry in the United States. That makes gambling bigger than the auto, steel, and oil industries combined.

The power of something for nothing is a strong motivator. As long as a consumer perceives that throwing away an entry is tantamount to throwing away the chance of a lifetime, sweepstakes will endure. The giant casinos of Atlantic City and Las Vegas provide testimony to the natural human gambling instinct.

All direct-mail tests indicate that the chance to win a dream will get envelopes opened and increase response dramatically. There's no evidence to support any decline. As in Las Vegas, it seems that each new sweepstakes purveyor simply broadens the total marketplace.

5
Law and Ethics

Robert Posch, Jr.
Doubleday Book & Music Clubs, Inc.
Garden City, N.Y.

As we look ahead to the business climate of the 1990s, it seems that database marketing will have a higher visibility to government than it had in the 1980s. The successful marketer will therefore be the one who reaches a targeted audience with the least intrusion from governmental regulatory bodies. Merely creating and fulfilling promotions will not suffice if this is done at the cost of excessive fines, legal defense fees, bad publicity, and government-dictated consent agreements affecting future policy. Finally there is increasing *personal*, civil, and criminal liability exposure.[1] To avoid this pitfall, the marketer cannot dwell in uncertainty concerning the regulatory environment.

This chapter will eliminate much uncertainty for you as to the basics. It directly addresses the fundamental compliance-test issues facing the direct marketer in areas of unique, primary impact. Because of space limitations, we must focus attention on areas of interest to all direct marketers. Therefore, we'll begin with and stress one key channel: the mails. This is important because no matter how rapidly your customer registers the desire to purchase your product or even pays (electronic transfer), you must contend with the delivery constraints of the U.S. Postal Service or some similar private carrier.

In reviewing these areas here and elsewhere, you'll see frequent reference to FTC "rules and guidelines." "Rules" and "guidelines" are *not* interchangeable terms but are legally distinguishable as to their effect on you and your business.

A trade regulation rule specifically defines acts or practices that are unfair or deceptive within the meaning of the FTC's mandate under Section 5. They carry the force of substantive law, and literal compliance is required. Examples include the rules for games of chance,[2] mail-order merchandise,[3] and negative option.[4]

Industry guidelines are administrative interpretation of laws issued by the FTC for guidance of the public in conducting its affairs in conformity with legal requirements.[5] These guidelines do not have the force of substantive law, though failure to comply may result in corrective action by the FTC. Examples include the Guides Concerning Use of Endorsements and Testimonials in Advertising[6] and the Guide Concerning Use of the Word "Free" and Similar Representations.[7]

CHANNEL COMPLIANCE

Direct marketers have little difficulty determining the length of the product marketing channel necessary to reach their markets. The channel is the U.S. Postal Service or certain specialized mail carriers. Intermediaries are few, though drop shippers may be used, and the DMA and Time Warner are dealers in alternative delivery. Formerly, the direct marketer was concerned mainly with postal regulations and their ensuing compliance costs and with physical distribution management. More recently, four major areas of compliance have arisen: the Thirty-day Rule, the Federal Unordered Merchandise Statute, "dry testing," and merchandise substitution.

With increases in costs for almost all aspects of mail-order selling (e.g., postage, printing, and the goods themselves), most companies have sought to cut back on inventories. As a result, they can't always fill incoming orders promptly. Furthermore, some marginal companies caught in the rise of inflation have sought to obtain interest-free, or "dry," loans, holding their cash flow vis-à-vis fulfillment for as long as possible.

The FTC and many states[8] have enacted thirty-day rules and laws. The latter must be consulted, especially as to the situs of the corporate domicile. Note 5 of the FTC rule specifically states that the FTC does not wish to preempt consistent but narrower state laws on point. Therefore, certain firms will find that they must comply with a narrower state law. For our purposes, we'll focus on the FTC's rules.[9]

THIRTY-DAY RULE

The FTC's mail-order rule was adopted in 1976; it will be enforced literally, and penalties up to $10,000 may be issued for each violation. Since it is only three and a half pages long, it is worth your time to review it. It is written for laypeople, avoids legalese, and boils down to three key areas:

1. Initial solicitation requirements
2. First and subsequent delay notifications
3. Internal procedures

INITIAL SOLICITATION

It is an unfair or deceptive act to solicit any order through the mails or by telephone[10] unless you have a reasonable basis (arrived at in good faith and with objective substantiation) to believe that you can fulfill the order within the time you specify or, if no time is specified, 30 days after the receipt of a properly completed order from the buyer.

What is reasonable is reflected by the variables of your industry, product, and market. This is a factual issue affected by the interplay of many considerations. We all know the value of a dollar in hand and the value of its retention. The FTC understands the "float" value of money too and doesn't want your customers providing you with interest-free loans. Your best protection as to your good faith and reasonable expectations at the time of solicitation is to maintain an organized system of written internal records that will validate your expectations objectively.

But bear in mind that you elect to become involved with the 30-day aspect of this rule. You can insulate yourself from problems here if you state at the outset a date you can live with clearly and conspicuously on the promotion piece. You might state, "90 days from receipt" of the order. Then there is no first-delay problem (see below) until 90 days have elapsed, not 30. The trade-off here could be a loss of "spontaneity," since customers may be discouraged by a long wait. However, the choice is yours.

You should note that the FTC's Mail Order Merchandise Rule is under review as this goes to press. As part of proposed revisions to incorporate sales made by telephone, it has been proposed that on credit card orders the 30 days begin to run when you have all the information needed (i.e., credit card account number) to process the order, not when you actually debit the credit card. This has not yet been finalized, but you may wish to check into this if it affects you.

You also elect to come within the provisions of this rule by accepting cash orders. Bill only by outside credit cards (this may help your bad-debt problem too) or by a system of internal credit adjustments or even COD. In none of these cases will you bill before delivery, and therefore you will not be affected by the Thirty-Day Rule.

Finally, there are methods to decrease potential legal problems as well as customer dissatisfaction. Remember, a customer complaint to the FTC, a state attorney general office, or the Better Business Bureau is not helpful even if totally unjustified. Such complaints attract unwanted attention to your firm and may accumulate. Examine the following ways to lessen complaints:

1. Don't wait until checks clear. The 30-day meter is running. Test whether this delay is resulting in 30-day shipment problems. If so, does the trade-off vis-à-vis your bad-debt picture justify this practice?

2. Test different post offices or even times of the day when you ship if this option is available. Your legal requirement is to ship, not deliver, within 30 days. Legally, your customer then must contend with the inherent delays in the U.S. Postal Service or some other similar system of distribution. However, your customer knows only that he or she is waiting. Maximizing your deliveries by finding the best post office will enhance goodwill and possibly avoid complaints to the regulatory agencies.

3. The 30-day meter begins only after you receive in house a properly completed order. If you write back to the customer, make sure you keep a record. You'd be wise to retain a copy of the incomplete order as well as refrain from cashing any checks. Customers may forget that the initial delay was not prompted by you but by them. When they complain to you or to an agency, it will be clear that once a properly completed order was returned, you fulfilled it and shipped it within the required time.

FIRST-DELAY SITUATIONS

The reality of any marketplace is that unanticipated delays occur—e.g., a welcome deluge of orders or a simple delay by your supplier. When you are unable to ship the merchandise within the applicable time (the specific time you stated in your promotion or 30 days if no time is specified), you have the option to cancel the agreement and so inform the buyer or attempt to preserve the sale. In a few states you can also offer substitute goods.[11]

To do this, you must send a postage-paid return notice to the buyer, clearly and conspicuously offering the buyer the choice to either cancel the order and receive a full and prompt refund or extend the time for shipment to a specified revised shipping date. Tactically, you have an advantage here, since inertia is in your favor. If the buyer does not answer at all, you get the delay. Silence is construed as acceptance.

Don't attempt to improve on the prepaid reply device (postal card or letter). You may feel that an 800 number is more spontaneous and actually of greater benefit in facilitating the customer's response. The FTC won't. Just make sure to use a prepaid response letter. The postage-paid factor is very important, since buyers must not have to exercise their rights at the penalty of even a first-class stamp.

MULTIPLE-DELAY SITUATIONS

As was discussed, you may obtain as much as 60 days' grace in fulfilling an order unless the buyer specifically returns the postage-paid notice requesting a refund. The buyer's silence is construed as an acceptance of the delay.

If after 60 days there remains some unanticipated delay (e.g., a strike), you still may be able to save the order. The rule will allow further delays in certain circumstances.

You must notify the buyer of the additional delay. You may request the buyer's permission to ship at a certain specified future date or even a vague, indefinite date. The buyer then may cancel or may affirmatively agree to extend the time for delivery. At this time, you must also notify buyers that if they consent to the delay, they still may cancel at any subsequent time by notifying the seller prior to the actual agreement. The buyer then may cancel or affirmatively agree to extend the time for delivery.

This situation is distinguishable from the first-delay situation insofar as silence by the buyer cannot be construed as acceptance. If the buyer remains "silent" (fails to return the postage-paid card), you must treat the order as canceled and return a refund promptly to the buyer.

What is a prompt refund? This depends on the payment option elected. If the buyer sent cash or check, the buyer is entitled to have a refund in full mailed first-class within seven business days. If a credit card or other form of credit adjustment is required, you have a full billing cycle from the date on which the buyer's right to a refund begins. All refunds are to be sent by first-class mail and returned in the form received where practical; for example, if cash is received, a return check is permissible and prudent. Under no circumstances are mere credit vouchers or scrip permitted.

INTERNAL PROCEDURES

The Mail Order Rule stresses the need for adequate systems and procedures to create a presumption of a good-faith effort present to satisfy customer inquiries or complaints. These systems and procedures also should be adequate to establish your good-faith basis on which to solicit the initial order to request a delay or delays.

The rule does not apply to negative-option forms of selling or to magazine sales (except for the initial shipment) or COD orders, orders for seeds or growing plants, and credit orders in which the buyer's account is not charged before you ship the merchandise.

DRY TESTING

We have stated that the social policy behind the Mail Order Merchandise Rule was to discourage the practice of dry loans. We also stressed that the FTC considers it an unfair or deceptive act to solicit an order through the mails unless you have a reasonable basis to believe you can fulfill the order within a certain time. In light of all this, can you still "dry test," or solicit for a product before it tangibly exists? Interestingly, the answer is yes in certain circumstances.

There is limited law on point, but you should be aware of FTC Advisory Opinion 753 7003.[12] Specifically:

> The Commission does not object to the use of dry-testing a continuity book series marketed by mail order as long as the following conditions are observed: (1) No representation, express or implied, is made in advertisements, brochures, or other promotional material, which has the tendency or capacity to mislead the public into believing that the books have been or will definitely be published, or that by expressing an interest in receiving the books a prospective purchaser will necessarily receive them. (2) In all solicitations for subscriptions and other promotional material, clear and conspicuous disclosure is made of the terms and conditions of the publication, distribution, and other material aspects of the continuity book series program. Such disclosure must provide adequate notice of the conditional nature of publication of the book series, i.e., the fact that the book series is only planned and may not actually be published. (3) If the decision is reached not to publish the book series, due notice is given to persons who have subscribed, within a reasonable time after the date of first mailing the solicitations for subscriptions. The Commission considers four months or less to be a reasonable time, unless extenuating circumstances exist. If the decision

whether or not to publish the book series has not been made within that time period, persons who expressed a desire to subscribe should be notified of the fact that a decision has not yet been reached, and should be given an opportunity to cancel their order. (4) There is no substitution of any books for those ordered.[13]

YOUR RIGHTS UNDER AN ADVISORY OPINION

The above discussion suggests a topic one hears about frequently: obtaining an advisory opinion from the FTC.[14] In 1979, the FTC substantially changed its advisory opinion procedures. The FTC will issue formal opinions on written applications by specified parties (unnamed parties may not receive a response) in the following areas:

1. Where the matter involves a substantial or novel question of law and there is no clear precedent.
2. Where a proposed merger or acquisition is involved.
3. Where the subject matter is of significant public interest.

Requests for advice and the commission's response are placed on the public record immediately after the requesting party has received the advisory opinion.

Any advice received does not preclude the commission's later right to reconsider, rescind, or revoke. However, the original requesting party will be notified.

If you are concerned whether an advisory opinion is still valid, call the commission at (202) 326-2222.

UNORDERED MERCHANDISE

We've reviewed the situation in which there are delays in getting your customer a desired product. Now let's review what happens when the recipient receives something unordered.[15]

The law[16] (Mailing of Unordered Merchandise) on point is short and should be read by all direct-mail marketing managers. This law forbids not just blatant sending of unordered merchandise but also sending of merchandise "on approval" without your "customer's" prior permission. The FTC specifically warned the mail-order stamp industry of this in 1979.[17]

Only two kinds of merchandise may be sent through the mails without prior consent:

1. Free samples, which must be marked as such
2. Merchandise mailed by charitable organizations

Merchandise mailed by charitable organizations is sent "on approval," however, and need not be paid for. Customers may return it or keep it but they need not pay for it.

Your best strategy is that when in doubt, don't dun. If an innocent error is made, (e.g., computer mislabeling), write off the order. The customer won't complain unless an effort is made to compel payment. Your dunning for unordered merchandise can be the trigger for unwanted involvement with the Federal Trade Commission or a state attorney general or simply bad customer relations. Dunning accomplishes this in two ways:

1. Billing or dunning for unordered merchandise is itself an unfair practice.
2. Many customers do not complain to a regulatory body until dunning begins, because they were not aware of the problem or violation.

What is the rule concerning the mailing of unordered merchandise, and how can you avoid problems with it? We shall review it paragraph by paragraph and then discuss its exceptions.

MAILING OF UNORDERED MERCHANDISE

(a) Except for (1) free samples clearly and conspicuously marked as such and (2) merchandise mailed by a charitable organization soliciting contributions, the mailing of unordered merchandise or of communications prohibited by subsection (c) of this section constitutes an unfair method of competition and an unfair trade practice in violation of Section 45(a)(1) of Title 15 15 USCS 45 (a)(1).

The paragraph clearly makes it a per se violation of the law to ship unordered merchandise, which is defined as "merchandise mailed without the prior expressed request or consent of the recipient."[18] The only ambiguity here is the reference to "mailed."

Because the original pronouncement referred to the Postal Reorganization Act, some thought that enforcement would be limited to marketers using the U.S. Postal Service. The FTC clarified its position in 1978 by stating that all unordered merchandise was included whether shipped by mail, United Parcel, other private alternative delivery, or any other carrier.

(b) Any merchandise mailed in violation of subsection (a) of this section, or within the exception contained there, may be treated as a gift by the recipient, who shall have the right to retain, use, discard, or dispose of it in any manner he sees fit without any obligation whatsoever to the sender. All such merchandise shall have attached to it a clear and conspicuous statement informing the recipient that he may treat the merchandise as a gift to him and has the right to retain, use, discard, or dispose of it in any manner he sees fit without any obligation to the sender.

It should be noted that it is a separate violation (apart from the initial sending itself) for anyone to mail unordered merchandise without attaching a clear and conspicuous statement informing the recipient that it may be treated as a gift.

(c) No mailer of any merchandise mailed in violation of subsection (a) of this section, or within the exceptions contained therein, shall mail to any recipient of such merchandise a bill for such merchandise or any dunning communications.

It also is a violation of this statute for any sender of unordered merchandise (including correctly marked free samples and merchandise sent by charitable organizations) to send the recipient any bill or dunning communication or suggestion of the same in connection with such unordered merchandise.

Again, your best strategy may well be "When in doubt, don't dun." A customer's complaint to a regulatory body or private action rarely will occur unless an effort is made to compel payment.

Now that we've reviewed the text of the law, a number of questions remain.

What are the penalties? The penalties for both firms and individuals are up to $10,000 per violation. State laws may carry varied penalties and also may be drawn more narrowly. You should review the law for each state in which you're doing business and monitor legislation and regulations in each state.

Must the consumer obtain a remedy by complaint to an agency? No, it was the intent of Congress to permit consumers to protect themselves under the terms of the Federal Unordered Merchandise Statute.

What if the customer denies the existence of an agreement? You are in a strong position if you have a signed order that unequivocally states the contractual relationship to which the individual is subscribing. If the signature was a forgery or was contested by the recipient in good faith, you should request that the customer return the item at your expense (postage).

Prior course of dealings, such as a call with follow-up shipment, is not a valid argument when dealing with a consumer on a one-shot basis. Under the Uniform Commercial Code (UCC), two merchants can develop such prior course of dealings. However, the UCC is not applicable to consumers. The fact that you have shipped before and the customer has paid for similar items by check or otherwise proves nothing in this instance.

If you dun, expect problems if the recipient complains to a public body. Your common-law implied contract probably will not be compelling to the FTC or a state regulatory body, though by all means argue it in order to establish good faith.

The weakest position of all is that of the telephone marketer making "cold call ordering."[19] In this case, without a prior business relationship, the seller ships an order with no confirming documents. There is little possibility of enforcing such a call against a complaint filed under the Federal Unordered Merchandise Statute. You have no acceptance proof at all of an order. Some ways you might consider to protect yourself include the following:

1. Send all orders COD so that unordered merchandise may be rejected up front.

2. Send a postage-paid envelope with the order so that recipients of unordered merchandise may be encouraged to return such goods immediately, at no cost to themselves, thereby saving the merchandise itself.

3. Comply with the cooling-off provisions as worded or provide your customer with a follow-up written confirmation that can be responded to in a positive- or negative-option manner (the former response probably will negate any problems as to cold calls).

4. Follow up all orders with a subsequent phone call confirming the original order. This provides still weaker protection (because it is oral) than the first two methods, but it is a procedure that may prove to an agency that you employ bona fide methods to avoid problems of unordered merchandise.

No matter what safeguards you employ, an oral order is not a provable order, and this must be considered at all stages, especially before you dun.

How does this statute affect negative option plans? During the commitment period and at all subsequent times, there is an ongoing business relationship subject to the FTC's rule on point.

Furthermore, the rule[20] permits the sender to ask for its return (but not bill) this one time. Any subsequent shipments after this one constitute unordered merchandise.

What about a continuity plan? Your rights are less clear because there is no rule on point. You could use a similar approach as to the one isolated shipment after cancellation, but I wouldn't dun.

What about substituted merchandise? The entire area is fraught with peril, even if the substitution is of equivalent or superior quality.[21] Artistic property by its very nature is too unique to be substituted for. If a seasonal surge or other unanticipated ordering deluge is overwhelming your inventory reserve, get expressed consent in writing before you substitute.

This will save your sale as well as satisfy customers who prefer the substitution to nothing when they need the item by a given date. Substitution without the prior expressed consent or request of the recipient falls within the literal terms of the statute and will be considered an unfair trade practice.

Finally, when a valid substitution is offered, the customer must be afforded the opportunity to return the item without a postage penalty.

A FINAL NOTE ON UNORDERED MERCHANDISE

The above is a brief review of the Federal Unordered Merchandise Statute. The law is written in uncomplicated language and has been reproduced here in its entirety. Most states have similar laws on their books, and some state laws are drawn more narrowly.

Whenever possible, coupons or order forms authorizing the shipment of merchandise to a consumer should be signed and laid out clearly in separate and distinct paragraphs. All wording should be in lay English, and the merchandise or purchase plan should be described in detail.

When a serious doubt arises as to the validity of your efforts to recover payment, don't dun.

THREE COPY HEADLINERS

You design your promotion piece to catch the viewer's eye both aesthetically and in terms of simple dollars and cents.

The former is primarily the work of the creative team, though they must be careful that all visual depictions convey a correct impression of the size and identity of the product. Deceptive mock-ups or those having a "tendency to deceive" are counterproductive. However, the major compliance issues arise when certain wording is used to capture the reader's interest. A thorough knowledge of the subtleties of "sale," "new," "free," and words of similar impact will assist your goal of maximizing reader interest while minimizing negative involvement as a result of deceptive wording.

SALE

From time to time, you'll wish to offer your customers special offers. The ad copy may at times signify the promotion as a "sale,"[22] "savings," or price "reduction." The most commonly asked questions are these:

1. What is a sale?
2. What discount reduction from our former prices is sufficient to constitute a sale?
3. Does every item featured in the promotion piece have to be on sale?

What is a sale? A sale is the offering of an article at a reduction from the advertiser's former price. If the former price is the actual, bona fide price at which the article was offered and sold to the public on a regular basis for a reasonably substantial period of time, it provides a legitimate basis of price comparison.

The objectively proved "sales test" is a necessary hurdle. Significant previous sales must be demonstrated in the same product and geographic marketplace to discourage the entry of an overpriced article (for which few if any sales are made) being "reduced" to its realistic market price and then being offered as a "sale."

What discount should be offered? You must take care that the amount of reduction is not so insignificant as to be meaningless. The reduction should be sufficiently large that consumers, if they knew what it was, would believe that a genuine bargain or saving was being offered. A nominal reduction — e.g., less than 5 percent — is unacceptable. Depending on the market, the ticket price, and trade practices, 10 percent or more would be a safe starting point. The alert customer may well be suspicious of a promotion claiming a large reduction or discount but not stating the actual amount of the reduction or discount.

Must every item in a sale promotion be reduced to satisfy compliance? Every item so designated in a "sale promotion" should represent a reduction from a former price that was openly and actively offered for a reasonable period of time in the regular course of business.

An item not reduced from a former price at which the same (not a similar) product was openly and actively offered for sale, for a reasonably substantial period of time, in the recent regular course of business, honestly and in good faith, has no business being offered in a sales promotion. Furthermore, you should not use language such as "formerly sold at X dollars" unless substantial sales at that price actually were made.

Therefore, the use of expressions such as "annual sale," "fall sale," etc., in catalogs, advertising, or other promotional pieces containing nonsale items without revealing in immediate conjunction with such representations that nonsale items were contained therein and without distinctively identifying such nonsale items is prohibited.

To conclude, a sale price must be a reasonable and honest statement of a valid former market price that is now reduced. All items advertised as being on "sale" in a sales promotion should represent an honest bona fide reduction from a previous benchmark price. You should be prepared to substantiate your claim that every item on "sale" was sold in the marketplace (and was not just "offered") previously. Items not on sale in a sales promotion must be identified and distinguished distinctively. If quantities are limited, you must disclose any limitation up front.

NEW

This is a relatively straightforward term. Merchandise may not be offered as new if it has been used or refurbished. This means that you may not clean or "improve" your returned merchandise in any way and then return it to your inventory. Unless you state otherwise, merchandise offered for sale must be new and may not have been used during a "trial period" or otherwise.

The word "new" also is used to promote a product which has not been introduced into the marketplace yet or has been "improved," enabling you to advertise the item as "new and improved." There is no particular usage period for an offer, but FTC Advisory Opinion 120[23] has indicated six months as a tentative outer limit. This suggestion is subject to certain variables. A new product should constitute the latest model in a particular product line and certainly not have been marketed widely elsewhere. In a bona fide test marketing of a new product that does not cover more than 15 percent of the population and does not exceed six months in duration, however, the six-months rule does not apply until the test period has terminated. Certain states have very exact disclosure requirements; therefore, make sure you ask counsel to review all state laws that have an impact on your operations and to monitor the legislatures. As always, you must consult state law and not be content with merely understanding the FTC's position.

FREE

There is one word any marketer knows will always prompt a second glance: *free*. Because of its ability to highlight and enhance the promotion piece, it is a highly regulated term of art both as to definition and disclosure. The following discussion will guide you through the regulatory thicket.

What is a free item? The word "free" indicates that a person is paying nothing for an article and no more than the regular price for the other article. Thus, a purchaser has a right to believe that the seller will not directly and immediately recover, in whole or in part, the cost of the free merchandise by marking up the price of the article that must be purchased or by the substitution of inferior merchandise.[24] Finally, shipping and handling charges cannot be built into or added to a free item. For example, if a free offer is sent as part of a total package for examination or trial, a prepaid mailing label must be included in the package to cover the cost of returning the item. If a return postage charge might burden the recipient, the item is not free.

Words of similar connotation (e.g., "gift," "given without charge," "no cost or obligation," "bonus," etc.) "which tend to convey the impression to the consuming public that an article of merchandise is 'Free'"[25] are held to the same standard.

What conditions must be disclosed? All the terms, conditions, and obligations (e.g., any credit limitations or qualifications, prepayment requirements, etc.) should appear in close conjunction (i.e., physically adjacent so that the elements are naturally read together) with the offer of the "free" merchandise. If there are conditions, the following rules pertain.

1. The type size in which any limitations are printed must be at least half as large as the largest type size in the introductory offer copy, exclusive of numerals.
2. I'd recommend a minimum type size of 6 to 8 points.
3. The qualification terms must be stated together in the same location in the ad, not separated by copy or graphics.
4. Disclosure of the terms of the offer set forth in a footnote of an advertisement to which reference is made by an asterisk or similar symbol does not constitute disclosure at the outset and will constitute noncompliance.
5. Finally, as to timing your free promotion, you should know that:
   a. A single size of a product should not be advertised with a "free" offer for more than 6 months in any 12-month period, and at least 30 days should elapse before another such offer is promoted.
   b. No more than three such offers should be made in any 12-month period.
   c. During this period, your sale of the product in the size promoted should not exceed 50 percent of the total volume of your sales of the product in the same size.

In summary, you may use the word *free* if your product is an unconditional gift or when a purchase is required. All the conditions, obligations, or other prerequisites to the receipt and retention of the free product offered must be set forth clearly and conspicuously in immediate conjunction with the first use of the word *free*, leaving no reasonable probability that the terms of the offer will be misunderstood. No "hidden" requirements are permitted. Ambiguity is no asset. Language that may be construed in favor of a free ad will be so construed against the creator of the ad.

To avoid copy clutter and redundancy, you should regard each promotion piece as constituting one component offer. To meet the "clearly and conspicuously" test, the qualifications merely need to be stated at the outset after the first use of the word *free*. Thereafter, the term *free* may be used as often per offer as you believe advisable regardless of how many items are being offered for sale.

USE OF CURRENCY AND FLAGS

You cannot reproduce currency (paper money, checks, negotiable instruments, and other obligations and securities of the United States) in any manner in its actual size. It should be larger than (at least one and a half times) its original size or smaller (three-quarters the actual size or smaller). The Court still feels these obvious differences are needed to protect "unwary and inattentive" people from accepting a photograph of money as the "real thing."

Black-and-white reproductions must always be used—the color ban remains. The Court believes this secures a substantial government interest in protecting against counterfeiting.

The reproduction of coins is allowed.

You can use a drawing or photograph of phony (assuming it is false) currency.

If you violate the law, your plates may be destroyed before their use is finished, all your outside printers may be subpoenaed, and you may incur heavy fines.

Commercial free speech is an evolving body of law, so be alert as to changes. However, as matters now stand, make sure your in-house and outside creative people comply with the law. If you're an advertising agency, you should keep the text of the law handy for reference if your client balks.

Major compliance issues arise when certain wording is used either orally or in print to capture the reader's interest or to break down buyer resistance. A premium is placed on clear and conspicuous accuracy. Ambiguity is no asset. A thorough knowledge of the subtleties of the words "sale," "free," "new," "at cost," "trial and examination," and other terms conveying similar meanings will greatly assist you in maximizing reader interest while minimizing the possibility of allegations of unfair and deceptive advertising.

Finally, all states as well as the District of Columbia have statutes prohibiting the use in advertising of their own flags as well as the U.S. flag.[26]

SUMMARY OF LAWS GOVERNING TELEMARKETING

- You can monitor an employee's call if it is done in the ordinary course of business for a reasonable business purpose. You cannot monitor a call for personal gain, gossip, or any other purpose.

- You can never tape a call without consent (or court order).

- In many states, you must review with your counsel whether the home-solicitation laws have incorporated telephone and if so at what threshold of sales level. If this is the case, you will have to comply with the applicable cooling-off periods.

- Most states restrict or ban automated selection or dialing calls.

- All states (and many localities) restrict the hours when you may call as well as what your script must and must not include.[27]

CONCLUSION

In this brief review of only a few salient areas of law affecting the direct marketer, we have not focused on horror stories. They abound, however, and a brief comment is warranted here:

When it comes to government regulations, following a policy of noncompliance either deliberately or through lack of knowledge is like playing Russian roulette. If you lose, the penalty can harm your firm and your career growth. But if you know the rules of the game, the decision about whether to abide by those rules is yours. Sometimes, however, after receiving advice of counsel, a marketer elects to make a "business decision" from legal sanction. You may subject both your firm and yourself to criminal as well as civil sanctions. Before electing to make a business decision that violates a law, you should consult counsel as to the law and the penalties imposed as a result of such violation. The penalties or fines generally are based on a number of factors such as number of infractions involved, previous warnings, size and financial status of the company, and public deception (even if not intentional in many instances).

The fines and other legal sanctions don't tell the whole story. The greater hardship may involve not the fine but the counsel fees, adverse publicity and loss of goodwill, and special measures that may have to be taken to counteract the "harm" that results from the violation. It is a sad reality that the cost in terms of both time and money of having to discontinue an ad or promotion that is not in compliance with federal or state regulations even when no fine per se is involved can be monumental. It's essential, therefore, not to dismiss the myriad laws and regulations that affect your profession.[28]

It is my hope that this chapter will prove to be a useful tool for direct marketers who wish to protect their firms from adverse visibility to government as well as to give their buyers a fair shake.

NOTES

1. Articles on point written by Robert J. Posch, Jr., for *Direct Marketing* are "Your Personal Exposure for Interoffice Communications," October 1988, p. 128; "Civil Personal Exposure in Common Corporate Settings," March 1989, p. 100; and "Personal Liability Exposure in Intellectual Property Areas," September 1989, p. 99.

2. 16 C.F.R. 419.

3. 16 C.F.R. 435.

4. 16 C.F.R. 425.

5. 16 C.F.R. 1.5.

6. 16 C.F.R. 255.

7. 16 C.F.R. 251.

8. For example, review New York State General Business Law 396 (m).

9. California, New York, and other states have added telephone to the Mail Order Merchandise laws, and the FTC will require it by 1992.

10. For example, see Sections 17538 and 175383 of California's Business and Professions Code.

11. "Dry Testing" and "Bulk Loading," a Continuity Book Series by Mail Order, 85 F.T.C. 1192-1197 (1975).

12. Ibid., pp. 1193–94.

13. 16 C.F.R. 1-1-1.4.

14. See also Robert Posch, "Legal Outlook: Avoiding the Pitfalls of Unordered Merchandise," *Direct Marketing,* January 1982, pp. 98–101.

15. 39 U.S.C.S. 3009. New York direct marketers might wish to review General Obligations Law, article 5-332.

16. FTC press release, May 24, 1979.

17. 39 U.S.C.S. 3009(d).

18. Such marketers should note that more than ten states have incorporated such calls into their respective home-solicitation laws requiring a three-day cooling-off period.

19. 16 C.F.R. 425.1(b)(1)(iii).

20. For example, see NYS General Obligations Law 396-m (3)(z)(i) and (ii).

21. 16 C.F.R. 233.

22. See also Advisory Opinions 120, 246, and 325.

23. 16 C.F.R. 251, 251.1.

24. Ibid., 251.1(2)(i).

25. *Regan* v. *Time, Inc.,* 468 U.S. 641, 82 L.Ed.2d 487, 104 S.Ct. 3262 (1984).

26. 36 U.S.C. 176(i).

27. See articles on point written by Robert J. Posch, Jr., in *Direct Marketing:* "Can You Monitor Employee Phone Performance," November 1981, p. 108; "Telephone Marketing: It Survived and Prospered," September 1982, p. 106; "State, Federal Phone Legislation Poses Threat to Marketers," September 1984, p. 118.

28. See Robert J. Posch, Jr., *The Complete Guide to Marketing and the Law* (Englewood Cliffs, N.J.: Prentice-Hall, 1988).

6
Multinational Direct Marketing

Richard Miller

Market Response International
North Chatham, Mass.

This chapter addresses the subject of extending your marketing reach to overseas locations while retaining control in your home base, presumably in the United States. Though there is necessarily some overlap, the chapter is not designed to address the requirements of companies wishing to locate marketing efforts within specific foreign countries. The distinction is important, as the requirements of the two systems differ in many respects.

U.S. companies exporting products, services, or ideas either have foreign-*based* divisions or operate multinationally from a U.S. base. In some cases they do both. IBM, for instance, is a true *foreign* marketer. They establish subsidiary companies in foreign countries, complete with manufacturing, distribution, and marketing support *within* the given country. *Mitsubishi* becomes a true foreign marketer when they set up a turn-key operation in the United States. McGraw-Hill, on the other hand, is an example of a true *multinational* marketer, in that their worldwide publishing operation is U.S.-based and most promotion, product, and customer service is *exported,* much of it via the increasingly sophisticated systems whose benefits have accrued to the multinational direct marketer. To enter the world stage as a foreign-*based* marketer implies saddling yourself with a large capital investment in foreign territory. Locating abroad requires an advance contingent, land acquisition or lease, manufacturing and distribution facilities, sales and administrative personnel, and all the baggage that goes with delivering the end product to a "local" market. Rather than assume this logistical burden, many companies have chosen to market abroad from their home base.

Through the increasingly sophisticated international printing, remailing, product exporting, and customer service networks, many companies are either selling directly from the United States or are paving the way for future foreign investment by *testing* products and services through multinational direct marketing techniques. By keeping the majority of their marketing and production control in the United States, they avoid the huge outlay that otherwise might be required.

One of the great contributions the direct marketing industry makes to the budding foreign marketer is the ability to act as a vanguard for his or her foreign aspirations. Target marketing can be used to identify plant location, market concentration, and prospect profiles; it can be used to develop and support salespeople and manufacturers' representatives; it is classic for lead generation, and perhaps most important of all, direct marketing techniques allow international entrepreneurs to *test* their products before committing to large high-risk foreign investments.

A number of developments have converged over the past decade to prompt a quantum leap in direct marketers' ability to reach large segments of the globe with relative ease and sophistication. They can tap into large international databases and communicate via international mail, fax, phone, and satellite. And they can do this in a freer, more dynamic trade atmosphere.

The handbook you are reading addresses many of the essential ingredients of a successful direct marketing campaign. To a greater or lesser degree, all of these factors come into play in the development of a *multinational* effort, plus additional considerations such as *culture, language, currency,* and *customs.* This chapter deals with some of the more important considerations.

RESEARCH

It is assumed that you have already made a decision to market multinationally and you are now ready for the strategical and logistical steps. Though a great deal of research may (and should) have gone into the basic decision to move ahead, your first step in preparing the direct marketing effort should be *more* research. It is imperative that you approach a foreign market with as much comprehension of its cultural and geopolitical background as you can reasonably assimilate. Just as it is important to know regional tastes and differences in your home country, it is doubly important that you know the cultural and geographic profile of your foreign target market. If you're based in the United States, you know instinctively that you might want to position an offer differently to a prospect in New England from the way you would present it to a prospect in Southern California; that one harvests lobsters in Maine and makes tacos in Texas; that Miami has a large Latin population and Peoria does not. This is the "common knowledge" that has to be learned about foreign markets.

There is a wide range of resources available to aid research of foreign markets; these include foreign trade and development offices, embassy commercial sections, foreign Chambers of Commerce, and professional research firms. It's very easy to ruin an otherwise well-conceived multinational campaign by the inclusion of a naïve cultural *faux pas*. It's far better to put the time in on research up front rather than find out when it's too late that the chrysanthemum you used to illustrate a product is the symbol of death in Asia, that the clever name you gave your product turned out to be slang for a contraceptive in Germany, or that the name of the insurance product you're promoting in France is gutter language to the Gauls. These examples are from actual case histories and are indicative of the ease with which one can fall victim to cultural ignorance.

STRATEGY

Multinational strategy should be based on well-researched facts and clear goals. Your strategy is going to be influenced by your knowledge of the marketplace, cultural considerations, lists and media, and all the elements of direct marketing that are or are not going to be available to you in your target market. A good grasp of these factors is essential to good strategic planning. It is equally important that the team charged with the multinational project has a clear consensus on goals, a sufficient budget, and agreement on acquisition allowances and break-even points.

Your strategy will flow out of your ability to answer certain basic questions:

Competition. How many are there ahead of me (either indigenous or foreign) and what is their share of market? In many of the developed nations, there is a direct marketing trade association that will be helpful in supplying answers to this and other questions.

Import regulations. What restrictions are there on the import of my product and what, if any, duties will be applicable? Import tariffs can vary from zero to 100 percent depending on product type. For specific tariff information, a good resource is the *Export Shipping Manual,* Bureau of National Affairs, Inc., 1231 25th Street NW, Washington, D.C. 20037.

Transportation and distribution. Will I be able to handle distribution with methods similar to those I use in my domestic market, or will I have to make accommodations? Most of the developed world can offer sophisticated levels of both ground and air transportation, with some notable exceptions. A good place to start research in your target country is with their foreign trade office or a reliable freight forwarder.

Political profile and economy. Am I going to be marketing into a stable political climate with a growing economy? Recessions sometimes affect one part of the world and not another. Political and economic indicators are published frequently by such publications as *The Economist* and should be reviewed on a regular basis.

Other pertinent questions you should be asking yourself are "What additional personnel will I need? Who will be responsible and are they qualified? Does this venture have the sanction of top management or will it be treated as a stepchild? How much money am I prepared to spend? To lose? Do I have a three- to five-year business plan?"

Perhaps more than in any other situation, an international entrepreneur must be ready to forgo short-term profits in entering the multinational marketplace. It is imperative that your domestic operation be of such size and stability as to allow for generous test funds and a deferral of profits for a longer period of time than you might generally be accustomed to. It is also ill-advised to look at the foreign marketplace as a panacea for domestic problems. An organization that is strong and stable and is ready to commit time, money, and patience will be more apt to reap rewards than the quick-hitting opportunist.

LISTS

As with any direct marketing effort, the research and study of appropriate target lists is crucial to a multinational effort. The subject is worthy of an entire chapter in itself, but space permits us to look at only the basic areas of consideration.

There are two main types of international lists, *national* and *multinational*.

National Lists

These are the lists that are held or compiled within a specific national border. Business lists tend to come from specialized periodicals, directories, telephone books, and association memberships. In some developed countries, consumer lists can be found in some of the same sources as in the United States, such as catalogs, magazines, insurance files, and credit cards; but generally speaking, customer lists are more tightly guarded than in the United States. There is a greater tendency to maintain security and forgo rental revenues. Ferreting out good consumer lists takes patience and is usually done in cooperation with a qualified international list broker or manager.

Multinational Lists

These are lists that cover a region or are even global in nature. They tend to come from world-class magazines, seminars, trade shows, and international directories. It should be kept in mind that the international list industry was really spawned by the publishing industry, particularly in the business-to-business marketplace. Trade magazines have been circulated worldwide for a century or more, and gradually these subscriber databases have been compiled into well-managed and profitable centers for many publishing companies. Leading multinational subscriber lists include *Time, Newsweek, Business Week, Harvard Business Review, The Economist, Fortune, International Herald-Tribune,* and *The Asian Wall Street Journal.* But there are hundreds of others from which to choose.

To illustrate the difference between *national* and *multinational* lists, assume, for example, that you are promoting a service to the computer industry or any other high-tech industry. You can target a particular *country* by reaching only Belgium with *Belgian Data News,* only Japan with *Nikkei Electronics,* or only the UK with *Computer Industry.* On the other hand, you can reach a Pan-European audience by renting the subscriber list of *Electronics Benn,* the *McGraw Hill High Tech File,* or the *National Computer Conference Attendees File.*

Case Example

One approach to locating international lists can be illustrated by an assignment in which the author was involved. The Acustar Division of Chrysler Corporation wanted to announce the availability of a multimillion-dollar line of electric-motor assembly machines. This was one-of-a-kind equipment to be sold at auction. It was immediately recognized that there would be a large potential market in newly developed countries (NICs) as well as developed nations. List research was approached with a three-pronged attack. Two list brokers were engaged, one with in-depth Asian experience and one with equal experience in Europe and the Middle East. Additionally, personal visits or contacts were made with foreign trade offices in the United States and at government reference libraries. The object was to identify manufacturers, suppliers, consultants, and trade organizations in the worldwide electric motor industry. Within two weeks, 40,000 names were identified (including multiple names in one company). Because of time constraints, Chrysler decided to waive a merge-purge run and risk some duplication. The lists were pared down to 30,000, and a lightweight illustrated brochure was created and mailed worldwide through a foreign distribution point, using a translation into five languages. The result was an immediate indication of interest from 60 companies around the world—about 5 times the amount expected. The leads were qualified and four bidders came to the United States for the final sale. The cost was about $60,000 for a sale of $10 million worth of manufacturing equipment.

Data Protection

One cannot discuss international lists, particularly in Europe, without considering the impact of data-protection legislation. In some European countries, data-protection constraints are severe and limiting. To a greater or lesser degree, European data-protection laws affect marketers in Austria, Denmark, Ireland, Finland, Germany, Greece, Iceland, Israel, Luxembourg, The Netherlands, Norway, Sweden, and the United Kingdom. Generally speaking, the laws tend to be more stringent in northern Europe. Germany requires registration of databases with the government, list brokering is virtually banned in Austria and Denmark, and some Scandinavian countries require a declaration of the list source on the outside envelope. It is beyond the scope of this chapter to detail data-protection laws, but *the direct marketer is well advised to become familiar with them.* As this chapter is being written, the European Economic Commission is preparing guidelines for a common set of data-protection laws, which will eventually apply equally to all EC countries.

List Cost

Expensive. That's the short answer to a frequently asked question. As to *why* lists are so expensive, there is no complete agreement. Obviously, the law of supply and demand plays a role. The universe has grown more slowly than the demand, thus tending to make it a sellers' market. And quite legitimately, the compilers and managers have had to spend more time (and expense) coaxing lists out of sometimes reluctant sources. Even where this does not appear to be the reason, however, costs are two, three, and even four times the cost of lists in North America. It is not unusual for a list to cost $300 per thousand.

Size of Universe

The first question a new multinational marketer might ask is "How large a universe am I going to be able to choose from?" The answer is: *very* large. Keep in mind that the United States represents only 5 percent of the world population. Admittedly, we are further advanced than most countries in the compilation and dissemination of list data, but it would be a mistake to assume that the rest of the world is far behind. Using the United Kingdom as an example, there are 200,000 company names available through just one list source, with another 300,000 in Europe (it may be helpful to keep in mind that the United Kingdom does not consider itself a part of Europe for purposes of many discussions). Size of universe can be a concern in highly specialized lists in the smaller countries. Whereas you might be used to dealing with 1000 widget manufacturers in North America, you might only find 50 in Spain. Obviously that will affect your direct marketing strategy if you are targeting only Spain.

The problem with international lists, particularly *national* lists, is not so much the size of the universe but access, organization, cleanliness, and speed of delivery. This varies widely, from *sophisticated* in locations such as the United Kingdom, Germany, and Denmark to *marginal* in such countries as Spain, Japan, and Brazil. There is rarely a management or delivery problem with recognized multinational lists, such as those cited at the beginning of the List section. But with national lists, it is important to have a clear understanding with the list owner, manager, or broker before ordering. In many cases, in both Europe and Asia, list owners will not deliver except to a local mailing house, in order to satisfy their security concerns. This can be frustrating and obviously requires patience and flexibility on the marketer's part.

Sample 1990 Lists and Prices	
List	Cost per 1000
International Management magazine	$238
Executive Travel magazine	160
Quelle catalog buyers	150
Fortune International magazine	240
Diners Club, Australia	145
Nikkei Computer	185
Singapore Institute of Management	250
Collin Street Bakery	185
Business Week International	220

In general, you have all the considerations in acquiring foreign lists as you do with domestic ones, with the addition of some special caveats. You must factor in higher costs, as high as three times U.S. costs. This is somewhat offset by the fact that foreign lists are less saturated and tend to produce higher response rates. You must allow plenty of time for delivery and be prepared to use a foreign lettershop if necessary. If you are not dealing with an experienced broker, you should get list samples with label formats displayed. Almost all countries will provide proper postal codes, but you must *ask* to have the country name line added if the supplier is not accustomed to having the list mailed from outside its national territory. And in the case of Asian names, you must be assured the printing is in Alpha. Because of the complexities and subtle nuances of the international list business, it would be a wise course to select an experienced international broker to assist. The foreign direct marketing associations—such as the British Direct Marketing Association or the European Direct Marketing Association—would be able to recommend appropriate list brokers and managers.

CREATIVE

Cultural Considerations

Packaging your promotional message for a variety of different cultures requires at least some fundamental understanding of national differences and a sensitivity to them. True, human beings are often motivated by similar stimuli no matter where they live, but they may react entirely differently to the manner in which the stimulus is presented. Americans tend to be open, gregarious, and informal, but this is not the case in many societies. Awareness of these subtleties can prevent the inexperienced multinationalist from making a serious error that could negatively impact response.

A frequently asked question is "Do I have to change the basic content of my U.S. control package?" Certainly the basic selling proposition may not have to change, but the way it is framed should be looked at carefully. For instance, some cultures would be offended by references to their families or an implied knowledge of their income or personal preferences. The use of first names in a salutation would offend in some countries and be acceptable in others. Until you are very comfortable with your knowledge of a given culture, caution should be used in framing an offer and message, with special attention paid to the choice of teasers, graphics, and personal information. A knowledge of local regulations is also imperative. The use of premiums, for example, is closely regulated in some countries.

Before you finalize your creative approach, basic questions of strategy have to be answered: Is my audience going to be targeted in one country or spread across an entire region? Is it monolingual or multilingual? (Switzerland has four languages.) Is my target universe a sales territory, a professional and trade strata, or a socioeconomic group? It's very possible that you will want to address a like audience (affluent auto owners, hardware store owners, or young mothers) who are motivated by the same desires but may have to be reached in different languages. On the other hand, with products such as trade magazines and technical equipment, which are targeted to educated internationalists, English will often suffice.

Translating

Whether or not to translate into a local language is greatly determined by your product and your audience within the target region. There are approximately 400 million English-speaking people in the world, and an unknown additional number who comprehend English, particularly technical and professional people. With this in mind, many business publications sold abroad from a U.S. base are sold without translations—or, in some cases, only certain elements such as instructions or the order form are translated. Consumer publications, however, are more apt to require translations. *Reader's Digest, Time, Newsweek,* etc., all have editions published in local languages, and the promotional material follows suit.

Where appropriate, dual, or multiple translations are sometimes used. This, of course, is very common in Canada, where French is mandated for most material used in Quebec. When designing for multilingual materials, keep in mind that different languages use significantly differing amounts of space for the same message. French and German, for example, require 10 to 15 percent more space than English.

Production

There is a long list of caveats in preparing for final production. Among the prime considerations is the *weight* of the paper stock. Most multinational mailings begin their journey in the air, and an extra gram or two can quickly tip a shipment over into a higher price bracket. Most international computations are based on the metric system, so it's helpful to keep a metric conversion chart handy. Allow for a larger envelope window, as foreign addresses often require more label and window space. Except for postcards, self-mailers are forbidden in virtually all international situations, so an envelope will almost always be required. To assist in this situation, most international remailers offer paper envelope or polybagging services at the U.S. departure city or foreign remail point.

In general, when devising your creative strategy, be sensitive to any possibility of offending. Study your market; talk with experienced "nationals" or consultants; check offers of premiums, sweepstakes, and similar "lift" promotions with appropriate regulatory sources; and above all, avoid the risk of appearing patronizing.

MULTIMEDIA

Print

As in the United States and Canada, there is a sophisticated network of print media available to integrate with a basic multinational direct-mail campaign. Many societies are accustomed to "off the page" direct-response advertising in local and national newspapers, and the use of inserts is widespread. In Europe particularly, ratecards are flexible, making it worthwhile to spend time in negotiation to arrive at a rate compatible with your marketing plans and budget. Most major world magazines and newspapers (and many business publications) have U.S. representation. Examples of world-class English-language publications are *The International Herald-Tribune,* the European and Asian editions of *The Wall Street Journal, The Financial Times, Newsweek, Time,* and *Business Week,* There are hundreds of other titles. Additionally, each major country has indigenous publications that will generally match a given customer target profile. A relatively recent development is the availability of lead generation via card decks, printed both in the United States and abroad using English and local languages.

Broadcast

Only recently has television as an advertising medium begun to make a mark in other parts of the world. Though advances in satellite communication do make it possible to reach large global audiences, the target marketer would more probably turn to local and regional programming. Broadcasting tends to be government-controlled, but there are commercial stations now emerging in most developed countries. The traditional techniques of direct-response TV used in the United States are still unfamiliar in most other societies.

Telemarketing

The medium of telemarketing, both outbound and inbound, is available in most developed countries of the world. Of particular interest to the U.S.-based marketer are the 800-type satellite systems offered by large companies such as AT&T and MCI. They are available at increasingly economical rates and allow for the same kind of prospect and customer interaction that you currently may enjoy with your domestic operation. More sophisticated systems include 24-hour multilingual operations, which receive orders, manage fulfillment, and handle customer service in Asia, Europe, South America, and other global points without leaving U.S. soil.

INTERNATIONAL MAIL DISTRIBUTION SERVICES

If you have made the decision to create and produce your promotional materials in the United States, the next question is "What postal delivery options do I have?" Multinational mailings would not be possible without the development of the economical and efficient distribution systems that have evolved over the past two decades. They are critical to a successful multinational promotion and differ significantly from the domestic mailing systems you may be accustomed to.

There are three basic ways to move your mail overseas: with the U.S. Postal Service via ISAL (International Surface Airlift), through an independent ISAL consolidator, or with a private "remailer." A knowledge of how these systems work is essential to the international direct marketer.

ISAL (International Surface Airlift)

This system was developed by the U.S. Postal Service. As the name implies, your material travels by a combination of air and surface transportation. The system is designed for bulk mailers and publishers and offers the least expensive way of moving your materials abroad. In order to qualify for the lower cost, the mailer must meet certain preparation requirements at the lettershop point and arrange for delivery of the materials to one of ISAL's acceptance points. The material is then airlifted to selected distribution points around the world and dropped into the surface mail stream in or near the target country. The minimum weight is 50 pounds and may include advertising material, catalogs, books, magazines, sheet music, and other publications. Rates (1990) range from a low of $1.92 per pound to the United Kingdom and some European countries, to a high of $3.60 per pound for more distant points. Delivery time is 7 to 14 days.

ISAL Consolidators

These are private companies who coordinate your ISAL shipment for you, sorting, bagging, and transporting the material to an ISAL gateway city. Consolidators are employed by shippers who either do not want to be burdened with the preparation arrangements or are unprepared or unfamiliar with the procedures involved. The chief advantage of consolidators is in providing a "turn-key" system, which can include labeling and inserting. In return they add a surcharge to ISAL rates. Delivery time is 7 to 14 days.

International Remailers

These are private distribution services. They differ from ISAL consolidators in that they negotiate private rates with airline cargo divisions and, in some instances—such as KLM, SAS, and Virgin—are owned by the airline. They can arrange a turn-key system, including pickup at your printer or lettershop, and offer efficient worldwide service. Some remailers also offer lettershop services abroad. Materials can be picked up at your printer, transported in bulk to an overseas distribution point, inserted, labeled, affixed with postage, bagged, and dropped into the appropriate country mail stream. Services can include customs clearance, return of undeliverables, address correction, tracing, reply handling (sometimes called "caging"), and currency transactions. Costs are higher than ISAL but include custom-designed services, and some remailers can provide quicker delivery. Unlike ISAL, however, a U.S. return address cannot be used with a remailer.

Variations on the above distribution systems include IPA (International Priority Airmail). This is another U.S. Postal Service system offering expedited air delivery and is designed for smaller shipments and for materials of irregular size and shape. For shipment of small parcels, shippers have a choice of Air Parcel Post, International Express Mail (U.S.P.S.), or a number of private courier services such as Federal Express, TNT, DHL, and other air express companies.

Following is an illustrated cost comparison for the international distribution of a typical direct-mail promotion using the three main distribution systems described above. We're assuming a mailing of 30,000 pieces, and a list cost of $200 per thousand. Printing costs are not shown. Each letter weighs one ounce and is destined for recipients in the United Kingdom, Germany, Switzerland, and The Netherlands:

	Option 1: ISAL	
List	$ 6,000	($200 per 1000)
Sorting/inserting (To ISAL specs.)	1,500	($50 per 1000)
Freight to Gateway	300	
via ISAL	4,162	(30,000 1-ounce pieces = 1875 pounds × $2.22 per pound)
	$11,962	

	Option 2: ISAL Consolidator	
List	$ 6,000	($200 per 1000)
Via Consolidator	$ 6,975	(Includes ISAL postage of $2.22 per pound, plus consolidator surcharge of $1.50 per pound for coordination, pickup, sorting, and delivery to ISAL gateway; total: $3.72 per pound)
	$12,975	

	Option 3: International Remailer	
List	$ 6,000	($200 per 1000)
Freight to Gateway	300	
Via Remailer	$ 6,900	($.23 each, including airfreight from gateway sorting, postage, bagging)
	$13,200	

The above are approximates and can vary depending on the exact services performed. The figures used are from 1990 published rates.

International Business Reply Service

A relatively recent development in worldwide mail services is the availability of International Business Reply Service (IBRS), created by the Universal Postal Union (UPU). Envelopes and cards may be distributed in a number of foreign countries for return to the United States without prepayment of postage. Postage and service fees are collected from the U.S. addressee at delivery. At this writing, the participating countries are only Great Britain and Northern Ireland if you are mailing from the United States. If you mail from a European point, however, the service is also available in Cyprus, Iceland, Norway, Switzerland (including Liechtenstein), United Arab Emirates, Ireland, and Sweden.

FULFILLMENT

Processing orders and moving products to foreign points is a major consideration and not one that can be addressed fully in one chapter. But a brief look at the basic options available may help set the reader on the correct course for further research. In addition to air mail and courier services, the transmission of orders has been greatly facilitated by the advent of the international 800 system and the facsimile machine. Where the logistical problem lies is in the actual shipment of the goods. To oversimplify, there are two basic methods:

Fulfilling from the United States

This is an option available to anyone who is dealing with manageable sizes and weights. Small parcels can be shipped via air parcel services offered by the U.S.P.S. and private services. Book publishers, catalogers, and suppliers of small industrial products and parts frequently use air parcel services. Delivery is quick and reliable but expensive. In some cases the order form will give the customer the choice of air parcel or a less expensive surface option.

A less expensive alternative is consolidated air freight. Here items are prelabeled and then grouped by destination in large air cargo containers for maximum economy. An agent at the foreign point of entry receives the shipment, clears it through customs, and arranges to put the items into the local delivery stream. Local parcel post can be used, and most developed countries have express surface delivery similar to, and sometimes in partnership with, major U.S. express parcel services.

The least expensive of all options is sea container service. It works exactly like air container service, but delivery time is measured in weeks rather than days. Ocean freight service is appropriate where delivery time is not critical to customer acceptance.

Fulfilling from a Foreign Point

Most manufacturers of large equipment, foods, and other high-volume, mass-produced goods tend to establish overseas warehousing and distribution points. These are either directly owned and operated by the company or are contracted for through agents and distributors. Goods are usually shipped via sea or air in high volume with enough inventory kept on hand at the foreign point to meet projected demand. The downside, obviously, is the risk of getting caught with too much or too little inventory.

In exploring fulfillment options, the advice of an experienced freight forwarder or "traffic" consultant is invaluable. They are familiar with the sometimes bewildering maze of international rules, documentation, tariffs, and customs procedures. It's important to remember that U.S. companies have been exporting for two centuries and efficient systems are well established. The direct marketer's task is to seek out the most appropriate and economical system for his or her situation.

PRICING AND PAYMENT

This is where the multinational marketer has to pay close attention. A simple mistake can depress response, upset conversion projections, and even doom a campaign before it starts.

Pricing

In addition to normal pricing considerations, it is important to factor in added costs specifically related to foreign sales. As we discussed earlier, these will include higher promotional and product delivery costs but may also include duties, customs brokers, and appropriate local value-added taxes (VAT). A fundamental decision has to be made as to how much of the forgoing to "build into" the price and how much to charge separately. Your price will also be affected by how regional or global your promotional reach is. If you are promoting multinationally with one price, it might have to be weighted for differences in promotional and delivery costs. If it is going to be *uni*-national, the task is simpler. Part of this decision will be tied into how well designed your product delivery system is. In the United States, major air express companies charge one price no matter where the package is to be delivered. But the price is arrived at only after very careful averaging and "weighting." The same process can be applied to foreign pricing.

Currency

Unfamiliarity with the vagaries of foreign currency has brought many a marketer to grief. It is something that requires a clear understanding and constant monitoring. If you think of the fluctuations just between U.S. and Canadian currency, a difference that can be as great as 25 percent, it may help put the discussion in context. Even well-run *Fortune* 500 companies have misunderstood the volatility of international currency exchange and had multimillion-dollar losses in international transactions. For the direct marketer, it means that he or she should be in a position to change pricing structures and payment options on a reasonably frequent and flexible basis. The best education is in practical firsthand experience by visiting abroad and dealing in foreign currency and in frequent monitoring of appropriate financial publications. Just as you would read the stock report to stay abreast of your investments, as a multinational marketer you should read the foreign exchange reports regularly.

Payment Methods

At some point in your international preparations, you are going to be designing the order form. There are a variety of considerations in choosing payment options with the least risk to you.

Credit Cards.   These are a great boon to the direct marketer in foreign as well as domestic markets. There are a number of U.S.-based international cards as well as foreign-based cards that can be offered. The most important advantage, other than convenience, is the fact that currency exchange is done automatically by the card company, which issues both parties a statement showing the exact currency conversion at the time of processing.

Foreign Bank Checks.   There are two types of foreign bank checks, those drawn on U.S. banks and those drawn on foreign. Foreign buyers generally prefer the latter, and it will increase the buyer's acceptance if the option of foreign checks is offered. Most banks will process foreign checks for a fee; there are several firms that specialize in foreign check processing at reasonable rates. Before offering the foreign check option, it is important to verify that the particular currency is convertible into U.S. dollars.

Giro.   This is a system prevalent in several European countries. In essence, it is a bank account with the post office. The customer gives the post office the authority to debit his or her giro account and deliver the funds to you.

Invoicing.   Though experience varies by country and product offered, "bill me" is a viable option. It is used particularly for high-quality publications and business products but should be used cautiously when dealing with the consumer market.

Agents.   Many industries, such as the publishing industry, are often represented by agents in the local country who perform a variety of tasks, including order processing and monetary transactions. The order form can be directed to their establishment and all transactions conducted on a local basis, with accountability to the U.S. company. The fee for this can be as high as 20 percent and would have to be built into the pricing structure.

Caging.   A number of airlines and freight forwarders offer a service whereby they will receive payments for you in local currency, transact the appropriate exchange, deposit the funds in a special account, and remit to you on demand, less a small fee.

SUMMARY

The international marketplace affords the direct marketer an opportunity to extend his or her reach beyond North American shores using increasingly sophisticated techniques. Venturing abroad is not without its risks, but neither is any ambitious domestic venture. Before taking the step, it's important to examine your motives, resources, and goals carefully. Following are ten questions you should be ready to answer:

- What is my objective in going into foreign markets?
- How am I going to fund the venture?

- How much am I prepared to spend on testing?
- How much am I prepared to lose?
- Do I have a three- to five-year expansion plan?
- Does this venture have the sanction of senior management or will it be treated as a stepchild?
- What additional personnel will I need?
- Who will be responsible and are they qualified?
- How am I going to distribute the product?
- Am I ready to put aside preconceived notions and approach foreign cultures with an open mind?

7
Privacy

Richard A. Barton

Direct Marketing Association, Inc.
New York, N.Y.

Privacy will be the principal public-policy issue for direct marketing in the 1990s. Postal rates and delivery, telemarketing regulation, taxes, and trade issues will remain very significant. But it will do us little good to be able to deliver our targeted advertising messages at reasonable cost and with as little regulation as possible if we cannot target our markets effectively. And that is precisely the danger facing us today. If some of the stronger recommendations now being made by some privacy advocates today are adopted, direct marketing as it has grown and prospered in America during the last 20 years could cease to exist.

This does not mean, of course, that direct marketing will grind to a halt. There will always be ways to reach a market and for customers to order directly. The genius of direct marketing in America, however, has been our ever-growing sophistication in targeting specific groups of consumers. Target marketing provides specific benefits to customers and companies alike. For customers, it reduces the chance that they will receive superfluous offers and thus reduces the receipt of unwanted mail. It enhances the chance that consumers will receive offers in which he or she has a specific interest. It increases opportunities for choice. For direct marketing companies, target marketing increases the efficiency of a company's operation, makes for a more satisfied customer, and allows companies to become more specialized and thus better serve a specialty market. In the final analysis, the ability to target markets allows us to serve the consumer more effectively and efficiently.

It is this ability that is now being challenged.

THE ANTECEDENTS

Privacy has always been a concern to Americans in both its principal manifestations: the desire to be left alone and the desire to protect confidenti-

123

ality in their personal affairs. Both concerns are of importance to direct marketers. Even though the two aspects of privacy concerns are very different, they tend to be combined in the minds of policymakers and citizens alike.

From a direct marketing viewpoint, the modern privacy debate came in the aftermath of Watergate in the 1970s. As we all know by now, the term *Watergate* does not refer simply to the aftermath of a burglary attempt at the offices of the Democratic National Committee but to the constellation of scandals involving the coverup of the attempt, illegal use of campaign money, and substantial invasions of privacy by the government for political purposes. In response to the latter, Congress created and President Gerald Ford appointed the Privacy Protection Study Commission in 1975. The primary focus of the commission was to study unwarranted invasions of personal privacy by government and to establish effective guidelines to protect the public. But the commission was also mandated to look into the compilation and use of mailing lists to determine if any regulations were needed.

The Direct Marketing Association immediately swung into action to educate the commission on the basic functions of direct marketing and list usage. The association had already anticipated the commission by several years with the establishment of the Mail Preference Service in 1971, a service that allowed consumers to have their names removed from all national mailing lists.

This service proved invaluable to DMA in convincing the commission that direct marketers had no desire to invade anyone's privacy and that the compilation and use of mailing lists, with protection built in by self-regulation, did not do so. Ultimately, the commission agreed with the DMA's position that no regulation was necessary, but strongly advised direct marketers to police themselves by making it clear that consumers could opt off of mailing lists and giving them ample opportunity to do so. The commission also emphasized that direct marketers must follow the principle that no information collected from or about a consumer for direct marketing should be used for any other purpose.

As soon as the commission's report was issued in 1977, the DMA went to work to be sure the commission's admonitions were heeded by direct marketers. The Mail Preference Service was advertised extensively in magazines and newspapers throughout the country and to a network of government consumer-affairs officials, consumer-issue editors and writers, and private consumer organizations. A major program was begun to insist that direct marketing companies that rented their lists disclose that fact to their customers and allow them to have their names deleted, and this is the norm in the business today. Also developed were Guidelines for the Protection of Personal Information, which has also become an industry standard, and the pamphlet *How Did They Get My Name?*, which explains mailing list practices in layman's terms and assures the public that there is nothing nefarious or threatening in the development of lists.

Thus, the late seventies established the fundamentals of direct marketing's response to privacy concerns. With some modifications, the same fundamentals will be the foundation of our response to the challenges of the nineties. These are: (1) No information gathered from consumers and other sources for marketing purposes should be used for any other purposes; (2) direct marketers must remove from their lists the name of any consumer who requests it; and (3) customers have a right to know if a company plans to rent their names to other companies. Direct marketers ignore them at their peril.

PRECURSORS TO THE PRESENT

While the privacy issue was relatively quiet on the regulation front for several years, three events in the eighties served as warnings of things to come:

First, in 1983, Congress began to work on legislation to deregulate the cable industry. Included in the proposed legislation was an obscure provision that would have prohibited cable companies from renting lists of their subscribers. Ironically, cable companies were unconcerned with the provision because they had not yet realized the added profitability that list rental could bring and because they were very anxious to achieve a law that prevented localities from dictating the amounts cable companies could charge. The Direct Marketing Association viewed the proposal with alarm, however, and began a lobbying effort to have the bill changed. After much consultation with the many participants in the development of the legislation, the DMA achieved a major part of its goal. Cable companies were allowed to rent lists of their subscribers. But they could not rent lists of subscribers to specific services or channels, and they had to inform their subscribers periodically that the lists were rented and give the subscribers the opportunity to opt out. This was the first time that the latter provision had ever been written into law. The former caused some concern because it placed a minor roadblock in the way of good target marketing and at least implied that some aspects of target marketing were suspect from a privacy viewpoint.

The second thrust came from the Internal Revenue Service. Again in 1983, the IRS approached some list brokers and asked to rent certain lists of upscale buyers. Their intention was to run these lists against their own files to try to determine if any had failed to file an income tax return. This directly violated the mandates of the Privacy Protection Study Commission (PPSC) to direct marketers, and the DMA issued a loud protest. Congress became very interested and conducted at least one hearing on the matter. DMA officials met with the IRS, including the commissioner himself, to argue that the action would be harmful to direct marketing and would not be useful for the IRS. Unfortunately, the IRS prevailed. While most list brokers and owners refused the request, the IRS did manage to obtain some lists. Fortunately, the experiment apparently was a failure. In 1990, however, the IRS was heard from again when it obtained some lists of contributors to at least one major cultural organization. The outcome of that program is still in doubt as of this writing. If governmental agencies such as the IRS persist in egregious violation of the government's own privacy principles, it will make it just that much harder for private enterprise to convince the public that it wants to respond positively to their privacy concerns.

The final warning came from the unlikely source of the 1987 Senate proceedings on the nomination of Judge Robert Bork to the Supreme Court. During the hearings, which ultimately led to Bork's defeat, an enterprising young reporter went to the video rental store patronized by Bork and received from an overly solicitous clerk a list of all the videos Bork had rented during the previous two years. A humorous article on some of his selections was printed in the Washington alternative newspaper *City Paper*. Fortunately, the list did not show any kinky or subversive tastes. Nevertheless, official Washington was outraged that such private data was so easily available.

Almost immediately, bills were introduced to correct the situation. While they differed in approach, the bills all generally banned the direct or indirect public dissemination of any information about the specific titles or the subject matter of videotapes rented or bought by individuals.

Our first reaction was that certainly these bills were not intended to cover direct marketing lists. After all, the problem had not been caused by a direct marketer at all, and there was not a shred of evidence that anyone had learned of the video preferences of any individual by looking at a mailing list. Anyway, it was virtually impossible and certainly highly impractical to glean such information from a mailing list.

We were disabused of these thoughts almost immediately. The drafters of the legislation had indeed intended to cover mailing lists. Further discussion with key staff, proponents of the legislation, and members of Congress confirmed this. We discovered that there was a deep suspicion about the nature and extent of personal data that went into the construction of a mailing list and a belief that at least some of target marketing crossed the boundaries into invasion of a person's privacy in both conceptions of the term. While several with whom we talked were aware of the industry's programs to meet privacy concerns and were highly complimentary of these efforts, there was a general feeling that the programs may not be adequate to meet current needs.

The Bork bill was the first opportunity that congressional privacy leaders had to express those concerns to us and do something about them. We were not dealing with an implacably hostile audience. They recognized the value of direct marketing and had no desire to do the business permanent damage. But there was a broad misunderstanding of how direct marketing operated. After a considerable education process and a certain amount of intense negotiating, an acceptable compromise was reached that may prove to be something of a landmark in the regulation of direct marketing.

In its final form, the Bork Bill permitted the rental by subject matter of lists of people who rented or bought videos. It forbade the rental of a list of buyers or renters of specific videos, however. Thus, a company selling videos could rent a list of buyers of Civil War tapes, but could not rent a list of *Gone With the Wind* aficionados. Moreover, the law requires a company to inform its customers that it intends to rent such lists and give them the opportunity to get off the lists. This is the law today (Public Law 100-618).

The Bork Bill was important for a number of reasons. First, it gave us an early warning about the depth of concern public policymakers have about privacy and direct marketing. Second, it is the first time any law states that the segmentation of lists by specific characteristics is not per se an invasion of privacy. Third, it also establishes that a negative checkoff to remove one's name from a list is an acceptable practice. This is far preferable to a system advocated by some that people should receive solicitations only when they ask for them, which is the practice in some European countries. Fourth, it shows that we can develop a positive relationship with those who would regulate us. Even if we do not agree on all occasions, we have credibility and access because of the positive approach we have taken toward privacy concerns.

THRESHOLD TO THE NINETIES

In 1989 we saw a new presidency, a new Congress, and several new thrusts on the privacy front. It was the seventies all over again, except there was much more of a concentration on privacy and the private sector. Government as Big Brother was receding, replaced in part by private-sector data banks. The initiatives begun in 1989 have exploded into the nineties and are both a challenge and a threat to direct marketing today.

A new spotlight on privacy came in the wake of the appointment of Bonnie Guiton as the President's Special Adviser for Consumer Affairs and Director of the United States Office of Consumer Affairs (USOCA). Dr. Guiton almost immediately moved the USOCA into the hitherto uncharted (for USOCA) privacy territory and declared privacy to be a major consumer issue. She embarked on a series of studies, briefing sessions, public forums, and numerous public statements and congressional testimony on various aspects of the privacy issue as they pertained to consumers. The subject matter ran the gamut from the use of credit bureau databases for direct marketing to the potential for privacy invasion by new telephone services such as Caller Identification and Automatic Number Identification (the commercial manifestation of Caller Identification).

Dr. Guiton is no stranger to direct marketing. In the mid-eighties, she served on the Postal Rate Commission for two years and learned a good deal about direct marketing there. She is no industry shil either, however, and is looking at the privacy issue with a balanced approach and with the individual consumer foremost in mind. She is also taking a major interest in European privacy laws, which are generally far stricter than ours, and in the move in Europe to develop pan-European privacy standards when European economic boundaries come down in 1992. Under Dr. Guiton's leadership, the USOCA is the closest thing we have now to a Privacy Protection Study Commission. This is threatening to the extent that it tends to focus disparate privacy concerns to an intensity that cool assessment might not warrant. It is important, however, that the public knows that its growing concerns are being addressed, and USOCA initiatives give direct marketing interests a good chance to educate the disparate players on the privacy field to the realities of our business. They also give us a better chance to understand the public perception of direct marketing and develop new programs to assure that we are sympathetic to the legitimate privacy concerns of the public.

Another general approach to the privacy issue is contained in a bill sponsored by Representative Robert Wise, a Democrat from West Virginia. Wise chairs the key privacy subcommittee of the House Government Operations Committee. Wise's bill, titled the Data Protection Act of 1989, would establish a permanent data protection board to monitor both government and private sector activities. The board would be advisory only, but as anyone who knows government will tell you, it is only a short step from an advisory board to a regulatory board. Wise's bill is a rehash of similar bills introduced several times by former subcommittee chairman Glen English, Democrat from Oklahoma. The English bill never went beyond the introduction stage, but the Wise bill appears to have a bit more push behind it. A hearing was held on May 16, 1990, that heard testimony from several significant groups favoring the establishment of the board and from some who were opposed. The proponents of the board, in a nutshell, testified that invasions of privacy were so pervasive and dangerous that it was imperative that some sort of watchdog agency be established. Dr. Guiton of the USOCA added a new dimension by pointing out that most European countries had similar agencies, and the United States should have an official group to interrelate with them. Opponents acknowledged some privacy concerns but opposed the establishment of yet another federal agency when existing agencies could do the job with congressional oversight.

The DMA was asked to testify not to support or oppose the bill but to describe in detail our self-regulatory process. We did not take an official position on the bill itself, but in the question period that followed the testimony we expressed doubt that another agency was needed. The testimony was very well received, though several of the proponents of the bill expressed grave doubts as to whether self-regulation alone would be adequate.

There is only a faint chance that a permanent data-protection board will be established anytime in the near future. The growing support of the concept, however, shows the depth of feeling many have about the privacy issue. It is more conceivable that Congress will increase its oversight activities or that a temporary study commission like the PPSC will be established. Regardless, we can expect growing interest on the part of legislators and regulators in privacy issues.

On another front, both the Federal Trade Commission and the House of Representatives Committee on Banking, Finance, and Urban Affairs Subcommittee on Consumer Affairs and Coinage in 1989 began a major examination of the administration of the Fair Credit Reporting Act (FCRA), which had become law 20 years before. Interest in this process from a direct marketing viewpoint is confined to two issues: prescreening for offers of credit and the use of credit bureau databases for target marketing purposes.

The FTC kicked things off in 1989 by announcing that it was rewriting its commentary on enforcement of the FCRA. A commentary is not in itself a regulation but a discourse on how the commission intends to enforce a regulation. After almost a year, the commission issued its final new commentary on May 4, 1990. As far as prescreening is concerned, the document was remarkably vague. In one place, it implies that in order for prescreening to be acceptable under the FCRA, the credit grantor must intend to grant credit when an offer is made. If a significant change in the creditworthiness of the grantee occurs after the prescreening, however, credit may be denied. This is how prescreening has worked ever since the practice started. But in another section of the commentary, the strong implication is that once a prescreened offer is made, credit must be granted. The controversy surrounding the commentary on prescreening will probably be resolved only by an official clarification or through litigation. The significance of the FTC action as regards the purpose of this chapter is that a time-honored practice of some direct marketers for many years is now being challenged for the first time on privacy grounds.

Of greater potential long-term significance than the FTC action on prescreening is the banking committee's reexamination of the FCRA. A kickoff hearing was held on June 12, 1990, which turned into a marathon session. While the use of credit bureau databases for direct marketing purposes was not initially a major focus of the hearing, it did receive a good bit of attention from some of the members of the subcommittee, particularly from Representative Charles Schumer, a Democrat from New York State. It soon became evident, however, that Mr. Schumer and others were not concerned only about direct marketing's use of credit databases but about all databases.

After the hearing, three bills were introduced. Mr. Schumer and Representative Matthew Rinaldo, Democrat from New Jersey, introduced bills that would prohibit prescreening and the use of credit bureau databases for direct marketing lists. Subcommittee Chairman Representative Richard Lehman, a Democrat from California, introduced a more moderate bill that would allow prescreening and the use of databases for direct marketing. But the bill would require the credit bureaus to inform those in their data bank that their names may be used for these purposes and give them a chance to opt out. Since the major credit bureaus have as many as 180 million names on file, this would be a prohibitive expense that would virtually put them out of the prescreening and direct marketing businesses.

Any list compiler has to look at this proposal and shudder. Major national list compilers use the Mail Preference Service very effectively. If they were required to contact every person on their lists, they would go out of business. So might many regional or local list compilers. List compilers cannot breathe easily because the proposed legislation does not apply to them. If the principle is established for credit bureaus, it could be but a short step to apply it to all list compilers.

The DMA has sent testimony to the subcommittee describing the self-regulatory programs we already have in place. While we agree with the principle that consumers should have an option to have their names removed from lists, we believe that the approach used in the Lehman bill would, in effect, put credit bureaus out of the direct marketing business and would establish a bad precedent. We offered to work with the committee to find better ways to notify consumers, which could include an expanded Mail Preference Service. A large coalition is working to amend the bill in various ways, and it will probably be two or three years before a complete package of FCRA amendments passes Congress. It will take a lot of work, however, to convince Congress that a different approach should be made.

Telemarketing is also the source of many privacy concerns. In most cases, telemarketing privacy issues are very closely related to privacy issues involving the mail, and in the case of list compilation and usage, the issues are virtually identical. No issue can better illustrate this symbiotic relationship than the debate surrounding Caller Identification and Automatic Number Identification services. Caller ID is the service now being offered to individual telephone subscribers that provides a screen on which the number of the caller is displayed. ANI is the commercial application of this service and is growing in popularity among direct marketers. The issue is whether or not the caller should have the option to block the display of the number.

Privacy advocates have had a field day on this issue and have split down the middle depending on whether they think the privacy of the caller or the callee should be paramount. Even telephone companies are split. The issue as far as Caller ID is concerned is complex and emotional. It is less so for direct marketing. The issue is whether a person calling to order something from or make an inquiry of a direct marketing firm should have the option to block the display of the calling number. The DMA has adopted the policy that the customer should where technically feasible, and where not, the company has the obligation to tell the caller that his number is being displayed and captured. We testified to that effect on August 1, 1990, before a Senate hearing on a bill sponsored by Senator Herbert Kohl, Democrat from Wisconsin, that would require companies offering Caller ID or ANI services to offer call-blocking services as well. This is another privacy issue that it is going to take a long time to resolve.

Developments in Europe may also have a profound effect on privacy laws in the United States. With Europe moving toward economic unification in 1992, transnational data-flow issues are coming to the fore and must be resolved by 1991. On July 18, 1990, a draft directive on privacy and data protection began to be circulated in Europe for discussion and possible action. If adopted, the directive would be binding on all members of the EEC and could seriously affect an American company's ability to do direct marketing in Europe. Conversely, the highly restrictive provisions of the draft could also form the basis for legislation in the United States.

In a nutshell, the directive would require each member nation of the EEC to create a data-protection board with regulatory and enforcement authority. It would also create a European controlling board, which would monitor the national boards. From a direct marketing viewpoint, the directive would forbid the processing of any personal data not received from a public source without consent of the subject. Consent is valid only if the person has been given "specific and explicit" information about "the type of data, the type of processing, and any recipients to whom they may be sent." Every time any data about an individual are to be transferred, the national board must be notified with full details about the nature of the transfer (e.g., the preparation and rental of a mailing list). Whenever a new name is added to a file, that person must be notified in each mailing and given an opportunity to get off the list. It could also prohibit the exchange of such information with any company from a nonmember nation unless that country had a data-protection board.

This directive may never become law, but it is being seriously considered and does to some extent reflect privacy laws already in effect in some European countries. Whatever privacy laws the EEC eventually adopts, there will be strong and perhaps irresistible pressure for the United States to do the same.

Finally, to those who say it can't happen here, there is the infamous California Assembly Bill 539. This is a bill introduced in 1989 by Assemblywoman Gwen Moore. Boiled down, the bill would require anyone collecting personal information about an individual to, within seven days, inform that individual of the exact nature of the information being collected and, if the information is being collected for a third person, the identity of that person. The bill would allow the compilation of a mailing list containing only names and addresses if the list compiler informs the individual of the source of his names and address and removes the name if requested. The bill contains many other restrictions on the use of data. If it is ever enacted, target marketing in California would virtually cease to exist.

AB 539 actually passed the California Assembly (the legislature's lower house) unanimously in June 1989, with virtually no debate or publicity. Since then, the bill has been stalled in the California Senate largely because of an information and lobbying campaign mounted by direct marketing and credit bureau interests. But the threat is still very real.

WHY NOW?

After a successful decade of warding off regulation, what has changed? Why are regulators taking a closer look at direct marketing? Why is the public raising new questions about how we operate? Is there really a problem?

The main change is an obvious one: technology. We can now collect so much more information now that we live in a different world from the one we lived in in the seventies. And we can use this information in much more imaginative ways. When George Orwell wrote *1984*, it was hard to imagine that the technology he described could ever exist. It does.

Orwell's novel was wrong, however, in assuming that technology must always be used in a threatening way. Generally, the opposite is true. Information technology has a much greater potential to expand our choices and enhance our lives than to destroy it. The public has become apprehensive, however, and direct marketers must be sensitive to this concern.

When the Privacy Protection Study Commission was created in the mid-seventies, the public was mainly concerned that government was on the verge of creating a universal data bank with a personal profile on almost every citizen. Actions of government officials then did nothing to allay their fears. Thus, the PPSC spent most of its time recommending legislation and regulation of government databases. Since then, however, there has been a major change in attitudes. A study sponsored by Equifax in 1990 showed that the majority of the respondents were more worried about private-enterprise data banks than they were about the government's. Private enterprise has now become Big Brother in the mind of the public.

Also, direct marketers have in the past 20 years emphasized the principle that data collected for direct marketing purposes should be used for no other purpose, and we have done a good job in protecting that principle. Nevertheless, the ground has shifted from under us. The public is now more concerned that information collected for other purposes may be used for direct marketing or any number of other purposes. While we have educated an entire generation of direct marketers not to use the information they have on file for nonmarketing purposes, we must now educate others on not using their information for direct marketing purposes.

The good news is that we are also the victims of our own success. Direct marketing has become one of the major forces in the American retail economy in the last 20 years. It was inevitable that direct marketing's competitors would begin to attack us (for example, newspaper campaigns against "junk mail"). We are also much more obvious to our customers and to others who receive our mail and telephone calls. Thus, more questions are asked about our marketing practices. This is more of a challenge than a problem, but direct marketers must understand that more intense scrutiny because of our success means that we have to do an even better job of describing to the public what we do and how we do it.

Finally, we must recognize that our own self-promotion sometimes gets in our way. All of us have seen advertisements from very fine list brokers and owners that overstate the amount and type of information they have on file. Sophisticated direct marketers know creative hyperbole when they see it, however creative the advertising may be. They also raise grave doubts in the minds of many nonspecialists, including government officials for whom regulation is a way of life. We need to be more circumspect in how we advertise our lists.

WHAT TO DO?

Fortunately, direct marketers enter the nineties with a good record of responding to the privacy concerns of consumers and an excellent reputation among regulators for promoting responsible approaches to privacy issues.

In January 1989, the DMA formed a blue ribbon Task Force on Privacy to examine issues related to the accessibility, transfer, and use of personal information for the targeting of customers. DMA president Jonah Gitlitz described the role of the task force in language that also sums up the theme of this chapter:

> The list business has changed significantly since the President's Privacy Protection Study Commission in the mid-1970s declared that personal information used for direct marketing posed no invasion of individual privacy. Now, sophisticated technologies have enabled new marketing opportunities, and, given the public's strong perception that individually identifiable information is easily accessible, it is time for our profession to re-examine the methods, practices, and guidelines we use in developing targeted customer lists every day and see if revisions are necessary....Self-regulation has been a trademark of DMA and the direct marketing field, both as an alternative to government intervention and as an initiative to place the interest of customers and consumers first.

The task force so far has supervised the revision of all DMA guidelines for ethical business practices as they pertain to privacy concerns. In addition to revisions to the Guidelines for Ethical Business Practice, substantial revisions have been made to the Guidelines for Mailing List Practices and the Guidelines for Personal Information Protection. New guidelines on monitoring and the transfer of data have been added to the newly designated Guidelines for Marketing by Telephone.

The task force also has spearheaded a reexamination of the Mail Preference and the Telephone Preference Services and the use of in-house suppression files to assure that the options to get off mailing lists are available to all American consumers.

Direct marketers, to meet the privacy challenge of the nineties, must first of all be sure that they are in compliance with all the appropriate direct marketing guidelines. Self-regulation can only work when all responsible direct marketers participate. They should also carefully follow all developments in state and federal legislation to assist direct marketing lobbyists in fighting unnecessary legislation and regulation. Finally, all direct marketers must be constantly aware of the privacy concerns of their customers and orient all their marketing activities toward alleviating those concerns. It should be easy because we are all consumers, and we are all concerned about our privacy.

PART 2
Databases and Mailing Lists

8

Database Marketing: An Overview

Jock Bickert

National Demographics & Lifestyles
Denver, Colo.

From AMEX to NYNEX, catalogs to cat food, diapers to diamonds, and buggies to Huggies, consumer marketers across an impressive spectrum of industries have discovered new ways to pick up the pieces left by the market fragmentation of the 1970s and 1980s. The new marketing approaches have a common theme: getting closer to the customer. They all depend on getting to know consumers better through their behaviors as well as through their demographic and lifestyle characteristics.

Thanks to computers, the modern repository for all that information is a *consumer database,* and the methodology used is *database marketing.* The direct marketing lexicon has expanded to include new phrases, ranging from high-tech mathematical and financial concepts such as "lifetime value" and "predictive modeling" to more Esalenesque, high-touch constructs that emphasize "bonding" and "relationship building."

Therefore, database marketing comes wrapped in many guises these days. Some people call it "relationship marketing." Lester Wunderman, the chairman of one of the industry's most prestigious direct-response agencies, uses the term "curriculum marketing." Grey Direct labels it "bonding," and other direct marketing practitioners refer to it as "one-on-one marketing," "interactive marketing," "dialogue marketing," or "micromarketing." This author has his own pet term: "relevance marketing."

Why a preference for relevance marketing? Because it's the only definition that spells out the benefits of the process for both the marketer and the audience. As Peter Drucker prophetically stated in 1973 during marketing's Bronze Age: "The aim of marketing is to know your customers so well that when your prospects are confronted with your product, it fits them so exactly that it sells itself." And that is the intent, either stated or implied, of every application in this chapter—to uncover the relevant information about individual consumers and apply that knowledge artfully to increase the probability of a desired response or purchase. The terms "relationship marketing" and "bonding" imply an underlying requirement of the relevance-building process: the need to establish sufficient trust with strangers so they willingly provide information that will eventually permit you to sell them something.

Semantic preferences aside, the public distaste for untargeted or poorly targeted mail and the attendant media delight in junk mail bashing are perhaps the most compelling reasons for emphasizing relevance in marketing. As the results of many surveys and focus group discussions have reiterated, unsolicited mail is considered junk mail only when it is irrelevant. The modest 70-year-old widow who receives an unsolicited catalog featuring revealing black silk lingerie from Harold's of Keokuk will be penning an outraged note to the local action-line columnist before her first blush has faded. And rightly so, since the mailing piece is irrelevant. However, the same unsolicited mailing directed to a recently married 30-year-old might be received with glee. Because the mailing is relevant, it is welcome, and action line never hears from the newlywed.

THE DATABASE AS A PRIVATE ADVERTISING MEDIUM

How many marketers might strike a Faustian bargain to own and control a major medium to the exclusion of all competitors? Would a Budweiser be at least somewhat tempted to sell its corporate soul for the chance to control every advertising—and better yet, every editorial—message that appears in *Sports Illustrated*? What might General Motors be enticed to do if it could dictate the advertising content and placement of every commercial on the NBC television network? What if Clairol or Levi's could own the commercial interruptions on the top-rated rock and roll radio stations in New York and Los Angeles?

This notion is not as farfetched as it might appear. In the past few years, many major consumer advertisers have been overtly or secretly building their own private media: their consumer databases. Many of these advertisers are aware of the ultimate power of the resource they're developing. Others, however, fail to see it as a medium at all, perceiving it only as a mechanism for collecting marketing information.

> **A fully functioning marketing database is a consumer database that includes both prospective and existing customers and, at its fullest range of applications, operates as a proprietary medium.**

Adopting a modern conceit used by many business writers today—using military metaphors and personages from Attila to Mao to illustrate marketing principles—a marketing database becomes the G-2, the intelligence-gathering apparatus that allows marketers to implement their marketing strategies most efficiently. Marketers covertly identify the mix of consumer, product, advertising, and media characteristics with the greatest probability of success, working in an environment sheltered from the inquisitive eyes of the enemy—the competition.

At the same time, this very database becomes a potent assault weapon, a blitzkrieg, allowing the company to precisely target and communicate with its audiences while the competition serenely sips champagne and nibbles *foie gras*, oblivious that a major attack has taken place. Even when the dust has settled after a database-driven quick-strike—used with increased frequency by packaged-goods marketers, retailers, and some savvy politicians—the competition is often unaware of the breadth of the assault (What market segments were targeted?), its depth (How many people did it reach?), or its effect (How many people responded or purchased?).

Contrast this privileged intelligence with the open nature of a network television campaign in which the content, placement, frequency, and timing are available to the competition. Even the effect of the TV campaign can be gauged by the competition as well as by the sponsoring company. However, those effects are often ephemeral, since neither side can accurately measure the true impact of such a campaign.

If, on the other hand, the strategy calls for drawn-out trench warfare because an immediate sale is improbable and thus either long-term customer retention or equally long-term prospect wooing is required, database marketing can assume a propaganda function. Leaflets, in the form of coupons designed to solidify customer loyalty or stimulate prospect trials, can be dropped on the targeted population for a protracted period. The generals of sales and marketing in their corner offices must be patient and willing to invest in the future, since long-term customer development is estimated to be three to four times more costly than attempting to consummate an immediate sale. However, the long-range payoffs can be enormous.

Marketers have a unique promotional advantage when their proprietary databases function as private media. For example, they can generate additional sales by promoting product A to other members of their database who resemble known buyers of product A. Or they can cross-promote products C, D, and G to their product A buyers because they know and can exploit their buyers' product and sales "hot buttons." Because they have proprietary knowledge of consumers' individual characteristics, marketers can test-market new products with target segments before making a full market introduction.

Perhaps the most critical long-range database application relates to the establishment and solidification of customer loyalty through ongoing relationship building. Several years ago, two direct marketing strategists, Ray Considine and Murray Raphel, developed a "loyalty ladder," a useful paradigm for viewing customer relationships. Rung by rung, it illustrates the process marketers should use to build the ideal relationship.

At the bottom rung of the ladder are the *suspects*, the universe of people you have identified as your potential customers. The next rung is occupied by *prospects*, individuals who have heard of your products or services but haven't yet purchased from you. Once someone has bought something from you, that person becomes a *customer* and moves to the next rung on the loyalty ladder.

Many companies' marketing efforts are geared only as far as making the sale and creating customers. This is a short-sighted practice because once someone has become a customer, you have the opportunity to nurture the relationship and transform that customer into a *client*. A client is someone who buys other products from you over a period of time, someone who selects your products over some other company's, someone who is loyal to you. With attention to product quality, customer service, prompt delivery, etc., you may be able to convert that client into an *advocate* on the top and most important rung of the ladder. Not only are advocates repeat buyers of your products, they also contribute to your total marketing effort by singing your praises to their friends.

Database marketing expedites the climb up the loyalty ladder. You can identify suspects and their subgroups, such as teenage males, young married couples, etc., through market research and database analysis and segmentation. Outside lists of prospects who have been identified through your segmentation efforts can be added to your database. Your database can store information about your customers' initial purchase behaviors and your clients' subsequent purchases. Correct use of that information assures that they will remain clients. Lists of advocates are more difficult to assemble. One technique: Have the company's database record the name and address of anyone who writes a complimentary letter and acknowledge those people now and then with a note or a special discount to protect that advocacy advantage.

IF DATABASE MARKETING ISN'T ALREADY A MEGATREND, IT SHOULD BE

Walter Martin of the Naisbitt Group states: "The emergence of database marketing is part of the process of increasing globalization and individualization. We believe that individualized relationship marketing will dominate all forms of commercial exchange in the years to come."

In their latest divination of our global future, *Megatrends 2000*, John Naisbitt and Patricia Aburdene predict that the 1990s will be characterized by heightened concern and respect for the individual. Empowered by the major personal technological advances of the 1980s—computers, cellular phones, and fax machines—home can be the workplace, and people can live anywhere they please. Naisbitt and Aburdene state that "the primacy of the consumer" will accompany this emphasis on the individual. Products will be customized to fit the needs of the individual, customization that is only possible with individual level information available through a database. Only a sophisticated database structure can store, analyze, and access sufficient information to facilitate the customization of products and services.

When embracing a marketing database orientation, users would be wise to heed an earlier Naisbitt caution. In his 1983 best-seller, *Megatrends*, he warned about the danger of depending on the quick adoption of high-tech products without introducing an accompanying high-touch component, stating they must go hand in hand for consumers to accept new high-technology products. In their latest book, Naisbitt and Aburdene attribute the rapid consumer endorsement of the fax machine to the familiar physical processes of cutting and pasting, copying, etc. Electronic mail, on the other hand, is likely to take much longer before it catches on because of its "high-techiness" and absence of "high touch."

The reminder for marketers is to assure that strong personal high-touch elements accompany the high-tech, automated, one-to-one access available through their databases. Individualized marketing can be offensive unless it's relevant and humanized. Individualized marketing should use such techniques as authentically personal letters rather than just personalized salutations and warm, real telephone operators rather than humanoids with carefully articulated synthetic speech. At the same time, marketers should not become overly familiar with their audiences. To be effective, the same sensitivity that goes into any important relationship should be applied to the database marketing process.

TYPES OF CONSUMER DATABASES

Any history of direct marketing would be remiss if it failed to label the 1980s the decade of database marketing, although the conceptual tools and various scattered database marketing applications existed prior to 1980. For instance, *Farm Journal* initiated its database-building efforts in 1973 and The Lifestyle Selector, the first true external database, began in the mid-1970s. By the early 1980s, seminars and conferences touting database marketing concepts were being offered to the direct marketing industry. Today, databases have become a panacea. Now, all list owners proclaim the wonders of their databases, no matter how humble their informational capabilities might be.

Not surprisingly, there is also a plethora of definitions for the term *database*. At the risk of picking a nit, this author believes that direct marketers would always precede the word "database" with a qualifier such as "individual" or "consumer," since, as Rose Harper, author of *Mailing List Strategies,* notes, "a database is a collection of data organized for rapid search and retrieval." In other words, databases do not have to be collections of information about human beings. There are databases of auto parts, baseball cards, and varieties of mosquitoes. This chapter, however, will address only direct marketing databases of individual consumers. This chapter is not concerned with business-to-business database marketing or any applications of nonhuman databases.

Stan Rapp, author of *Maximarketing,* defines a database as "a computer file of names which have, and are selectable by, other bits of information attached to them." On the other hand, John Stevenson of Krupp Taylor describes a database as "a list of known facts which may include names and addresses." He places his emphasis on the information in the database rather than on the name of the individual in the database, which may disappoint many list owners who like to think of their unenhanced name-and-address files as databases.

George Orme of David Shepard & Associates may have come up with the most appropriate definition. He defines a marketing database as "an organized collection of data about individual customers, prospects, and/or suspects that is accessible and actionable for marketing purposes." Using Orme's definition, it is not necessary to identify a specific name and address as long as the "collection of data" is accessible and actionable. In other words, a unique ID, social security number, or bar code would suffice in the absence of a name and address.

INTERNAL DATABASES

Marketing databases come in two varieties: internal or customer databases and external or noncustomer databases.

Internal databases result from the relationship-building process between marketers and their customers and/or prospects.

At its most primitive level, an internal database would consist entirely of information about the behavior of customers or prospects. Marketers might want to record, for instance, if a customer responded to September's direct-mail promotion, purchased more than $300 worth of merchandise in 1989, or redeemed a coupon at Kroger's for All detergent on April 4, 1990. At its most elegant, an internal database would be enhanced by individual data from other sources, such as age and income information obtained about specific customers through an overlay process with an outside data source.

An internal database is truly a proprietary medium. It consists entirely of customers and/or prospects and has been purchased by the marketer or developed in the course of establishing some sort of business relationship with consumers. Traditionally, the internal database consisted of a customer file of names and addresses to which summary transactional information was appended.

The most commonly captured and the most useful transactional data are: (1) recency (When was the last purchase made?), (2) frequency (How often does the customer purchase?), and (3) monetary value (How much money did the customer spend over the past year?). These data elements are usually referred to collectively as RFM.

As data storage costs have decreased and computer access to multiple and complex data elements has improved, the breadth of internal data variables has increased dramatically. The following list contains data elements which might appear on a marketer's internal database:

- Customer identification
- Name and address (both billing and shipping)
- Telephone number
- Dates of promotions to prospect/customer
- Responses to those promotions
- Source code indicating the medium from which the original customer response was obtained (telephone solicitation, print ad, direct-mail solicitation, coupon offer, etc.)
- Date of first purchase
- Dates of subsequent purchases
- Date of last purchase
- Frequency of purchases
- Item(s) purchased by product ID, category, or department

- Distribution outlet from which purchase was made (name of retailer, type of retailer, catalog, etc.)
- Items returned
- Purchase amounts
- Average purchase amount
- How purchase was made (telephone, mail, in person, etc.)
- Method of payment (check, cash, type of credit card, etc.)
- Bad debt history, if any
- Personal information generated by transactions with the company (Many bank transactions ask for personal data, such as age, income, home value, marital status, ages of children, occupation, and automobile ownership.)
- Personal information obtained from other sources (See "External Databases" below.)
- Product usage information obtained from records of customer transactions (Airlines can identify customers on their frequent-flyer databases by the number of miles flown with that airline, destinations by number of trips, etc.)
- Product usage information obtained by merging formerly disparate databases within the same corporate entity (Time Warner has created a 29-million-name megadatabase by merging all the subscriber files to its consumer publications, Time-Life Books, Book-of-the-Month Club, record clubs, and cable operations.)
- Product and/or purchase information obtained from questionnaires (Many manufacturers of consumer durable and soft goods package questionnaires with their products. When the products are purchased, buyers complete the questionnaires and return them to the manufacturers. The questionnaires are designed to capture valuable marketing information, including reasons for purchase, effect of specific media on the purchasing decision, competitive products considered or owned, intended use of product, etc.)

Which transactional data elements are selected for storage obviously depends on the business collecting them. Supermarket transactions are different from catalog sales, which, in turn, differ from banking transactions. Each of these businesses also has different marketing needs, dictating which data elements are to be captured, stored, and used. The selection of data elements must be made judiciously because, although data storage costs are lower today than they were 10 years ago, they are still significant. Cost considerations force marketers to make "need to know" versus "nice to know" data selection decisions.

EXTERNAL DATABASES

External databases are collections of consumer characteristics, attached to specific individuals, that can be accessed either by name and address or by some other specific identifier.

Examples of external databases are R. L. Polk's X-1 file, Metromail's National
Consumer DataBase, and The Lifestyle Selector®, owned by National Demographics & Lifestyles. Neither the U.S. census, geodemographic systems such as
PRIZM or ClusterPlus, nor conventional consumer surveys qualify as true external marketing databases because they do not contain collections or lists of individuals that marketers can access.

A List Does Not a Consumer Database Make

To protect individual privacy, the U.S. census does not report individual household information. Instead, it reports aggregate data, summarized information
about the people who live in a specific geographic area. Therefore, access to
census data is at the aggregate level by census tracts, block groups, zip codes,
etc. Although these levels of aggregation continue to shrink in the direction of
individual households or people, a marketer is still unable to first specify a particular set of census characteristics and then designate a list of individuals from
within the census files who match those characteristics. At best, marketers must
first seek census descriptions of geographic aggregates that match their target
market characteristics and then select the names and addresses of individuals
who live within those specified geographic aggregates from other list sources.

Geodemographic Systems

Geodemographic systems suffer from the same limitations to individual access
as the U.S. census. These systems are actually clustering and segmentation techniques, not databases of people. The marketer must go to another list source to
obtain individual names and addresses. However, such systems offer a significant improvement in segmentation capability over the census. Through a statistical technique known as cluster analysis, these systems have grouped units of
geography (block groups or zip codes) according to their demographic similarity, hence the term *geodemographic systems*. The four systems of consequence—
PRIZM, ClusterPlus, VISION, and ACORN—have produced between 40 and
48 groups or clusters and have given each cluster a unique designation.

The pioneer system, PRIZM, developed by the Claritas Corporation, offers
not only the most exotic taxonomy (PRIZM's clusters have names such as Shotguns and Pickups, Blueblood Estates, and Norma Rae-Ville), but also emphasizes the underlying assumption of all geodemographic systems: birds of a
feather flock together. That basic hypothesis states that people with similar demographic characteristics tend to bunch into relatively homogeneous neighborhoods which can be defined by block groups, zip codes, etc. The smaller the
geographic entity, the greater the degree of homogeneity. For example, block
groups are more homogeneous than census tracts or zip codes.

Given that demographic homogeneity exists, the system further hypothesizes
that an accompanying homogeneity exists in other characteristics as well, such as
purchasing behavior and media habits. Consequently, these cluster systems have
been linked with consumer behavior data provided by market research firms such
as Simmons Market Research Bureau, MRI, and Stanford Research International.

Therefore, individuals who live in a Blueblood Estates neighborhood, a very affluent PRIZM designation, have been found to be more likely to purchase luxury cars,
to consume gourmet frozen foods, and to participate in golf.

The systems also contend that other neighborhoods falling within the same
cluster designation, no matter how distant they are geographically, share similar
consumer characteristics. In other words, residents of Blueblood Estates in
Darien, Connecticut, Bloomfield Hills, Michigan, and Beverly Hills, California,
not only share common demography but are also likely to share an affinity for
LA Law, designer cat food, and Gucci loafers.

Research Surveys

Mistakenly, conventional market research survey samples have also been labeled
databases. But in most survey samples drawn solely for market research purposes, respondents have been assured that their answers will be kept confidential. In compliance with that promise, survey research firms refuse to link any of
the survey data to individuals by name and address. Therefore, it is impossible
for marketers to gain access to individuals with specific survey-generated characteristics, such as people who are impulse shoppers or those who prefer a particular brand of diet soda.

The exceptions are questionnaire-bred databases in which consumers are informed when they are presented with the questionnaire that they will be identified and their answers will be used for purposes other than research. Such
questionnaire-generated databases are discussed in detail later in this chapter.

Another common error is the mislabeling of the VALS system as a consumer
database. VALS, the psychographic brainchild of the late Arnold Mitchell of
Stanford Research International (SRI), is a consumer segmentation scheme that
categorizes individuals according to a combination of attitudinal, behavioral, demographic, and decision-making variables. The current version, VALS 2, is a
retooling of the original version, which had a history of inconsistent marketing
applications.

SRI administered a 30-item questionnaire to an initial national probability
sample of 1635 adults and used the responses to identify eight distinct groups.
Each group is described on two dimensions: (1) resources, which include income, education, intelligence, health, and self-confidence, and (2) orientation,
which distinguishes whether the individual's behavior is guided by principle,
status, or activity. For example, the Achiever group has abundant resources and
is guided by the actions of others (how SRI defines status). Achievers, therefore,
are considered likely to prefer established prestige products that convey a message of success to their peers. Wallowing at the bottom of the barrel are the
Strugglers, who are not only the oldest VALS group but also its least affluent.

The VALS 2 system is a survey-determined segmentation mechanism, which
is not a database. It has been wedded to the PRIZM system in a psychogeo-
demographic marriage, allowing marketers to analyze neighborhoods in terms
of their psychographic composition. However, the only VALS 2 application to
individual targeting is a prediction that an address obtained from a compiled list
has a higher-than-average probability of housing an individual with certain
VALS/PRIZM-defined attributes.

True External Databases

There are four basic types of true external databases: (1) mass-compiled, (2) financial, (3) questionnaire-generated, and (4) amalgams of the first three types, known in the industry as multisourced enhancement files. Three companies own mass-compiled databases: R. L. Polk, Donnelley Marketing, and Metromail. Their basic data sources are public records (automobile and auto license registrations, telephone directories, birth records, etc.). This information is often supplemented with other data elements obtained from household canvasses or geodemographic coding of individual addresses.

In the late 1980s, two credit-granting giants, TRW and Equifax, made their credit files available for market analysis and list rental. Their primary attribute is financial information obtained from consumer credit records.

The first questionnaire-generated database appeared in 1977. Currently, there are three such databases of consequence: BehaviorBank from Computerized Marketing Technology, The Lifestyle Selector from National Demographics & Lifestyles, and Shareforce from Donnelley Marketing. The common thread through all of these databases is the distribution of large numbers of questionnaires to consumers to capture demographic, lifestyle, and behavioral information about individuals. The fourth type of external database, the multisourced enhancement file, is typified by Infobase Services. As of mid-1990, Infobase had assembled a massive file of individuals from several of the first three types of external databases.

EXTERNAL DATA ELEMENTS

In the mid-1970s, the data found through external sources was so limited that no self-respecting list compiler would have had the audacity to label the resulting product a database, even if the term had been widely used or accepted. Most owners of compiled files considered themselves fortunate if they were able to provide age data. Household income was estimated by applying algorithms based on aggregate census data. The most powerful information at that time was the automobile ownership data compiled from auto registrations by R. L. Polk. Variables, such as the number of automobiles owned and their makes, models, and years, constituted an early precursor of soon-to-be-introduced lifestyle data.

By the end of the 1980s, there was an abundance of external data to be used by marketers to perform segmentation analyses and select targeted mailing lists. There are four basic types of external data elements: demographic, geodemographic, psychographic, and behavioral.

Demographic Data

Demographic variables describe the physical attributes of an individual, the human being unadorned. Demographic variables are the meat and potatoes of the U.S. census. Among the 73 demographic variables measured by the Census Bureau in 1990 were gender, age, income, marital status, education level, and occupation.

Geodemographic Data

Geodemographic data are clusters of demographic variables collected through the U.S. census. These clusters are then used to categorize units of geography. These composites are much less unwieldy than the 73 census variables and have been useful to infer other behavior—the propensity of Blueblood Estates residents to consume 3.3 times more mineral water than the national average, for instance.

Psychographic Data

Psychographic variables describe the state of the individual's psyche. They include ephemeral data such as attitudes, beliefs, opinions, traits, and values—the fabric in which the demographic individual is clothed. Marketers have recognized the importance of psychographic information for decades but have rarely been successful in making it work in marketing applications. In many instances, psychographic factors have been very product-specific, and a set of psychographic variables discovered to be predictive in one situation often fails in subsequent applications, even after costly surveys and analyses.

The VALS 2 system, a true psychographic system, holds high promise but does not allow marketers to identify individuals of known VALS types. As an example, let's say you know your target group consists of Achievers. The problem is that there is no list of known Achievers available. Marketers will persist in their pursuit of the psychographic grail as markets continue to fragment and as unaccompanied demographics continue to weaken in their ability to generate relevant segmentation.

Behavioral Data

Behavioral data could prove to be the hottest category of the 1990s because it presents marketers with an opportunity to measure prospects' willingness to buy. By collecting transactional data on retail purchases through product-scanning devices at the checkout counter, marketers can build and maintain a record of individual purchase behaviors and then use that information to predict the likelihood of future purchases of specific products. Behavioral history gathered through questionnaires can also provide a reliable estimate of purchase willingness.

Donnelley Marketing and Computerized Marketing Technologies' Select and Save are two of the companies that have been distributing millions of questionnaires each year and asking consumers to report specific product use. Their clients, primarily package-goods companies, use this information to reward their current customers and to encourage users of competitive brands to test their products.

Lifestyles are another extremely valuable aspect of behavioral data. Lifestyles are often regarded as psychographic in nature since they are related to a person's attitudes and values. The motivational component of any given lifestyle is certainly psychographic. For example, a person may be an avid downhill skier (activity/behavior) to experience the thrill of speed (attitude/value). However, lifestyles are described and operationally defined in terms of specific activities and behaviors, observable manifestations of those attitudes and values. Therefore, lifestyles fall within the behavioral dimension. People with an outdoors lifestyle are enthusiastic about fly fishing, enjoy cross-country skiing, or spend weekends trail biking. As you can see, lifestyles have no definition or meaning without activities or behaviors.

People's lifestyle activities and behaviors define who they are. Individuals describe themselves as serious golfers, bridge nuts, or movie addicts. What they are passionate about, committed to, and make time for tells more about them than age, occupation, whether they own or rent, or how much money they make.

Lifestyles also function as an effective link in social interactions. More often than not, people gravitate toward other people with similar lifestyles. Initial and subsequent bonding takes place on the basis of those similarities. In the early 1980s, *Psychology Today* surveyed 40,000 of its readers as part of a study of the components of friendship. Aside from shared traits such as sense of humor, loyalty, etc., the most frequently mentioned components of friendship were shared leisure and nonleisure interests: in other words, common lifestyles. Those commonalities were found to be much more important in the relationship process than were shared demographic characteristics such as age, income, or education.

Because lifestyles are so significant to the bonding process, they should be of paramount interest to many marketers. Marketers can use lifestyles to identify and communicate with consumers. When you know someone's lifestyle, you can make other inferences about that person's behavior and how and what to communicate to that person as a consumer. Lifestyle data gives a marketer the correct language to use to relate to a squash-playing theatergoer in Manhattan and another vocabulary to use to establish a relationship with a trail-biking, fly fisherwoman who lives in Montana.

Because lifestyles are an integral part of an individual's public persona—the face a person chooses to present to the world—collecting this information and using it in the marketing process is less sensitive than compiling other types of behavioral data, especially from financial transactions. To the woman in Montana, acknowledging her interest in fly fishing and trail biking reinforces her positive self-image. Acknowledging her bank balance, however, even if it is healthy, is likely to evoke a different and probably hostile response.

MASS-COMPILED DATABASES

R. L. Polk & Co.

R. L. Polk's principal mass-compiled file, X-1, was introduced in 1973. By the beginning of 1990, the file contained more than 87 million households—96 percent of all households in the United States—79 million of which are addressable by name and another 8 million of which are addressable as "resident." The X-1 file is produced by cross-referencing more than 1 billion names from 22 information sources six times a year. The richest and largest of those information sources are:

- 103 million current auto registrations
- 17 million current truck registrations
- 23 million households contacted by R. L. Polk's door-to-door canvassers
- 66 million residential telephone listings
- 22 million new car buyers
- 53 million records with known birth, high school, and college data
- 64 million known direct-mail respondents
- 52 million homeowners
- 140 million credit card users
- 27 million questionnaires
- 13 million members of the National Demographics & Lifestyles database

Up-to-date deliverability of Polk's X-1 file is maintained by monthly updates of all moves and address changes as reported through the U.S. Postal Service National Change of Address (NCOA) system. Selections from the X-1 file can be made at any level of geography: state, county, zip code, census tract, census block group, U.S.P.S. carrier routes, and, of course, individual households. Examples of the most numerous selection factors are estimates of household income, the gender of the head of household, the type of dwelling unit, home ownership, marital status, occupation, telephone ownership, and current market value of the motor vehicles owned.

Donnelley Marketing

Donnelley's master compiled file, DQI^2, contains information about more than 84 million households and is drawn from two sources: (1) the Donnelley Marketing Telephone List compiled from 4000 telephone directories and updated daily, and (2) the Donnelley Auto List compiled from motor vehicle registration departments in 37 states.

External data sources are used to verify the ages and genders of household members. These sources include birth records, lists of children's book buyers, student lists, drivers' licenses, and voter registration lists. Additional data comes from the Donnelley Shareforce questionnaire, mailed twice a year to between 30 and 45 million households as part of the Carol Wright couponing program. This program yields demographic, lifestyle, and product usage data that are appended to 8 million names on the DQI^2 file every year.

Further file enhancements come from almost 100 census variables and from ClusterPlus, Donnelley's proprietary geodemographic clustering system. ClusterPlus categorizes neighborhoods—census or postal divisions—into 47 unique groups. Each group is enhanced with market research data from a number of major national syndicated research suppliers.

Both the raw census variables and the ClusterPlus groups provide marketers with estimates of individual household characteristics but, because they represent aggregates rather than individuals, marketers cannot be assured that any specific household actually has those characteristics. And this is the inherent weakness of all geodemographic systems that incorporate aggregated census data.

The major drawback to using aggregate data as opposed to individual data is that you are never certain what the data is telling you. To illustrate, suppose you are a new head basketball coach and all you know about your new team is that its average height is 6 feet, 4 inches. That height information is based on aggregate data. As it turns out, two of the team members are 7-footers, one person is 6 feet, 4 inches, and two others are 5 feet, 8 inches. That individual-level information is much more helpful than the aggregate data, which described one member of your new team accurately and seriously misrepresented the other four. The same misrepresentation is possible when aggregate census data are used to describe a collection of individual households, particularly in heterogeneous neighborhoods.

Metromail

Metromail's National Consumer DataBase is a compiled file that includes more than 83 million households and 185 million individual names and addresses. Metromail was acquired by R. R. Donnelley, the world's largest commercial printer, in 1987. Prior to that acquisition, Metromail had purchased two proprietary data sources, Market Development Corporation and Dataman Information Services. Those acquisitions and other data purchase agreements have given Metromail the ability to enhance its National Consumer DataBase with information about new home ownership, new movers, families with recent babies, and households with either high school or college students.

Metromail's access to Donnelley's Selectronic printing and binding technology allows the company to offer many vertical marketing applications, similar to the capabilities provided by *Farm Journal* magazine, which is described later in this chapter. Metromail assures the currency of its database by updating it 65 times a year.

FINANCIAL DATABASES

TRW

TRW, one of the "big three" credit bureaus, has added a variety of services to become a more extensive provider of consumer information services. The company maintains PerformanceData System, a database of 143 million individuals, that stores consumer credit history and demographic data.

TRW's data sources include public records (census aggregates, birth records, voter registration, vehicle registration, etc.), financial institutions (accounts receivable of banks and finance companies), and retailers (accounts receivable of department stores). The massive compilation includes 300 demographic and 400 financial variables. Because of the sensitivity of its financial information, TRW uses a third party, usually a mailing company, when it rents mailing lists and provides list renters with only names and addresses devoid of all other individual information.

Equifax

Equifax, one of the largest U.S. credit bureaus, owns the Equifax Consumer Marketing Database, compiled from financial institutions, retailers, the U.S. census, public records, and VISION, a proprietary geodemographic clustering system owned by National Decision Systems, an Equifax subsidiary.

The Equifax Consumer Marketing Database of 135 million individuals is used to screen names for direct marketing purposes and is a source of consumer mailing lists. As with TRW, individual financial data elements are not available to mailing-list renters. Many Equifax customers are credit-oriented companies, such as financial institutions, insurance companies, and retailers.

QUESTIONNAIRE-GENERATED DATABASES

BehaviorBank

BehaviorBank, a product of CMT Data Corporation, is a 25-million-name questionnaire-generated database with more than 150 selections. Questionnaires and accompanying co-op product couponing inserts are mailed to consumers several times a year. The questionnaires ask for product usage behavior, primarily in the packaged-goods area. Demographic and lifestyle data, mail-order propensity, and political tendencies are also gathered. Direct marketing companies rent BehaviorBank lists to customize their mailing efforts. Companies can also participate in the package-insert program.

The Lifestyle Selector

The relative youth of database marketing is illustrated by the fact that the granddaddy of questionnaire-generated databases, the first to offer marketers lifestyle data for both list selection and overlay profiling, made its public debut in 1978. By 1990, The Lifestyle Selector database, owned by National Demographics & Lifestyles, contained 27 million names with demographic and lifestyle data, none of which is more than 24 months old.

The information is gathered from consumer questionnaires packaged in consumer goods produced by more than 80 major manufacturers. Most of the products are durable goods (photographic equipment, consumer electronics, large and small appliances, home furnishings, housewares, and sporting goods).

Generally, the questionnaires accompany other print materials, such as product information booklets and warranty statements. Product buyers complete the questionnaires, providing information about the purchasing decision as well as household and individual demographic and lifestyle information.

Every questionnaire contains a statement informing consumers that the information will be used for both research and direct marketing purposes. If, however, consumers do not want their personal data to be used for direct marketing mailing lists, they can opt out by checking a box. Less than 7 percent request that option.

National Demographics & Lifestyles receives approximately 15 million completed questionnaires a year. The information is merged and deduplicated to create The Lifestyle Selector database. The manufacturers' proprietary product and purchase behavior information and the names of the people who "checked the box" are not included on the database.

The Lifestyle Selector data elements consist of 10 demographic items (gender, exact age, marital status, occupation, home ownership, family income, number and ages of children, and credit card usage) and individual participation in more than 50 lifestyle activities and interest areas (tennis, foreign travel, gourmet foods, etc.).

Direct marketers use The Lifestyle Selector for highly targeted list selections, choosing either a combination of individual selections or scored lists. The demographic and lifestyle variables can be selected individually or in constellations of related lifestyle activities (outdoor, active sports, high-tech, etc.). The scored list selection process uses predictive modeling to rank the names and addresses of prospects according to the likelihood of response. Other uses of The Lifestyle Selector include internal database enhancement and the profiling of data-poor house files.

Shareforce

Donnelley Marketing's Shareforce database contains approximately 17 million individuals who are described in terms of their demographic, geographic, and lifestyle characteristics. Data is obtained by means of a questionnaire packaged in the Carol Wright co-op direct-mail program mailed twice a year to 45 million households. In addition to the questionnaire, each co-op package contains an assortment of direct marketing promotions and cents-off coupons.

The Shareforce database is designed to give direct-response mailers segmentation capabilities through a number of data elements, including occupation, presence and age of children, hobbies and interests, and detailed financial information. Shareforce clients, primarily in the packaged-goods industry, can also sponsor specific questionnaire items, which entitles them to exclusive rights to the gathered information and the corresponding database of respondents.

MULTISOURCED
ENHANCEMENT FILES

The Infobase database is a unique multisourced enhancement file called Infobase Premier. It includes data from R. L. Polk, NDL, Database America, Equifax, SmartNames, American Student List, U S WEST, and Donnelley Marketing. By mid-1990, this huge database contained 200 million American consumers, 95 percent of all U.S. households, with more than 170 data elements. When the contributing data sources are merged and duplicates are eliminated, only the most current data elements are retained. Infobase's primary businesses are analysis and enhancement. The match rates for most enhancement processes range from 45 to 60 percent; the Premier file match rates generally fall between 60 and 80 percent.

Initially, Infobase developed the Premier file to assist large credit card issuers to screen names rented from credit bureaus more effectively. However, the need for more overlaid data elements by database marketers led Infobase into providing enhancement services for retailers, financial institutions, publishing, insurance, catalogs, and nontraditional direct marketing organizations, such as telecommunications companies.

BUILDING THE BRIDGE TO FULL DATABASE MARKETING APPLICATIONS

The manipulation of information on internal databases to improve customer response has gone on for years. The recency-frequency-monetary value (RFM) paradigm has proved its worth over and over.

With wider circulation of advanced statistical techniques, such as logistic regression and discriminant analysis, the ability to optimize customer response by using internal database information has increased dramatically. For many companies this capability has been a gold mine. They have branded, segmented, and appropriately coddled their most responsive, most extravagant, and most loyal customers. Their internal database machine purrs like a Silver Cloud.

But no matter how efficiently that engine operates, attrition takes place. Customers die, move, or enter new life-cycle stages where old products become irrelevant, or they succumb to the promotional seductions of competitive products. At some point there is a need for companies to promote new customers to fill the void. Prospective customers—prospects—are "out there" somewhere, perhaps waiting patiently in an external database where they can be identified and accessed.

However, the old-style Gonzo marketer wouldn't have a clue about which prospects to approach. He'd have some educated hunches about the characteristics of the people who were currently buying his products. Those intuitions would point him in the direction of certain lists to either test in incremental stages or retain or discard through a lengthy trial-and-error process.

The meticulous modeling of RFM variables would be of little use in the prospecting situation because there are no RFM variables "out there." RFM models only work on known customers. Since prospects are not yet customers, they do not yet have any recency, frequency, and monetary value characteristics that can be used to identify them as likely new customers.

The database owner who has collected only internal transactional data about current customers is stuck without a Get-Out-of-Jail card and can't go prospecting because there's no linkage between the owner's internal database and external prospect sources "out there." A bridge is needed—a set of matching variables or data elements that exists in both locations.

Let's say you own an internal database and you've gathered other information besides transitional data. You know the ages of your customers and can determine the age range of your best customers. Since age appears as a data element on almost all external databases, you can now select prospects from external databases whose ages fall within the age ranges of your best customers. In this vastly oversimplified example, age is the bridge variable between your customers and your prospects.

The first bridges were constructed in the 1980s, using demographic variables as the unifying link. Marketers used a common name and address matching process, a merge-purge, to overlay external databases onto their internal customer files. Demographic data from those external sources were then tagged — appended — to the names that matched in both files.

The match rates between house lists and large compiled databases generally range from 50 to 65 percent. The match rates for questionnaire-generated databases usually range from 10 to 20 percent, depending on the size of the external database.

In either case, the match sample, the names that appear on both the internal and external databases, is sufficiently large to accurately profile a marketer's entire customer file as well as important subsegments. Those subsegments might consist of frequent flyers, big-ticket buyers, or reluctant pays. The process is similar to a large customer survey, except a survey sample rarely numbers in the hundreds of thousands as these do.

Once you have the information from the overlay, you can venture "out there" with confidence to promote customer look-alikes, those individuals who have the same demographic characteristics as your most valuable customers.

With the advent of questionnaire-generated databases, the overlay information goes well beyond demographics. Now, behavioral and lifestyle data elements can also be appended to internal files, expanding the possibilities in the quest for customer look-alikes.

A more sophisticated and powerful variation on the process involves the development of statistical models using the internal, enhanced database elements to point you in the direction of the best prospects. Such models can be produced by using a number of statistical techniques, most commonly a regression technique or discriminant analysis.

The models score prospects according to their resemblance to the profile of the criterion segment (frequent buyers, most loyal customers, etc.) and then rank all prospects from highest to lowest resemblance. Rankings are often grouped by deciles, increments of 10 percent, or by duodeciles, increments of 5 percent. A model prepared for Eddie Bauer might very well rank our Montana fisherwoman and trail biker in the top 10 percent of the prospect list and the Manhattan theatergoer toward the bottom.

The modeling process has led to significantly improved performances by prospect databases. Future improvements will depend on two factors: the modeling methodology itself and the data used.

Today's modeling methodology is relatively sequential and limited in its handling of complex interactions between variables. Recent advances in pattern analysis may produce response models that take many more variables and their complex interactions into account. In other words, the modeling process has been very left-brained and needs to become more right-brained in the future. But more of that later.

Just as we have witnessed a dramatic jump in the nature and quality of external data elements in recent years, we can also expect that more and better data will become available in years to come. It's unlikely that an extremely large number of variables will be necessary for improved modeling performance. What will be necessary is that the variables must be more relevant to the model. For example, marketers could benefit from greater understanding of the dynamics of response, if only to be able to identify the key variables that will help them predict it.

In the past, direct marketers have been correctly described as wanting to know only *what* works with no real interest in behaviors—*why* something works. But with the need to specify the correct predictors of behavior and improve the efficacy of the prospecting process, future marketers will need to have a better understanding of why consumers behave as they do.

THE DATABASE MARKETING
APPLICATIONS BOOM

In 1986, the Marketing Council of the Direct Marketing Association conducted a survey of 1000 direct marketers to identify their current and anticipated future database marketing applications. The use of the customer's name within the mailing piece itself was the only application that received more than occasional mention in the survey. The customization of mailings according to customer profiles and the use of geodemographic classification of mailing lists were also mentioned. Hardly acknowledged at the time was the use of lifestyle lists to classify potential customers or customer profile analysis to create new products or customize catalogs.

Even the most forward-thinking industry analysts failed to envision the rush to the database Klondike that would take place in the next 4 years, particularly in the area of computer modeling to identify prospective customers. Another surprise has been the interest shown by previously skeptical packaged-goods marketers whose former direct marketing activities had consisted of indirect mass distribution of coupons and samples.

AUTOMOBILE
MANUFACTURERS

Buick has used a survey of attendees of auto shows to develop the prospect characteristics for a showroom traffic-building promotion. By profiling the 68,000 survey respondents, Buick created the income and car-buying demographics of owners of targeted automobiles. From this process, Buick created a master list that was matched against lists of country club members, golf equipment buyers, and subscribers to special-interest golf magazines. The match process produced a multimillion name target list which had appropriate car ownership characteristics and demographics and included people with an interest in golf.

The subsequent promotion, known as the Winning Putt Sweepstakes, was designed to generate showroom traffic in conjunction with two Buick-sponsored golf tournaments. Buick estimated that the final response rate was close to 25 percent. The company expected to sell 31,000 automobiles as a result of the promotion, a very handsome return on an $8 million investment.

That same year, Chrysler countered with its own successful $10 million dealer-traffic promotion. Chrysler used sophisticated analytic techniques from R. L. Polk to identify households with the greatest likelihood of purchasing a new vehicle. The targets for the promotion, the prospects, were identified by predictive modeling techniques that used auto ownership data as well as demographic and lifestyle variables. Chrysler mailed the prospects invitations to a private screening hosted by Lee Iacocca via satellite transmission at more than 4000 dealerships.

Foreign auto manufacturers have also benefited from database development and applications. Alfa Romeo began its database program by running direct-response ads in consumer magazines that appealed to auto enthusiasts, men, or people who lived in a particular region. The audience profiles of the selected magazines conformed to Alfa Romeo's target audience profiles of well-educated, affluent males under the age of 55.

Several weeks later, Alfa Romeo ran direct-response spots on seven cable networks. All of the advertising featured an 800 number. Respondents were directed to the nearest dealer for a test drive of an Alfa 164S and a gift of a specially designed Alfa Romeo paperweight. The campaign generated nearly 2000 calls a week.

CATALOG MAILERS

Because of the richness of purchasing information and the long-term loyalty potential of their customer base, catalog mailers — especially those in the medium to large categories — have been long-time and active proponents of database marketing, even before the recent database fervor. For many years, catalog applications used only RFM variables, particularly when catalogers discovered how intelligent manipulation of their product mix and mailing schedules to their house files could generate significant improvement in overall response. Their success at orchestrating known buyers muted catalogers' interest in prospecting efforts to outside lists.

When catalogers became aware of the rich potential of maximizing the lifetime value (LTV) by using their customers' prior buying behavior to predict which offers they should make to which customers at what time, they began to capture as much purchase data about their customers as possible. Nevertheless, a 1988 survey by *Catalog Age* indicated that fewer than 20 percent of all catalogers were even calculating LTV.

But as new catalog companies proliferated and existing catalog companies generated line extensions, a situation called catalog glut developed. Meanwhile, fewer direct-mail buyers were entering the marketplace. In their fascination with known direct-mail buyers, catalogers had turned their marketing efforts inward. As a result, everyone was mailing to the same target group with increasing frequency.

Fortunately, with the appearance of rich external databases with opportunities for efficient linkages to prospect sources, the prospecting process has become more attractive. Catalog companies know they have to expand their markets beyond existing customer files and realize that prospecting efforts cannot be evaluated by short-term profitability.

The relatively recent appearance of relevant data and effective analytic tools to access it has encouraged a burgeoning of database-marketing applications within the catalog industry. In fact, some observers suggest that the catalog companies that do not implement a successful database strategy will disappear from what is a highly competitive marketplace. To avoid that scenario, many, if not most, of today's catalog mailers must move beyond their current operational use of customer databases for better and faster order processing, as an example, to more extensive marketing applications.

As discussed earlier, the existence of overlaid externally resourced data such as demographics, lifestyles, and competitive buying behavior permits much more useful segmentation of consumers than RFM data alone. In this regard, catalogers are advanced in their thinking. For example, Sears Catalog Group uses advanced segmentation techniques to classify their customers and noncustomers and targets product offerings to conform to known characteristics. Important in that targeting process is the determination of lifetime value, using modeling methods. Saks, Talbots, and some other catalogers use similar methodologies to customize offerings to specific segments they have identified through variables on their databases.

Relationship Building and Lifetime Value

The very use of a term like *lifetime value* implies the existence of a significant relationship between a mailer and a consumer. The mailer's database can serve as the information resource through which the relationship maintenance function is maximized. Catalog mailers can strengthen their relationships with their customers through shared values and demonstrate a corporate orientation that transcends the profit-making motive.

Two diverse catalog companies, Swiss Colony and Spiegel, contributed a portion of their profits to environmental causes to show their sensitivity to their customers' concerns in an interesting relationship-building application. In the past, Spiegel has encouraged customer participation in charitable enterprises by featuring certain charities on the pages of its catalogs, tracking the donations which ensued, and matching them. Other charitable programs that carried similar messages were the disaster relief efforts supported by Bedford Fair and Talbots following the devastation caused by Hurricane Hugo. These efforts manifest each company's commitment to long-term relationships with their customers that go well beyond an interest in simply making the next sale.

Embarking on programs that center on customer LTV represents a tough, upfront corporate decision because there's no assurance that the margins reaped from future sales to those customers will offset the costs of the relationship-building efforts.

To establish and nurture the customer-company relationship in today's database marketing environment, the company must know as much as possible about each customer. That sort of information is gathered from customer surveys or by appending information to the house file from external databases. Neither alternative is cheap or a one-time phenomenon, and the data must be updated regularly to remain relevant.

Several observers have made a distinction between contractual and noncontractual relationships with customers. Marketers of continuity programs, such as book and record clubs, establish contractual relationships with their customers at the program's inception. The customer might agree, for example, to buy four compact discs during a 2-year period. Since the customer can opt out at any time, continuity marketers need to minimize turnover by constantly wooing or teasing their customers with discounts or promotions geared to future sales, such as buy one, get one free offers, half-price sales, etc.

Catalogers, on the other hand, do not have contractual relationships with their buyers. The customer treats the initial sale as a test. If the merchandise or service fails the test, a repeat sale is unlikely. In fact, even if the purchase experience is entirely satisfactory, the buyer may still be lured away by a clever competitor. Therefore, catalogers must use their database information to maximize retention. They use any number of techniques, from attempting to solidify the relationship through newsletters to special promotions targeted specifically to valuable customers.

Line Extensions

Another database application which is becoming increasingly popular, especially among catalog mailers, is the introduction of line extensions based on segmentation analysis of the information on file. For years, Lillian Vernon produced a core catalog aimed primarily at well-educated middle-aged women. The company identified the women on their file who had purchased children's items in the past and who were also known to be young parents, thereby isolating a subfile to which a brand-new Lilly's Kids children's catalog will be promoted. Lands' End and Talbots have also mined their customer databases. Based on analyses of their customers' demographic and purchasing characteristics, both companies developed children's catalogs.

CHILDREN AND TEENAGE OFFERS

A presentation by *American Demographics* magazine in the spring of 1990 identified 25 "particle" markets, the metamorphosed market segments of the 1980s and the latest series of supernova caused by the Big Bang market fragmentation of the late 1970s. The fragmentation is so intense that there are stepfamily, grandparent, and anti-aging senior citizen particles. (Presumably, this last particle is made up of people who are more than 50 years old and refuse to act their age.) One particle that has been embraced by direct marketers most enthusiastically of late consists of adolescent and preadolescent children.

Although some adults have become sufficiently jaded so as to resist the blandishments of many third class mail offers, not so their kids. There are 20 million impressionable American preadolescents who love to receive personally addressed mail and who have an uncanny knack for influencing the purchasing decisions of their parents.

Although marketing to children is hardly a new phenomenon, the upsurge in children's databases is. In many instances, the marketing objective is to sell products today. But in some cases, marketers are actually attempting to establish brand loyalty at the earliest possible age, thus giving even greater meaning to the term "lifetime value."

For some companies, such as Lillian Vernon, new children's catalogs represent product-line extensions generated from their existing customer databases. For other direct marketers, specifically Time Warner's *Sports Illustrated for Kids,* the database was built by tapping into outside lists. This monthly magazine, with a median readership age of 11.1 years, has a subscription base of 800,000 children. A survey of these young readers revealed, to no one's surprise, that they significantly influenced the family's purchase of bicycles, sneakers, and cereal. However, more than 70 percent of the children surveyed also claimed to influence the family's vacation plans, and an unspecified percentage influenced the family's automobile purchases. Time Warner's anticipated line extensions include books, calendars, and school products.

Even Barbie has become a member of the database generation. Barbie's manufacturer, Mattel, Inc., launched a continuity promotion with the objective of building a database of 300,000 young girls within the first year. The core of the program is a club that offers premiums, including small television sets, telephones, and Barbie accessories. The premiums may be obtained through the redemption of Pink Stamps packaged in all Barbie products. In addition to name and address, the database will carry the types and number of purchases and the types of premiums selected.

Future plans call for the addition of the names and addresses of the child's parents and the names and ages of other children in the household. That information will enable Mattel to communicate more relevantly with Barbie's admirers and their families in future direct-mail promotions.

Maybelline, the cosmetics company, is also engaged in targeting teenage females, for now and forever. The company is building a database of personal information generated from coupon responses. The target market is females between 12 and 17 years old. They are asked to provide name and address, date of birth, hair and eye color, and skin tone. In return, respondents receive a customized beauty care kit. Girls are also encouraged to join the Buddy Plan and to enlist two or three peers in the program.

The objective of the campaign is twofold: to cross-sell within the teenage product line and, by reinforcing the natural brand loyalty of teenagers, to create brand-loyal customers for the next 50 years. That relationship-building objective is more ambitious than most marriages.

LEGO Systems is an unlikely entry in the database game. In 1986, the company launched a LEGO Builders Club to establish long-term customer relationships. After analyzing shelf space movement, LEGO developed a geographically generated database from which to solicit club members. The club members receive newsletters, the *Bricks Kicks* magazine, and special product offers. It's reasonable to assume, however, that LEGO will use the resultant database for current promotions and, unless the company is planning to go into the executive toys business, has no intention of promoting lifelong LEGO use.

FINANCIAL OFFERS

A major deterrent to database marketing by financial institutions has been the pro-liferation of customer information files, each based on unconsolidated individual accounts. For years, research consultants who had just been hired to help a bank solve its marketing problems would ask, "How many customers do you have?" The inevitable response was, "We don't have any idea. However, we do know we have 170,000 checking accounts; 87,000 savings accounts; 120,000 CDs...." Since no one understood the nature of multiple-account relationships, there was no serious effort made to cross-sell the many products in the bank's portfolio.

The first step entailed what is now known as "householding," combining mul-tiple nonintegrated systems (checking accounts, installment loans, etc.) into a single database of individual customers, thus appending the disparate account activity of each individual to a name and address. Once that task was completed, many banks were surprised to discover that each customer had an average of fewer than two account relationships and that for every dollar on deposit with the customer's primary bank, that customer had $1.20 on deposit with other fi-nancial institutions. In addition, the banks found that 10 percent of all affluent consumers change financial institutions annually.

All of this information awakened many banks to the need to strengthen rela-tionships with existing customers instead of pursuing less lucrative prospects. This refocusing of marketing emphasis prompted many banks to recognize the enormous potential of cross-selling their many product lines. The services most frequently cross-sold by direct mail are checking accounts, installment loans, credit cards, other credit services, money market accounts, home equity credit lines, CDs, and IRAs.

The variety of account relationships offers fertile territory for the capture and retention of information about financial behavior. These data items include size of deposits, average balance, most recent deposits and payments, and the way in which transactions are made. Other data elements, such as age, occupa-tion, assets, annual income, and even the ages of children, can be obtained from mortgage loan applications. Such behavioral data can be supplemented with de-mographic and lifestyle information from external databases.

By applying credit-scoring techniques to the information on the resulting da-tabase, banks can predict high-risk individuals. Response modeling is used to predict likely customer response to cross-selling promotions. (It's somewhat par-adoxical that individuals who score lowest as credit risks often have the highest response likelihood scores and vice versa.)

Chase Manhattan has been one of the most sophisticated cross-sellers of its prod-uct lines through database marketing. Using internally generated and externally purchased data, Chase has segmented its customers into several dimensions of af-fluence, such as wealthy households (households with incomes in excess of $250,000 and investable assets in the range of $1 million), affluent households (in-comes between $75,000 and $250,000), and mass-market households. Chase de-cided to focus its cross-selling attention on the first two groups, particularly since wealthy households produce an average annual profit of $5500.

One example of Chase's success is the direct-mail sales of private banking ser-vices to wealthy customers. Another successful direct-mail promotion involved marketing a gold Visa card with tiered credit lines. Chase's response rates in

1990 averaged 10 percent across the board, and bank officials hope to increase those rates to 12 and 15 percent through better database tracking of customer awareness, attitudes, and purchase intent.

Successful bank database marketing applications have not been the sole province of giant corporations such as Chase Manhattan. Sooner Federal in Tulsa used its customer database to identify nonmaturing CD customers who also had liquid funds of less than $1500. The bank developed a new product especially for this target group, a jump-rate CD. The promotion resulted in over $45 million in new deposits within 60 days at a very low acquisition cost.

American Express has been a pioneer in database marketing, dating back to John Stevenson's tenure with the company in the late 1970s. By using transactional data combined with income estimates, AMEX has developed models that rank customers by their likelihood of response to specific promotions. This approach has helped AMEX eliminate excessive mailings.

PaineWebber has produced millions of dollars in incremental revenue by cleverly excavating its 10-year-old database, Profiled Prospects. The system generates sales leads for its individual brokers and provides PaineWebber management with valuable strategic information, such as cost per account, conversion rates, and dollars generated per account and promotion.

Actually, PaineWebber uses two databases. One database of prospects includes transactional history and some demographics. The second database includes broker characteristics, such as length of time with the company and product strength. Prospects are matched to those brokers who have the greatest likelihood of generating a sale. By using the customer transactional database, PaineWebber has tripled its revenue by cross-selling clients who were identified as likely to be receptive to a particular offer. The cross-selling program also helps reduce client attrition and strengthens the total institutional relationship.

LIQUOR DISTILLERS

In the last 10 years, whiskey distillers have seen a major exodus from brown to white liquor consumption, as the whiskey-drinking public started buying more vodka and then moved to white wine as their alcoholic beverage of choice. Several distillers have attempted to reverse, or at least stem, that trend by building databases of brand-loyal consumers.

The distiller of George Dickel Tennessee Sour Mash Whisky, Schenley Industries, Inc., has developed a customer database by obtaining individual information through a club membership program and a newsletter. The George Dickel Tennessee Whisky Water Conservation Society has 100,000 members, primarily located in the Southeast. The newsletter contains a questionnaire inviting recipients to become charter members of the society and to supply information about selected demographic characteristics (marital status and occupation), favorite interests, favorite drinks and brands, and weekly liquor consumption. The newsletter also offers premiums, such as a tasting kit which allows the user to sample and compare George Dickel with its chief competitor, Jack Daniels. Future promotions will be able to target drinkers of competitive brands and reward loyal George Dickel customers.

The use of databases is not new to Seagram. In 1986, the distiller began collecting data about drinkers and their individual tastes. The information has been collected through promotions for various Seagram brands, as well as from inbound telemarketing, in-package promotions, and magazine surveys. Seagram, unlike many other database builders, has avoided incorporating any names generated by magazine sweepstakes, apprehensive that they would mar the integrity of its database. Because of Seagram's heavy reliance on surveys, the database is extremely rich in specific category and brand behavior information.

Because liquor advertising is not permitted on broadcast media, Seagram benefits from database marketing. As Ashleigh Groce of Leo Burnett points out, Seagram qualifies as a natural database user because of its broad spectrum of brands. For its Glenlivet single-malt scotch, a fairly complex offer package of gifts, rebates, and cassette tapes was used to increase awareness and brand-attribute recall. Cross-selling mailings were used to stimulate the trial of other Seagram brands.

One objective of a database-driven promotion for Chivas Regal was to overcome the brand's premium-price image and increase its use among scotch drinkers familiar with the brand. One of the techniques Seagram used was to establish a Chivas Class, which, through promotional tie-ins with airlines and hotels, reinforced the first class image of Chivas. Seagram introduced a campaign for Crown Royal, a Canadian whiskey, to increase brand awareness. The Seagram database effort is given added potency through sophisticated modeling techniques, allowing the company to predict likely users of a liquor category with remarkable precision.

Easily the most unusual and provocative database-building effort has been attempted by Johnnie Walker Red. The company conducted tests in Los Angeles and San Francisco where 18 strategically located billboards featured an attractive woman who urged viewers to fax her at a featured number if they drank Johnnie Walker Red. Respondents were then faxed a provocatively worded reply. The campaign blended two unique media, billboards and fax, to establish a dialogue with consumers.

PACKAGED GOODS

During the heyday of the mass-marketing approach, when most advertisers were enamored with the television networks' favorite market segment—adults 18 to 49—packaged-goods manufacturers eschewed targeted marketing as unnecessary. The potential for intimate, relevant relationship building was abused by mindless, one-shot, mass distribution of millions of coupons, the net result of which was millions of dollars spent with no lasting customer relationships to show for it.

When the database marketing movement took off in the 1980s, packaged-goods manufacturers, as represented by the brand managers, initially looked askance. Database building was perceived as both difficult and costly. Besides, many products could not be differentiated on the basis of demographics alone, and useful segmentation needed additional data elements.

Until the advent of Donnelley's Carol Wright, JFY, CMT's Select and Save, and other similar programs, there were no external databases that addressed individual consumption by brand. Most brand managers, faced with small margins and the pressure to show short-term profitability, were scared off by the costs associated with direct-mail campaigns generated from a consumer database: postage, list rental, file enhancement, database management, and printing. Also present was the natural inertia that usually greets any change in the established way of doing things. Besides, no one could guarantee that the very difficult database marketing process, with its many unforeseen potholes, would ever pay off. A commitment to the concept of customer lifetime value, by definition, calls for risky, visionary leadership.

With the passage of time, however, more and more packaged-goods marketers are becoming true believers in the potential of database marketing to build brand loyalty. They understand that database marketing can create a lifetime return to the manufacturer worth hundreds of dollars from brand-loyal customers, far transcending the immediate sales value measured in cents.

Packaged-goods marketers are also beginning to realize that the database process has more immediate benefits, including (1) developing alternative channels of distribution, (2) testing new products, and (3) establishing a relevant bond with consumers by customizing communications to match their brand usage, demographic, and lifestyle characteristics.

Indeed, for some companies, such as cigarette manufacturers whose total media access has been attenuated bit by bit, year after year, database marketing may eventually be the only available medium. R. J. Reynolds has spent $100 million to develop a database composed of 50 percent of the 55 million smokers in the United States. The effort appears to have been worth every cent. Some of Reynolds database-driven direct marketing programs have achieved response rates of 30 to 50 percent. Compare that to the response rates of 3 percent obtained from earlier direct marketing efforts that were not database-driven. Philip Morris has turned to a database marketing approach, driven by 12 million subscribers to a magazine published by the company.

General Foods began a massive database building effort in 1985 by collecting all of the names and addresses provided by its premium buyers, sweepstakes entrants, and coupon redeemers. The company enhanced the transactional data on those files by mailing customer questionnaires through National Demographics & Lifestyles. The questionnaires solicited information about specific brand use across a number of product lines and gathered demographic and lifestyle attributes. In 5 years, the General Foods database grew to 30 million consumers and has been in continual use.

One extremely successful database-directed promotion was aimed at households with children aged 3 to 12. The company began by building a special database of known users of Kool-Aid (a General Foods product), users of other General Foods beverages, users of a competitive soft drink, a General Foods list of heavy users of presweetened cereals, and several outside lifestyle lists. Through regression modeling, the database was culled to 4 million households likely to respond to the promotion. General Foods used television commercials to arouse kids' interest in a concept called Wacky Warehouse. The company used involvement mechanisms (direct-mail packages, premiums, and a comic book). In conjunction with Field Publications, General Foods produced an educational magazine for kids, *What's Hot,* and mailed it to 2 million households in the database. In addition to educational articles, the magazines contained free posters, a page for parents, brand premiums for T-shirts and mugs, and coupons and ads for a variety of General Foods products.

In one campaign designed to increase the category share of Post presweetened cereals and to stymie brand-switching to competitive products, General Foods targeted households with children aged 6 to 12 who preferred presweetened cereal. Each target household received books and games designed to build brand image.

The campaign was successful in producing incremental purchase behavior, with an 8 percent lift across all of Post's presweetened brands. The campaign measured three times more successful than General Foods norms for direct mail. In answer to some critics of advertising to children, 90 percent of the mothers in the targeted households indicated that they would welcome additional mailings.

Another General Foods database-driven campaign aimed at increasing the use of Kool-Aid products also used the combination of magazine, free offers, and bar-coded coupons. This effort succeeded in increasing sales by 33 percent and coupon redemption by 88 percent.

Not to be outdone, Quaker Oats has launched Quaker Direct and targeted 18 million promotionally responsive households for three successive direct maildrops. The drops primarily contain Quaker product messages and coupons that have been tailored to each household's known demographic and purchasing characteristics. Each coupon is assigned a unique household number, so that its redemption can be tracked and product use can be linked to the identified characteristics. That number is entered into a sweepstakes whenever a redemption occurs, thereby creating an incentive. According to Quaker spokespersons, the program has short- and long-term benefits by adding value to the customer's shopping experience and providing one-on-one brand bonding.

Although Quaker Oats uses direct mail to build its database, many companies have used other media effectively. Dr. Cookie gourmet cookies has developed a 30,000-name database through an 800 number on every cookie package. Respondents have the opportunity to purchase a Dr. Cookie cookbook as well as aprons and T-shirts with the company's logo.

Holly Farms used a 30-second television commercial inviting viewers to call an 800 number to receive a free chicken. More than 200,000 calls were received, and Holly Farms will use the resulting information to maintain an ongoing relationship with its customers.

What about databases of almond aficionados? Absolutely possible in today's marketing environment. Blue Diamond Growers, a cooperative of almond farmers, has participated in a joint promotion with Ralston Purina to advertise the Almond Plaza catalog on Almond Delight cereal boxes. The objective of the promotion is to sell almond items from the catalog at an average order size of $65 and to build a database for future direct-mail promotions.

If you can build an almond lovers database, can popcorn be far behind? The makers of Smartfood, a cheese-flavored popcorn, mailed a whimsical package to a targeted group of innovators and early adopters as a first step in constructing a popcorn-specific database, more highly targeted than parent Frito-Lay's larger database. The mechanism for database development was a light-hearted questionnaire.

Although there is no known database which includes the names of Goofy and Garfield, there are databases that list the names and addresses of dog and cat owners. Once the people in Carnation's pet foods division learned that more than one-half of the households in the United States own a cat or dog, they set about gathering the names and addresses of cat owners through rebates and coupon redemptions.

Carnation mailed the feline fanciers a package of coupons and a questionnaire that captured buying habits. The same individuals have been assigned unique ID numbers so their coupon redemption and buying habits can be tracked. By using its database to target its mailings, Carnation has received response rates in the 30 percent range. Carnation is also using its database to introduce new products, a new premium dog food sold exclusively by mail order, for example.

Manufacturers of skin care products have discovered how helpful database marketing can be in securing preferred in-store shelf placement and increasing sales. Using four-color ads in magazines read by their target market of girls and young women, 15 to 24 years of age, marketers at Clairol have built a marketing database to supplement the 2-million-name database of their parent company, Bristol Myers. The target prospect group was challenged in the magazine ads and in point-of-sale displays to find an 800 number printed inside packages of Sea Breeze lotion. Each caller was entered in a sweepstakes. The campaign helped Clairol place 1.5 million Sea Breeze packages in 50,000 drugstores and 40,000 supermarkets.

Revlon has also developed a sweepstakes-generated database for its Clean and Clear product line, and Dove Soap is building a database of women who maintain a 7-day diary about the effect of Dove on their skins. The objective of Dove's campaign was to switch brand use from competitive soap products and promote continuity purchases of Dove Soap. Initial results indicated that repeat Dove purchases rose 110 percent.

Huggies disposable diapers, a division of Kimberly-Clark, has used database marketing to attain brand leadership in its product category. Since the average product lifetime of the disposable diaper market segment is less than 3 years, Huggies' mission was to instill brand loyalty in the mother at the earliest possible moment in her infant's life. Huggies created a database to capture the names and addresses of new parents and the date of birth of the newborn. Every 3 months, the company sent the parents a pamphlet that offered advice and information on child development and parenting, appropriate for the particular stage in the infant's life cycle. The campaign successfully positioned Huggies as the brand leader by "bonding" with the parent.

Several years later, Huggies demonstrated its database expertise again, this time in new product development. A free-standing insert (FSI) appeared in national newspapers, offering parents a tape of lullabies that had been personalized with their baby's name. Huggies received more than 100,000 leads through calls to a 900 number that cost each prospect 45 cents a call. In this instance, customers shared the cost of database development with the company.

SUPERMARKETS

The data-capturing capabilities of the checkout scanner have awakened super-market retailers to the potential benefits of database marketing. Whereas a publication may have at least one or two interactive contacts with its customers each year and a catalog mailer may have four to five times that many transactions with its best customers, consumers visit their favorite supermarkets an average of twice a week. Those visits represent a possibility of more than 100 data-capture opportunities annually. Supermarket retailers are just beginning to capitalize on that potential. They are organizing frequent-shopper programs that reward their regular customers and attract new ones.

Ukrop, a supermarket chain in Richmond, Virginia, has developed a frequent shopper program, complete with a Valued Customer Card issued to 160,000 customers in its trade area. The program was launched in 1987, promoted by radio commercials, billboards, direct mail to households in Ukrop's trade areas, shopping bag announcements, and in-store presentations. Each customer card has a unique UPC ID that permits the electronic capture of coupon discounts at the cash register. Every cardholder receives a monthly mailing announcing that month's electronic coupon specials.

Ukrop's monthly mailing costs are covered by the participating manufacturers. The Ukrop program has been a win-win situation. Customers can save up to $500 a year in discounts, and store sales have increased 10 to 15 percent since the program began. In addition, the database was used effectively to stem attrition when a competitive chain opened a store in the area.

Other supermarket chains, including King Kullen, Grand Union, and Vons, have also initiated customer loyalty programs that use purchasing behavior captured at checkout. Through electronically acquired and analyzed individual data, the supermarkets are able to emulate the personal attention to their customers that was typical of the neighborhood mom-and-pop grocery store many years ago. Perhaps the checkout clerk will never be able to duplicate the traditional grocer's customer knowledge to know enough to ask how Billy likes Dartmouth, but the store's ability to customize its offers will go a long way to strengthen the supermarket-customer relationship, help the store keep its customers, and sell more products.

Another giant step in the database marketing process involves the third-party brokerage of a marriage between supermarkets and packaged-goods manufacturers. That relationship has often been strained because manufacturers must compete for shelf space, and their ability to get their products in front of the consumer is controlled by the individual stores. However, third parties such as Citicorp, Donnelley Marketing, and Catalina Marketing are providing data acquisition and analysis systems with simultaneous benefits for manufacturers and retailers. By wedding questionnaire-generated demographic, lifestyle, and behavioral data with transactional information about purchases and coupon redemption, these systems allow both manufacturers and supermarkets to reward, as well as change, consumer behavior.

The systems, although differing in technology, methodology, and specific benefit packages, have the collection of individual transactional data in common. The eventual goal of the Citicorp point-of-sale (POS) system is to create a massive database of 40 million households, or 44 percent of all households in the United States. Every supermarket transaction for every brand or product will be recorded and linked to the purchaser's name and address and to other questionnaire-developed data. Participating consumers are invited to submit an application for a card with a scannable UPC label or magnetic strip which contains a unique household identifier.

Demographic characteristics and financial data are also collected during the application process. By providing this information, consumers can participate in some or all of the following benefit programs: (1) a frequent-shopper loyalty program in which customers receive rebates, coupons, and free products or points customized by the retailer; (2) a rebate program, Reward America, in which members receive a monthly rebate check based on their purchase of specific brands and announcements about upcoming rebate opportunities; (3) an electronic couponing program that eliminates many of the current abuses of printed coupons; and (4) an electronic payment system linked to various credit card alternatives.

The advantages to consumers lie in cost savings and convenience. The benefits to both manufacturers and retailers include short-term targeting of coupons and promotional offers to the most likely buyers and the establishment of long-term brand or store loyalty.

Donnelley Marketing has joined with Procter & Gamble to introduce the Vision 2000 frequent-shopper program. This system, known as APT, uses a smart card containing a microchip that records all transactions and stores personal information. The same card is used in the financial transaction for direct debit or credit granting. Vision members are rewarded for their purchases with points to use in purchasing items from the Vision catalog.

Catalina Marketing Systems was an early entrant in this same area when it introduced an in-store coupon distribution system in 1983. Individual purchases received appropriate coupons at checkout. The system was refined in 1989 to include a continuity program based on a scannable identification card. Members of this frequent-shopper program earn rebates when they purchase participating products and receive quarterly rebate checks. The consumer behavioral data is shared with the participating manufacturers. Manufacturers and retailers are able to identify their best customers and their corresponding purchase behaviors, allowing them to target and customize future offers.

As these programs mature and are "debugged," they will likely be extended beyond the current business base of packaged-goods manufacturers and supermarkets to include other types of manufacturers and retailers.

GENERAL RETAILERS

Some general retailers have embraced a database approach. With a few exceptions, however, retailers are not using external data to the same extent as some of the large supermarket systems. The potential for relationship marketing that matches a store's personality with its customers may be much, much greater for many general retailers than it is for most supermarkets. The similarities of product offerings, in-store layouts, and advertising present supermarkets with limited opportunities for differentiation in the eyes of the consumer. A Vons in Los Angeles looks a lot like a Safeway in Denver which, in turn, seems very much the same as a Grand Union in New York City. Contrast that, however, with the real or perceived differences in image between a Nordstrom, a Neiman Marcus, and a Sears.

Greater customer differentiation in transactional behavior is possible among general retail marketers because of three factors:

1. There is a wide variance in frequency with which consumers shop at any particular retailer. It's unlikely that the average retail shopping frequency approaches twice a week as is the case with supermarket shopping.
2. The expenditure patterns may vary widely among retail shoppers—from $4 to $4000 at some stores.
3. Sales by category or department will show greater variability; for example, Neiman may be patronized for evening wear, Nordstrom for lingerie, etc.

These transactional differences provide an opportunity for greater customer segmentation and, consequently, for greater personalized relationship enhancement between store and customer. Provided they have the data available, retailers can maximize the relevance of their advertising and promotions communications to their customers.

A case in point is the use to which the Sears Merchandise Group puts its 30 million household database. The database system has been developed by capturing point-of-sale transactional data from those customers who use a Sears or Discover card. This mechanism links the transaction to a name and address. The system provides Sears with customer profiles for any Sears vertical business (home furnishings, automotive), all departments within those businesses, and all product lines within departments. The profiles are enhanced with externally generated and overlaid demographic and lifestyle data.

The Sears system functions as both a decision-support tool and a targeting mechanism. It tracks changes in shopping dynamics in much the same way an internal database is used by many catalog mailers. For example, changes in shopping frequency or average purchase amounts can be monitored by business, department, or product line.

By segmenting customers into similar groups on the basis of shared demographics, lifestyles, and transactional behavior, the relevant advertising can be created and targeted to address the specific needs of each group. The effect of those differential promotional activities can be evaluated by monitoring subsequent buying behavior. The profitability of direct mail can be maximized by predictive modeling. And cross-selling opportunities become more apparent.

Because of the widespread use of its specific credit mechanisms, the Sears or Discover cards, Sears operates a much more effective system than stores with either no captive credit mechanism or stores that share card use with nonproprietary cards such as Visa or MasterCard.

Nevertheless, some retailers have been successful in establishing relationship marketing programs with their best customers by imbuing their in-house charge card with status elements. Neiman Marcus initiated the In Circle Club for customers who spend at least $3000 a year with the store. Neiman issues members a special card that identifies them to sales clerks for exclusive treatment. Members also receive a newsletter, special shopping evenings, personal shoppers, and other favored-customer privileges.

Retailers' database marketing efforts are not limited to upscale apparel retailers like Neiman Marcus or Saks Fifth Avenue, another store that recognizes the value of identifying and targeting its best customer segments (Saks' database records more than 1000 customer characteristics). During an 8-year period, Helzberg Diamonds, a large jewelry retailer, developed a database of 900,000 customers. Traditional RFM transactional variables were recorded, as were some overlaid geodemographic data. Helzberg's database use leans more toward decision-support applications whereby sales trends by markets are analyzed to determine where more advertising support is needed.

As sophisticated methods develop to link transactional information to specific purchasers, more and more retailers will be able to take advantage of highly targeted promotional opportunities and gain access to advanced relationship-building capabilities. Some preliminary approaches have already begun.

REACT, a new software system announced by Direct Marketing Technologies, allows retailers to program their cash registers to record a customer's telephone number, if it is offered, with each transaction. Through a reverse directory, Direct Tech later translates that phone number into a name and address using its database developed from the white pages. Some externally derived data, such as age, income, and dwelling type, can also be appended to the resulting customer file. The file can be segmented and used for subsequent direct-mail offers or to establish a continuity program for favored customers.

Although the willingness of customers to supply the retailer with a correct telephone number is as yet undetermined and the transaction-to-address matching process permits only a 65 percent match rate, the system represents an exciting opportunity to extend database marketing capabilities to a new group of retailers.

PUBLICATIONS

No discussion of database marketing in the publishing industry can omit the *Farm Journal* story. This most unlikely practitioner of an extremely sophisticated technology has led its own industry and every other as well in terms of innovative database use and true relevance marketing.

In the process of reaching its goal of being relevant to its readers and advertisers, *Farm Journal* purposefully reduced its circulation from a high of 3 million in the late 1960s to a figure of approximately 850,000 in 1990. However, during that same time period the magazine's advertising revenues increased to $25 million.

In the early 1950s, *Farm Journal* management recognized the beginning of the fragmentation of its market by both size of farm and type of product. As a result, a magazine that had once tried to be relevant to all segments was becoming relevant to none.

Management decided to collect information about subscriber characteristics and use that data to target editorial content. The requested data included type of crop, size of acreage, type and quantity of livestock raised, annual agricultural income, computer ownership, etc. The information was also used to begin to cull those farmers with fewer than 50 acres and annual agricultural sales of less than $10,000, the waste circulation which was of little interest to major advertisers and for which they were not willing to pay top advertising dollars.

Farm Journal management discovered four consistent and different segments and developed four special-interest subsegment publications (Top Producer, Beef Extra, Hog Extra, and Dairy Extra) at only 25 percent of the cost normally involved in launching new publications. Because they have the ability to analyze subscriber demographics, the magazine's management can isolate a segment and approach the advertisers who want to reach only that segment. *Farm Journal*'s regular advertisers are so cognizant of the magazine's targeting precision that they willingly pay for specially produced advertising and editorial supplements because they know *Farm Journal* delivers the readers they want to reach.

In 1979, *Farm Journal* began to use the selective imaging and binding capabilities of R. R. Donnelley & Sons. As the magazine moves through the printing process, computerized equipment adds the editorial and advertising pages that are appropriate to an individual subscriber's demographic profile. The result is a totally tailored magazine that is relevant to the advertiser and the reader.

The high point of this operation occurred in May 1984 when *Farm Journal* printed 8196 versions of that month's issue. The Selectronic Binding system meets the objective laid out by Dale Smith, *Farm Journal*'s president: "delivering to the individual reader the information that matters, while eliminating the information that doesn't matter." Smith might have added that the magazine also delivers to the individual advertiser the reader that matters, while eliminating the readers that don't matter.

In the course of making 390,000 annual telephone contacts to update the individual demographic information, solicitors obtain a 98 percent compliance, an unattainable figure in any commercial survey effort and a measure of the relevance of the publication to its readership.

Aside from advertising revenue, the circulation database also generates other revenue streams, some of which are unusual. On the more conventional side is the profitable list rental business. Not so conventional is the magazine's ability to assist marketers who wish to target specific segments by direct mail. Because of the publication's exhaustive coverage of the serious farm market, it can overlay its demographic database on the marketer's house file and isolate only those individual farmers who meet the marketer's exact specifications. *Farm Journal* will also assist with the mailing and is often able to include its own material.

Another unique target marketing service is offered by the magazine to marketers who have a very small list of buyers, too small to constitute a viable mailing list. Using the overlay technique, *Farm Journal* profiles the company's buyers and then delivers a group of *Farm Journal* subscribers with that identical profile, either as an advertising buy within the magazine or as a target group for a direct-mail solicitation.

The difficulties in building a rich database and the high costs associated with Selectronic binding technology means that fewer than 20 publishers have developed their own variations on the *Farm Journal* theme. However, the merger of Time, Inc. and Warner Brothers created a 29 million-name merged mega-database of purchasers and subscribers to all of the corporation's products and has led to a sophisticated database venture. The Time Warner magazine group has created a printing program, TargetSelect, combining database marketing, selective binding technology, and ink-jet printing. Advertisers will be able to place their ads in specific Time Warner magazines to which their target market segments subscribe, such as recent movers or senior citizens.

Isuzu was the first advertiser to participate in Time Warner's new Target-Select program. A glossy card personalized with the subscriber's name and address and the location of the nearest Isuzu dealer was inserted in issues of *Time, Sports Illustrated,* and *People* magazines. The subscriber was invited to visit the dealer for a test drive and to present the card to receive a premium, which served as a response analysis mechanism.

Newsweek magazine has tested a selective binding process and is prepared to offer advertisers space in editions which have been specifically targeted to preselected market segments. Subscribers can be addressed by name and directed to local advertisers.

Among special interest magazines, *American Baby* magazine has been using selective printing and binding since 1986. The magazine has created five main editions and as many as 139 different versions. In an example of finely tuned advertising targeting, Gerber baby foods used *American Baby* to successfully reach only women with babies between the ages of 2 and 3 months.

As printing technology catches up with the sophisticated possibilities of database marketing, publications in every area of interest will be offered to advertisers and readers. For example, magazines and catalogs have only recently been able to produce horizontally printed personalizations within the ads themselves.

TRAVEL

Travel marketing is especially amenable to a database approach since, by most marketing standards, its target segments are small and, once identified, can be profitably exploited through cross-selling. We know, for example, that tour operators who offer a variety of packages can obtain three to five times the response rates from prior passengers than from rented lists or lead-generation programs. Using statistical modeling techniques, those same multidestination tour operators or cruise lines can accurately predict what any prior passenger's next destination is likely to be.

The data elements most frequently found on travel-oriented databases are past travel history, preferred time of year to travel, and demographics and lifestyles obtained from external sources. This latter information is particularly useful for promoting vacations or tours centered around a special interest, such as opera tours, golf vacations, etc.

The Royal Viking Line has successfully mined its 100,000-member, worldwide database for a number of years. One result has been that the company has been able to avoid open discounting in its trade advertising, a practice many cruise operators are forced to use. Royal Viking cleverly positioned one particularly undersubscribed cruise to its database members as a once-in-a-lifetime opportunity. The promotion was successful to the tune of $1 million in revenue, with attendant marketing costs of only $50,000 and no discounting. The success of the effort lay in Royal Viking's continued relationship building with its past customers.

Exploration Cruise Lines has also been effective in tapping into its past passengers. Their ongoing communications medium is a newsletter, the *Explorer Gazette*. The newsletter highlights the attractive and interesting features of upcoming destinations, followed soon after by direct-mail promotions offering special premiums. Again, the key is relationship building.

Several motel and hotel chains have discovered the advantages of promoting customer loyalty. Holiday Inn formed a frequent-traveler club known as the Priority Club. After a modest beginning, the club has become an effective tool for strategic positioning and decision support. Holiday Inn can cluster its Priority Club membership into eight separate value groups based on spending levels. Each group receives its own special promotions aimed at strengthening its relationship with Holiday Inn.

Another hotel chain, Days Inn, originally developed a database of senior citizens to fill a slack time in room occupancy. By 1990, the ensuing organization, the September Days Club, had grown to 300,000 members, each of whom pays a $12 annual membership fee for a package that includes a magazine and discounts on a variety of products and services, everything from reduced room rates to discounts on food, pharmaceuticals, car rentals, and insurance. Reaching senior citizens through newsletters and direct-mail promotions has been more effective than any other advertising medium, including newspapers, magazines, broadcast, and package inserts.

The major objective of many of these travel services providers is to establish customer loyalty. In addition to Holiday Inn and Days Inn, major hotel chains, such as Hilton, Hyatt, and Marriott, have established frequent-guest programs that award points in a fashion similar to the airlines' frequent-flyer programs.

CONSUMER GOODS MANUFACTURERS

Quietly and without much fanfare, consumer goods manufacturers have entered the arena of database marketing—not with the elan of many traditional direct marketers and, somewhat surprisingly, not with conventional direct marketing applications either. Instead, many manufacturers of durable and soft goods, primarily apparel, have built large databases of their product owners to gather information to assist their marketing decision-support functions. They collect the information through questionnaires packaged with the product, along with product information and warranty material. Consumers return a sufficient number of the completed questionnaires to allow many manufacturers to build databases containing more than a million of their customers.

The questionnaires are rich in personal data: purchasing motivation, competitive brand ownership, media use, importance of specific product features, and individual demographic and lifestyle characteristics. Most of these questionnaire-generated databases have been developed for manufacturers by National Demographics & Lifestyles. Some have been developed in-house by the manufacturers. Most questionnaire-generated databases lack the transactional complexity of the retail databases currently under development. But since purchases in the area of consumer durables occur with less frequency than those of packaged goods (the purchase of a new dishwasher may occur twice in a lifetime, whereas a dishwasher-detergent purchase occurs monthly), transactional information is less important.

Many manufacturers are still hesitant about engaging in full-blown database-driven direct marketing. Their reluctance stems from a long-standing caution about fueling retailers' fears that manufacturers will use their databases to circumvent dealers and sell their products directly to consumers. In general, then, manufacturers use their databases on a fairly limited basis, primarily to provide strategic information for a wide variety of marketing applications.

KitchenAid, for example, uses its database to guide or reinforce product development decisions. Consumer questionnaires confirmed that KitchenAid had a significant market presence in the 50-50 segment: those consumers who are over the age of 50 and have incomes in excess of $50,000. However, the questionnaires also indicated that those consumers marched to a different tune than the one played by many American and European manufacturers who are designing integrated appliances that blend or disappear into their environment by using smaller knobs or smaller graphics. KitchenAid customers said they prefer easy-to-use designs, large, comfortable oven knobs, graphics that are easy to read, and controls in front of their refrigerators instead of in back.

After a moderately successful launch of a 37-inch projection television in the early 1980s, Philips Consumer Electronics was able to use the information on its consumer database to reenter the market with a much more successful product. The company learned that buyers of projection television units were older, more stable, and higher-income families who wanted full-featured models.

Philips listened to its consumers and several years later introduced 41-inch and 46-inch models with features such as expanded surround-sound and remote control on-screen graphics for tuning. At the same time, Philips was able to raise its pricing structure by appealing to consumers who were more interested in features than price. In this low-incidence market, a questionnaire database provided answers the company needed, answers that would have been impossible to get otherwise, except through an enormous market survey.

When Skil Corporation introduced its cordless power screwdriver, The Twist, the company's database uncovered an unexpected market. Skil had originally suspected that the do-it-yourselfer was its new product's prime target market. However, a substantial portion of the early buyers were elderly people for whom ease of operation was a chief advantage. As a result, Skil began advertising The Twist in publications geared to older Americans.

Amana discovered, quite accidentally, that purchaser profile information generated by its database could assist in making direct sales. An independent distributor of Amana products in Florida learned that the enormity of Amana's database made it possible for him to obtain a profile of the Amana purchasers within his territory. The distributor examined the data and realized that the high-end profile of the Amana purchaser matched the prospect profile for a major South Florida housing developer. The distributor convinced the developer to use Amana products in his kitchens.

Database applications used to strengthen the manufacturer-dealer bond are becoming more prevalent. By knowing its customers better, W. L. Gore & Associates, the manufacturer of GORE-TEX fabric brand, created a successful program to drive consumers into stores carrying its products. Using its NDL-developed database, Gore sent a 74-page, full-color GORE-TEX product directory to a targeted group of 100,000 of its best purchasers.

The purpose of the mailing was to promote the brand and show the breadth of products made with the material. A dealer listing of stores in the consumer's local area was included with each directory. To monitor response to the directory, the company offered a free GORE-TEX headband to those people who received the directory and purchased a GORE-TEX product at their local retailer. Consumers were required to mail in the receipts for their purchases with the promotional cards from their directories.

Initial response from consumers and retailers was so strong that a second mailing of 100,000 was made. It's not surprising that GORE-TEX had to reorder headbands. Gore mined its database to establish brand awareness with a significant number of its customers. An independent, follow-up survey found that one out of four consumers purchased a GORE-TEX product, and approximately half of those purchases were directly attributable to the promotion. Gore's stature also increased with its retailers.

Honeywell used its customer database for an unusual dealer development program. From its questionnaire-generated database, Honeywell discovered that purchasers of its electronic air cleaner had learned about the product from either a doctor, friends, relatives, or advertising—but rarely from a dealer. Honeywell found that furnace and air-conditioning dealers were recommending the product to less than 10 percent of the homeowners for whom they were installing equipment, and those recommendations were highly selective to upper-income and mature homeowners.

Honeywell met with its top dealers and distributors in each market to let them know they were missing out on a huge market. Honeywell's database information indicated wide consumer acceptance of the electronic air cleaner, especially among lower-income homeowners.

Panasonic, the electronics.company, used its database for a more conventional direct marketing application. Panasonic set out to help small-to-midsize retailers increase store traffic, using its database information to target specific areas near dealer stores.

In a radical step for the consumer electronics industry, which has rarely looked beyond mass-marketing approaches, Panasonic used co-op dollars for an ambitious dealer support direct-mail campaign. The mechanism was a sweepstakes promotion. Consumers were offered a chance to win prizes, including a vacation in Hawaii.

Panasonic allocated approximately 25,000 flyers for each of its 122 participating dealers. The target geography was an area within a 3- to 5-mile radius of each dealer. Each dealer's database began with Panasonic's own customers in the target area. Panasonic's database was used to profile its product buyers, and the profiles were used to draw lists of non-Panasonic customers from The Lifestyle Selector and the Polk X-1 file.

The program was successful, driving Panasonic customers and qualified prospects into the stores and encouraging most people to stay and buy. Panasonic used the program to develop its relationship with its dealers. The costs of the sweepstakes, displays, and printing and distribution of the imprinted flyers would have been beyond the financial reach of the individual retailers, who could see for themselves that the company was committed to dealer support.

Action Industries manufactures recliners. An enterprising Action Industries salesman from Cincinnati used the company's consumer database to help one of his biggest retail accounts, Swallen's Furniture, a six-store chain in the Cincinnati area. Swallen's had traditionally blanketed the northern Kentucky-southwestern Ohio area with 430,000 advertising circulars three times a year. However, those efforts had not proved to be cost-effective.

The Action salesman persuaded the Swallen's stores to rank in descending order the zip codes in which most of their customers lived. Action used NDL's OASYS system to analyze those zip codes to see which ones had the highest percentage of households that matched the profile of the Action customer and, therefore, had the greatest potential to respond to an Action advertising circular. A test mailing of 53,000 sale circulars was made to the targeted zip codes for one store.

The results were dramatic: an increase of 55 percent in recliners sold compared to the results of the same sale a year before when there had been a blanket distribution of 422,000 circulars. As a consequence of that test, the distribution list was fine-tuned to 149,000 circulars, which were delivered to the high-potential zip codes for all six stores—another example of the efficiencies attainable through highly targeted database marketing.

Unfortunately, there are only a handful of direct marketing database applications by consumer goods companies at this time. Perhaps they are still too immersed in the multifaceted applications in the decision-support arena, where durable-goods manufacturers have been extremely inventive. They use their databases to monitor market position, identify the strength of key competitors, and measure sales performance.

Some companies use their database information to identify opportunities for increased sales, set sales targets, and allocate sales resources. Manufacturers schedule production, inventory, and media based on what their customers are telling them. They perform sophisticated gap analyses to pinpoint under-penetrated consumer market segments for existing products and identify market needs for new product development.

But manufacturers rarely communicate directly with the buyers of their products through the medium of their databases. Perhaps there's a clue in the parlance used by durable-goods manufacturers when they describe their markets. When manufacturers talk about their customers, they're usually referring to their distributors, not the consumers, the people who buy their products and take them home. Given that orientation, it's not surprising that many manufacturers have not yet perceived what a powerful medium their purchaser databases could be to help them build long-term relationships with consumers.

It's ironic that so many packaged-goods manufacturers are spending millions of dollars to build proprietary databases because they already have applications in mind, while so many durable-goods manufacturers consistently underutilize the multimillion-name databases they built at such a low cost.

THE FUTURE OF DATABASE MARKETING

Given the lightning-fast technological advances of the past decade and the rapid deployment of applications by a potpourri of users, it's foolish to try to predict the future for database marketing applications. However, some educated guesses can be made. Current nonuser industry segments will come alive. For example, durable-goods manufacturers will recognize how their databases give them enormous capabilities to speak meaningfully to their many market fragments, slivers, niches, segments, or whatever the segmentation buzz words of the 1990s will be. Manufacturers with multiproduct lines will see the wisdom of establishing the lifetime value of their customers and maximizing it through well-informed relevance (or relationship, loyalty, curriculum, or one-to-one) marketing.

The increased power and lower cost of micro- and minicomputers, combined with increasingly user-friendly applications software, will make database marketing more accessible to a new breed of users. Those users will range from destination resorts, with highly targeted loyalty programs tied into local retail participation, to issue-oriented nonprofits, who will move well beyond their donors' contribution histories to include attitudinal data and willingness to assume varied levels of advocacy.

Larger and richer external data sources will make the possibilities for additional applications even more exciting. Most current external databases are static when it comes to individual data elements. Seldom do they contain historical information about individuals, the exception being R. L. Polk's historical database of auto ownership dating back to 1962. Now, however, large transactional databases are being constructed by packaged-goods marketers and supermarkets. Information about a person's purchasing history is being captured. But how much of that data will be made available as an external resource, rather than remaining proprietary, remains to be seen.

Because so many of the external databases have been constructed in the past few years, historical demographic and lifestyle data has not been available. Identifying individuals immediately following a significant change in their personal status has not been possible. In Lester Wunderman's holy trinity of ability to buy, willingness to buy, and readiness to buy, it's the readiness factor that's elusive. Historical demographic and lifestyle information can close that gap. For example, the consumer who moves from a $50,000 income to $75,000 in a year is a much different spender from the person who has reached the $75,000 level through $4,000 increments over several years. The first person suddenly has disposable income which didn't exist before and is very likely to be a big buyer.

That same sudden propensity to buy can occur when an individual discovers a new activity. For example, someone who has never before appeared in a lifestyle database as a golfer suddenly emerges as someone who lists golf as a favorite activity. That person is a "lay-down" for offers for golf vacations, instructional videos, and even expensive clubs (particularly if they promise to substantially improve the beginner's game).

Several external databases, particularly The Lifestyle Selector and Shareforce, have existed long enough to have accumulated histories on people who have bounced in and out of their databases over the years. That historical information could open up a whole new dimension of external database applications.

One of the most significant advances in direct marketing during the 1980s was effective manipulation of data through computer modeling that increased response rates and permitted mailers to target rather than mail to huge universes. Modeling technology will continue to improve. Recent advances in neural computers will lead to the examination of the individual consumer as a "gestalt," a whole person who is more than the sum of his or her parts.

Sequential examination of characteristics leads to a false, additive process for defining market segments. For example, the DINK category (dual-income, no kids) is constructed first by searching for married couples, then searching for those couples in which both partners are employed, and finally searching for the final criterion, the absence of children. That sequential process, no matter how many variables are added, cannot do justice to the uniqueness of the individual. Complex pattern analysis, through neural computing, will improve modeling performance by looking at the whole individual and making reliable predictions about future behavior.

The database marketing of the near future will do a better job of marrying the medium to the message. Not long ago, many direct-response agencies first developed the offer and then designed the graphics and wrote the copy with little indication of who the final recipient might be. The end product was the list.

At long last, the process is being reversed. First, the marketer's internal database is analyzed to determine the number and characteristics of its various market segments. Then, research is done on each segment to determine the positioning, copy, and graphics likely to cause individuals in each segment to respond or purchase. The individual is no longer an afterthought. By using psychographics and more sophisticated personalization techniques within the process, database marketers can speak effectively to consumers on a one-to-one basis.

As a last word of caution, the current data avarice, which is leading marketers to seek out and capture more and more personal information, has a definite downside. The more effective the information gathering, storage, and retrieval process becomes, the greater the tendency will be to encroach on individual privacy.

The very information marketers need before they can hope to approach a reasonable probability of predicting individual behavior accurately is the same data that is certain to arouse the concern of privacy watchdogs. For example, health care marketing could become very efficient if personal medical information were available. And the public availability of certain financial and credit information would certainly improve the effectiveness of a wide range of offers. However, in each instance, effectiveness is gained at the expense of individual privacy.

At some point, marketers are likely to bump their heads on an effectiveness ceiling, where responsiveness increases no further without the addition of personal sensitive data to the analysis process. Maintaining the balance between information and individual privacy will be one of the important challenges in the 1990s.

9

Selecting and Testing Response Lists

Steve Roberts

Edith Roman Associates, Inc.
New York, N.Y.

Want to dramatically increase the response to your next direct-mail package or campaign *by as much as tenfold or more?* This chapter can help you achieve that goal. This success method is based on the following observation:

> **A brilliant copy approach might double response. The same for a new format or unusual design. But the identical letter mailed to the right mailing list can pull more than *10 times* the response of that same sales letter mailed to the worst list.**

For direct marketers who sell products and services directly from their mailings, the right lists are response lists.

WHAT IS A RESPONSE LIST?

Lists that are available commercially for sale or rent fall into two basic categories: compiled lists and response lists. *Compiled lists* are lists of people or businesses compiled from published sources, such as industry directories or telephone books. *Response lists* are lists of people who have bought products or services through direct-response offers. They are called response lists because the people on the list have responded to an ad, direct-mail piece, or television commercial and bought the product or service advertised. There are several categories of response lists.

Mail-Order Buyers

These are people who have bought a book, gadget, gift, or other item through the mail. If you're selling a book on transcendental meditation, for example, your best bet would be to send your mailing to a list of people who have bought books, herbs, crystals, and other New Age products through the mail.

Inquirers

A company with a list of mail-order buyers is likely to have a list of inquirers. These are people who requested more information on the product (such as a brochure or catalog) but did not buy—in other words, leads that did not convert to sales. When you rent a list, you can choose to rent buyers or inquirers or both. Buyer names almost always work best, are most desirable, and consequently cost more. Inquirer names, while less effective, are still sought after because these people have at least expressed *some* interest in the product.

House List

The house list is your own list of buyers (customers) and inquirers (sales leads). These are people who have either bought from you or at least requested more information on your product or service. House lists frequently pull double or more the response of even the best-performing outside response lists. Indeed, one of the main goals of your direct-mail program, aside from generating immediate revenue, may be to build a bigger house list of customers to whom you can sell related products and offers. Mailings to house lists are often highly profitable because the overall response is higher. Also, the cost of mailing is cheaper since you do not pay a list rental fee.

Attendee, Membership, and Seminar Lists

These are lists of people who belong to an association or professional society or have attended an industry event—a conference, seminar, or training program. Such lists can be considered response lists when the conference registration, group membership, or seminar attendance was solicited and paid for via a direct-mail promotion.

Subscription Lists

Magazine and newsletter subscription lists are considered response lists because the subscriptions are obtained through direct-mail letters or packages. There are two types of subscription lists: controlled-circulation lists and paid-circulation lists.

Controlled-circulation magazines are sent free to qualified people within an industry or profession. To get the controlled-circulation magazine, the subscriber must fill out a questionnaire (called a "qualification card") that gives the publisher a lot of information about the subscriber: job title, company, job responsibilities, purchasing authority, size of company, types of products purchased, and so on. This information enables the list user to select those portions of the list that are pertinent to his or her needs. For instance, a valve manufacturer renting the subscriber list of a chemical industry trade journal might be able to select only those people who buy or specify pumps.

A paid-circulation magazine is a publication the reader pays to receive. In a sense, the paid-circulation subscriber list is more purely a response list because everyone on the list has bought a product (the magazine) through the mail. On the negative side, paid-circulation lists usually have fewer selection factors than controlled-circulation lists.

Donor Lists

A donor list is a list of people who have contributed money to a nonprofit organization, charity, or other worthy cause. These lists are used primarily by fund-raisers, although they may have other applications. For example, people who have contributed money to an animal shelter might be good prospects for pet-related products sold by mail.

Credit Card Holders

Credit card holder lists are highly desirable for several reasons. First, a large percentage are mail-order buyers. Second, credit card holders are somewhat upscale, as they earn enough money to qualify for a credit card. Third, credit card holders will often buy big-ticket items, while cash-only buyers tend to limit purchases to the amount of cash available. And finally, you can boost your response by including a toll-free number for credit card orders (prospects without a credit card can't order through your 800 line unless you accept bill-me's over the phone).

Merged Database Lists

These are master databases or lists of most or all prospects in a given category. They are created by merging a number of similar lists, then eliminating the duplicate names. An example is the CMP High Tech Database, a master list of 638,343 executives in wholesale, manufacturing, retail, and service industries derived from highly selective qualified trade publication subscriber lists.

The advantage of merged databases is twofold. First, they allow list users to reach a large portion of a specific market without having to spend time on obscure, hard-to-find, or poorly managed lists. And second, they can be enhanced with "overlays" (we'll discuss this shortly) to add more information and selection factors than were available on the original lists. When considering a merged database for a mail-order offer, make sure the source lists are all *response* lists. A mixture of compiled and response lists will lower your response.

WHY RESPONSE LISTS ARE SO VITAL FOR MAIL-ORDER OFFERS

In direct mail there are two basic selling methods: one-step and two-step. In the one-step method, the prospect orders the product directly from the ad, mailing, or catalog. This is what is traditionally known as "mail order."

Magazine subscriptions are a good example of a product sold this way. You get a package from a magazine publisher. The envelope contains a four-page letter, a brochure, some additional inserts, and an order form. You send a check or provide credit card information and they can begin your subscription. You can't "think about it" or "ask for more information" or speak to a salesperson. You either order the product or you don't. That's true one-step mail-order selling.

In the two-step method, which is generally used for higher-priced products and most services, the mailing package says, "Here's our product or service, here's why you should be interested, and if you'd like more information, mail back the reply card." The reply card typically has two boxes you can check: either "Send a free brochure" or "Have a salesperson call." They don't give you the price of the product or service, and you can't order it directly from the mailing. You can only get more information. This is the two-step method, commonly known as "lead generation."

For the two-step method, you can use either response or compiled lists. In fact, compiled lists are usually preferable for lead-generating mailings, because they are more likely to reach the bulk of your target market. For example, if you are offering accounting services to attorneys, you can rent a compiled list of all attorneys in your city or state. A response list is likely to contain only a small percent of these attorneys, because the majority of attorneys have not responded to mail offers.

On the other hand, for a one-step mail-order offer, response lists will generate the highest sales and profits virtually every time. The reason is simple: Not only do the people on the response lists have the right characteristics, they are proven mail-order buyers. And that's important. Research shows that approximately one-third of the people in the United States do not buy through the mail. Therefore, if you use a compiled list, you are automatically dooming yourself to sending one-third of your costly packages to people who will not respond to your offer, no matter how good it is, simply because they don't like to order by mail. With a response list, on the other hand, everyone on the list is a proven mail-order buyer. So they are much more likely to order your product or service through the mail.

Test after test confirms this. As one seller of audiocassette albums says, "Compiled lists of targeted market names don't buy. Only *buyers* buy. If you're selling books or tapes, mail to lists of proven mail-order book or tape buyers. It's the only thing that will work."

When selling via mail order, use response lists only.

FINDING AND RENTING RESPONSE LISTS

Where do you find response lists? The one place *not* to get them is in the opportunity-seeker and mail-order type magazines or from mailings from mail-order operators selling lists of opportunity seekers. These lists are generally worthless. How can you spot a phony? One sign is price. Today response list rental costs $80 per thousand names and up. Any ad or mailing offering 1000 names for $10 or $15 is suspect.

Legitimate response lists are generally available from list owners, list managers, and list brokers. A *list owner* is a mail-order entrepreneur, direct-response marketer, publisher, seminar sponsor, or other firm that makes their customer list available on the commercial list-rental marketplace. For instance, if you want to rent a book publisher's list of mail-order book buyers, you could contact the publisher directly. A *list manager* is an individual or firm that manages and markets the list owner's mailing list for a fee. If a list is handled by a list management firm, the owner would probably refer you to that firm. A *list broker* is a third-party agent who rents mailing lists. Unlike the list manager, who works primarily for the list owner, the broker works primarily for you, the list user.

Which source should you use? Approximately 80 percent of all list rentals are made through brokers. Brokers act as consultants to you, the list user, advising you on what response lists are available and which would most likely work for your product and offer. List managers, on the other hand, are more likely to recommend only the lists they manage, while list owners only know the lists they own.

Therefore, brokers have the broadest knowledge of the many lists that are available and will be the most candid and objective in their recommendations. Many mail-order marketing experts suggest getting list recommendations from at least three different brokers initially, until you find a broker you are comfortable with and whose advice has been proven to work for you.

Many list brokers and list managers advertise regularly in such publications as *Direct Marketing, DM News, Target,* and *Direct.* There is also a list of mailing-list brokers in *The Direct Marketing Market Place,* published by Hillary House Publishers, Inc., 980 North Federal Highway, Suite 206, Boca Raton, FL 33432, phone (407) 393-5656.

MATCHING THE LIST TO THE MARKET

To successfully select the right response lists for your offer, you must come up with an accurate description or profile of your target market, then select lists of people who most closely fit this profile.

Most mail-order experts agree that the ideal response list is a list of people who have bought a product similar to the one you are selling, at a similar price. For instance, if you're selling a $49.95 cassette album on successful selling techniques, your best lists would be people who have bought books and cassette programs on sales, success, marketing, business, and similar topics.

Contrary to what common sense would indicate, a compiled list of professional salespeople would probably *not* prove profitable for this offer. The reason? Although the people on the compiled list qualify by occupation, they are not proven mail-order information buyers. Many don't buy by mail, and many are not interested in books, cassettes, or self-improvement information. Having the common characteristic of "salesperson" is not enough. You need a response list of the right people to succeed in mail-order selling.

Unfortunately, there are often not enough ideal response lists on the marketplace to make your business venture profitable. So you need to research and find other response lists that, while not a sure thing, may prove profitable and should be tested. This is why the expertise of a list broker is needed.

For instance, if you wanted to promote an expensive financial advisory service, you would want to mail to lists of wealthy people, right? But which lists would work best? A list of doctors is one obvious possibility. A list of corporate CEOs is another. But what about people who own power or sail boats 40 feet long or longer? Or how about people who own twin-engine private airplanes? Or people who subscribe to expensive stock market newsletters? It's not always obvious which list is right for your offer. Sometimes it takes creative, intuitive leaps—or knowledge based on years of experience—to make the connection between offer and list selection. Again, that's where choosing and using the right list broker can make the difference between success and failure.

RECENCY, FREQUENCY, AND AMOUNT

For response lists, three key factors determining success are recency, frequency, and amount. *Recency* refers to how recently the people on the list made their last mail-order purchase. The more recent the purchase, the better. This seems like common sense—to a point. After all, you can see where a list of mail-order buyers who bought within the last 12 months would be better than a list of people whose last purchase was 5 years ago. The people who bought within 12 months are likely to still have an interest in the type of product purchased (or at least the benefits it offers), while the people who bought 5 years ago may no longer be interested and probably don't even remember buying it.

But people often ask, "What about the prospect who just bought last month or last week or yesterday? He or she has just spent a lot of money on a product similar to mine, so isn't he or she less likely to buy?" This seems to make sense, but in practice, it isn't so. Testing confirms that there is virtually no limit to the dictum, "The more recent, the better." That is why, when you donate funds to a charity, you immediately get a follow-up letter (and often a second and third and fourth letter) asking for an additional donation. The fund-raisers know that the person who just made a donation is the one most likely to respond to a request for additional funds. And so it is with mail-order product selling. The person who just bought (whether from you or from your competitor) is the one most likely to respond to your current offer.

So look for lists of people who have *recently* purchased products by mail. In the list sales literature, the data card (a standard format for presenting list information) will frequently specify "last 12 months buyers" or "last 24 months buyers," indicating that everyone on the list bought within the specified time period.

Recency is so important that many list owners and managers rent separately the portion of their list containing buyers who have bought very recently, that is, within the past month, 3 months, 6 months, or 1 year. These names are called "hotline" names and generally are more expensive to rent than the list as a whole. Hotline names often generate substantially more profitable results for circulation and other mail-order promotions than regular response lists.

In addition to recency, frequency and amount are also important. *Frequency* refers to how often the prospect buys through the mail. Most experts agree that lists of "multibuyers"—people who have bought more than once—will usually outpull lists of one-time-only buyers. Many list owners and managers rent the multibuyers portion of their lists separately at a premium.

The third key factor in evaluating response lists is amount. *Amount* refers to how much money the prospect on the list has spent on a mail-order purchase. Many data cards provide a dollar amount figure for "average order," representing the average dollar amount spent by people on the list per purchase. Ideally, you want a response list of people who have spent an amount similar to the price you are charging for your product. For example, if you want people to attend a $495 two-day business seminar, people who have paid only $20 or $30 for a subscription to a business magazine have not demonstrated that they are willing to part with a far greater amount of money through the mail, even though they might have a proven interest in your topic. You would be better off renting response lists of people who have registered by mail for seminars on similar topics, for comparable registration fees.

ENHANCING RESPONSE LIST INFORMATION AND SELECTIVITY

Years ago, the information available on response lists was the recency, frequency, and amount discussed above. Yet there may be other factors you want to know about your target audience. Do they have a credit card? Are they parents? How old are they? How much money do they make?

Through a technique called overlays, this information is becoming available on many large response lists. In an *overlay*, a response list is run on the computer and matched with a larger master list of people; the larger list contains a fuller demographic and descriptive profile of each person. For each person on the response list, the information is taken from the large master list and added to the response list. As a result, you now know a lot more about the people on the response list and can even select portions of the list according to various demographic criteria gained as a result of this overlay of information.

On a consumer response list, these selection criteria can include marital status, sex, age, type of dwelling, religion, ethnic background, number of people in the household, ages of children in the household, credit card status, lifestyle, income, catalog buyers (whether the person orders from mail-order catalogs), sweepstakes participants (so you know whether they're likely to respond to a sweepstakes offer), and many others.

On a business response list, data that can be added through an overlay include number and sex of employees in the firm, sales volume, job function or title of the prospect, industry, Standard Industrial Code (SIC), and phone numbers. Selections by specific characteristics are relatively inexpensive (usually $5 per selection per thousand) and, in our experience, usually pay off in terms of higher response.

SELECTING THE RIGHT RESPONSE LIST

In addition to the factors already discussed, there are some other important criteria for selecting response lists.

Product Purchased

Try to select response lists of mail buyers who have bought products similar to yours. For instance, if you're selling collectibles, you want lists of people who have bought collectibles by mail. If you can't get a list of people who have bought similar products, you at least want a list of people who have bought *related* products or services. For instance, someone who is on the Value-Rent-a-Car list and is therefore a proven traveler would likely respond well to offers for travel and entertainment products and services, financial and insurance offers, consumer publications, vacation packages, leisure activities, general consumer mail order, resorts, and other offers that appeal to responsive, creditworthy people who travel.

Location

Most mailing lists can be segmented by state and zip code. However, geography is usually not a big concern when selecting response lists because, unlike retailers and service firms, most mail-order firms serve a nationwide market. If you sell fruitcakes by mail, you can just as easily sell a fruitcake to someone in New Jersey as you can to a buyer in California.

Geography becomes more of a factor with some offers, such as regional publications, seminars, and conferences. You might then select only that portion of the response list within a certain radius of your location. For instance, a New Jersey–based firm offering public seminars in "How to Publish Your Writing" regularly rents the New Jersey portion only of the *Writer's Digest* magazine subscription list.

Demographics

As discussed previously, many response lists and databases have been overlayed with a wide range of demographic information, including age, sex, income level, ethnic background, interests, and family status. Although not as important as actual buying behavior (recency, frequency, and amount), these are still useful selection criteria for many mailers.

Psychographics

This term refers to the psychological makeup of the prospects on the list. For instance, one psychographic characteristic might be "people with an interest in writing." But aside from subscription lists to writer's magazines, how do you select a list with this characteristic? "An interest in writing" will *not* be found as a selection criteria on response list data cards. Here's where creativity comes in. You must ask, "What type of person is likely to be interested in writing?" You might decide, for example, to test the membership list of the AARP (American Association for Retired Persons) on the theory that many people may want to write but only retirees have the leisure time to pursue it.

List Size

Response lists range in size from under 10,000 names to 1 million names or more. The traditional approach in mail-order direct mail is to select a number of lists for testing, invest in a test mailing, and then, based on the results, mail to the rest of the names on those lists that proved profitable.

If you test 5000 names, and the list has only 10,000 names, there's limited potential because of the small size. For this reason, many mail-order marketers whose products have broad appeal prefer to test larger lists only. Their reasoning: If the test is successful, then they have a large lucrative market to tap into.

However, mail-order marketers with products that appeal to specialized audiences and narrow vertical markets may find that the only lists available are small lists. Before you launch a mail-order venture, you should make sure the total number of names available is large enough to make the effort worthwhile. For instance, successful newsletter publishers generally capture 5 percent of the total market as subscribers. Therefore, if the response list contains 10,000 names, you must determine whether selling 500 subscriptions at your annual subscription rate will generate enough revenue to pay your costs and make a profit.

Cost per Thousand

List rental typically represents 20 to 25 percent of the total cost per thousand of the mailing. While compiled lists typically rent for $50 per thousand, the price of response lists ranges from $80 to $100 per thousand. It generally costs $5 per thousand to select portions of lists by specific characteristics: sex, age, multibuyers, hotlines, etc.

As discussed earlier, beware of firms offering "bargain" lists renting for $5 or $10 per thousand; often they are worthless. One firm, for example, compiles its so-called mail-order buyer lists by writing to mail-order companies and paying 25 cents for the discarded envelopes in which these mail-order operators receive checks and orders. This list is nearly worthless since you have no idea who the people on the list are, what they bought, or what they spent.

List Description

Ask mailing-list brokers to send you a data card on each list they recommend. Data cards contain the basic information on each list, including price, number of names on the list, multibuyers' behavior, selections of buyers versus inquirers, average dollar amount of sale, state counts, minimum order, and so on.

Most data cards contain a few paragraphs of narrative describing the list. Read this carefully. It gives you a good idea of who the people on the list are and whether they fit the profile of your target prospect. Data cards will often suggest types of offers the list is good for, but you should ask brokers whether they think the list will work for *you*.

List Usage Report

One of the most important facts about a response list is who else has used it. Specifically, have marketers with offers similar to yours tested the list, and if so, were the results favorable or negative? Although confidentiality may prevent the broker from revealing the names of the actual firms using the list, a good broker can tell you whether the list has proved successful for products and offers similar to yours. If it has been successful for them, then there's a good chance it will work for you, too.

Cleanliness

When list users ask "How clean is the list?" they mean "How current are the names, and how frequently is the list updated?" Some list owners, such as controlled-circulation publications, regularly update and clean their lists annually. On the other hand, many smaller mail-order firms never do so. A list that is handled by a professional list manager is likely to be clean.

Making sure the names are current and that the list is frequently updated is important. One out of five Americans moves every year, so lists that are not updated regularly become dated quickly. Names that are not current should be removed at least once a year.

Many list brokers and managers guarantee their lists to be reasonably clean and will refund a portion of the mailing costs if the nondeliverable mailing pieces (called "nixies") returned to you by the post office exceed a certain percentage. For instance, a mailing-list broker that guarantees "93 percent deliverability" will pay you some set amount (typically 25 cents or so) for each nondeliverable piece in excess of 7 percent returns.

Format

Most mailers prefer to get their mailing lists on cheshire or gummed labels. Gummed labels are selected when the labels are to be affixed by hand; cheshire labels are used when labels are to be affixed using automated equipment available in most modern letter shops (a letter shop is a company that specializes in assembling, stuffing, collating, and preparing mailing pieces for the post office).

However, if you want to personalize your mailing, you need to get your list in computerized form—typically on magnetic tape or a floppy disk. Check with your broker to make sure these formats are available. If you want to follow up your mailing with a phone call, ask if a duplicate of the list, including phone numbers, can be provided on cards or in a computer printout form.

TESTING RESPONSE LISTS

If you find a good list of 100,000 potential buyers for your product, it would be foolish to immediately send your direct-mail package to all 100,000—for two reasons.

First, you don't know that this list will work. Just because you *think* the people on this list will buy your product doesn't ensure that they will. So it makes sense to mail to a small portion of the list as a test. If the test is successful, you can mail to a larger portion of the list knowing, with relative certainty, that your mailing will work.

Second, you cannot be certain that the list you think is best will generate the greatest response. As we said at the beginning of this chapter, the worst list can pull less than one-tenth the response of the best list. If you have the budget to mail 25,000 pieces, it's better to mail 5000 to five lists and find out which works best rather than mail all 25,000 to one list and discover that you picked the wrong one.

How many lists should you test? We recommend you test between five and eight different lists initially. The biggest mistake mailers make is to test too few lists—or to not test lists at all. Remember, the list is the factor that can make the greatest increase or decrease in response. So it's foolish not to test it.

How many names should you test? Table 9-1 can be used to determine how many pieces you must mail to get a statistically valid test result. There are two factors to consider: percent decline and confidence level. The numbers in the other columns show the number of replies you must get back (*not* the number of pieces you must mail) to achieve the desired confidence level and percent decline.

Let's say you want to design your test so that when you "roll out" (mail to a larger portion of the list after a successful test), you know with an 85 percent confidence level that the response to your mailing won't decline by more than 25 percent (roll-outs typically have lower response rates than tests).

According to Table 9-1, we must get back 14 replies for the test to give us that confidence level. If we anticipate a 1 percent response rate, we must mail a test quantity of approximately 1400 pieces *per list being tested.* Therefore, if we mail 1400 pieces, and get back 14 replies, we can be 85 percent certain that the roll-out on that list will generate a minimum response of 75 percent, that is, no more than 25 percent decline from the test result of 1 percent.

To round things out, and to anticipate a possibly lower than 1 percent re-

Table 9-1. Number of Pieces Needed for Valid Test

Confidence level	Percent decline			
	50%	25%	12½%	6¼%
75%	1.8	7.3	29.2	116.8
85%	3.5	14.0	56.0	
90%	6.6	26.2	104.8	
95%	11.0	42.8		
99%	21.7	86.9		

SOURCE: Adapted from Ed McLean, *The Basics of Testing,* etc. Reprinted by permission.

sponse to the test, we generally recommend testing 2000 names per list. Therefore, if you are testing eight lists, your total test quantity would be 16,000 pieces.

How do you know which replies came from which response lists? First, describe your test plans to your list broker. The broker will key each mailing label with a special code identifying which list the label came from (the cost of key coding is only $1 or so per thousand names).

Second, design your mailing so that the label comes back to you when the prospect responds by mail. For instance, you can affix a cheshire label directly to the order form and have the label show through a window on the envelope. For phone orders, ask callers to read you the identifying code number from their labels.

How many names can you roll out to if your test is successful? Our rule of thumb is that the maximum roll-out quantity should be no more than 10 times the test quantity. Therefore, if you test 2000 names, you can roll out safely to 20,000 names. If you get a good result from mailing to the 20,000, you can roll out to 200,000. And if the results are good from the mailing to 200,000 pieces, you can roll out to 2 million.

MERGE-PURGE

Merge-purge is a computerized process through which duplicate names on the various lists you are mailing to are eliminated. For example, if "Steve Roberts" appears on three lists, the merge-purge process eliminates two of the duplicate labels; as a result, you mail Steve Roberts one package, not three.

Since the duplication factor on response lists can be high, doing a merge-purge can save you a lot of money on printing, letter shop, and postage costs. However, the list broker or computer service bureau charges a substantial fee for this service. Generally, merge-purge pays off on mailings of 30,000 to 50,000 pieces or more; on tests of 30,000 or less, it may not make sense.

COMPARING THE PERFORMANCE OF RESPONSE LISTS

Many novice mail-order operators measure the success of a mailing by percentage response, say, 2 percent or 2.4 percent. But that's a mistake. The true measure of which response list is best is the *cost per order*. For instance, list X may pull a slightly greater number of orders but may be much more costly to rent than list Y. Therefore, list Y generates orders for you at a lower cost per order and is overall more profitable.

To determine and compare the results of testing lists, you can use the following 12-step formula (the results of these calculations are displayed in Table 9-2).

1. **Write down the name of the list you tested.** In our example, we'll call the first list "A."

2. **Key.** The key indicates the priority sequence, if any, in which duplicates

were eliminated from lists during merge-purge. To obtain an accurate measurement of list effectiveness, merge-purge should be done on a random basis, not according to priorities.

3. **Invoice.** Write down the amount of money paid to the broker for rental of this list. This is the total invoice amount, not the cost per thousand.

4. **Quantity.** Write down the total number of names rented from this list.

5. **Cost per thousand.** The cost per thousand is calculated by dividing step 3 by step 4 and multiplying by 1000.

6. **Quantity received.** Of the total names rented, the quantity received indicates the number of names shipped to the computer house for merge-purge. Often, during tests, mailers rent a larger quantity (because of typical minimum-list rental requirements of 5000 per list), split the list, and use only a portion of the names rented in their initial test.

7. **Quantity mailed.** These are the names remaining from step 6 after merge-purge is run and duplicate names are eliminated. This is the quantity of unduplicated names from the list actually mailed. In the example in Table 9-2, only 489 unduplicated names from list A remained after the 3007 names received were merge-purged against the other 43 lists tested. That means 84 percent of the names on this list were duplicated in the other lists at least once! You can see why merge-purge is so important; without eliminating duplicates, you'd be mailing a huge quantity to a small audience. There would be tremendous waste, and you'd get a much lower percentage response.

8. **List adjustment factor.** This number represents the factor by which duplicate elimination scaled down the list. To calculate, divide step 6 by step 7. For example, for list A, we selected 3007 names to mail (quantity received). After duplicate elimination, we were left with only 489 names (quantity mailed)—approximately one-sixth of the original quantity. List adjustment factor is 3007 divided by 489, or 6.15.

9. **List adjustment cost per thousand.** This is the *real* cost per thousand for the mailing list after elimination of duplicate names is accounted for. To calculate, multiply step 5 by step 8. For list A, we multiply $85.23 cost per thousand times the list adjustment factor of 6.15. This gives us an actual cost per thousand of $524.13. Is this accurate? Yes, since we have paid for 3007 names, but are left with only one-sixth that amount, our real cost per name mailed is approximately six times higher than the actual rental fee. This is the key factor that many mail-order marketers do not take into account in evaluating list performance. Yet, failure to factor in merge-purge duplicate elimination when evaluating list tests can result in inaccurate analysis of a list's ability to generate orders cost effectively.

10. **Adjusted total mail cost.** To calculate, add step 9 to the cost per thousand for the other elements of the mailing (these are printing, postage, and letter-shop fees). Then multiply this sum by step 7. This "adjusted total mail cost" tells you what it actually costs to send all the pieces mailed to this list after taking elimination of duplicate names into account.

Table 9-2. Comparison of Cost Per Order

List name	Key	Invoice by line	Invoice qty.	Cost per M	Qty. received	Qty. mailed	List adj. factor	List adj. cost per M	Adj. total mail cost	Number of response	Cost per order	Percent of response
List A	DJ60	784.07	9,199	85.23	3,007	489	6.15	524.13	365.34	30	12.18	6.13%
List B	DJ89	504.23	5,050	99.85	4,938	458	10.78	1076.52	595.18	61	9.76	13.32%
List C	DJ50	305.27	1,756	173.84	675	454	1.49	258.47	218.58	24	9.11	5.29%
List D	DJ52	576.97	6,648	86.79	2,047	348	5.88	510.51	255.26	29	8.80	8.33%
List E	DJ40	1,390.97	15,605	89.14	9,846	3,027	3.25	289.94	1552.63	179	8.67	5.91%
List F	DJ46	816.23	8,234	99.13	2,800	1,163	2.41	238.66	536.90	63	8.52	5.42%
List G	DJ74	330.90	3,059	108.17	449	276	1.63	175.98	110.11	13	8.47	4.71%
List H	DJ83	885.26	8,437	104.93	1,381	773	1.79	187.45	317.27	38	8.35	4.92%
List I	DJ57	1,566.81	16,888	92.78	5,720	2,664	2.15	195.20	1124.73	141	7.98	5.29%
List J	DJ46	1,047.00	10,400	100.67	1,204	769	1.57	157.62	292.69	37	7.91	4.81%
List K	DJ37	1,890.66	20,143	93.86	5,863	1,948	3.01	282.50	984.70	126	7.82	6.47%
List L	DJ25	1,604.06	18,513	86.55	6,397	1,104	5.79	502.05	800.45	110	7.28	9.95%
List M	DJ61	764.18	10,531	72.56	3,674	1,551	2.37	171.89	612.46	87	7.04	5.61%
List N	DJ90	546.09	5,213	104.76	530	128	4.14	433.75	84.06	12	7.01	9.38%
List O	DJ70	373.01	5,047	73.91	271	153	1.77	130.91	54.15	8	6.77	5.23%
List P	DJ51	3,383.27	36,154	93.58	18,172	8,580	2.12	198.20	3613.78	535	6.75	6.24%
List Q	DJ75	1,045.75	15,166	68.95	6,679	1,502	4.45	306.62	795.47	118	6.74	7.86%
List R	DJ62	700.48	9,621	72.81	3,615	2,098	1.72	125.45	731.03	109	6.71	5.20%
List S	DJ73	765.43	7,075	108.19	1,700	761	2.23	241.68	353.61	53	6.67	6.96%
List T	DJ45	170.84	9,920	17.22	495	187	2.65	45.59	50.22	8	6.28	4.28%
List U	DJ85	1,306.21	12,689	102.94	3,751	1,841	2.04	209.74	796.65	129	6.18	7.01%
List V	DJ44	631.12	6,872	91.84	2,480	1,570	1.58	145.07	577.86	94	6.15	5.99%
List W	DJ61	880.12	8,183	107.55	1,944	1,029	1.89	203.19	438.54	72	6.09	7.00%
List X	DJ38	900.06	10,186	88.36	2,615	711	3.68	324.99	389.61	65	5.99	9.14%
List Y	DJ78	1,077.92	10,383	103.82	2,355	1,144	2.06	213.71	499.59	84	5.95	7.34%
List Z	DJ54	647.17	10,660	60.71	1,952	542	3.60	216.65	239.37	43	5.57	7.93%

11. **Number of responses.** Write down the number of replies (orders) produced by mailing to this list.

12. **Cost per order.** To calculate cost per order, divide step 10 by step 11. If you wish to determine the percentage response produced by the list, multiply step 11 by 100, then divide by step 7. Note that while list A pulled a slightly higher percentage response than list C (shown two lines down)— 6.13 versus 5.29 percent—list C generated orders at a much lower cost per order: $9.11 per order versus $12.18 per order for list A. Thus, all else being equal, list C performed better for this offer.

The key point is that if you're looking at percentage responses only, you're not evaluating your list tests correctly. Another example: list B produced a 13.32 percent response—which sounds great—but has the second-highest cost per order, which indicates that it is one of the two least profitable lists of the lists tested.

These calculations can be performed manually with calculator and pencil. Software programs that automate the 12-step procedure described above are also available. Lists can be ranked according to cost per order, from highest to lowest, or by adjusted list cost per thousand, quantity mailed, percentage response, list adjustment factor, number of responses, and source (list broker).

10
Fundamentals of List Management

Dee Kendall

Marketry Inc.
New York, N.Y.

Next to your product, your mailing list is your most valuable asset. It is the life-blood of your business. It is the vehicle by which you deliver your product. Without it, you would be out of business. How, then, can you effectively market your mailing list to gain a new or auxiliary source of income? Whether you are managing your list in-house, or choose to have a list manager do it for you, here are the fundamental strategies for cost-effective list management.

BUILDING A LIST FOUNDATION

Once you have accumulated a list of your product buyers, identify and code according to source as much of your customers' demographic and psychographic information as possible, either from your return order card or by other methods, such as a customer survey. The information you gather about your customer and how you make that information work for you and a potential list client can make additional corporate revenue.

Using your return order card, ascertain your customer's full name, sex, address, city, state, zip, age, income, home and/or business phone number, method of payment, number and ages of children, etc. Once you have this information in a database, you will be able to select your customers by specific characteristics for your own or a list client's use. *The key is to find out as much as you can about your customer*. The more selections you can make available, the more marketable your list will be; hence, the more money you will make on list rental sales, because mailers can focus in more sharply on their target audience. What you are trying to give the potential list client is maximum penetration so that they can hone in precisely on the audience they need to reach to make a sale. Mailers need demographic and psychographic selectability for cost-effective promotional mailings. When you make those selections available, you can charge an additional fee above the base list rental price for them.

Establish a base list rental price for the list, as well as prices for all the selections that you are making available, including the method of addressing (cheshire labels, pressure-sensitive labels, magnetic tape, manuscript, etc.). You might want to find out what your competitors are charging to get some idea of what the market will bear. Find out what your computer department or service bureau will be charging you to set up and maintain your list. Make sure you are covering those costs and adjust your list rental sales prices accordingly. Most list owners charge from 30 to 50 percent over and above the computer department or service bureau costs. A word of caution: Don't overprice your list. Don't think that by charging more than your competitors, you will make your list seem more valuable to potential clients, who will therefore pay more—they usually won't. Mailers are only looking at their bottom-line costs. Unless you have a very rare list product, you're better off keeping your overall prices competitive. You'll get more list volume usage by more list clients and, in the end, make more money than if you had priced the list too high initially. Mailers will only return for more names if they can make better than break-even sales from your list.

UPDATING YOUR LIST

For subscription products, most list owners update once a month (or once a quarter, depending upon subscription-purchase volume), adding new buyers, deleting bad pays and nonrenewals, correcting addresses, etc. For general products, update about once a quarter or once every 6 months depending on whether your product is seasonal or not. Some list owners only update once a year; this can seriously impact the list rental usage because many variables change in a file in one year. There is a higher percent of people who moved, didn't renew, didn't pay, etc. If you think that by updating only once a year you'll save on your computer service updating costs and still make your list sales revenue goal, you're wrong. If your list names are not kept "clean," mailers will not get the desired response and will not return to use your list names again. If you spend the money to update your list file, you will make more money from list rental usage.

WHAT INFORMATION TO INCLUDE ON A DATACARD

Potential list users will need to know the following:

1. Current and overall list quantity available
2. Recency available (last 3 months, 6 months, year, etc.)

3. Base list rental price

4. List profile or description: information about what your product is, demographic and psychographic information about your customer, etc.

5. Selections available and additional costs for each

6. Source of list: direct mail, space ads, warranty cards, store sign-ups, contests, telemarketing, directories, registrations, public records, rosters, etc.

7. Unit of sale: dollar cost of what the customer paid for the product

8. Gender/sex ratio of the file

9. List format: cheshire labels, pressure-sensitive labels, magnetic tape, etc.

10. Label key coding charge

11. Any other additional charges: set-up fees, rush fees, etc.

12. Restrictions and terms in using list

13. State counts

It is time- and cost-effective to include state counts on the list datacard since it will save hours of time giving those counts out to regional mailers who may want to use the list.

HOW TO MARKET THE LIST

You must have heard or read the quotation "unseen is untold is unsold." That's exactly the point in successfully marketing a list.

Most list owners or list managers use various and integrated methods to get their sales message out to potential list users. The marketing mix is usually a combination of the following:

Direct mailing to list brokers, mailers, and advertising agencies with "direct" arms, at least on a quarterly basis

Space ads with a coupon cut-out in standard trade publications in issues where the editorial articles focus on list conventions, special topics covering direct mail, etc., at least six times per year

Telemarketing campaigns to list brokers, mailers, and advertising agencies with "direct" arms at least once a quarter.

Convention booths are another way to advertise and get your message out there, and for you to have contact with existing and potential list clients. Schedule booths for major direct marketing conventions which usually are well-attended and represent a cross section of the direct marketing community. This will maximize and augment your other sales and promotion efforts during the course of a year.

It is extremely important to develop a list rental promotion list. When you mail your list datacard and promotional literature and who you mail it to can determine how much exposure the list is getting. You can rent the list of people who are actively involved in direct mail from most of the trade publications initially if you don't have a promotion list at all. When you start getting list rental orders in from list brokers, mailers, and advertising agencies, record their name, company, address, and phone and fax number on a computer database and update at least once a quarter. Make sure you are not wasting your promotional literature by mailing to a wrong address and/or to a person or firm that no longer exists. Keep this list as current as possible. You will need it to further promote your list. *You only want to put your sales message in the hands of people who can buy.*

INTERNAL REPORTING AND OPERATIONAL SYSTEMS

Once your firm receives a list order, knowing where that list is at all times is critical. Having a tracking system which can monitor the status of every order from the time it leaves your hands for list rental fulfillment through invoicing and payment is essential.

First of all, you will need a corporate purchase order form, which will be used for list rental fulfillment, accounting purposes, client confirmation, client usage, etc.

Mailing list sales are an important and profit-making part of your business. Knowing how a client should order is part of it. Incomplete order information will cause unnecessary delays in your list order fulfillment process and cost you money and time. Make sure you get the following information when you receive the initial order:

1. Mailer name, address, phone and fax number, contact person.
2. List broker or agency name, address phone and fax number, contact person.
3. Exact name of the mailer's offer.
4. Complete promotional sample of what will be mailed.
5. Exact title of list to be ordered.
6. List quantity ordered.
7. List selections requested.
8. Geographic selections requested.
9. Whether mailer wants an "nth" (cross section of list file) or not.
10. Whether the order is a test or continuation.
11. How the mailer wants the names supplied: cheshire labels, pressure-sensitive labels, magnetic tape, etc.
12. Key code, if any, on labels supplied.
13. On continuation order, does the mailer want to omit the prior order. If so, what is the prior order number, date, quantity shipped? (You will need to give this to your computer department or service bureau for proper omission.)
14. Methods by which list is to be shipped.
15. Person to whom list is to shipped.

16. Any special instructions on marking the outside shipping package.

17. Any special instructions of how the list should be run. For example, does mailer want selection run in a certain geographic order?

18. The date list is to be received.

19. The mail or call date. It is important that mailers adhere to their scheduled mail dates and notify you in writing of any changes.

20. Method and terms of payment.

Time is money. Going through the above checklist before an order is fulfilled is smart business.

It will be necessary to verify all prices or any corrections or changes on any incoming order. Call and then fax order verification corrections immediately before you place the order for list rental fulfillment. (Usually after you call client, they will fax or mail all changes in writing on their corporate letterhead.)

Your corporate purchase order will contain all the information that you have received from the client's purchase order. In addition, you should note:

1. Your firm's purchase order number

2. Any special instructions to the computer department or service bureau on list rental fulfillment and/or any special instructions to your accounting department: whether the order is taxable, what commission percentage is given to the list broker or agency, terms of payment, and so on.

When you receive the client's order, you will also need to verify the list title and all selections and prices on the incoming order. Immediately call the client if there are any discrepancies or incorrect prices or if the due date cannot be met. If all information is accurate, transfer the order information to your corporate purchase order form, and then get the mailer's offer approved for list rental fulfillment.

Next, give the list order to the computer department or service bureau. Any changes from the original order must be transmitted in writing to the client who ordered the list. For example, often a list order with certain selections may either fall short of or be over the quantity requested. You must inform the client who ordered list for the "runned quantity approval" and then instruct the computer department accordingly so they know whether they can ship the "runned quantity" as is or if there will be further adjustments they will need to make in order to comply with the client's quantity needs. In other words, your staff must constantly communicate with the computer department. This type of customer service will win you many happy list clients.

The computer department will need to supply the following shipping information:

1. List title

2. Mailer name

3. Exact quantity shipped

4. When and how shipped

5. Shipping cost

6. Your corporate purchase order number

Additionally, make sure your computer department/service bureau is properly marking the outgoing list package with mailer name, any requested identification number, list title, etc. The outgoing list itself should also be marked with the list title, quantity shipped, any identification number, and any list usage restrictions or terms that your firm or list owner has established.

Once you have completed and verified your corporate purchase order and have given a copy to the computer department for list rental fulfillment, it will be necessary to monitor the status of the list for on-time delivery, quantity ordered versus quantity run, correct selections, and so on.

Regarding the quantity ordered versus quantity run, the client should be told if it varies by more than 10 percent either way so that the mailer can approve the new quantity for shipment. Some mailers will not pay for an overage if it is shipped to them without approval. The additional running charges from your computer department will be billed to your firm. It is better to call the client at once to authorize any overage than to try and collect it through invoicing later on. After the order is run and shipped, call the client and give them the shipped quantity, date, and shipping method. Let your customers know you are concerned and appreciate their list order.

After the order is run and shipped, you should note it in your list rental logging records. This log will allow you to keep track of the total quantity a mailer is using over a period of time. If a mailer is using your list heavily, you might be willing to give them a quantity discount over a certain number of names used or rented. This cuts the cost of the mailer's expenses and makes your list more profitable to the mailer. Additionally, there are some large mailers who use your list for more than one offer, and you will need to know the volume used per offer as well as who the list was ordered through. A simple form with the headings indicated below would be more than adequate.

1. List title ordered

2. Date ordered

3. Your firm's purchase order number

4. Quantity ordered

5. Mailer name and purchase order number

6. Mailer offer

7. List broker or agency name (if not a direct order from the mailer)

8. List broker or agency purchase order number (if not a direct order from mailer)

9. Shipped quantity

10. Shipped date

11. Date invoiced

12. Date paid

Keep a record of which list broker or agency was used by a mailer. Often a large firm will use more than one for various offers. You need this for prior order omits. Additionally, some mailers may use a few list brokers or agencies in general. Some list brokers or agencies may owe your firm money from prior mailer usage. You will need to know which order came through which in order to know not to process any new order for a given mailer until *all* prior orders are paid in full regardless of the list broker or agency the order may have been placed through. On the positive side, you will also be able to ascertain which ones are giving your firm the most business. You might want to work more closely with the list brokers or agencies who might be able to give you more business than what you've been getting from them. Be sure and thank the list brokers, agencies, or clients who are giving you a lot of business. Tell them of your appreciation.

COMPUTER DEPARTMENT/SERVICE BUREAU OPERATIONS

List order fulfillment can make or break your list rental program. Whether your firm has an internal computer department or whether you use an outside service bureau, certain functions must be strictly adhered to. When assessing a service bureau's performance, the following should be points of concern for your firm:

1. Pricing (watch out for hidden charges)
2. Correctly processing list rental fulfillment initially
3. Turnaround time
4. Hardware-software capabilities
5. Package and list output labeling
6. Staff assignment

Your service bureau should know your list file thoroughly. There should be one account supervisor and a backup person exclusively assigned to handle and oversee your list rental fulfillment. Not only should they be reading your list rental order fulfillment specifications *before* the order is run, but they should be checking the output as well to make sure those initial instructions were met. The account supervisor should fully understand the coding and specifications of the particular file. If the specifications are incomplete or inaccurate, the output will be as well. It is extremely important that the account supervisor understand the makeup of the file and how to extract what is required by the order. The account supervisor should inspect the "layout and dump" to make sure the list was correctly run. The computer technician should properly be labeling the list with the list title, output quantity, mailer name and offer, and special identification mailer requests so that when it is received by the mailer's requested "ship to" firm, that firm will know exactly what mailer and program it is for. All list rental restrictions should be clearly labeled on the list itself so that the mailer will have no question as to the list owner's policy.

The shipping department should be following the mailer's requested "ship via" instructions (UPS Regular, Red, Blue; Federal Express Regular, Priority 1, etc.) since the mailer is paying for the shipping.

If you are not getting the above, your chances of having multiple problems with orders fulfilled are high, and this will affect the overall list rental revenue. Incorrectly running the list specifications initially and not delivering on time can severely hamper the mailer's future use of the list. Standard turnaround is 10 working days or less.

It is a good idea for you to meet with the service bureau on a regular basis to talk with the people working on the file. Their input can offer you some insights. Ask them what types of problems they have encountered, what suggestions they can make to run the list or properly streamline the procedures between your firm and theirs. Then meet with upper management and include the account supervisor in that meeting. Communicating with both levels will allow for list fulfillment adjustments (if necessary), result in continually improved service, and keep you abreast of new developments.

The service bureau should provide shipping information within a day or two after the shipping date. For accounting and invoicing you will need the following in writing:

1. Mailer name

2. Mailer, agency, or list broker purchase order number

3. Quantity and date shipped

4. How shipped

5. Your firm's corporate purchase order number

6. Shipping cost

Your list rental customer service representative should promptly relay this information to the client. Often, the initial quantity requested is different from the quantity shipped. The client will need to know this in order to have the proper number of the mailer's promotion pieces ready for mailing. The shipping information should also be given to your invoicing department. You will need to keep your arrears to a minimum. *The quickness with which invoicing can be executed and payment received by your firm will affect your corporate cash flow.*

Communication, investigation, and interacting with the service bureau's staff enhances customer service to your clients. *Without thoughtful customer service, your list rental revenue can be hampered.* Be sure that you are meeting your client's needs as best you can.

LIST TURNOVER

The number of times that your file is used (turned over) a year should be determined early. There are many firms, especially subscription firms, who want to limit outside list rental because they are also mailing to these names for renewals and other internal product offers during certain times of the year. Usually, during these periods, the list rental department will be instructed to limit not only the number of mailers renting the list but also the type of offer being used. The premise is to give that company's primary business (its product) first use of these names for potential new purchasers and renewals.

List rental is considered auxiliary income; therefore, mailers using the list or the list rental volume rented can be limited or "capped" during certain times of the year. There are, however, other list owners who are not particularly concerned about the volume size rented or the time of year in which the outside promotion will be mailed, and do not necessarily impose any restrictions. This is an internal decision and, as stated, should be made early in the year and adjusted if necessary during the course of that year.

It should be noted that there have been debates for decades about whether it is better to undersell the list or to allow list rental sales volume to reach a very high level. On the latter, it can usually be detected if renting out the list too much is hurting the firm's sales or those of your list clients. If outside mailers who have used the list heavily and who have consistently received a good response, using essentially their same promotion package offer, begin to experience a significant drop in *their* response rate, then you might check to see if you need to impose some list rental volume usage restrictions. You will need to keep an eye on this periodically throughout the year. *It is better that your list works for a few mailers than for it not to work for any.*

LIST RENTAL AGREEMENTS

Some list owners insist that the mailer sign the list rental agreement for every order before the list is processed or even shipped. This agreement states certain restrictions the renter must adhere to. It protects the list owner's list from misuse and abuse and holds the mailer responsible for any infractions. What it usually contains are the following clauses or stipulations:

1. List rental is for one-time use only for the approved mailer/offer on a certain mail or call date. (It is extremely important that the mailer adhere to the mail or call date. If the mailer changes that date, he or she must inform you in writing of the change and you must get that new mail or call date reapproved.)

2. The list shall at all times remain the sole property of the list owner.

3. The mailer will not transfer, attach, copy, disclose, enhance, or retain all or any portion of the list in any form or manner whatsoever nor permit any third party, agent, employee, or contractor and their agent and employees to do so.

4. The mailer agrees that no telephone solicitation to or telephone follow-up of the list be permitted or made and that no method will be employed to add telephone numbers. (This clause is not valid nor should be included if the list owner makes its telephone numbers available to the public.)

5. The mailer agrees to indemnify and hold the list owner harmless from any

and all claims, damages, losses or exchanges, however incurred, by the use of the list.

6. The mailer understands and agrees that the list has been and will be monitored with "decoys" (seeds) or by other methods to prevent improper and unauthorized use of the list.

7. The mailer agrees to pay the established fee by an agreed-upon date, including the appropriate tax, if applicable.

8. The mailer's order cancellation must be transmitted to the list owner by phone, then followed up in writing within a certain time. The mailer agrees to pay any cancellation fees incurred.

9. The mailer agrees to allow the list owner, if desired, access to the mailer's own list, either by rental or trade.

10. This agreement shall not be modified, except in writing, by either party and as agreed to by both parties.

11. The mailer agrees to notify the list owner of any mail or call date changes by phone and follow up in writing as soon as the mailer knows of the change.

12. The mailer agrees to return or not return the magnetic tape, according to list owner's wishes.

13. The mailer will not employ any method to detect the list owner's "decoys" (seeds) or alter or eliminate such.

14. The mailer or its service bureau may not manipulate merge-purge programs to give improper weight to any list. The merge-purge operation will be used for the sole purpose of eliminating duplicate names and addresses. Computer verification of net names mailed will be provided with remittance to the list owner within a certain period.

15. The list owner makes no warranty or representation of any nature as to the accuracy of the list. (This is at the list owner's option since there are some lists which are telephone-verified as well.) The list owner may not be responsible for undeliverable names unless the list owner specifies in writing to the mailer that credit or other arrangements be made to the mailer.

DMA MAIL PREFERENCE SERVICE

It is the list owner's responsibility to protect the wishes of its customers. The Direct Marketing Association's *Guidelines for Mailing List Practices,* Article 6, states:

> Every List Owner who sells, exchanges or rents lists should see to it that each individual on the list is informed of those practices, and should offer an option to have the individual's name deleted when rentals or purchases are made. The List Owner should remove names from its List when requested directly by the individual, and by the use of the DMA Mail Preference Ser-

vice Names Removal List. List Brokers and Managers should take reasonable steps to assure that List Owners and Compilers follow these practices.

LIST DATA PRIVACY

An ever-increasing concern of consumers is their right to privacy. It is the responsibility of all involved in direct marketing to adhere to the wishes of individuals. The Direct Marketing Association's *Guidelines for Mailing List Practices*, Article 8, states:

> All list Owners, Brokers, Managers, Compilers and Users should be protective of the consumer's right to privacy and sensitive to the information collected on lists and, subsequently, considered for transfer, rental, sale or exchange. Information such as but not limited to medical, financial, insurance or court data and data that may be considered to be personal and intimate in nature by all reasonable standards should not be included on list that is made available for transfer, rental, sale or exchange when there is a reasonable expectation by the consumer that the information would be kept confidential. Any advertising or promotion of list being offered for transfer, rental, sale or exchange should reflect a sensitivity for the individuals on the list. Promotional methods and language that tend to portray characteristics of those individuals in a disparaging way should be avoided.

The need for strict adherence to the guideline should be vehemently enforced as it does involve our personal rights as citizens. People buying the products that we offer allow us in direct marketing to operate and make a profit for our business. To abuse individual privacy wishes would be foolish to say the least. It should be a top concern for all those involved in direct marketing.

LIST PROTECTION

Your list is the vehicle by which you deliver your product. You will need to stringently protect it. It is also *your* responsibility as the list owner for the protection of the list data. Unauthorized access, alteration or distribution of the list data cannot be tolerated. Certain safeguards should be employed to do such. One of these methods is to "decoy" (seed) your list. How is this done? Your computer department service bureau should be consulted for advice on the best way in which to do this for your particular file. Usually, a false or altered name with a deliverable address is implanted every so many records throughout the file. An additional measure would be to hire an outside service, such as the U.S. Monitoring Service, who will, for a fee, provide names and addresses in any or every geographic location you desire. These decoys should be included in each list rental order fulfillment run by your computer department/service bureau. Decoy names should periodically be changed but the address should remain the same. In that way, if you have an "old decoy" name which was rented to a mailer and that name is no longer valid and the mailer mails more than one time, you will be able to detect misuse or abuse rather quickly. For added protection, change your decoy names once a quarter.

Once the decoys are received and returned to you they should be checked to make sure that the mailer/offer and the mail/call date were adhered to by the mailer. If the mailer has violated what the list owner initially approved, the mailer must immediately be notified and questioned for misuse or abuse. Most mailers are honest and do not abuse or misuse the list. Most cases of misuse or abuse stem from mailers who are new to the direct marketing industry and who are not aware of all the rules, guidelines, restrictions, and terms. As stated, it is a good idea to mark each list shipped with the list owner's particular restrictions and have the firm's order confirmation state these as well. Most misuses or abuses can be worked out without resorting to legal measures. Remember that the list owner is responsible for its own list's protection. Make sure that a system and policy is worked out before a list is put out for list rental.

LIST OVERLAYS

There are some list owners who choose to "enhance" their mailing list selections by doing an overlay of the list file. How is this done? There are a few direct marketing firms who will either supply demographic and psychographic information on magnetic tape to you or, for a fee, will do it for you. If your list has very few selection criteria either for your own use or for a mailer's use, you may choose to have this done. Most list owners do not do it or have the capability to do it; therefore, hire a service that can. All you have to do is supply your house master magnetic tape to the service. They will identify and "overlay" the demographic and psychographic information onto your file and "flag" or "mark" it for selection extraction. The result of this overlay allows you to glean more information about your buyer. You can extract any criteria flagged in order to be able to pinpoint more accurately who these people are on your file. You might want to market a particular or new product to them. It also allows the mailer to more finely target the audience they need to reach for them to make a potential sale. You can charge an additional fee for overlay information extraction for a mailer's use, and hence, make additional money.

The overlay information is gathered from many sources, including census tracking, automobile registration, and various public records. It is matched by zip code, cluster codes, and census tract to your file. The information is then moved into your file and "flagged" or marked for extraction. Some firms are further refining their list by using expanded zip + 4 codes because some zip areas are too broad for accurate identification.

The benefit of overlaying is that you as the list owner will get to know your customers better and be better able to market to them. Mailers using your list can further penetrate into the market areas they need; hence, you not only can make more money by selling more products, but you receive more revenue from list rental.

LIST RENTAL INCOME AND EXPENSES

The challenge is obviously to make more money than what you are spending. You will need to know exactly what you are making and spending, at least on a monthly basis, to strategically administer and manage your budget. Your accounting invoicing department should be providing the following reports:

1. Invoicing: Statement of the month's billed list rental activity

2. Payment: List of invoices paid during the month

3. Adjustment: Information concerning a change of a previously reported invoice

4. Sales activity: List of each order entered for the month

5. Financial and aging: List based on invoice date of accounts receivable still outstanding

6. Profit and loss statement: A listing by line item of all expenses and revenue month-to-date and year-to-date and calculated for profit and loss.

These reports should be provided to you, as stated, at least on a monthly basis with a year-to-date analysis. Additionally, you will need to have reports structured so that you can do a month-by-month versus year-by-year analysis. You will need to track "month/year-to-date versus month/year-to-date" in years in order to ascertain which months are the largest volume and revenue producing for your list. There are some lists which can work year round. Most, however, have a season in which the incoming volume is higher. This is mainly due to the mailer's mailing schedule for the individual product. It is important for you to get to know your mailer's product offer and when they usually order and mail. This will allow you to try to get other types of mailers to use your list in the slack time. *Your goal is to effect year-round list rental volume sales.* There will always be months that are slow, but with a smart marketing schedule, you can probably get most of the months booked for list rental activity.

Watch your promotional budget carefully. Measure it against the monthly incoming list rental revenue or list volume ordered. Adjust your promotional schedule accordingly. You don't want to be overspending on list promotion if you don't have to. Your cash flow is extremely important to the health of your overall list rental program and should also be uppermost in your mind.

SHOULD YOU MANAGE YOUR LIST IN-HOUSE OR HIRE A LIST MANAGER?

Some list owners prefer in-house management while others want a list manager focusing full-time on making list rental revenue for their firm. The expenses of in-house management including staff and various overheads must be weighed against paying a list manager anywhere from 10 to 20 percent management fee for doing all the work. What must be emphasized is that *list owners do not lose any control over their list at all if they choose to hire a list manager*. They still must approve each and every mailer and their offer for every list rental order submitted. The list manager does not make any money unless your list file is rented out. Therefore, it is virtually at no cost to the list owner to try a list management firm. The list manager pays for all expenses of staff, marketing, promotion, printing, space ads, conventions, office space, etc. The list owner receives monthly reports with a check. List management contracts between a list owner and list manager can be tailored and refined exactly to the list owner's requirements and terms. A list management firm can be an international bridge by which a list owner's list is sold since many list managers interface with firms in other countries who might possibly use the list owner's list, thus making more potential list revenue.

Making the decision to keep the list in-house or to have an outside list management firm representing and selling the list comes down to this: If you feel comfortable in being able to make auxiliary revenue without it being a detraction from the main product of your company, and if you are willing to make a sizable budget investment in marketing, promotion, training, and staff, then perhaps you might want to manage your list in-house. If, however, you feel that you need to make a full corporate commitment to expanding your main company's product, having a solid list management firm who can and will meet your firm's list rental revenue goals would be a good business decision.

CONCLUSION

Running a smart business means choosing the right team players whether you choose to manage your list in-house or have a list management firm do it for you. List rental revenue will enhance your corporate profit. The strategies and systems by which you can make that corporate profit are extremely critical. Having a good list is not enough. How it is structured, marketed, and administered is equally important in maximizing the profitability. Making money on your list is determined by the effort put forth by you and your team players, and your company's willingness to make a commitment.

GLOSSARY

Computer Service Bureau: An internal or external facility providing general or specific data processing services.

Cross Section: A group of names and addresses selected from a mailing list in such a way as to be representative of the entire file.

Decoy: A unique name specifically inserted into a mailing list for verification of list usage. Usually it is in the form of an order number or unique spelling of a name at a deliverable address which indicates which order it was used for. Also called a *seed* or *salt*.

Demographics: Socioeconomic characteristics pertaining to a geographic area.

Dump: A printed display of the contents of a data file; typically a magnetic tape or a portion of that data file for purposes of review of the data.

Duplicate: Two or more name and address records which are found to be equal by basis of comparison.

File: A collection of records on a single storage device.

Geographics: Any method of subdividing a list based on geographic subdivisions.

Key Code: Alphabetic and/or numeric letters on a label or order form that indicate the source of that name or segmentation of a mailing. Assigned to a specific list by the list user to facilitate the tracking of responses and analysis of a given list's effectiveness.

List Broker: The agent of the list. The broker conducts research, suggests lists, makes recommendations regarding marketing strategies, analyzes and evaluates results, acts as an intermediary between the list owner and mailer, places, monitors, invoices, and collects for list order purchases and transactions.

List Cleaning: The process of correcting and/or removing a name and address from a mailing list.

List Maintenance: Any manual, mechanical, or electronic system for keeping name and address records updated on a mailing list.

List Manager: An employee of the list owner or an outside agent who is responsible for the use, by others, of a specific mailing list. List manager's responsibilities include list marketing, promotion, sales, list clearance, record keeping, monitoring the status of each order at any point, maintenance and exchange of records, credit checking, invoicing, collections, and payments. List manager generally provides various monthly reports along with monies collected to the list owner.

List Owner: A person or firm who, by promotional activity or compilation, has developed a list of names having something in common or has purchased such a list from the developer.

List Rental: An arrangement generally made by a list broker (or a list owner), in which a list owner furnishes names to an approved mailer for an approved offer on a one-time basis unless other arrangements are made in advance.

List Source: The media or other data sources used to generate names for a mailing list.

Magnetic Tape: A storage device for electronically recording and reproducing by computer defined bits of data. Commonly supplied in the output format of 9 Track 1600 BPI.

Mail/Call Dates: Dates on which the list owner and list user have agreed for the list user to mail or call to a specific list. No other date is acceptable without written request for change and approved by list owner.

Mailer: An individual or firm who uses direct mail to promote a product or service using its own or other list owners' mailing lists.

Mailing List: Names and addresses of individuals and/or companies having a common specific interest, segmentation, activity, or purchase.

Merge-Purge: Combining two or more lists in a computer format for the purpose of eliminating duplicate names and identifying multibuyers among the lists being used. Reports are issued to the mailer and/or list owner documenting, by list, the number of unique names, interfile and intrafile duplicates, assigned multibuyers, and other pertinent information.

Need By or Due Date: The date specified on a list rental order that the list material is required by the mailer so that the mailer can mail the promotion message or offer on time.

Nth Name Selection: A fractional unit that is repeated in sampling a mailing list.

One-Time Use: All list rentals are for one-time use only unless special arrangements are made with the list owner and/or list manager prior to the initial mailing.

Overlay: The process by which information is added to a main or master file to enable a more specialized selection.

Pressure-Sensitive Labels: Self-adhesive labels in continuous form, four labels across and usually eleven down which can be applied manually or mechanically to a mailing piece.

Psychographics: The attributes, characteristics, or qualities used to denote the lifestyles or attitudes of customers and prospective customers.

Sample Package: The actual mailing piece of the list user or mailer which will be mailed to a particular list. The sample must be approved by the list owner. If the sample is changed after approval, it must be recleared with the list owner.

Source Code: Unique alphabetical and/or numeric identification for distinguishing one criteria or media source from another.

Tape Dump: A printout of data on a magnetic tape for checking correctness, readability, consistency, editability, etc.

Tape Layout: A written field-by-field description of the data contained in a record, typically describing each field as to its length, beginning and ending positions, name, editing characteristics, and data format.

Test/Continuation: A test indicates that it is a first-time use of a mailer's promotional offer measuring the responsiveness and effectiveness of a particular list or a particular section of a list. A continuation is subsequent times that a mailer is using a list for the same approved promotional offer.

Turnaround Time: Elapsed time between submission for an order for processing or list rental fulfillment at the computer department service bureau and the delivery of a specified output to the mailer's ship-to address.

Update: The adding of recent transactions and current information to the master or main list along with any deletions, name or address changes, etc., reflecting the current status of each record on the list.

Zip Plus 4: The addition of four additional numbers after the five-digit zip code to facilitate in sorting mail more finitely and defining a geographic area more precisely.

11
Business Lists

Mary Ann Kleinfelter

MISCO, Inc.
Holmdel, N.J.

While business lists share some attributes common to consumer lists and lists in general, there are significant differences. Once again, as traditional wisdom dictates, how you manipulate these differences to your advantage will be determined by your direct marketing strategy.

The information and selections available on a business mail-order list are more limited than on a compiled or subscription list largely because the order form is what dictates the information on the file. Generally speaking, because mail-order companies are attempting to close a sale, they ask very few questions on the order form, feeling that the most important job of the order form at this point is to explain the product, sell it, and do any credit checking that's necessary. However, some of the typical types of information you can get pretty readily off the order form without complicating the selling process too much would be:

1. The individual's title
2. The individual's gender (if they give their first name)
3. Whether or not they are credit card holders
4. What kind of card they have
5. What types of products they purchase
6. How much they can spend

Because so little information is captured on the order form, a mail-order marketer will often have his or her list matched by any of the different enhancement capabilities that are out there. These can be done on a business address and range from telling how many employees are at that location, to Standard

Industrial Classification (SIC) coding indicating what industry the company is in and so forth.

Just as consumer address lists can be broken down into types or categories, business address lists can be characterized according to one or more of the following groups:

1. **Responsive buyers.** These lists are composed predominantly of buyers who have chosen to purchase as a result of a solicitation received via direct mail or some other form of alternative direct marketing media. They can be further subdivided.
    a. **Merchandise buyers.** These buyers bought a specific product, such as a computer supply from MISCO or a book from McGraw-Hill.
    b. **Magazine subscribers.** These buyers paid for a subscription to a magazine, such as *Inc* or *Fortune*. This type of list must be distinguished from controlled-circulation subscription lists, for which the respondent must answer questions to qualify to receive the magazine but does not actually pay for it. As a result, controlled-circulation lists may contain much valuable information, which may be selectable, but do not indicate a purchase. An example of a controlled-circulation list would be *Hardware Age* from *Chilton*. The subscribers to a controlled-circulation list are typically called *recipients*.
    c. **Buyers of services.** These buyers purchased a service, such as a seminar from National Seminar or a membership in an association, such as the National Association for Female Executives (NAFE).
2. **Inquiry names.** This type of list contains names and addresses of individuals who have inquired about products or services, sometimes as a result of a lead generation offer received through the mail. They can be subdivided into two major groups: paid and nonpaid inquiries. An example of paid inquiries is a list such as Balwin-Cooke, and an example of nonpaid inquiries would be Dictaphone. However, some lists, such as Dictaphone, may be small and contain a mix of both buyers and inquiries. This is typical of many business-to-business lists.
3. **Compiled lists.** The world of compiled lists is varied, but they all contain one common thread: the names were "compiled" (thus the terminology) from some source, such as the Yellow Pages, census data, credit data, or association rosters, and therefore do not imply any kind of propensity toward mail-order purchases. An example of a compiled list would be Dun & Bradstreet or Trinet. Compiled lists can contain business addresses with or without individual names.

HOW TO SELECT A
MAIL-ORDER LIST

Many years ago, there was a generally accepted feeling in the direct-mail industry that if you were buying a mailing list to promote a product you could only use a list which contained mail-order buyers. Fortunately, for the widening of the potential universe that old adage has been proved to be incorrect. List buyers today are able to use a wide variety of lists other than just merchandise buyer lists. Instead we now talk about a variety of characteristics that a direct-mail list should have when we attempt to match it to the product we're selling. For example: If your product is selling for $20 or less and you want to make an outright sale of the product, then you may be able to purchase a list either with an average unit of sale of around that amount or make a product or dollar selection on a list. If you are selling a product with a very high unit of sale, as in advertising specialties or a catalog of big-ticket items where the unit of sale may be in excess of $200 or $300, then you want to do one of two things:

Either you may want to try a list with a very high unit of sale or you may want to try a two- or three-step lead generation. Lead generation is accomplished as follows: (1) Rent a list which may include both inquiries and buyers or inquiries only. (2) Mail an offer to inquire or receive more information about your product. (3) Turn inquirers into buyers of the product either by direct mail or by a combination of telemarketing and direct mail.

In general, when choosing a list to test, it is safest to start with a profile of your customer house file. This profile should reveal key characteristics of your customer type that should help you select lists which contain prospects that look like your present buyers. This fact has contributed one rule of thumb to the direct-mail industry: the higher the degree to which a prospect (rented) list duplicates your house file, the better it will perform. Examples of key characteristics to watch for are gender, geographic skews, density of SICs, and company size. In addition, you can choose to test lists that bear some resemblance to your historically most responsive lists, or ask your broker to provide usage on lists you are considering. Remember, when asking for usage on a list, you really need to know what kind of mailers are continuing, not just those tested. Once again, it is probably more important to find out what kind of mailers the list works for than asking for specific mailers by name (which is a sticky ethical question for some list suppliers).

All this advice will help you pick test lists with the least degree of risk. Unfortunately, in some cases, that also means the least degree of payback in the long term. Obviously, your best list would be buyers of products competitive to your own. Surprisingly, these names and addresses are more often available to you than you may think—if you are willing to negotiate, pay more, and/or make your names available to them. However, by picking lists like these, you may get better response but you are not expanding your potential universe of prospect names.

For this reason, the general rule of thumb is to set aside between 15 and 20 percent of the names for every mailing to test new lists. Obviously, not all tests will work so it is necessary to observe this testing discipline even during periods when the economy at large is soft. Remember, while you may prefer a great response on a test list, a list that performs poorly also delivers some very valuable information that, once analyzed, can help you avoid choosing similarly unsuccessful lists in the future.

Another pitfall to avoid is using test lists on test mailing packages, thereby introducing too many simultaneous variables that may render results for both package and lists statistically unreliable. Many direct-mail professionals are too quick to abandon test lists that perform poorly. The consequences of such a decision can be especially dire when there is a marked scarcity of good prospect names from which to choose. If you have a very sound reason for why the list should perform well and it doesn't, then you should look into it. Perhaps you did not receive the selection—or even the list itself—that you ordered!

Often people ask how many names should be taken from a list for an accurate test. There are as many answers to this question as to the equally famous query: What is a good response rate? You should attempt to strike a balance between fitting into your mail plan as many tests as you can afford and making sure you go as deep as possible into each list to extract a good cross section for a test.

The rate of response you expect must also be taken into account. For example, if your response rate means that a 5000-name test will yield only 25 orders (some of which may be incorrectly coded or not even recorded by your internal data processing system), you may not have the confidence in just 25 responses to determine that this list performs well enough to roll out, while another test list that yields only 23 responses should not be used again.

SIC CODING

To the newcomer, perhaps no other selection unique to business lists seems so baffling as trying to use the Standard Industrial Classifications (SIC) selection. Recent improvements in SIC coding may initially appear to compound the confusion but in reality can make targeted marketing more precise.

Even today, few business response lists offer an SIC selection. Most often, the coding is available on compiled business lists and controlled-circulation lists of business publications—and, by means of overlays, on public business list databases. When deciding which list to test, be sure to ask how the SIC was assigned. For some compilers, like Dun & Bradstreet, this assignment is based on how much of the particular company's revenue is generated by what part of that company's business. On some compilations, the assignment of SICs is left to the discretion of whoever is doing the compiling, perhaps even a data entry clerk.

Controlled-circulation lists can be equally problematic because they often depend on the respondent to indicate a company's appropriate SIC on the order card the respondent must complete and return to qualify to receive the publication. It is a startling but true fact that many employees from the same company answer this question differently. So whether you are testing compilations, controlled-circulation lists, or a public business database, be sure to inquire as to the method for assigning SICs.

In today's business atmosphere of mergers and acquisitions, a legitimate question arises regarding the SIC coding of subsidiaries and branches. Dun & Bradstreet assigns SIC codes to subsidiaries and branches based solely on the activities performed at that branch or subsidiary. Obviously, many companies are engaged in more than one line of business. So in all compiled lists, there will be duplication between SIC codes. Dun & Bradstreet attempts to assign SIC codes for all lines of company business that produce 10 percent or more of the company's revenue. Nowhere is the discrepancy between these methods more noticeable than in the determination of a primary SIC code (a company's central business) versus its secondary SIC code (a subsidiary business). Today some compilers, like Dun & Bradstreet, can offer SIC selections of two, three, four, six, or eight digits.

The SIC system begins with these major two-digit groups, which divide all U.S. economic activity into 10 major divisions:

Title	Two-digit group
Agriculture, forestry, and fishing	01–09
Mining	10–14
Construction	15–17
Manufacturing	20–39
Transportation, communication, electric, gas and sanitary services	40–49
Wholesale trade	50–51
Retail trade	52–59
Finance, insurance, and real estate	60–67
Services	70–89
Public administration	91–97

Dun & Bradstreet publishes an excellent manual, as I'm sure others do, which devotes a section to each of the major SIC groups, such as 15 (Building construction). Within this two-digit SIC, they break down to three-digit (such as 152, General building—residential) and four-digit (such as 1521, General contractors for single-family houses). Within this subgroup, you can ask for only those involved in townhouse construction (9903). Here is an example:

15	Building construction
152	Building contractors—residential
1521	Contractors—single-family houses
1521 99	Single-family housing
1521 9903	Townhouse construction

Using the appropriate SIC can tremendously enhance your ability to market, especially when your product has a specific application exclusive to a specific industry. Obviously, the danger in this method of marketing is its potential for limiting an already limited universe. Therefore, different lists, different SIC coding methods, and different SICs should be tested routinely.

When selecting compiled lists to test SICs and other selections, be aware that there are essentially two kinds of compiled lists: those derived in great part from company credit histories, such as Dun & Bradstreet or TRW, and those compiled from the Yellow Pages and other directories. These include ABL, Compilers Plus, Trinet, and Database America among others.

Whichever you choose, remember that when the government revised the SIC codes in 1987, there were some significant changes to the 1972–1977 codes. Please make sure to have your compiler and/or list broker review these changes, especially in those industries to which you market.

BUSINESS ADDRESSES

Sometimes when a business product has broad-based appeal, selecting by SIC is not enough or even effective. Other selections are required. Whether or not you use SIC, the first decision business mailers must face is whether to market to individuals by name at business addresses or to businesses without individual names. The result of this decision will seriously affect which business lists are used and the marketing challenges to be faced. Recently, a third alternative has arisen. With the increase in businesspeople working out of their homes, and a corollary increase in the number of corporations encouraging employees to by-pass the corporate mailroom for third-class mail delivery, more and more businesspeople are using a combination of their names, their company names, and their home addresses.

Obviously, removing duplication from and among these home-business addresses and true business addresses presents an almost overwhelming challenge for present data processing methods. In addition, there are almost always some true home addresses on a business list, whether selectable or not. Realize that the old distinction becomes blurred between a three-line address (which can be an individual at home or a business with no individual) and a four-line address (which can be an individual at a true business address or an individual at one of the pseudo-business-home addresses described above).

Business Addresses without Individual Names

When you choose to mail to a list that contains business addresses with no individual names, you may sidestep the issue of how many pieces to mail into a business at a single business location. These types of lists usually contain fewer duplicates because they do not contain several individuals at one site. However, even such lists may contain duplicates as many businesses are opting to use "prestige" addresses. These addresses may not even be at real physical locations, but at addresses that enhance a company's image and are familiar only to the addressee's local postal worker.

Even if you mail to business addresses without individual names, it may be advisable to include an attention line, for example, "Attn: Vice President of Marketing." This simply makes the mail move more smoothly through the mailroom and helps to direct it, thereby taking the decision of how to route it out of the hands of the mail clerk. By using different attention lines, you can also multiply the number of pieces you are mailing into one company's physical location. For example, you may choose to mail three solicitations into a single company site:

1. Attn: Chief Executive Officer
2. Attn: Vice President of Marketing
3. Attn: Purchasing Agent

However, you may want to take into account the average size of the companies on the lists you are using. Average size is usually expressed in sales volume and/

or number of employees. For example, if you're mailing to mom-and-pop retail stores, usually with a workforce of under 10 people, you really don't need to address it to the attention of the purchasing agent, as they most likely do not have one.

Business Addresses with
Individual Names

When you decide to mail to a list of individuals at business addresses, the decision of how many pieces you are mailing into a single physical location takes on an even more interesting dimension. Some large business lists are so dense, you may find you are mailing as many as 800 or more pieces into one location after you have completed a large merge-purge containing many rented lists. So, how do you reach the individual you are seeking? Many business-to-business list owners may not even keep track of or select out the number of buyers their house list contains at a single site.

SELECTABILITY

Unlike large consumer lists, business lists tend to be smaller and offer fewer selections, such as those mentioned before—number of employees, sales volume, recency, etc. Some do not even differentiate between buyers and inquirers. Many do not offer title selections, and the unit of sale shown on the datacard is an average, which is not offered as a selection.

Although the practice of appending data provided by overlays to rented names is even less common than overlaying customer files, the advantages, especially for a business-to-business mailer, may outweigh the disadvantages. Many business-to-business catalogers offer a wide variety of products sold through several different kinds of promotional vehicles. Of course, these efforts deliver various units of sale, which you can segment to boost your response. By overlaying information, you can refine and create selects on small lists, where there was none available for rental. You may be able to target various product offers to appropriate segments. A list that once was marginal for a single offer can become profitable for two different offers, each tailored to a segment. For example, if a business list has a mix of buyers and inquirers, or high- and low-ticket buyers, you may not be able to make the entire list pay for a high-ticket catalog offer. However, if the list can be broken into segments, the inquiries may be profitable for lead generation, while the high-ticket buyers can produce outstanding sales for the catalog. List owner rental revenue is enhanced, because a mailer can order the entire file with minimum risk. The mailer can even negotiate with the list owner, giving the owner the benefit of the enhancement that was done on the names. This type of segmentation can be especially effective when a mailer uses a multiple number of offers. As the universe of good-response names shrinks, making marginal lists work becomes the single greatest challenge for direct marketers.

Net Names and Other Special Arrangements

While business-to-business mailers tend to realize better nets after they perform merge-purges than comparable consumer mailers, the small size of the lists available to them often makes list owners less likely to negotiate favorable net name agreements. This is a strong argument for creating and using business-to-business databases. After you remove duplicates, incorrect addresses, bad zips, undeliverables, keying errors, DMA preference no-mails, deadbeats, etc., only 50 percent of the original names may remain to mail. You may be billed for 100 percent of the names rented.

PURCHASING AUTHORITY

When you consider that unit of sale in a business-to-business environment indicates the purchasing authority of the individual, you can see how difficult it is to reach the appropriate individual without any such selection. An alternative way to reach this individual would be by title, a selection also not offered on the usual business list. The inability to pinpoint individuals by title or purchasing authority makes the decision of how many pieces of mail to send to a particular company per site especially difficult. With so little information, which individuals do you select to mail and which to omit? A popular method is to stagger the number of mailing pieces, but this alternative requires the mailer to exercise a great deal of timing and control over arenas not within his or her venue—that is, the U.S.P.S. and corporate mailrooms. When a business list does include individuals with titles, some mailers choose to mail to a certain number and limit it to that: for example, the top three titles. As we all know, titles, and their relative importance as to purchasing authority, not only differ widely from company to company, but even within the same organization. Often, the name and title of a purchasing agent or secretary may be captured on a business list, but he or she is not the ultimate user of the product purchased—or even the specifier.

DELIVERABILITY

Deliverability of the names and addresses on business lists was once thought to be a nonissue. For that reason, and the relative small size of business lists in general, the selection of recency was not much in demand. However, increased activity in mergers, acquisitions, and bankruptcies of companies, compounded by issues mentioned before (incorrect addresses, prohibitive mailroom policies, etc.), has caused industry experts to speculate that up to 40 percent of the business community may experience change annually. Nowhere is this problem more evident than in the business list with an individual name. The individual may have been promoted, transferred, or left the organization. To some degree, this unique characteristic of business lists is offset by the high rate of pass-along a piece of promotional mail may enjoy in an office atmosphere. Many wise mailers of consumer products rent business lists simply to enjoy the benefits of this pass-along they cannot achieve at a home address. Recent developments in data and postal processing can help the mailer rid a business list of certain kinds of undeliverables, such as poor or nonexistent zip codes. However, the challenge of locating successors to job positions remains unanswered.

SUMMARY

The characteristics of the best consumer lists are still similar to ones found on consistently high-performing business lists. One of the most elemental is source, that is, the way names were acquired. Although business lists were traditionally considered to be largely direct-mail sold, even the most conservative mailers are venturing into alternative media. Also, some business product purchases are surprisingly seasonal, as they are dictated by the requirements of the buyers' fiscal years. Some business mailers have certain offers only during these "peak" seasons and discount offers at other times, changing the compositions of their buyer file throughout the year. So, it is wise to monitor the composition of even your most responsive business lists on an ongoing basis.

As mentioned before, selections such as unit of sale, recency, frequency (multibuyers), gender, and cash versus other payment methods are generally not offered, even if they are present on business lists. For this reason, and owing to small list universes, public and private databases of business lists have proliferated. A debate rages on as to whether zip-based models and overlays have real value when applied to a business-to-business database. Undoubtedly, especially for a mailer limited by geography or a specialized product, the data shared among lists on such bases can be invaluable in terms of more precisely targeted marketing and substantial cost savings.

Finally, whether testing a business mail-order buyer list, a business subscription list, business inquiries, or a business database, follow some tried and true words of wisdom: Look for a list of names and addresses that shows evidence of dynamic growth, a universe potential that is healthy, and TLC (Tender List-owner Care).

12

List Selection Criteria

Ed Burnett

Ed Burnett Consultants, Inc.
Montvale, N.J.

MAIN CRITERIA IN SELECTING LISTS

Criteria determine the ways one list varies from another, as well as the ways one list segment within a list varies from another segment in that same list. Thus criteria are the *essence* of selectability and thus the *essence* of what makes one list segment produce a different response.

Criteria can be and often are selected as single entities, lists of say, $50 buyers, new moves, or those who buy by American Express. However, as mailers begin to delve into the wealth of options open to them, more and more selections are based on one criterion within another, for example, $50 buyers who have made a mail-order purchase charged on the American Express card in the last six months.

Some mailers that order lists by multiple criteria tend to forget that each "cut" of a criteria by the part represented by another criteria reduces the size of the list segment available. After two or three "cuts" a list selected in this way may be too small to warrant using or testing.

From the book, *The Complete Direct Mail List Handbook,* by Ed Burnett © 1988. Used by permission of the publisher, Prentice-Hall, Inc./a division of Simon and Schuster, Englewood Cliffs, N.J. 07632.

To illustrate this point consider the following:

In zip code XXXXX there are	10,500 homes
Of these homes 63 percent have family incomes of over $25,000, leaving	6,600 homes
Households headed by females are 15.5 percent and are to be eliminated, which leaves	5,600 homes
Those owning two or more cars are 28 percent, which leaves	1,600 homes
Of these, 22 percent have purchased a car in 1984 or 1985, which leaves	350 homes

In this case, by selecting one criterion within another, only 350 names within a universe of 10,500 are utilized.

We will now look more closely at the main criteria for selectability.

Demographic

The major *demographic* criteria for a consumer list (data on who the individuals are and where they live) are:

- Individual data:

  Income (usually family income)
  Age (usually of head of household, if for a family)
  Education (usually for head of household, if for a family)
  Family size
  Age and sex of children

- Household data:

  Type of dwelling (single-family or multifamily)
  Length of residence
  Value of home
  Geographic location

- Telephone/car registration

  93 percent of families have a telephone
  70 percent of families have a *listed* phone number
  23 percent of families have an *unlisted* phone number
  7 percent of families do not have a phone
  70 percent of families have a car in an available list

Psychographic

The major *psychographic* characteristics (what people do, how they live, and their lifestyles) are disclosed by:

- What books and publications they buy (and read)

- What products they buy
- What they *do* with their leisure time
- What organizations or clubs they join
- What charities or groups they support
- What political party they register for
- What petitions they are willing to sign

Three Factors That Influence the Capacity and Willingness to Buy

Demographics and psychographics, but particularly the latter, are remarkably impacted by three influences that must not be overlooked:

The first is literacy.   An adult functional illiterate cannot read a road sign, menu, or headline. Sad to note, 25 percent of *adults* in America are functional illiterates and another 35 percent are completely illiterate. This leaves 60 million of 130 million or 135 million adults who *can* read and comprehend a newspaper, magazine, book, or direct-mail offer.

The second major influence is discretionary income.   Twenty-five million of the 96,000,000 families in America live well enough (above the cost of living and of taxes) to have extra income that they can spend by choice and not by necessity. While a number of direct-mail response offers are deliberately aimed at those without discretionary income, the majority of solo direct mail (including catalog mailings) is aimed at those who have income over which they have discretion as to how they spend it and for what.

The third major influence is a tendency or willingness to buy by mail.   To paraphrase Gertrude Stein, a mail-order buyer is a mail-order buyer is a mail-order buyer much like a rose is a rose is a rose. There are now over 2 billion names of mail-response customers commercially available. If we assume that the average size of a purchase from prospecting mailings is in the $30 range, then new transactions (first-time orders on a list from direct-mail prospecting, much of it among mail-order buyers found on other lists) total over 700 million transactions. Customer mailings, where the average order may be closer to $60, will add 600 million transactions to this. A billion or more transactions produce over $50 to $55 billion of gross sales from direct mail. These billion plus transactions come from a total universe which numbers only 240 million people of which roughly 140 million are adults. These adults reside in 96 million households and work in about 10.5 million establishments including 2 million farms.

If the $55 billion of direct-mail sales were spread equally over each individual, then the average individual (both adult and child) would buy approximately $230 through direct response in the course of a year. However, surveys indicate that not over 40 percent of adults (or families) will buy anything by mail. If that is true then the universe of buyers from direct mail is limited to 40 percent of the 140 million adults (about 56 million) who in essence are likely to live in 40 percent of the 96 million households (about 38 million). Using these figures, the average known mail-order buyer spends an average of $1000 per year on mail offers. Based on these figures each family that buys by mail order is then responsible for an average of $1450 per year of mail-order purchases.

There is a great deal of redundancy on lists because the average mail-order buyer can be found on a number of mail-order buyer lists. The closer the lists are psychographically (as to what is purchased and at what price) the greater the likelihood of interlist duplication. Mailers who use multiple lists go through a merge-purge process to eliminate such duplication.

Such duplication is particularly apparent in cultural lists — lists of buyers that are lovers of books, magazines, theater, opera, art, interior decor, and music. A merge-purge of half a million names from, say, 10 such lists will disclose and eliminate 25 percent of the records inputted and will provide a list of unique, unduplicated names and addresses for one-per-individual or one-per-family mailings.

Thus far this discussion has provided the key data defining demographic criteria and psychographic criteria, as well as the three major "outside" influences. Without any doubt these outside influences will also influence response rates.

Mail-Order Characteristics

The third major set of criteria are mail-order characteristics — in other words in what ways a given segment in a list of mail-order buyers varies from another segment or, what is more true in practice, in what ways a given segment selected on the basis of multiple criteria varies from another segment also selected on the basis of multiple criteria.

A mnemonic to aid recall of mail-order characteristics is RF$USISM. This stands for *Recency Frequency Dollars Item Source Method* of payment. There are a number of cells or "cuts" within each one of these.

R stands for recency, which measures the last order placed on the file for a given customer, donor, or subscriber. Recency can be measured by the last week, last month, last quarter, the last 6 months, or the current year.

F stands for frequency — which is how often the customer has purchased from the company on whose list his or her name is found. Frequency includes one-time buyers only, two-time buyers, or more than two-time buyers. It should be noted there is a difference between a one-time buyer from last week and a buyer who has not bought since a first buy 2½ years ago.

$US stands for dollars. However, there are different kinds of dollar data, and they provide different data to understand and test. There are variances in size and consistency, as well as highest dollar amount in a given order, and cumulative dollars:

- Size of orders may vary in amounts ranging from $1, $5, $10, $25, $50, $100, and over $100.
- Highest dollar may be based on the latest order, earliest order, or first order.

- Cumulative dollars may convert a recent buyer who spends only $5 into a regular customer who has spent more than X amount of dollars over the last two or three years.
- A review of purchases by period (quarterly, semiannually, annually) will disclose those who buy regularly, semiregularly, sporadically, every two or three periods, and so on. Each pattern discloses a different type (and cell) of buyer as far as the mail-order company is concerned.

I stands for item or the products or services that have been purchased. It is common to code a large number of different items generically into group classifications, perhaps 10 to 20 in number. In this way statistical analysis is possible, along with selection of buyers of one product who might then be good prospects for an allied product.

S stands for source. There is a distinct difference between customers who buy from space ads or electronic media and customers who buy through direct mail. Similarly a buyer from one list may be different than a buyer from another list. It is imperative to code every effort and attempt to record every order by its source, and never to lose the initial code.

M stands for method of payment. A person who pays by cash is different from one who pays by check. They both differ from a person who pays by money order or credit card. There are also differences in response, which can sometimes be subtle or significant, between those who pay by travel and entertainment (T&E) cards (Amex/Diners Club) and bank cards (Visa and MasterCard). There can be a difference in response between buyers who use T&E cards and mail in their orders as opposed to a group that phones in their orders.

Physical Characteristics

The fourth basic type of criteria is *physical*. Lists can vary physically by such factors as:

1. List data as a whole
2. Deliverability
3. Selectability
4. Format
5. Means of reproduction
6. Accessibility

We will now explore these variances in greater detail.

List Data as a Whole

Size.   Perhaps the first fact needed about a given list is the number of names it contains. Lists available for rental range from a few hundred names to tens of millions. Other factors (age, source, reputation of owner, accessibility, means of reproduction, for starters) being equal (and they rarely are) the list with the greater quantity will be preferred. Tests are made to locate lists that can be continued at a profit. Limits that are small may not be considered for test purposes because there is "no place to go" if a test is successful.

Completeness or coverage (the proportion of the universe available for the classification or type). In compiled files the element of completeness has particular importance. For example, there are at least 20 lists available of architects and architectural services. Most of them contain about the same number of establishments or professionals. A list half the size of these complete files will have little chance in the list marketplace. (A list of architects who buy by mail should not be expected to include all architects. Those who buy by mail from one supplier represent a special segment of the universe of architects available from compilers.)

Sometimes, however, the smaller list may embrace a greater portion of the known universe than a larger list. For example, an industrial magazine file of recipients, averaging, say, 1.7 records per plant may be matched with a compiled list consisting of the same number of records. The compiled list, if representative of one record per plant, will cover a higher proportion of the totality.

Deliverability

1. Cleanliness of the list—the methodology and timing of the cleaning and purging process
2. Duplication factor—the proportion of names that are duplicated
3. Updating cycle—when the list was last updated and when it will next be updated
4. Feedback for updating—the gathering of data on expected lack of deliverability
5. Zip code status—the proportion of good zip codes; utilization of zip code cleaning passes
6. NCOA—when the list was passed against the national change of address

Some mail-order lists have value even though they are many years old. (Members of a Humphrey Bogart book-buying fan club, for example, might well outpull other lists several years after the death of the star and the operation of the club.) In any case it is important to find out when the data were put on file and when they were last mailed and cleaned.

The deliverability of compiled files is inversely proportioned to their currency. The latest compilation (providing the source is current) will have the greatest deliverability. In this field two questions should be asked about any list being considered: (1) What is the source? and (2) When was the data updated or cleaned?

There are *no* secrets in the list business. If a compiler will not or cannot give you a reasonable answer to these two questions, the best thing to do is find another compiler to deal with.

At the present time most telephone registrants are being compiled by converting data from both alphabetical and classified (Yellow Pages) published listings. These data are aged before they can be obtained. Meanwhile, back at the phone companies up-to-date data are continuously available. Thus a list coming from a phone company tape, which is now slowly beginning to happen, is far more current than data converted from printed phone books.

Selectability

1. Individuals
2. Company names
3. Titles
4. Codes for titles

Format

1. Layout of data and discipline followed
2. Fixed versus variable length fields
3. Sequence in which the list is maintained
4. Sortation fields (if any)
5. Sequencing of crutch files (if any)

Means of Reproduction

1. Cheshire
2. Tape
3. Diskettes
4. Other
5. Cost factors of reproduction

Accessibility

1. Time requirements (on demand or scheduled)
2. Approval process
3. Who has access
4. When maintained

Physical Constraints

The aspect of deliverability is dependent on the currency of the file. However, the accuracy with which the data have been placed on tape and the accuracy of the zip codes, have a good deal to do with deliverability as well. Two lists compiled from the same source at the same time in which currency is not a factor can be far apart in deliverability because of the difference in the "physical" handling of conversion and zipping.

It is more than likely that the average list in America has a zip-error percentage of 4 to 5 percent. Every last zip error results in undeliverability by third-class mail.

Some years ago the method of reproduction had a great deal to do with how the list was judged by the list-using community. Lists on plates or cards, or particularly lists on 33-up labels (requiring moisture to adhere) were used but somewhat reluctantly. Now with costs dictating the necessity for merge-purging of duplicates prior to mailing, lists for rental must be on tape and be available on tape. Availability of tapes is a restraint because some list owners will provide labels for rental but not on tape even for computer letters or merge-purge.

On almost every merge-purge consisting of more than five lists, one or two will almost inevitably show up days (sometimes weeks) after the merge-purge final date for acceptance of data has passed. Because a list is on the market does not guarantee its owner or computer service access in the time frame desired.

One major provider of business lists is notorious in this regard. It is rare for this company's list to come in until all other lists, compiled, magazine subscribers, and mail-order buyers alike, have been on hand for several weeks. Because this firm has data very difficult to obtain from any other source, mailers continue to order—and hope.

Foreign lists, even Canadian lists, pose a problem of accessibility. Occasionally a desired list withholds its data from the market for a period of time for its own use. (The two compilers serving *Time* and *Newsweek* magazines, for example, are ordered to halt their services several months each year so that outside offers to college students cannot be mailed.) Also occasionally, a list is unavailable due to some upset at the company or a serious glitch in the computer servicing the list. Usually in such cases there is a reasonable alternative solution.

Some lists are available only if the owner or his *dedicated* service bureau does the addressing and mailing. Once a common practice, this is now reduced to only a handful of particularly valuable files. Where the need for such specific names is so great, the mailer must "heel" and send his or her pieces for mailing.

Almost all mail-order buyer lists of all kinds have no phone numbers. In addition many owners will not permit outsiders adding phone numbers for teleprospecting, or in the case of subscription renewals, telemarketing sales.

With the tremendous growth of word processors and PC users the market for lists to be placed on floppy disks is growing apace. Until recently the problems inherent in providing data on floppy disks have deterred compilers from providing their data in this form. The establishment of the DOS operating system for most floppy disk operations has now changed this. The Burnett operation now not only provides data on floppy disks at moderate costs for the conversion, but for the same price includes a program (also on a floppy disk) that permits the list user to sort, or copy, data and produce it in hard copy form on sheets, cards, envelopes, or pieces.

13

List and Database Maintenance

Tom Zukas

Namebank of America, Inc.
New York, N.Y.

The term *database* has for the most part superseded the term *list*, although technically there's a significant difference between a list and a database. Mailing lists are now rarely just names and addresses used for mailings; rather, they are repositories of extensive data about the actions taken by customers, and sometimes prospects, over a period of time. Whether you're building a list or a database, it is important that you follow certain procedures so that the product that you ultimately end up with is one that you can use as you intended.

I will not discuss software or hardware products, but rather data use concepts. Defining all the data elements that you possess or eventually will be able to use and how you want to maintain and use that information are the primary goals. The subsequent research into the software and hardware that would be most appropriate for your needs is not the subject of this text.

Additionally, there is another factor that doesn't fit within the logical flow of developing a list or a database but often can determine its success or failure. That component is corporate politics. In the sixties and seventies the power base of many corporations and businesses belonged to the person who controlled the data processing. Because of the mystery and complexity involved in data processing, the MIS people were able to wield a lot of political power and influence. This was especially true in matters related to budgets and strategy.

The new political power base resides with the database managers or the information managers. These are the people controlling the development, maintenance, and flow of information through the organization. Many well-

226

developed databases built at great cost and over lengthy periods of time can become little more than underutilized data files. Oftentimes this is due to major political conflicts within the organization. Corporatewide involvement and co-operation in the database design and building process is a way of ensuring the development and use of a quality product. Once the database is complete, sharing the information across all applicable areas will ensure that the database becomes a positive rather than a divisive force for your business.

There are three major segments in the process of developing your database: building the database, maintaining the database, and using the database.

BUILDING THE DATABASE

The building of the database can be broken up into several subcomponents.

- Defining your objectives
- Data identification
- Data use

Defining Your Objectives

The prime objective here is to focus on your ultimate goal throughout the database-building effort. Here you will define whether you want the system to interact with and/or support other subsystems such as a territory database, dealer network, customer service, or any system with which you may need to interact. You must determine in the beginning how you need each of these subsystems to interface with the main list database. If you plan to use the database as a stand-alone solely for marketing to customers and supporting all the marketing efforts related to that customer database, I would rethink your goals. Databases are powerful information tools that rarely should exist in isolation from other systems.

Data Identification

Defining the data elements that will go into the database is a critical step. If not done correctly, the cost to change at a later date could be steep. There are two schools of thought regarding the retention of customer-related data. One is to keep only what you think you can adequately use for segmentation or for building models. The other is to save everything you possibly can regarding every single contact you have with your customer. I lean toward keeping as much information as possible while still trying to be practical. My reasoning is that as time goes on there may develop new relationships between data or new concepts not currently used which will add value to such data.

A good place to begin defining your data elements is to review all information you currently receive about a customer through purchase transactions or any other type of interaction. Include contacts such as inquiries, refunds, complaints, and customer service calls. All these transactions have value. Other sources of data might come from accounting, fulfillment, or any department that has recorded information about your customers. The next thing to look at is the information you do not now retain but you may be able to in the future because of systems changes. And finally, consider what outside information is available to enhance your file that may be useful in the future. Leave room for enhanced or acquired data. When looking at data elements, try to compile a complete list of the data you do have and everything that you will most likely get in the near term. Meetings related to identifying data elements should involve as many people as possible who are aware of the information sources in your company. Leave latitude for the length of time you ascribe to doing this particular part of the database. I've been in meetings that went as long as three or four days before everyone identified all available data components. This does not include fully determining where the data will come from, who will supply it, and its value. Not giving enough time to this part of the database build is one of the most common mistakes in the building process.

Table 13-1 is not meant to be all-inclusive, nor is it meant to be specific to any one application. It is meant to guide your thinking when you look at your data or any potential data that you may bring into the database.

Data Use

Having identified your objectives and data, you then determine how you're going to use the data. What type of reports will you want, and what strategies have you implemented or do you expect to implement? What is the database going to do for you in the way of a capability that you do not already have? It is important to get as many people involved as possible in structuring the question, how will we use the database? Very often the completed database is capable of serving only some of the needs of marketing and a few other departments when, with careful planning, it could have served the needs of everyone.

MAINTAINING THE DATABASE

Maintenance of a list or database can be categorized into two distinct functions: data verification and updating.

Data Verification

Once all of the data elements have been identified, the next step is converting and editing the information. The converting process will take transaction data from various sources such as from your product fulfillment, customer service, or data entry. This information will be converted into a common processing format that will feed into the next step, which will be the edit process. *Note:* The convert-and-edit process can be one process. The purpose of the edit program is to edit all input transactions. This is a critical step in maintaining the integrity and quality of data on a database. If information is not verified as correct at this point, it will reside on the master file and eventually produce erroneous reports,

Table 13-1. Potential Database Data

Data field	Description
	Customer Data
Name, title, company name	Free-form name
Care-of address	Care-of name or address data
Street	Primary address
City	City name
State	State code
Zip	Zip code
Customer ID Number	Unique record identifier
Do-not-mail flag	Customer does not want to receive your mailings
Do-not-rent flag	Customer does not want you to rent their name to other mailers
Creation date	Date customer was added to the file
Transaction date	Date of last customer activity regardless of activity type
Credit card flag	Flag indicating an order was paid via credit card
Change-of-address date	Date of latest change of address
Delete-flag date	Date of latest delete transaction applied
Gender code	Male/female/unknown
Account number	Account number
Telephone number	Area code and number
Credit status code	Bad pay or credit risk indicator
Score	Recency/frequency/monetary value or specified scoring model
	Transaction Data
Date	Date of transaction
Source code	Transaction source code
Dollar amount	Total order dollar amount
Payment code	Method of payment code (credit card, check, cod, etc.)
Media code	Vehicle used to make offer to prospect (direct mail, space ad, television, telephone, etc.)
Response code	Vehicle used by customer to order (mail, telephone, etc.)
Transtype code	Type of transaction (purchase, inquiry, etc.)
Product category	Similar products group code
Product code	Specific product code or number
Product quantity	Number of units purchased for this product code
Product dollars	Amount spent on this product

incorrect selections, and completely misrepresented data. Basic edit routines should include checking to see that zip code and state are correct, all alphanumeric fields in fact contain alpha and numeric information, and all codes match valid code tables. These tables are maintained and updated separately. The edit can also contain default information if certain information is missing; for example, if a transaction has an invalid date but you know it was processed during a specific time the edit would automatically slug in that information. The edit program will also access name tables to identify such things as whether a first name is male or a female, whether a record is a company or an individual, whether a record contains a title, what code should be used for that title, and any other information that is possible to verify in the edit process.

Any transaction that is rejected by the edit should be reviewed manually to determine if an error has occurred that may affect other transactions. The source of particular errors must be isolated and a decision made about the possibility of reentering the transactions that were rejected. This is your last chance to protect the integrity of your database. Going back and correcting mistakes that have been made earlier is often impossible and at the very least costly. Invest the time now to ensure that your edit system is doing a quality job.

The next process in building the database is taking transactions that have gone through the edit and creating a master file. This is usually referred to as an update process.

Updating

The update process is complex. Records have to be matched to the existing file so that transactions for existing customers can be applied to a particular customer's history. If the customer for a transaction does not exist, a new customer master-file record is created. There are several methods for determining whether or not records exist on a master file. One method is to use a matching formula, whether it be a match code or some other algorithm. The other method is a straight account number match, but this requires knowing the account number of a record prior to the transaction coming into the update. This would therefore require some sort of clerical or human intervention each time a transaction occurred without an account number. In some cases, a combination of both might be used. Very simply, the update's purpose is to keep all the information related to a customer in one logical unit or, depending on the technology, set up so that all information points to its original source record. All the logic involved in updating a master record would take a book to describe. Highlighted are some important issues relating to updating a master file and the logic to consider in applying certain transactions.

The update process in general performs the following functions:

Generates the match code for the transactions and the master file to be used by the system for matching to identify duplicates.

Decides which records are duplicate names and which records are unique names.

Processes changes of address and changes the address of a master record.

Updates existing master records with new transaction data or creates new master records.

Applies transactions and merges master records. Master records are merged if two or more master records can become one master record as a result of such factors as change of address. The history related to each record is combined, and all transactional history is retained on that one surviving master record.

Create a variety of update reports or select new files. In a tape-processing environment, you would get a new updated master file. In a dynamic database environment, your master file would be updated as often as data entered the system.

There are some critical issues related to an updating system's capability and some issues related to the logic it uses. One such item is that when addresses are changed, it is important to allow the history to follow to that new location. Additionally, very often when a change of address occurs, there may be location-related information such as a phone number that should be reverified or deleted. It may be inappropriate to carry that old phone number to the new address without reverification.

Additionally, when processing delete transactions, don't physically delete the data. Consider that records be flagged or coded as deletes but not removed from the file for a specific period of time, perhaps 6 to 12 months. Very often a record might have moved and left no forwarding address, but a month or two later a change of address will come in. Now you have a record which can be reactivated and has not lost any of its history. Another reason for keeping records on the file is the history related to that record, even though it cannot be mailed. From a statistical point of view, if you're doing source analysis or other types of reporting, more complete statistical information would be available. A shortcoming of many list maintenance systems (primarily tape-oriented systems) is that there is a limit to the amount of information you can carry. These systems have fixed-length records and you are limited to the amount of data carried by the length of a record. Therefore, at some point you must delete or cumulate data but lose the specific detail. Most of these restrictions do not exist in a variable-length record environment or in a dynamic database environment.

Reviewing your data element checklist will give you a basis for reviewing how the update system you are using will handle each of those data elements in the update process.

USING THE DATABASE

This is the point when data becomes transformed into information. This is also usually where one or all of the following will happen:

You find now that you have so much data retention flexibility that you are developing uses for which you have not developed procedures or applications software.

You want to use certain data but neglected to include it in the database design.

You want to access the data for a variety of selections, reports, and what-if scenarios but have neglected to tell anybody or didn't realize you wanted to until you saw the richness of the information that you now have available.

The database master file will now have to be accessed for a variety of reasons. Typically those reasons are as follows:

To make selections for customer mailings

To make selections for statistical analysis

To score your customers using regression analysis techniques

To get reports of just about any type out of the database, more commonly known as ad hoc reporting.

To create what-if situations which help you decide who to mail what, when, and with what offer.

Each of these applications has their own logical needs. It's generally more cost-efficient to use leased software report packages or a high-level language like SAS to help in developing reports and manipulating the data. Often data is downloaded onto PCs from a mainframe so that multiple users can play with the data. Often at this point when the database is complete and people are now trying to access the data it becomes apparent that not enough consideration was given to specific applications.

Here are some basic lessons that I have learned from my past database development experiences.

The building of a database, which includes planning through to conclusion of the first update, usually takes twice as long as the original plan.

You cannot fully grasp the scope and complexity of the project until you're halfway through the project.

Developing your own system is always more expensive than buying or leasing, assuming you can get what you want from an outside vendor.

Companies fail in building their database because of politics, underestimating the scope of the project, reducing their commitment as time goes on, not having a true need, or not having the resources.

14
List
Segmentation

Barry Hauser

Barry Hauser & Associates
East Meadow, N.Y.

INTRODUCTION

The ability to specifically identify, qualify, promote to, and track individuals within the marketplace is at the very core of direct marketing. However, the process of communicating directly with individual consumers is an increasingly expensive one. Therefore, it is critically important to segment the market precisely in order to develop and maintain a profitable business. Poor list segmentation practices can undermine an otherwise powerful marketing program. While pinpoint targeting is an advantage of direct marketing media, it is also a mandatory skill—a two-edged sword in this respect.

The information universe continues to grow at a rapid rate, spurred on by conceptual and technological improvements in computer systems and media. These developments have made it practical to capture, retain, and exchange an increasing amount of data about individual consumers. The potential for effective use of the information has spawned major databases specifically created to support the direct marketer in further segmenting the market. This growth has expanded into industries previously considered to be outside the realm of traditional direct marketing, to the extent that there has been a redefinition of direct marketing versus marketing-at-large.

Conventional market segmentation is typically accomplished through analysis of industry statistics, census, and survey data. The basic tasks include sizing the overall industry, researching consumer needs and wants, and assessing market share of one's own company versus the competitors. However, the process of marketing to the consumer outside of direct marketing is largely at arm's length, through layers of wholesale and retail distribution.

Immediate and direct contact with the end consumer fosters availability of individual prospect and customer data, which, in turn, provides feedback to the marketing process with the information needed to promote new and repeat business. This is a highly detailed and ongoing segmentation function, not limited to an occasional research survey or special project to reassess the market.

A DEFINITION

List segmentation refers to the process of defining groups of individuals according to future potential response and profitability. It is an essential step in successfully targeting promotions to those most likely to buy. There are usually two distinctly different versions of the process, one for the customer list and another for list prospecting. Much of the difference has to do with the nature of the information available for the two.

THE BASICS

Segmenting Prospects

List rental prospects come "presegmented" to some extent. Heading the logical hierarchy is the source type, defined largely by the method of acquisition. These include:

Mail-order buyers: People who have actually bought something from a particular company.

Subscribers: Those who have subscribed to magazines, newspapers, or some form of service.

Retail and other buyers: These are typically compiled from warranty registration cards for appliances, etc.

Club members: Members of book and record clubs, etc.

Inquirers: Consumers who have requested catalogs or product information but have not actually purchased anything.

Compiled lists: Names gathered from phone and other directories, auto registrations, and any other preexisting source. These are frequently enhanced with demographics and overlay data to provide useful segmentation.

Survey and coupon databases: People who have responded to surveys or incentive offers specifically designed to generate names for rental.

Financial sources: Sources such as Equifax and TRW, which were originally designed for credit-screening purposes but have also provided names on a list rental basis.

Sweep No's: Consumers who have opted to enter sweepstakes without opting to order.

Of course, there is also the specific company source—company A, company B, etc. Further, there are more detailed segments as offered by the list owners and brokers such as 6-month repeat buyers, hot lines, product-oriented classifications, etc. These elements together form the traditionally defined segments of list prospecting, at the level of depth expressed on the brokers' list cards.

In recent years, list enhancement resources, such as demographic and psychographic overlays, credit screening, and other information-matching techniques have become more commonplace. Internally generated statistics are also used to improve segmentation of prospects. For example, previous mailing history can be applied to suppress prospect names which have been repeatedly promoted without a response. The coincidence of names between individual list sources and the customer list can be used to create valuable segmentation factors. This kind of information is often incorporated within a full-blown database marketing system.

Segmenting Customers

Customers, as distinct from prospects, are defined as those who have bought at least once in the past and are usually grouped according to purchasing history. The variables most often applied include recency of the last order, number of orders, product groups, amounts purchased, payment history, original list source, and customer service activity. While some of these variables parallel those used in list-prospecting segmentation, the information available for customers is generally more extensive, directly relevant to the immediate business, and higher in predictive power.

Customers are often subject to a primary split: one-time buyers versus repeat customers. For customers, the "magic number" appears to be two. A customer is not considered to be a real customer until a repeat purchase has been made. In some situations, the second order is called the "conversion." One-time buyers fall in the middle ground between prospects and repeat customers. While they reside on the customer file, relatively little data is available for them, and the segmentation design will generally reflect this. The one-time customer will be segmented primarily by the age of the order (recency) and the amount and type of purchase. They may also be clustered according to the type of original source, the number of mailing or telemarketing campaigns they received prior to ordering, credit factors, and so on.

Repeat customers, on average, have considerably more in the way of promotion and purchasing history as a basis for selection. The interval between the first and second orders tells much about the customer's propensity to buy, as does the number of promotion efforts. Beyond two orders, true frequency measures become increasingly effective.

List enhancement can also be of great value when applied to customer files, especially for large volumes of names with little history—old (nonrecent) one-time buyers, for example. There is a "theory of relativity" that applies to list segmentation: The less you know about a customer or prospect, or the more dated the information, the greater the potential for external data to be useful in identifying differences.

THE GOALS

Broadly stated, the aim of list segmentation is to determine which prospects and customers to promote, and when to promote them to achieve business objectives. Strategy may vary over time, and therefore the segmentation scheme should be flexible enough to handle the range of possibilities. At first, company objectives may center on building a large, highly responsive customer base as rapidly as possible. Later on, the focus will probably shift toward generating higher profit margins. In many businesses, it is virtually impossible to make a profit on the first sale, therefore the prospecting goal is to minimize the cost per order (or new customer acquisition cost) while maximizing the quality of the customers that are produced.

In promoting repeat business from customers, the goal is more often in the realm of profit taking rather than investment. However, the customer base also requires cultivation to maintain its vitality from year to year. This often calls for marginal promotions to certain groups of low-response customers to yield higher-quality upgraded names. Turning the house list this way is essential to maintaining its long-term value.

The ultimate, if imaginary, goal in list segmentation is to select only those people who will order. If only 4 percent of those mailed will order, then that group is ideally the only segment to promote. The trick is to weed out the 96 percent who will not respond. This is the Holy Grail of the list segmentation crusade. It is highly unlikely that it will ever be achieved.

CONSIDERATIONS IN SEGMENTATION DESIGN

Targeted Promotion Strategy

The task of list segmentation goes beyond answering the promote/don't-promote question. Fully expressed, the task is to determine who to promote, when, and with what marketing vehicle and offer. To fully realize the potential of the business, and support future business expansion, targeting strategy should be continuously and periodically overhauled.

On one dimension, there is the makeup of the list rental universe and customer base with all the relevant segmentation variables. Along another dimension is an array of environmental factors and potential marketing actions: promotion frequency, seasonal timing, the offer, media mix, and creative presentation.

Promotion Patterns

The "mailing pulse" or promotion schedule refers to the overall array of planned campaigns. For most direct marketing companies, this evolves over time based on the accumulation of a great deal of test results and experience. A major factor is seasonality—the best times of year to promote for a given product category. For example, August to October is a peak period for many catalogers. On the aggregate, potential response rates are highest at these times and therefore support peak promotion volumes.

Typically, all the viable list segments will receive primary seasonal campaign. All but the weakest live segments will get the second-strongest effort, and so on, down the line. The limit on the overall number of campaigns per year for a company is usually governed by the volume and response levels of the top-quality customers. For example, if you can identify 250,000 customers who can profitably sustain 10 mailings per year, then the tenth mailing is justified if 250,000 is a practical level for creative and production economics. If not, the total number of campaigns might be set at nine, or fewer. In this example, the various customer list segments would be scheduled for anywhere from one to ten mailings per year.

When planning customer campaigns, it is important to view response by segment over a 6- to 12-month period, or even longer. When a particular segment is given an additional mailing, there is a ripple effect. The added promotion effort negatively affects response in the following efforts. Not all of the response of the added mailing is incremental to the business. A large part of what initially appears to be added business may represent sales which have merely been displaced to an earlier point in time, from one promotion to another. Some marketers refer to this effect with the colorful term "cannibalization."

Segmentation design should be relevant to both the global marketing environment and the nature of the customer base. The greatest part of the precision should be placed where the weight of the promotion frequency decisions are likely.

To be effective, segmentation should be sensitive to response differences, yet consistent and stable enough to support accurate planning. For example, in the attempt to be superselective, a segmentation scheme can be overly aggressive in detail, resulting in the formation of many small cells (under 5000 in volume). The statistical noise level inherent in these unstable readings will tend to undermine the attempt at precision.

Planning

Segmentation is integral to the planning process for direct marketing campaigns. Therefore, an essential consideration is the practicality of the segmentation system where planning is concerned. In other words, effective segmentation thrives on planning accuracy as much as it does on raw sophistication. Two or more alternative levels of detail may be needed—one for planning, one for execution, and perhaps yet another for analysis after the fact. Of key importance in planning is the ability to accurately predict volumes as well as response levels. Volume forecasting typically does not assume the equivalency concept that applies to predicting response levels. Equivalent list segments do not necessarily materialize at consistent volume levels year-to-year. Information such as input from list owners and brokers, order volumes, transaction volumes, and so on must serve as vital factors in forecasting volumes.

The importance of accurate volume forecasting cannot be overstated. An otherwise sophisticated segmentation design can be seriously flawed with respect to volume planning support or poor forecasting methods. This can result in some very nasty surprises. For example, you might need to backfill a campaign with weak segments because the actual volume selected was lower than expected. On the other hand, when volume exceeds expectations, this signifies lost opportunity. Volume variances, and the quick fixes needed to counter them, can defeat a large measure of segmentation effectiveness.

Practical Aspects of Segmentation

There are important practical considerations in segmentation design. One concerns the sheer number of segments that can be effectively handled. Capacity tends to increase over time with enhancements in computer resources. However, statistical confidence is a factor, no matter how many segments can be physically tracked and forecasted. If the system produces segments of very low volume, the response readings will not be reliable over time.

One saving grace: In the process of creating segments, or cells, we have many surrounding cells that are related, so "flukes" or "sports" can be weeded out or smoothed over to read through the noise level. In addition, the results can be summarized to the next level up, providing the segments were keyed appropriately or a database system permits resegmenting on a post hoc basis. Therefore, we can work to segment volumes lower than the minimums required for promotional testing.

The Human Factor

Another consideration in designing and working with a segmentation system is the human factor—the ability of your company to work with the information. On some level, dry data should be translated into flesh-and-blood descriptions. This allows the creative group to communicate with the numbers marketers well enough to productively interact—to more fully participate and take advantage of the knowledge base. Parameters built into the design should embrace creative and product factors. The creators of the promotion should be able to understand the makeup of the prospecting and customer base. Segmentation groupings and descriptions should support meaningful dialogue and exchange of ideas.

SEGMENTATION DYNAMICS

Correlations

Segmentation variables tend to be correlated. If you mix enough variables together, you'll see that many are redundant and that the principle of diminishing returns materializes. Those very redundancies may tell you something.

Therefore, the benefits are not simply additive. If one parameter discriminates to the extent of 10 percent and another, when independently measured, yields 5 percent, using both will produce a combined discrimination of something less than 15 percent.

Changes in the promotional environment can occasionally be profound enough to upset the constancy of selection variables. These might include low-ticket introductory offers, sweepstakes, massive changes to promotion schedules, and so on. While some variables will be immune, others, such as monetary (dollar amount purchased) can become inconsistent with history. For example, a low-cost introductory offer can dramatically change the definition of a one-time buyer. When a major promotional or environmental change is anticipated, additional segmentation may be needed to prepare for the probable impact.

The Equivalence Assumption

In order to plan effectively, we need to be able to rely on a high degree of constancy. The basic presumption is that list segments equivalently defined will perform at the same response level from one year to the next. Recency is the lynchpin of equivalence. For example, everything else being equal, 1-year-old customers should perform at the same level from year to year. The quality of 60-day hot lines from a particular source should respond consistently from one year to the next (unless an up or down trend is evident). Table 14-1 shows a simple illustration for customer segments.

The response of this 1-year-old group indexes at 100 from year to year. However, the 3/93 group on a same-segment basis "rolls off" from 100 to 80 from year to year. Of course, there are many other elements to consider, but the basic presumption is that names of equivalent age will perform equivalently. Most other segmentation variables can be dealt with on an absolute basis. Some, however, need to be updated or indexed to maintain equivalence. For example, any dollar definitions need adjustment for inflation periodically. Planning adjustments are needed to account for changing conditions and mailing patterns.

To take advantage of the equivalence principle in planning and analysis, it is very important to build the overall segmentation system with this in mind. List segments should be consistently defined from year to year to permit direct comparison and scaling. The same applies to list rental prospects, although repeat mailing dynamics, for the most part, do not apply.

Roll-off Dynamics

Customer segments vary in terms of their sustained response levels over repeated mailings. At one point, two different segments may respond at the same level; however, the response of one may drop off by 20 percent and the other by 35 percent in the next campaign.

Table 14-1. Customer Segmentation

| Campaign | October 1994 | | October 1995 | |
	Last order	Response index	Last order	Response index
Segment A	3/93	100	3/94	100
Segment B	3/92	80	3/93	80

Profiles of Names: The List Mix

The volume patterns of customers and prospects by segment, in and of them-selves, provide a major indicator of business conditions. Any trends in the vol-umes of major groups—in addition to their response levels—can have an im-pact. Therefore, the segmentation design you employ also should serve as a research and strategy tool. It can make sense to add additional variables, or seg-mentation within existing variables, to further support strategic decision mak-ing, even though this may be unnecessary for direct use in the actual selection process.

In Table 14-2 list volume forecasts were made to determine trends by quality level of customers. The news was not good. What is the impact? Table 14-2 shows what can happen if we assume that the relative performance for the groups will remain constant—indexed at 150, 100, and 75.

This change in the mix implies a 5 percent drop in overall response for future campaigns.

RFM

For many years recency, frequency, and monetary factors have been the main-stay of direct marketing segmentation. In simple terms the key factors are how recently the customer last ordered, how frequently he or she has ordered in the past, and how much was purchased. The basic presumption is an empirical one: People behave consistently with their past behavior. Of course, customers change over time, but slowly enough that their purchasing history is an accurate basis for predictions. The approach taken by the direct marketing industry is not unlike that of the experimental psychologists who employ the scientific method and statistical analysis.

The following is a brief summary of some of the many customer variables in current use:

Recency: Most often, recency is driven by the date of the last order, but can also apply to other transactions as well. For example, older customers who have recently placed an inquiry or a sweeps entry may be more responsive than those who have not.

Frequency: Technically, frequency refers to orders placed over time; how-

Table 14-2. Trends by Quality Level of Customer

	Year 1		Year 2	
Quality level	% of volume	Response index	% of volume	Response index
High	25%	150	17%	150
Mid	50%	100	55%	100
Low	25%	50	28%	50
Overall	100%	100	100%	95

ever, there is a great deal of variety in the operational definitions actually used. It is important to set the time slice for the frequency definition. The simplest is lifetime frequency—the number of orders placed since the customer started. However, consumers' buying habits are subject to change, so it usually makes sense to place an age limit on the measure—for example, orders placed in the last 5 years. Frequency can also be inverted and viewed in terms of time intervals between orders.

Monetary: Customers vary in terms of amounts purchased. This can be grossly defined as total lifetime purchases or applied to a timing or number-of-orders cutoff, for example, average amount purchased in the 3 years ending with the last order, or average purchased for the last three orders. If measured in currency, monetary factors need to be periodically adjusted for inflation and changes in offers. To avoid this, an alternative parameter can be devised, and these seem to discriminate every bit as well as, if not better than, raw dollars. For example, some catalogers use number of line items per order as a measure of order size.

Historical response or profitability: In some ways a derivation of frequency, this measurement takes the number of prior promotions into account. How customers perform is not only the result of their inherent propensity to respond, but is also governed by the number of opportunities to order that their history reflects. This can be defined as orders over efforts: in effect, an individual response rate. To incorporate order size, currency or number of items purchased can be used in the equation. Again, as with the other variables, it makes sense to apply time slices to qualify the data. Promotion schedules and patterns change over time, such that long-term customer history can reflect a distorted amalgam of old and new situations.

There are many additional segmentation possibilities, which are dependent on the specific business and market. For example:

Payment history: Many of the primary variables in use for selecting customers for promotions are front end-oriented. Where the company offers credit, payment history is also important in using segmentation to control profitability.

Customer service activity: In most cases, a complaint well handled is a positive indicator and may identify customers with response rates higher than those of their basic segment. However, as with all selection variables, this needs to be tested and verified. It may be necessary to cluster this activity by type of customer service transaction to make it useful as a selection tool.

List coincidence: The fact that subsets of customers appear on outside lists can be useful in segmenting them. This data may be captured as part of merge-purge processing. One caveat: It is important to consider list rental agreements in capturing any of this data. Often, simply generalizing list identification is sufficient to comply.

Product and offer type: Where there is a variety of product choices or offer types, these can be important factors. For example, customers who respond to introductory offers, deep discounts, or premium offers may not be as responsive in the future as those who buy with less inducement or incentives. Many catalogers have a variety of books with differing emphasis or product selections. It makes sense to identify customers by product types purchased and therefore have the ability to custom-select for each campaign.

ANALYSIS AND TESTING

Statistical Technology

Just a few selection criteria with several ranges each can produce hundreds, if not thousands, of segments. For example, 10 recency levels by 6 frequency levels by 5 monetary/line item levels would produce 300 segments. Add another five-level variable and there will be a total of 1500 segments. While this example reflects customer selection, a similar progression in the segment counts also applies to prospecting.

While it may be practical to manually track and plan 1 to 200 segments, it becomes increasingly difficult to work with much more than that before some computerized assistance is needed. Complex segmentation designs also call for more advanced statistical methods. A wide range of approaches and techniques are currently applied to the statistical and planning requirements of list segmentation.

The simplest general approach is to define the groups and individually track and project them. Response forecasting is accomplished by viewing the history and projecting it forward in time, typically on a straight-line basis. Volume forecasting may apply order volume projections and input from list owners. This process can be computer-aided with spreadsheets or a database management system on the PC or a custom system on the mainframe. However, what is in common to the variations is that the individual segments are previously and constantly defined. Most often, someone is viewing and deliberating on all of the data at the maximum level of detail.

A logical extension of this approach is the computer model. Usually there are separate models for the customer and prospecting bases. In effect, the task of dealing with all of the segmentation data is highly automated. A truly sophisticated modeling system goes beyond simple percentage scaling and may incorporate regression techniques and complex mathematical sequences to handle the effects of changing mailing schedules, etc.

On a somewhat different tack is the indexing method. These should be based on a thorough statistical workup involving multiple regression and other multivariate techniques (which are beyond the scope of this chapter). Factors are developed to represent the implications of every applicable criteria. Based on this factoring, clustering of customers and prospects are rated, as expressed by an index which translates to relative response. The names are then selected according to index scores. While indexing systems offer a way to deal with many variables and gradations, they can be tricky. With certain schemes, equal indexes can be generated for very different kinds of people when their response levels are projected to coincide. If something happens to change the assumption base, and the indexing system lacks provision to detect it, this can result in a massive error in selection. When building systems of this kind, it is critically important to go the full distance in providing the special analysis and planning support tools that are needed.

Statistical tools used to analyze segmentation and response data range from simple correlations to multiple regression, TREE, AID/CHAID, and factor and cluster analysis. It makes sense to run a sophisticated analysis of this type periodically, to support general marketing strategy development as well as input to segmentation design. It pays to know as much about your customers and prospects as possible. However, when conducting a project of this kind, know-how is very important. Statistical analysis software packages available today make it possible to run complex analyses without much knowledge of what the various procedures mean. In some cases, the cookbook approach to higher statistics can produce results that are dangerously misleading.

Another potential problem with sophistication in segmentation is the increasing distance it can place between marketing management and the analysis, planning, and actual selection processes. The worst manifestation of this is the black-box effect: No one truly knows how the system works. However, the great potential for improvement in segmentation makes this a problem well worth solving.

List Testing

List testing takes two different forms for customers and prospects. For the latter, this means renting an nth name sample of the list rental offering and merge-purging it into a mailing or phone campaign. Although there are formal statistical methods for determining minimum volume to test, the actual number is mitigated by budgetary, practical, and risk constraints. The first result can be evaluated before the campaign is launched — how the test list duplicated against other lists, the customer base, and any suppress files. These hit rates will be understated for small samples at first; however, they can serve as a pre-roll-out indication. Where prospects are concerned, a large part of the evaluation concerns to what degree the addition of the source will be truly incremental to the prospecting program. Then the front- and back-end response rates are evaluated when the results come in. On a longer-term basis, assuming the list goes to higher roll-out volumes, a full source analysis should be run several years after the fact to determine the number and quality of customers produced, that is, the long-term profitability of the source.

There are additional variations on this theme. For example, the list can be tested with and without enhancements. One major consideration in prospect list testing is the merge-purge logic of the system. Many systems employ the hierarchical concept in which higher-ranked lists get credit for any duplicates between lists. The customer list is given the highest rank, followed by the best outside source, followed by the next best list, etc. The rationale for the hierarchy is that the duplicates among the better lists would mail even if the lower-ranked list were eliminated. Therefore, the higher-ranked list deserves full credit.

While this approach makes sense, it is, to some extent, a circular and self-fulfilling prophecy. Prospects that turn up on two or more lists at the same time tend to be higher in performance than otherwise similar names. By virtue of higher positioning in the hierarchy, a given list will arbitrarily receive credit for more of these names. When testing a list, it must be placed *somewhere* in the hierarchy to start, even before anything is known about its quality.

A solution to this problem is found in the practice of additionally reading results by list source for unique names only. Better still is a system that will provide a full cross-tabulation of interlist duplicates. Periodic analysis of this kind should be conducted to validate positioning of a hierarchical system. Some merge-purge systems prorate credit for duplicates among the lists that share a multihit name. That avoids one problem in exchange for others. In any event, it is important to recognize the influence of merge-purge logic in list test results.

Customer list testing takes another form. Although historical results may exist for all segments for a single campaign, some repeat-mailing situations may have no historical base at all. In other words, if a segment has not been mailed in a particular slot before, extra steps are needed to forecast response. If the group in question is closely related to segments that have been promoted before, then a reasonable estimate can be developed by projecting from known segments. However, a major change in selection should be based on testing to minimize risk. To provide for future opportunities, it is wise to have an ongoing program of customer list testing. This is accomplished by including test segments in virtually every customer campaign, partly to provide a basis for future projections and partly as a back-test of existing selections. Test segments should be chosen which are solidly outside the realm of the standard selection but not so out of range that their low response would represent a major cost. Information can be maximized while minimizing cost by using nth-name selections rather than full-scale segment volumes.

Sourcing

List-prospecting economics are frequently evaluated based on front-end response versus promotion cost. The factors typically include consideration of list rental fees, processing costs, promotional materials, and postage, as well as bad debt loss, order processing, and other direct expenses. However, to fully evaluate and compare various prospecting sources, what really counts is the long-term perspective. Sourcing, in the context used here, refers to the tracking of profitability over a number of years, based not only on front-end response but also on the volume and future productivity of customers that are generated. The basic questions are:

How many viable customers were initially produced up front at what acquisition cost?

What was the profile of quality of those customers?

How many repeat orders were generated?

How many efforts were required to generate those repeat orders?

What was the profit per customer after acquisition costs are deducted?

Depending upon the specific business situation, sourcing is performed on a 5-year basis or longer. It takes a number of years for the information to mature and the differences to surface. A sourcing analysis of this type can produce a

wide range of results. The long-term profitability of a list source may correspond to its relative front-end performance — or it might not. What appears to
be a mediocre list source may well prove to generate exceptional customers, or
the reverse could be true. What you might find is that the long-term list hierarchy is directionally consistent with front-end response; however, it shows a
wider or narrower range.

On one side of the dynamic, higher-response lists simply produce more customers per thousand prospects promoted. This influences the long term. On
the other side, targeting promotions to customers may tend to have a leveling
effect, effectively counterbalancing and thereby reducing much of the long-
term differences between the various lists and media sources. Surprises are not
uncommon.

Database and systems design should provide the extra measure of customer
history necessary to P & L sources over the long run. Obviously, to support this,
the system should capture original list or media source identification for each
customer. In addition, repeat promotion and cumulative response data are also
necessary.

The whole process of sourcing also relates to the task of determining the lifetime value of a name. Each name added to the customer base has a future value
in terms of long-term profit. When you perform a full financial sourcing analysis, the productivity for all sources combined yields the value of a name added
to the customer inventory as of a given point in time. That valuation is then
projected forward in time, adjusted for inflation in sales and costs, and net
present value mathematics, to provide a more relevant current number. This is
used as a guide to determine reasonable acquisition cost goals and as a general
barometer of the health of the company.

A full-blown sourcing analysis views customers as of various stages to track
any trends that may be developing. These are usually performed on an annual
basis. If results indicate that the overall value of a name is declining, this signifies serious implications for the long-term outlook for the company. In some
cases, this may reflect expansion, with the introduction of lower-quality customers at the bottom of the spectrum. Conversely, stable or increasing valuations
indicate a solid future base.

DATABASES AND DATABASE MARKETING

In one sense, the technology of list segmentation has grown to become an even
larger part of direct marketing and is evolving into a new marketing form altogether. Development of promotional strategy and the very running of the business has become customer-driven rather than product-driven.

This concept is mixed up with some unclear notions revolving around the
much-abused term *database*. This means different things in different circles —
but all are connected to the developmental windstorm of the last decade. Each
of the alternative meanings are important to us, if confusing at times.

The broadest definition simply refers to any body of information. In this context using the term database occasionally qualifies mere word magic. Your

Rolodex file is a database. The ABC Hot Lines List became a database overnight.

Another meaning refers to the process of gathering valuable information for its own sake, for example, for sale. These applications include consumer and industrial databases such as Compuserve, Lexus, Nexus, Census Data, etc. Essentially, the distinctive value is that these are all available in computerized form, usually on-line for instant access with frequent, if not continuous updating. This has real meaning for direct marketers in the sense of increased opportunity for practical use of existing information...and the availability of *new* forms of information. Some of these involve psychographic or demographic data; others represent behavioral data such as coupon redemption, or surveys, specifically designed to generate useful prospecting and segmentation data.

The most intense rendition of the term occurs within computer technology. There are various kinds of data storage and retrieval systems, the most popular of which is now the relational database management system. In simple terms, these systems have the logic and wherewithal built in to handle relationships between various types of data. They usually go hand-in-hand with fourth-generation computer languages (4GLs), which essentially meet the programmer and user more than halfway in systems development and ad hoc inquiries. The roots of this technology, which span more than two decades, apply to a broader range of administrative, industrial, and scientific applications—from the IRS to NASA. However, it has special significance for direct marketers. Along with the increases in raw computing power at lower cost, relational database techniques make it possible to more effectively cope with large volumes of data at various levels of detail.

Database marketing embraces practically all of these meanings and goes a step further. The marketing strategy of the company now emerges from the process of capturing, assembling, compiling, analyzing, and modeling a large array range of consumer data from multiple sources. Markets are identified and "mined" from this amalgam of information. In effect, the long-term strategy of the company becomes customer-and market-driven rather than purely product-driven. In an aggressive database marketing environment, the questions What business *are* we in? and What businesses *should we go into?* are asked more frequently.

THE FUTURE OF SEGMENTATION

In many ways, the technological basis for the future is already with us. Many of the building blocks exist and are in use in one form or another. The rate of progress is dependent more on the speed of refinement and integration of the tools, rather than the outright inauguration of new ones.

For example, the means for targeted, personalized promotion mailings and telemarketing scripting are available in the form of ink jet imaging, laser printing, and sophisticated phone support systems. High-volume laser printing is available only in monochrome; however, ongoing improvements in color xerography will change this within a few years. It will then become practical to target graphics as well as copy to the various customer and prospect segments within a campaign. Currently, the outcome of creative tests are usually decided based on the "greatest good." The package that wins on an overall basis may not be the strongest for all recipients. With this degree of segmented marketing, it becomes possible to optimize the "hot buttons" for diverse groups of consumers.

While much is said about fourth-generation database management systems (4GL/DBMSs), there are a number of serious limitations. All of the increased capability comes at a price—generally slower performance than custom-refined third-generation systems. While current DBMSs may be fine for analysis, they can present throughput problems when applied to production volumes. At least two things will serve to overcome this. The major software suppliers are developing high-speed transactional modules to streamline their systems. Secondly, continuing improvements in the hardware technology will provide the raw processing capability that is needed.

Artificial intelligence (AI) software is still in its infancy. However, it could have a major impact on segmentation in the not-too-distant future. AI techniques can be employed to maximize the value of statistical information in automating the selection of individuals for promotions. Fuller implementation will allow the system to "learn" from its own "experience" and make course corrections for future campaigns.

Even now, as this is written, it's possible to run a state-of-the-art merge-purge on a laptop computer in flight at 30,000 feet (not that you would *want* to do this). The same database and high-level statistical software can be installed on your mainframe, minicomputer, or desktop PC, and these can be configured to work together as part of a distributed system. A wealth of segmentation data can be captured via Touch-Tone responses through ACD equipment. These are impressive capabilities, yet all of these examples already qualify as "old technology." Of course, the technology is old as soon as the ink is dry on the first batch of brochures.

The real challenge to advancing the art and science of list segmentation lies in learning to assemble and profitably apply the tools we already have, as well as those which are yet to come.

15
List Processing

Arthur Blumenfield

Blumenfield Marketing Inc.
Stamford, Conn.

Today's direct marketer has to deal with a number of economic pressures. Almost every cost involved in selling a product or service has continued to rise. Postal increases, higher printing costs, growing costs for labor and all of the other costs of doing business are putting increased pressure on the bottom line. As a result, if there ever was a motivation for efficient list processing, today's economy provides ample reason for doing so.

The days of simply capturing, storing, and using names and addresses in a helter-skelter fashion are gone. A simple mailing list can be a liability rather than an asset. In this day and age, you have to think in terms of a database which retains not only name-and-address data but also sufficient information to permit the intelligent use of the file.

Fortunately, the development of the computer has more than kept pace with the other changes that have taken place in the direct marketing industry. Today's hardware and software make it possible to capture, store, and retrieve the data that is so vital to successful direct marketing.

To fully appreciate the concept of utilizing a database, it is useful to imagine yourself as a 12-year-old setting out to sell magazine subscriptions to your neighbors.

You might start at one end of your street and go to each house in sequence. However, you know that Ms. Smith goes to work and her mother (who doesn't speak English) is home, so you skip that house. Ms. Jones just bought a subscription from you a month ago, so it's unlikely she'll buy another now. Mr. Brown is only interested in fixing cars, so he won't be interested in the type of magazine you are selling. So, armed with this knowledge, you pick and choose your prospects. And, because you know something about each one, you alter your sales pitch to try to appeal to their specific needs and desires.

In effect, this is what we try to do with database marketing. By providing as much information as possible, we try to let the computer decide which of the records on the file are likely prospects. We also can attempt to use what we know to alter our offer so as to enhance our success rate.

Improving this response rate is accomplished by trying to identify those characteristics that seem to point to both recipients who will respond and nonresponders. Then, using this information, one would mail to as many of the positives as possible while eliminating the negatives.

Therefore, the function of good list processing is to provide the data, hardware, software, and techniques to permit this to be done.

In the past, databases of any significant size were maintained on mainframe computers. However, the developments in the computer field have advanced to the stage where it is possible (and practical) to have large databases on every type of hardware ranging from desktop PCs to huge mainframes. The concepts and techniques are fundamentally the same no matter what type of hardware is used. The capacity of the particular system will determine the amounts of data that can be stored and the speed with which it can be retrieved.

WHAT DATA SHOULD BE CAPTURED?

Database decisions are based upon the information that is available about each person, household, company, etc., on your file. Much of this data is entered by you. Some of it is added (overlaid) from other data sources. Other data might be implied.

When determining what data should be captured and retained, it is important to consider the following points:

- Will this data be of value, either now or in the future?
- Could I add this data at a later date?
- Is the data time-sensitive?
- Is there a privacy risk (might the data be misused)?
- Can the data become wrong (like a married person getting divorced)?
- Is the data objective or subjective?
- In what form will the data be most useful?

DATA ENTRY

The process of entering data into a computer has changed as direct marketing has matured. With current computer hardware, data entry can be made faster and more accurate. Accuracy (particularly in the address data) is extremely important since those mailing pieces directed to addresses which contain even minor addressing errors or omissions are often not delivered. Consequently, any steps that can be taken to ensure accuracy and completeness in the recording of addresses will pay large dividends as the record is used and reused.

Where the data being entered is handwritten (as is the case on many coupons), errors can easily crop up. In some cases, these can be eliminated by referring to accompanying data. For example, if a check is enclosed, the name and address are often printed on the check. Here are some suggestions as to things to consider when entering name and address data.

Name

Name data includes the prefix (Mr., Mrs., Ms., Dr., Rev., etc.), given name and/ or initials, surname and suffix (Jr., M.D., etc.). Besides the obvious irritation that misspelling of a person's name will cause, there are a number of factors that should also be considered regarding this data.

The prefix not only is useful for sending personalized mailings but also permits the determination of the gender of the individual. However, since there are numerous gender-neutral prefixes (like Dr., Captain, The Honorable, Senator, etc.), it is a good idea to record the gender of the person in a separate field to the degree possible. Genderization can be done fairly accurately by computer (by referring to files of names that are coded as male or female). However, it is often as accurate (and as fast) to have the male/female/unknown code determined by the operator and entered.

It is uncommon today to find situations where the retention of initials only rather than the given name is more practical. The most common form of this data is the retention of the first name and any middle initials.

Suffix data (Jr., M.D., etc.) is an important element of a correctly addressed mailing piece and should be kept in a separate field so that it will not "tag along" with the surname in those cases where personalization is used.

Another factor to be considered in the entry of this data is whether to enter it in UPPER CASE or Upper and Lower case. It takes more time (and is more error-prone) to use upper-lower case, but if you are going to print personalized letters or similar documents in the future, this is a pertinent consideration. It is possible to convert from all upper case to upper/lower by computer. The accuracy of these conversions is very high (better than 98 percent) except for company names on which the accuracy varies to as low as 80 percent. Keep in mind that a computer program cannot know whether MacDonald or Macdonald is the preferred or whether MR. OHARA is Irish (O'Hara) or Japanese (Ohara).

Many computer programs utilize some of the name data to permit an operator to retrieve a desired record to the screen. If this is the case, the way in which the data is to be stored must take into consideration the retrieval capabilities of the hardware and software. For example, if your retrieval routines are case-sensitive, they will not find MacDonald if you enter Macdonald. Where this is the case, it is sometimes practical to store an all-caps version of the name in the record and use that field for retrieval purposes. (Conversion to all caps is 100 percent accurate!)

Company Name

The most significant problem associated with the entry of company names is their length. While the computer programming can be set up to store company names of any length, one is often faced with the restrictions imposed by the size of standard address labels. Even though you may not utilize these, it is worthwhile to consider their size since others using your file (list renters, swappers, etc.) may do so.

Standard mailing labels have a restriction of 31 characters per line (when printed at 10 characters per inch, which is the most common print density). Therefore, most name-and-address formats try to limit the length of the name-and-address lines to 30 characters.

Company names longer than 30 characters can be made to fit by abbreviating some of the words (be sure to use proper abbreviations: for example, Assoc., not Ass.). In those cases where abbreviation does not work, the splitting of the company name into two lines is an alternative.

If you provide for this capability, it is often most efficient to permit the operator to enter the entire company name as one long field and have the computer break it into two lines. Also, remember to have the routines that print the address "squeeze out" the second line if it is unused (as well as any other unused address lines) to avoid blank lines in the middle of the name-and-address block.

Street Address

The importance of thoroughness and accuracy of this element cannot be stressed enough. The U.S. Postal Service has indicated that problems in this element of the address cause the bulk of the nondelivery problems. It is important to understand and follow the U.S. Postal Service rules and use only their approved formats and abbreviations when entering address lines.

One complication that affects your ability to comply with these rules is that the data you are entering is supplied by the respondee, who does not know what the rules are. In many cases, people write their address down in a form that is undeliverable. So it is important to build your computer programs and train your operators to recognize these incorrect elements and correct them to the degree possible. Standard abbreviations should be used wherever possible. More sophisticated computer systems can be programmed to recognize the "invalid" versions and automatically replace them.

The design of your order form or coupon can often enhance your chances of getting better data. For example, the Postal Service requests apartment numbers for multifamily dwellings. By specifically asking for this data (and providing a space for it), you can ensure that you will get this data more frequently. Also, provide sufficient space on the coupon or order form for the various elements. All too often the space provided for one or more of the address items is much too small for the data that must be written there.

City, State, and Zip Code

Errors in the city and state fields can often be eliminated by entering the zip code and letting the computer supply the city and state from a file (which is available from the Postal Service). If using this technique, it is a good idea to have the operator enter one or two characters of the city name from the input document and have the computer compare those against the corresponding characters in the city name supplied by the computer. This will help to prevent the errors which would otherwise occur if the operator enters the zip code wrong (or if the respondee has written a wrong zip code on the coupon).

In those cases where the respondee is using an alternative (but acceptable) city name, the computer can be programmed to permit the operator to override the computer and input the respondee's data.

This approach not only reduces the number of entry keystrokes (as well as entry time) but also ensures a very high degree of accuracy in the data as well as compliance with Postal Service standards.

If your computer has sufficient data storage capacity, you can load the full zip+4 file. This will enable the computer to determine the full 9-digit zip code for most of your entries. It will also identify some addresses as being invalid, thereby helping you find some data entry errors.

If your computer system has very limited capacity and cannot hold the zip/city name file (which contains about 40,000 entries), you can still program it to verify that the zip code you enter falls within the range for the state.

Country

It is becoming increasingly common to have to handle foreign addresses. Therefore, the provision of a separate data field for the country name (blank for the United States) is often worthwhile. Keep in mind that the way the city/state/zip line is formatted varies from country to country. If you anticipate having significant foreign volume, you should take this into consideration.

ADDITIONAL DATA ELEMENTS

In addition to the name and address, there are a number of other data elements that should be considered for inclusion in the database. Some of these can be captured at entry time. Others are generated by the computer system as a by-product of other tasks. While these vary from project to project, they often include several of the following:

Entry Date

This can be automatically supplied by the computer. It serves a number of purposes, not the least of which is to provide a starting point for various marketing computations. The date on which a customer's first contact took place is used in many ways in database marketing techniques.

Source Code

The source code is the code of the effort that stimulated each response, order, inquiry, etc. (also known as the key code).

Type of Remittance

The method by which a payment is made (personal check, company check, money order, credit card, etc.).

Telephone and Fax Numbers

The uses for telephone numbers would seem quite obvious. They not only provide a means for contacting an individual to resolve a problem, but are increasingly being used for outbound telemarketing efforts. The enormous growth of fax installations has made it quite practical to capture fax numbers as a potential marketing tool.

Recency, Frequency, Money

These criteria have been used by direct marketers for many years to select or reject individual records for specific marketing efforts. In their simplest form, they require the retention of the date of a customer's most recent order, the total number of purchases they have made to date, and the monetary total of the purchases.

However, by capturing more detailed information about each order or promotional effort, the selection process can be far more effective. Remember, decisions can only be made on the basis of the information available. The more information that can be considered, the better the selection capability.

Detailed Sales Information

The details of each sale (or inquiry) provide important information. In the case of sales, this data would include the date of the sale, the items ordered, the amounts involved, and the source code of the offer that prompted the order.

Detailed Promotion History

It is often useful to record how many times an individual record is selected for a promotional effort, the type of promotion sent, the date, and the costs of the promotions.

Please note that by keeping track of the money spent in promoting to an individual and comparing that to the revenue received from that individual, decisions can be made as to whether or not to continue to send what appear to be marginally effective promotions.

Transaction History

In addition to sales and promotional data, there are a number of other transactions that can add to the decision-making process. These include returns, bad checks, claims of payment or nonreceipt, and complaints (correspondence). This information, whose primary purpose is often to support customer service, can also be used in constructing the selection algorithms.

DATA OVERLAYS

Significant information can be added to the data you capture. This addition is done by matching the data on your file to that on large marketing databases and, when matches are found, adding the information contained in those databases to your file.

Several organizations offer these list-enhancement services. The data they can provide can range from simple things like telephone numbers, numbers of children, and types of cars owned, all the way to detailed profiles of the individuals, including estimated income, education level, hobbies, particular lifestyle characteristics, magazines read, product preferences, and so on.

Other service companies have developed methods for grouping individuals into homogeneous groupings that are more meaningful than those used by the Census Bureau. This coding can be added to your file. Then, by measuring the effectiveness of your efforts on these different groups, you can imply that other groups that share the same characteristics might react similarly.

For business addresses, it is often useful to add such information as SIC code, number of employees, annual revenue, and so forth.

In summary, it makes sense to explore the various data overlays that are available for your file and determine which of them make sense to pursue.

SELECTIONS

Given the complexity of the data that one has to work with, the task of making selections from the database is no longer a simple one.

In the past, when we had very little data to consider, a selection could be specified quickly and often with nothing more sophisticated than good seat-of-the-pants judgment.

While that kind of selection can still be done, today's economics call for something far more involved. Sophisticated computer analysis programs are available that can read through the data you have accumulated and generate statistics, which can then be used to create the selection algorithm.

Using techniques like multiple-regression analysis, cluster analysis, and similar methodologies, it is sometimes possible to determine some criteria which, by their presence, seem to indicate that the individual is more likely to be a buyer or, conversely, a nonresponder. A further description of these techniques will be found elsewhere in this book.

However, these selections can only be as good as the available data permits. And it is through proper list-processing procedures that you will build and maintain your list in a manner that facilitates this selection process.

MERGE AND PURGE

Our office often receives calls from individuals who have decided that they no longer want to receive any more advertising mail (they use a somewhat different term for it). They ask to be deleted from "The List." Their assumption is that there is just one list somewhere and if they get their name off it, all of those envelopes and catalogs will stop coming. (We refer them to the DMA's Mail Preference Service.)

However, there are very few mailings today that use just one list. And when more than one list is used, the likelihood is that there will be a degree of overlap (duplication) between the lists.

This duplication factor is, obviously, a waste. In addition, it creates a very unfavorable impression, particularly in this day and age where ecology has become an important consideration.

That is where the technique referred to as merge-purge comes in. This computer technique reads in all of the records from all of the mailing lists that are to be used for a given mailing and identifies the duplicate names and addresses.

It isn't as simple as it sounds. The programs that do this task have become increasingly sophisticated over the years and can now be said to be one of the leading areas where artificial intelligence is utilized.

There are a number of computer service companies that offer this service. In addition to identifying the duplicated records, these systems turn out reports which provide important and valuable information regarding the files they have processed.

In addition, some of these service companies can simultaneously match the addresses against the Postal Service's National Change of Address (NCOA) file. This permits the computer to automatically identify households that have moved and provide either the new address or indicate that there is no forwarding address. In either case, a mailing to a nonexistent address is eliminated.

Even though these systems are highly capable, their accuracy and thoroughness is increased if your list is maintained and supplied properly.

For example, they all work by breaking apart a name and address into its various elements and then analyzing those. These elements include the first and last name, house numbers, street names, and zip codes. So to make your list as easy to work with as possible, it should be maintained in such a way as to make it easy to locate and extract these elements.

Keeping the first name, last name, and zip code in separate fields is easy. However, it is in the address area that attention should be paid.

The most important thing to consider is consistency. Where there are multiple address lines, try to always enter the street address on the same line all the time. Don't put it on one line in one record, then another in the next record.

For example, if you allow two address lines, skip the first line if only one address line is required. Use the first line for company names, care-of addresses, etc. The computer can be programmed to squeeze out the blank line when printing the address.

The reasons for this care become evident when you examine the process that is involved in a merge-purge run.

The first step involves getting all the various names and addresses standardized into a common format and then into some specific sequence. This conversion process is one of the most difficult steps in the procedure. It is not uncommon for the various lists included in the program to have widely varying characteristics. For example, they may have been produced on different computer hardware and as a result have different technical specifications (800, 1600, or 6250 bytes per inch; ASCII or EBCDIC coding; etc.).

In addition, the way the data are recorded on the file (the format) usually varies from file to file. As a result, fairly sophisticated programming often is needed to permit the location and extraction of the various elements required by the matching process.

To give you some idea of the magnitude of the problem, consider the task involved in telling a computer how to find the last name and street name in an address like this one:

> Mr. A. John Van Sickel, VP Finance
> A. Wattenstein and Assoc. Inc.
> 117-119 Avenue A West, Suite 27
> Anycity, NY 12345-6789

The computer should be able to identify "Van Sickel" as the surname, "A" as the name of the street and "117" as the house number.

The conversion program also must standardize many variable words which appear on the address line, such as Box, PO Box, PO Drawer, Post Office Box, Drawer, Bx, etc. In addition, it must recognize various abbreviations and spelled-out numerics so that it can equate MT. with Mount, ST with Saint, One with 1, etc.

Once it has isolated and standardized the various data elements, it then uses its proprietary matching techniques to determine the likelihood of duplication.

Merge-purge programs can be analyzed on the basis of their thoroughness and their accuracy. Thoroughness is the measure of how many of the duplications that exist in the various files they find. Accuracy is the measure of how many erroneous matches they make. These two factors often work against each other. To find the most duplicates, one would permit a greater degree of allowable difference. To eliminate erroneous matches, one would reduce the allowable difference. This is often referred to as tightening or loosening the matching criteria. So it is important to determine in which direction your project is best to lean and to instruct the merge-purge service bureau appropriately.

However, despite the sophistication of the matching logic, the real key to the success of a merge-purge program lies in the thoroughness of the conversion process, not in the trickiness of the matching algorithm. The way in which your list is provided is an important factor.

Even though your file may be maintained in a very complex and long record format, provide a simple format for extracting the file for inclusion in merge-purge runs. When sending it, include an accurate file layout and a "dump" of several pages of data.

Paste a label on the reel identifying the file, the number of records, the coding "language" (EBCDIC or ASCII), the block and record size, and the track and density of the data. Where possible, identify the mailing for which the tape is intended. Your file may be going to a service bureau that is performing many different merge-purges simultaneously.

NET-NAMES ARRANGEMENT

A *net-names arrangement* is one of the things that you get involved with when you are part of a merge-purge, either as a mailer or as the supplier of a list. It is a process which came about in the early days of duplicate identification when mailers who were renting several lists found the same name on more than one of these lists and objected to paying each list provider for that name even though it was only being mailed once.

A technique was developed whereby the list owner from whose list the name was retained was paid for the name and the other list owners (from whose lists the name was dropped) were not paid. However, a maximum deduction (typically 15 percent) was imposed, as were modest charges for the costs involved in selecting the name onto the supplied tape. These arrangements are very common and very negotiable. Some list owners allow no net-names deductions. Some are more liberal than others.

As a list provider, it is important to remember that the person renting your list will or will not come back to rent it again based upon the way it works. The method of determining the value of a list usually involves comparing the income derived from the list by the cost of the list. So if you take actions which either reduce the effectiveness of your list or raise the cost of the mailed names, it will affect this computation.

Consequently, a list owner who supplies 100,000 names, has 20,000 of them dropped as duplicates, but allows no net-names allowance will have increased the cost of his or her names by 20 percent. The remaining names will have to be even more responsive to overcome the increased cost or they will suffer in comparison to other lists in the program.

A fair net-names arrangement would, therefore, seem to be one which takes the long-term value of a list renter into consideration.

LIST USAGE

When discussing list-processing techniques, it is important to keep in mind the various uses to which your list will be put. Knowing how you (and others perhaps) will be using the data will make it easier for you to see why the data should be structured in specific ways.

LABELS

One very common output format is labels. These are generally printed either 1-up or 4-up (four labels across the page). For large-volume mailings, it is customary to have the labels affixed by a labeling machine into which the unburst computer printouts containing the labels are fed. This machine cuts the labels apart and glues them to the envelope or mailing piece.

The labels can be printed either on plain computer paper or on pressure-sensitive peel-off labels. If printed on pressure-sensitive forms, they can be affixed by hand (for small-volume mailings) or by machine. When affixed by machine, they can be affixed by being cut out along with the backing paper and glued onto the mailing piece so that the label itself can then be peeled off by the recipient and affixed to the reply device.

The most common labels are approximately 3.2 inches wide by 15/16 inches high. The amount of data they can contain depends upon the characteristics of the computer printer.

The most common computer printers print 10 characters to the inch horizontally and 6 lines to the inch vertically. They are thus able to fit 5 lines of up to 31 characters each on a label.

Newer printers have the ability to vary the size of their type and the number of lines per inch. Laser and ink-jet printers can print in a number of fonts. Thus, while it is still important to keep in mind the 31-character by 5-line format, it is becoming increasingly common to be able to print longer addresses.

BAR CODING

The Postal Service has indicated that it will be able to automatically process bar-coded mailings and will provide a discount to mailers that submit such mailings.

Their new machinery will be able to read the code if it is printed in the proper place within the address block. (Formerly, it had to be printed just above the bottom edge of the envelope, making it impractical to print along with the name and address label).

Consequently, when designing a list-processing system, particularly when determining printers, it is advisable to consider the possibility of printing bar codes on your labels and getting the appropriate hardware and software.

INK-JET PRINTING

Current equipment available at many lettershops today includes devices which, instead of pasting a label onto a mailing piece, print the name-and-address data directly onto the piece. This permits a mailer to send the names and addresses to the lettershop in magnetic tape form rather than on labels. The process is fast, efficient, and usually less costly than labeling. (Do be sure your forms are printed on appropriate paper. Some papers, particularly those with a glossy finish, do not lend themselves to this process.)

The ink-jet process can print other information in addition to the name and address. In some situations, particularly catalogs, an entire "personalized letter" can be printed as part of the printing and binding process, thereby eliminating the need for labeling the catalogs after they have been printed.

The requirements for this process are similar to those for merge-purge. You should be able to provide the printer or lettershop with a magnetic tape (or diskette) file in a clean, easy-to-use format along with the appropriate documentation.

PERSONALIZED FORMS

The computer-personalized letter has been around for many years, and it still works. Not in every case, but often enough to make it an important format for you to consider. Variations of it are used extensively by companies offering sweepstakes. These mailings include not only a personalized letter but numerous other personalized pieces.

When doing computer personalization, certain data elements become very important. For example, the gender of the individual is desirable. Without it, one has to write to "Dear A. Blumenfield," a very impersonal and awkward form of address.

The ability to distinguish between individuals and nonindividuals becomes important. (We once sent a letter to "Dear General Motors." The General did not respond.)

However, given these factors, you should be able to see the range of possibilities that you can take advantage of when you combine the personalization capabilities of the computer with the data in your database.

Not only can you use the database to determine which individuals to write to, you can alter the text of your message as well. The offer can be modified based upon the characteristics of the recipient. Theoretically, every individual could be getting a unique offer.

With laser printers, it is possible to produce high-quality personalized mailings at a speed that was unavailable a few years ago. These printers can print upside down, sideways, in varying fonts, in different colors; they can add signatures and do a myriad of other tasks.

The outputs can then be combined with other personalized forms (printed in the same sequence!) and automatically matched and inserted into mailing envelopes.

It is when one is doing computer personalization that the impact of entering and maintaining your data in upper and lower case becomes important. Unless you want to print the name and address in all-caps, you will have to convert it to upper and lower case if you don't enter it that way. Such conversions can be done by the computer with a very high degree of accuracy, but the conversion is not perfect. There are a few names that just can't be converted by machine. And company names are more difficult. However, it is faster (and, therefore, cheaper) to enter name and address data in all caps, so if you are willing to put up with a small degree of error, you might wish to make this trade-off and save money.

CUSTOMER SERVICE

One by-product of a well-designed list-processing system is a system which facilitates good customer service. The ability to quickly retrieve a customer's data and answer any questions is enhanced by good database design.

A well-designed system will permit an authorized user to find customer records by searching on their account number, name, zip code, phone number, purchase order number, or your invoice number.

Once found, the system should display the dates of the various transactions that have taken place, the dates orders were entered and shipped, the method of shipment, details of payments received, any back-order information, returns processed, etc.

Some of this information will be of little use other than to support such customer service inquiries. In this case, the system can be designed to delete (purge) this data after a fixed time has elapsed. In some cases, this time period is measured from the date on which the transaction is paid for in full rather than the date it was entered or shipped.

Your own experience with inquiries should be used to determine what data to retain and how long to retain it.

LIST RENTALS AND EXCHANGES

For many direct marketers, the key to their continued success is the availability of new and responsive names. They get these names either by renting mailing lists from other companies or by exchanging their list for the other company's list.

Another aspect of this process is the fact that the income derived from renting their mailing list is a major contributor to the profits of a large number of direct marketers.

So if you are planning to rent your list or exchange with other list owners, here are some things to keep in mind.

In today's economy, the more ways you can segment and select names from your list, the easier it will be to rent. The selections that most list renters will want will, necessarily, be less complex than those that you will make for your own use. However, you will need to be able to select names by a number of common criteria. These include zip codes, sectional centers, states, and nth name selections. An nth name selection is used to extract a statistically relevant subset of the file. It is done by dividing the number of names on the file by the number of names desired. The resulting number (dropping any remainder) is "n." By reading the file and selecting every nth name, you will wind up with the desired number of records. For example, if your list contains 275,530 records and you wish to select 5000, divide 275,530 by 5000, yielding 55.106. Drop off the .106. Then choose every fifty-fifth record. This will give you 5009 records, which represent a cross section of the entire file.

Continuations are another thing you must provide for when supplying names to others. These come about when a renter rents a portion of your list (often for a test mailing) and then comes back to get more of the names. You should be able to suppress any of the names that were included in the previous list supplied to them when you select the names for this "continuation" order. And, if they come back again, the names from both previous orders should be suppressible.

The simplest method of providing for this contingency is to retain a list containing the IDs of the records supplied to a list renter. This file need only be generated for those renters who indicate that they want you to provide for a continuation and need only be kept for that period of time during which you offer to suppress previous orders (commonly 6 months). Since the list you are retaining only contains IDs, it will not take up much space. It will, however, provide you with the ability to accurately and easily suppress previously rented names.

LIST SECURITY

The entire concept of list rentals rests on the assumption that records supplied by a list owner will be used only one time and in accord with the specifications agreed upon. This concept is undergoing great examination in light of the developments in computer technology which make it possible to extract and retain either names or information from a rented list without a trace.

The Direct Marketing Association has set up a special task force to address this area and to come up with guidelines which cover the new technologies and their ramifications. This group, the List Practices Committee, has published a series of guidelines after much review.

What makes the list rental marketplace work is the fact that the vast majority of the organizations involved in it are honest and ethical and will not jeopardize their reputation by misusing a list. As in so many other areas of endeavor, the best list security is based upon knowing to whom you are renting your list and getting references for any organizations with whom you are not familiar. This task is made easier by the fact that the vast majority of list rentals are made through the offices of list brokerage companies who are in position to do most of this checking for you.

Nevertheless, there are a number of procedures which should be followed to provide a means for detecting misuse of your data. This misuse can occur both outside your company and inside it.

To start with, it is important that all individuals in your company who have access to your files be made aware that the data is proprietary. They should know that they are not permitted to turn the data over to anyone or use it in any way that they have not been duly authorized to do. Many companies affix a brightly printed sticker on each reel of tape which indicates that the data it contains are confidential.

Next, it is important to include on your file certain unique names and addresses. These should be designed in such a way as to be deliverable, but instantly recognizable.

In the event your list is used for some unauthorized purpose, the mailing pieces bearing these unique names will serve to alert you to that effect. Obviously, these "salt" or "seed" names should be kept confidential to prevent their being removed by someone who wishes to misuse the file.

Whenever a copy of your list or a selection of it is created for another company's use, the selection program should insert a series of unique "salt" names into that file. These "salt" names should vary each time a new list selection is made and a record kept of each variation.

The inclusion of these unique names provides the following benefits to you:

Samples of the actual mailing will be received, providing a means of assuring that the mailing is in accordance with the specifications of the order in terms of content and mailing time.

Misuse of the list (mailing a different offer, multiple mailings, or mailing at a different time) will be detected.

Theft of a list is deterred since misuse is likely to be detected.

The actual date on which mailed pieces arrive is determined and can be used in measuring response activity as well as post office efficiency.

Misuse of a list is documented by being able to show several different "salts," all of which were included only in the specific list delivered to a renter.

MAIL PREFERENCE SERVICE

As a mailer, you have a vested interest in the continued availability of mailing lists as well as in seeing to it that few, if any, restrictions are imposed on your right to mail. Therefore, it is important to recognize that some people (thankfully not too many) do not wish to receive advertising mail and are quite vociferous about it.

Your system should provide a means whereby you can code such individuals' records so that you will be able to suppress mailing to them or exclude their name from any list rentals or exchanges that you create.

In addition, you should participate in the DMA's Mail Preference Service (MPS). This is a program in which the DMA provides those individuals who do not wish to receive such mail with a means of diminishing the amount of mail they receive. Their names are put on a special list which is made available to direct marketers. These names then can be suppressed from any mailings.

If you rent lists from other list suppliers, it is good practice to request that they suppress any names which appear on the MPS list. If you supply names, you should automatically suppress any such names, as well as the names of any individuals on your list who have requested that you not send them additional mailings.

Experience has shown that if they are given that option, a very small percentage of individuals will request that their names not be rented or reused. As a result, it is highly recommended that mailers follow such a procedure as well as other practices which, from time to time may be recommended by the List Council of the DMA. Doing so will help all of us to continue to operate in an atmosphere as free of crippling regulations and restrictions as possible.

PART 3
Alternative Media

16

Media Tactics: An Overview

Brent John Bissell

McCann-Erickson Direct
Troy, Mich.

Traditional wisdom in the direct marketing community held the following definition as unshakable:

> **Mass, or general advertising communication, addresses broad, diverse audience groups according to the single thread of commonality uniting them. Direct marketing communication seeks to detect the differences among mass marketing constituencies and to address them specifically, within a niche orientation.**

East was East and West, West. Polarization was the practice. While this broad definition is still largely accurate, society and many other conditions have changed the way consumers receive and perceive marketing communications and, more importantly, the way they act upon them.

This section will provide an overview of these market conditions and explore their impact on the delivery of marketing communications to appropriate targets. Your message delivery is conveyed through media, and today can both address broad diverse audience groups and simultaneously detect and address the differences in various consumer segments. The difference between image and direct response messages has begun to disappear. Polarization is no longer a fact of our advertising life.

Naturally, the accomplishment of the strategies established to meet program or corporate objectives is of primary importance. The selection of the proper medium or combination of media to target the right audience for your message contributes 50 percent of the success equation. You can't produce a sale without first putting the right message before the right person. That message, delivered by the right medium, must convey the right selling appeal and much more.

To accomplish this the business world today stands on the threshold of an integrated marketing system that must utilize *all areas* of marketing specialization in a simultaneous, cohesive, and powerful way. The traditional differences between image advertising, direct marketing, sales promotion, packaging, event marketing, and point-of-sale materials blur as marketers focus on building equity under a strong umbrella of a cohesive company image. While going about the business of getting the sale today, marketers must bank an investment in the consumer's mind for eventual future purchases.

These objectives can be accomplished and their impact quantified through the synergistic use of the full spectrum of the media of direct marketing: television; radio; magazines; newspapers; inserts; take-one's; outdoor and direct mail. Increasingly, direct marketers of the next decade will have uncommon media to choose from, including video cassettes, computer discs, and interactive cable. I have even seen brown grocery bags with an offer and a call to action via an 800 number. (Can sky writing be far behind?)

Mail has traditionally been the workhorse medium of direct marketing. However, the technological advancements of the recent past (computers, satellite dishes, Cable television, WATS lines, and fax machines) and those of the foreseeable future (interactive television, "smart homes," voice-activated telecommunications, and affordable International WATS) will continue to vastly enrich the arsenal available to direct marketers. Accordingly, we forecast that the share of work borne solely by direct mail will decline and never again reach the dominance it once enjoyed.

Legislated privacy laws restricting data access and information sharing, coupled with increasingly prohibitive postal costs, will combine to change forever the face of direct marketing as it has been practiced until now. Overreliance on single-digit response rates mined from large-scale mailings will soon give way to more tightly monitored, purchase-timed, database-marketing-driven efforts. And these efforts will combine a number of direct marketing and corporate image strategies into a powerful multidimensional selling thrust. Harvesting the consumers' sale at the moment of ripeness will be the order of the day.

Consumer retention strategies will no longer be subjugated to a defensive tactic some marketers use in an eroding sales environment. Rather, consumer retention efforts will assume offensive postures seeking to secure at-risk customer segments in advance of their defection.

Propensity to buy, coupled with affinity to the brand or company image, will prove to be the marketer's edge in moving sales ahead in the increasingly jaded consumer sales arena. Since the leaders in the business-to-business sales arena—purchasing managers, presidents, and administrators—are consumers as well, we can assume a rapid and complete transference of this effect to the business-to-business marketplace.

A primary acknowledgment must be made: that every organization in business today, regardless of the nature of that business, possesses a brand or company image position (i.e., an overall position of core values and standards). This recognition logically extends to the equity inherent in the company/customer relationship. Even mail-order giants, such as the L. L. Bean Company, have embarked upon emotional image-building mass media advertising campaigns. They understand and value a clearly expressed company image. Further, these campaigns acknowledge equity of image beyond obtaining today's sale. That means investing in tomorrow's customer as well.

It has been argued by those who observe the evolution of modern society that the computer revolution holds greater power to reshape human organization and perceptions than did the advent of the wheel. The rapid increase in computerization and power, coupled with the equally rapid fall in the cost of that technology, has set the stage for management of individual company-customer relationships on a mass scale. It is this same "computer revolution" that has set the stage for the utilization of a number of media, rather than the overreliance on what once worked well.

Thanks to this "computer revolution," you can be armed with an understanding of the individuals who represent your best customers and you can begin the search for new customers that "look and act" like current ones, all the while expanding and extending that important company-customer relationship with those who believe in you.

The array of media we direct marketers have at our disposal now makes practical the cultivation of the multidimensional relationships we've just cited. The development of these relationships depends on the introduction and continuation of a dialogue in which buyers, free to act on their own initiative, can lead you in the direction of real marketplace movement. The sellers then have direct and timely access to experiential data that paves the way for truly market-tuned communications and products.

In the era of the individual, it is only through the direct participation of the consumer that equity in the relationship between seller and buyer will occur. This participation is best exemplified by the purchase dynamics of information obtained from customers and prospects as they voluntarily respond to radio, television, newspaper, magazine, or other media communications. Few of your customers or prospects will object to your asking three or four questions during the course of a transaction.

With the preceding points made, it is clear that we are moving away from the view of media as solely a conduit for the delivery of communications. The combination of factors cited makes obvious the fact that communications media are now required to deliver a message and simultaneously harvest market data and return it to the marketers. Thus even the broadest media vehicle becomes both transmitter and receiver, closing the distance between seller and buyer.

There are a number of factors to examine before we can begin to understand what is behind this force of change. Once we recognize these underlying factors, we can better accept their inherent challenges and put them to work for us.

NO LONGER BUSINESS AS USUAL: THE FOUR FACTORS OF CHANGE

Four primary factors are behind the case for direct marketing utilization of both targeted and broad-reach media in combination. The need for these adjustments in our marketing practice as we approach the next century stems from:

- Information overload
- Marketplace congestion
- Globalization
- The targeting of the individual

The dynamics of the marketplace have combined to form new marketing challenges at a pace never before experienced in such a short span of time. The marketing challenges now before us are equalled only by the opportunities and rewards to be gained by the individuals and firms who successfully understand and manage the change now upon us.

The four factors of change will also open new opportunities for pinpoint marketing to the individual. Uncommon media choices will open to direct marketers and require our receptivity to testing fresh approaches.

Information Overload

World population rates are not the only numbers reaching unheard-of levels. So too are other barometers of today's society. Clutter has become a way of life. According to the Direct Marketing Association, in 1989 *alone* over 13 billion catalogs were mailed to American consumers. That figure is *just* catalogs. The U.S. Postal Service estimates that in 1990 the average American received over 740 pieces of mail. Of that estimated volume, over 40 percent was theoretically comprised of third class mail.

According to the *Gale Directory of Publications,* in the past decade the number of U.S. magazines grew 16 percent to a 1989 total of 11,556 titles. Since 1980, SRDS has been adding an average of 78 new titles per year.

In today's information-rich business culture and personal environment, each of us is inundated with all types of data. Daily we receive letters, memos, computer-screen and voice-mail messages, and spoken presentations from co-workers and associates. Welcome and unwelcome information accosts our senses through radio, television, telephone, fax, books, video and audio tapes, newspapers, and magazines. It seems that we are the subjects of relentless pursuit by veritable battalions of salespeople.

Clearly, it is not even more information that we desire. It is, however, *relevant* information *edited* to meet our needs and *dispensed at the appropriate time* to gain our attention and action.

When faced with volumes of material to sort through, it's no wonder that individuals struggle to discern what is most relevant, noteworthy, and beneficial. For the most part, marketers and advertising agencies do realize this problem and are working to simplify and unify messages to ease consumer consumption. Every effort should be made to be part of the solution and not part of the problem.

The Center for Advertising Services, the information facility of the Interpublic Group of Companies, Inc., issued a white paper entitled *Advertising in 1990—And Beyond.* This report illustrates the importance placed by one of the world's largest groups of advertising agencies on helping its clients assist consumer understanding of their marketing messages:

The growth of family (or umbrella) brands can provide one solution to the problems of clutter. Consumers use brand core values to reduce risk in the purchase of product extensions. This leads to more segmentation with fewer brands.

Another move toward less clutter is narrow targeting of both the product (or service) and media. Special editions of magazines, direct marketing (including telemarketing), cable TV options, and event marketing all illustrate the shift toward narrow targeting.

But by far the broadest attack on clutter is in aggressive integration of the entire consumer program. Promotions, packaging, retail co-op ads and displays increasingly are seamless with image advertising. Line extensions of brand authority and R&D improvements increasingly are seen as powerful consumer communications in and of themselves.

The report continues, noting that creative excellence is necessary to cut through clutter to communicate the necessary points of differentiation to the target market.

The whole premise of aggressive integration of the entire consumer program and the utilization of multiple direct marketing media has been proved many times. The more you add reinforcing interactive marketing channels, the more you cut through the clutter and boost response. Examples abound:

- The oil company that followed up a direct-mail credit card offer with an outbound telemarketing effort reported a nearly 700 percent lift in response.

- Publisher's Clearing House airs a television schedule to announce its direct-mail drop and to show you the package creative and offer you should be looking for. Their major annual promotion usually achieves a response from three out of every four people it mails to.

- The business-to-business marketer, Kroy, runs a consumer television schedule to support its direct-mail and telemarketing efforts when the density of targeted businesses reaches sufficient levels to assure effective reach and frequency.

- Buick Motor Division of General Motors wraps the Buick Classic and Buick Open PGA Golf Tournaments in a two-month-long national multimedia sales event that utilizes just about every media available.

Advertising and direct marketing are not mutually exclusive. A message that creatively supplies both an understandable company position and a means for helping consumers fit offerings to their requirements is received positively. Allowing satisfaction through a response mechanism builds the requisite bridge between seller and buyer. Even more, it truly helps the consumer to organize the clutter in the marketplace and obtain satisfaction.

Let us not forget one of the basic tenets of sales success: dispense information to customers in carefully measured amounts—neither too little nor too much. There is equal peril in inadequate, mistimed, and excessive information.

Marketplace Congestion

Competition in the marketplace and for a share of the consumer's mind is intensifying. From 1977 to 1984, before the more intense escalation of recent years, 40 percent of the 175 new products introduced in supermarkets were extensions of established brands. It is easy to understand this concept of extension when you consider the following perspective:

Type of Extension	Example
Repackage product in a different form	Jello Pudding Pops
Distinctive taste or ingredient component in the new item	Haagen Daz Cream Liquor
Natural companion product	Log Cabin Pancake Mix
Extend customer franchise	VISA Travelers Checks Cartier Dishware
Expertise	Honda Outboard Engines and Lawn Mowers Remington Hunting Boots
Benefit/attribute/feature owned	Ivory Shampoo and Hair Products
Designer image/status	Pierre Cardin Cologne and Accessories Ralph Lauren Home Furnishings

After reviewing this list, I'm sure you can add dozens of your own examples of extensions. As brands and their offspring, extensions, proliferate, so do promotional efforts and direct mailings to support them.

The Quaker Oats Case Study. A leading cereal marketer, Quaker Oats, has made a major commitment to databased marketing. Rather than utilize the traditional free standing insert (FSI) newspaper media, they recently embarked on a carefully designed alternate delivery strategy, mailing to ten million households.[1] This is an extremely broad use of direct mail as a medium. It was, however, a fundamental first step toward implementing their databased marketing strategy.

Subdivide the universe of ten million households by the 250 coupon offers tested and you'll get an understanding of their database construction process. The tests sought to differentiate current customers from competitive prospects; to discern cereal type purchased; and to ascertain consumption frequency and serving size. The last two items, frequency of use and serving size, establish an important parameter for future direct marketing use — determination of the repurchase interval. The rollout was to 18 million homes defined as promotionally responsive according to the models derived from the test phase.

Each coupon was coded to allow Quaker to track redemptions by household. Creative, product, and offer were all versioned according to individual household composition and purchase history. Typically, response levels will be increased by a factor of from five to ten times, solely from the timely use of customer knowledge.

Once you know your customers it is easy to sell that knowledge to other noncompeting firms. In effect, that knowledge can become a product itself and generate profit independently.

CBS Tie-in to Quaker Direct. CBS became the first television network to use direct mail when they participated in Quaker's fall 1990 direct marketing effort. Having built upon earlier database construction efforts, the Quaker customer and prospect file now reaches over 18 million households. Three mailings go to the complete file over a 12-month period.

CBS joined the mailing because Quaker could clearly portray the household profile and composition through their past data acquisition and enrichment efforts. The network was able to promote new and returning shows in its fall programming to demographically and psychographically matched household segments.

"Quaker Direct provides CBS with mass circulation on a target basis, enabling us to become highly focused in reaching our audience with program promotions aimed specifically at family households," says George F. Schweitzer, senior vice president for the CBS Broadcast Group.

This is yet another case for media diversification of communication efforts. Even those who control a major network of a dominant medium realize that the era of the massed market has passed. Individual faces now appear via databased marketing where once only broad "audience segments" stood.

The importance more and more companies now place on customer data acquisition is evident in the increasing use of package-goods discount coupons with a sweepstakes overlay. This combination allows for both instant gratification of the customer and acquisition of the purchaser's name, address, and other information for later marketing efforts.

To the efforts of those discovering the power of databased direct marketing and increasing their importance, add the names of Seagram, R. J. Reynolds Tobacco USA, S. C. Johnson, General Motors, AT&T, Marion Merrill Dow Pharmaceuticals, and many others. These firms now stand side by side with such mail-order stalwarts as L. L. Bean, Sharper Image, J. C. Penny, Lands' End, Sears, Stark Brothers Nurseries, and over ten thousand others.

As this direct marketing "ship" grows larger and larger, so will the wake that follows each industry movement. The end result will again be clutter. As the integration of direct marketing techniques continues—as well it should—into even more business-to-business, package-goods, and brand-development programs, all direct marketing media will reflect the congestion we anticipate.

Effectively reaching and selling to individuals requires knowledge of who buys what; when they have bought and intend to again; as well as what creative approaches and media they respond to best, wherever they may live.

Globalization

Surely you've seen it in your own neighborhood: traditional American, German, and Italian restaurants surrounded by scores of Indian, Vietnamese, Thai, and Middle Eastern restaurants. And all have at least three "Mexican" entrees. Everyone seems to cherish ethnicity.

As the world evolves toward an open and unified marketplace, the tool of computerization will give direct marketers the ability to manage the global data. It is precisely this technological edge that will allow us to access and adjust to the vast global environment as easily as if it were the neighboring state.

For most marketers there is promise of reward for taking the time to understand the differences that *unite* otherwise diverse audiences. This is where the tracking ability of direct marketing comes into its own. Faced with the opportunity of expanding markets and untapped potential, the global marketer is obligated to define tastes, product trial and purchase preferences, application, and needs. This information is valuable and best captured up front, through a variety of response channels, to discern responsiveness by medium. The use of this data in subsequent marketing efforts will, of course, lead to more segmentation.

Dick Hodgeson tells this story of a global direct marketer expanding to meet an unanticipated opportunity:

> A major Dutch-based catalog company already distributing in West Germany, England, and the U.S. sought to expand its circulation into East Germany at the time of the Wall's destruction. They fielded a large team of young adults to circulate catalog request forms, one on one, to those who came across to the West. Within approximately one week several hundreds of thousands of request forms were distributed. The acceptance forms and subsequent orders flooded in. Extreme and unforeseen troubles occurred when it became obvious that the East German postal service was not used to direct mail marketing and the resulting volumes of correspondence.

While media and the information dispensed and collected through it are globalizing, those forces will be heavily dependent upon local know-how. The local factors become visible when you consider postal regulations, cultural diversity, language dialects, production resources, and acceptance of the direct marketing process.

Technology now allows one-on-one selling across the nation and across the globe. No single medium can be depended upon to deliver prospects and customers alike. Clearly diversification of media and selling message are required as we approach the individual as a marketing target. An interesting paradox faces you: broader and more global markets countered with the growing force of individualism.

The Targeting of the Individual

In times past, people took comfort from being part of the whole. There was safety in numbers, and often those who were different from the rest were treated as subnormal.

Certainly there was a high value placed on conformity and togetherness in the decade of the 1950s—right up to the mid-1960s, in fact. You remember: families were supposed to be structured like the one on *Father Knows Best*. Programs like *Ozzie and Harriet, The Donna Reed Show, Captain Kangaroo,* and *Our Miss Brooks* taught us the values of self-control and unanimity. We were all expected to conform. Group-think was the order of the day.

The late 1960s and early 1970s changed all that. Sensing the strength to be found in divergent viewpoints, and recognizing that humankind is truly a sum of its separate parts, toleration began to replace suspicion and exclusion. Archie Bunker let us view our worst points from afar, even as Mister Rogers invited us all to be his neighbor. In the years since, as the president and CEO of the Estee Lauder Companies, Leonard Lauder, has observed, we have increasingly become a "niche-itis" society. As people seek greater involvement with more specific aspects of their lifestyles, less mainstream media is required. Consumers are demanding more tailored programing and more specificity from advertisers before they form opinions or respond.

This trend toward greater segmentation is precisely why direct marketers must use an array of media in combination to seek out special tastes and address them with goods and services tailored to satisfy them. Consumers cannot be standardized, either in terms of products, or styles of advertising communication, if they are to be expected to respond.

Megatrends 2000 proclaims the period from 1990 to the year 2000 as heralding ten new global movements. One of the prominent trends is termed "The Triumph of the Individual." If the prediction is correct, we can assume that the beginning of the next century will be greeted with an even greater celebration of self. Perhaps we will appreciate the sum of the component parts that makes each of us unique. If so, the circle will be joined when individuals, sure of their uniqueness, begin to see that through our individualism we are all truly parts of humanity as a whole.

A concise statement of the wisdom behind a direct marketer's use of synergistic multiple media was offered by Ron Fusile, manager of sales promotion and direct marketing for the Buick Motor Division of General Motors. He makes an analogy between the direct marketer and a teacher; the consumer and a student. Professional educators, he reasons, have long known that subjecting students to a combination of lectures, reading, and writing exercises leads to higher retention of learned data than would any of the stimuli alone.

Behavioral psychologists cite the following percentages of retained information: 20 percent retention when a person only hears a message (radio exposure); 30 percent when a person only sees a message (print exposure); 50 percent retention when a person both sees and hears a message (television exposure); and 90 percent retention when a person sees *and* hears *and* responds.

Mr. Fusile has effectively utilized this strategy to leverage the combined Buick Classic/Buick Open PGA golf events into a major national automobile sales event. To promote this, he utilizes television and radio; national, regional, and local newspapers; magazines; inbound telemarketing; national and local direct mail; and the in-dealership POP, which reflects the coordinated theme and graphics.

Once again direct marketing basics are proved solid: *the success of a program depends on properly addressing the right person with the right offer of the right product at the right time.* Knowledge of your current and potential customers then allows effective media planning and selection. Once you know the details of how your current customer or prospect lives, consumes, and forms values you can examine their media habits as well.

As consumers are discovering unique aspects about themselves, they are equally willing to tell you what they've learned. For the reasons examined earlier—information overload, marketplace congestion, and globalization—today's consumers will tell you about themselves in some detail. They will do this with the hope that the information supplied will aid the relevance of the marketing communications that are aimed their way. They are essentially saying: "Tell me only what I *need* to know and spare me the rest."

UNCOMMON MEDIA CHOICES

The case for looking beyond sole reliance on direct mail is a compelling one. There is an astounding array of direct marketing channels to explore, even to the point of testing the "pulling power" of the in-house VCR player and home computer.

In 1990 the home video cassette player/recorder surpassed basic cable-serviced households in terms of penetration by over one-third. From 1985 to 1990 alone, VCR penetration climbed from 28.7 percent to 68.6 percent, an increase of two and one-third in just five years.

No five-year period up to the year 2000 is predicted to match the explosive growth the home VCR industry experienced in that period. However, VCR households will continue to grow over 1990 levels by one and one-third by 2000 to the level of 92.5 percent penetration. Over the same period, basic cable will rise from 49.7 percent in 1990 to 63.7 percent of all households by 2000. (All data from U.S. Census and LINK Resources.)

The reasons for this growth in VCR penetration are easily explained: Increasing technology, decreasing cost, and the fact that they put the task of programming for individual tastes in the hands of the viewers. It is, therefore, little surprise that many of today's direct marketers are utilizing home video tape packages in their marketing curriculum: Nordic Track, marketer of home exercise equipment, offers a free video tape in inquiry-generation advertising efforts. Nordic Track then follows prospects through three or more outbound telemarketing and direct-mail efforts.

Buick Motor Division has used a home video tape presentation to show qualified prospects the care and attention that goes into building their limited production Reatta luxury two-seater. Prospects are qualified and their purchase intention is established in advance of the prospect being placed into one of six sequences of direct marketing action. Each sequence then defines the applicable mix of media, communication pacing, and appropriate amount of follow-up activity to harvest the sale.

Throughout the U.S. numerous direct-to-home entertainment, information, and home shopping services are testing both the limits of what can be practically offered and the consumers' willingness to participate and pay for them. Among these services are:

- Sears/IBM's Prodigy, an on-line subscription video text service accessed by home computer.
- J. C. Penney's Teleaction, a cable-service home shopping service.
- GTE Main Street, a hybrid interactive cable shopping concept utilizing a telephone inquiry system; it also allows electronic mail and a reservation service.

Computers, VCRs, and cable service are not the only means of home-based interactivity. Nintendo has announced that its product expansion plans include home banking and stock market information access among others.

Have you ever considered the *home* itself as a force for consumerism? Home automation is expected to become such a force by the year 2000. As we mentioned earlier, message clutter is very real. Individuals now seek to expand control over their environment and separate "the relevant" from "the noise."

In the foreseeable future, programmable "smart homes" will communicate with "smart products." (I.e., home computers linked to electronic news services or shopping networks will "shop" for preprogrammed products or data.) Your marketing net must be wide enough to capture these opportunities, and the media and methods of even 10 or 15 years ago just will not do.

Before you discard this prediction as impractical consider this: two trade associates are at the center of the development of the home automation movement. The Electronics Industry Association favors a form called a "consumer electronics (CE) home bus" and the National Association of Home Builders (NAHB) is advancing the "smart home" concept. The technology is in development and on its way.

As part of this rethinking of the American home, you will probably see a rewiring of American homes and businesses as well. This will occur as fiber optics eventually replace "twisted pair" telephone lines and cable's coaxial wire. This factor alone will open new channels of interactivity.

Fiber optic lines can provide conventional and enhanced phone service, interactive pathways, and up to 100 channels of full band width video delivery. This technological improvement will open up direct-to-consumer ordering of virtually every product. Videophones could be practicable, with controllers allowing the viewer to zoom in or pull out to examine specific details of the product being offered for sale.

As this capability expands, so will the interactivity occurring directly between buyer and seller. Payment for items ordered will be made by electronic funds transfer, or entered directly on your phone bill. Perhaps magnetic strip credit card readers will become a fixture on the phone or television set of tomorrow.

It is this vision of our society tomorrow that is driving technological innovation to speed the delivery of what we want as consumers, precisely when we want it, with an absolute minimum amount of inconvenience. Therefore, direct marketers must keep an open mind about adapting this technological innovation to selling and servicing. Being first on the block to test new alternative media is to be applauded. Innovation, boldness, and decisiveness will be rewarded by increased market share.

HOW TO GET STARTED

The case for the direct marketer's use of a diversity of media is a compelling one. The fact that this book includes a substantial section on the use of alternative media clearly demonstrates the growing recognition by leading direct marketers that new strategies for growth must be adopted. They know that new rules must be established to meet the challenges and opportunities of our time and that media alternatives previously beyond consideration must be tested.

Equally clear is the fact that due to all of the forces we've touched upon in this interview it is no longer "business as usual." Direct marketing and its experienced practitioners will be required to assume both expanded and more complex roles in their companies and industry segments in the years to come.

The adoption of database as a marketing strategy shows no sign of abating. However strong the power of multivariate regression modeling may be, we still lack enough individual-specific information to precisely understand the psychology of buying.

Sophisticated techniques of data interpretation still stop short of letting us know specifically when a purchase will take place. In short, knowledge of future buying intentions by individuals can only come from specific information supplied in a timely manner from our prospects and customers. Without this data we are unable to scientifically and effectively deliver the right message, correctly worded, at the right time.

Apart from creative and impact/response considerations, there are financial aspects that make the use of many media in combination attractive. The use of broad-based media (radio/television/cable/print) to communicate your message will cost you an average from 1 cent to 10 cents per person. Direct mail will cost you from 25 cents to several dollars per person on average. Telemarketing contacts will cost you from $3 to $10 on average. Video tape or computer disk efforts will cost you approximately the same as for a telemarketing contact.

The issue of budgeting for testing the use of alternative media is hard to address in meaningful terms unless you currently know the following:

1. **Current customer acquisition cost.**   How much does it currently cost you to find a customer through your traditional prospecting efforts? For instance, if $3000 in advertising nets you 300 prospects and you end up converting 20 percent (or 60 people) to actual purchase, your cost per lead (CPL) is $10. Your cost per order (CPO) is $50. This historic data ($10 for CPL and $50 for CPO) now becomes the yardstick by which you will evaluate future customer acquisition efforts.

2. **Average first order/gross sale and profit amount.**   Customers obtained by various offers communicated through many media will demonstrate different ordering patterns. Therefore it is necessary to code each respondent as they are obtained, with the originating media source and offer types. This will allow you to compare order behavior by group (i.e., print-generated orders as compared to broadcast-generated orders). Since order frequency, volume, depth, and product variety differ by media source, a profit analysis prior to rollout will project the most profitable media through which to obtain a customer. Naturally this analysis should be performed as an ongoing process for all media used.

3. **Lifecycle value.**   Once the evaluation of customer profitability by media source is understood, you will have the framework for understanding the value of customer groups over time: how much was spent to acquire this customer; how quickly and to what extent was this customer profitable; and how long did he or she remain an active purchaser? Just as direct marketers value the "winning" creative or package approach, so too must we value the most profitable medium, or media combination.

Once you've come to understand the three dimensions just reviewed, you will have a firm fix on the past, present, and future profitability of your database of customers. You will also have gained market-sensitive data about how your future customers will find and respond to you by media channel.

No radical departure from your tested primary lead generation media should be undertaken without sufficient sampling of alternative media. If, for instance, you have traditionally prospected by mail, why not test cable television for lead quality and quantity against your "control" mail package? If you have traditionally sent out an envelope mailing, why not try a version of that message delivered on video cassette, if appropriate to your market. Telemarketing before or after your mail drop will effect response. Do you know its place in your next campaign for maximum effectiveness? The answers to these questions must be found.

Clearly the use of alternative media is prudent for direct marketers in the 1990s. Change is upon us and this is a resilient strategy. Using and measuring uncommon media *and* traditional media in combination will pay off. It will also provide your company with the communications flexibility to change media "gears" as conditions change.

The sections that follow will go into specific detail on important alternative media. You will even read about how to tailor the creative approach to each medium for maximum impact. Just continue reading: the world and its challenges await you.

NOTE

1. Midyear 1991 saw the Quaker Direct effort put on indefinite hold. Corporate spokespeople acknowledged that a lack of "outside interest," coupled with internal management change precipitated the action. However, other package-goods companies, such as Hanes, the Coca Cola Company, and General Foods, maintain their premium on database development. Pharmaceutical firms such as Marion Merrill Dow, Inc., have begun strategic consumer database development as well. Clearly, the trend is building.

17

Newspapers and Magazines

Maxwell C. Ross

Maxwell C. Ross and Company
Kansas City, Mo.

Before plunging into the field of magazine and newspaper space advertising, let's get oriented by taking a look at some essentials:

1. The ad must ask the reader to do something. It must make a definite offer or request of the reader. Most ads don't work hard enough.

2. If you are attempting to make a sale, there must be enough information to make a decision.

3. If you are mainly interested in getting an inquiry that you will follow up by mail or with a personal sales call, you want to guard against telling the whole story in the ad.

4. Your ad will work far better if there is a response device—a coupon, a pointed request to write for more information, even a bind-in form where possible. (If a bind-in form can be used, the response may be four to six times as great as an on-page coupon, for example.)

5. When you can use an 800 number, do so. The response will be enhanced, the time span will be shortened, and your reader will be more likely to close in the case of an inquiry.

6. Magazines that carry a heavy volume of direct response will usually (about 95 percent of the time) outpull those who don't. The same is true of newspapers (the *Wall Street Journal*, for example).

Back in the 1960s many publications began to slam direct mail and direct marketing. They seemed to be afraid that the success of direct mail might cut into their advertising revenue. Instead, they would have done better to encourage the happy combination of the two—a combination that made it possible for Old American, the insurance company where I was advertising director for many years, to appear in more than 800 newspapers and something like 125 different magazines.

Along the way we learned some mighty strange and interesting things, and I'll show you in the pages that follow just how the things we learned influenced the space advertising results we obtained:

1. Audience characteristics
2. Cost (i.e., the proper pricing per 1000 readers delivered)
3. Editorial climate
4. Editorial adjacency
5. Physical position in the publication
6. Physical position on the page
7. The advertising copy itself
8. Scheduling, timing and market testing

AUDIENCE CHARACTERISTICS

When we worked with newspapers, audience characteristics were not significant because the sheer size of the circulations made detailed audience profiles impossible. In contrast, as the number of special-interest magazines grew by leaps and bounds, *their* audience characteristics became extremely important. By 1990 the number of magazine titles had nearly doubled (to 1,937) in little more than a decade.[1]

COST

The best results in newspapers generally came from those papers which delivered the most readers per dollar spent. Our best was the *New York News* because of its extremely low rate per thousand (at that time). We took great care to tally the results correctly, and the correlation between cost per inquiry from the space and the cost of the space itself was remarkably clear. In other words, the best results in newspapers came from those papers that delivered the most readers per dollar spent. To a lesser extent, cost was an important barometer in our work with magazines.

Good records are vitally important and these are the main points on which we scored a publication:

1. The number of inquiries produced
2. The number of applications that resulted from these inquiries
3. The number that converted from our introductory offer to a full premium, and therefore to a permanent basis.

Obtaining Discounts on Space

Many magazines will sometimes extend discounts on space (called special mail-order rates) because they know that a great many companies who use direct marketing cannot possibly come out if they have to pay for space at higher general advertising rates. It's simply a fact of life.

In rare instances, you may be able to establish such a friendly relationship with a publisher that it can work to your mutual advantage—something along these lines:

1. Using a specified number of insertions (6-time, 12-time, etc.) at a lower rate. Often, these can be established at better-than-frequency discount rates.

2. Through your contractual use of "remnant" space (space left over at closing date through cancellations).

Remember, it's important for you to do your part in maintaining such a relationship. Once the publisher sees your actual costs and is fully aware of the cost breakdowns involved, he will often come through on your behalf. But trust and honesty in these cases are very, very important.

Just How Important Is Cost?

It may very well be the most important classification you have available to you. We found this especially true in the field of newspapers.

Cost may explain why weeklies and semiweeklies don't fare as well as one would think they should. To be in business at all, their cost figures have to be high. They usually cannot match the costs per thousand of the giant circulation newspapers. This is just as true for magazines. For example, we did well in the fraternal field—in magazines like *Eagle* and *Moose* and *Elks*—and in *American Legion* and *VFW*. But *Kiwanis* and *Rotarian* did not do so well, despite the fact that both magazines were extremely well edited and that both reached high-quality audiences. What went wrong was that the cost per thousand was nearly twice that of the other magazines.

It should be pointed out that some publications pull enough inquiries, but not enough sales result from them. Farm newspapers and farm magazines fell into this category for us.

EDITORIAL CLIMATE

Editorial climate might best be defined as the mental or psychological atmosphere in which readers find themselves when reading a given publication. An obvious example is *Popular Science* or *Popular Mechanics*. We tried Old American in both, but had trouble breaking even—simply because our advertising message wasn't in the right editorial climate.

One point especially worthy of mention is that so-called "special" issues (issues devoted to one subject) did not do well for us. One magazine devoted an entire issue to "The Romantic World of Art," and response hit an all-time low for us.

Business magazines have high costs per page per thousand, but in our case most of them, like *BusinessWeek* and *Nation's Business,* did not seem to deliver the reader page-traffic we needed. One staff analyst expressed an opinion that these magazines do not generally get a thorough, lingering readership. Business people are busy, and that's probably why.

We also had problems with sports magazines. And again, this may have been because of the editorial climate.

One of our all-time failures was a misguided venture into paperbound books. For a while there were a number of bound-in insert cards in the paperbacks. We picked four titles which should have delivered a mature audience. Yet we got virtually nothing in the way of response. We were pretty sure the editorial climate was wrong—but it may just have been that the idea's time had not yet come.

Before we move to another subject, I should mention how disastrous foreign-language newspapers were for us in those earlier days. Maybe the climate for them has improved; let's hope so.

EDITORIAL ADJACENCY

It stands to reason that one thing governing the traffic on any given page is the editorial material that appears on that page, particularly in magazines. Keep in mind that you have very little control over the editorial material that will appear on the same page as your ad, so there isn't much you can do about it in advance. You *can* make a request; just don't be too unhappy if the request isn't granted.

Any position alongside a cartoon has a chance of bringing benefits. One classic example occurred in *LOOK* magazine, when a little dog seemed to be walking right out of a cartoon and into our ad. The results were double anything else we ever experienced in *LOOK.*

Generally speaking, positions on the table of contents page were not good for us. Evidently not enough readers focus on this department. Once we tested an ad farther back in the book against that table of contents position, and it worked far better farther back.

There was some evidence that being alongside an editorial feature with a color tint block behind it was a good sign. Certainly any editorial mention of your product will help. See if the magazine you are considering has a Reader's Service department. It can work, but be sure to watch your percentage of closure.

Again, let me emphasize that you must track your results very carefully. This is particularly true if you are tempted to run your ad in a "special issue." (The same rule applies equally to newspapers and magazines.)

PHYSICAL POSITION IN THE PUBLICATION

Try to avoid magazines that group all their ads in one section of the book, as *National Geographic* does. I used to think we were alone in this discovery, but as the years went by I met dozens of others who felt the same way. Grouping all the ads in one section of a magazine is like grouping all the television commercials that appear during daytime and evening hours in one segment. The audience would be long gone in a hurry.

Try, in most cases, to avoid the directory section. This is especially true in business magazines which sometimes publish a directory issue. Put this among your specifications if you face such a proposition.

Positions alongside a classified section can be suicidal. Not always, but usually. A shopper's section, on the other hand, can be fairly good. Positions near a publication's house ad can be surprisingly productive. But as you might expect, it does depend on what the house ad is about.

We found that an inside front cover is not as good as the inside back cover, and we had considerable experience to back this up. (As a point of information, some magazines may give you inside coupon space when you are using cover advertisements, with this thought: "In case you don't want to mar the cover of your magazine, use this coupon to reply to the ad on the back cover.")

PHYSICAL POSITION
ON THE PAGE

When your ad doesn't pull its quota of responses, search for a possible answer. Often we found that such an ad was badly buried. If that was not the problem, we could see that the reader's attention was perhaps distracted by something else on the page.

Color appearing anywhere on a two-page spread always seemed to help. Every time we were placed opposite a full-color ad we enjoyed success.

If you are running small space ads, it may pay to buy the necessary extra space for a ruled line above, to keep your ad from becoming part of the ad over yours. Once *Life* magazine put a popcorn ad on top of us so that the words the reader saw were JOLLY TIME PEOPLE 50 TO 80 CAN APPLY FOR LIFE INSURANCE. But in *Retirement Life* there was nothing to separate our ad from the editorial material immediately above, and the results were outstanding.

One of our ads in *American Legion* ran directly under a shoe ad with the toe of a shoe pointing directly to us — and the ad pulled fantastically. In an issue of a religious magazine there was a pattern of vertical dots leading the reader's eye down to our ad. The pull was phenomenal. We wished we could attribute it to sparkling copy, but not so. Once, with an issue of the *Detroit Times,* we were amazed at the fine results. The checking copy turned out to have a reducing ad next to ours, arranged in such a way that the attractive posterior of an attractive model pointed directly at our ad.

THE ADVERTISING COPY ITSELF

By now you probably have a fairly clear idea of just how little control you have over your destiny when it comes to newspaper and magazine advertising positioning. But with the right kind of strategic copy, you can bring the odds into play on your side.

Here are a few things that one of the world's all-time great advertising men, David Ogilvy, has said about magazine and newspaper copy:

> There is no law that says advertisements have to look like advertisements. If you make them look like editorial pages, you will attract more readers.

Roughly six times as many people read the average article as read the average ad....

If you are lucky enough to have some news to tell, don't bury it in your body copy. State it loud and clear in your headline....

All my experience shows that for a great many products, long copy sells more than short. I have failed only twice with long copy, once for a popular-priced cigar and once for a medium-priced whisky. In split-run tests, long copy invariably outsells short copy.

How Much Difference Does Copy Itself Really Make?

Let's look to the words of another great, the late John Caples, who created the world-famous advertisement, "They Laughed When I Sat Down at the Piano."

> I have seen one advertisement actually sell not twice as much, not three times as much, but 19½ times as much as another. The advertisements occupied the same space. Both were run in the same publication. Both had photographic illustrations. Both had carefully written copy. The difference was that one used the right appeal and the other used the wrong appeal.

And speaking of the right appeal, it may help to include this list of human wants and needs, culled from my booklet "How to Write Successful Direct-Mail Letter Copy":

1. To make money
2. To save time
3. To avoid effort
4. To be comfortable
5. To be healthy
6. To be popular
7. To be in style
8. To avoid criticism
9. To conserve possessions
10. To escape physical pain
11. To gratify curiosity
12. To satisfy appetite
13. To protect reputation
14. To purchase wisely
15. To have beautiful things
16. To attract the opposite sex
17. To save money
18. To be individual

19. To enjoy life
20. To be clean
21. To be appreciated
22. To protect family
23. To emulate others you admire
24. To avoid trouble
25. To take advantage of opportunities

There is every evidence that unless an ad appeals to one of these human wants and needs, the copy will not achieve maximum results. It was the well-known advertising consultant Richard Manville who wrote:

> Advertisements that give people what they want outpull advertisements which present those things which people do not want as much — or do not want at all.

Manville points out that people want not only food, shelter, and adornment; they want to love and be loved, they want to assert themselves, and they want to feel "adequate."

When we first began our space advertising campaign to America's senior citizenry, we learned quickly that straight-type ads proved to be the best format. We tried all manner of visual art devices, but the "reader ad" style always came out ahead. Our tests, under perfectly controlled conditions — with exact-split runs in three major newspapers, seven insertions for each — were clear and unmistakable. *Without exception,* the type copy format outpulled the more visual art device format by two to one.

Larger ads usually worked for us, but generally they did not pull at the same low-cost figures as our small-space ads. But tiny ads (one inch or so) were not at all cost-efficient.

We learned to be conventional, to stick to the tried and true, to stay away from a school of thought prevalent at the time of running ads upside down, standing on end, or with any other bizarre treatment that long-suffering art directors could come up with. In short, we learned not to do anything that made it difficult for readers to get our message firmly planted in their minds.

Think in terms of what your reader wants. When you have to make your decision on a pair of headlines, decide in favor of the one your *reader* wants most. For example, here are two: CUT THREE STROKES OFF YOUR AVERAGE SCORE BY WEARING THESE XYZ GOLF SHOES, and YOUR PAIR OF XYZ GOLF SHOES WILL OUTWEAR ANY OTHER BRAND EVER MADE ! Any real golfer will gladly buy a new pair of golf shoes every summer if it will improve his or her game. The wearing quality of the shoes is only secondary.

Think things through. Visualize your prospect sitting quietly with your ad in front of him. These are the questions that most likely will be running through his mind:

1. What will you do for me if I pay attention to your story?

2. How are you going to do this?

3. Who is responsible for the promises you make?

4. Who else have you done this for?

5. What will it cost?

To this highly successful "sales formula," used by Jack Lacy for training sales-people, we have added one more question, "What do I do next?" The formula works—remarkably well. Try it!

Still Another Formula That Can Work Its Magic for You

So many copywriting techniques depend on a certain amount of practice before you can be successful with them. But here is a secret you can put to work at once:

> **For every 100 words you write, make sure that about 75 percent are words of five letters or less.**

Few men of our time have had such a deep effect on the trend toward clear writing as Dr. Rudolf Flesch. From the moment he turned his Columbia University Ph.D. thesis on readability into the bestselling *Art of Plain Talk,* his impact on modern writing has been unmistakable.

Among other things, he gave the world two formulas: one based on "reading ease," the other on "human interest." In his book *The Art of Readable Writing,*[2] Dr. Flesch explained how to pick writing samples, count the number of words, figure the average sentence length, and then count the number of syllables, arriving at a "reading ease" score by joining lines across a bar graph. You found your "human interest" score by counting the number of personal words and personal sentences.

So why not use the formulas as they were originally designed? That's fine if you have the time. But for most of us, the formula concept is a bit too complicated to use. The original formula for reading ease needs to be used by the greatest possible number of people. So here is a shortened version of Dr. Flesch's fail-safe formula:

1. Take the copy draft and count the number of words.

2. Omit any proper names used.

3. If there are numbers in the copy, count any with five digits or less to your credit.

4. Now determine how many words there are with five letters or less.

5. Divide this total by the number of words in your copy draft and you have your score.

If you are in the vicinity of 75 percent, you are all right. Anything in the 60s can be a danger signal.

Using this formula actually puts you in pretty good company. Shakespeare, the Bible, Lincoln's Gettysburg Address—they all measure out.

You see, Dr. Flesch championed the belief that *it is long words that cut down readability,* especially when they are strung together in a monotonous fashion. Short words can be combined, for the sake of rhythm, with an occasional longer word, to come up with just the right combination. Through the years, interestingly enough, sales promotion letters using this formula consistently outperform those that don't.

Combining Color and Copy

You may wonder about using color. Start off with these points in mind—(1) Almost every publication makes color available, but (2) you must pay for it through an increased space cost and the increased production costs you will run up.

Generally speaking, adding a single color does not pay for itself (although you can experiment with tint blocks, lines or words in color, and so on). But the use of four-color can pay out handsomely. Before you go off the deep end, though, test wisely. There are publications that permit a split-run involving a test of four-color against black-and-white. Much, of course, depends on your proposition and whether or not you have the right piece of art available or shootable. When you calculate your costs, be sure to include the usually heavy production costs that go hand in hand.

We have mentioned elsewhere that color appearing anywhere on a two-page spread in a magazine always seemed to help, and that every time we were placed opposite a full-color ad, it meant success. You may want to use your ingenuity to capitalize on these findings.

Before we leave this topic, let me emphasize how important it is to be careful with your execution. Get the most for your money. Don't take any more chances than you really need to. Your goal is not to win art awards; it is to sell.

SCHEDULING, TIMING, AND MARKET TESTING

Insofar as scheduling was concerned, we did plan a whole year at one time, but the secret of getting the most out of the money we budgeted was to review the budget studiously frequently—every 3 months as a rule.

This careful scrutiny of our quarterly forecast gave us a chance to turn on a dime, if that was necessary. Every magazine and newspaper insertion had to carry its weight, or else we would stop it quickly.

Monday seemed to be the best day of the week for us to run—even better than Sunday on a dollar-spent basis.

Seasonal variation for space ads is about the same as for direct mail, with January and February our best months. One somewhat isolated oddity was that there were several magazines that would pull for us *only* in certain months. We were never sure what the underlying reason was; it seemed to vary with the particular case.

Through the years we did a lot of experimenting with certain geographical and economic factors. For example:

- We found that inland and west coast towns in Florida did better than the east coast resort area. Fortunately, we could use almost all of Florida for the older age market, but it was a good thing to know which coast to favor when budget money became tight.
- The oil field areas of Texas showed up especially well.
- In South Dakota we tested space in newspaper towns where a hospital was located versus those without. There was a considerable advantage to advertising in the former.
- More prosperous farm counties in Iowa didn't show up any better than a random selection. (This may have occurred because the Des Moines metropolitan newspaper pretty much blanketed the whole state.)
- The western half of Tennessee did better for us than the eastern half. We didn't know why but we accepted the results for what they were worth.
- The southeastern diagonal section of Arkansas did better for us than a predominantly mountainous northwestern slice.
- Towns adjacent to metropolitan areas worked slightly better than those further removed. (Perhaps nowadays towns close to a U.S. interstate highway have a better chance of working than those farther away.)
- In Midwestern and Plains states we learned the wisdom of seeking out county seat newspapers.
- Larger metropolitan cities did better for us than small or medium ones. But the reason, we were sure, was the better break on advertising rates.
- Sometimes outsiders felt that we tested too many factors. Maybe so. No need to deny it. But what we learned opened many eyes (and pocketbooks).

And a final piece of advice. When it comes to determining the longevity of space ads, you can use these figures for rule-of-thumb calculations:

- Monthly magazines can be expected to pull 50 percent of their eventual total response after 1 month.
- For a weekly magazine, the ad should pull about 50 percent of its total at the end of 2 weeks.
- The span on daily, semiweekly, or weekly newspapers is proportionately shorter.

USING NEWSPAPER PREPRINTS

Joel Feldman, in a previous edition of this handbook, aptly defined *preprints* as being "Advertising materials which are printed in advance and then delivered to the newspaper for insertion in a specific edition."

The preprint phenomenon came about and developed fast during the last decade. By the mid-1980s the Newspaper Advertising Bureau of New York estimated the number of preprints at close to 50 billion. An early user was the Columbia Record Club, followed by Time-Life Books and many others soon after.

Preprint sizes range from *TV Guide*-size to a full tabloid dimension. Costs are lower for large metropolitan papers, so if your market is small-town, preprints may not fit into your picture.

Many advertisers find it profitable to use television support for the appearance of their preprints in Sunday or weekday papers. One word of caution: Be sure to test your use of preprints gingerly to make sure your costs are in line. Likewise, test carefully to make sure that your use of television support can pay out for you.

HOW MUCH SHOULD YOU SPEND TO GET A CUSTOMER?

No discussion on space advertising would be complete without returning to this important question, perhaps the most important question of all.

Usually cost projection and cost analysis formulas are quite complicated. They don't get used as much as they should. So I'd like to present a single simple idea to help you in your business: Concentrate on finding a formula with the help of your accounting specialists that will not merely tell you *how much* you *can* spend, but one that will show you how much you *should* spend to get a customer.

Consider that once your prospect becomes a customer:

You can sell him more of the same product.

You can sell him other products you have to offer.

You can secure referrals from him.

And often you can get him to give gifts.

Not all of these possibilities apply to every company. But—with variations—they come close.

Your customer will buy from you again and again at percentage rates so much higher than cold prospects that you will be astounded. How much better will a customer buy than a prospect? Answers vary, of course, by product and service categories, but the range could be from 10 times to 25 times as great. But the wonderful secret is that you can mail to that customer many times.

Once your company has gone through the arithmetical calculations involved, there are some other questions to answer:

1. If my Selling Price is to be $_____, what is my Cost of Merchandise or Service? $_____. (A rule of thumb should be that cost should not be greater than one-third.)

2. What will it cost me to handle the order? (Make sure your estimates are ample, including Preparation for Shipping $_____; Postage and Handling $_____; Taxes $_____; and Allocation of Overhead $_____.)

3. Will I get any merchandise back because of dissatisfaction or other reasons? And what will my Cost of Refurbishing and Return Postage be? $_____.

4. Will there be a Loss on Bad Debts? (If you sell on credit it is wise to build in a small amount per thousand.) $_____.

5. What is the physical Mailing Cost of outgoing mailings, including Addressing, List Cost (actually space cost in this particular instance), Printing of Components, Inserting, and Mailing? $_____

NOW ENTER THE TOTAL HERE $_____

Looking at #1, you will know how many items per thousand you will have to sell in order to come out even. "Even" may be the incorrect word. Built into your sales allowance formula is the extra margin that actually amounts to a cushion.

If your universe is at all limited, you will want to obtain as many customers from that universe as you possibly can. To get more, you may have to make less money.

After all, that customer has a long-range value to you far beyond what you may have anticipated. So you may want to increase arbitrarily the amount to, let's say, half as much again. If your figures show that you could spend $25 to get one new customer, your accounting department may have demonstrated that this amount could be upped to $37.50, for example. (I know of one case in which a marketing director determined that $100 was a proper allowance to get a $1 introductory sale into his records and keep it there. So this is not a subject to dismiss lightly.)

So, once again, as an epilogue to this chapter on selling through newspaper and magazine space advertising (where you so often find your total potential audience limited), think in terms of how much you *should* spend — not how much you *can* spend.

NOTE

1. I'd like to pay tribute here to a section in Bob Stone's excellent book, *Successful Direct Marketing Methods*. 4th ed. (Lincolnwood, Ill.: NTC Publishing Group, 1988). His tables 9-1 and 9-2, pp. 196–206, represent a gold mine of information about U.S. consumer magazines.

2. Rudoff Flesch, *The Art of Readable Writing*, rev. ed. (New York: Macmillan, 1986).

18
Broadcast Media

Dana Vogel

Nash/Wakeman/deForrest
New York, N.Y.

For the last ten years, direct-response television has been one of the fastest growing media in direct-response advertising. It has an unmatched ability to provide immediate revenue—revenue that can be reinvested in the proposition more quickly than in any other medium currently available.

Direct-response television offers direct marketers a viable distribution channel for marketing products directly to end users. More than any other mass market medium, television provides the marketer with immediate, quantifiable, and justifiable results that build brand equity. Television also offers a broad range of creative format variations, enabling the marketer to spend as few as 30 seconds or as many as 30 minutes selling a product.

MEDIA PLANNING

Before outlining the details of your media plan, stop and ask yourself these questions:

1. Does my product represent a unique selling proposition?
2. Is my product unavailable at retail?
3. If my product is available at retail, does my offer represent a unique value in excess of the retail price?
4. Is my product priced at a point where it is affordable to the largest potential market?
5. If my product and offer are geared to a narrower market, is there media potential for this audience segment?

If the answers to these questions are all "yes," direct-response television awaits. You are ready to proceed.

Outline your media test plan by setting objectives. These should include:

1. Determining the viability of generating cost-efficient leads or orders

2. Establishing an acceptable CPL (cost-per-lead) or CPO (cost-per-order) range

3. Determining the quality of the leads through conversion analysis or the lifetime value of the customer through reorders of the product and any and all product extensions

4. Fine-tuning the test variables for a rollout campaign

Each media plan should indicate the market, station, and dayparts being tested. The plan should show the total households reached by station and by daypart. A cost-per-thousand (CPM) for each of these should also be included in the plan so that the marketer can compare his cost per order against it.

CPMS AND CPOS— WHAT ARE THEY?

When the offer is geared toward a mass market audience, rates can be based on households reached per station. If a given rate represents $1.50 CPM on households, then you are probably paying the right cost per spot for your offer to pay out. If an offer is targeted toward a specific demographic segment, then you might try to negotiate the rates based on a $3 CPM. While the comparison of CPM to CPO is not an exact science, it is clear that the more households available per airing, the greater potential for increased volume.

The frequency allocated by daypart and by station should be combined with the cost per spot to calculate the total budget for each station. In order to get the reading on the offer during the test, you need to book approximately 15 spots per week.

A prospective user has a variety of research tools available to assist in media decision making and developing media plans. Mediamark Research, Inc. (MRI) measures product usage among various demographic segments. Nielsen provides ratings per daypart and programs measured for rating. Arbitron provides household coverage numbers for broadcast markets and stations. But even with the statistical information at hand, a station's previous performance is the best indicator of future success.

KNOW THE COMPETITION

Knowing what the competition is doing is a helpful research tool in developing your own media plan. There are several ways to measure this. *Barcume Reports* is a quarterly publication that calculates media dollars (television and cable) by advertiser and product. Dollar expenditures are broken down by month and the total expenditure (year-to-date) is updated with each report. And you can watch television. During first and third quarters keep a log of what you see. Note when you see, where you see, and how often you see a direct-response commercial on television. Try to make note of the company, product, length of spot, and price of offer. Make a special note if you notice any new or different direct-response techniques being utilized.

KNOW YOUR AUDIENCE

Because direct-response television can target various types of consumers, it is important to determine your primary and secondary audiences when airing on broadcast and/or cable television. Define your target by considering the following: male/female; age; urban, suburban, or rural; household income. Ideally your offer should appeal to the largest segment of television viewers. That will enable you to utilize more dayparts, thus lowering your media cost per spot and potentially increasing your response.

When selecting a broadcast market, stations, and/or cable networks, their prior experience with similar offers should count heavily. Since direct-response buys are combinations of availabilities and rates, your main objective in selecting stations is the lowest possible rate and the best opportunity to generate response at a desirable cost per order.

The target audience and demographic profile of your customer is also important in selecting the stations. For example, if your offer carries a high price point, you may want to consider cable networks that have a higher concentration of upscale viewers than broadcast stations.

What is probably the most important element in negotiating—and renegotiating—direct-response schedules is what is called the "friendship factor." If you asked the most established and experienced media buyers in the field what the key is to generating successful direct-response programs, they would say (off the record) relationships! These relationships are formed and strengthened because of the following factors:

- Rotation of various commercials
- Offers that produce high volume and that have mass appeal so that broader dayparts can be scheduled
- Low-maintenance schedules
- Quality commercials that enhance a station's on-air appearance
- Payment of bills on a timely basis

All these factors contribute to building ongoing relationships with stations so that you become established as a major, reliable, and credible direct-response player.

TESTING

Spot market stations and cable networks sell direct-response time at substantially reduced rates during soft seasons to corporate, retail, and package-goods advertisers. Therefore, the very best seasons for direct-response advertising are first and third quarters. It is in these quarters you want to buy as much time as possible.

When do you test? It may sound strange, but it's wiser to test your offer during second and fourth quarters. True, rates are higher and availabilities are lower. True, you may air in dayparts where your least desirable customers are found. True, your cost per order may come in over your allowable margin. But equally true, and more important, you will be able to determine what time periods don't work for your offer and the rates you need in order to pay out. This provides you with the basis for renegotiating rates with stations for your rollout. Since direct-response television is an ongoing process of testing and refining, learning what doesn't work is almost as critical as learning what does.

For example, if the early morning daypart doesn't work for your offer on one station, you now know not to book that daypart for other stations that have similar audience and programming profiles. However, the same early morning daypart might produce more favorable results if the station has a larger household coverage and/or if the programming scheduled during that daypart attracts a larger number or different kind of viewer.

If you are going out in the market with a new product at an untried price, it would be wise to reserve some of your test budget for price testing. While it is difficult to set up precise price testing cells on television, the following criteria need to be used in order to read the results in any way at all:

1. Select two matched markets in broadcast (TVHH, programming, and similar audience profiles).
2. Schedule similar dayparts.
3. Schedule equal frequencies per station, per daypart.
4. Test one price on both stations during the same 2-week period.
5. Select markets that air at the same price.

Repeat this test with two other markets at a different price for another two weeks. This gives you a total test flight of 4 weeks. Instead of running for 4 weeks at one price, you now have information for two price points. Rollout with the best results.

If you are not testing for price, a different direct-response test usually lasts 3–4 weeks. A typical test scenario would include the following:

1. Three broadcast markets—two stations within each market. This allows you to test two independent stations within each market to determine which performs better. Budget $20,000 for each of these six stations.
2. One or two cable networks. Budget between $20,000 and $30,000. This brings the average test budget to $40,000–$50,000.
3. Frequency per station—at least 15 spots per week. In second and fourth quarters where preemption is high, you'll have to overbook testing frequencies by 25–35 percent so that the schedule clears 15 spots per week.
   There are times when you can test offers during first and third quarters

without losing the value of these quarters for surefire rollout winners. If you are placing one or more rollout campaigns, stations will often allocate testing flights for untried direct-response offers. While stations tend to look for 13-week advertisers during first and third quarters, your relationship with the station will help you achieve testing frequencies at lower rates.

THE LONGER THE BETTER?

The question of how long a direct-response commercial ought to be in order to successfully relay its message and produce results is an ongoing debate among professionals in the business. In some cases, the longer format commercial is necessary if the product requires demonstration or if the offer is one that requires a lot of explanation. One of the more traditional direct-response offers is the record collection offer. This category has been tested in both the 60-second and 120-second length. Results have shown that viewers need to see and hear more music selections before they make a purchase decision. Additionally, products like kitchen appliances, that require demonstration, require a longer commercial so that all the relevant information about the product and the offer is conveyed.

Stations have sought to discourage the 120-second advertisers by pricing the inventory at a very high rate. In some cases it's impossible to schedule a 120-second commercial in a daypart other than early daytime and overnight. However, a 120-second commercial can still prove effective, especially when aired in conjunction with a 60-second commercial.

Sixty-second direct-response commercials have proved successful for many advertisers. The shorter length spot allows the advertiser to book more frequency at lower rates, and go for overall volume as opposed to efficiency per spot. Today 30-second direct-response commercials are being tested.

THE ROTATION GAME

The majority of direct response airs on a run-of-schedule (ROS) basis. Spots scheduled from sign-on to sign-off offer the lowest direct-response rate. When booking an ROS rotation, request a minimum separation of 2 hours between airings to reach a more varied audience. Some stations only promise 1 hour, some only a 30-minute separation. That's a point for negotiating. Use ROS as a negotiating tool to give the station more business. Offers that appeal to the mass market do well on ROS schedules, and stations have an easier time scheduling direct response on an ROS basis.

When ROS proves inefficient, it might be time to schedule your commercial in broad daypart rotation, perhaps 9 a.m.–5 p.m. Rates will be approximately 30 percent higher than the ROS rates. The more narrow rotation allows for greater narrowcasting of the television audience and a potentially higher response because the offer will target the intended primary market.

To better understand the concept of dayparts, you should know that 9 a.m.–4 p.m. constitutes daytime; 4 p.m.–7 p.m. is early fringe; 7 p.m.–8 p.m. is prime access; 8 p.m.–11 p.m. is prime time; 11 p.m.–1 a.m. is late fringe; 1 a.m. to conclusion (cc) constitutes overnight.

For ever more selective target marketing, direct response can also be scheduled within narrow dayparts, e.g., 4 p.m.–7 p.m. Rates will be approximately 15 percent higher than broad daypart rates. This allows your commercial to air in early fringe.

PREEMPTION

Clearance, or preemption percentages, will vary based on the quarter of the year, as well as the time in the quarter in which you place your buy. In first and third quarters the average preemption rate is 15–25 percent. In second and fourth quarters the average preemption rate is 25–60 percent. When you begin a test schedule, you will usually begin to see your clearance increase as you proceed. It will reach a certain point and then start to drop off. This usually happens at the same time that your orders start declining on a particular station. This is the time to give your commercial a rest so that you have time to regroup your media strategy and air on other stations.

In terms of how many viewings it takes a viewer to respond to your offer, there's no magic formula. The industry dictates that it takes two times for the message and offer to sink in. By the third viewing the caller should be motivated by need, desire, or impulse to pick up the phone and order.

TELEVISION'S FLEXIBILITY

Television certainly provides flexibility. There is no other medium that can provide the direct-response advertiser with as quick a turnaround in getting on and off the air, or making immediate sales or not. With the ability to refine dayparts, renegotiate rates, and cancel schedules altogether, television is not a one-shot proposition. Even an unsuccessful offer, after all attempts to make it work have failed, leaves the marketer with a certain amount of sales to help recoup a portion of the expenses.

There is also no other medium that enables the advertiser to recycle revenue faster. Much of this is due to the billing cycles of the stations. Stations bill based on a broadcast month. Station affidavits are received during the middle of the next month and are due 30 days later. Therefore, money from orders received is captured before media money is due to the stations. This money can be reinvested without having to invest more of your own financial reserves.

TELEMARKETING

When direct-response television advertisers were given the opportunity to tag their commercials with 800 numbers, the financial configuration of running a direct-response television campaign changed dramatically for the better. This single critical addition created major benefits that made doing television possible for many advertisers.

The 800 number not only benefited the advertiser but the customer as well. Because 800 numbers were toll-free, customers no longer had to pay postage for mailing their orders. Customers received their orders more quickly. This in turn reduced the amount of cancelled and returned product. Reorders were achieved more quickly and in higher quantity.

Advertisers were able to capture larger orders more quickly. This allowed for a faster media reinvestment, which increased order volume on an overall basis. In addition, the ability to use an 800 number instead of, or in addition to, a post office box address, enabled the commercial to be produced in a shorter length. This not only saved the advertiser production costs, but also provided for lower media costs and more frequent runs.

The addition of telemarketing to direct-response television also enabled the advertiser to learn much more about his customer during the front-end marketing process. The front end provided an opportunity for direct-response advertisers not only to capture orders for the product being advertised, but also to "upsell" the customer to multiple orders or a higher-priced product extension item.

There are several considerations to evaluate before you decide on a telemarketing company. Ask the sales representative from the company about the size of the inbound facility. Determining the square footage of the service will give you some idea of how many operators they accommodate.

Ask lots of questions about their software capabilities. It's important that you become aware of the industry's latest technological advancements, such as downloading capabilities, so that you can request that they be applied to your program. This eliminates the need for the telemarketing company to fax you the daily source reports. Instead, all the results for each station can be electronically transmitted right into your own computer system. This will make formulating your weekly cumulative reports much easier.

Once you've selected a telemarketing company, ask for a request for proposal (RFP) for your program. Provide them with whatever information is available about your product, the offer, price structure, accepted payment methods (credit card, bill-to, COD, etc.), the estimated volume based on the media you will be running, and any upsell offer you want to make on the front end.

As a guideline, the basic cost of capturing name, address, city, state, and zip code is about 80–95 cents per call. If you ask the telemarketing operator to request a form of payment and capture credit card information, you can expect to pay 25–35 cents more per call. So, your estimated cost per call is between $1.25 and $1.35.

If you are using the same telemarketing service for several inbound programs, you may be able to get a volume discount on the cost-per-call rates. In some cases it is advantageous to use the same telemarketer for several programs. If they are reliable, cost-efficient, and familiar with your type of programs, you can expect better service. However, it is equally important to establish relationships with other telemarketers in the industry. You can vary your service and provide a backup if need be.

You may decide to change or add some information in your telemarketing script following the initial media test. For example, you may decide to capture the phone numbers of those customers who chose not to pay by credit card. This will enable you to use followup outbound telemarketing to try and convert these people to a sale. Or you may wish to add an upsell question to the script. Since adding an upsell will add an additional 25–35 cents per call, it is advisable that you only offer an upsell to customers who use credit cards for payment.

When using a telemarketing service, remember to allocate a different phone number for each television or cable station on which your commercial is airing. This will enable the telemarketing company to properly allocate the orders that come in to the correct station. This, in turn, will help you determine the viability of the offer on each station. There are some cases where the same 800 number can be used on more than one station. If the station signals are at least 200 miles apart, there should be no problem with station allocation.

800 VERSUS 900 NUMBERS

The basic difference between an 800- and a 900-number call is that the first is free, the second is not. While more and more advertisers are making use of 900 numbers, consider very carefully before you install this kind of program, because at present they seem to have more disadvantages than advantages:

Advantages

900-number programs defray the cost of telemarketing.

900-number programs produce income

900-number programs lower overall media cost per order.

Disadvantages

Callers don't truly understand the cost structure.

Some phone companies have abandoned charging their customers for these calls due to previous misallocation problems.

Investigations into some 900-number adult services have discovered that children are calling these numbers.

Many stations won't accept 900-number programs due to viewer complaints.

AT&T requires that the advertiser show value for including a 900 number in the commercial.

The cost of the call or the service cannot exceed set price points.

It is important to remember that telemarketing companies play an essential role in your ongoing direct-response television campaign. Not only do they provide you with daily source reports that show you how many orders each station achieved, they can also help to increase the average sale per order and enhance the very important customer list you will be building. By asking additional questions and capturing useful information, telemarketers can help build the foundation for future back-end promotions.

EVALUATING TEST RESULTS

In evaluating results, you're looking for three things:

1. How well a particular market performed in comparison to other markets
2. How well various stations performed in relation to each other

3. How well each daypart or ROS rotation you purchased delivered in terms of
   your target CPO.

Prepare a daypart analysis after you've received your exact times and results,
which are provided weekly by the station. You should be able to call stations
between Tuesday and Wednesday to get the exact times. Calculate your analysis
to determine the CPOs achieved in each daypart and on each station overall by
totalling orders received in each daypart from the telemarketing source reports.

Begin by totalling the money you've spent in all the dayparts you've bought
for each station. Allocate the orders you've received in each of these dayparts.
Typically you should take the number of orders that come in with each spot
plus the next two hours worth of drag. *Drag* is defined as additional orders that
are reported on the daily source reports 2 or more hours after a spot has aired.
To calculate the cost per order for each of these dayparts, divide the number of
orders by the total dollars spent. The stations with CPOs at or below your allowable should be booked for rollout immediately. The stations with CPOs 10–
30 percent above your allowable should be able to be renegotiated to breakeven
or below. With those 50 percent above allowable you can attempt to renegotiate,
but you will probably have to drop them from the media plan.

Your cost per order enables you to figure out the following: what rates you
need by station; what rates you need by daypart to make the offer pay out; how
increased or decreased frequency will affect your CPO. These questions and
their answers will take you back to negotiate a lower rate, a narrower or broader
rotation, or additional or reduced frequency.

The media test influences your original media plan in determining what return you are going to need to start producing a profit. Look at the percentage
of credit card orders versus CODs versus prebills. Credit card is self-
explanatory. COD, used by advertisers for many years, requires a lot of paperwork and administrative followup. Since the potential for undelivered merchandise exists, COD usage has decreased.

Prebilling affords the caller who chooses not to pay by credit card or to send
a check to a particular address, the opportunity to order by first receiving an
invoice. Once payment is remitted, orders should be shipped within 2–4 weeks.
The key to making this two-step payment method work is for the advertisers to
send out prebills within 48 hours of receipt of order.

It costs a bit more to send out a communication before you receive an order.
But in cases where you experience a 30–40 percent prebill percentage on your
total orders, you can convert 15–30 percent of your orders if you prebill
quickly.

Since credit card orders can be turned into immediate cash, it is advisable to
deposit the credit card money as cash as soon as the product is shipped. This
will cut down on the amount of merchandise that is returned or orders cancelled. Customers don't like to be billed for orders they've not yet received. So,
either ship within a 72–96-hour turnaround, or hold off depositing credit card
slips until you ship the product.

Stations that generate a high percentage of credit card orders should be
weighed as significant stations during a rollout. Plan on spending more on these
stations as the rollout progresses.

If you have a mail-to address tag – usually a PO box number that appears at the spot's end — it's important to evaluate the percentage of orders that come in through this channel. In some cases, it could be 2–3 percent of your total orders. If you are reaching that percentage, you may want to make a quick revision on the tag that enlarges the address or reads it out in audio so that more viewers can register the address more clearly and use it to mail checks. That way you're not paying telemarketing charges to capture customer information and sales.

In renegotiating rates, if the station won't lower the rate prior to rollout, perhaps you may be able to negotiate a certain number of bonus (free) spots. These can offset a high CPO and help a program pay out. The station benefits because it won't lose the scheduled revenue.

One of the biggest advantages of direct-response television is that there are many things that can be done with a station before deciding to cancel that station altogether. Here's a list of strategies to attack before cancelling a station:

1. Renegotiate to achieve a lower rate.

2. Ask for bonus spots.

3. Narrow the rotation. This often means that the rate will go up, but it may help target your audience more exactly, which may prove more efficient in the long run.

4. Broaden the rotation. Perhaps your offer may appeal to a wider market, and broadening the rotation will afford you a lower rate.

5. Request additional frequencies so that you can get more separation between spots.

The process of testing provides you with the information you need to help you refine your stations for rollout. While the words *test* and *rollout* have different definitions, it is important to understand that even during a rollout you will always be testing something. Whether it's a different rotation, a lower or higher rate, or an additional frequency, the process of testing never truly ends until you reach a point where you attain your cost per order objective.

ROLLING OUT

In planning a rollout, first decide which of the test stations are applicable in terms of how they performed during the test and then decide on the best way to allocate your budget.

You need to determine how long a flight you'll run. If possible, schedule a rollout for no less than 13 weeks. Anticipate a hiatus during second and fourth quarters and concentrate most of your frequency during first and third quarters.

If you have a product or offer that's date-sensitive, e.g., anniversaries of certain events, elections, dates of historical significance or sports events, your key selling time will usually be centered around the date of the event: 4 weeks before and 4 weeks after. The time you spend in building the frequency is also critical, so be sure to test early when it comes to planning for event marketing offers.

For most traditional direct-response offers, run your commercial and increase spending up to the point at which you see the results begin to level off. Then pull back on spending and only air in dayparts and on stations that produce the best results. Plan a hiatus to give your offer a rest. Viewers don't like seeing the same spot run all the time.

If a campaign is doing well, it can run longer than 13 weeks. While it is valuable to understand the importance of giving your commercial a rest, it is equally important to understand that this is not necessarily true for all offers at all times.

If you are running a campaign that seems to be improving as the weeks go on and you can see no foreseeable drop in orders, there is no reason to pull it. However, start testing other stations so that you can increase your market share.

ONGOING EVALUATION

Ongoing evaluation of results is critical to a program's success. One of the single most important considerations is the monitoring of results. For clients new to direct response, you may wish to consider preparing daily estimated reports based on telemarketing dailies. These reports would include how many spots ran, based on the spots noted on the dailies, with a cost per spot for each airing. This will enable you and the client to see what the daily clearance rate is and what the trend of orders is.

While this kind of daily reporting often requires more time than a buyer might want to devote, it can save time in the long run. Advertisers new to direct response won't read test results the same way you will and will want to know what to expect from day to day. Instead of spending hours on the phone explaining how a test works, it might be better to put some hard data in their hands. It means spending more time and asking the test stations to provide you with exact times earlier than they would ideally like to, but that can be a requirement of the test prior to implementation. Be sure to make appropriate comments on your reports so that your clients not only read the numbers but understand what they mean.

More experienced advertisers will be content with weekly cumulative reports following each week's airing. Listed by station, this report includes columns for the total dollars booked by station (based on exact times); total dollars cleared; percentage of clearance; orders per spot; credit card orders; COD or other method of payment for orders; total units sold per order; upsells sold; and average sales per order.

Daily monitoring of each station for the first few weeks of the rollout is essential. Once the cost per order reaches the allowable margin, you can report weekly and monitor a bit less closely.

As previously mentioned, one of the best ways to become an established direct-response advertiser is to book schedules on a 13-week basis. Stations like low maintenance schedules and they get to know you by the length of time you air on their station. If you have several programs that you plan on testing you can always insert one of them if your rollout program doesn't achieve the results you need. This will keep you from cancelling the buy and leaving the station to resell the inventory.

Knowing when to renegotiate is important. Don't start calling the station after the first spot airs. Let the spot air at least three to five times before you begin talking with the station about what to do next. Ideally, it's best to let the entire test run as scheduled, analyze, and then renegotiate.

If, after renegotiation, the offer still isn't doing well, go through your renegotiation steps. If after that, the CPO is still too high, pull the plug.

Reconsidering the structure of your offer should be your last effort in trying to make the offer work. If you have the money in your budget, spend it on refining the offer. Very often changing the price of your offer can give you a 30–50 percent lift. Other things to consider include adding an incentive, such as a premium or dollars-off reduction for those who order within a specified time period. Also try putting the phone number up sooner and for a longer period of time.

Another way to help make direct-response television more efficient is to take a look at your telemarketing script. Is it working hard enough? Is it converting buyers to the upsell? Think about offering some kind of incentive to customers who order your product for ordering multiples of the product or taking the upsell. Very often these two things make the program work on its own.

CABLE

Cable affords advertisers an opportunity to narrowcast the offer. The demographics of cable viewers suggest they are more responsive to direct marketing offers. Research shows that the average cable household is a more upscale household than the noncable household. Research also shows that cable viewers are better educated, hold more managerial and professional jobs, have higher household incomes, and spend more discretionary income than noncable viewers. MRI states that cable viewers spend 60 percent more on goods and services than viewers in noncable homes. The demographic profile of the cable viewer is an inviting proposition for the direct-response advertiser.

If cable is part of your media mix, it should be considered and used as a frequency medium—especially if your test objective is volume. Since most of the major cable networks (USA, TBS, CNN, MTV, ESPN and The Family Channel) cover 55 percent or more of all U.S. television households, you can literally test your offer nationally at affordable rates. To test an offer nationally on broadcast would mean running on network television—and we all know what that costs. Cable affords the advertiser the opportunity to read an offer nationally and build frequency because of its affordability.

If you are selling a product that seeks an upscale, educated market, cable should definitely be a consideration. Cable networks have achieved sufficient growth over the past three years. Table 18-1 represents the growth of total subscribers by cable network 1988–1990.

Typically the kinds of offers that have pulled major volume on cable include: record offers, books and magazines, various children's products, big-ticket items such as cosmetics and upscale European household appliances, financial services, and long-distance services.

The credit card usage among cable viewers is high, and therefore your average sale per order from cable might be higher than from broadcast.

As with most things in high demand, supply often depletes much faster than

Table 18-1. Cable Subscriber Growth, 1988–1990*

| Network | July 1988 | | July 1989 | | July 1990 | |
	% U.S.	Viewers (in millions)	% U.S.	Viewers (in millions)	% U.S.	Viewers (in millions)
A&E	39	30.1	44	40.0	50	46.4
BET	23	20.4	26	23.9	30	28.0
CNN	53	47.0	57	51.1	60	55.4
Discovery Channel	38	33.7	48	43.3	56	55.4
ESPN	53	47.0	57	51.9	54	49.8
Family Channel	47	41.6	50	45.4	37	33.7
FNN	34	30.1	34	30.7	47	43.1
Headline News	37	32.8	41	37.4	54	49.7
Lifetime	45	39.9	48	43.7	56	49.7
MTV	48	42.5	52	46.9	56	51.9
Nickelodeon	47	41.6	52	46.7	56	51.8
Nick-at-Nite	42	37.2	52	46.7	56	51.8
TBS	51	45.2	55	49.5	59	54.5
TNN	46	40.8	50	45.6	55	20.7
TNT	—	—	32	29.0	52	47.8
Weather Channel	40	35.4	42	38.3	49	45.2
USA	51	45.2	53	48.2	58	53.0
VH-1	32	28.4	35	32.0	41	37.7

SOURCE: Nielsen Media Research Coverage Tracking Report

you had planned. This is true of cable. In 1984, time was plentiful. Direct response advertisers had their pick of the lot. PI (per-inquiry) opportunities were plentiful and you could buy a paid spot for $100–$200. Today the pickings are rather slim. PIs are few and far between. Those networks that do accept them are asking 30–35 percent of the retail value of the offer. Paid spots in daytime, early- and late-fringe are still affordable. It's best to place your buys in advance of first and third quarters to lock in the best rates. Be sure to leave enough time to schedule your tests during second and fourth quarters so that you can secure the lowest rate possible in the more expensive quarters.

One indication that times have changed for cable advertising is the strong upfront market that cable experienced for 1991. Package-goods advertisers, corporate sponsorships, and spot packages are all cashing in on cable's upscale market—early. No longer are general advertisers waiting for network and spot television to underdeliver on their guarantees. These advertisers are applying more than just the incremental budget to cable. They are now scheduling dedicated budgets to the major cable networks.

What this means to the direct-response advertiser is that less time will be available on the major cable networks. Rates will continue to increase. The smart direct-response advertiser will keep this in mind when formulating the offer and producing the commercial. Since the major cable networks are seeing more activity from general advertisers, cable networks such as Lifetime, A&E, The Discovery Channel, MTV Networks (which include MTV, VH1, Nickelodeon, and Nick-at-Nite), and Headline News are seeing more advertising dollars.

These "secondary" cable networks are growing at a fast pace and offering programming slanted toward different and profitable market segments.

INFOMERCIALS

Infomercials are paid programming announcements that are 15 or 30 minutes long. They are one of the newest and most profitable forms of direct-response television today.

If you were to turn on your television early in the morning or stay up past your bedtime during the week, you would no doubt catch one of the latest infomercials airing on independent television stations and perhaps on national cable.

You may not have known the term *infomercial*, but you've seen the format. Or perhaps you've seen the demonstration formats—someone showing you the very latest in cleaners that removes "even the toughest stains," or electric kitchen utensils that can do every cooking chore imaginable. Perhaps you've spent time watching and learning about techniques that can turn you into a real-estate mogul with "no money down," or educational and study tips that can help your child get better grades in school. You may have also witnessed remarkable cosmetics and face-care products that promise a more beautiful, wrinkle-free, and healthier skin, and diet programs where the only gain is in customers, not pounds. These are infomercials.

The products may differ, but there is a string of common elements in all these programs. First, if budget permits, many producers of infomercials will have a well-known celebrity host the program, usually someone a bit past his or her prime, but recognizable, credible, and effective all the same. There will usually be one or more guests who will come on the show and explain their success with the product being sold. These infomercials even have breaks so that a 1–2-minute commercial "wrap up" can air. This commercial usually restates the product benefits, explains the offer, and tells you how to order.

Today you'll see infomercials that sell products with price points from $39 to more than $2000. The initial reason for producing infomercials was to sell a product or service at a price higher than the normal impulse price point of $9.95–$29.95. Infomercials have the time to persuade the viewer to spend more than the impulse price normally offered within a 60-second, 90-second, or 120-second spot, so the higher price can be justified.

There are many advantages and reasons for producing infomercials. The time allotted provides the audience with a lot of background on the product. Through testimonials from customers who have used the product, and interview-format programs, viewers get firsthand knowledge of how the product works. The credibility of the product and of the company selling the program is proved, and viewers feel satisfied that they are purchasing a reputable product.

Another benefit of infomercials is that they can provide a back-end marketing plan not only for additional orders, but also for bounce-back offers on product extension lines and cross-promotions.

There are also disadvantages to infomercials that advertisers should be aware of when placing infomercials on television. There have been some companies that have used the format of an infomercial to promote products that simply don't work. Because of this viewers have become somewhat wary of some of the products sold through infomercials. But there are ways to overcome objections:

1. Be sure to include disclaimers throughout the program. State that this product is a paid commercial announcement and that the views expressed are solely those of the advertiser, not the station.

2. Be clear on any product claims being made. For example, in selling products like cosmetics, make sure the viewer knows that results are not guaranteed.

3. Be sure to list—in supers—the price, the shipping and handling costs, and any other cost or payment method applicable in the offer.

4. Offer a money-back guarantee.

5. Include as many case histories, demonstrations, facts, and testimonials as possible. Viewers like to see that other people like themselves have bought and liked the product.

In testing infomercials, it's important to realize that each infomercial will literally build its own audience and customer base. Every market has the potential to succeed and every station can work, provided you know the formula. The basic rule of thumb in negotiating rates for infomercials is to rank stations based on the total households delivered in a given half-hour segment and the resulting CPM. Obviously, dayparts that deliver more households provide more of an opportunity to gain customers.

Since the cost of buying infomercial spots is high, it is not possible to gain as much frequency as from a traditional direct-response spot. However, it is important to gain frequency within a particular daypart so that you can continue to build your own audience. Following your test, rollout by scheduling five to seven shows a week.

Stations tend to sell infomercial time during the following times:

1. Weekday late night: 12:30 a.m.–conclusion

2. Weekend early morning: 7 a.m.–10 a.m.

It has become more profitable for the station to sell infomercial time to direct marketers than to schedule programming during dayparts to sell to general advertisers who could not afford the station premium rates.

The costs for half-hour infomercials vary from $200 to $30,000. It all depends on the market, the station, and the households delivered during the daypart being sold.

Telemarketing can play a large role in capturing front-end customer information and orders. Operators should be trained to answer more questions about the offer and also to work harder to try to upsell each customer. This will keep down your media costs per order.

The future of infomercials is promising. Without doubt, this is the largest and fastest area of growth in direct-response television today. If you have a unique story to tell about your product, are offering it at a valuable price point, can show value through testimonials and demonstration, can afford a celebrity host for additional credibility, can offer a unique product new to the marketplace, and have enough back-end offers to develop lifetime customers, you are an excellent candidate for an infomercial.

CONCLUSION

With the increased amount of direct-response advertising and the number of companies, including start-ups, getting into television, what kind of future will direct-response television have in terms of being able to be a viable distribution channel for selling products?

If we've learned anything from the past, it's that history has a way of repeating itself. In length and content, today's 15-minute infomercials resemble the direct-response spots of the 1960s before the Federal Communications Commission banned the long commercial format. As a next step, direct-response advertisers began experimenting with 2-minute formats.

So experimentation seems imperative for the successful direct marketer in the 1990s. Breakthroughs will be seen not only in infomercials but in shorter length direct-response formats. As more and more consumers turn to video as well as to television for their entertainment, additional opportunities to generate buying opportunities may result in this allied medium.

The sophistication of databases will make it logical to target customers with specially-prepared video infomercials delivered right to the home. As a result, the back end for these products has the potential to grow dramatically.

Increasing narrowcasting opportunities on cable will also encourage advertisers to zero in on consumers with specific lifestyles and interests and relate those lifestyles and interests to specific new products.

The aging of the baby boomers, with their increasing needs for service opportunities, will provide an opportunity for industries previously not involved in direct response.

As computer technology refines interactive systems, new opportunities will arise for what has traditionally been considered broadcasting. With new electronic media choices, advertisers will be able to fashion commercials of varying lengths. The cost of placing them will also be reminiscent of days gone by.

A few constants will remain. An increasingly sophisticated audience will continue to demand the highest quality production values. Additionally, while the product will certainly continue to be important, the offer must be appealing. Increasingly, advertisers who are able to appeal to the desire for quality will be able to garner new sales and see improvements to their bottom line.

Whatever commercial formats prevail, the ultimate purpose of direct response will stay the same—to make the offer and close the sale. And the ultimate success in direct-response television will always result from the art of negotiation.

19

Co-op Mailings and Package Inserts

Leon Henry, Jr.

Leon Henry, Inc.
Scarsdale, N.Y.

The direct-mail industry has always looked for and found alternative media to use. As the postal rates have climbed, so has the number of alternative media. Two that have had a greater-than-expected impact on the industry are co-ops and package inserts.

Package inserts should be considered the more viable medium because their availabilities are greater. The growth of co-ops, which were once in the same class of expansion as package inserts, has been inhibited by a number of factors, making it unlikely that they will continue to grow beyond the current market.

Package inserts originated in a casual way approximately 30 years ago. At that time, several advertisers who were placing their advertisements in mail-order packages on a direct basis were approached by an entrepreneur who wanted to use his expertise to make the appropriate connections, do the paperwork, and see the jobs as they then existed through to completion. Among the original advertisers were some of the bigger names in the direct-mail field: RCA Record Club (now BMG Record Club), Nashua Photo (then called Best Photo), and GRI World of Beauty.

The distributors of the inserts (which were not then called "inserts") were many of the same companies. They were, in effect, trading among themselves through several "brokers." (The list brokerage fraternity was not involved then.) Pricing was in the $15 per thousand range. The number of participants was limited, as were the number of inserts placed. Several entrepreneurs were exploring various other avenues of activity: one was in the retailer statement area, another in supermarkets, and another in toys and games.

Competition brought greater recognition to the emerging medium. Several additional developments resulted in the next level of activity. The medium worked satisfactorily enough for repeat usage. The repeaters were more conspicuous, thereby drawing in more users. Some of the users were very heavily involved in the new medium and needed more outlets than were in existence. The new outlets required more than one or two insert users and put pressure on the fledgling insert brokers to come up with even more users. Finally, the first in the current series of postal rate increases made the emerging medium more viable to all concerned.

The co-op market went through a similar evolution. The low price of third class postage made this medium more viable in the beginning and less so as time passed. Eventually, the costs of most co-ops became too high to allow the requisite profit for the entrepreneurs involved, so the co-op market began to move in the direction of "ride-alongs," with the original mailers accepting others in their mailing to amortize their costs. This is how most of the co-op market operates today. (An exception is the Carol Wright Co-op from Donnelley Marketing.)

WHAT IS A PACKAGE INSERT?

As the name implies, package inserts are advertisements, either from the company selling the product or from outsiders, inserted in packages being delivered to customers. Depending on the way in which the purchase transpires, the packages—and the advertising inserts therein—are delivered to mail-order or retail buyers. The packages naturally vary in size, weight, and method of delivery (which can be via the U.S.P.S., UPS, retail delivery, or take-home). The packages originate with such well-known companies as Spiegel, Fingerhut, and Drawing Board, and such exotic ones such as Adam & Eve (contraceptives), Atlas Pen (pencils), Wecolite (kitchen gadgets), Wine Enthusiast (bar accessories), etc.

The number of inserts enclosed varies from four to eight, with the most common number being six. They will be loose or contained within a folder, catalog, or envelope. There will probably be "house inserts" if the package is from a mail-order company.

The conventionally packed and mailed or UPS-delivered packages allow for variations in the number of items ordered. This leaves space available for inserts. The insertion usually takes place as the merchandise is being packed. This gives the insert more of a chance to be seen by the customer as he or she unpacks the merchandise. Of course, the excitement of opening the purchase can minimize some of the impact of the package inserts. Large furniture items, for example, need packing material to protect them during shipment, and inserts placed in this type of package can be lost.

The mailer has to be alert to the variations of packaging and at the same time should only provide one insert format for all of the variety of package insert situations. Otherwise, the mailer's costs will be too high, and the added expense will reduce the probability of success.

By asking the insert broker to check with the distribution facility, the insert advertiser can find out how the inserts are packed. The problem is that at any given time the number of inserts and the participants will vary. Therefore, advertisers have to expect some variation in response to their offers, depending to some extent on the number of other inserts and their strength relative to their offer.

Since the one unwritten rule of the insert business is that there will be no category duplications, the advertiser who gains a place within the package can stay as long as it is economically feasible. And you may be sure there are advertisers who occupy categories *beyond* their economic viability in order to preserve their place in the package-insert program.

Retail distributed packages, which are a growing force in the package insert industry, have their own peculiarities. These can best be described as the problems inherent in the retail distribution cycle of the particular product involved. For example, the manufacturer of diapers who offers a package insert program has to have the inserts collated at an outside mailing house, then have the inserts moved to his packing line, where they are inserted. And this is still only the beginning of the distribution cycle, because, even after the inserts are in the package there is some storage time in the plant before the goods are moved to the various retailers selling the diapers. If the goods go to a wholesaler as an interim step, the time it takes for the inserts to reach the consumer will be that much longer. If the inserts go directly from the plant to a high-volume retailer with rapid turnover, the inserts will be distributed more quickly. The insert advertiser dealing with the retail distribution of his inserts must be prepared for the time it takes to distribute the goods.

Television-generated merchandise has its own peculiarities. Since television-marketed merchandise is often for COD delivery, there is the problem of unsold merchandise. An understanding of the nature of the distribution function will avoid the problem of undelivered merchandise and, accordingly, of undelivered inserts. Be sure to find out what happens to the undelivered merchandise and inserts.

Another problem with television- or radio-sold merchandise is the life span of the merchandise. These products often have a short life cycle. The advertiser has to be alert to the timing of the product. Too many inserts delivered with a product with a short life cycle can produce an overage of inserts, coupled with an invalid reading on the keying of the inserts.

WHAT IS A CO-OP?

A co-op is a noncompetitive group of advertisers mailing together to reduce costs and reach the same prospective customers. If the co-op mailing is run by a company whose primary purpose is to mail a catalog or announcement and it carries outside inserts, it should be called a ride-along.

Co-ops have had a spotty history. The main reason for most co-ops' lack of continuity seems to be the increasing costs faced by the organizations sponsoring them. This reason also seems to be behind the increase in ride-alongs.

Pricing for ride-alongs tends to be less than for co-ops, because any contribution by the participating advertisers lowers the expense of the sponsor. With a co-op, all costs have to be covered before the first dollar of profit is earned. Because the results are diluted by the increase in the number of participants, a circular situation tends to develop, diminishing the number of co-ops (at least currently).

One method of offsetting the increased number of mail-order participants is to substitute non-mail-order advertisers, such as couponers or local advertisers.

The problems with this system are that major couponers need very large distributions for their coupons and that the number of co-ops that fit this need (as the Carol Wright Co-op does) is very few. Non-mail-order industries (like the travel business), which have some experience with insert production, cannot seem to grasp the full potential in the co-op field; hence, the lack of non-mail-order inserts within co-ops.

Ride-alongs are more assured now than co-ops, because by definition the sponsor of the ride-along must have his catalog or mailing out by specified dates. It doesn't make sense to have a mailing for Christmas greeting cards except in August and September. Therefore, a ride-along from a company offering this product is sure to be delivered as contracted for. A major problem for co-ops has been postponement of the delivery date while the sponsor waits for the sale of, and then the delivery of, the inserts. Of course some advertiser is always ready to come in for a lower price at the last minute, which is advantageous to that advertiser and provides a potential problem for the sponsor.

Ride-alongs (like the Columbia Record Club's) with a membership bulletin or announcement have all the benefits the insert advertiser seeks: reliability of delivery, volume of recipients, reasonable cost, and reasonably assured readership. The major problem for the advertiser who has not used these vehicles before is the heavy prior commitment made by those participants who have had successful experience and who therefore may already occupy the category the new advertiser is seeking. An excellent example is the mail-order photo-finisher category which is next to impossible to obtain in most ride-alongs.

WHAT KINDS OF ADVERTISERS USE PACKAGE INSERTS AND CO-OPS?

At this point in the development of the medium, there are many major categories of advertisers:

Book and record club application forms

Mail-order photo finishers

Clothing offers

Catalog inquiries

Magazine subscription offers

Jewelry and other merchandise offers

Collectible offers

Credit card applications

Insurance applications

Historically, the medium has been dominated by the photo finishers, magazine clubs, jewelry groups, catalog inquiries, and credit card offers. These have been the medium's heavy users — the advertisers who take all the insert space available in the programs that is appropriate to their offer. A mail-order photo finisher, for instance, would want to be in all the consumer-directed package-insert and co-op programs, especially those that target the young homeowner. A magazine produced for young parents would want packages and co-ops that are going out to young families. A magazine reaching an older audience would be interested in the insert programs directed to buyers of vitamins and other merchandise frequently ordered by older persons. Similarly, so-called grand-parent programs have been effective with such offers as Christmas gifts.

It used to be that advertisers whose products are limited to a specific audience had to inquire if there were enough package-insert programs to consider par-ticipating. There are still many categories of programs that are not extensive enough to produce an insert. For example, there are very few scientific pro-grams. (Edmund Scientific is the best known.) An advertiser looking for the young boy who buys by mail (or for his parents) will find very few insert pro-grams, but at least enough to build a media schedule.

Efforts to enlarge the industry have been undertaken by the major brokers whose growth has paralleled the postage rise. But these efforts seem to be in the program categories that offer the most participation by advertisers. The indus-try is heavily weighted toward the woman mail-order buyer. Efforts on the part of the most active brokers seem to be in her direction.

An increasing number of advertisers are using the insert medium, a natural development given the publicity generated by the field in the last few years and the constant rise in postal costs. The newer entrants are encountering some problems, however, starting with their lack of experience in the direct-mail in-dustry. Since the principles of the industry dictate the success of the insert seg-ment, it is vital to know what to expect before using the medium.

Looking for too-rapid results and success on every effort also seems to be common among the newer advertisers. An unwillingness to understand the test-ing procedure and a failure to grasp the mathematics of direct mail are addi-tional problems to be overcome by the newer entrants.

Many of the newer insert advertisers seem to have financing difficulties as well. The insert medium appears to be a haven for new entrepreneurs, who are enticed by the low cost of entry and the ability to conceal this kind of advertising from potential competitors. Usually, the undercapitalized entrant is requested to pay up front for participation by most programs.

INSERT FORMAT AND PREPARATION

The basic industry format is a 5 1/2-in × 8 1/2-in, one- or two-panel, four-color advertisement. The second basic format is that which fits a statement situation. These are generally 3 1/2 in by 6 in. The two common ways of accommodating this situation are to create an insert for this size only or to fold the larger insert to fit the smaller situation. There are some sound reasons for the second ap-proach. First of all, there are fewer small-size distributions. Secondly, there are many examples of the folded insert being used to cover all situations. Perhaps the best known are magazine inserts, which are prepared in only one size and then folded where necessary to fit smaller-size distributions.

The insert must be prepared in such a way that it is machine insertable. By this we mean that the printer must pack the insert material in such a way that it is readily available to the inserting vehicle. Since most collating is done on a Phillipsburg or Bell & Howell inserting machine, the insert material must be banded in uniform amounts of approximately 200 pieces. When the material is to be stored in cartons, care should be taken to ensure that it does not slip in the containers. Each carton should be marked with the amount contained and the key code of the inserts. There should be a notification on each carton of the total number of cartons included in the shipment. Shippers should obtain signed receipts from the receivers.

RETURN VEHICLES

The use of a return vehicle is taken for granted in the insert medium. How it is used depends on the offer, of course.

There are two standard formats for return vehicles, the first being the business reply card, or BRC. Though the business reply card is usually part of the format, it can be interleaved with the insert. The price of inserting is always quoted on a per thousand basis, so that it is better to provide one, *and only one*, insert to the inserting house. With two separate pieces, you stand the chance of an increase in price and the possibility that the second insert will be lost or not distributed.

The other return vehicle that is commonly used is the business reply envelope, or BRE. With the development of the Webcraft envelope, cash-with-order offers can be accommodated in the insert medium. Heretofore, the mailer would have had to provide an additional envelope in order to receive cash or checks.

New Formats

Lately, there have been several new format developments. One is the extremely lightweight and/or smaller insert. The second is the heavier and/or bulky insert. In each case, creative mailers are looking at the distribution problem and seeing if they can bend the rather simple pricing structure to their own ends. The lightweight insert offers the broker a good reason for negotiating lower prices. There are some justifiable uses for the smaller insert, among which are inquiries, ads for very low-priced products, and very simple offers. The combination of lower pricing costs and sometimes lower insert costs can give this approach a viability that some other inserts do not have.

The heavier or bulkier insert can usually only be used in packages that are large enough to accept them and in cases where the packing is done by hand. The advantage to the mailer is that a considerably larger amount of copy (and thus a more powerful sales message) can be distributed for the same or a proportionately lower price. Even if the program charges more than the normal pricing, the heavier insert is ahead of the game.

The usual weight of inserts is 1/4 oz or less. A few programs have lately begun to price their programs on a 1/10-ounce basis. There is almost always a surcharge for overweight inserts. Statements have the closest weight tolerances due to the first class nature of the distributions.

Oversize or nonfolded inserts create a problem in that the majority of insert programs are those which accept the 5 1/2-in × 8 1/2-in format. When dealing with a 6-in × 9-in envelope, the mailer who provides a small insert loses visibility within the program. The outsized insert is not always acceptable, thereby reducing the number of insert programs available to the mailer.

WHAT ARE THE COSTS OF PARTICIPATING?

The medium has two major costs: distribution and printing. Printing prices are determined by the format used, the quantity of inserts ordered, the keying, and the delivery charges. The cost of inserts has risen along with everything else. You can use $20 per thousand for a rough estimate in computing the cost of printing.

Prices are set by the programs since the distribution facilities vary widely. The determining factors are the popularity of the program, the number of inserts per package, the number of packages or mailings per year, the competitive situation, and the availability at any given time. Just as yesterday's empty airline seat has no value, the package that goes out without the requisite number of inserts is not producing the anticipated income that the owner intended to receive for providing the service.

As of mid-1990, the average cost of package inserts is $45–$55 per thousand. The average cost of co-op and ride-along mailings is edging above the $30-per-thousand mark. The overriding concern to the mailer should be the number of orders or inquiries and the translation of these into cost per order or cost per inquiry, depending on the measurement of success for his participation. Naturally, rising prices do not portend rising results. But responsive package insert programs are the name of the game.

When testing—which is the first step any direct mailer takes—the cost of printing will be higher than for rollouts. Be sure to evaluate results by determining the cost of the printing on a rollout basis and not on the test quantities. The same situation will occur with distribution prices. When the mailer negotiates through his broker for rollouts, many prices are reduced somewhat. The profit and loss determination for each distributing program will be influenced by the lower prices obtained.

WHAT ARE THE RESPONSE RATES?

This is by far the most common question asked of any package-insert broker, and it is the most difficult question to answer. There are a number of valid reasons for not being able to be definitive in answering this question. First of all, most mailers consider the package-insert medium a small part of their marketing program. Its costs are less than mailing and the attendant risks are less, so that most brokers are given less information than they would receive in a list selection, with its higher costs and risks.

Secondly, most mailers are not working exclusively with a broker. The state of the industry is such that most mailers still use more than one broker and presumably keep privileged information to themselves. In any event, the real question is not what are the response rates, but what is the cost per order (or inquiry)? If the responses, divided into the costs as outlined previously, are such that they are viable, then the response rate is only part of the equation—an important part, but only part.

Let's look at an example:

Cost of inserts	$20/M
Cost of distribution	50/M
Total costs	70/M
Needed cost per order	$10.00

In this case, a response rate of seven orders per thousand is acceptable. Below that the cost per order is too high and above that there is an increasing profit to the mailer.

Each distribution has to be analyzed in a profit and loss just as each mailing has to be gone over. In a two-step situation, the mailer has to know the allowable backend as well. For example:

	A	B
Cost of inserts	$20/M	$15/M
Cost of distribution	40/M	35/M
Total costs	$60/M	$50/M
Responses at 0.4%	4/M	4/M
Cost per order	$15.00	$12.50
Response rate at 0.5%	5/M	5/M
Cost per order	$12.00	$10.00

Therefore, at a lower response rate, the costs of either the insert and/or distribution will have to be lowered by $10 per thousand to make an average and successful use of the particular package insert or co-op program.

WHAT ARE THE ADVANTAGES OF USING PACKAGE INSERTS?

As marketers well-versed in the field already know, there are numerous advantages to using package inserts. Those of you who are just beginning to explore the field will want to know that package inserts will enable you to accomplish the following:

- **Keep initial costs low relative to benefits.** For under $6000, the average mailer can have a well-diversified and correctly constructed test of the package insert and co-op medium. This would include five tests of 10,000 each for package inserts and two tests of 25,000 each for the co-ops.

- **Test multiple copy approaches.** Once a successful format is in place and several programs are producing the desired results, adventurous mailers can refine their strategies by testing various copy formats within the successful programs. Under no circumstances should the format be tested before the medium is tested. Among the tests that can be run are copy, format, and offer.

- **Keep exposure to competitors to a minimum.** You have to receive a package to see your competitor's insert. The brokerage fraternity is reasonably good about keeping secrets, so the promotion can remain reasonably confidential.

- **Build up a strong, profitable mail-order business.** While this is not always the case, it has and is being done. As in any marketing effort, more than one medium should be used. Each should be used for its benefits.

- **Test mailing lists.** In doubt over the use of a particular list? Try the insert route. If you have developed correlations among your list and package-insert results, you can interpolate the list results from the package-insert results. Quite obviously, you are reaching a hot-line buyer when you use package inserts. You can also consider giving up some of the list expense and substitute lower-cost package inserts.

- **Preempt your competition.** Since only one insert or product per package is the normal rule, you are in the package until you decide to leave, if you are the first one in.

- **Supplement your advertising campaign.** The insert medium can sometimes be localized so that the insert advertising supplements the general proposition.

- **Determine whether you want to sell your product through catalog houses.** There's nothing to prevent you from broadening your line to include direct sales through the very catalog houses inserting your insert. You can also test a new product or publication inexpensively.

- **Test a new market or create a larger market for your product.** If you feel that your offer will work in markets other than the staple ones, this low-cost medium can provide the answer. A good package-insert broker will continue to try and develop more programs to be used. If your offer is general in nature, you can expect to have more places to put your insert. It pays to have extra insert keys available for tests.

- **Revive a product.** If your product is on a downward slope through your conventional media approach, the low-cost insert route may breathe life into it for some additional time.

- **Test a publication without advertising in it.** Many publications offer insert space in their statements. You can get a feel for the publication through the responses received from inserts.

- **Expand your cash flow.** Since most inserts are billed at the completion of the job, you can receive orders before you pay for them.

WHAT ARE THE DISADVANTAGES OF THE INSERT MEDIUM?

Most of the disadvantages of using the medium come from not understanding the insert process or from expecting more of what was purchased than can be delivered. The insert medium once had as its major problem the unreliability of the distributing program. Today this is relatively uncommon. Most responsible package-insert brokers employ checkers who monitor the flow of inserts and invoice accordingly.

- **Correct keying lies at the heart of successful insert use—and at the root of most unsuccessful experiences.** Keying simply involves assigning one or more codes to each program distributing your inserts. Most printers suggest key blocks that are too large to be useful. Even with retests and continuations, the alert user will have sub keys within the master block. Programs tend to have fluctuations in the number of products sold at any given time. Correct keying will let you analyze the number of inserts going out. The same thing is true of co-op distributions. A co-op mailing to 500,000 should have several keys within it, to be sure that all keys were used. The temptation is not the problem, but the temptation is removed.

- **Any time you forget to key your insert, you risk the chance of error.** It is important that every insert used has one key (or more) and that the broker insist that the program provide a sample of the insert received prior to inserting.

- **Package-insert programs have different lives at different times.** The most active time for many products is pre-Christmas, so insert users benefit from heavy distributions at that time; the same program can be nonexistent in January. A question to the broker will produce monthly or weekly counts to help you avoid this problem.

- **You must allow for the packing process at each distributing program.** Some "packages" are 3–6 weeks in advance, and allowance for delivery by your printer is necessary. Be sure your broker provides for delivery to coincide with expected distribution.

- **Media usage by programs can change without warning.** What did well for you in the test can be disastrous in the retest or continuation if the program's advertising changes radically. The same turnabout can be observed when the distribution goes to a different geographical area or to a different type of buyer.

- **You are to some extent the partner of the other insertees.** If your offer is not strong enough, you can be "knocked off" by another insert. It is rarely the number of inserts in a package that reduces the response but one or more of the variations mentioned above.

- **If your insert is not visible, you can also suffer lack of response.** Since you are paying the same as the other inserts, why not get as much visibility as possible for your money?

- **The lack of correlation among advertiser and program can be devastatingly unprofitable.** It pays to test—with a pretested and successful insert. Be prepared for some surprises.

SUCCESS FACTORS:
WHAT ARE THEY?

There seem to be two stages to reaching success in this medium. The first is the test phase. The second is the rollout phase.

Tests come first, because without a successful test, there can be no rollout. Most of the new insert users will have to create an insert. As simple as this may seem, it can be the turning point in the success or failure of the effort. The new insert has to be pretested to avoid the problem of determining the cause of failure, i.e., if the tests are not successful, is it the medium or the message? The best way to overcome this problem is to run enough tests so that a range of results will be available for analysis. We feel that a minimum of ten tests is necessary in this initial stage.

Successful insert users analyze their responses the same way they would in a direct-mail or space campaign. That is, a "p and l" is done to determine the cost per order (or inquiry) of each program used. The analysis determines the ability to move forward and/or the adjustments to be made before committing more funds to the medium.

As each distributing category is costed out, the user should expand in two directions. The first is within the individual program. This is called a retest or confirmation. The increase can safely be between 2 1/2 and 5 times the initial test. If the initial test was statistically reliable, the rollout should reconfirm the test results. This will lead to the continuation phase.

The other direction to follow is to use additional distribution programs similar to each successful test program. For example, if yours is a consumer product aimed at mothers, and you've tested a package and co-op mailing to recent mothers, you should have your broker look for additional co-op mailings to recent mothers. At the same time, you should be considering additional programs, such as those to be found by exploring age, geographic, and media selections.

Success in the insert field in the rollout phase is tricky. Done with moderation, however, it can be profitable. Here is what the really successful users advise:

1. **Key in such a way that you can read the results quickly.**   This ensures your ability to reorder new programs and therefore reserve your category. It also enables you to see if the program is holding up. Earlier, we discussed the many ways programs can deteriorate. Small key blocks, while more expensive, keep all parties alert.

2. **Test for copy and format adjustments only within proven programs.** Too much testing can be self-defeating and expensive in any phase of direct mail, including the insert medium. Finding ways to cut costs and improve response should be done only within the confines of programs that have proved themselves.

3. **Take advantage of what's new among distribution programs.**   This is important when you have decided upon a format that works. Since this is still an emerging medium, the advertisers will have a considerable number of selections brought to them by alert brokers. Knowing that your insert works gives you confidence to use the programs that come along. There are two theories on new programs: test and rollout. Each has its merit.

4. Negotiate for price.   More prices are negotiable than ever before. Prices are rising, so rollouts are a way to "leverage" the price in your favor.

5. Act where you think you are right.   The really good programs fill up. However, lately there has been a trend toward booking and not fulfilling the contract. Naturally, just as with no-shows on airlines, something has to be done.

6. Look beyond the obvious.   Once your testing is done, move into collateral areas of distribution. The opening up of business-to-business packages to women-oriented offers is an excellent example of using a program category that on the surface did not seem to be viable until tested. Some of the alert book clubs and inquiry seekers are finding that nearly every program available works for their offers.

7. See if the program has additional areas of distribution available.   Ask your broker to check this out. Among the possibilities: inserts in the catalog of a successfully used program if there is one, and inserts in the bills if they are sent.

8. Pay promptly.   The industry is suffering from too many slow pays. There will be a place made for the known prompt payers. See to it that your broker remits your money promptly.

9. Decoy your insert.   If you can afford to, buy a package from every product distributing your inserts. One advertiser who does this uses the purchases as gifts at Christmas. In the meantime, he knows who is in the package with his insert. Be sure your broker decoys the co-ops. There is no way that you can be sure of the other participants in the package insert program without purchasing products.

10. See that your insert dominates the others.   Good graphics can be better. Good copy can be better. Size can be increased within limits.

11. Monitor the flow of inserts.   It changes depending upon the season, the advertising done by the package insert distributor, and a variety of other factors.

12. Look closely at other successes.   There is much to be said for copying. It is the sincerest form of flattery. It also can get you into trouble if not done with flair.

WHAT'S NEW NOW AND IN THE FUTURE?

The co-op end of the insert medium is headed toward ride-alongs for economic reasons. However, there does seem to be an increase in the number of mailings that will accept outside inserts at an increased price. For example, in the mail-order photo-finishing industry, nearly every major finisher has accepted inserts in their mailings.

The package-insert field will see an increase, perhaps even an explosion, in popularity, spurred on by the aggressive activities of the brokerage fraternity, by continuing postal increases, and by the obvious need for reduction in general costs. The retail end of the package-insert field is barely touched. There are more insert distribution categories than are being used. One reason why the number of insert programs grew slowly for a long time was the relatively low postage rates. Each increase has encouraged the creation of more package-insert programs. The "me-too-ism" within industry groups tends to accelerate this trend.

There will be an effort to increase the number of inserts within the more popular insert programs. One way this will be done is by using envelopes directed to interest groups within the packages. For example, in the business-to-business mailer category, it is possible to have an envelope with inserts inside addressed to the Boss or the Office Manager.

Small packages have an obvious difficulty in accepting additional inserts. Someone who is creative will develop an insert to take advantage of this area of the medium.

Multiple offers from different advertisers in an "all-of-1" format will be developed. There have been several attempts at this so far, but none seems to have been completely successful. One was in a preprinted format with a number of advertisers sharing the cost of the production and distribution. Another effort has been in the direction of providing collated inserts within one envelope to take advantage of the per-1000 distribution rate. Personalizing offers to match the distributing program is another technique that is catching on. After all, each package or statement accepting an insert is, in effect, already endorsing the product featured on the insert.

20

Outbound Telemarketing

George T. Bradbury

Bradbury & Associates, Inc.
Southport, Conn.

The telephone. It's easy to take this common communication tool for granted, because we've all grown up having it at arm's reach. Each of us has used it in our personal and business life to deliver messages, ask questions, make arrangements and appointments, offer advice, initiate contact, solidify a relationship, or sell an idea or product. For most of its history, the telephone has been used as an individual means of communicating, and it is only within the past 20 years or so, with the dramatic advances in the telecommunications industry, that businesses have recognized and begun to utilize the telephone as a powerful marketing medium.

The scope of outbound telemarketing is limited only by our own imaginations. After all, the nature of the medium gives us the ability to test a concept, immediately measure the results, and refine our techniques. This chapter will explore the burgeoning outbound telemarketing industry, define the requirements for implementing successful telephone marketing campaigns, and challenge the reader to come up with innovative new ways to use its marketing power.

THE SCOPE OF TELEMARKETING

Outbound telemarketing as part of the overall direct marketing mix is fairly commonplace among businesses now. But it wasn't always so. It took technological telecommunications advances and their positive economic implications to spread the use of telephone as a mass-marketing vehicle.

Telemarketing's phenomenal growth really began in the early 1960s. At that time, only a small number of companies were testing the medium, and for the most part, their tests were limited to lead generation for a company sales force.

A dramatic impact on the industry occurred in the late 1960s when wide area telephone service (WATS) was introduced. WATS provided flat monthly rates for fixed numbers of hours based on geographic coverage. This service significantly reduced the cost of both inbound and outbound calling, opening up telephone marketing across the board to companies for which the medium's cost had been hitherto prohibitive.

Although outbound telemarketing began to grow in the 1970s, it wasn't until the 1980s that telephone marketing mushroomed into a multibillion-dollar industry. Divestiture of AT&T and the resulting entry of new long-distance competitors into the marketplace further reduced telephone costs and helped to spread the use of telemarketing.

Other economic factors also helped to make outbound telemarketing more attractive. The energy crisis, brought on in the mid-1970s by OPEC and its oil-producing member nations, helped push the cost of a personal sales call over the $200 mark. Escalation of the price of paper and the ever-spiraling cost of postage have had profound effects on direct-mail package costs, forcing marketers to explore alternative marketing channels.

Lastly, we've all been linked closer together with the proliferation of fax machines, cellular telephones, answering machines, voice and data networks, etc. The speed of communication and the intensity of competition in business—both domestic and foreign—are helping to fuel the use of the telephone in marketing campaigns.

The cost-effectiveness and profitability of the medium have been proved time and again and the signs are there for accelerated growth through the 1990s. More service bureaus are opening up. Automation is changing the nature, scope, and reach of telemarketing. More companies, large and small, both service- and product-oriented, are more and more often beginning to include outbound telemarketing in their strategic marketing plans.

TELEPHONE MARKETING

The telephone is a powerful tool. It has the ability to create a truly positive image by the nature of its personal interaction with a customer or prospect. Therefore, as in any other medium in the marketing mix, it is important to carefully weigh and evaluate all the variables when devising an outbound telemarketing strategy:

- What is the objective?
- How do I achieve this objective?
- Who is my audience?
- What is my budget?

- How do I measure results?
- What do I do with these results?

Once these questions have been addressed and it has been determined that an outbound telemarketing program will be part of your marketing campaign, you need to plan how to implement an effective telemarketing effort.

LISTS

A campaign, whether direct mail or telemarketing, is only as effective as the list used. You can have the best product or service in the marketplace, but the list will drive the results. Therefore, it's imperative that the list, or lists, be carefully selected.

Customer Lists

These customers are the people with whom you already have a relationship; they have responded to your previous campaigns and now exist on your database. These customers will, therefore, have a higher propensity to respond positively to another offer or service from your company.

The customer profile of the people already on your list will also guide you as you mine the vast lists available on the market for likely new prospects. Database analysis of your customer file, either in-house or with the assistance of an outside service, can yield the characteristics you need to know when devising new products or services, as well as telling you which prospective customers will be most likely to respond to those products and services.

Assuming that you have asked for phone numbers during previous transactions, the telephone enables you to reach your customers to offer new products and services, but that is merely one aspect of its total value. As least equally important, if not more so, is the customer service side of the telemarketing coin. Nothing can compare to the direct interaction between two living, breathing human beings. In this regard, the medium can be used to cement the customer-supplier relationship. For example:

A customer buys an expensive new car. Several days after the purchase, he or she automatically receives a call from the automobile manufacturer inquiring about the purchase experience. With one telephone call, the company has conveyed a caring, responsible image to its customer, increasing the likelihood of a repeat purchase.

A customer purchases several items from a catalog. The cataloguer, after the anticipated delivery date, calls the customer to make sure that the shipment was received and that the order was correct. Aside from creating a positive company image, the call also opens up the potential to make additional sales.

The value of the customer database, therefore, cannot be measured in terms of numbers alone. It is your most important asset. These customers deserve and require your utmost attention, for it is this base from which your company will grow.

Outside Lists

There are countless lists on the market, and new ones become available every day. Not every list owner automatically allows telemarketing against its customer file, so permission must be granted before beginning an outbound telemarketing campaign. Moreover, some lists do not have phone numbers available. However, there exist companies that will append phone numbers to a supplied customer or prospect list. Adding phone numbers to either consumer or business lists can be done in two ways:

Manual telephone number look-up. This is a time-consuming, costly method of acquiring phone numbers through directory assistance which can cost up to 45 cents per number found. Thus it is advised for use only with very small lists. This method generally has a 65 percent match rate.

Computer match of the list against a compiled database of households or businesses with telephone numbers. This process usually yields about a 50 percent match rate with a cost ranging from 3 cents to 6 cents per number matched and a turnaround time of about a week.

Outside lists are segmented by numerous demographic, geographic, and psychographic characteristics. You should select your test lists based upon your existing customer database characteristics and your projected target market. The only way to know if a list will really perform is through the testing process.

SCRIPT PREPARATION AND IMPLEMENTATION

You must have something to say! The cornerstone of every successful telemarketing venture is the script. Without a well-structured, carefully written, highly interactive script, your message will not reach its intended audience. You will be left with a list of targeted names and a warehouse full of product.

The key to script writing is to keep in mind the audience you are talking to; the language and tone of a script will be determined by who is listening. For example, the script used for a business presentation will be more formal than a call made to a consumer at home.

Another important element in successful script writing is to construct an interactive conversation between the communicator and the contact. This involves strategically placed questions that allow the prospects to feel that they are not simply listening to a programmed pitch, but are actively involved in a conversation. By soliciting continued responses from the prospect, you increase the chances of getting a positive response.

The script should be written by a team of skilled communicators who also have in-depth knowledge of the product or service being offered. This ensures that the most important benefits will be presented in the most effective way. Scripting is a constantly evolving process in which the script is tested, rewritten, and fine-tuned even before the first telephone call is made. Role playing among the marketing team is an excellent way to discover problems in a script and correct them before it is introduced to the actual telephone sales representatives (TSRs). Some key elements to keep in mind when script writing:

- Clearly identify the caller name, company name, and the reason for the call.
- Verify that you have reached the target prospect or someone who is responsible for making the decision.
- Be prepared with scripted answers to a variety of possible questions or objections that might arise during the conversation.
- Remember the KIS rule: Keep It Simple! Don't give the prospect too many choices.
- Keep the script to a reasonable length. Let the offer speak for itself as much as possible.
- Be clear and to the point. Don't use ambiguous terms that mask the true benefits of your offer.

Once your team has self-tested the script and is satisfied with the results, the next phase involves training the supervisors and the TSRs responsible for making the actual calls.

Strict script adherence by the TSRs is important, for reasons of both quality control and results measurement. If the TSRs vary script presentation, the results will be an inconsistent company image and customer dissatisfaction. Additionally, it will be difficult to determine exactly how or why your offer was accepted and impossible to project future results. For this reason, ongoing call monitoring is essential by you, the client, and the on-line supervisory telemarketing team.

Telemarketing offers immediate results. You can know whether a script is working after the first few hundred actual calls and adjust it as needed. This means that you are constantly monitoring and evaluating both positive and negative customer responses. As in the preparation process, the script should continue to evolve and improve during implementation until you feel it has reached its peak level of performance.

Remember that you can use telemarketing to its best advantage by constructing a program that allows you to vary the script in order to test not only telemarketing itself, but also some of the variables necessary for determining the direction of future campaigns—that is, list tests, price tests, incentive offer tests, product feature tests, etc. Analysis of the test results will help guide your future marketing efforts.

QUALITY AS A CONCERN

Although no direct marketing tool can match the cost-effectiveness, flexibility, control, and speed of the telephone, it takes more than just telephones to get quality results. It takes qualified TSRs who have been well trained to use the telephone as a marketing tool. Successful training involves proper voice inflection, listening skills, persistence, and patience. A TSR should also possess an even temper, an outgoing personality, and a responsible attitude with a desire to succeed.

The training program, conducted by an experienced training supervisor, begins upon hire and continues throughout the TSR's employment. New programs require new product training and new scripts demand rehearsal. Aside from developing the skills to close a sale, particular attention must be paid to the specifics of data gathering, because a sale is only as good as the information supplied.

OUTSIDE HELP

Up to this point, we have outlined many of the requirements to help you establish an in-house telemarketing effort. If, however, you decide that you do not have or do not wish to allocate the necessary resources for an internal campaign, or feel that you will be better served by a more experienced team than you can provide, or have a sudden increase in the volume of work beyond your internal telemarketing staff's ability to handle, you have the option of employing one of many qualified outside telemarketing service agencies.

There are several advantages to using an outside service agency for an outbound telemarketing program. These include low initial investment, fixed and predictable operating costs, rapid start-up capability, ability to adjust quickly to the market, and an operation experienced in the business. There are a multitude of service bureaus which vary in size, capability, technology, and experience. In order to determine which vendor is right for you and your specific program, you must consider the following questions:

1. Does the agency understand and have experience in your type of business?
2. Is the agency the right size to handle your project?
3. How serious and focused is the agency in the area of quality?
4. What are the agency's quality controls and how are they implemented?
5. What are the recruitment, training, monitoring, and supervisory standards?
6. Who writes the scripts?
7. Is the agency manual or automated, and which method would be best suited for your application?
8. How are the TSRs paid? (salary, commission, bonus, etc.)
9. Is the workplace conducive to productivity?
10. How responsive is the agency to the individual needs of your company?
11. Can they customize your reports?
12. What are the backgrounds of senior management?
13. What is the employee turnover rate?
14. Does the agency have full-service capabilities, including mail fulfillment, tape formatting, and data processing?

A legitimate service bureau will address each of your concerns openly and without reservation. If questions are not answered to your satisfaction, seek another agency.

Once you have established a relationship with a particular vendor, it is wise to periodically test the resources of that agency by comparing results against another test site. Also, keep in mind that very large programs may need to be split among several vendors in order to get the best results within your specified time frame. Excellent sources for listings of telemarketing service bureaus are *Telemarketing Magazine* and *Inbound/Outbound Magazine,* both of which annually publish issues on the top service agencies in the business.

THE IMPACT OF AUTOMATION

As the telemarketing industry continues to grow, companies have looked to automation in order to increase productivity. The primary aspects of an operation improved by automating a telemarketing center are campaign and resource management, both having a direct impact on productivity and back-end results. Computers assist in overall management by creating a paperless environment, while at the same time offering accurate and up-to-the-second individual TSR and total campaign results.

Automated systems can also input, access, and retrieve an unlimited amount of customer information. By using computer work stations connected to a main database, telemarketers have an abundance of information at their fingertips, accessible before, during, and after the call. Specific product information, appropriate responses to objections, and competitive product comparisons can be programmed to appear on the screen in an instant.

PREDICTIVE DIALING

In a manual operation, a TSR spends approximately 12 to 18 minutes per hour in actual talk-time speaking to prospects. The rest of the hour is spent waiting for calls to connect, listening to answering machines, busy signals, no-answers, and wrong numbers. Predictive dialing equipment, the most technologically advanced system on the market, completely eliminates this wasted time. It automates the dialing, call-recognition, and transfer process, thus increasing TSR talk-time to approximately 38–43 minutes per hour.

Calls that do not result in a live answer are sorted according to predefined call outcomes. Busy signals, answering machines, and no-answers are recirculated for later dialing and wrong numbers and disconnects are removed from the calling list. Only "live" prospects are transferred to TSRs sitting at computer terminals, the prospect voice being transmitted into the TSR's headphone and the associated prospect information appearing on the screen.

The net results of this technology are that more quality calls can be dialed, more prospects can be reached (up to 90 percent of a list versus the 65 percent that can be reached manually), and therefore that more well-informed sales presentations can be made.

This technology does not suit every purpose, however. Today, it is specifically geared toward the business-to-consumer market, especially for large volume programs. Business-to-business programs, which require longer scripts and routine call-backs in order to reach decision makers, are best served by a manual environment.

CASE HISTORIES

Here are four case histories which illustrate how outbound telemarketing can be used successfully.

Business-to-Business—Company A

A *Fortune* 500 company introduces a new machine for its standard product which it wants placed in small-to-mid-size offices and in departments of larger companies across the country. This market, which represents more than one million offices nationwide, has largely been untapped for direct sale of this product, either by this company or its competitors.

The company recognizes that it has a substantial business opportunity, but understands that it needs to create a general awareness of and interest in this new product in the general and targeted business community. The company also knows that it must depend on its nationwide network of independent distributors to place the machine, once demand for it starts rolling in.

To test the different segments of its identified market and generate leads for its distributors, the company places direct-response ads in business magazines and stages a series of targeted direct-mail campaigns, the object of which is to generate leads for the distributor network. A sophisticated lead processing system is established; the distributor is notified of the inquiry for follow-up machine demonstration and placement, and the lead receives a thank-you letter acknowledging that a contact will be made by an identified distributor. This process is completed within a short time of receipt of the inquiry.

The initial direct-response program is successful, generating several thousand leads per month. However, due to the large number of leads, the company has difficulty determining if the distributors are actually following through and getting machines placed. In essence: Are the distributors doing their job?

An outbound telemarketing program to business responders is implemented with a dual purpose; to get customer feedback on the machine (customer service contact) and to check on follow-through by the distributor network. The leads are segmented by month of response.

The results of the outbound test reveal a good deal and substantiate much of what the company already believes:

1. When placed in an office, the machine is well received by the customer.

2. A sizable percentage of the leads have never been contacted by a distributor (but most are still very interested in the machine).

3. Many businesses have been told they were too small.

4. The company can depend on only a few distributors out of its total network to follow through.

Recognizing that there is substantial interest in its machine, the company is being forced by its telemarketing results to seek an alternative method of distribution to leads being generated through its direct-response campaigns. This alternative approach will be tested in the next phase of the total campaign.

Business-to-Business—Company B

A major business publication wants to build its controlled circulation base to a specific number before the next magazine audit. It has built a substantial database of targeted businesses, but exact names are not available for all the positions earmarked for a free subscription, nor are there sufficient prospects available to reach the subscription-number goal.

The publication chooses outbound telemarketing as the medium to achieve its objective for two reasons; reach and timing. The datebase is segmented by parent company and divisions within the parent company for ease in controlling and monitoring the project. Key corporate and marketing positions are identified as a calling base, and a very upbeat, interactive script is developed. Since it's been determined that the publication will fall short of its circulation goal with just the available names, a referral element is incorporated into the script. In other words, those who accept the complimentary subscription are asked to provide a name or names of others in similar positions within the company (perhaps a division not identified) who might benefit from the publication.

The telemarketing program is very successful. The publication achieves a controlled circulation beyond its goal, and the first issue of the complimentary subscription is in the hands of the recipients before the audit.

Business-to-Consumer—Company C

A major regional bank card issuer, very successful in building its portfolio in its own backyard, seeks to go beyond its regional boundaries and market its gold card on a national basis. Although the bank has identified its target prospects demographically and psychographically by an analysis of its existing customer base, it is uncertain which market areas and what incentive offer will yield the best results.

Like other card issuers, the bank has experienced a fall-off in mail response over time and has thus decided to test the outside market waters via outbound telemarketing. Aside from the substantial benefit of the personal interactive nature of the medium, outbound telemarketing will enable the bank to know rather quickly if it can establish a card presence outside its own territorial boundaries within an acceptable cost per order, based on past experience and current market trends.

The bank's lists are selected to include prospects from several states that it feels are worthy of testing. A fairly complex test matrix is constructed in order to sample the different market areas and different introductory offers. The list is segmented into the test cells in preparation for calling via predictive dialing equipment. This equipment allows the telemarketers to reach more prospects on an hourly basis, thus allowing the test to be completed in a rather compact time frame. It also allows the capture not only of the quantitative results, but also of certain qualitative information that the bank can use to guide future marketing efforts.

The test program yields sufficient positive results in several of the market area test cells to warrant ongoing outbound telemarketing efforts into these areas. Based on the test results, several market areas are eliminated from the bank's marketing plan. Additionally, the bank is able to glean the most responsive incentive offer, an offer which continues to be used.

The bank continues to market its card predominantly via outbound telemarketing as it continues to produce an acceptable cost per order. But always included in the telemarketing rollout are new market area and offer tests that enable the bank to fine-tune its marketing efforts and find new areas of distribution.

Business-to-Consumer—Company D

A large specialty retailer with a substantial, well-respected presence in its market area has identified a specific audience segment to which to market its credit card. The audience is particularly suited to the products offered by the retailer. However, the mission is to reach this target audience within a very tight time frame for two purposes: (1) to offer the store credit card, and (2) to draw these hot prospects into its stores ahead of the competition.

After using solo direct mail for several years with diminishing results, the retailer seizes upon outbound telemarketing, a medium with immediate impact, to use for its marketing efforts to these highly targeted prospects. A strategy is devised to call all available prospects with predictive dialing within a week of the names becoming available. A very attractive and highly colorful mail piece is sent to those names without phone numbers and to people not contacted from the prior calling effort.

Outbound telemarketing proves very successful. Acceptance of the card by the prospects is overwhelming, with the retailer generating a large number of new accounts each month. And the retailer has found that the calls serve an effective customer service function as well, even to those who refuse the card; these people are also very receptive to the retailer's calls and want to engage the telemarketers in conversation extolling the retailer's merits.

LEGAL ISSUES

As always, with rapid growth comes abuse and the temptation to push the medium beyond its legitimate limits. Those of us who make our living from the industry and those of us who use the telephone effectively recognize the need for self-policing and regulation to protect our interests.

Across the country, restrictive legislation relating to telemarketing has either been passed or is pending. Some of the legislation, like that restricting the use of sequence dialers or automatic dialing and recorded message players (ADRMPs) is welcome. Other legislation may seriously affect the ability of the industry to conduct its business. Associations like the American Telemarketing Association and the Direct Marketing Association are working to protect the interests of the industry without neglecting the rights of the general public.

Standards of self-regulation have been established by the Direct Marketing Association in its Guidelines for Telephone Marketing. The industry would be best served if we all adhered to these standards and practices:

1. Telephone marketers should promptly disclose the name of the company and the nature of the call. Telemarketers should not make offers or solicitations in the guise of research or survey when the real intent is to sell products or raise funds.

2. Telephone marketers should be clear, honest, and complete in their presentation. There should be no attempt to use advertisements or claims that are misleading, fraudulent, deceptive, or untrue, or which disparage the competition.

3. Telephone marketers should disclose the cost of the product or service and all associated terms, conditions, and additional costs.

4. Telemarketing calls should be made during reasonable hours.

5. Taping of telemarketing calls should only be conducted with all-party consent or the use of a beeping device.

6. Telephone marketers should remove the name of any contact from the phone list when requested to do so. (The DMA has a Telephone Preference File which is available by subscription and lists all those who do not wish to be contacted by telemarketing companies.)

7. Telephone marketers should not market to minors without adult consent.

8. Telephone marketers should avoid calling telephone subscribers who have unlisted or unpublished numbers unless a prior relationship exists.

9. Telephone marketers should operate in accordance with federal, state, and local laws governing advertising, marketing practices, and the transaction of business by telephone.

CONCLUSION

As general advertising becomes less effective because of the need for advertisers to target specific marketing messages to segmented audiences, direct marketing, and especially outbound telemarketing, will continue to expand in both breadth and importance. Advances in technology will enable companies to reach large constituencies cost effectively. This will enhance the relationship between supplier and consumer, thus giving an increased value to each marketing dollar.

Both in business and in our personal lives, time is becoming a limited commodity. Those companies that can offer their products or services in the most direct, expedient, and simplified manner will be able to compete most effectively. Outbound telemarketing in conjunction with other targeted direct marketing channels will help to secure your company's place in the future.

21

Inbound Telemarketing

Eugene B. Kordahl

National Telemarketing, Inc.
Home, Kans.

Inbound telemarketing (TM) is growing by leaps and bounds as the industry expands to meet an ever-widening variety of customer and prospect needs. And as the field expands, the professional marketer is flooded with all kinds of information. In this chapter we'll try to put that information in some coherent order by taking a look at the way inbound got started, exploring the different uses of 800, 976, and 900 services, reviewing the major strategies used today, and zeroing in on the critical issues involved in choosing a telemarketing service bureau.

INBOUND HISTORY

It is said that it takes 25 to 40 years for a new technology to reach acceptance at the public level. The truth of this is borne out by the story of the fax machine, which was invented in the 1950s and is only now beginning to be widely used by the business world. The theory is even better demonstrated by the story of inbound calling, which also started 40 years ago and—after a turbulent history—is only just beginning to hit its stride.

The First Inbound Services

In the postwar era of the fifties, the telephone company introduced several services designed to stimulate toll-call business. The plan was simple: All the services depended on the subscriber to pay for incoming calls. The first service,

Foreign Exchange (FX) was a dedicated telephone line that stretched from another location, say a distant city, to the location of the budding "telemarketer," thereby giving the impression that he or she had an office in that city. (By the way, the term "telemarketing" wasn't being used then. That word was first introduced by C. Dicky Dyer, III, an eminent management consultant, in an article entitled "How to Use the Telephone to Build Sales — And Cut Sales Costs" in the May 29, 1967, issue of *Modern Distribution Management*.)

The phone company's second type of inbound service was a "code number" associated with an actual telephone number whose subscriber had agreed in advance to accept all collect calls (without the word *collect* being used). This system was called the WX or Enterprise service. The caller would simply ask the operator for a WX or Enterprise number, and the call would be placed on a collect basis to the subscribing company. This form of inbound service gave rise to a number of strategies still in use in inbound services today. Marketers placed ads in the Yellow Pages indicating which of the services they were using. These ads drove in new accounts, existing accounts, inquiries, and customer-service calls. Customers liked the idea of doing business long-distance "for free."

What Do You Mean, "Toll Free?"

Things went well in the inbound business until 1967. The outbound technology of wide area telephone service (WATS) had been introduced slowly during 1965–66, and WATS was just beginning to be perceived as a bulk-calling discount from the regular long-distance charges that a company could generate each month. At this point, it became obvious to the Bell System that a complementary inbound service, IN-WATS, could also be offered. But interestingly enough, the introduction of IN-WATS fell on deaf ears. The concept of "toll-free" dialing by customers and consumers was just too novel and was greeted with skepticism by both sides. The Telco subscriber was asking, "Won't we get a lot of nuisance calls if we allow people to call in free of charge?" And the consumer was asking, "What's the gimmick? Nobody gives me a free telephone call without expecting something in return." As a result, the 800 number was launched by the Bell System to a resounding silence. No one used — or understood — the new offering. Even the sales personnel in the Bell companies didn't know how to sell the new service, other than to reduce the cost (if appropriate) of the FX lines then in use by the Bell customer.

THE 800 BANDWAGON GETS ROLLING

The earliest users of the 800 WATS Service were the visionary marketers at the Sheraton Corporation in Connecticut. They were the first to recognize something that even Bell didn't realize. The Sheraton identified the huge potential in the needs of the traveling public — people who needed lodgings on a speedy basis, people who might be stranded somewhere without coins and needed to make emergency accommodation changes. The Sheraton's existing customers found the 800 toll-free number very valuable, and the toll-free service enticed many new customers to open an account with the Sheraton. The rest is history, of course—at least for the Sheraton and its famous jingle imploring us to dial "Eight-oh-oh, three-two-five-three-five-three-five."

This first triumph of the inbound, together with the competitive nature of the 800 service, changed the travel and leisure industry almost overnight. Hotels, motels, airlines, limo services, travel agents, and even baggage-locating services all jumped on the 800 bandwagon. Interestingly enough, the vast majority of other businesses in the United States were slow to pick up on this new technology. Just as in the case of the fax and the computer, the time simply wasn't ripe to explore this new marketing tool. It wasn't until 1978 that the first (rather half-hearted) advertising campaign about the use of the 800 service was started by the old Bell System. Two years later, in 1980, AT&T went all out with an advertising campaign designed to emphasize the 800 service and the "new" word *telemarketing*.

Featuring the football legendary Fran Tarkington, known as the "Scrambler" for his running dexterity, commercials on all the media extolled the virtues of calling toll free with AT&T. It was suggested that the businessperson on top of the business game would "scramble" in order to hear more about using the service in his or her business. The campaign was a roaring success, and inbound telemarketing hasn't been the same since. Look at any printed material or listen to any media and you will find the ubiquitous 800 number everywhere. But if "free" was good, just how much better for the telephone company coffers would "pay-per-call" be? The answer was not long in coming.

THE STORMY HISTORY OF 976

In 1982, through a fluke in the awarding of the new 976 service by some of the local Bell companies, a few states such as New York and California were forced to give the pay-per-call service to some firms that were engaged in offering "adult," otherwise known as "dial-a-porn(ographic)" communications. A ruling by the FCC ordered that the local telephone companies stop providing recorded messages and allow private companies to offer these "enhanced services." On January 1, 1983, the publishers of the adult magazine *High Society* and Carlin Communications began their service in New York. Callers could pay for several different messages each day describing various sexual acts in the most explicit terms. An outcry from angry parents was heard when consumers were billed for enormous long-distance tolls to the 976 "dial-a-porn" lines. The grapevine of the younger generation had spread the news about the 976 numbers very quickly on a national scale.

In February 1983, Suffolk County in New York filed a suit to have the operation run by Carlin Communications stopped. Their suit was based on the 1934 Communications Act, which prohibited the interstate transmission of obscenity by means of telephone. Both the Department of Justice and the FCC juggled the responsibility for a while, and in the ensuing years, rules were made, revised, struck down, and rewritten. As of this writing, they have still not clearly defined how calls coming into a 976 number can be effectively blocked.

Of particular interest to the younger set (and to some older folks, too) were the controversial 976 chat lines and the "one-on-one" conversation lines. (In fact, all 976 numbers except AT&T's Dial-A-Channel, are now interactive.) The caller-cost of these lines varies from state to state, but the costs incurred by some of the younger users have been truly astronomic in some cases, adding more fuel to the 976 controversy.

Meanwhile, other firms, offering such 976 services as prayers, horoscopes, wake-up services, jokes, weather, health awareness, diet lines, and sports scores have grown apace, undeterred by the storm. (Not so lucky was the famous "Easter Bunny" line that was child-oriented and very popular. Many parents refused to pay, and the uncollectible charges spelled the end of the service.)

976 Dating Lines

Dating, conversation, and confession lines are rapidly becoming the mainstay of the 976 industry. A current example is the singles' "chat line" and "dating line" service offered by Arden-Lee, Inc., of Temecula, California.

The objective of any 976 or 900 line is to keep the caller on the line. To this end the marketer attempts to keep the caller engaged as long as possible so that the call rate goes up. This requires that the marketer be innovative enough to provide options and interests to the average caller that will keep that person on the line. Arden-Lee is not only a leader in this field, it is trying to help the 976 industry become more professional. To get away from the controversial side of the market, it uses target-marketing direct-mail campaigns to increase its response rates. In fact, it sends out over 300,000 direct-mail pieces a month to known users of 900 and 976 numbers.

Specialized 976 Carriers

By 1990, interactive offerings were becoming more popular and sophisticated. Indeed, the industry had grown to the point where it had its own long-distance carriers specializing in 976 numbers in each state. One such carrier, TELESPHERE, of Oakbrook Terrace, Illinois, has expanded from Chicago to cover several Midwest cities and even New York. A number of magazine publishers are currently looking at ways to use 976 services to tie their advertisers into an interactive service providing more information about ads that appear in their magazines.

The image of the industry is improving as the truly professional marketing opportunities become known. Gradually, as the industry cleans up its act, the legal questions will diminish and the service will become easier to establish and use. The toughest battles regarding the pay-per-call business were about its pornographic uses. This has been changing, and the course is set for more consumer services that will be of value to us all.

976 Enters the Big Time

A number of magazines and newspapers have begun using 976 lines as an enhancement to their normal boy-meets-girl service. Some of the publishers have claimed that the menu-driven 976 lines have created a new profit channel and have increased readership significantly. Such papers as the *Boston Phoenix* the *New Times* in Phoenix, and over one hundred similar voice-messaging systems from New York to San Diego have made this service one of the fastest-growing legitimate offerings in the field. Why? The 976 lines are making huge profits for them.

Here's how: Some of the newspapers receive up to 1000 calls per day. The average duration of a call is 4 minutes (though some callers have been known to stay on the line for up to 50 minutes). Let's say that a 976 line were to receive 500 calls per day. It would receive $495 per day in revenue from the line. In a 30-day month, that would total $14,850. Deduct the line charges of $800 per month for 16 lines, $50,000 for the interactive voice response system, and $1,200 for the telephone set-up fees, and you have a profit of approximately $110,000 per year. Is it worth investigating 976? You bet!

THE 900 NUMBER ARRIVES

It is said that over the next few years, many companies will make the switch from 800 toll-free services to 900 pay-per-call services. This will certainly make for changes in the way that advertising campaigns and direct-response budgets are put together.

The 900 industry got started with hardly a squeak from its parent, AT&T, with its Dial-It-900 service in 1981. This service only allowed the caller to listen to a live or recorded program. The caller was unable to interact by speaking or by touch-tone. Interactive pay-per-call had to wait till 1987 before the more innovative and aggressive marketers could start inventing applications the carriers hadn't thought of. It was then that AT&T, quickly followed by MCI and SPRINT and a new player, TELESPHERE, of Hinsdale, Illinois, began to offer the interactive service. Then the rush began. Imagine—a promotion campaign that not only delivers the message, increases response, and pays for itself all at the same time....

Service with a Dial

The interactive and caller-paid-for 900 lines provide the services customers are hungry for. No more "sorry, I don't know" or "that's not my department." People are willing to pay for real services and qualify themselves for even more marketing offers by simply paying for the telephone call.

The general public is getting used to the idea of interactive lines and is looking for some very specific things from 900 numbers—namely, better and higher-grade service from the sponsors. Yes, the caller is going to pay for the call. And yes, the caller can expect to get quicker, cheaper, and more accurate information and service this way than can be obtained elsewhere. As more consumers become willing to pay for this type of service, more businesses are willing to migrate from the 800 to the 900 services. It's a neat package, once it is understood by the general marketplace. People are realizing that there are costs associated with service, and they are choosing to pay those costs. For their part, the sponsors benefit from not having to pay the toll, and are able to charge a fair rate for the added services.

The cost of the call varies. Sponsors, called information providers (IPs), set the rate they wish to charge the caller. The telephone company charges their base rate for its service and remits the balance of the charge to the IP on a monthly basis. Programs that are considered successful are the ones that generate thousands of calls per day. This of course eliminates the need for live operators. Some of the new automated inbound telemarketing systems can process up to 500,000 calls per day. In 1989, the caller-paid services grossed $1 billion in revenue to the IPs. MCI has predicted that 900 services will account for $2.25 billion in the United States by 1992.

Some 900 Service Innovations

By getting an audience involved with trivia games or some type of entertainment, such firms as Pepsi-Cola, Procter & Gamble, Revlon, and Clorox are already reaping the benefits and profits of using the 900 inbound telemarketing services.

How are others using the 900 services? There are plenty of representative examples to choose from:

- Mothers Against Drunk Driving (MADD) used a bowling contest to create the first national database of seven million bowlers. This raised funds for their cause and emphasized MADD's position regarding bowling and drinking. Bowlers reported their top scores each week. Approximately 70 percent of the revenues went to the MADD coffers.

- Pre-Paid Legal Services of Ada, Oklahoma, has introduced their Justice 900 service offering low-cost legal information using a 900 number. Callers dial the 900 number and are simultaneously billed $9.00. They are connected with a live operator who refers them to a toll-free 800 number with an access code that identifies a prepaid client to an attorney in the caller's state. The prepaid fee entitles the caller to 30 minutes of consultation. The service, which began in the spring of 1990, has already enrolled over 900,000 people.

- The Madison Square Garden Network, a regional sports cable network in the New York area, ran a "Yankees Greatest Moment" sweepstakes in which fans called a 900 number to vote for the greatest moment in Yankee history. An all-expense-paid trip to Los Angeles to see the Yankees play a game against the California Angels, as well as instant prizes, were the incentives. The proceeds from the 900 number, after the cost of producing the sweepstakes, went to the benefit of the Amyotrophic Lateral Sclerosis (ALS) Association (Lou Gehrig's disease).

- The Republican party has used their first 900 number in conjunction with a 200,000-piece direct-mail fund-raising campaign. This campaign, which began in July 1990, offers the donor the opportunity to donate and pay directly by telephone. The party earns $7.75 of every $10 in donations, with the balance going to pay for the services of the telemarketing agency and the cost of AT&T's service.

- Even Warner Bros. Collection, celebrating the 50th birthday of Bugs Bunny in 1990, used 900 services in a very unique way. The text of their catalog ad said: "Say the word and Bugs Bunny will phone anyone you want—friends, kids, co-workers—with a special greeting. He'll address them by name. Wish them your choice of Happy Birthday, Happy Anniversary, Get Well, or Congratulations. Even sing to them." To order the service, callers were instructed to call 1-900-VIP-BUGS. Some simple questions were asked and the time and day you wanted Bugs to call was arranged. You could even leave a recorded message of your own. And all this cost only $6.95. As the ad pointed out, "it's automatically charged to your phone bill. No Checks. No credit cards. No hassle."

- In Larchmont, New York, the American National Bank introduced a secured credit card program featuring a 900 number to be used to apply for its program. The 900 number was advertised in print ads as well as on broadcast and cable television. Customers paid the $10 per-call fee to apply for a credit card. Though the response was lower than requests to other secured card offers by others, the response was "profitable," according to the bank's chairman.

- Digital Publications, Inc., of Atlanta, Georgia, a computer software firm, is selling and delivering software via a 900 telephone number. They claim that it is the first such use of the technology in this fashion, and our studies bear this out. In this innovative program, the charges for the software and for an additional on-line information program are directly billed to the customer's AT&T monthly bill. A 900 call costs $1 for each minute, or about $36 for a 266,000-byte program. The market is made up of businesses which include direct marketing and telemarketing firms.

But All in 900 Land Is Not Rosy

In December of 1989, Revlon announced its first 900-number direct-response campaign as part of a $2 million dollar sweepstakes aimed at 52 million households. It was pointed out that Kimberly-Clark, Lever Bros., General Foods, and Gillette were using 900 numbers as well. A one-day free-standing insert was included in 220 general circulation newspapers nationally. The target market was women between the ages of 18 and 49. Respondents were given the choice of either a $2 caller-paid 900 number or a mail-in coupon. It was felt that the promotion would "attract many Sunday impulse buyers who are seeking 'instant gratification.'"

Revlon expected a 1.8 percent response "virtually all within the first week," and a 3.7 percent response on the coupons. As an additional incentive to respond, a portion of the revenues would be given to a charity, the Juvenile Diabetes Foundation, strictly on a percentage basis of calls received. It was felt also that consumers liked public-spirited promotions. The results of the 900 campaign were nowhere near what had been expected. The response was reportedly less than one-tenth of 1 percent with only 40,000 to 45,000 calls generated from the 52 million households. In the wake of this experience, the marketing vice president left Revlon, and the Juvenile Diabetes Foundation reported that Revlon donated "about $2,000" to the charity.

Fortunately, according to Revlon, the costs of the campaign were covered. A former head of the telemarketing service bureau handling the incoming calls blamed the low response on the ad copy. He reported that Revlon had learned

337

that it was easier for people to write in using the coupon "because of the way the ad was written." There is a world of truth in that statement. Direct marketing copy writers have yet to learn that the copy, in order to be telemarketing-sensitive and effective, cannot be written in the same style or even quantity as that of the direct-mail ads they are so competent at writing.

A footnote of importance to this campaign: One of the promotion managers involved with another Revlon 900 response sweepstakes stated that response was better when its target market of 14-to-21-year-olds mailed their names and addresses "on a piece of paper." She pointed to the failure of the 900 campaign as evidence of the reluctance teenagers feel about asking their parents if they can make a pay-per-call contact.

THE 11 MAJOR 900 TELEMARKETING STRATEGIES

The numerous firms using 900 services usually employ proven strategies from past telemarketing experience. There are 11 basic strategies employed by the telemarketing professionals who use the telephone in planned programs integrated with traditional marketing methods and techniques. Here are the 11 strategies in which the use of a 900 service should be considered:

1. Sales programs to handle existing accounts

2. Opening of new accounts

3. Add-on and upgrade of sales on incoming calls

4. Qualification of prospect lists

5. Activation of marginal, old, and forgotten accounts

6. Introduction of new products or services

7. Lead generation

8. Tie-in to outbound call campaigns

9. Follow-up to direct-mail campaigns

10. Full account management by telephone

11. Coordination with telesales, order entry, and customer service procedures

Innovative use of 900 services is opening many new marketing windows for the sharp marketer. The use of experienced 900 service bureaus, such as TELESPHERE, Matrixx, and WATS Marketing, will enhance the planning process and do much to avoid the pitfalls that others have fallen prey to.

CHOOSING A TELEMARKETING SERVICE BUREAU

Planning is the key to your inbound telemarketing success if you decide to use a telemarketing service bureau (TSB) to handle your 800 or 900 responses.

Just how do you find the right bureau? First let's look at the TSB industry's background for a moment. According to the *Annual Guide to Telemarketing,* there were 632 TSBs in the United States in 1990. This figure was down from 1,870 in 1985. What's happening? Well, in the early 1980s, everyone with a telephone and a card table who had a pleasant voice and dreamed of some fast, easy money, opened a TSB.

By 1985, the industry had started to experience the fallout of all the nonprofessionals. That is why we now have only 632 left. It is interesting to note that of the 632 TSBs in the United States, 132 are 4 or more years old and the balance of 500 are less than 4 years old.

One glance at the reasons why so many TSBs have failed points up the need for the purchaser of these services to be on guard. Almost all TSBs go under because (1) the firm has experience but no capital, or (2) the firm has capital and no experience. (Either way, the clients or customers have had to pay for the learning curve.) Many of the firms have started out as answering bureaus, hardware manufacturers, software designers, or direct-mail firms. Of the 132 "older" TSBs in the country, only 24 or 25 could be considered professional.

So how do you avoid getting into trouble? Prepare a request-for proposal (RFP) in which you ask for specific things to be done by the agency that you would expect any telemarketing firm to do. If you need a checklist of things to ask for, you are already in need of help; don't delay conferring with a telemarketing consultant before you do anything else. One way the consultant can help you is by giving you instant access to TSBs with experience in the field. The consultant can also ensure that the TSBs that receive your RFP can take your program from start to finish without employing a third outside contractor. As you can see, the telemarketing consultant can save you time and money in the learning curve. If, on the other hand, you are confident that you know what you want, then you are ready to meet with the top three respondents to your RFP.

Meet the respondents at their place of business. It's amazing how many sound great on paper but fade upon in-person inspection. Prior to meeting them, however, use reference contacts supplied with the RFPs to determine whether or not your candidates can deliver what they say they can. When talking to firms that are customers of your targeted TSBs, you will want to ask some questions. The following is not a complete list, but should put you in a good position to establish that the TSB in question can protect and meet your interests.

How many full-time personnel do they have?

What kind of management information do you receive?

What kind of telephone equipment does the TSB have?

Do you know the TSB's capacity (in numbers) of incoming and outgoing lines? And *how many are being used?* (This will tell you if the reference has done their homework.)

How did the TSB train their personnel in your product or service?

What is the agent turnover rate?

Where does the TSB recruit its agents?

After talking to the references, you will be ready to talk to the TSB salespeople themselves. The questions you will want to ask may seem obvious but they must have answers or you may find yourself in hot water later. Be sure to ask them if their computer is electronically compatible with yours. Have their technical representative talk to yours; this is critical and is a real must. Since you are the client, you must define the database and let the TSB meet your needs. Don't let the TSB define how the program will work, as you will then have to conform to their design of a database that may only be competent to handle the simplest of programs. You need that data received in your office and formated in the way that your system works. Don't accept anything less. And speaking of database issues, find out if the TSB can perform such functions as inventory status, credit card verification, product information, and answers to technical questions.

You should be sure to ask whether they have performed any programs like yours before. If so, ask whom you should talk to at that company. You will want to know what kinds of clients this TSB has. (Are they working with reputable firms, or are they representing questionable firms only interested in quick contacts and even faster sales?) You don't want to hire a TSB that has developed bad habits in their work.

You will want to know about the TSB's telephone service capabilities. How many work stations do they have? Are they all computerized? What is the average abandon-call rate per hour? How many contacts per hour can they handle?

And finally, the big question: How much is this all going to cost you? Presumably this has been answered in your RFP response. But—and this is important for you to know—they have quoted on your RFP, but in the conversation that has now followed, additional charges that they didn't realize belonged in the quotation have arisen. Get all the monthly charges and minimums, the program implementation charges, and the cost to handle each contact. Then ask if there are any other charges you must be responsible for. If the answer is satisfactory to you, you are now ready to make an in-person visit to the TSB. Visits to no more than three TSB's usually produce a fine selection for your new vendor.

WHERE IS INBOUND TELEMARKETING GOING?

The industry is definitely in an explosive growth period. The dozens of applications of toll-free programs testify to the success of the 800 service. The 976 service will continue to grow on the local scene and will become a network of services nationwide. The 900 service was expected to triple its size in 1990 alone, with a growth of over 200 percent expected once again in 1991. More than 2000 dial-it programs were added in 1990, for a total of 5,767 dial-it programs in the United States. It is further predicted that over 54,000 dial-it 900 service lines will have been purchased by the end of 1991.

WHAT IS THE DIFFERENCE BETWEEN INBOUND SERVICES?

One of those things we can easily take for granted is that everyone knows the difference between the 700, 800, 900, 976, and 222 inbound calling prefixes offered by the interstate and intrastate carriers.

The 900 and 700 prefixes are known as special access codes (SACs), and are area–code-like. The prefixes 976, 550, 540, and 556 are known as specially designated local exchange (SDLE) prefixes. Just for the record, let us clarify the differences:

700 SERVICE: This is a national special access code, which in addition to the 900 service, will carry special pay-per-call services such as information, entertainment, or other audiotex services. The firms that offer these services are called information providers or IPs. The IPs collect their fee by receiving a portion of the charges that are billed to the caller by the telephone company.

800 SERVICE: A nationwide or just statewide service in which the caller is not charged for the call. Used mainly as a channel of communication for response-to-advertising and direct-mail campaigns. Both business-to-business and business-to-consumer programs use this service heavily. Advanced features such as call forwarding, etc., are available. Offered by AT&T, MCI, and SPRINT.

900 SERVICE: A nationwide service in which the caller is billed a predetermined fee for the call. This fee will appear on the caller's telephone bill from the telephone company. Used mainly for consumer programs such as fund-raising, subscriptions, polls, sweepstakes, and as "rap lines" for singles. Information-offering services such as therapy, legal advice, and accounting advice are popular. This service has unfortunately been identified with the "dial-a-porn" industry, but is finally coming of age for other services. Offered by AT&T, MCI, SPRINT, and TELESPHERE.

976 SERVICE: A statewide service offered by the local telephone company. Used mainly for consumer services such as fund-raising, subscriptions, polls, sweepstakes, and provision of information such as "rap lines" for singles, and offerings for therapy, legal, and accounting services. The service gained notoriety for its introductory phase, during which the "dial-a-porn" industry was allowed to start and grow. Planned for future use in the pay-per-call prefixes in addition to 976 are 550, 540, and 546.

222 SERVICE: This is a local telephone company offering which provides a toll-free call for persons wanting to access local information on sports, lotteries, weather, etc. The "sponsors" get to promote their particular product or service before giving the sought-after information.

PART 4

Creative Tactics

22
Creative Methods: An Overview

Joan Throckmorton

Joan Throckmorton, Inc.
Pound Ridge, N.Y.

We're always pretty free with comments like "It's not creative," "Make it more creative," "Where's the creativity?" "Wow—that's creative!" *But what does "creative" mean? Really* mean? In ad land we make these judgments ourselves a million times. If something is creative, we assume it does its job persuading the market. It's easy to recall. It gets people to act; it influences and impresses them. "Creative" advertising in the broad, general sense helps move goods and services.

But when we talk about direct-response advertising, we go a bit further. We ask our advertising to get out there and bring in a bona fide, bottom-line response, be it inquiry or order. We want to measure our advertising precisely, apart from any awareness-raising or image-building it may inadvertently do. So then, can we only say something is really creative when it gets good scores? When the numbers say so? Is that the measure of our creative function? Recall be damned? Impressions ignored? It certainly used to be our yardstick. Pure and simple. "Creative" was sort of synonymous with "control" or test-winner. Or high marks on the order forms returned. Or a large number of telephone calls coming in.

TOMORROW'S MANDATE

Well, things are changing. We no longer exist in our own private little vacuum of bottom-line, CPO, ROI measurements.

Today even the staunchest old-line direct marketers are talking glibly about such things as integrated advertising, combined impressions, image advertising, multimedia and, dare I say it, working closely with general advertising (thanks to some of the early leaders in this field, like Speigel, Lands' End, and American Express).

Actually, it all started when general advertising got interested in *us*, the direct marketers. Grossly oversimplified, the history at the agencies went something like this:

1. Let's get our agency into direct-response advertising. Put a coupon on that ad!

2. OK, so we have to invest in direct marketing and do it their way. But don't ask for any of *my* client's budget.

3. So now we have a direct-response division; the client thinks it's great. Well, who am I to say no?

4. You know, it's really all the same thing. It's part of the big picture and direct marketers have a role. (Hey—even David Ogilvy said direct marketing was a top training ground for real advertising!) But don't take any of *my* budget...

As we gradually come closer together and some reputable agencies even feature *integrated* services and "relationship marketing," it becomes a complex creative question of (1) general advertisers and direct marketers walking hand in hand into the sunset; or (2) one marketing methodology totally smothering the other and simply absorbing it, period. Right now, it's a standoff.

There's no big problem if direct response is introduced *after* a general agency has done its thing. Or in a small company where there is no agency of record *except* the direct-response agency. But there can be fireworks and power plays when the two forms of advertising try to work together from ground zero on a mutual client.

What it signifies is this: most of us now readily agree that, while you work to build a direct-response customer base, you also build image and awareness, whether you try to or not. If you can work positively at both functions together, you'll get something more effective than either of you would get in working alone. But producing harmony may not be easy on the agencies. Or the clients.

On the client side, many traditional direct-response users draw back and express concern that image advertising is a dubious expenditure because it can't be precisely measured or evaluated. On the other side, large newcomers to direct response focus on projected returns and breakeven, totally neglecting creative testing to increase response. ("Why test? We got 1 percent and that's what we needed." or "How can you do *creative* testing with an integrated creative theme?") Good questions.

Nor does this new attitude of recognition mean that all users will now embrace direct marketing equally or in the same way. It's still "different strokes for different folks." For example, it allows very large consumer product companies—those who look for fast builds and market share—to indulge in direct marketing (along with other forms of advertising in their mix) as:

1. A way of pretesting new products

2. A market entry test for new product pricing, packaging, and positioning

3. A means of follow-up customer research on new products

4. A tool for influencing or persuading other channels of distribution regarding a product's pretested viability

5. And, just recently, a way to reach prime purchasers regularly, to influence small pockets of customers in repeat sales, or increased sales, and/or to introduce them to other product lines via a database. (As such, these are not considered "distribution channels" because of their insignificant size.)

On the other hand, direct marketing allows smaller or medium-size companies to establish entire new channels of distribution through the development and cultivation of a prime customer database. In the case of small, special-interest, highly targeted companies, it simply enables them to survive and prosper.

As direct-response conflicts and agency differences impact on our creativity, our creative dictates continue to say, "Emphasize benefits; benefits sell." But now we often add: "Incorporate current advertising. Use it as fully and as well as its own adherence to benefit orientation allows." If, for example, the general advertising campaign emphasizes the strength, reliability, and safety of the product, and does this with the symbol of a child in protective arms, direct marketers would do well to pick it up, adapt it—graphics and all, and run with it. If, on the other hand, the current campaign emphasizes a meaningless line like "Listen to baby coo—it loves our product, too," direct marketers would have to switch such advertising to a secondary position and build a strong benefit-oriented case that would segue into or rationalize the general advertising's "baby coo."

It's not always easy to combine creative themes or approaches, but direct marketers, knowing full well the rules of their creative trade, can indeed work constructively and productively in doing this, even if they cannot always work as well as they'd like with general agencies.

Ideally, direct marketing planning is worked in at the start as an integrated aspect of the overall creative strategy. It's not added on as an afterthought. Direct-response creatives must bring their own special creative knowledge to the project from the beginning.

THE RULES AND TECHNIQUE

Describing creativity or "teaching" creativity in direct marketing is a relatively new endeavor. As far as I can determine, it really got going in the 1940s with John Caples's *Tested Advertising Methods* and Vic Schwab's *How to Write a Good Advertisement* (although neither gives direct marketing much recognition). This was primarily direct-response print advertising—how to do it successfully. And it represents our first attempts to be analytical and to *explain* our creativity.

A funny thing happened here. It seemed a lot of our creativity was simply technique or, frankly speaking, good market research applied. "If you want a winner, be sure to put a big FREE in your headline...use illustrations...give news..."

We studied the sins of the past (so we wouldn't be bound to repeat them), and

thanks to direct-response advertising's ability to measure, a vast body of rules developed (and has gone on developing, growing, and changing, even as I write).

If the customer or prospect is king or queen, if the customer votes each time,
then we have a totally reactive form of customer-driven advertising with a
sound research basis. And we must use it.

What's more, look carefully and you'll find within our body of rules at least
three different kinds of rules that pertain to the creative function:

1. The Big No-No's (or Yes-Yes's, as I call them).   You don't question or
test these. You just *do* them. (Or don't do them.) To tamper is to reinvent the
wheel. Most are simply good common sense, like "Make it easy to order"...or
"Don't test silly little things that people don't notice—the color of the BRE, for
example."

2. The Prospect Market's Rules of Current Appeal.   These are the guidelines on what's working right now, what's getting good response. They center
largely on motivators, incentives, formats, designs, and offers that are enjoying
current popularity. These wear out, they come and go, so we have to be watch-
ful and test (or take the temperature of our market) regularly to keep tabs on
them. For example, one Big Yes-Yes is to involve your prospect with devices
that let him/her participate in the process. Interaction: that motivates response.
Under "what's hot and what's not," however, you might find that direct-mail
tokens don't work well—not half as well—today, as peel-off labels. Tomorrow?
Well, maybe tokens again.

3. Customer Rules.   This third group of guidelines is one that should be
more important now than ever before. Here we have a valuable body of names
in a database—people with certain similar distinguishing characteristics. Our job
is to talk with them politely, lovingly even, to find out what they want and exactly how they wish to be treated. If we do this and do it well, we will be richly
rewarded by their support.

And from this, we develop a set of customer rules. Not just *universal* customer rules, mind you, although they're a part of it, but quite highly individualized customer rules that allow one of us to say, "My customers love premiums.
One small gift, and they double the size of their order!" Another to respond:
"Really? Not *my* customers. Premiums actually depress response from my
customers..." and so on.

Right you are. All this ain't exactly creativity. It *can* substitute for it, however,
when necessary. And it is, in fact, pure technique based on the finest market
research in the world.

In passing on our experience—in formalizing it—we find that we have developed a vast body of formulas, constantly shifting and changing shape like a row
of sand dunes between us and the sunrise of our creativity. We have to learn to
negotiate this terrain of shifting techniques before we can go running off into
that sunrise. So rules come first, and every person determined to write great
direct-response copy, or teach it, or evaluate it, or design formats for it has to
understand this. How we apply our rules, matching the primary benefits of our
product or service to what we know of our target market's needs, desires, and
aspirations—that's where our real creativity comes in.

CREATIVE CONCEPT DEVELOPMENT

Put technique aside for a moment (or assume you've mastered it), and let's move on to the creative stuff. The creative process itself can be structured and formalized. Sort of. Partially. Up to a point. And up to this point, I'm even suggesting that it can be done by several people working together as a team.

When blind inspiration strikes, it is beautiful and wonderful and magical. But consciously or unconsciously, certain organizational processes, involving highly cognitive skills, are going on in the head, or on paper, at the same time.

I have attempted to illustrate and order some of the basic steps in that process, irrespective of whether they amount to conscious or unconscious actions. In trying to trace the steps that move us forward in the creative process, I have also worked backward from the finished creative product to the original creative source.

Before any writing or design begins, there must be a certain amount of constructive cooperation on any creative project. That's the teamwork, and it includes concept development and copy strategizing. It's how we prepare ourselves so that our creative results, inspired and imaginative, communicate the message that the marketing director, product manager, creative director— client—all agree *is* the message. This is not tampering with the muse, but rather helping to make sure that the muse shines its light properly on the work in question.

Assuming that our technique (rules and formulas) is ever present in our thinking, sound research on product and market precedes any kind of creative work. And I mean it. You'll want the creative team (composed of the writer, the designer, the marketer or product manager, and even a media person and a production person) to follow this research with an objective evaluation of the total proposition. What precisely is the product's positioning? Is the offer competitive? Unique? Justifiable in light of the product's positioning or the market's level of awareness? (An entirely new product that does revolutionary new things is priced and promoted to a high-end market in one way, for example, while a well-known mass product is competitively priced and promoted against its competition in quite a different way.) Discuss it.

Once you understand fully what you've got, who it's going to, and how it's going to be perceived, it's important to make sure you're comfortable with the findings. Now is the time to tamper and to question management and/or the client if everyone isn't happy with the answers. Go for consensus.

By the way, team leaders, or "creative managers," as I call them, can be any of the following (depending on the kind of creative operation and the size of the advertiser): company presidents, promotion directors, product managers, account executives, marketing directors, creative directors—you!

And you, as a creative manager, can do a lot more than just encourage and inspire good work. Through a series of creative strategy meetings before the writer and the designer walk off into that sunrise to create beautiful direct-response advertising—surefire, effective winners—you can work with your creative group to make sure you're all on the same wavelength. You can make sure *you* communicate and interact with them on every single aspect of the project.

Too often a writer and a designer carry a job through copy and layouts only to discover at presentation that they are way off track...or that you, your managers, or your peers had never conveyed certain vital information. Or simply that these creative artists saw it in a new or different light—one that you were not prepared for. Or more simply still—that *you* weren't clear, and *they* didn't listen!

Some of the smartest creative managers I know have several meetings *before* any copy or design work begins. After initial agreement on the basic feasibility of the product and the proposition, creative people need a chance to think. Then comes the first strategy meeting—a meeting to discuss the overall creative concept or the big benefit and the tactics for getting it across.

As we all know, every product or service has a multitude of benefits. Some are big, some are small. On which benefit shall we hang our proposition? Which benefit or benefits will have the strongest appeal to our market, based on the things we already know are important to this particular market (its desires, aspirations, fears)?

Which benefits are next important? Which can come later? How should this be conveyed? What assumptions or hypotheses are we making?

Here, you and your team build a sandwich. Take your primary benefits, overlay them on your market and its primary desires, aspirations, or fears...match up benefits and market traits, then draw up an assumption or hypothesis and wrap it around the benefits. For example:

Your product is a facial creme that, used regularly, helps soften rough skin, smooths out small wrinkles—even makes some wrinkles disappear.

Your market is primarily middle-aged, affluent women—largely business women. (The creme is very expensive.)

Your hypothesis is that everyone looks older than he/she feels. Many women do not want to show their age. For real and imagined reasons they are insecure, afraid they'll be unattractive, or that they'll be viewed as "out of the action" and less desirable in both their business and their social life.

Your big benefits, assuming FDA approval, are clear. The creme will "take 10 years off your life and you will again look as young as you feel. This means men will find you more attractive...your friends will be impressed...and you will be more confident in everything you do."

It's a very good idea to have *consensus* on this benefits and hypothesis point before the writer and designer go off to do their thing. No matter how many meetings it takes!

Another area of consensus is production and budget limitations. I'm not suggesting that production be allowed to dictate tight restrictions on creative design and format. Only that *some* agreement be reached—particularly in the case of direct mail, due to all the limitations (budget and otherwise) imposed by the U.S. Postal Service. Without agreement, creative people in their enthusiasm are likely to return with copy and layouts for an execution that far exceeds the practical limits of the budget.

One other aspect of the creative development should be discussed and firmed up at this stage. I call it "recommendations." It involves signing off on all the details, and includes wrapping up a lot of loose ends and answering some big questions that can have an important effect on your creative work. Using direct mail as an example:

1. Who's the spokesperson? When the writer does the letter, who does he or she represent? What (based on the most *logical* spokesperson) is the writer's point of view? Is the writer the president of the company? The technical director? Head of research? A designer? A sales manager? Each of these individuals speaks from a different point of view. Each has his/her own *voice*.

2. Is there a good reason to have a lift letter? Is there a *second* point of view to reinforce or strengthen the main speaker? (For example, with a series of cookbooks, the publisher might introduce the series in the main letter, but the head of the test kitchens would do a lift letter to explain all that goes into finding and testing a new recipe for the books.) A lift letter is, in effect, a *second* salesperson.

3. How will credibility be reinforced? What qualifies you to go into people's homes with this offer? Are testimonials needed? An endorser—someone well known to the market? A distinguished board of advisors? Illustrations of the plant, assembly line, offices, customer service reps, or fulfillment? Awards and ratings earned? Growth stories? Sales curves, number of customers?

4. Is a deadline feasible? Certainly it's desirable. But how specific can the writer get? Naturally the best, most credible deadline is an exact date in the reasonably near future. But sometimes this isn't possible.

5. How about guarantees? What are your legal parameters here? What are you allowed to say? What would be the strongest/best guarantee? Will your management accept it? Your lawyers?

6. How about involvement devices? Do your creative people feel that there will be logical opportunities for strong ones? What kinds? Will they make sense to the chosen market? On what basis have they been selected? Make relatively sure the involvement device—be it peel-off label, token, stamp, scratch-off or plastic card—is likely to justify itself by increased return on investment.

Whether direct mail, print, or broadcast, once a creative strategy is determined and mutually accepted (to include proposition testing, concept/hypothesis development, production parameters, basic recommendations from which creative development will flow) your writer and/or designer are ready for that walk into the sunrise. And you, the manager, can sit back and rest (so to speak). After all this input and strategizing, however, your creative people owe you something in return.

A MANAGEMENT CHECKLIST FOR EVALUATING CREATIVE WORK USING DIRECT MAIL AS AN EXAMPLE

On presentation, your creative people owe you an introduction with an exposition *of* and rationale *for* the creative approach as executed through both copy and art. This includes a clear explanation of what has been done, with the underlying creative strategy carried out through copy and comps.

In addition to the strategy—since a good direct-response writer must also be a good technician—there must be a *reason* for every element, every copy approach—the very structure of the package or ad. If you ask your writer, "Why do you use a headline (or subhead or lead) like that one, or why is this illustration so small, etc., the answer should always begin, "I'm glad you asked that question..."

The resulting creative work should show adherence to and full incorporation of agreed-upon data: correct and complete product information and a fully developed offer.

It should be fully and clearly explained to you, the manager, or to the client *why* anyone will stop and open the outer envelope (or read the ad, if print, or listen or watch, if broadcast).

On reviewing the copy, ask yourself: "Does the sales story come across clearly, dramatically, and convincingly the *first* time I look at it or read it or hear it? Is the offer up front? Is it stated so clearly everywhere that even a child can understand it?" If not, watch out. Your prospects will either be confused, become impatient, or lose interest immediately. *They're* not going to give it a second chance. Why should you?

The Outer Envelope

The outer envelope is *the* most vulnerable (and important) part of your direct-mail package. Most envelopes, I contend, never even *get* opened! Be hard on yourself and your creative team. Will your envelope copy and design tease, force, intrigue your prospect to find out what's inside? Or will it allow your recipient to give it a glance and a toss (into the waste basket)? Would you open it if the envelope appeared in a stack of *your* mail? Many an outer is killed by too much talk. Don't let your prospect make a decision until they get inside. Remember this: an envelope that says nothing is stronger—by far—than one that says too much.

Some Specific Guidelines for Evaluating the Letter

1. If the outer envelope teases or promises, does the letter pick it up immediately, give your prospect answers, and carry it forward?

2. Would the all-important letter *lead* be stronger if the letter started with the third or fourth paragraph and just skipped the first two? You can't imagine how many good leads get buried halfway down the first page. (We've *all* been told this many times. It's true. Try it!)

3. Is the approach used in the letter the strongest possible approach and, if not, can you suggest a better one? Suppose, for example, that an invitational approach is used throughout on all components. Perhaps the letter, while maintaining the invitational graphics, might be strengthened by starting it with the question approach, or by using a quotation for the testimonial approach.

If the business approach of "Be a Hero" is used in the promotion, might adding a story approach lend greater interest to the letter?

If a package seems to fall short (even when the creative team has adhered to the strategy), understanding and recommending approaches is an excellent way of critiquing. (I explain twelve of these approaches and how to apply them in my book *Winning Direct Response Advertising*.)

4. Is the writing wordy, with long sentences and convoluted ideas? Can you cut it and make it clearer? If so, then the writer must do likewise.

5. Is there a "pet word" syndrome? (A word that the writer repeats over and over?) Explain that "no pets are allowed" on this project.

6. Are paragraphs short (five lines, or two sentences maximum)? Are margins wide?

7. Are there good bridges? Is the reader carried forward from one paragraph to another? From one idea or concept to the next?

8. Is typewriter type used for the letter? This is *required* by the pros—not to fool the prospect, but to flag the prospect by announcing that this piece of paper represents a one-on-one message, a letter!

9. Is there a P.S.? It's one of the most important positions in the letter because so many people look there. Its job, therefore, is to catch the prospect's interest and pull him/her back into the letter.

If You Use a Brochure, Make Sure It Does Its Job!

Ask yourself: Does it *dramatize* the benefits as well as show the features? Be careful here. More and more I find that brochures merely tout the data. Check the main head. Is it a *feature* or a benefit headline? For example, "These Beautiful, Graceful Figures Are Sensitively Hand-Carved with Lifelike Faces," is a *feature* headline, while "Let the Beauty and Sensitive Grace of the Figures Enhance Your Home and Give You Pleasure" is a *benefit* headline.

Does the brochure track? That is, does the layout and copy draw you into the brochure and open up the story or promotional theme gradually, along with *each fold*, right to the grand finale on the inside spread?

Is the type style consistent, easy to read, bold and dramatic on the headlines? Make sure that there's a minimum of reverse type in the brochure, that no type is printed over colors or tints (like blue or gray sky). And that all pictures that aren't immediately self-explanatory carry captions. *And* that there are no blank white surfaces on the back of an order card or brochure panel. (If there are, at least tell your reader where to go with an "Over, please" or an arrow.)

The Order Form Is Important, Too

Does it fully restate the big benefit and offer? Does it look important? Is it involving—with things to check, paste, peel, tear off? Is it easy to use? Have you made your 800 number prominent? Does the form carry a reply address?

Is the Package as a Whole Really Dramatic?

Or just like all the others? Is the brochure folded in a new and different way? Is the type strong and readable? Does it use action colors (gold and black)? Modern colors (magenta or fuchsia, flamingo, turquoise, pink)?

Does the entire package track? Does it *control* the prospect, take him/her by the hand from "open here" on the outer, to "over please," right on to "drop this in the mail today!"?

And while we're talking about color and design, don't forget that this kind of creative review includes, or should include, the designer as well as the copywriter. Good creative work requires teamwork, the kind of teamwork that relies on all of you who manage creative staff, hire or train creative staff, or interface in any way, be it ad agency, freelancer or in-house promotion staff.

You pull the strings. If you're creatively aware and open-minded, if you bring high expectations and make sure that sound planning precedes each assignment, you'll get good work, winning work.

SOME THINGS TO WATCH FOR IN THE YEARS AHEAD

Since change is indeed our only constant, I feel compelled to point out a few significant developments now taking place that will affect your marketing—and that can at the same time impact positively on your creative strategizing and resulting creative efforts in the years ahead.

Major Market Shifts

There's no question about it: our population is changing.

Mature Market. We all know that the mature market will soon be bulging, that the number of grandparents will soar, and that we'll be storehousing the millions of adults living well past sixty as never before.

My suggestion: For older eyes, see that your people use large type. And use very straightforward selling and little hype; this market eschews shouting and is naturally suspicious of the fast talker. (Well, aren't we all?)

Shift in Values. Our marketers have also been seeing a major consumer shift in values as time becomes money. Affluent, working consumers (including women workers) demand time-saving (as opposed to money-saving) products and services. They demand prime service—and they're willing to pay for it.

Convenience and speed in ordering and fulfillment should be emphasized in copy, along with aspects of your product or service that help save time or make life easier. In short, focus on "time-saving" as a major benefit.

Illiteracy.   Population increases, extremes of wealth and poverty, and our faltering national education network have fostered a tremendous increase in semi-illiteracy and functional illiteracy. At the same time, the audio/video medium and the computer screen are fast becoming a primary form of mass communication *and* education at all levels of society.

Brief, simple copy with words of no more than two syllables will be the rule for writers who want to communicate. Many companies, among them a major financial institution, already employ a computer copy checker that allows no words above eighth-grade-English level to be used in their customer communications and advertising. In print, lots of illustrations will be needed, too. You might want to consider a form of comic book graphics for a lot of your products and services.

Ethnic Markets.   Impressive growth in the ethnic sectors of our population is creating a significant new Hispanic market made up of peoples from Central and South America and the Caribbean, newcomers and first-generation Americans who bring customs and language from a variety of Latin countries.

Learn Spanish. It takes a lot of living in Latin countries to write copy in the idiom. But to understand the advertising and manage a creative budget in the Hispanic market, every one of us would do well to get a better feeling for the people and the language. "¿Pues, cómo no? ¡Sin duda!"

Media Shifts

Everything we know about market trends and media costs (and, in the case of direct mail, always-looming postal problems) makes one thing perfectly clear: the most cost-effective media for reaching many new markets is going to be electronic carriers.

If you're looking for impulse response in a market where people are too busy to read (and/or simply can't read), you may find that a lot of your initial selling efforts are moving to television, video cassette, and various interactive electronic methods.

As this happens, creativity will not necessarily go through any great upheaval. We're already into television sales and support. We have video cassettes and infomercials as well. Our technique remains. Our emphasis on benefits endures. Our creative process still requires creative strategies, concept development, and good dialogue. Our best copy, as a matter of fact, *is* dialogue. The dialogue between two correspondents in the mails need not be too different from telephone dialogue or broadcast dialogue and dramatizations.

If and when this shift in prospecting occurs, direct mail will survive and prosper, certainly, but largely in highly targeted, specialized marketing areas that are not efficiently reached by most forms of mass electronic media. You'll find excellent applications for it—matchless applications—in cultivating current customers. Direct mail linked with the telephone will become our most effective tool for influencing customers and establishing a good dialogue.

The one big problem with this probable shift in media could be a demise in creative testing. And that will be rough, because we already have far too many practitioners cutting back on creative print test budgets, and still more new practitioners ignoring this area completely. Budgets that are regularly allocated to media and offer testing are seldom increased to include scientific copy and concept testing. Yet this is an area where tremendous strides can be made in increasing media efficiency simply by attracting more prospects, increasing response.

Those companies that do invest in such creative testing, that are committed to a creative budget and time frame, will be able to use media far more productively. You'll see, too, that even when such budgets start small, they multiply rapidly simply because creative testing is so profitable.

The Customer as King/Queen.   In conjunction with changing markets and new market demands will come a surge in customer service. At every level of sales, the customer rules today. And those of us who neglect this little point will be left behind.

Creatively speaking, this gives you, as a response advertiser, a wonderful opportunity to express your dedication and service to your best prospects and customers at every contact level, in word and deed. Instead of "Dear Reader," make it "Dear Friend;" instead of "Dear Customer," make it "Dear Valued Customer." Warm, friendly, caring copy from *real people*.

If direct mail, because of its costs, is used less for prospecting and more for customer communications, our writers will have to learn to speak warmly, to deal with the customer with sincere interest, asking for his/her opinion and using the resulting data to serve the customer better.

You'll want to recast your best writers in a newly defined role: as your best customer communicators as well as your best customer service reps. You may want to plan more frequent communications—opportunities just to say "thank you," special efforts to apologize if mistakes occur, chances to update customers on new products and services, exclusive customer offers tailored to personal customer history and demographics as they are recorded in your customer database. Now is the time, as never before, to begin using your database constructively. And "constructively" leads me on to our next point.

Privacy.   This is bound to be a big issue in the next decade, especially with global marketing and our ability to start computing international data on our customers everywhere. There are already strict rules on privacy in Europe. Now we too will have to monitor ourselves more carefully, especially when we carry what we know from our database to our customer copy.

We must draw a fine line between data that compliments and involves the customer and help us fine-tune an offer to his/her interests, and data that oversteps the bounds with offensive familiarity—the kind of familiarity that can lead us right into public sector attention and government controls. ("Aha, Mrs. Smith, so you're overweight and you'll be sixty-five next Friday!")

I know this is hard to believe, but I've seen personal data handled improperly on several occasions recently by companies which, because of the nature of their business, have unusually extensive databases (the kind of customer databases we all dream about). Too much customer information, poorly handled, not only walks a dangerous line in the privacy area, but also makes for promotions that are cold, uncaring, even downright unfriendly. Tossing in meaningless raw data about the prospect's life or the prospect's company is more than an invasion of privacy, it can be threatening to them, like a letter from the IRS. It takes real creativity to use data well, and sometimes, less is more. Use the data to better understand your prospect or customer, then write from the heart.

Green Consciousness.   It's here, it's big, it's global and growing, and you can bet it will impact on everything we say and do—and the way we advertise—in the years ahead.

From the youth market to the retiree sector, everyone is "concerned." These concerns range from air pollution, acid rain, and the greenhouse effect to conservation, waste management, and organic farming. The Green movement is growing and so is environmental marketing right along with it. Every aspect of your creative work is going to have to take this into consideration in the years ahead. The way you run your company must reflect it in word and deed, and so must the way you present your products and services.

The benefits underlying our selling platforms should begin by incorporating environmental issues when they are honestly reflected by the products or services themselves. In customer relations you'll want to emphasize positive corporate actions and corporate policies regarding environmental issues. Just demonstrating that you print and ship on recycled paper won't be good enough.

Look for honest opportunities. Help create them. An ever-growing number of catalog companies are already involved and contributing to the Green movement from sales profits—and making sure their customers and prospects know about it!

One final thought: whether your future creative efforts involve direct mail, television and radio, magazines, newspapers, coupons, 800 and 900 numbers, interactive electronic kiosks, or other means, as a direct marketer you have one wonderful creative tool that, to the best of my knowledge, no other form of advertising or marketing has ever mastered: dialogue.

Despite integrated advertising, relationship marketing, and all those other hefty terms, good direct marketers bring something very special to the table: the ability to be a *good listener,* to ask our prospects and customers what pleases them and to react accordingly. No other form of marketing, no other advertising techniques can replace our most effective creative persuaders, our one-on-one conversations that build considerate, friendly, enduring relationships.

23
Psychological Appeals

Alan Rosenspan

Bronner Slosberg Humphrey
Boston, Mass.

You arrive home one day to find two different envelopes in your mailbox. One is plain, white, and businesslike. The other has a question on it. But it's the kind of personal question you'd ask only a longtime friend:

DO YOU CLOSE THE BATHROOM DOOR EVEN
WHEN YOU'RE THE ONLY ONE HOME?

Which envelope would you open first?

This provocative package was created by writer Bill Jaymee in a famous direct-mail solicitation for—what else?—*Psychology Today*. The question was written on the outside of the envelope. And if you wanted to know what your answer meant, you had to open and read the package. Hopefully, you would then subscribe to the magazine.

When Mr. Jaymee wrote this famous headline, it was very appropriate to a magazine that appealed to people interested in people and how they behaved. However, it took advantage of a more general and important advertising principle: It grabbed, intrigued, and involved the reader by using a powerful psychological appeal.

Psychological appeals are a critical factor in direct marketing. In fact, because we don't have many of the other tools of general advertising, such as repetition (viewers may have to see the same commercial 12 times before it makes an impression on them) or music (as the saying goes, "If you've got nothing to say, *sing* it"), the psychological appeal may be the single most powerful weapon we have at our disposal. And in the private, personal, *targeted* medium of direct mail, we can use psychological tools in very potent and leverageable ways—ways that might not be appropriate in mass media.

OUR PATH IS HARDER

The nature of direct marketing is different from general advertising. Our goal is action. While other advertising is seeking a "share of mind," we are looking for a *show of hands*. We want people to do something after they've received our message: to clip a coupon, fill in a response device, place a telephone call. But we not only demand that they act, we have the temerity to demand that they act *now*. Not when they feel like acting, nor when it's most convenient for them, but right now, at this very moment.

> **When Brutus spoke, people listened. But**
> **when Anthony spoke, people *marched*.**

How can you get significant numbers of people to march? It's important to know at the very beginning that you *can't*. Many direct marketers would be extremely satisfied with a 5 percent response. But that still means that 19 out of every 20 people turned it down. So even on our very best days, we fail most of the time. But that leads us to a very important point; one that should always be kept in mind: you are writing or designing to reach that *one* person out of 20. Just the one. So you don't have to be all things to all people. You can write with one particular person in mind; the one you think is most likely to respond.

Other chapters in this book will discuss how to *find* that person, using lists and/or predictive modeling. Trust me, they can be found. What we will be discussing here, however, will help you to communicate with that one person in a psychologically compelling way.

HOW TO SHIFT THE ODDS
IN YOUR FAVOR

The chances are fairly good that you, like me, are not a professional psychologist. However, as a direct marketer you must become a star student of human behavior. You must learn where the pressure points of motivation are and become as familiar with the anatomy of a sale as a surgeon is with the intricacies of the human body. The important point to recognize is that psychology is the study of the individual. It involves understanding the way he or she thinks, makes decisions, and ultimately acts. It's precisely this kind of knowledge that you'll need to use every time you develop a direct marketing piece. But unlike a lawyer having to influence a jury of 12, or a politician having to persuade the masses, you need to convince only one person to act. Better still, you need only one out of 20 and you will be considered a great success. Sounds easy, doesn't it? Fortunately, a lot of our work has been done for us by pioneers in the worlds of both direct marketing and psychology.

CLIMBING THE HIERARCHY OF HUMAN NEEDS

When considering psychological appeals, most people begin with *motivation*. After 20 years of clinical practice, Dr. Abraham Maslow developed a hierarchy of human needs. Dr. Maslow's hierarchy has five distinct stages, beginning with our first and most basic physiological needs—for air, food, and water. The second stage is our safety and security needs—for protection, order, and stability. Next come our social needs—the longing for affection, friendship, and a feeling of belonging to something. The fourth stage is ego needs—our desire for self-respect, success, and feelings of accomplishment. And the final stage—which most of us never reach—is the need for self-actualization, for the conviction that we are doing our best and fulfilling every aspect of our potential.

From a strictly psychological point of view, Dr. Maslow's list may represent the evolution of man's needs from cave to supermarket. And you might suppose that the higher the need, the more effective the appeal to it. This is not necessarily true. In fact, the reality is very different: the strongest direct marketing package is usually the one that zeroes in on the needs about halfway down Maslow's list. In other words, while an offer of self-actualization may sound just great—humanistic and uplifting—the offer of a free calculator is more likely to get you a response.

THE HOLE-IN-ONE APPROACH

For our purposes, I would like to describe human needs in terms of another metaphor: a round of golf. The first nine holes are the primary needs, those that are required to sustain life. There's not a lot that direct marketing can do to affect those first nine holes, and that's not where the game is won or lost, anyway. It's on the back nine, the secondary or acquired needs, that a direct marketing approach will succeed or fail, or fall somewhere in the rough. These "holes" include prestige, affection, power, learning, greed, self-esteem, competitiveness, fear, and getting something for nothing. Here, the right direct marketing approach can result in a hole in one. But first, you'll need to have a thorough knowledge of the clubs you have in your golf bag. You'll need to know which approaches will work best in which situations. You'll need a working knowledge of your course, so that you'll know all the sand traps and rough spots. And, of course, you'll need to learn the game.

THE MARKETING PHILOSOPHY COMES OF AGE

In the past 50 years, the marketing needs of companies have shifted dramatically. They began with a *production* orientation: the name of the game was who could produce and distribute the goods, and a product was sold primarily because it could be made. But after the 1950s, the sales front began to move forward, from simply selling what was made, to developing marketing techniques that sold what was made *more effectively*. The era of mass marketing took off, with radio, television, and national magazines carrying the banner. Then came the computer, which allowed us to analyze mass marketing with a depth and level of detail never before possible. Suddenly we could see beyond the forests and focus on specific trees. The result? Today's marketing philosophy, which demands that a company be able to determine the needs and wants of a variety of specific target markets and deliver the desired satisfaction better than the competition.

Enter market segmentation, a "science" that is simpler in theory than it is in practice. Let me give you a quick but illuminating example. The $1.3-billion vitamin market is segmented by age (adults, children, older adults); gender (male, female/pregnant female); place of distribution (drugstore, supermarket, health food store, mail order); formulation (multivitamins, liquids, tablets); and price (premium, generic). Although all segments of the market may use the product for the same reason, each segment may best be targeted by an entirely different approach. And that approach will change over time. However—and note this—*the basic psychology of the buyer of those vitamins, or indeed of virtually every other product, has* not *changed.*

A fascinating study was done of "Motives in Male and Female Adults." According to the study, they include, in no particular order:

appetite	curiosity
love of kids	efficiency
love of parents	respect for deity
health	sympathy
sex	protection of others
ambition	hospitality
pleasure	warmth
bodily comfort	courtesy
possessions	play/sport
approval of others	control
competition	fear/caution
cooperation	style
personal appearance	humor
safety	amusement
cleanliness	shyness
rest/sleep	teasing
economy	domesticity
social	distinction

A complete list? Pretty much so. A *recent* list? Hardly. It was first published in *Principles of Advertising* by Daniel Stard back in 1923. And Daniel Stard wasn't creating any new motivations. He was merely cataloging what was already old hat. The truth is that people's wants and needs haven't changed much over time. From the very beginning, there have been only a few basic psychological motivations for human behavior. What *has* changed are the vast number of *choices* we each have today—the sheer variety of products and services that our grandparents could never even have imagined. And just as those products and services have proliferated, so has the marketing challenge multiplied to a mind-boggling degree.

WHY ARE THERE ONLY 10 COMMANDMENTS?

The old joke has Moses coming down from the mountain on his third trip and saying, "I have some good news and some bad news. The good news is that I've gotten Him down to only 10 Commandments. The bad news is that adultery is still on the list."

The joke that there's been no need to "update" the 10 Commandments underscores the point that people haven't really changed very much. They may *know* more, mainly because of such technological advances as the printing press, radio, and television. But the same basic driving forces exist, and probably always will.

WHAT HAPPENS IF I ACT NOW?

When you consider what people want, you must also take into account what they are willing to do to get it. And that brings up one of the most important elements in direct marketing: the psychology of *risk*.

Denny Hatch, publisher of *Who's Mailing What?*, and a brilliant direct marketer, uses a telling analogy when he compares direct marketing to other ways of buying products. He says, "Suppose you went down to your corner newsstand and asked to take home a magazine to read, with the idea that you wouldn't pay for it unless you liked it. And even then you wouldn't pay full price, you'd pay half." Would any newsstand or retailer allow you that liberty? Would they be in business for long if they did? But that's how virtually every magazine subscription, book club, record club, CD club, and video club actually operates.

Many people see direct marketing, however, as a tiger of a different stripe. They are reluctant to buy anything that they can't hold in their hands at that moment. So for them, direct marketing has a number of *risks* associated with it that regular marketing or selling does not. You should be aware of these perceived risks as you develop a direct marketing package, advertisement, or offer, and be prepared to address them.

The risks fall into six different areas:

Type of risk	Questions that must be answered
1. Functional	Will it work? Will it last?
2. Physical	Is it safe?
3. Financial	Is it worth it? Am I getting a good deal?
4. Social	Will other people approve? Is is appropriate to my peer group?
5. Psychological	Do I deserve it? Will it make me feel good? Will it impress others?
6. Time	Will I get it in time? Will I have to return or exchange it?

Some direct marketers have minimized these risks for the potential buyer by offering a money-back guarantee, a test drive, a "no obligation" offer, or by relying heavily on the reputation of the brand they are selling, or the company that makes it. Other direct marketers have used these perceived risks to their advantage by acknowledging them openly and showing potential buyers that there really is no risk involved.

One book club enclosed a mailing label to be used to return the book being offered if the buyer so desired. They put the mailing label in a special pouch outside the package and assured the buyer that he or she didn't even have to *open* the package to return it. The result: people felt less afraid to open it and assess the enclosed book. Orders went up—even though the club had made it easier than ever *not* to order.

Still other companies have used their money-back guarantees as marketing weapons. Nobody does it better than L. L. Bean:

> All of our products are guaranteed to give 100% satisfaction in every way. Return anything purchased from us at any time if it proves otherwise. We will replace it, refund your purchase price or credit your credit card, as you wish. **We do not want you to have anything from L. L. Bean that is not completely satisfactory.**

Would you worry about ordering from a company like that? They've developed a multimillion-dollar business just by getting people to *trust* them.

WHAT HAPPENS IF I *DON'T* ACT NOW?

The other side of the coin is equally powerful. Most successful direct marketing packages carry a caveat. But it's not "Let the buyer beware." It's "He or she who hesitates is lost." After you have laid out your most powerful selling proposition, after you've asked for the order three different times, it is imperative to remind readers what could happen if the *don't* act. The possibilities include their not being able to take advantage of a time-sensitive offer; their not being able to take advantage of it at all (a limited-edition offer, often used by collectibles companies); or worse, having their lives somehow diminished by their failure to take action. A tough sell, but a winning argument if you can carry it off.

Sometimes the threat is implicit, and sometimes it is used as the entire basis for the package. One powerful package now in circulation has an outer envelope that reads, "Things the airlines won't tell you. Things the IRS won't tell you. Things the government won't tell you." The package is for a book entitled *The Book of Information*. A deadly dull title, but a brilliant direct marketing approach that uses risk to the hilt. And perhaps even a little fear.

THE VALUE OF TRUST

The three most important words in real estate are "location, location, location." In direct marketing, the three vital words are "credibility, credibility, credibility."

If you can't get people to believe you, there's absolutely no way to convince them. Worse, *one unbelievable claim* in direct marketing campaign is an almost unsurmountable barrier to success. General advertising can get away with what is legally known as "puffery." For example, advertisers can almost always say their product is the best in the world, because their claim rests on how they choose to define "best." You can do the same thing in direct marketing—but only once. Customers will never buy from you again. And, unlike the claims made on 30-second television spots that are usually forgotten a few seconds later, your claims are right there in black and white, to be picked up and read again, and sometimes even carefully studied, before a consumer decides to act.

Credibility can be gained or lost in your choice of paper stocks, your use of postage, the decision to go with photography or illustration. (Hint: if you *can* photograph it, do so. People like to see what they're getting.) And credibility will also dictate some of the language you use, or choose to eliminate. Here is where the restricted use of superlatives and adjectives must be judiciously imposed.

The finest biographies ever written about the greatest people who ever lived...introduced by the most noted figures of our time.

This is the subhead used by one book publishing company in their four-page direct marketing advertisement. Even if it is true, I suspect that most readers would at least hesitate before reading on.

It is important to accept that credibility is not to be confused with actual truth. As everyone knows, truth is often stranger than fiction. But unless something *sounds* credible, rather than incredible, today's consumer is unlikely to act. William Bernbach, the creative genius behind Doyle, Dane, and Bernbach once said, "Nothing can kill a bad product faster than great advertising." In direct marketing, nothing can kill a great sales pitch, or a compelling offer, faster than an overblown, unsubstantiated, or unbelievable claim. One false note casts doubt on the contents of the entire package.

YOU CAN'T BUY NOW...I HAVEN'T FINISHED MY SALES PITCH!

A good salesman knows to stop talking once the customer is sold.

One of the problems in direct marketing is that you never know when to stop, or when one last bit of argument might sway a prospect. But the thing to remember is this: You're still only talking to one out of every 20 people. Chances are, that person is a *very good prospect* for your product or service (after all, they've read this far into your package, haven't they?). If you don't treat them like good prospects, and anticipate and answer every question they may have, you may be losing that sale.

The only exception may be lead generation, where your objective is to give your reader just enough information to *tantalize* them into asking for more. Here you don't want to tell the whole story, or have your prospect make a decision; you just want them to be sufficiently intrigued to respond.

BUT WAIT...THERE'S MORE!

What about those late-night commercials with the "too good to be true" offers; the ones that keep increasing what you get to such a point that you find it hard to believe they can make a penny's worth of profit?

There's no question that they work when it comes to creating sales. But the proper practice of direct marketing lies in creating *customers*; people who will buy from you again and again, and even recommend you to their friends, because they've trusted you and you haven't let them down. Now there are some businesses that don't care about building customer relationships. All they care about is that large, one-time sale. Typical among them are most time-sharing companies, who are willing to offer you big prizes just to get you to show up for a 3-hour tour. And you're guaranteed to win something of value. You can imagine the huge margin a company like that must work on. But even time-share companies are beginning to see erosion in response figures and actual sales. You *can* fool some of the people all of the time, but you can't really build a business on it.

DAVID OGILVY'S WIFE

Before we go deeper into the tactics of psychological appeals, I urge you to heed David Ogilvy's advice: "The consumer is not a moron, she's your wife." In a sense, we all qualify as "wives." Before we are direct marketers, we are also consumers. So the first thing you should do before you send out any package or advertisement is ask yourself the really tough questions:

"Do you believe it?"

"Would it make you act?"

"Does it sound like a good deal?"

"Does it sound too good to be true?"

And finally,

"Would you recommend it to your best friend?"

If your answer to any of the above questions is "no," that's probably going to be the extent of your response. Writers and designers reveal too much of themselves in their work. No matter how professional you are, or how many years of experience you have, your sincerity or insincerity will show through. One of the dangers in direct marketing is that we are so well versed in presenting any side of an argument that we can often convince *ourselves* of things we'd never believe from anyone else. The best packages are created and approved by people who have the perspective and the courage to stand aside, and who answer these questions the way the potential prospect would. Better that a package die nobly in the word processor or conference room than suffer an expensive and unnecessary death in the mail. As Franklin P. Jones put it, "Nothing's so apt to undermine your confidence in a product as knowing that the commercial selling it has been approved by the company that makes it."

WHAT'S IN IT FOR ME?

But I am being unfair to the reader. You may have turned to this chapter with a direct-mail package due next week, or even tomorrow morning. You may be staring at a blank piece of paper or word processing screen, and saying, "This is all very interesting, but I need an angle." And so, having established some of the strategic underpinnings of psychological appeals, I will now get down to brass tactics.

The first question that any prospect will ask, perhaps on an unconscious level, is, What's in it for me? Or, more explicitly, Why should I bother to:

1. Open your envelope...read your headline...watch your commercial?
2. Seriously consider your proposition?
3. Accept your offer?
4. Take the steps necessary to follow through on that impulse—i.e., get up from my comfortable chair and call your toll-free number, or complete and mail your reply card?

Why *should* the consumer choose to respond to *your* communication when he or she is assailed by so many others each day? Going back to Dr. Maslow's hierarchy of human needs may provide an answer. But the best words of advice I've ever read are by Bill Jaymee, the man whose headline began this chapter. Bill said, "The subject of any direct-mail piece is *you*"—and by "*you,*" of course, he means the recipient, the potential buyer.

Whether the direct marketer is selling fresh fruit by mail, or complex technological systems, the copy has to make absolutely clear what the product or service will do for the consumer. And what he or she wants to know is:

- Will it make me smarter?
- Will it make me money?
- Will it save me money?
- Will it save me time?
- Will it help me get ahead at work?
- Will it make me more attractive?
- Will it make people like me?
- Will it give me more control?
- Will it make me feel good about buying or using it?

Please remember that potential consumers don't give a hoot about what your product actually does. It's what you say it will do for *them* that will motivate them to buy it. And chances are, the things they'd like it to do for them are somewhere on the list above. These things are not features of the product.

They're not even benefits of the product. They're personal benefits that consumers can derive from *using* the product, or even by simply *owning* it. (Do you want proof? Research has shown that over 25 percent of all individuals who own a Steinway piano can't play.) If you can't make them smarter, richer, more attractive, more powerful, or more productive...or if you can't make their lives easier, more enjoyable, more rewarding, or more fun—consumers would just as soon listen to someone else who can.

Does this apply to business-to-business communications? *Even more so.* Because business is even more demanding of the individual's time, and your message has to work harder and faster to get through. If you want to tailor your message to the individual's specific business or job function, you will probably improve response. But the key question must remain the same: What's in it for me?

There are some packages that give the reader value just for reading. They provide information. Or they entertain. Or they tell a story. But to get people beyond the communication, to get them to actually respond, you have to give them something more. Revlon puts it best when it says, "We don't sell cosmetics. We sell hope."

THE SEVEN DEADLY SINS AND HOW TO USE THEM

Suppose you or your competition have tried every reasonable approach (and a few unreasonable ones) and you just can't crack a 2 percent response? The time has come to take a slightly different look at human motivation, and to turn to a higher source of inspiration.

There are dozens of excellent books on consumer motivation, direct marketing, and how to write and design powerful and compelling advertisements. But probably the world's most valuable and pithy guide to human nature—and, by extension, to effective psychological appeals—is the Bible's famous no-nonsense list of human frailties, the Seven Deadly Sins. To refresh your memory, the seven deadly sins are sloth, envy, anger, pride, gluttony, covetousness, and lust. There are many minor sins as well, but we'll leave those for the people who are satisfied with a 2 percent response. We're after bigger game.

Let's take each one and show how it can be applied to direct marketing.

Sloth

The first of the deadly sins, of course, is *sloth*. It means laziness, and most of us are guilty of it. There are at least two ways to make sloth work harder for you. The first way is to make it as easy as possible for people to act. This includes giving them a choice of calling your 800 number or mailing in a postage-paid reply card. It also includes being as simple and specific as possible in showing and telling people what you want them to do. Countless packages interest, intrigue, and then falter in the stretch, because they aren't crystal-clear on what action they want the reader to take. Nor do they make it easy enough for them to do it.

There's another, more insidious, way to use sloth, and that is through what is called a "negative option." This is commonly used in magazine subscriptions and book and record clubs, and it works like this: We're going to keep sending you merchandise on a regular basis; if you like it, do nothing (except pay for it, but that comes later). If you decide not to keep it, just send it back. What could be easier? But how may people, victims of simple sloth, find themselves *keeping* the item because it's just too much trouble to send it back? The marketers have actually succeeded in making it easier for people to buy than *not* to buy. How many readers of this chapter have joined these clubs to take advantage of a great introductory offer and promised themselves they would never order anything else again? And how many have failed to keep that promise?

Envy

Envy has always been a very workmanlike sin. John Caples used it with great success in his famous advertisement, "They laughed when I sat down at the piano...but when I started to play!" My favorite paragraph in this advertisement, which ran for 25 years and paid for itself many, many times over, is this: "How my friends carried on. People shook my hand—wildly congratulating me—pounding me on the back with delight." If that's not the way *you* were treated at the last party you attended, envy may hold a special place in your heart.

Envy has also been used for products as rational and unemotional as *The Wall Street Journal*. Their famous subscription letter tells the story of two men who graduated from college at the same time, and now return for their 25th reunion. One is the manager of a small department; the other a company president. The difference, of course, was *The Wall Street Journal*. This package has been their control for many years. But I have to believe that it works better with *middle* managers than those at the top. It is also interesting to note the singlemindedness of the communication. It doesn't push the argument any further. For example, we never learn what kind of car the more successful man drives, where he vacations, or anything else about him. He made it. The other guy didn't. If you want to make it, you still have time to order the *Journal*. Why? Envy...

Pride, Prestige, and Persuasion

There is some dispute about this next deadly sin, because, properly utilized, it can be a great virtue. One example is the pride in a job well done. Another can be the pride of belonging to a great and noble institution...like American Express, for example. For over ten years, their control letter began with this haughty introduction:

> **Quite frankly, not everyone is invited to apply for the American Express®
> Card. And not everyone who applies is accepted.**

Pride, or as they define it, *prestige,* is one of the most powerful and persuasive benefits of American Express. Other charge and credit-card companies have found that their most effective technique is to *pre-approve* people. This technique capitalizes on the fear that many people have of being rejected. If you can reassure them that they won't be, or that the chances are very slim, they're much more likely to apply.

Pride also works well in what has been called "member-get-member" programs. Basically, this is a communication that goes to your *existing* customers and involves copy that reads something like this:

> As a person of high standing and good taste, you probably know other people of similar stature. Don't you think they might enjoy some of the privileges and advantages that you already have with our product?

What they *don't* say is: "Wouldn't you just love an excuse to rub their noses in it?" Porsche has had extreme success with "member-get-member" programs, because it gives the Porsche owner an opportunity to show off his or her ownership of the car in a socially acceptable situation.

The Glut of Gluttony

Whether or not multimillion-dollar state lotteries have helped develop and nurture this sin, it seems to be more popular than ever before. In the last few years, sheer, naked greed has been as effective a selling tool as anything else you can name. Publishers' Clearing House and American Family Publishers have practically co-opted this one. In fact, you have to read their packages very carefully to find out that they're actually selling magazine subscriptions. But it is my belief that these highly professional packages would work no matter what product or service they represented. They are certainly successful. After all, how many businesses could afford to give away ten million dollars year after year after year?

A good rule of thumb: If you're going to use gluttony in a package, *drench it* with gluttony. The people to whom it will appeal will appreciate it all the more; the people who would have thrown it out couldn't possibly do so any faster.

Covetousness, Lust, and Anger

The three remaining "deadly sins" will be covered together in this section because of their relatively limited usage.

Covetousness is a specific form of gluttony practiced in the realm of material things. Once again, I have always found it more effective to sell not the product itself, but what it does for you. The best example is the collectibles companies, who urge you to buy right away because "only as many statues, dolls, plates, etc., will be made as are ordered!" (You have to think about that one for awhile.)

Lust can also be used, but only in a very creative way. My favorite example is an advertisement that had a totally black picture covering three-quarters of the page. The headline read, "Ever wonder why most people make love in the dark?" The advertisement was for Marcy exercise equipment.

Last but not least among the sins is anger, which can be an extremely powerful tool of persuasion. Perhaps that's why it's mainly used for fund raising. We can all get good and angry about lots of things, however, including poor service and bad products, so perhaps this is the most untapped "deadly sin" of all.

The Writer Atones

Now that I've unleashed the seven deadly sins, it behooves me to step back and issue a word of caution. The sins are techniques, not ideas—not even good substitutes for ideas. David Ogilvy once wrote that, "If your advertising is not based on a big idea, it will pass like a ship in the night." In direct marketing, the ship will vanish without a trace. So before you rush to apply any of the suggestions presented in this chapter, give it the "big idea" test. Ask yourself, "Is this a new way of looking at the product that hasn't been tried before?" Or, "Is this compelling enough to get me to try it?" If your answer falls short, so will your response rates.

A FEW FINAL TIPS

The following psychological appeals don't fit squarely into any category, but the author has found them extremely successful.

Getting people to interact.   Several years ago, I did a mailing to all fleet managers. I included a P.S. that told the manager that we had sent the exact same mailing to the president of his company. An interesting thing happened. The mailing didn't get discarded quite so easily—because the fleet manager *never knew when the president would come in with some questions* about the mailing. Response rates soared.

Honesty is the oldest trick in the book.   A major retailer had overstocked men's suits. My letter began, "When our buyers make a mistake, they make a big one. They've stuck us with over 3,000 winter suits that we *have* to get rid of before the new season." We sold out in two days.

Beware the power of direct marketing.   A car company came to us after running a sweepstakes for people to come in and test-drive a new car. The first few people who walked into the showroom were treated like royalty, until the sales force discovered there were no real prospects among them; they had just come for the prize. By the time genuine prospects began to show up, the salespeople were just handing out entry forms and going back to their newspapers. The sweepstakes ended up costing the company more than just the prizes.

Personalization plus.   Here I'm not talking about printing your own name and address in 32-point type, or using it throughout the mailing. I am advocating the *creative* use of personalization. An insurance company wanted policyholders to increase the amount of money set aside for their retirement. We knew the name of each person, the amount of their policy, and when they first took it out. From then on, it was easy. My letter began:

Dear Mr. Sample:

When you first took out your retirement policy in 1979...

A new home sold for $85,000. Today, the average home is $165,000.
A quart of milk cost 65 cents. Today, it is $1.25.
A movie ticket cost $3.00. Today, it's $7.50 and climbing.

The sad fact is that inflation, which used to nibble at your retirement funds, is now taking bigger and bigger bites. And the money you provided for *will probably not be enough.*

WHICH PSYCHOLOGICAL APPEAL WILL WORK BEST?

As the saying goes, there are different strokes for different folks. But the right psychological appeal can mean a leap in your response; It can literally make your business. The best way to discover it is to test, and test aggressively. I'd much rather test two different positionings or copy approaches than whether a self-mailer outpulls a closed-face envelope. But then, I'm interested in putting up big numbers on the board, not improving fractions.

If you can't test, take Harvey Mackey's advice: Go out and talk to ten customers, or ten potential customers, or ten of your competitor's customers. You'll soon know what makes them tick, and what makes them ticked off.

24

Broadcast Creative

Robert Santangelo

Nash/Wakeman/deForrest
New York, N.Y.

Creating a successful direct-response television commercial is far more challenging than is commonly assumed.

A general-awareness spot can use ingredients from outside arenas to help enhance the brand imagery being associated with the product. In putting together a certain Pepsi spot, for instance, the copywriter and art director needed to give the product an identity that talked directly to the 13-to-24-year-old market. The creative team pulled information from every relevant direction: current trends in music, videos, movies, fashion, and the celebrity world. Each of these active ingredients, by embodying "what's in," helped create an image for the product. Throw in Michael Jackson, a huge budget, a high-priced director, and a cast of a hundred or so hot young people. The result? A spot for Pepsi that was memorable enough (hopefully) to move people to buy Pepsi the next time they felt like a soft drink.

The goal of any commercial—direct-response or general-awareness—is always the same: to sell a product or service. However, direct and general commercials achieve that goal differently, by utilizing tools that have been developed for each discipline.

Like all creative efforts, direct-response broadcast must respect the time-honored "AIDA" formula:

1. **Get *A*ttention.**   You have to look great to get the door opened.

2. **Create *I*nterest.**   Follow up with a great line, to keep the door from being slammed on your foot.

3. **Create *Desire*.** Now that you are in, have the sell be intriguing enough to pique the prospect's interest.

4. **Elicit *Action*.** Show the prospect what's in it for him/her. Make it easy to sign on the dotted line.

Similarly, a great direct-response commercial should begin with the copywriter and art director aiming for the same level of quality found in outstanding general-awareness spots. (That should be a given. After all, copywriters and art directors shouldn't be paid to do a mediocre job in any area of advertising.)

Devising a creative concept, hardworking copy, and compelling visuals relevant to the product and the prospect: this is the place to start. But the challenge doesn't stop here. The complex nature of direct-response television also involves creating a need, a sense of urgency—and including the facts (phone number and supers) required to make the actual purchase an easy decision. It should all be right there—as clear as can be—for every viewer to see.

In order to achieve the desired results, direct-response commercials must also pave the way to signing on the dotted line. Specifically, this means rushing the prospect to the nearest phone. But here's the challenge: a successful direct-response spot must be the result of careful strategy, taste, and creativity.

THE CHALLENGER SPOT: AIMING FOR THE MOON

Let's take, for example, an extremely successful direct-response spot for the Marshall Islands commemorative medallion honoring America's reentry into the space shuttle program. After the space shuttle *Challenger* exploded on take-off in 1986, the program came to an abrupt halt. After 2½ years, space shuttle *Discovery* was launched. A $5 medallion was issued, commemorating the "rebirth" of the space shuttle program. A 60-second spot needed to be written.

The creative team was put to the test. Because of the circumstances surrounding the tragic end of the *Challenger,* the copywriter and art director had to walk a very fine line between creating a relevant, timely message and veering into bad taste. It was decided that the *Challenger* disaster was a negative emotional "hot button" for the viewer and that he/she did not need to be reminded of it. Of course, if the creative team could take the negative association and turn it into a positive one, so much the better. But no negative reference to space shuttle *Challenger* could be made in the spot.

THE RIGHT SPOKESPERSON: A CRITICAL ELEMENT

It was also decided that using a positive, relevant spokesperson would not only take the sting out of any association between the new launch and *Challenger*'s, but also help to sell our product. After an extensive search for the right spokesperson, we asked former astronaut Buzz Aldrin, a true American hero, to do the spot. The use of this particular spokesperson did more than simply bring credibility to our product. It surrounded our message with a sense of optimistic anticipation and hope—emotions that are a far cry from the ones surrounding the *Challenger* disaster.

The presentation of Buzz Aldrin included a beautifully lit set and textured backdrop. He talked into the camera about the rebirth of America's shuttle program—never once mentioning *Challenger*. The camera alternated between Mr. Aldrin and the medallion, with the 800 number prominently displayed throughout the spot.

Since the launch of the space shuttle was fast approaching, media placement of this spot was crucial. The commercial began to run about 5 weeks prior to the launch and the medallions sold at a brisk rate. On the day of the launch, a network placement was made for the spot. The commercial ran simultaneously with the launch. In that one day, 22,000 medallions were sold. Over the next 5 days, another 37,000 were sold. Over one million medallions had been sold by the end of the commercial's run.

As this example shows, recognizing a winning direct-response television proposition doesn't take 4 to 6 months. Results can be evaluated immediately—thanks to an 800 number prominently displayed and solid telemarketing backup.

The success of the medallion commercial also demonstrates that a powerful direct-response spot need not scream at the viewer, be shot on tape with garish lighting, or be wildly jazzed up. Quite the contrary. Creative standards were made a top priority. The prospect was carefully studied. Interest and desire were created through moving copy. The actual shooting of the medallion was very carefully considered. Intelligent media buys were placed. All of this attention to detail enabled this spot to be both high-quality and successful.

CREATIVE: A STEP-BY-STEP PROCESS

Before the copywriter and art director begin burning the midnight oil in search of that award-winning idea, they have to ask things like:

1. Who am I talking to?

2. What do I want them to know?

3. What do I want them to do?

4. How will I get them to do it?

These questions pertain to the prospect—the person to whom you'll be selling your product or service. But in order to find the answers, you have to have the facts:

1. What is the benefit?

2. What is the support for the benefit?

3. What or who is the competition?

4. What key facts, negative or positive, about the product or service could determine the outcome of the advertising?

Once the answers to these questions are in place, the copywriter and art director should be ready to go.

CONTENT: ALL THIS AND BE CREATIVE TOO?

In direct-response television, it's a safe assumption that a phone number will need to be supered along with a few other important facts that might or might not be in the final audio. This should have no bearing on how conceptual, how exciting, or how innovative the direct-response commercial can be. Many creative people in the business are intimidated by the sheer number of bits of information that need to be communicated in 60 or 120 seconds. In all too many cases, the ultimate priority — delivering a superior creative product that sells (supers and all) — falls by the wayside.

BUDGETS: CHECK EVERY CORNER

You're on your way back from the client. They loved the spot. They've never seen anything like it. The copywriter and art director are in the back of the taxi trying to decide who will accept the award at the shows next year. The account person leans back smiling, content with a job well done.

Your get back to the agency. People come in to congratulate you. "This spot is going to be the best the agency has ever done," says someone who's been there a week. You're still reeling from all the attention when you hear a knock on your office door. You look up and see the agency producer. "We can't do this spot for the money," she says. After you're helped to your feet by concerned coworkers, you may notice a rise in temperature. This is probably because you are now in hot water.

Before doing any spot, it is the creatives' responsibility to know the budget. This is especially important for direct-response television. Traditionally, production budgets for direct-response commercials are low in comparison to those for general. A successful direct-response spot will make up the production costs with sales in the first week. The lower the production budget, the lower the liability if the spot is not successful.

Before sitting down to create a commercial, the copywriter and art director must have a realistic working knowledge of the budget and what things cost. If the creatives do not, they should be able to talk to a producer for realistic guidance.

One of our art directors designed a board with a cast of five, a full living room set with windows and walls, a special-effects television set, and product shots in a different setting. To top it off, he wanted to shoot the whole thing on film with sound effects, music, and announcers. We took the board to the client, who approved it with open arms. But when the art director got back to his office, he discovered that the budget was only $14,800. Now anyone who knew anything about what things cost would know that $14,800 was absurd for what we'd planned. (It's even low for direct response.) Nonetheless, that was the final figure. After we got up off the floor, the producer and I called a friend of ours who happened to be a director. After promising him my firstborn, my house, and anything else we could think of, he agreed to do the spot for the money.

But no creatives should ever get themselves into this situation. It can jeopardize your relationship with clients, your working relationships with suppliers, and, most importantly, your job.

TALENT: SEEK AND YOU
SHALL FIND

Even if a 60- or 120-second direct-response commercial has been meticulously designed and written with everything well thought out in advance, including the budget, I can guarantee that money problems will still arise.

When selecting directors for your direct-response spots, always search for quality regardless of budget. If it's a slow time in the industry, you might be able to get a top-notch director for your money. Unfortunately, most high-priced directors are reluctant to have anything to do with direct-response television, primarily *because* of budget. (I once called on a director friend to shoot one of my spots. After he found out that I was now working in direct response, I never received a return phone call.)

Finding a director who shoots direct-response commercials should be easy. Finding one who is going to bring to the spot the level of quality you're looking for is a more difficult task. But don't let anyone tell you that because it's direct response, you can't get good talent. That is simply not the case.

The same holds true for postproduction. Film editors, tape houses, recording studios, and dubbing facilities are all in business to do business, and the business of direct-response television is just as important to them as any other venture.

HOW LONG SHOULD A
COMMERCIAL BE?

Just as direct mailers long ago put aside the debate about whether letters should be a certain length, so direct-response broadcasters should end the debate about commercial length. The answer is similar to the one in the classic Abraham Lincoln story: When the unusually tall candidate was asked how long a man's legs should rightly be, he replied "Long enough to reach the ground."

So just how long should a commercial be? Long enough to present the story in the most effective manner. Products aimed at general audiences are often more effective in 60-second or even 30-second spots, in order to get placement in better dayparts. Seniors, who are more prone to watching late at night, are often more responsive to the longer, 120-second format. And some products simply need the longer format in order to tell the whole story. As soon as I complete this, I will be shooting a spot for the "Responder" Personal Response System in both 60-second and 120-second lengths, because our agency management has decided and the client has approved the testing of both lengths.

One of the most exciting developments in direct-response broadcast is the emergence of the "infomercial"—a 30-minute format similar to those used in the early days of television. Once used only for cooking or beauty products, these are now routinely used for a variety of self-help, investment, and other direct-response broadcasts which require the added time to educate viewers, a more complex process than simply selling them. I have been engaged in a wide variety of infomercials and find the format one of the most satisfying, as well as best response-getting, techniques in the field.

WHEN IS AN INFOMERCIAL APPROPRIATE?

Since it's a long-format spot, an infomercial should be used when the product or service has strong news value, is multifaceted, and/or is well suited for a series of demonstrations. This type of commercial can take on the identity of a talk show, news program, variety show, or anything else for that matter. If a creme were invented that, in 30 seconds, removed wrinkles, that would be big news. Since such a product would have obvious news value and would also require demonstration (for nonbelievers), it would be an ideal candidate for an infomercial. There would simply be no sufficient way to tell the whole story, or create the necessary credibility in a 60- or 120-second spot.

After the decision is made to produce an infomercial, the "executional concept" should be decided on. Depending on what's being sold, the actual executional concept of the show, whether it's a talk show or news program, relies solely on the product. Let's say, for instance, that you had to sell a tablet that helped balding people restore their hair. Like the creme for wrinkles, this tablet would have tremendous news potential. A news format, therefore, would be the appropriate format. This would also provide the sell with a feeling of seriousness and professionalism. Remember: the people you would be targeting take baldness very seriously.

If you had to sell a machine that built a house in one day, your executional concept might take place on an empty lot outdoors. Certainly one would want to demonstrate such a fantastic product. Therefore, ample room would be needed. And what better place than an empty lot?

The point is, locations, sets, and the executional concept must each relate directly to the product for the infomercial to have a sensible orientation and an effective delivery.

WHAT GOES INTO AN INFOMERCIAL?

All the professional assortment of concepts, copy, lighting, sets, and talent utilized for a 60- or 120-second spot should be summoned for an infomercial. Rather than having a mere minute or two, the writer and art director have the luxury of a full half hour to tell their story. The one catch is that they have to be good at knowing what to put in and what to leave out. (The temptation, of course, is to put too much in.)

DO IT PROUD OR NOT AT ALL

When setting out to do direct-response television, the goal should be greatness. All the parts and intricacies of direct-response television should be viewed as important steps and challenges to creating not just a commercial that the copywriter, art director, agency, and client can be proud of, but a commercial that really moves the product.

The essential elements of quality direct-response television (infomercials included) could be listed as follows:

- Begin with what's fascinating (or at least relevant) to the prospect and feature the product or service as solving a need.
- Relate the product to the prospect.
- Demonstrate the benefits to the prospect.
- Communicate immediacy.
- Make it easy for the prospect to order with clear, simple supers.
- Do all of the above with an original concept, clear copy, and effective visuals.

Every spot should contain all the necessary techniques and tools of direct-response television. The supers, phone numbers, addresses, money-back guarantee, etc., should all be used judiciously. The commercial should "show the merch" (merchandise or product) dramatically. The product and the benefits of buying it should be shown in a relevant way to the prospect. All the immediacy of traditional direct-response television should be present. What should also be there is simplicity, a great deal of finesse, and a concern for the creative product that is obvious to anyone who views the spot.

25
Personalization

Ed McLean

McLean Creative Services
New York, N.Y.

A SUBJECT OF CONTROVERSY

Few subjects dealt with in this handbook are as controversial as personalization in direct marketing. (There is even sharp disagreement about what personalization is and what it is not.)

For every manager who raves about the consistently excellent results gained through personalization, you are sure to find another who has only one disaster after another to report. You are also likely to discover a third body of opinion, one that views personalization as neither a panacea nor an expensive-but-disappointing gimmick. Managers in this group look upon personalization in the same way they assess sweepstakes — as a promotional tool that can be useful in some situations and of no help at all in others.

THE USES OF PERSONALIZATION

Personalization has been in use in direct marketing since long before computer-generated letters, impact printing, laser and ink-jet technology came on the scene. But right from the beginning there has been disagreement about the most productive ways to use it. Sixty years ago, for example, most companies used personalization only to make their mass-produced mailings appear to be typed individually rather than printed. But by the time Frank Egner's classic, *How to Make Sales Letters Make Money,* appeared in 1936, there was a movement afoot to use personalization for something more important to many mailers: to seize the reader's attention and encourage him or her to read on.

Egner, who was then McGraw-Hill's mail-order marketing chief, gave many examples in his book of mass-produced sales letters with filled-in salutations or the name of the recipient reproduced at the end of an all-cap letter headline. But he also showed examples of personalization as attention-getter.

In one example, he reprinted a one-page letter he had received from a hotel restaurant. There was a standard personalized all-cap headline leading into the letter's opening paragraph:

IT CAN BE A REAL PLEASURE, MR. EGNER

Above this headline, however, there was a line drawing of a plump, smiling man wearing a chef's brimless cap. Inside a cartoonist's balloon coming from his mouth were three lines of what appeared to be hand lettering:

MR. EGNER,
YOU'LL FORGET THE HEAT
IF YOU LUNCH WITH US!

This balloon and the picture of the chef dominated the one-page letter. It certainly got the attention of the reader and encouraged further reading.

Lettershop expert Lee Epstein studied the illustration in Egner's book and concluded that the second and third lines of copy within the balloon were printed at the same time as the picture of the chef and that the name personalization was done later by hand. The lettering expert at the hotel's lettershop simply copied the name given in the all-cap headline that opened the letterhead. Since Egner worked two short city blocks from the restaurant, it is likely his name was on a relatively small list of past customers, making this quite "personal" personalization entirely feasible. (Today, this same task could be accomplished for a much larger list at great speed using laser or ink-jet processes.)

Undoubtedly, the personalization in this letter caught Frank Egner's attention. And, if it had failed, there was a powerful P.S which promised that the hotel's bartender would fix your favorite mixed drink at the 1936 price of just 25 cents a drink.

The influence of one person — Leo Yochim — in exploiting name personalization as an attention-getter must be recognized here. While others tried to use the new computer-generated letters as personalized versions of typewritten sales letters (just as an earlier generation of mailers had), Leo Yochim, then of Printronics Corporation, told all who would listen that the most effective use of this new technology was as an attention-getter, not as a rather expensive automatic typewriter.

Yochim's message was eventually heard and heeded. Soon companies were vying with one another to find new ways to seize the reader's attention with data from his or her own profile. Fortunately for the industry, cool heads prevailed and the temptation to stray into an unacceptable familiarity via personal data in customer records was suppressed.

PERSONALIZATION IN SHORT-RUN CORRESPONDENCE

There is a place, still, for the skillful use of personalization in letters to members of the business and professional communities. In conducting extensive research for this chapter on personalization, nearly three dozen firms were contacted nationwide. Samples of their processed materials were received and studied. The high quality of name personalization in business and scientific/professional correspondence is quite evident in almost all the samples studied.

Advertisers who target certain business/professional lists and send printed direct mail to them would do well to look into the possibility that their mailings could have far greater impact if well-produced personalized correspondence were mailed instead.

THE PLEASURE OF PERSONALIZATION

Sometimes it may be good strategy for the copywriter and/or designer to go beyond attention-getting with personalization by using the same technology to give a flush of pleasure to the mailing's recipient — with a bit of fun tossed in. *Golf Digest* magazine did exactly that when it showed a "scorecard" for a golfing foursome through a window in the outer envelope, to the left of the address window.

The technique worked this way: Let's call the addressee "A. Recipient" and put his name on the scorecard in this slightly abbreviated way, while spelling it out in the address area to the right of the scorecard as "Albert Recipient." Let's then add the surnames and first initials of three world-famous golfers to the same column on the scorecard as A. Recipient. On this scorecard, J. Nicklaus, A. Palmer, and L. Trevino have not had as good a day on the course as A. Recipient. While he shot a 62, they are all in the high 60s.

This mailing pulled extraordinarily well. And *Golf Digest* received many photographs of the "scorecards" taped up to lockers at golf courses across the country. Personalization can get attention and increase readership for a mailing. It can also give the recipient pleasure and a little fun, too.

Recently, cartoonist Stu Heinecke has given thousands of recipients of direct mail the same kind of name-recognition pleasure with his unique, personalized-caption cartoons. Working with Howard Strome of WX Wordtronics, the talented Mr. Heinecke has demonstrated to many companies how powerful the pleasure of name recognition can be.

Imagine a *New Yorker*-style cartoon on an outer envelope of a mailing to be sent to physicians. An eye-catching cartoon by cartoonist Gahan Wilson shows a patient checking in with the receptionist at a doctor's office. In the personalized caption below, the receptionist is reassuring the patient: "Don't you worry, Mr. Kranitz. Doctor [insert name from mailing list of physicians] will give that streptococcus of yours the old one-two."

Think of a drawing by cartoonist Lee Lorenz of a lavish yacht splashing along on the high seas. It is visible behind an acetate window in a mailing from a local bank. A man in the stern section tells a crew member: "Get me the ship-to-shore, Phillipe. It's time [insert name from list of homeowners] learned what a home equity loan can do."

For a book-club mailing to former members, cartoonist Eldon Dedini depicts a scene in a high-class restaurant. In the foreground, one tuxedoed waiter is saying to another: "A big red wine, steamed truffles, three bestsellers for

$1 million...[insert name of former member] won't settle for anything less than the very best!"

Do doctors, homeowners, and former book-club members get a kick out of seeing their name in these personalized cartoons?

Test one in your next mailing and see for yourself!

IN CONCLUSION

Personalization can be a valuable promotional tool for direct marketing professionals. Used as an attention-getter, for the pleasure of name-recognition, or as a means of personalizing special mailings to business, the use of computer-generated impact printing, laser in-sheet-fed or continuous form, or ink-jet printing can give you the speed and quality you will need to get the results that justify the additional investment.

Don't look for miracles. Everything in direct marketing develops in its own time and often requires adjustments to the original plan. Proceed slowly. And good luck!

PART 5

Production Methods

26
Production: An Overview

John L. Rosenthal

Queens Group New Jersey, Inc.
Edison, N.J.

THE PRINTING AND MAILING FUNCTION

Function, as applied to the printing industry, is the process of guiding the work flow through the plant from the time the order has been placed to the time of delivery (in the mail). Its purpose is to control the work flow to ensure it is delivered on time, accurately, and with the proper quality control.

The printing industry is primarily a communication business. All printed material is reproduced so that someone can read or see someone else's thoughts or ideas. A company producing the final material is following instructions, as a printing press doesn't know or care what is being reproduced.

This chapter will take you through the various operations in a printing plant or lettershop and explain what is expected at each of the various stages of manufacturing.

WHO HANDLES THE FUNCTIONS

The person responsible for these manufacturing functions usually has the title of production manager, production supervisor, production operator, or customer service representative (CSR). This person is located at the plant where the job is being manufactured. Many companies have a salesperson at a regional office who acts as a liaison between sales and manufacturing. This person generally has no control over the various production operations that occur at the plant.

383

The CSR is on duty, though not necessarily at the plant, the entire time the plant is open. Most companies run a two- or three-shift operation and must have someone available to answer questions.

The job is a technical one, requiring an extensive knowledge of the printing industry. There must be a system of checking work-in-process on a regular basis to ensure that everything is on schedule. Many jobs may be in process at any one time, and therefore the systems to track each job must be in place as they go through the plant.

INFORMATION REQUIREMENTS

The production team must have a good working knowledge of layouts, film, manufacturing, and mailing requirements.

It is important to know how the finished product will be used. Will it be mailed, inserted in a magazine or newspaper, or used as a store handout? Will the piece have a shelf life, or will it be looked at once and discarded? The more that production knows about the finished product, the better they are able to find the most efficient and cost-effective means of producing the job.

Production must also have some knowledge of estimating, as it is their responsibility to review a job as it comes into the plant to make sure it is properly quoted. They do not necessarily need to know cost, but they must understand how the job is manufactured to assure that all time is accurately accounted for. Very often, a project will come into a plant with changes from the original estimate. Production must be able to recognize these changes and ask for a new quote. This quote will then be forwarded to the sales department so that the customer is informed of any changes.

A knowledge of bindery operations is necessary to make sure the job will be finished properly. Packing and shipping instructions are also important. If the job is to be mailed, additional information to spell out the mailing requirements must be gathered and included.

As you continue reading through this chapter, you will see how each of the various functions can have an impact on work flow. You will see, for example, how the size, stock, or weight of a mailer can have a major influence on the method of manufacturing or distribution, whether it is mailed or distributed by some other method.

SCHEDULING

One of the most important aspects of any printing job is its schedule. Nothing is done until the mail drop has been set. This is usually the first decision reached by the client; it is at this stage that the client's goals or objectives are determined. Once the method of distribution has been decided on, then a production schedule is made to assure that the job will be produced in its proper time period.

As a job is scheduled, special attention is paid to all of the different processes necessary to create the finished product. No one person can take a project from concept to finished product. Designers, artists, photographers, writers, prep departments, film houses, printers, bindery, lettershops, and mailers all help deliver the finished product. At each stage, proofs, instructions, checks, and followthrough are all important ingredients to get the best and most accurate product possible. Therefore, the instructions in the beginning must be clearly understood.

Whenever someone else's thoughts or ideas are assumed, a mistake is waiting to happen. It becomes very important to communicate everything accurately to reduce wasted time, effort, and materials.

A joint effort on the part of all departments must be maintained. Communication between the various operators is critical to make sure that all of the functions are being properly treated. Everything is riding on the project being in the customer's hand on a certain date. Every day that the mailer is late, money is lost. In some cases, the mail piece could be tied into a television campaign or newspaper promotion. If the mailer is not at the right place at the right time, millions of dollars could be lost. Just imagine a game with a dated coupon attached. The coupon has no value if it is delivered to the consumer at the end of the promotion campaign.

INTERNAL FORMS

Every organization has internal forms to establish the work flow and keep the manufacturing process under control. These forms are communicators and record keepers all in one. Therefore, it is very important that all the information necessary to produce the job is there and that the information entered is orderly and accurate.

Every organization has its own system. One plant may have a prep department, while others may have a bindery. A small printing company could have one press, while some of the larger companies can have 40 to 50 presses. The combinations are endless as to the type of product being produced and ancillary equipment necessary to provide a company with its specialty within the industry. Therefore, the forms each uses may differ, but all have the common goal of getting the job done right.

Order Entry Form

The information entered onto the various forms comes from an *order entry* form, usually submitted by the sales department. When you realize all the forms that are generated from this order entry, you will see how important it is to be as accurate as possible. All of this information is critical to the operator. A typical order entry will have the following information:

1. Customer's name, address, and phone number
2. Contact
3. Job description
4. Quantity

5. Size of finished piece

6. Paper stock

7. Press work, including number of colors and any special instructions (in-line folding, die cutting, perforating, gluing, remoisting glue, numbering, fragrance, scratch-and-sniff, latex rub-off)

8. Bindery folding or stitching

9. Prep work and film requirements

10. Kind and quantity of proofs

11. Number of samples

12. Delivery date

13. Packing and/or mailing information

14. Shipping instructions

15. Copy of the estimate

16. Price

From this order entry form, all other forms for all the departments will be created. Usually the production operator writes the job ticket or job jacket. This job jacket is most often an envelope so that copies of all other forms of information can stay inside. Press sheets, finished products, and all other information from every department are placed in the job jacket. This way, there will always be one central place to maintain all information as the job proceeds throughout the plant.

Stock Requisition Form

The person who is responsible for stock control must make sure that the correct paper is at the press just prior to the press date. This could mean taking the stock from inventory or purchasing it from an outside paper merchant. This form tells the paper warehouse how much paper is required for an upcoming job.

Template or Layout Form

This form not only tells the prep department what to do, it often shows them by means of a drawing or layout. The layout indicates where all the trims, margins, and folds are positioned and any special treatments, such as die cutting, perforating, or gluing. When catalogs are being produced, it shows the imposition of the pages on a press sheet for both the front and back.

Sample Requirements Form

Picking customer samples is very important, as it is usually the first time the client will get to see the finished product. Also, clients usually request samples for their approval prior to shipping.

FOUR-COLOR SEPARATIONS

Color printing, known in the industry as four-color printing, is based on old and simple theories we learned back in school. Two easily understood concepts are used together to produce a complex image.

1. All pictures are reproduced by putting a series of dots together. The dots are extremely small, and when placed close together on paper in a specific pattern, they create an image.

2. The inks used in four-color printing are transparent so that when two or more colors are mixed together, other colors are created. For example, when you mix yellow and blue, green will appear. By using different amounts of three primary colors—yellow, magenta, and cyan—you can create all the colors necessary to reproduce a photograph or color art. Black is added for details and definitions which are not produced by color alone.

The shape of the dots may vary, particularly since the introduction of electronic scanners, but for simplification, we will assume the dots are round. (It must be noted that this is far from accurate. However, the shape is unimportant for purposes of understanding this concept.)

Before discussing four-color dot printing, let us focus on how a black-and-white print is made. A camera transfers the image onto a negative. This negative is referred to as a continuous-tone negative (no dots) and is similar to what one gets from a 35-mm camera at home. This negative is sandwiched with another negative, with a screen in between. The screen creates a dot pattern on the second negative. The sharpness of the picture depends on the number of dots per inch. The more dots, the sharper the image. Sometimes, on very fine printing, 200- or 300-line screens are used, but the most common are 133 to 150. A newspaper will typically use an 85-line screen.

The importance of understanding line screens is to help you choose the appropriate one when you are having a picture reproduced. You should understand that *a dense area does not have more dots, but only larger dots.* As the dots become larger, they start to fill up the area until it becomes a solid. Conversely, in a lightly colored area, the dots are smaller, almost to the point where they are nonexistent. We now have what is referred to in the printing industry as a *halftone.*

This concept of dots is the same when reproducing a four-color subject. However, it is done four times, once each for yellow, magenta, cyan, and black. That is, to create the yellow halftone, a special filter is placed between the negative and the original art which takes out all of the colors except yellow. The same process is done for cyan, magenta, and black, leaving four halftone films or negatives. Note that these negatives are creating a reverse image; that is, the dark areas will be light while the light areas will be dark. These negatives are used to create a plate which is a positive image, the same as the one we see on the finished product.

Color has not actually been used yet to create a color image. All the negatives and plates look similar. The actual color image appears when the appropriate ink is transferred from the plate to blanket to paper. As each color is placed on top of the preceding color, the image takes on a new appearance, until all four colors are printed, reproducing the original subject.

A dot etcher can make the dots larger or smaller within a specific area on each individual color film. This will enhance or reduce the intensity of an area to improve the accuracy of the overall image.

In the 1980s the process of making separations changed drastically, but the concepts of dots and four colors mixed together remain the same. In most cases, the use of screens has been replaced by computer technology. Four-color art is read by a scanner, an electronic machine that scans the subject and digitizes the information in a computer (all four colors at the same time). The dots are then reproduced on a negative through electronic impulses. An image is first shown on a television-type picture tube. The dot size can be changed electronically to make the necessary color corrections before the halftone film is made. Later on, if additional corrections are necessary, the image can be brought back up on the tube and the corrections can be made.

This process is faster, more accurate, and easier to control and eliminates many of the steps and unnecessary film once used to achieve the final product. Also, additional sets of film, sizes, and changes can all be made simply and quickly with no need to start over. The scanners also offer such things as major color changes, movement of parts of pictures from one place to another, exact duplication of part or all of a subject, silhouetting subjects (even with extreme details) quickly and accurately, and changes of shapes and sizes with relative ease. All of the corrections and changes are done without ever producing film, but rather by viewing the subjects on the monitor. Also, the information can be stored on computer disks, thus saving space. Today's technology can even transfer the information from one plant to another and will shortly be perfecting the ability to make plates electronically, bypassing the use of film altogether.

PROOFING REQUIREMENTS

A customer may have special requirements. The customer will usually route the proofs to several people for approval. The customer signs off on proofs and returns them to the plant. The printer is expected to match the proofs on press. It should be understood that color proofs are only used as a guide to achieve what the customer wants. Whenever there is a question of color interpretation, the customer will usually go to the plant for a press approval. Proofs can come in many forms: a one-color proof (blue line) for type and copy only or a four-color proof with Cromalins, matchprints, press proofs, and color keys. It does not matter which proof you supply, as long as your plant has the ability to reproduce it accurately. The color proof and blue line must be signed and returned so that the customer's approval can be verified.

LETTERSHOP REQUIREMENTS

This information will vary depending on whether this function is being done within your own plant. If it is an outside function, additional information will be needed. The people handling this process must have complete information, including

- Customer
- Job number
- Description
- Drop date
- Material-received date
- Number of items in package (including description, size, and number of pages of each item)
- Rotation
- Samples
- Addressing specifications
- Weight of the complete package
- Qualified mail: carrier-route presort, five-digit presort, first class, or bulk rate
- Type of addressing: ink-jet, laser, impact, or labels

PRINTING EQUIPMENT

The production operator must determine what type of equipment is best suited to manufacture a particular project. The length of the run is usually the most important aspect in determining whether a project should run on a sheet-fed or web press. This must be decided early in the planning stage, usually as far back as the estimate, so that the project is not produced on the wrong equipment.

Sheet-Fed Press

A sheet-fed press will run at a rate of 3000 to 12,000 sheets per hour. The press prints one side at a time. Then the sheets must be turned over and printed a second time to produce an image on the back side. Factors that will determine running speeds are the age of the press and the size and weight of the stock. If the weight of the stock is very light or very heavy, the press must run at a slower speed. The process of printing on two sides of a sheet can be slow but still cost-efficient when the press run is approximately 25,000 sheets or less. Paper waste is about 3 to 5 percent and the number of make-ready (start-up) sheets can be held to as few as 100 sheets.

Web Press

Once the run length starts to get larger than 25,000 sheets, a web press might be considered. A web press will print from rolls instead of sheets. The press speeds range from 15,000 impressions an hour to as high as 65,000 impressions an hour on some of the newer presses. The press will print both sides of the paper at the same time. The roll then goes through an oven for drying and into a folder or sheeter (converts rolls into sheets), depending upon the final product. There is a great deal of paper waste during a web press run (as much as 15 to 20 percent).

Even with all of the waste, this method is considerably more efficient than using a sheet-fed press for the following reasons:

1. Paper is less expensive when purchased on rolls
2. Because of the high speed of production, the average unit cost is greatly reduced once you pass the break-even point. (To determine the break-even, you have to estimate the cost for both sheet-fed and web.)
3. Folding and finishing costs are usually cheaper on a web press because they are handled as part of the whole printing process, not as a separate operation, as with a sheet-fed project.

IN-LINE FINISHING

Over the last 20 years, technology has added new features to the web equipment. Now you can perforate, die-cut, number, add remoist glue, fold, apply fragrances, or add a latex rub-off in one operation while the press is running. In some cases, you can combine two different presses into one folder or one in-line finishing line. All of the above-mentioned features are used to produce a specially designed product and have the piece come off the press completely finished, thereby requiring no additional off-line binder.

You can easily see the tremendous savings in both time and money when this process is used for long runs. Simple math shows how quickly a product is produced when you deliver a finished product at a rate of over 100,000 pieces per hour. One full day of productivity on one press could produce as many as 2,400,000 pieces. (This number will vary depending on the number up on a press form, but for discussion I used 3 up with the press running at 33,000 impressions per hour.) The speed will vary depending on the number of applications you are applying, the stock weight, and the complexity of the finished piece. As you add features, the process slows up. If the press rate is approximately $500 an hour, the manufacturing cost for one day's worth of work would be around $12,000 (500 × 24 hours). A similar project on sheet-fed equipment might take a month and the cost would be prohibitive.

THE LETTERSHOP

A lettershop is where products are assembled into their final package for mailing. This shop will handle the mechanical details of mailing such as imprinting, inserting, addressing, and mail sorting. The lettershop is the final stop before an item is mailed.

It is critical that all of the mailing functions are understood to ensure that as much as possible of the mailing program is delivered. For the best possible results, the lettershop must

1. Be familiar with size and weight regulations, proper placement of bar codes, and FIN codes, and proper placement of name and address lines.
2. Have a working knowledge of the different methods of personalization (ink-jet, laser imaging, and impact printing).
3. Understand match mailing. That is, if there is more than one item that is addressed, what kind of guarantee is there that everything matches?
4. Track and reenter lost names. During every mailing, a certain percent of names are not properly entered. These names are either lost or must be reentered into the system. If the names are placed back into the list, they must go back in so as not to impact zip code sequence or they must go on the end of the list.
5. Acquire postal receipts and verification of the dropped mail. This gives the customer an accurate handle on the quantity mailed, one of the most important bits of information to analyze the mailing properly.
6. Bag, sort, bundle into mail sacks, and attach the proper bag tags.

Mail should be addressed with the correct carrier route presort and 5-digit presort. Either magnetic tapes or pressure-sensitive or paper labels may be used. A magnetic tape stores information, which will be electronically entered onto the mailer—usually a name, an address, and possibly a personalized message. A pressure-sensitive label can be removed and placed on another location (usually for the reply vehicle). Each item must have a source code or key code. This is a unique identification mark for distinguishing one list from another.

All of the elements must be under tight control through the whole manufacturing process. A mailer cannot go out unless all the elements are available at the same time. This includes not only all of the components but the mailing list as well. A dummy package should be put together earlier by the supplier to ensure that the lettershop has all of the elements to complete the package. If a package is more complex, it is a good idea to have a quality-control person at the lettershop who is familiar with the package to approve it before it goes into the mail. This will reduce the risk of finding an error after the components have already been inserted or, worse, after they have been mailed.

COMPUTERS

In recent years, computers have added a new way of processing work and information throughout a plant. Many companies have installed computers for recording information. For example, you are apt to find a computer terminal at a press, in the prep department, in the bindery near the folders, and in the office of the production manager. Computerized records make possible

- Up-to-date status reports
- Ease of billing
- Accurate, immediate cost accounting
- Material inventories (paper, ink, film, cartons, etc.)
- Layouts and templates

The use of computers to manage the work flow is becoming more and more important. The requirements of each company will vary, which will help determine how extensive the system should be. There does appear to be a relationship between the size of a company and the uses it finds for a computer. The bigger the company, the more applications there are and the greater the need for constant controls.

IMPORTANCE OF GOOD MECHANICALS

One of the biggest additional costs a printer has is waste, whether in the form of materials or time. Passing on additional charges can become very expensive and usually can be avoided when the proper information is conveyed. Wasting time is money and must be reduced to a minimum. This situation puts an emphasis on the importance of a good mechanical.

A mechanical is an art board prepared by a designer or mechanical paste-up artist. It is designed to show what the finished product will look like. It is done in black and white with overlays indicating color breaks.

It does not matter how you mark the boards, as long as the printer can read and understand them. Every time a color is not marked, or type has to be repositioned or redone, additional charges are incurred. Whenever a blue-line proof is marked for corrections, it costs time and money. These errors are usually a result of incomplete information on the mechanicals. Often a mistake is made by the film house because they did not follow the instructions, but sometimes even though the instructions are correct, they may not be very clear. Pages must be marked properly, color breaks must be clear, position and sizes of the halftones must be clear, and the overall appearance of the boards must be clean and neat to help reduce errors. Everyone expects changes and revisions, as no business is perfect. However, if all the information available is accurate in the beginning, chances are the changes will be easier and not confused with corrections.

When mechanicals are done neatly, correctly, and clearly, you can be assured that the prep cost will be reduced and mistakes will be minimal. In the long run, everyone will gain, but especially the purchaser, as he or she usually ends up paying for the corrections some way or another.

One of the best ways to eliminate, or at least reduce, errors is to have the mechanicals looked at by the printer and prep house before sending them out. At that time, they can ask questions pertaining to any areas which may be unclear. This can save hours of time. Another important suggestion is to refer to the book used in the printing industry on standard marking of mechanicals.

Knowing the proper notations helps make markings clearer and consistent. In this way everyone will be speaking the same language.

Remember, we are in a communication business and every phase of communication must be clean, accurate, and easy to understand if we are to keep time and money to a minimum.

SELECTING THE RIGHT PAPER

Selecting the right paper can be a simple task when you understand your objectives. Not knowing one's objectives can make this process complex. Usually, the better the sheet, the more expensive it is. However, one does not always need a better sheet. The following will try to explain some of the differences in paper and why you would choose one over another.

Probably the easiest decision is whether to use *coated or uncoated stock.* Coated stock has a gloss finish and a smooth surface and, for the most part, will reproduce a brighter, cleaner, and more accurate product. An uncoated sheet is more absorbent. This results in a flat-looking product with less detail. As explained in the section on color separations regarding dots, the screen value on an uncoated sheet will often be coarser than on a coated stock. Often a 133-line screen is recommended instead of a 150-line. You will never see higher than 150, as the dot gain is too great, causing a blotchy look.

Paper grade is important. Papers are graded from 1 to 5, 1 being the highest quality. The characteristics here are determined by brightness, surface coating, and smoothness. Generally, number 4 and 5 sheets are considered groundwood sheets. This means the wood impurities in the sheet are still visible. Number 1, 2, and 3 sheets are free sheets, which means they have been processed sufficiently to give a clean look. For example, a newspaper has a great deal of impurities, whereas a catalog is brighter and cleaner. If you compare the catalog to a high-quality art book, you will note another drastic change.

The next major decision is *the weight of the paper.* Weight usually coincides with thickness: the thicker the sheet, the heavier it becomes. Usually a thicker sheet is more opaque, has more bulk, and, therefore, becomes stiffer. When a sheet is too thick, it becomes brittle and can crack on a fold. Heavier stock will slow down a press speed, become more difficult to fold, and increase the overall cost. As paper is sold by the pound, the more pounds you have, the more money you will spend. Also, heavy stock could mean increased mailing cost. When a mailer is over a certain weight, the post office will increase the cost. On the other hand, a business reply card must weigh a minimum of .07 points or the post office will not accept it. That is why magazine reply cards are printed on card stock. When paper is too light, other problems occur. Often there is too much see-through and a product becomes difficult to read because the printing on the other side of the sheet interferes. It also becomes harder to print and will slow down a press, causing additional costs. It will often not even go through a folder because it is too flimsy.

Text stock offers another option. Here the surface of the paper has a very noticeable texture. These papers are not usually used in the direct-mail business because of the higher cost. However, they are available for special projects.

Color stock is also available. Once again, there is a very specific application when one chooses to use a colored stock. Here, the cost does not create a problem, as a colored sheet has only a very minimal up-charge, and often this charge can be less expensive than using ink to change the color of the sheet. Usually, the art director is trying to create an impact or attract attention to a specific item within the mail package. If you choose a colored stock, don't use one that is too dark or you will have a difficult time reading the copy. Also, make sure the color of the ink is carefully selected because, as mentioned, the mixing of transparent ink on a color stock will change the reproduced color. For example, yellow ink on blue stock will turn green.

Today, there has been an increasing demand for *recycled paper*. Recycled paper is stock that has previously been printed on, collected, washed, rebleached, and processed once again into usable paper. Because this collection process is very expensive, the recycled sheets are usually more expensive. Also, be aware that these sheets are usually not 100 percent recycled (50 percent is the most common), but they will satisfy the needs of environmentalists. The primary reason these papers are made is to help remove solid waste from landfills. Originally, the benefit was to save the forest, but that issue has become a secondary one.

RELATIONSHIP BETWEEN CLIENT AND PRINTER

It doesn't take very long to learn that no one knows everything about every aspect of the printing business. There are many types of paper needs, film requirements, and equipment variations from one company to another. As a buyer of printing, it is your job to purchase the best possible value for every project. To make sure that this is actually happening, a relationship between the buyer and printer must exist so that a qualified printing salesperson can act as an adviser or consultant to the purchaser.

A truly good printing salesperson will turn down projects that are not suited for their plant and will even advise the buyer about who could handle a specific project. Many projects are produced on the wrong equipment because the salesperson doesn't want to give up a project, and the buyer doesn't know where else to go. A relationship of trust must be established. For example, if a project that has been ideal for a sheet-fed press suddenly increases in quantity, such that it would be more cost-effective to run it on a web press, it is the obligation of the initial printer to inform the buyer where he or she will receive the best value.

Many times, the buyer innocently does not convey all of the necessary information for an accurate quotation. After the job is awarded, additional information may be presented which changes the price. These charges should be passed on to the purchaser, but often the buyer will not accept them because he or she has already submitted the budget for the job. This is an awkward position and, depending on the amount of money involved, could create a major dispute. Everyone should have as much information as possible or at least have a good working relationship with the supplier so that these types of situations can be worked out to everyone's best interest.

Many buyers have a phobia about telling a printer who their competition is on a particular project. They also do not like to let a company know by how much they lost a bid on a project. It is this type of information that will help a supplier determine whether or not to continue soliciting business from a company. This information can help both the purchaser and the supplier when new quotes are submitted. For example, when a printer knows he is constantly being underbid by 25 to 30 percent, he must come to the realization that he cannot compete for this type of work at this company. However, if his prices are 3 to 5 percent higher, he can now determine whether or not he should reduce his pricing structure by this margin in order to secure future work.

It is also important for the buyer to supply the printer with as much information as possible. Different things are important to different companies. For example, some projects require better quality and the buyer is not looking for the shortcuts to reduce the price. Schedules can have an effect on the price: Whereas some projects have an excess amount of time to be produced, others never seem to have enough. Sometimes there is even a benefit to inform the printers quoting on a project of a budget. In this circumstance, the printer can start making suggestions immediately as to how to get the project in the budget without going through the quoting process over and over again. Many times, different suppliers will come up with different solutions to get a project within an appropriate cost. The buyer can analyze the different methods of approaching the problem and choose the one that best satisfies her needs. Look at changes in stock, size, and color when trying to reduce cost. Even special packing can have a major impact on the price.

Also, new suppliers should always be considered. One never knows when a new piece of equipment has been developed that might help reduce cost for your specific type of work. For example, new types of folders can deliver different products. Sometimes this will offer new opportunities for designers and their company.

CONCLUSION

As you can see, the printing and mailing functions are extremely important to ensure that a successful mailing program has been properly manufactured. Each stage requires a degree of technical knowledge, and each function relies on the success of the preceding one. The cost of every campaign can determine the success or failure of the program. Even if the projected results have been reached, if the costs are too high, the project will fail. Therefore, the way to keep costs in line is to keep every stage of manufacturing under tight control. One bad instruction or poor communication can have a chain reaction, either causing the whole program to be late, which creates loss of business, or to be incorrectly produced, which creates extensive additional charges.

27
Printing and Formats

David G. Rosenthal

Webcraft Technologies, Inc.
North Brunswick, N.J.

THE INDUSTRY IN PERSPECTIVE

The printing industry in the United States is the world's largest single print market in terms of value added, demand and consumption of products, and number of operating plants. It is also large in comparison with other American manufacturing industries. With 1989 sales of $73.4 billion and more than 800,000 employees, U.S. printing is

- Largest in number of manufacturing sites — 51,617 to be exact
- Second only to automobiles in number of employees
- Growing in employment faster than computers and outpaced only by plastic products and aircraft

In addition to size, the industry is strong, stable, and diversified. Over the past 15 years, growth in industry sales has outpaced the gross national product by about 30 percent.

Printing is the most geographically dispersed manufacturing sector. There are fewer than 1000 printing employees in only five states, while in all but a dozen, commercial printing ranks among the top 10 manufacturing industries. This dispersal is one factor contributing to the industry's relatively low profile. There is not one but a number of printing industries; it is at once national (long-run web processes), regional (medium-size commercial companies), and local (thousands of small shops).

One asset of printing that is underrecognized is the diverse nature of its plants and their primary products. While three-fifths of the industry falls under the heading of general commercial printing, the remainder is an array of specialized shops of all sizes that cushions ups and downs in specific areas. It is this size and market spread serving basic print buyer needs that gives printing its broad and stable base.[1]

The focus of this chapter is *not* to discuss the chemistry, process, or technique of applying ink onto paper. Rather, this chapter will discuss specifically in-line manufactured printed products, capabilities, and other print-related issues that affect direct marketers.

READY, FIRE, AIM!

Let's assume that you understand *your* business extremely well. You have done all the research. You have chosen merchandise that's sure to sell and selected the best lists, you have prepared written copy that's sure to keep your prospect's interest through the offer and an art package that is creative and award-winning. Now, the art and mechanicals are prepared and ready to go to the printer. Of the 36,000 printing companies in the United States, which one do you choose? Which can best serve your needs?

Vendor Selection: Make Your Printer Your Partner

Vendor selection is critically important. Many direct marketers' only vehicle to their market is direct mail. As such, your printer is your partner and can make or break the success of your promotions. To be an effective partner, your printer must understand the dynamics of your business, the purpose of the promotion, and any additional functions or operations that will interface with the printed format.

Your printer must have the appropriate equipment, and also the desire to support your needs. Vendor selection considerations must include the printer's equipment compatibility with the requirements of your work. Does the printer have adequate capacity to accommodate your needs, especially in seasonal peaks. Is the printer capable of producing to the quality expectations that you have articulated? In the business of producing data-driven mailings, does your printer have a working knowledge of data management and usage for direct mail? Does your printer have a working knowledge of the U.S. Postal Service? Does your printer develop new ideas featuring improved methods or new printed products to enhance your business by improving your sales and reducing your costs?

The point is, especially in today's economy, you are responsible for increasing earnings concurrent with reducing your operating costs. Postage costs continue to escalate, placing greater pressure on your bottom line. As printing costs usually represent a significant portion of the direct marketers' costs, choosing the most interesting and cost-effective format produced by the most capable printer can assist in the goal of earning improvement and cost reduction. Additionally, the experienced direct-response printer will generally have a broad base of exposure and experience gained by working with other direct marketers. That experience will help to perpetuate successes, develop new processes and products, and troubleshoot potential problems.

Do It Right the First Time, Every Time

Mistakes are expensive. The printer is manufacturing a custom-made product each time he goes to press. If the product is made incorrectly for any reason, the likelihood of it being used by you, or sold to someone else is nil — remember, it has *your* name on it! Further, in the manufacture of database-printed materials, the attention to detail is even more important. In addition to printing, other considerations must include:

- Personalization technique: Ink-jet, laser, impact?
- Fit: Will personalized (variable) copy fit into the designated space?
- Data availability: Is the required data contained in the file?
- Font selection: Is font (type face) compatiblé with end-usage expectation?
- Proper entry into U.S. Postal Service: Proper presort, discounts?
- Data security

Bar coding and/or additional copy that will be scanned must be produced in compliance with the end-user requirement. Remember, the materials should always be produced in compliance with U.S. Postal Service regulations (see Chapters 28, 29, and 30). Also, consult your direct-mail printer or lettershop and/or U.S.P.S customer service representative to assist in the planning of your mailings to make certain that you are in a position to maximize every cost-saving opportunity. Any missed detail can cause additional unnecessary expense, mailing delays, and high frustration levels.

IN-LINE FINISHING

The offset lithographic printing process was invented in 1796 by Aloys Senefelder and is the most widely used commercial printing process in the United States. The quality of offset printing has continually improved for a number of reasons: today's presses can maintain tighter tolerances and run at speeds nearly twice as fast as the most efficient presses of only 10 years ago; improved prepress operations now include plates, chemistry, films, and inks; and scanners now link the art director to the color separator to a much greater degree. Peripherally, desktop publishing has profoundly changed the typesetting industry as we knew it only a few years ago and has changed the link between client and printer. All of these process improvements yield a sheet of paper that will probably have been printed faster, at a higher level of consistency, and perhaps with fewer people hours than was previously possible.

In parallel with these printing (ink-on-paper) process improvements, a complementary process was being developed which, when linked to a web press, gave direct marketers the tools with which to produce larger quantities of "unique and interesting" printed formats quickly and efficiently.

This process, called in-line finishing, has been one of the most innovative segments in commercial printing on paper in some time.

As the direct-mail marketplace grew, in-line finishing and its format capabilities and creative possibilities did also. The era of junk mail of the 1960s became direct mail of the 1970s; in the 1980s the term was *direct marketing*, while the sobriquet for the 1990s seems to be *niche marketing*, or *micromarketing* — that is, highly targeted marketing to a specific user of a product or service based on specific knowledge of that consumer. The continually increasing level of sophistication in printed formats demanded by the direct marketer has stimulated further evolution and development of the process.

As the competition for the reader's attention — "clutter in the mailbox" — continues, the creative format capabilities give the direct marketer opportunities to make his or her packages different — certainly more interesting, unique, and cost-effective.

The Tools

In-line finishing is a revolutionary and time-intensive evolutionary process. It is the process that has eliminated the need for timely and expensive additional finishing operations. In-line finishing is the process that starts with one or more webs of paper and concludes with a completed direct-mail package or finished component that may be used as part of a package. This process encourages creativity of formats and enhancements that could not be produced by any other method, or certainly could not be produced in a timely or cost-efficient manner.

The web travels through a series of stations, which include:

- Printing
- Perforations and score
- Die cutting (cutting windows or shapes)
- Glue applications to include pressure-sensitive and remoistenable
- Personalization of the document
- High-security scratch-off (games, sweepstakes, and lotteries)
- Folding and slitting
- Envelope conversion and insertion
- Embossing
- Fragrance application
- Tip-ons (labels, cards, tokens, etc.)
- Affix-product sample
- Affix credit card
- Lettershop (sort, tie, bag)

Each of the stations may be used independently or in combination with one another to "build" a custom-engineered product made of paper with ink (and other materials) on it.

Use of these tools might be as follows: An automobile manufacturer opts to do a high-impact mailing to owners of 3-year-old models of their make and also to owners of the 3-year-old competing make. Their ad agency has developed a concept that will include a full-color brochure on number 1 grade coated paper, with a highly personalized letter on a laid-finish stock. Additionally, part of the brochure will contain a three-dimensional pop-up of the profile of the car. As the reader opens the brochure, the silhouette of the car pops and the door opens—emitting the fragrance of a brand new car! Part of this package includes a scratch-off game sweepstakes enticement which may be validated and redeemed at the dealership upon presentation by the prospect. Rebate and/or incentive vouchers with the prospect's name, the dealer's name and sales representative, and a map illustrating the location of the dealership will be part of this format. Voucher redemption and other traits will easily be tracked by utilizing a bar code. The quantity is 3.5 million pieces and the allocated production time is 4 weeks.

In the above example, the job is easily doable in a cost-effective manner. In-line finishing offers the capabilities, features, and benefits that would not be readily available through alternative processes. Using conventional methods, the multitude of operations required to produce this format in the allocated time and the high cost would probably eliminate the viability of executing this concept.

Micromarketing in the package-goods industry via targeted variable-offer couponing is now available. Rather than offering discount coupons to users of your products, package-goods marketers want to know who uses their brands and who buys their competitors' brands, as well as frequency of purchase, size of purchase, and other purchasing traits. With this information, company packages are now being distributed with variable-information-inducing, variable-offer coupons to each household. They use sophisticated data and technology, in-line personalization and converting capabilities, and highly customized packages which include the selective insertion of product samples at high speeds. These packages can be produced in polybag and/or paper envelopes.

The Formats

In-line finished formats may be somewhat esoteric, as in the previous example. However, in-line formats may also be quite simple. A format as basic as an 8½-by 11-inch letter with two folds to fit into a number 10 envelope, previously produced in sheets, cut, then folded, are now routinely printed, folded, cut, and finished using the in-line process. Bind-in order-form envelopes, the essence of direct marketing, are routinely produced using the in-line process.

Other in-line finished formats include:

- Closed-end mailing packages
- Open-end mailing packages
- Cosmetic and fragrance samplers

- Airline ticket jacket envelopes
- Game pieces
- Scratch-off lottery tickets
- Stamp sheets
- Product samplers
- Paste-bound minicatalogs
- Paper premiums, such as slide rules, wallets, paper airplanes, etc.

Applying the in-line capabilities — the tools — to attain your specific business objectives promotes high levels of flexibility and creativity.
Features and benefits of the following format options represent:

- High quality
- Low cost
- Unique, interesting, open-ended creative possibilities
- User-friendly benefits
- Payment with order
- Size flexibility
- Large quantity produced quickly
- Rapid production turnaround

How Do I Get Started?

In-line engineered and enhanced formats have many applications that may promote creativity and save time and cost. Most important, in-line finished formats are extremely versatile and unique; as a result, it may not be possible to produce them using any other manufacturing method.

To explore general and/or specific format options, contact the printers who have targeted their business to serving the needs of the direct marketing community. Match their capabilities to your needs. Explore the options and benefits of converting your conventionally produced formats to in-line. Compare features, benefits, time schedules, and bottom-line cost. Ask your vendor to prepare folding dummies of the proposed format options. When you are ready to prepare art and mechanicals, always ask your vendor to prepare an exact size template indicating print areas, variable copy areas, postal copy locations, and clear areas. Always make certain that whatever is required downstream is engineered into the product and process upstream.

You're on your way.

NOTE

1. Peter Johnson, "The Geography of Print," *Graphic Arts Monthly*, January 1990.

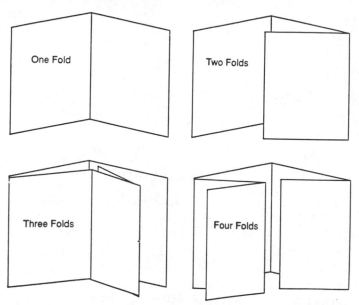

Figure 27-1. Format diagram 1: Folding. Formats may be folded in many configurations to accommodate and fulfill a specific purpose or function. An enhanced in-line press offers the creative user a multitude of sizes, shapes, and format options. (*Webcraft Technologies, Inc.*)

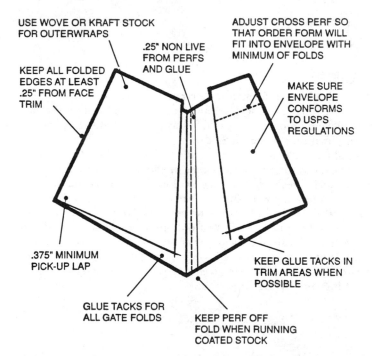

Figure 27-2. Format diagram 2: Bind-in order form/envelopes and outerwraps for use in perfect-bound and saddle-stitched publications. (*Webcraft Technologies, Inc.*)

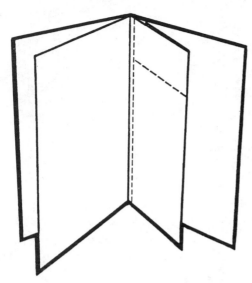

Figure 27-3. Format diagram 3: Mini-catalogs. Versatile, multipage formats with or without a built-in reply envelope. Available with 6, 8, 10, 12, or more pages in either digest or maxi size. Suitable for distribution by mail, as a take-one, a package-stuffer, or a magazine/newspaper insert. (*Webcraft Technologies, Inc.*)

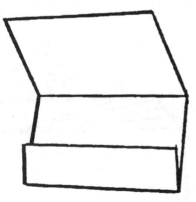

Figure 27-4. Format diagram 4: Long-flap mailer, the display carrier. (*Webcraft Technologies, Inc.*)

Figure 27-5. Format diagram 5: Round-trip mailer, the dual-purpose envelope. (*Webcraft Technologies, Inc.*)

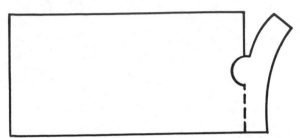

Figure 27-6. Format diagram 6: Snap-pack mailer, the easy-access envelope. (*Webcraft Technologies, Inc.*)

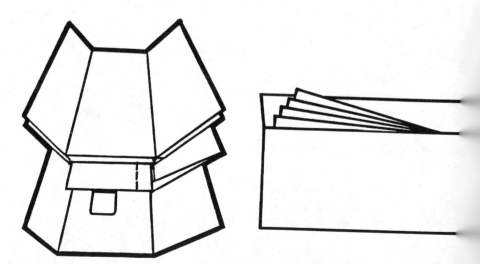

Figure 27-7. Format diagrams 7 (open-end mailer, left) and 8 (closed-end mailer): Both are economical, personalized web formats with closed-face or open-window envelopes. Match mailings are easily accomplished using the in-line process. Process colors, various grades of stock within a package, product samples, pop-ups, and fragrance applications are some of the capabilities. Format configurations are designed for the specific user. (*Webcraft Technologies, Inc.*)

28

Lettershop Processing

Robert H. Jurick
FALA Direct Marketing, Inc.
Melville, N.Y.

In years gone by, the term *lettershop* meant a company that would address envelopes; fold and insert letters; and seal, stamp, and deliver the mail to the post office. At that time, almost all methods for producing lettershop services were done manually, Today, modern technology has made lettershops rather diverse organizations. Some operations still need to be done by hand, but planning and technical expertise have changed the industry.

In the past, a well-rounded lettershop had an addressing department, a mimeograph-multigraph printing department, a folding department, and, of course, an inserting department. Today these departments still exist, but almost all have been mechanized. However, every shop still requires some experienced personnel to do work that cannot be done by machine.

SELECTING A LETTERSHOP

There are certain basics to look for in determining whether a particular organization can provide the services you require. Meeting the people who run the shop is a prime requisite in selecting a lettershop. From the salesperson to management to the production team, the machine and hand operation and the receiving and materials-handling personnel add up to a team that must have the ability and experience to produce your project.

The sales personnel who work with you in starting a project are the key. Experienced salespeople who are fortunate enough to have started in the plant have the technical ability to help you organize all or part of a mailing project.

Their production experience can often make the difference in saving dollars in postage through the recommendation of a minor size or weight change.

Who are the backup people to the sales executive? Are they knowledgeable people, capable of answering your questions when the salesperson is on another call? Can they help make proper production decisions?

The equipment in the lettershop is, of course, the next key area to be checked. If your product is a mailing of 1 million or more, the equipment required will be more substantial than it would be for a mailing of 25,000. The lettershop you are seeking must have the equipment necessary for two or three times the quantity you require.

What type of equipment does a lettershop require? First, it needs materials-handling equipment capable of taking your printed materials from a truck and storing them in the facility, whether Hi-Lo, pallet trucks, or dollies. Also look for some kind of storage area that is neat and well marked as to skid or carton position.

Basic equipment for a lettershop should also include a burster for separating computerized forms, a burster and folder for separating and folding the forms, and folding machines to fold letters and brochures. Folding machines are important as backup in case an additional fold is necessary or an element of a mailing received requires a fold.

A shop's labeling machine must be capable of affixing 1-up labels, 3-, 4-, or 5-across labels, or even cut labels in various sizes. The attachments for this equipment should be examined when you visit the shop.

Inserting machines are a necessity. There are two types: 6 inch by 9 inch and 9 inch by 12 inch. Note the number of stations the machines have. Generally, most lettershops have six-station machines. How many inserts does your mailing have? If six or fewer, a shop with six-station machines is adequate. Ten or eleven inserts create a difficult problem. If your mailing quantity is under 100,000, a double pass on a six-station machine is possible. If it is in the millions, the shop should have machines capable of inserting all eleven pieces in one pass. For estimating purposes, always use 2000 or 2500 inserts per hour (depending on the package) for determining the length of production time on a machine.

A shop should have minimum equipment equal to three times the quantity you require. For example, enclosing 50,000 of four inserts into a 6-inch-by-9-inch envelope would take 25 hours (2000 an hour × 25 = 50,000 units). If the plant works an 8-hour day, it would take 3 days to complete on one machine. If you are thinking of millions of pieces, the same formula will work. However, lettershops that mail millions of pieces generally work a minimum of two shifts (if not three). The minimum number of machines to look for would be twelve.

It is also important to know that a plant has good mechanics (the people who set up the machines) and a capable repair staff in case there is a breakdown.

Larger shops may have mail-sorting departments. Most shops today will sort the mail at the end of the machine cycle. If you're seeking a major mailer, it is important that they have a post office operation on the premises. This is an asset because you now know your mail will move more rapidly. If small mailings are required, this is not a necessity. Smaller mailings generally are delivered to the local post office by the lettershop. It is important to know where the post office is and whether your vendor has in-plant loading.

Basically, all this equipment is found in the up-to-date lettershop. Many shops also have data centers, fulfillment centers, and printing plants which augment and round out the lettershop services.

Once you have seen the people and the equipment, how do you select the lettershop best for you? To do efficient work, a lettershop must be neat and tidy. An inspection tour will give you this input.

Next, ask for three customer references with work similar to your type. Make the calls and find out how long they've done business with this firm, the type of work performed, and the record for on-time service.

After completing your investigation, you'll see how your materials were received and reported. You'll discover how you're notified as far as deliveries and mailings are concerned, and you will see how you're billed for the project at the end, along with reports about the surplus material.

Postage is always required in advance. Whether it is an advance deposit to the permit number at the post office or a check to the mailer, the monies always should be delivered at least 5 to 7 days before the mailing date to allow for clearance of the postage check. An industry rule prevails: No mailing without postage on hand. The lettershop does not earn a profit on postage.

SIZE OF THE MAILING PROJECT

There is no magic number. Through the years, the quantity that has separated the volume-mail class of work from the smaller or hand operation has been 25,000. Over this quantity, plan on making use of machines; under 25,000, be prepared to produce manually. How the smaller quantity finally is produced is not really the question. The planning approach should assume that this project will be done at a much lower rate of production than the higher quantity.

TIMING OF THE VARIED PARTS

Whether you are producing the project in your facility or are using a lettershop, the information that is required will make for an easier production schedule.

When will the material to be used in the mailing be delivered to the lettershop? Most direct-mail companies will not schedule the production of the project until all the materials have been received. Planning with your envelope manufacturers, printers, and list houses certainly can make the difference between success and failure. A commitment from a reliable vendor in each of these areas allows the mailer to set the tentative schedule.

SCHEDULING THE MAIL DATE

After you review the delivery of each of the components, the mail date for the project should be scheduled. The rule of inserting 2000 pieces per hour should be your means of double-checking the scheduling by your lettershop. Most lettershops will give you the number of working days to produce a project from the time all the material has been received. Don't forget that this refers to working days. Do not include holidays, Saturdays, or Sundays. Always add an extra day to any schedule. If that timing does not work out, you know you'll have to spend overtime charges on the printing to get your project to the mailer so that it can drop on the proper mail date.

TYPING OF LISTS

The lettershop must know what they will receive so that they know what equipment they'll need to affix labels (if that is the source). They may have to plan for addressing by typewriter.

As soon as you know how the project is to be done, get this information to the lettershop. Make it easy. In your instructions, indicate the following:

1. Type of label to be used: 1-up, 3-up, 4-up, or 5-up

2. List format and typing, if any: for example, list to be typed on number 10 envelopes

3. Type of insert: for example, a computer letter form 2-up, $17\frac{3}{4}$ inches by 11 inches, that must burst to $8\frac{3}{8}$ inches by 11 inches and two parallel folds, copy out, to fit in a number 10 window envelope

These are only a few of the ways to clarify the input on types of lists to be used for the project.

NUMBER OF ENCLOSURES

It is also important to notify the mailer as to the number of inserts or enclosures. For example, there will be four inserts into a number 10 envelope or six inserts into a 6-inch-by-9-inch booklet envelope. Where possible, make up a dummy using the actual paper if the printed samples are not yet available. This will serve a twofold purpose: (1) It will verify that the pieces are machine-insertable, and (2) the weight of the package will help determine postage costs.

METHOD OF MAILING

With the weight and size available, the class of mail can be determined. If the weight is very close and you're still in the planning stage, you still may be able to trim a unit down in size slightly or change the weight of one stock.

It is important to give a dummy to the lettershop in advance. Their scales generally are attuned to the postal requirements. When in doubt, most shops will walk the dummy package directly to the post office and verify the weights. The shop can give you the weights and tell you the postage costs for both third-class and first-class postage so that you can make the decision.

KEY ITEMS TO DISCUSS IN PLANNING A MAILING

Envelopes

The envelope is the carrier of the contents of your mailing project. It should be sturdy enough to get your package through the mails so that it arrives without damage.

Size. Every mailing package may require a different size. Below is a list of the most common envelopes and their basic size. Give the dimensions at the same time. Not many people give this information, yet it is of great assistance to the mailer.

Envelope	Size	Envelope	Size
Monarch	$3\frac{7}{8} \times 7\frac{1}{2}$	$6\frac{1}{4}$ envelope	$3\frac{1}{2} \times 6$
Check	$3\frac{5}{8} \times 8\frac{5}{8}$	$6\frac{3}{4}$ envelope	$3\frac{5}{8} \times 6\frac{1}{2}$
Number 10	$4\frac{1}{8} \times 9\frac{1}{2}$	Number 7	$3\frac{3}{4} \times 6\frac{3}{4}$
Number 11	$4\frac{1}{2} \times 10\frac{3}{8}$	Number 9	$3\frac{7}{8} \times 8\frac{7}{8}$

Booklet or Open End? It's very simple to recognize the two basic types of envelopes once you've seen them. A booklet type, with the flap on the top or bottom of the long side, is machine-insertable. The open-end type, with the flap on the narrow edge, is not machine-insertable. Even when you plan to hand-insert a job, check with the lettershop as to which type, booklet or open-end, they would prefer for the project.

Window or Regular Envelope? This is one of the easier pieces of information to determine. Where are you addressing? If directly on the face, use a regular envelope. If on a reply device, a letter, or even on the reply envelope, use a window envelope.

There are basic types of windows: with or without glassine and with or without poly. Some areas for windows can come die-cut for position with nothing pasted behind. Again, this is a decision for you to make, but it should be specified to the mailer.

Paper Envelopes. Two basic types of envelope material are used today. Envelopes made of paper, of course, have been the standard for years. However, plastic envelopes have been popular in recent times. Which type you use is important to the lettershop. Not all lettershops have the ability to handle plastic. Let them know early which you plan to use.

Inserts. Flat, folded, fan-folded, booklets, single sheets, thick, or thin? It would be helpful for the lettershop if you could give them the proper dummy of the entire project as discussed above, but sometimes this information is not available. You should, however, very explicitly, describe the number of pieces in the package and what they are physically: a single sheet (one-page letter), two sheets (four-page letter), and so on. Bulky pieces or unusual folds should be pointed out.

Will the lettershop have to fold one or more elements? What size will they be and how will they be folded?

Number of Inserts.   How many inserts? Let the lettershop know the exact number of inserts and the size of each.

Inserting.   What is the sequence of the pieces as they go into the envelope? List the pieces as you count them, inserted from the flap to the front of the envelope. Be specific. Don't leave anything to chance. Will the package be hand-inserted or machine-inserted?

Self-Mailers

Self-mailers fall into a category of their own. You must do everything to a self-mailer that you do to an envelope package except the inserting.

There are certain things you must tell the lettershop.

1. What is the size of the self-mailer — and is it a simple card, folder, brochure, or catalog? Knowing the weight is helpful both for postage and for proper handling.

2. Does the self-mailer have a preprinted indicia? This is advisable, but sometimes it doesn't happen. If there is no indicia, it will be necessary to meter or stamp the unit.

3. How many lists are going to be used for the mailing? If third-class or catalog rate, are the lists in zip sequence? Does the quantity indicate a presort or carrier route?

Weight, size, and number of pages are all key pieces of information for the mailing house. With this information in advance, they can better help to schedule and plan the project and can get the best possible postage rate.

Addressing

Today we use two distinct categories of addressing: noncomputer and computer. Our industry, of course, started without computers. Today, we still use many of the older methods, but computer addressing is dominant.

Noncomputer Addressing.   We can go from the very basic handwritten means of addressing to one of the mechanical methods of addressing. From the handwritten, we go easily to the typewritten. Type the address directly onto the envelope. Type the name, address, and salutation onto a preprinted letter. Use that unit in a window envelope or type-address a matching envelope. If your lettershop is to do the job, they should know exactly what method you want used.

Typewriting led to many mechanical addressing systems: Speedomat, Addressograph, Scriptomatic, Elliot Stencils, etc. Based on quantity and data to be maintained, determine how your mailing list is kept and on what system. However your lettershop is handling your mailing, the form in which the list gets to them is important.

Computer. Generally, lists of 20,000 or more are maintained on computers. That was almost a rule when computers came into being. Today, with all kinds of minicomputers and word processors, lists of all sizes may be maintained on the computer. Regardless of the size of the computer, almost all are capable of producing labels in any number of formats: 1-up, 3-up, 4-up, 5-up, etc.

The computer produces these labels on varied stocks. Cheshire stock is the ordinary computer paper (basic 50-pound stock): pressure-sensitive, peel-off pressure-sensitive, and gum stock. These labels are produced on continuous forms by either the Kirk Rudy or Cheshire labeling machines, which most lettershops have.

The computer also produces computerized letters, either full or match-fill. These too can be used as an addressing vehicle.

Finally, laser printers can produce labels and letters and can even be part of web printing equipment, addressing catalogs as they are being printed in multiple colors at high speeds.

How the list comes to the mailing house, when it arrives, and the format and sequence are of key importance. The more information given to the vendor or to your own production facility, the better chance you have of getting the quality and results you seek.

IMPORTANCE OF SUPERVISION

Earlier it was suggested that you check into the supervision of the lettershop. Now that you've selected the shop, the first job you do will tell you a lot about your decision. It is important to follow through on this job from start to finish.

You've done your job. You gave the lettershop the dates material would be received. It's their turn now to show you that they are the company they claim to be.

Material starts to arrive at their door. You should be informed with some type of receiving report within a day of the receipt of your material. This report should tell you the following:

1. Name of vendor that delivered the material

2. Number of cartons received or skids of material

3. Weight of carton or skid

4. Number of pieces received per shipper's report

5. Estimated quantity based on weight

6. Condition of the material

7. How it compares with the dummy you submitted

8. Samples of the material (a minimum of two)

This information is important in case you have any kind of problem in the future.

If you receive this report, you can be assured that the same information has been passed on to the production department of the lettershop. This is the point where the team effort pays off. As material comes into the receiving department, the production department should check it out to see if it clearly meets the specifications you discussed in the original planning of the project. This is the time to catch an error.

The production department's efficiency and knowledge will be apparent at this point. When they receive the samples, their promptness in reviewing the sample against the actual piece will be indicated.

There is nothing more frustrating than being informed on the day of a mailing that a printed piece that arrived days earlier does not meet your requirements. Situations like this certainly would change your opinion. However, your experience will always tell you how good the performance is in the firm you chose.

COMPUTERIZED FORMS

You may be shipping your lettershop fully computerized forms from an EDP company. In almost all cases, computerized forms will be shipped in the same cartons in which the forms printer delivered them. One additional piece of information should be on the cartons: the sequence number of the production of the form (carton 1 of 40, carton 2 of 40, and so on). Receiving the material with this simple information on it will save many hours of work that would otherwise be wasted. If a program was in zip sequence and the cartons were not numbered, it would create a problem in sorting the work.

Samples from a number of different cartons should be pulled. Some of these samples should be shipped to the client so that they can double-check that all is correct.

COMPUTER FORM MAIL PRODUCTION

Your computer forms have been received at the lettershop. You've received samples from the lettershop along with the receiving report.

It is a good idea to have a carefully ruled-out form delivered to the lettershop so that they can set up their equipment to burst, trim, or fold the form in question. This rule-out is a key element in the proper handling of any computerized job.

If the form, for example, is a 2-up, one-page letter measuring 17¾ inches by 11 inches, the rule-out pictured in Figure 28-1 will be most helpful and will save time and eliminate any chance for error.

On the 17¾-inch-by-11-inch, 2-up letter form, the rule-out tells the lettershop to perform the following steps in preparing the project.

1. When the form is burst, take off ½ inch of holes on each side.

2. Halfway across the sheet, slit so that the form when cut measures 8⅜ inches wide.

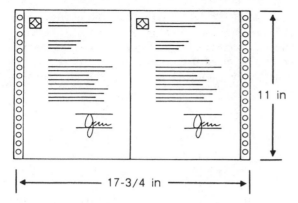

Figure 28-1. Sample ruled-out computer form.

3. The sheet on the right must interstack behind the sheet on the left.
4. It folds in thirds, copy out, so that the personalization shows through the window envelope.
5. Make a hand-cut dummy of the piece.

These steps will help eliminate any chance for error. In an instance where the computer form may have been produced incorrectly, you would know about the inaccuracy before any work is done. If an error did occur, you would have the opportunity to make minor alterations to salvage the package.

INSERTING

Regardless of whether the machine work is 9 by 12 or 6 by 9, the basic input that should be known is the same. We saw the dummy when we estimated the job. We must now produce the project.

Machine Inserting

Once the components of the project are all in the shop, a good management team will make up two basic dummies: one for you and one for the plant. The two samples are made so that you can check the estimated package and also double-check, in the case of machine inserting, that all pieces meet the machine requirements.

It is suggested that a six-insert job, for example, have a sample piece hung above each station of the inserting machine that is producing the job. These samples should be numbered and dated along with the time. Management in the lettershop should check these samples and, of course, check all samples every hour from every machine.

In essence, this step gives the lettershop the security of knowing that the work is being performed accurately. The chance of any major error is now limited.

On multiple-pass jobs, an envelope should be taken each hour from each facet of the job. These hourly checks protect the lettershop and also show the client that the work was performed accurately. These checked samples should be retained, although some clients want all the material to be mailed. In that case, on the last day of handling, all the samples pulled during production also would drop.

Inserting by Hand

There is no difference between the procedures for hand and machine inserting. Each rule followed by the shop for machine inserting should be followed for hand operations.

One of the major differences in the work is, of course, the envelope that you can use for hand inserting. It is not required that you use the booklet-style envelope; the open-end envelope may be used. In fact, the reason why you are doing the project by hand might be that you had certain envelopes on hand or wanted to use an open-end envelope.

In most cases, doing handwork is because the quantities are too small for the machines or because an insert or two is not machine-insertable.

Again, it's most important to mock up the dummy package for the lettershop. Number the pieces from the flap side of the envelope to the face or address side. The hand-collation department should also display — near where the work is being done — samples of the inserts in the proper sequence. This eliminates the need for the operator to exercise judgment or interpret specifications. If there are similar pieces in the package, the shop supervisor should explain the difference to the inserters. Usually the pieces to be inserted have key codes which help to identify each. These should be pointed out and written in large letters on the display near the work station.

Another portion of hand work occurs when you've designed personalized packages. For example, the outer envelope has the name and address as follows:

> Mr. John Sample
> 110 Sample Street
> Any City, NY 00000

The letter in the package may be personalized as follows:

> Mr. John Sample
> 110 Sample Street
> Any City, NY 00000

Dear Mr. Sample:

The response device may be personalized with a list code, mail date using the Julian calendar, the account number, and the name and address, as follows:

> AB-001-000000
> Mr. John Sample
> 110 Sample Street
> Any City, NY 00000

Other inserts may also be included in the package. If none is related to the personalization, you have two personalized inserts to match with the outer envelope. In a job of this type, it's most important to mark the trays of completed work with the inserter's or operator's number or name so that you can check the accuracy of each person doing the work.

When planning match jobs, it's always good to give thought to how the job will be assembled. Always try to leave the address portion on the side of the piece that is facing out. This will make it easier to check.

When match work is performed, it is suggested that it not carry a preprinted indicia. Instead, use either stamps or a meter imprint. The client is spending added dollars for the hand assembly to get a more personal-looking package, and the postage method should support this image.

In a final review of this work, thought should be given to attempting to make it machine-insertable. Sometimes it is possible that the letter, the order form, or even the envelope be done by computer. This can simplify the whole project. Of course, quantity plays a major role. If possible, review the project with the lettershop sales executive prior to designing the mailing. These salespeople can offer good suggestions to save dollars and speed production.

PERSONALIZATION: VALUE YOUR PROJECT!

Many direct-mail users are confused about the issue of personalization. Here are some questions to ask yourself.

Does personalization increase response? As one expert on direct marketing has observed, "A fundamental axiom of the direct mail business is that the more you can personalize the message and the package you send the prospect, the greater the probability that the prospect will respond."[1]

Is personalization appropriate for my particular mailing? It depends on the market, the mailing list, the product, and the offer. One area where personalization is especially effective is in mailing to the house list of existing customers with whom you have established a relationship.

What methods are available for personalizing direct-mail packages? Most common methods of personalization today are continuous laser, sheet-fed laser, impact printing, and ink-jet imaging.

LABELING

In simple terms, a label is a piece of paper that contains the name and address of the recipient, which can then be applied to a mailing piece or envelope for use as the address vehicle. There are many different kinds of labels.

Cheshire labels involve specially prepared paper: rolls, fan fold or accordion fold, continuous form papers used to reproduce names and addresses to be mechanically affixed one at a time to a mailing piece. These labels generally are available in 1-up, 3-up, 4-up, and 5-up. The stocks that are available include:

1. Plain paper, generally 50-pound white offset (called Cheshire stock)
2. Davac gum stock, which is paper that will stick to the piece when moistened
3. Pressure-sensitive stock, which is paper that can be affixed by machine, peeled off by hand, and affixed to the mail piece

North-south labels are mailing labels (1-up) that read from top to bottom and can be affixed with label-affixing equipment. This product is usually generated by processes other than computer.

Peel-off labels are self-adhesive labels attached to a backing sheet which is attached to a mailing piece. These labels are designed to be removed from the mailing piece and attached to an order blank or card. They are another form of a Cheshire label.

All other labels can be designed to any specifications one desires. For anything other than the labels listed above, always give the size and quality of stock of the label. The size of the piece and the type of label selected will determine how the label is to be affixed.

Much depends on what order the list is in. Is it...

Alphabetical by name?

Alphabetical by company?

State order?

Zip code order?

Presorted for postal savings?

Carrier route on large quantities?

No particular sequence?

The order the list is in has a lot to do with what postage will be spent to mail the job. If it is a national list in zip code order, you could probably sort for the cheapest postage, whether first- or third-class. If not, the relative costs of sorting and postage for each class of mail should be determined.

First-class presort.   As of September 1991, specifications for first-class presort call for 50 or more pieces to a zip code being kept together in trays, for the special rate of 26 cents each instead of 29 cents each. The minimum quantity allowed for this mailing is 500 pieces. Where there is a great quantity, the postage requires a printout giving exact quantities of all mail by qualified portion and also a report on counts that do not qualify for the reduced rate.

Third-class bulk rate.   The minimum quantity for this mailing is 200 pieces. Such a mailing must be sorted by zip code, and the postage rate is .198 cents each, or $198 per thousand.

Third-class five-digit zip sort.   The minimum quantity for this mailing is 200 pieces or 50 pounds of mail, presorted to five-digit destinations. Each piece must be part of a package of 10 or more pieces to the same five-digit zip code, and the postage rate is .165 cents each, or $165 per thousand.

Third-class carrier route. The minimum quantity for mailing under this regulation is also 200 pieces, but the ruling calls for large mailings broken down by carrier route, rural route, etc., with the imprint or endorsement of "Carrier Route Presort." The postage rate is .131 cents, or $131 per thousand.

Nonprofit. All carry the same rulings as the bulk rate. The following are the postage rates for each class.

Regular third class	.111 cents each, or $111 per thousand
Five-digit presort	.098 cents each, or $98 per thousand
Carrier route presort	.074 cents each, or $74 per thousand

A labeled job does not always have to be mailed. It may be intended for distribution to an office, plant, or school. The job would then be packed and marked in sequence. A cover sheet would tell the client what sort is covered in each carton.

WHAT LIABILITIES MUST BE CONSIDERED?

The following are excerpts from the trade customs as revised by the Mail Advertising Service Association (MASA) International, February 1989.[1]

1. **Quotations.** Subject to acceptance within 30 days. Quotations are based on the cost of labor and materials on the date of the quote. If changes occur in cost of materials, labor, or other costs prior to acceptance, the right is reserved to change the price quoted. Subsequent orders will be subject to price revision if required. Quotations do not include applicable taxes, shipping costs or deliveries unless specifically stated.

2. **Cancellation.** Orders may be cancelled by the customer at any time by notice in writing with the understanding that the mailer will be compensated in full for any work or services performed prior to cancellation, plus the cost of any goods or services purchased for the order.

3. **Alterations/Specifications.** Prices quoted herein are based upon our understanding of the specifications submitted. If there is a change in specifications or instructions resulting in additional costs, the work performed will be billed at the current rates and the mailing date may be delayed.

4. **Delivery Schedules.** Mailer will make every effort to meet scheduled delivery and mailing dates, but accepts no liability for failure to meet any requested delivery dates. In addition, mailers have no control over U.S. Postal Service delivery schedules and cannot guarantee when mail deposited will be delivered by the Postal Service. All orders are accepted contingent to fire, accident, act of God, mechanical breakdown, or other case beyond the mailer's control. Since the time element is an integral part of our business, quoted prices are based upon a specific set of time schedules for completion. Any requested deviation from the schedules described or agreed upon by both parties at commencement of order may alter the quoted price. Late material may affect the completion date of the order by a greater degree than the actual elapsed time the material is late.

5. **Materials.** The mailer assumes in all quotations that all material provided will permit efficient handling on automated equipment, and meets equipment manufacturers' published specifications. Materials furnished that are within manufacturers' specifications, but which are not up to acceptable operational standards due to poor folding, facing, trimming, packing, sticking together of material, insufficient leeway between enclosures and envelopes, square envelope flaps or other causes, will be subject to pricing at special rates. Customer will be notified when a deficiency is discovered and approval will be obtained for handling at special rates before proceeding with work, and a new delivery schedule may result.

6. **Acceptance of Order.** The customer agrees that the mailer may refuse at any time to mail any copy, photographs, or illustrations of any kind that in the mailer's sole judgment he believes is an invasion of privacy, is degrading, libelous, unlawful, profane, obscene, pornographic, tends to ridicule or embarrass, or is in bad taste, or which in the mailer's sole judgment is an infringement on a trademark, or trade name, service mark or copyright belonging to others.

7. **Errors in Mailing.** Mailer shall be liable only to the extent of remailing a correction or corrected job as soon as possible to rectify the mistake, and allowable damages shall be limited to the value of the work performed. In no case is the mailer liable for loss of business or implied damages.

8. **Postage.** Quotations do not include postage. Payment of postage in advance is required on all orders. Postage should be paid 15 days prior to mailing date or by cashiers check.

9. **Spoilage.** All direct-mail handling and processing involves spoilage. Allowances for spoilage should be taken into consideration in ordering material. Every effort will be made to handle customer's material with frugality and to prevent undue spoilage. Nevertheless, the mailer cannot accept responsibility for shortages of material as a result of normal spoilage in processing. All stock and materials belonging to a customer will be held and stored only at the customer's risk, and the customer shall be responsible for insurance on his material.

10. **Mailing Lists.** Customer's mailing list(s) in the mailer's possession, for storage or otherwise, is the exclusive property of the customer and shall be used only at his instructions. Mailer assumes responsibility for replacement of such lists in the event of loss by fire, vandalism, theft, or other such causes, only if the customer has a duplicate list or has the source material from which the list was compiled, and then only to the extent of the costs involved in replacing the list lost. The mailer does not accept liability or responsibility for compiling such lists nor for an intangible or special value attached thereto.

GENERAL SPECIFICATIONS CHECKLISTS

Once you've worked out everything, write down detailed specifications; don't count on the layout being sufficient. Again, I prepared the following list of questions that should be asked by sales representatives when writing up orders for printing, computer, or mailing services.

General Printing Specifications

1. Name or subject matter of the job?
2. What is the quantity?
3. What is the size? If a book or booklet, number of pages and the trim size of the page? Does it bleed?
4. What is the paper stock?
   a. Brand name if required.
   b. If brand name, can an equivalent sheet be used?
   c. What weight sheet?
   d. What finish is required—glossy, vellum, smooth, etc.?
   e. If a book or booklet, is there a separate cover? If a separate cover, what stock, weight, and finish?
   f. Color of stock?
5. How many colors, how many sides?
   a. If two colors, are they two colors, not black or black and one color?
   b. If two colors on two sides, are they the same two colors?
   c. If four colors, is it four flat colors or four-color process?
6. What type of art?
   a. All line, ready for camera?
   b. Bendays—how many and what size?
   c. Halftones—how many, what size, square or silhouette?
7. Is it process color?
   a. Size of process area or areas?
   b. What art will be supplied for process areas—chromes, wash drawings, continuous negatives?
   c. If chromes, what size and are they all in the same focus? Are they separate units or assemblies?
   d. Do the process areas print on one or two sides?
8. What is the approximate ink coverage, in percent—50 percent, 80 percent, 100 percent?
9. What kind of proofs are required?
   a. Blueprints?
   b. Color keys (or Cromalins)?
   c. Press proofs?
10. What type of binding?
    a. Saddle stitch? How many wires?
    b. Type and number of folds?
    c. Perfect bind?
    d. Stitched or glued?
    e. Die cut?
    f. Embossing?
11. What type of packing? Skids, cartons, pallets, banded? Moisture-resistant? How should cartons be labeled?
12. Delivery. Where? Is delivery additional? Date of delivery? Receiving department hours? Method to be used?
13. Are overruns acceptable? If so, is there a percentage or quantity limit?

General Computer Specifications

1. What type of job? What is the quantity? Computer letter, list maintenance, labels?
2. How is it to be run? Impact, ink-jet, laser? On continuous forms or cut sheets?
3. Is it a computer letter?
    a. Match fill-in—how many lines?
    b. Full computer letter—how many lines?
    c. Should everything be spelled out, abbreviated, or exactly as on tape if tape is supplied (e.g., Ave., St., State, etc.)?
    d. If prefix is not on tape, what are the rules for Mr., Miss, Mrs., Ms.? Should we look up female names on table?
    e. Type style—standard courier, wide courier, 10-pitch, 12-pitch, or other?
    f. Proof and artwork information?
4. Computer forms information
    a. Type—1-up or 2-up?
    b. Trim size of letter, excluding pin holes?
    c. Weight of stock, color?
    d. One- or two-sided printing?
    e. Bindery—perforations, die cuts, or tip-ons?
5. Labels
    a. Type—1-up, 3-up, 4-up, or 5-up?
    b. Type of stock—regular Cheshire, gummed, pressure-sensitive?
    c. Should match code, source code, or other information be printed on label?
6. List maintenance
    a. How will client submit changes?
    b. How often is list to be updated?
    c. Will list be used for rental? If so, should test tapes of various quantities be kept "hanging"?
7. Tape information
    a. How many bytes per inch (6250, 1600, 800) EBCIDIC, etc.?
    b. What track—nine or seven?
    c. What is the blocking factor?
    d. What is the record size? Is the field fixed or variable?
    e. Are tape layout sheets, explanation of codes, sample printouts, or "dumps" available?
8. Tape information, if conversion required
    a. How much information will go onto tape—codes, dollar amounts, references, dates, etc?
    b. What purpose will the tape be used for—letters, labels, etc.?
    c. Will the client be doing "dupe" elimination?
    d. Will the list be used for rental?

General Mailing Specifications

Having been involved in the direct-mail business for over 35 years, I've made up a list of basic questions to help sales executives determine what work has to be performed.

1. What is the quantity? Under 25,000 is lettershop; over 25,000 is volume mail.
2. When will material be received and what is the mail date?
3. Envelopes
    a. Size? Booklet or open end? Preprinted indicia?
    b. Window or closed (if window, open or cello)?
    c. Paper or plastic (polybag)?
4. Addressing
    a. If labels, what kind—Cheshire, pressure-sensitive, gummed?
    b. If labels, affix to envelope, BRC, etc.?
    c. If computer forms, do we burst and trim? Size of forms, number up, trim size?
    d. Type of address? What font? To what piece? What is the source—directory, cards, galleys, handwritten?
5. Mailing
    a. Is list provided in strict zip-code sequence?
    b. How many lists and what size, from small to large?
    c. Class of mail (first class, third class, bulk, etc.)?
    d. Is indicia preprinted? Do we meter or provide meter strips?
    e. Do we stamp and, if so, what kind—regular, commemorative, bulk rate, United Nations?
6. Self-mailer: same questions as in item 5.
    a. Size?
    b. Number of pages or thickness?
7. Bursting and folding
    a. Size of full finished sheet?
    b. Number up (1 or 2)?
    c. Number of folds and type of fold?
8. Shipping
    a. Where?
    b. Method (what carrier)?
    c. If packed in cartons, material supplied?
    d. Should shipping be included in price? Additional?
9. Incidentals
    a. Tipping, stapling, clipping, etc.?
    b. Keying: separately or while labeling? How many different keys and number of each key (approximate)?

Check with the U.S. Postal Service. Always check for postal acceptability and new regulations. Don't presume tolerance, understanding, or common sense. An extra fraction of an inch on a reply card can increase your business reply postage costs. An error in postal indicia can lead to the refusal of an entire mailing. Go by the book, or they'll throw it at you.

GETTING ESTIMATES

Once the specification sheet is prepared, getting estimates is simple. Specification sheets are simply attached to a request-for-bid memo and given to various suppliers.

Ideally, three suppliers should be asked to bid on each part of each job. One should be a tried-and-true supplier who helped you plan the job. Another should be an alternative supplier who is sometimes used by your firm. The third should be a new supplier who has been soliciting your work.

Unless the savings are substantial, the supplier who has been working with you and helping you should get the job. It's only fair. The alternative supplier should get occasional jobs or parts of the overall job because you don't want all your eggs in one basket. New suppliers should be tried occasionally to keep prices where they should be. If the job is exceptionally important or difficult, you won't want to work with a new supplier, but if they brought in a low bid, add them to the list for future bidding and break them in on simpler jobs.

It isn't cricket to play one supplier against the other. You'll drive the prices down in the short run, as a hungry printer will meet the price, but you'll pay for it in quality shortcuts or last-minute additional charges or by putting the supplier out of business. Most likely, you'll also suffer by not getting the job done on time. If you get a printer to do a job for less than cost just to keep the presses busy, your job is the one that will get bumped if a normal-profit job comes along while yours is in progress.

There are other bidding methods if you have a trained production person on your staff or an acting consultant. Some advertisers place their printing on a cost-plus basis—a fixed-percentage profit margin over the actual costs of the job. To do this, however, requires that you know estimating and are able to calculate press time, setup time, ink coverage, bindery, and lettershop functions in the same way that the supplier would estimate the job.

Other advertisers act as their own printing brokers, buying the paper directly, dealing with the separators and platemakers, and buying press time (including labor) from printers around the country. Some firms regularly canvass printers or lettershops for idle machine time to make deals that will show significant savings. Here again, you have to have trained personnel who can manage the entire job through each individual graphic process, and you have to be willing to take the full responsibility for the finished job.

It usually costs no more to work with a printing broker or to let your ad agency handle everything. Not only do they supervise and take responsibility for the entire job, but often they get trade prices, which enables them to charge the same as if you had bid on the job directly.

Award the job in writing, with the specification sheet appended and all details of price, overruns, delivery, etc., worked out in detail. The suppliers should be asked to sign an acceptance of the detailed order.

AVOIDING ERRORS

There are two ways to avoid errors. One is to check everything yourself. The other is to be sure that the client, or the senior executive in your organization, sees and approves all details at every stage.

Don't count on proofreaders. They check the various stages against the original copy. If the copy is wrong, the finished job will be wrong, too. A proofreader once "corrected" Barbra Streisand's name to "Barbara" at the last minute, causing understandable consternation at her record company. To avoid problems like this, a proofreader must be given a detailed list of do's and don'ts, including spelling of proper names; styles for numbers, grammar, and punctuation; and preferred usage.

Whenever anything is corrected, don't just check the one area that contains the correction. I once saw a piece of copy prepared on a word processor that retyped a revised paragraph and plugged it into an entirely different piece of body copy. On the revised copy the changed paragraph was perfect, but everything else described an entirely different product.

The most critical obstacle to cost control is revisions, whether made by agency, designer, or client. The way to avoid excessive revisions is to be sure to obtain all approvals at each and every step of the creative and production process. A copy change on a press proof can cost thousands of dollars; on a blueprint, hundreds; on a mechanical or type proof about $50; on typed copy, nothing. Obviously, the earlier that changes are made, the less they will cost.

Be sure that everything is checked. Don't count on a client or a senior executive to know what to look for. If a layout isn't clear, or a mechanical pasteup is confusing, be sure to point out exactly what illustration goes where and what color.

NOTE

1. Mail Advertising Service Association International, 1989.

29

Emerging Lettershop Technologies

Richard D. Haugan

Richard D. Haugan & Associates
Seattle, Wash.

INTRODUCTION

Recent years mark the arrival of new technologies that offer lettershops and the direct mailers that use them more flexibility and capability when producing their mailings. These new technologies produce two major benefits:

1. *Cost savings* through efficiencies realized with "single-stream" assembly of direct-mail components (collating, folding, inserting, franking, and sealing), which result in achieving maximum levels of postal discounts and minimal splitting of the mail into smaller cells (caused by production constraints).

2. *Creative flexibility* for the direct mailer, which allows more options for envelope quality and size and for variability of the contents in direct-mail packages being produced.

The new technologies either are mechanical in nature (for example, the ability to produce a multipiece mailer, inserts, and envelope from one press sheet) or are achieved as a by-product of the integration of computers into inserting equipment. It is expected that the integration of computers into inserting equipment will have as pronounced an effect on the direct-mail industry as the personal computer did on the business community in the last decade. Similarly, advancements in paper-handling technology result in clever ways of creating mailing packages at minimal cost.

Database Marketing Changes

Probably the single most significant underlying cause for change in the lettershop industry today is the expanded use and understanding of database marketing techniques. The trend is now toward "one-to-one," or highly personalized, direct-mail advertising. Marketers have figured out how to segment a large group into significantly smaller subgroups, or "clusters." However, until recently, this information was used mainly to purchase additional mailing lists with identical attributes or inferred similarity.

Now, the application of database analysis is being used to create direct-mail packages that are more personalized and that should, therefore, achieve greater response and/or cost-effectiveness per inquiry or sale. In the past, traditional lettershop methods have constrained the business, because these methods prevented the efficient assembly of variable components (such as multiple-page letters, variable combinations of inserts, and variable postage rates, because of the different weights of each mailer).

A good example of this process is the relatively new point-of-sale data collection performed in key supermarkets. This process involves the collection of all of the detail on the cash register receipt, which is matched to a specific individual in a megadatabase for subsequent use as a source of target marketing. For example, if a consumer buys brand X dog biscuits, it is not to the marketer's benefit to offer a discount coupon to a person who is ordinarily willing to pay full price. Rather, the objective would be to gain sales from a competitor's product, cross-sell or upsell one's own, or maintain customer loyalty. The combination of products and offers that could be used in this example is very hard to effectively target-market using conventional means and therefore requires new methods of mail production that are technology-driven.

Application of technology is the key to achieving new breakthroughs. The current special report commissioned by the Direct Marketing Association, entitled "Impact of Technology on Direct Marketing in the 1990s," states that: "One does not need a crystal ball to see that the *future of the direct marketing field* and the *survival* of many of its current players will be dictated by the use, or the ignorance, of technology." The report goes further, stating two key findings:

1. ...the direct marketing industry has not widely absorbed important technologies.

2. ...if there is a common thread tying together the important technologies, it is the *concept of a database.*

As a group, direct marketers are slowly adapting to new technologies—probably because most people are not aware of the options available. Descriptions of these technologies are included in this chapter.

Data Processing Technologies

Data processing has been fully integrated into all areas of direct-mail production, with the exception of mail-inserting equipment, which is in the process of catching up. The following table shows major direct-mail segments and how data processing is currently applied:

Segment	Application
Creative (e.g., graphic arts, ad copy)	Desktop publishing
Mailing lists	List management
Research	Regression analysis, clustering, etc.
Letter production	Mail management programs
Name and address hygiene	Merge-purge, Zip+4 appendage
Lithography	Computerized presses

Lettershops are ripe for technological change. In-house lettershops serving transaction mailers (e.g., producing monthly statements for banks) have been using new technologies for the past 3 years, but these techniques have not yet migrated to direct mailers.

Mechanical Technologies

Direct mailers are innovators by trade and have become expert at finding ways to perform unconventional tasks on conventional machines. An example of this would be a mailing package consisting of a letter and inserts put into an envelope, all of which are created from a single press sheet in a complex in-line process (e.g., "LOPES"). Frequently, these applications are not universal or standard off-the-shelf products but are one-off technologies developed for a specific purpose.

DESCRIPTION OF NEW TECHNOLOGIES

Collating

The requirement to collate documents is not new; several methods have been employed, including hand-collation and mechanical equipment that takes one or more continuous webs or continuous forms, interleaves them, bursts them, and ultimately stacks them as collated sets. Sometimes these collated sets need to be bound or stapled, which requires another off-line operation. Now, there is a new process available to direct mailers called *intelligent collation*. Intelligent collation varies from other types of collation in that it allows a wide variation in the ways in which sets of documents or letters are assembled and controlled by a computer.

Traditionally, the most common way for a direct mailer to produce a mailing piece is to have every letter the same length. The words or copy may vary, and key personalized elements may be inserted (such as name and perhaps account balance), but the length of the letter would remain constant (one page, two pages, etc.). Furthermore, there is a practical limitation as to the number of pages that can be produced. You'll see very few mailers that consist of more than two or three pages of personalized information, owing to constraints of production.

A technology that has been in use for at least 3 years was developed to enable transaction mailers to produce billing statements (for example, the bank statement). In these operations, every individual's statement will contain a different number of pages, depending on the complexity or the number of transactions made in that particular cycle. Direct mailers can now use the same process, but it varies slightly, depending on whether a continuous form or a cut sheet is used.

If a continuous form is used, generally, the preferred format is to produce a 2-up continuous letter. The web is then fed into the inserting equipment and slit down the middle, the edge is trimmed, and the pages are interleaved one on top of the other. They are then cut or burst, producing a stack of documents that is essentially the same, as if you have produced them as individual sheets. Even letters produced on continuous forms can vary in both the length and the number of pages, owing to the ability of the equipment to deal with this variance. The preferred imaging method is either laser (hot or cold fusion) or LED-type imaging.

Once a collated set of documents is assembled in a stack, the problem becomes one of identifying where one set of documents ends and the next set starts. This is accomplished by one of three methods; the most typical is the use of a process called an optical mark recognition (OMR) code, which uses a binary code representation to control functions. Most phone bills today contain these OMR codes, which are horizontal half-inch black lines (usually on the right side of the statement), configured in a relatively low vertical density of five marks per inch. Each bar represents an on-off type of switch and can be used for different purposes. For example, in the case of collating, one of these codes would indicate end of collation; this code is sensed by the computer, which commands the inserter to send the accumulated set of documents to the next station, where additional inserts will be assembled.

The second method, which offers more flexibility simply because it carries more information, is the utilization of the "code 3-of-9" (also called "code 39") bar code. This code is similar to what you will see as inventory codes on packages bought at the grocery store but is much more dense and can contain 13 characters (any representation of alpha or numeric characters) per inch. Hence, much more information can be carried—a sequence number, job number, and other control information. If the details of a job require exact matching to ensure that no material is collated out of sequence, code 3-of-9 is preferable to OMR coding. Also, code 3-of-9 can be read more reliably than an OMR code.

The last method is the newest and is optical in nature. Optical Character Recognition (OCR) has been available for years, but not until recently has it found application in mail-finishing and -inserting equipment. Utilizing this technology comes closer to reading documents as a human being would do. Somewhere on the document, there will be either a sequence number or other identifying mark that can be read optically, which is aesthetically more pleasing than having either OMR or code 3-of-9 codes on the document.

There is one final piece of technology that gives added value to the direct mailers. Once the OMR, code 3-of-9, or optical code is read, if it is written on the edge of a document, it can be trimmed off in the process so that the finished product is a codeless, perfectly matched set of documents. The recipient will not be able to tell that they were machine-produced.

These are the two major benefits of intelligent collating:

1. A machine, rather than people, will assemble the mail; this improves accuracy and decreases labor.

2. The direct mailer has much greater flexibility in constructing one-to-one personalized messages without regard to the length of the copy.

Envelope Addressing

Over the years, direct mailers have produced many methods of imaging envelopes, including individually on a word processor, imaging on continuous-form or flat sheets and then postconverting the envelope around the already imaged piece, and special in-line processes that form an envelope around the contents. All of these methods are restrictive in nature and are relatively expensive; as a result, producing "normal" personalized envelopes with a high-quality font has been a problem.

New technology is now perfected that will allow conventional, preformed envelopes to be lasered, the only restriction being how well the toner takes to the paper stock (a problem common to all Xerographic processes). However, through new technology, "already-formed" conventional-type envelopes can be fed directly into the Xerox 9790 laser in almost any normal size, from Monarch up to 9 inches by 12 inches. This saves direct mailers several production steps and allows them to produce a package using a font consistent with that used on the inside materials. There are some problems with this process, however. Critical considerations must be observed when it comes to the grain of stock on the envelope, the amount of curl in the stock, and the positioning of the flap on the envelope, as they must be fed to the laser in a "flap-open" configuration. Not all Xerox Model 9700 lasers are configured in the same way, which also adds an element of variation, but the process can be accomplished. It is not possible to feed individual envelopes on any continuous-form laser.

Lasering normal envelopes can be beneficial because:

1. Lasering creates a better image. The package looks less like advertising mail and more like regular correspondence.

2. Lasering is more cost-effective, because manual handling and several production steps are eliminated.

Franking and Manifesting

Applying postage to envelopes produces a special set of problems, but the process has been enhanced by technology. A typical application might require that different segments of the mailing stream be given varying postage amounts. A mailing that calls for multiple discount levels (owing to different postal-sort levels, for example) would require separate setups and runs through the lettershop to ensure that the correct postage is affixed. The use of computers on inserting equipment helped to solve this problem, in that mail packages of different weights (which require different postage amounts) may be kept in a *single stream,* as long as the mailing stream is manifested in a way that is accepted by the post office. Different discount levels may be presented and accepted into the postal system, although such a procedure is not commonplace. The process is facilitated by having two or more postage-affixing machines (or meter bases) in-line on the inserter. The weight of each mail piece is calculated and the appropriate meter selected to apply the proper postage. Since meter heads can be interchanged with stamp heads, alternating stamps (as well as meter indicias) can be applied in the same stream. Multiple stamps and/or multiple stamps with different denominations may also be applied.

Another franking method that is not yet widely used by mailers is called *manifesting.* Manifesting utilizes the same process described above but produces a "key line" printed at the bottom of each envelope. The numbers and letters in the key line show the unique identification number, the weight, the level of sorting, and the amount of postage for each piece. In addition to this information, a manifest report is prepared that identifies all pieces in the mailing and the proper amount of postage for each. The manifest report is presented along with the mail and is given to the post office to provide a 100 percent audit of what is being mailed. Manifesting is produced in conjunction with a mailing permit, and the manifest report serves as the basis for paying the post office the correct amount due.

The benefits of maximizing postage discounts are an important by-product of making the entire production-mail process as efficient as possible through single-stream processing.

Inventory Control

Technology can help to facilitate lettershop functions through computerized inventory control. As material is used, it can be accounted for on a precise basis and manipulated in a computer program, rather than relying on an individual to properly reset and read a manual counter. The opportunity is compounded if multiple inserting machines are working on the same job, as a computer network consolidates this information. The technology is developing to the level where computerized inventory is on-line and accessible to the customer on an on-line basis.

Benefits include greater control over a common problem area, which will reduce hidden costs and provide better quality control (that is, the correct insert will go into the correct package).

Match Mail

One of the most significant benefits of utilizing computer technology on mail finishing and inserting equipment is the ability to produce match mail, or mail that has a closed-face outer envelope matched to its personalized letters and inserts. All components are matched by computer rather than manually. In the past, commonly used methods have been the manual, or "blind match," which involves batching or checking every nth package manually. The assumption is that if the sample is correct, the rest of the run will be correct.

A second version of mechanized match mail is the freeze-frame camera operation. To control the production process, a video camera stationed at critical matching points on mail-processing equipment will freeze every nth piece so that an operator can visually check to see that all pieces of a particular mailer are matched. Because of human limitations, difficulty is encountered when there are variable numbered pieces or when the requirement is to have every piece 100 percent matched. This can only be done by a computer, because of the complexity and the speed at which the machines operate.

The processes used for matching are identical to those presented in the collation section, with a few differences. It is common practice to hide the visual code under the envelope flap so that when it is sealed, the sequence number disappears. Yet, before the envelope is sealed, it is easily readable by the operator on the inserting equipment. A secondary method is use of the OMR codes or other match code, placed underneath the stamp that is placed on the face of the envelope. This is fine as long as one is using a stamp, but if a meter is used, the code would be obvious and undesirable. Occasionally, the OMR code will be totally visible on the back of the flap.

A new method, again utilizing computer technology, involves the use of optics, in which the name and address are read, much like the U.S. Postal Service uses its equipment to read and code its mail. This process doesn't require any external codes but reads it as a person would, matching it to what the computer has identified as the other contents of that package. Direct mailers are used to producing most of their direct mail in window envelopes, not as a matter of choice, but as a matter of convenience and practicality; it has been the most efficient way to produce mail. When direct marketers are looking for ways to be different and/or avoid the advertising-mail look, computerized match mail offers the promise of conventional-looking mail at a more affordable price.

The benefits of codeless match mail (especially where intelligent collating and selective inserting are also used) are:

1. Better image
2. Better response rates

PostNet™ Bar Coding

The process of applying the PostNet bar code is relatively new and, as of this writing, applies only to letter mail; flat mail will follow suit. If the lettershop does not apply the PostNet bar code, the post office will. The advantages of having the lettershop put on the PostNet bar code are twofold:

1. If the mail has a zip + 4 code appended, significant postal discounts will be achieved.

2. The mail will be delivered more quickly, since major presort operations at the post office are bypassed.

If closed-face envelopes are lasered, the PostNet bar code is easily attached today. With the introduction of "wide-area" bar coding, mailers will be able to put the bar code at the top line of their address, which can show through the window envelope and be mailed. To some, however, this identifies the package as advertising mail; the method of preference is to put the bar code where the post office would — in the lower-right-hand corner of the envelope. Again, technology has been introduced to direct mailers to allow this process to be used on mail-inserting equipment, on either an off-line or in-line basis. This is accomplished by optically reading the address on the envelope (it can even be read through a window), picking up or calculating the zip + 4 code and, finally, formatting the PostNet bar-code representation of the zip + 4 code in the lower-right-hand corner of the envelope. Of course, the advantage to doing this in-line on the inserting equipment is that it results in one less operation, resulting in efficiency and cost savings.

Sampling

Sampling and quality control have long been issues for both the lettershop and the customer. Typical methods involve pulling samples manually from the mailing stream or having samples prepared at the beginning or end of a production run. The difficulty is that the samples may not be representative of what's really going on in the mailing stream.

Again, through the application of computer technology, in-line sampling can be done on a very controlled basis. At the time that the mailing stream is created, a dummy record or duplicate record can be added to the mailing file. This record will serve as a special code that will flag the document as a sample (the special code being an OMR, code 3-of-9, or optical code). The sample may then be outsorted before postage is affixed. In this manner, a live sample from the mailing stream is produced automatically, which facilitates verification that the mailing is accurate.

The benefits of in-line sampling are:

1. Better assurance of the quality and integrity of the mail
2. Production of representative "historical" samples

Selective Inserting

The concept of selective inserting is not new. In fact, direct mailers have long been using selective inserting by setting up multiple cells or runs. (The same is true of catalog houses, to whom selective binding and inserting is old hat.) For example, in a mailing, if half of the recipients are sent brochure A and half are sent brochure B, the run is typically split into two groups and then processed through normal inserting equipment. Through the adaptation of computers into the mail-inserting equipment, duplication is avoided. Inserts can be selected through computer programming and the use of the OMR, code 3-of-9, or optical codes.

Even multiple inserts of a particular type may be selected. For example, customer A could receive three coupons, while customer B might receive only one. Conventional methods of processing would require multiple lettershop runs to accomplish this, but adding intelligence to selective inserting allows the process to be dynamic. It is also possible to maximize the number of inserts selected based on the available weight (that is, the difference between the weights allowed for the postal class and the cumulative weight of the package). In other words, inserts may be selectively added without jumping to the next-higher postal rate. Intelligent inserting, too, was developed by transaction mailers, enabling them to identify and assemble a variable number of personalized checks for banking statements.

The benefits of selective inserting are:

1. Reduced waste of superfluous material

2. More highly targeted mailings

3. Maximum inclusion of inserts within postal-rate constraints

SUMMARY

New technologies are constantly being developed and/or adapted, dictated by direct mailers' needs. The key is utilizing the power of the computer to drive mail-inserting equipment and to process the mail in a single stream, rather than mechanically separating operations into smaller, less cost-efficient groups. Following the golden rule of data processing—"Do it once"—the in-line process promises greater control, greater flexibility, and cost savings from the efficiencies of running and handling materials one time only. It also offers creative flexibility to the marketing people producing the packages. There are no longer conventional constraints as to the number of inserts, the number of pages, or the size of the package. Monarch sizes are handled as easily as Jumbos.

For many marketers, the ultimate goal is to produce "normal" mail that doesn't look or read as if it was mass-produced. One-to-one personalized marketing is the driver of the 1990s in technology, and the lettershop will be the key to facilitating that process.

30

Postal Regulations

Lee Epstein

MAILMEN Inc.
New York, N.Y.

This chapter will acquaint you with the U.S. Postal Service rules and regulations in order to make you knowledgeable about the various classes of mail and their specifications. It will enable you to determine the most economical rates for the level of service you require based on the type of material you wish to mail.*

A BRIEF HISTORY OF THE U.S. POSTAL SERVICE

In 1789, Congress created a government agency called the Post Office Department. Its purpose was to set up a universal communications and delivery system which would provide for the delivery of mail to all citizens, regardless of location or distance, with the same postage rates for everyone. The private express statutes mandated that this agency would have a monopoly on the delivery of letters. Congress would set postage rates and provide the necessary funding; the Postmaster General would be a member of the President's cabinet. At that time, there were 75 post offices.

A postal system was created by the Continental Congress in 1774, with Benjamin Franklin as the postmaster general. In 1847, the first postage stamp was issued. In 1970, Congress discontinued direct control over rates and wages and passed the Postal Reorganization Act, which established the U.S. Postal Service

*All figures used in this chapter are copyrighted and reproduced with the permission of the U.S. Postal Service, whose cooperation is greatly appreciated.

as an independent government operation. This act permitted the U.S.P.S. to negotiate directly on wages with its employees and, through the Postal Rate Commission, establish postage rates which eventually would permit the U.S.P.S. to break even.

THE CURRENT RATE-MAKING PROCESS

When the U.S. Postal Service feels that it needs more revenue, it makes recommendations for rate increases to the Postal Rate Commission, based on cost studies. The commission then conducts its own studies and hearings on revenue requirements in which not only the U.S.P.S. but any association or individual can participate as intervenors. The Postal Rate Commission in turn must recommend to the board of governors of the Postal Service its conclusions and recommendations for rates within 10 months. The board of governors then can accept, reject, or resubmit its case to the Rate Commission for reconsideration. In the interim, the U.S. Postal Service can put in place temporary rates until the case is resolved. After the third rejection of the Rate Commission recommendations, the board of governors can modify these rates as they see fit. Since 1970, rate increases have taken place every 3 years.

CLASSES OF MAIL

There are four basic classes of mail: first, second, third, and fourth. Each class services a different product line and has different levels of service as well as different mailing requirements. Within each class there are subclasses, such as priority mail for first-class, controlled magazines for second-class, nonprofit mail for third-class, and special fourth and library rate for fourth-class.

In discussing each class of mail, I have specifically avoided mentioning rates, since rates are subject to periodic changes. Check with your mailing service or the U.S. Postal Service for the latest rates.

First-Class Mail

First-class mail is a preferred category. It receives expedited handling and transportation and delivery. Postage may be paid by meter, preprinted indicia, or stamp, and any mailable matter up to 12 ounces may be sent. It receives free forwarding and return service and may not be opened for postal inspections. Postal cards, personal correspondence, or typewritten bills and statements of accounts must be mailed first-class. Delivery may be expected in 1 to 3 days, depending on the distance. (See Figure 30-4, page 444, for delivery standards for all classes of mail.)

Priority Mail

First-class mail over 11 ounces is called priority mail. Postage is determined by weight and by zone distances. The maximum weight permissible is 70 pounds. Pieces weighing less than 11 ounces may be mailed at the priority rate.

Second-Class Mail

This class is used by newspapers and magazines issued at least four times a year. To qualify for a permit, a publication must have request (controlled) or paid subscribers and must not be designed primarily for advertising purposes.

Second-class mail generally receives speedy delivery. Daily and weekly publications are entitled to newspaper or "red tag" treatment.

Third-Class Mail

Third-class mail consists of advertising circulars, brochures, booklets, catalogs, and other printed matter (for example, letters, order forms, reply envelopes, etc.) weighing less than 1 pound. Small parcels and merchandise under a pound also can be mailed in this class. There are two subclasses.

1. The single-piece rate does not require the zip code and needs no mail preparation for acceptance. Delivery is slower than for first-class, and it receives no free forwarding or return privileges.

2. Bulk rate is by far the most popular class for solicitation or prospect contact. A permit is required as well as an annual bulk-mail fee. A minimum of 200 pieces or 50 pounds is required. All pieces must be zip-coded. The mail then must be separated by ZIP code and tied and bagged before being presented to the U.S. Postal Service for mailing, along with a statement of mailing. Postage may be paid by preprinted indicia, meter impression, or precanceled stamp. Since this is a deferred category of mail, its delivery can run from 3 to 30 days, depending on its level of sortation and density.

Fourth-Class Mail

Parcels weighing 1 pound or more are mailed as fourth-class or parcel post up to a maximum of 70 pounds. Some post offices are restricted to 40-pound packages. Postage is computed by weight and by zone.

Fourth-Class, Special. This subclass is used to mail books and records weighing 1 pound or more. It is a subclass with postage computed by weight regardless of zone.

Fourth-Class, Library Rate. This subclass is for items weighing 1 pound or more mailed for or to recognized schools, libraries, and nonprofit organizations.

Fourth-Class, Bound Printed Matter. This is fourth-class matter weighing between 1 and 10 pounds, including advertising, promotional, directory, or editorial matter. It must be bound securely and does not permit loose-leaf binders.

There is also a special bulk rate for bound printed matter when 300 or more identical pieces are mailed.

PRESORT PROGRAM

The U.S. Postal Service has developed lower rates for first-, second-, third-, and fourth-class mail when the mailer performs the preparation and sorting functions. These work-sharing programs can result in significantly lower rates when there is sufficient density and volume. There are three tiers to the presort program.

Carrier Route Presort

To qualify for this rate, the address on the mailing piece must be carrier-identified, must have at least 10 pieces to a carrier route (6 for second class), and must be tied and bagged by carrier route and placed in the proper five-digit bag. The U.S. Postal Service will provide a mailer with computerized carrier route tapes, which then can be used (with the proper computer software) to identify the carrier route number for your name-and-address file. Labels or computer letters then are printed with the carrier route number as part of the address.

Five-Digit Presort

For this discount level, you must have at least 50 pieces or 10 pounds of mail for a ZIP code, and each ZIP code must be put in a separate sack. You may combine certain three-digit codes.

ZIP+4 (Nine-Digit ZIP Code)

The U.S. Postal Service has introduced the expanded ZIP code program to automate the sorting process and eliminate the manual processing of first-class mail. The process involves scanning the address and imprinting a bar code on the envelope. Mail which qualifies is processed by bar code readers that sort the mail at high speeds directly to the letter carrier.

Automation

The Postal Service has embarked on a total updating of its mail processing equipment through the use of optical scanners and bar code readers. When fully implemented, it should dramatically speed up the processing of mail at a much lower unit cost. Up to now, most mail processing was either done manually or by mechanized equipment.

Bar Coding

To further their automated mail sortation, the U.S.P.S. scanners will read the address, city, state, and ZIP code, and spray a bar code interpretation of the address on each piece of mail. These bar-coded pieces can then be read by bar code sorters, which then separate the mail to its proper post office or carrier route automatically. Additional discounts can be earned if the mailers can apply the bar code themselves.

Work Sharing

This is an essential industry-U.S.P.S. concept which enables industry to perform certain mail processing functions in the preparation of mail. The U.S.P.S. cost avoidance is then shared with industry, resulting in lower rates.

Basic Rate

All mail that cannot qualify for the carrier route or five-digit rate falls into this category. Presorted mail may be presented and paid for by preprinted indicia, meter, or precanceled stamps. Minimum quantities are required, which differ for each class of mail. It is now possible to commingle first-class presorted mail from more than one mailer. There are first-class presort services in many cities that will take your daily mail and merge it with other first-class mail, thus achieving greater density and greater discounts, resulting in additional savings to the mailer. Your customer service representative can supply you with the names and addresses of firms offering this service.

NONPROFIT RATES

For organizations which qualify as nonprofit, Congress annually provides appropriations to the U.S. Postal Service to permit it to charge lower rates. The amount of the subsidy Congress appropriates each year determines the rate and is known as "Revenue Forgone."

BUSINESS REPLY MAIL

Another service to business enables mailers to include in their solicitation postage-paid reply mail (envelopes or cards) to be used by recipients to send orders and payments back to the mailer. The mailer then pays the U.S. Postal Service the first-class rate and a surcharge for this service. A permit is required which is used only for first-class mail. Cards must be at least 0.007 of an inch thick, and specific formats and markings are mandated for the face of reply mail (see Fig. 30-1).

OCCUPANT MAIL

It is possible to mail without the use of an individual's name, with only the address and a line which says "Occupant" or "Resident." This technique is used primarily for saturation mailings by supermarkets, penny savers, local retailers, and companies wishing to send samples of merchandise.

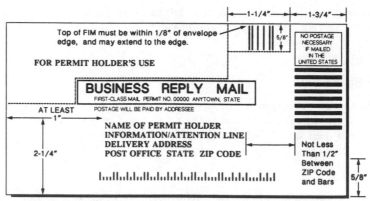

Horizontal identification bars must be at least 1-inch in length, and must not extend
vertically below the delivery address line.

Exhibit 917.52c, Business Reply Mail Format Requirements

Note: Both FIM and Barcode must have at least 30 percent print reflectance difference and the combined effects of positional and rotational skew must be limited to ±5 degrees from the FIM or Barcode to the top or bottom edge of the mailpiece.
Exhibit **not** drawn to scale.

Figure 30-1. Business reply mail. (*U.S. Postal Service*)

PERMIT IMPRINTS

For mailers who choose not to meter or use live stamps on their mailings, permit imprints may be used. These are indicia which are preprinted on the mailing piece at the time the envelope, catalog, or self-mailer is being printed. Figure 30-2 illustrates some of the variations in style that are acceptable to the U.S. Postal Service.

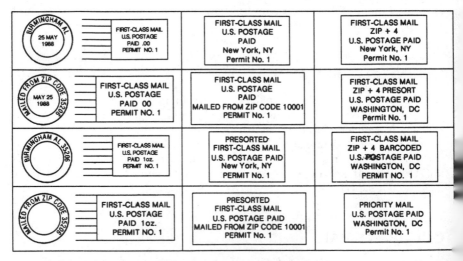

Exhibit 145.41a, Formats for First-Class Mail

Figure 30-2. Formats of permit imprints. (*U.S. Postal Service*)

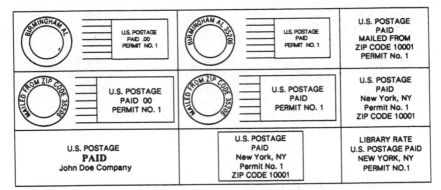

Exhibit 145.41b, Formats for Third- and Fourth-Class Mail (Date and Class of Mail Omitted).

Note: When this form of permit imprint is used, the markings required by 629.6, 725.1, or 760 must appear below or to the left of the permit imprint on the mailpieces or as otherwise specified.

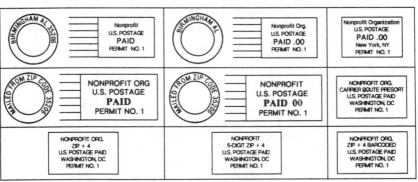

Exhibit 145.41c, Formats for Third-Class Mail (Regular Single-Piece and Bulk Rates)

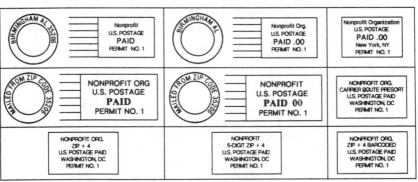

Exhibit 145.41d, Formats for Third-Class Mail (Special Single-Piece and Bulk Rates)
(Authorized Organizations Only)

Figure 30-2. *(Continued)*

Exhibit 145.41e, Formats for Fourth-Class Bulk-Rate Mail

Figure 30-2. (*Continued*)

AUTHORIZED SERVICE ENDORSEMENTS

Address Correction and Mail Forwarding

This service is for direct marketers who wish to clean their lists by receiving changes of address. If mail is not deliverable as addressed, they can have the piece forwarded or returned to the sender. Various endorsements can be printed under the corner card (return address) in the upper left-hand corner of the mailing piece. If there is no endorsement on a mailing piece and it cannot be delivered as addressed, third-class mail will be deemed "of no obvious value" and will be destroyed.

If you wish to receive additional handling, the following options are available.

Address Correction Service

First-class mail bearing the endorsement "address correction requested" will be forwarded to the new address, and a Form 3547 will be sent to the mailer with the new address. For a fee, third-class mail will be returned to sender with the new address if it is under 2 ounces. If it is over 2 ounces, the U.S. Postal Service can use Form 3547 or return the piece.

Forwarding and Return

Undeliverable-as-addressed third-class mail bearing the words "Forwarding and Return Postage Guaranteed" will be forwarded to the addressee at no charge. Mail that is returned to the sender will be charged the single piece rate multiplied by 2.4.

Return Postage Guaranteed

As used by third-class mailers, this will not get you the new address, but you will get your piece back at the single piece rate.

The endorsement rules vary for each class of mail (see Figure 30-2) and should be checked carefully before you print your envelopes to determine which service you may want or not want. House lists should be cleaned regularly, whereas outside lists (rentals) are usually for one-time use and are not to be cleaned by the list user. (See Figure 30-3 for an explanation of treatment of endorsements of undeliverable mail for all classes of mail.)

Exhibit 159.151c

Treatment of Undeliverable Third-Class Bulk Business Mail Weighing 1 Ounce or Less (Forwarded up to 12 Months)

Mailer Endorsement	USPS Action
No Endorsement	No forwarding or return service is provided.
Do Not Forward	No forwarding or return service is provided.
Address Correction Requested	No forwarding service is provided. Return entire mailpiece with address correction or reason for nondelivery; charge the first ounce single-piece third-class rate, do not charge the address-correction fee.
Forwarding and Return Postage Guaranteed	Forward at no charge. If mail is not forwardable, return the entire mailpiece with reason for nondelivery; charge the appropriate third-class weighted fee.[1]
Forwarding and Return Postage Guaranteed, Address Correction Requested[2]	Forward at no charge. If separate address-correction notice is provided, charge the address-correction fee. If mail is not forwardable, return the entire mailpiece with reason for nondelivery; charge the appropriate third-class weighted fee.[1]
Do Not Forward, Address Correction Requested, Return Postage Guaranteed[3]	Do not forward. Return entire mailpiece with the new address or reason for nondelivery; charge the first ounce single-piece third-class rate, do not charge the address-correction fee.

[1] The weighted fee is the appropriate single-piece third-class rate multiplied by a factor of 2.472. The fee is used during months 1-12 when forwarding is unsuccessful and the mailpiece is returned to the sender. During months 13-18 charge this fee on mailpieces endorsed "Forwarding and Return Postage Guaranteed" or "Forwarding and Return Postage Guaranteed--Address Correction Requested."

[2] The authorized abbreviation for this endorsement is "Forward & Address Correction." This abbreviation is authorized in those limited situations where the full endorsement cannot be accommodated.

[3] The authorized abbreviation for this endorsement is "Do Not Forward--Address Cor--Return Guar." This abbreviation is authorized in those limited situations where the full endorsement cannot be accommodated.

Note:
These regulations apply to mail associated with a customer's change of address. Do not provide temporary change-of address information at any time. When necessary, more than one line may be used to print the mailer endorsement.

Exhibit 159.151d

Treatment of Undeliverable Third-Class Bulk Business Mail Weighing Over 1 Ounce (Forwarded up to 12 Months)

Mailer Endorsement	USPS Action
No Endorsement	No forwarding or return service is provided.
Do Not Forward	No forwarding or return service is provided.
Address Correction Requested	No forwarding service is provided. Address correction is provided via Form 3547 or Form 3579; charge the address-correction fee.
Forwarding and Return Postage Guaranteed	Forward at no charge. If mail is not forwardable, return the entire mailpiece with reason for nondelivery; charge the appropriate third-class weighted fee.[1]
Forwarding and Return Postage Guaranteed, Address Correction Requested[2]	Forward at no charge. If separate address-correction notice is provided, charge the address-correction fee. If mail is not forwardable, return the entire mailpiece with reason for nondelivery; charge the appropriate third-class weighted fee.[1]
Do Not Forward, Address Correction Requested, Return Postage Guaranteed[3]	Do not forward. Return entire mailpiece with the new address or reason for nondelivery; charge the appropriate single-piece third-class rate, do not charge the address-correction fee.

[1] The weighted fee is the appropriate single-piece third-class rate multiplied by a factor of 2.472. The fee is used during months 1-12 when forwarding is unsuccessful and the mailpiece is returned to the sender. During months 13-18 charge this fee on mailpieces endorsed "Forwarding and Return Postage Guaranteed" or "Forwarding and Return Postage Guaranteed--Address Correction Requested."

[2] The authorized abbreviation for this endorsement is "Forward & Address Correction." This abbreviation is authorized in those limited situations where the full endorsement cannot be accommodated.

[3] The authorized abbreviation for this endorsement is "Do Not Forward--Address Cor--Return Guar." This abbreviation is authorized in those limited situations where the full endorsement cannot be accommodated.

Note:
These regulations apply to mail associated with a customer's change of address. Do not provide temporary change-of-address information at any time. When necessary, more than one line may be used to print the mailer endorsement.

Figure 30-3. Treatment of endorsements of undeliverable mail for all classes of mail. (*U.S. Postal Service*)

Exhibit 159.151e
Treatment of Undeliverable Third-Class Mail,
Single-Piece Rate (Forwarded up to 12 Months)

Mailer Endorsement	USPS Action
No Endorsement	No forwarding service is provided. Return the mailpiece to the sender at the single-piece third-class rate, with the reason for nondelivery or new address; do not charge the address-correction fee.
Do Not Forward	No forwarding or return service is provided.
Address Correction Requested	No forwarding service is provided. If the mailpiece weighs 1 ounce or less, return the entire piece with the new address or the reason for nondelivery; charge the third-class single-piece rate. Pieces over 1 ounce will receive an address-correction notice via Form 3579 or Form 3547; charge the address-correction fee.
Forwarding and Return Postage Guaranteed	Forward at no charge. If mail is not forwardable, return the entire mailpiece with reason for nondelivery; charge the appropriate third-class weighted fee.[1]
Forwarding and Return Postage Guaranteed, Address Correction Requested[2]	Forward at no charge. If separate address-correction notice is provided, charge the address-correction fee. If mail is not forwardable, return the entire mailpiece with reason for nondelivery; charge the appropriate third-class weighted fee.[1]
Do Not Forward, Address Correction Requested, Return Postage Guaranteed[3]	Do not forward. Return entire mailpiece with the new address or reason for nondelivery; charge the appropriate single-piece third-class rate, do not charge the address-correction fee.

[1]The weighted fee is the appropriate single-piece third-class rate multiplied by a factor of 2.472. The fee is used during months 1-12 when forwarding is unsuccessful and the mailpiece is returned to the sender. During months 13-18, charge this fee on mailpieces endorsed "Forwarding and Return Postage Guaranteed" or "Forwarding and Return Postage Guaranteed--Address Correction Requested."

[2]The authorized abbreviation for this endorsement is "Forward & Address Correction." This abbreviation is authorized in those limited situations where the full endorsement cannot be accommodated.

[3]The authorized abbreviation for this endorsement is "Do Not Forward--Address Cor--Return Guar." This abbreviation is authorized in those limited situations where the full endorsement cannot be accommodated.

Note:
These regulations apply to mail associated with a customer's change of address. Do not provide temporary change-of-address information at any time. When necessary, more than one line may be used to print the mailer endorsement.

Figure 30-3. (*Continued*)

Exhibit 159.151f
Treatment of Undeliverable Fourth-Class Mail, Including
Parcel Post (Forwarded up to 12 Months)

Mailer Endorsement	USPS Action
No Endorsement	Forward locally at no charge; forward out of town postage-due. If undeliverable or addressee refuses to pay postage, return mailpiece with new address or reason for nondelivery; charge both forwarding (where attempted) and return postage.
Do Not Forward, Do Not Return	No forwarding or return service is provided; mailpiece is disposed of by the Postal Service.
Forwarding and Return Postage Guaranteed	Forward locally at no charge, forward out of town postage-due. If undeliverable or addressee refuses to pay postage, return mailpiece with new address or reason for nondelivery; charge both forwarding (where attempted) and return postage.
Forwarding and Return Postage Guaranteed, Address Correction Requested[1]	Forward locally at no charge; forward out of town postage-due. If forwarded, provide a separate address-correction notice; charge address-correction fee. If mailpiece is undeliverable, or addressee refuses to pay postage, return mailpiece with new address or reason for nondelivery; charge both forwarding (where attempted) and return postage.
Do Not Forward, Do Not Return, Address Correction Requested[2]	No forwarding or return service is provided; provide a separate address-correction notice; charge address-correction fee; mailpiece is disposed of by the Postal Service.
Do Not Forward, Address Correction Requested, Return Postage Guaranteed[3]	No forwarding service is provided; return mailpiece with the new address or reason for nondelivery; charge return postage.

[1]The authorized abbreviation for this endorsement is "Forward & Address Correction." This abbreviation is authorized in those limited situations where the full endorsement cannot be accommodated.

[2]The authorized abbreviation for this endorsement is "Do Not Forward or Return--Address Cor." This abbreviation is authorized in those limited situations where the full endorsement cannot be accommodated.

[3]The authorized abbreviation for this endorsement is "Do Not Forward--Address Cor--Return Guar." This abbreviation is authorized in those limited situations where the full endorsement cannot be accommodated.

Note:
These regulations apply to mail associated with a customer's change of address. Do not provide temporary change-of-address information at any time. When necessary, more than one line may be used to print the mailer endorsement.

NONSTANDARD MAIL

First-class mail weighing 1 ounce or less is nonstandard if its length exceeds 11½ inches, its height exceeds 6⅛ inches, or its thickness exceeds one-quarter of an inch. A surcharge is levied on each piece of nonstandard mail.

Third-class bulk mail does not have maximum size limitations. The only exception is carrier-route mail, which cannot exceed 11½ by 13½ inches and cannot be more than three-quarters of an inch thick.

MINIMUM SIZE STANDARDS

For all classes of mail, any piece under 3½ by 5 inches will not be accepted by the post office. Mail which does not have sufficient postage also will be returned to the sender as short-paid mail.

SERVICE STANDARDS

Figure 30-4 can be used as a guide for estimating average delivery time for any class of mail. Note that the U.S. Postal Service does not meet these standards in all cases. When planning for home delivery dates, allow additional time, particularly for third class, which is a deferred category. As of press time, service standards were being revised, and the U.S.P.S. did not have the new chart ready to include here. To find out about a specific standard, it would be wise to call your local post office.

SPECIAL SERVICES

Express Mail

This is an expedited service for high-priority shipments within the United States and to selected foreign countries.

Mailgram

This is an expedited message service using Western Union for the message transmission. Mailgrams are delivered by a letter carrier the next business day.

Attached Mail

A recent change in regulations permits the attachment or enclosure of incidental first-class mail with other classes of mail, with postage paid on the combined piece at the applicable rate of the host piece. This applies to second-class mail, third-class merchandise including books but excluding merchandise samples, and fourth-class mail. In practical terms, this means that an invoice, statement of account, or renewal notice can be included in a mailing without paying first-class postage.

WORKING WITH THE POST OFFICE

Every mailer has a customer service representative (CSR). This individual should be consulted on any question you may have concerning rules and regulations, postage rates, and services. The CSR also can be consulted for approval

UNITED STATES POSTAL SERVICE
SERVICE STANDARDS
(ZIP CODED MAIL ONLY)

EFFECTIVE 5/15/85

	OVERNIGHT	OVERNIGHT REQUIREMENTS	2nd DAY	3rd DAY	4th DAY	5th DAY	6th DAY	7th DAY	8th DAY	9th DAY	10th DAY
EXPRESS MAIL NEXT DAY SERVICE	OVERNIGHT NATIONWIDE		(SEE DIRECTORY)								
FIRST CLASS	LOCALLY DESIGNATED CITIES AND SCF's	UP TO AND INCLUDING 5:00 P.M. COLLECTIONS	LOCALLY DESIGNATED STATES	REMAINING OUTLYING AREAS							
PRIORITY MAIL	DESIGNATED CITIES	STATED AT MAILING POST OFFICE	NATIONWIDE								
SURFACE PREFERENTIAL*	UP TO 150 MILES	5:00 P.M. MAILINGS	300 MILES Zone 3	600 MILES Zone 4	1,000 MILES Zone 5	1,400 MILES Zone 6	1,800 MILES Zone 7	OVER 1,800 MILES Zone 8			
BULK BUSINESS MAIL	AS DEVELOPED LOCALLY		INTRA-SCF (for 5:00 P.M. CARRIER PRESORTED MAILINGS)	DESIGNATED SCF's AND NON-PRESORTED INTRA-SCF	UP TO 150 MILES Zone 2	300 MILES Zone 3	600 MILES Zone 4	1,000 MILES Zone 5	1,400 MILES Zone 6	1,800 MILES Zone 7	OVER 1,800 MILES Zone 8
PARCEL POST			SEE SEPARATE STANDARDS ISSUED FOR EACH BULK MAIL CENTER. This form is available at local Post Office.								

*Includes 2nd class, special handling parcel post and special delivery.

Figure 30-4. Service standards of the U.S. Postal Service. (*U.S. Postal Service*)

of your direct-mail package to make sure that you conform to the regulations for acceptable mail.

POSTAL SERVICE PUBLICATIONS

Domestic Mail Manual

This manual includes all postal regulations and information. Revisions are issued quarterly. It can be bought for a fee from:

> The Superintendent of Documents
> U.S. Government Printing Office
> Washington, D.C. 20402-9371

Postal Bulletin

This is for mailers who need advance information relating to U.S. Postal Service changes in rules and regulations. Subscriptions are available from the Superintendent of Documents for an annual fee.

Memo to Mailers

This newsletter is issued by the U.S. Postal Service monthly at no charge. It covers various items of interest to users of the mail. To get on the mailing list, write to

> Memo to Mailers
> U.S. Postal Service
> P.O. Box 999
> Springfield, VA 22150-0999

ZIP Code Directory

A complete listing of all correct and current ZIP codes can be purchased from your local post office.

PART 6

Fulfillment Planning

31

Fulfillment Planning: An Overview

Stanley J. Fenvessy

Fenvessy Consulting
New York, N.Y.

THE IMPORTANCE OF CONVENIENCE IN BUYING DIRECT

Customer marketing questionnaires, telephone surveys, and focus groups repeatedly indicate that shopping convenience is the single most important reason why consumers and businesses buy direct. And it is the fulfillment process that delivers this sought-after convenience and satisfaction.

What comprises fulfillment? After the customer's order is received, the merchandise or publication must be delivered promptly, completely, and in good condition. The final step in the fulfillment process is customer service, which involves answering customer telephone and mail inquiries, responding to complaints, and effecting adjustments for disappointed customers.

THE BENEFITS OF SUPERIOR FULFILLMENT

The unique advantage of direct marketing is the personal relationship between the marketer and the customer, which carries with it all the potential for goodwill inherent in such a relationship. Lester Wunderman, one of the deans of direct marketing, describes it this way: "Direct Marketing converts a product into a service. After a product is chosen and the order placed, a customer expects to be personally served in terms of either a delivery or a dialogue."

In addition to providing convenience and fostering a personal relationship, a superior fulfillment function affects the success of a direct marketing business in four ways: competitive advantage; improved profits; increased reorders and reduced returns; and fewer consumerism problems.

Competitive Advantage

Top-notch fulfillment may be one of the answers to the much-talked-about catalog glut, which is the overissuance of catalogs to the same potential customers. Providing customers with outstanding service may distinguish a company's catalog or promotion from those of its competitors and thereby achieve a competitive advantage. Also, if the customer promptly receives everything ordered, there is a strong likelihood that the customer will continue to order and not regularly shop other catalogers or retailers.

Improved Profits

Direct marketers who provide superior service have learned this valuable corollary about fulfillment: the faster and more proficient the service, the lower the fulfillment cost. It doesn't cost more to better serve the customer. The disciplines, controls, and systems necessary to process an order efficiently also produce these cost-effective benefits: work simplification, elimination of unnecessary operations, and high worker-productivity.

Increased Reorders and
Reduced Returns

If customers receive their orders quickly, there is a strong probability that they will reorder, and repeat buying is the lifeblood of direct marketing. If it takes weeks for a product to be received, customers may change their minds and purchase similar items elsewhere. Further, studies have shown that fast order-turnaround substantially reduces returns.

Fewer Consumerism Problems

The very nature of direct marketing, in which a customer is asked to buy "blindly," based on a picture and description, makes it impossible to make all customers 100-percent happy. Problems can result from the sheer volume of transactions or from sources outside the control of the direct marketer. A small number of these disappointments result in contacts from governmental agencies, the Better Business Bureau, the Direct Marketing Association, consumer advocates, and action-line newspaper columnists. Consistently good fulfillment will keep these agencies and advocates at bay.

THE 12 PHASES OF THE FULFILLMENT PROCESS

Today, customers who buy direct are better educated and more demanding. They firmly believe that they are entitled to quality service in terms of order completion; they expect the order to be totally, accurately, and promptly filled and to arrive in perfect condition. They believe equally firmly in their right to customer service; they feel that any disappointment or dissatisfaction should be promptly, fairly, and courteously resolved. The achievement of these customer expectations and the development of management information and controls to fulfill them involves twelve basic steps—each of them precise and some of them quite complex.

1. Order Receipt

This step comprises the receiving of orders by telephone, by mail, and by fax and the initial clerical and data entry processing tasks. The telephone has become the major source of orders for most direct marketers. For example, the giant catalog companies, such as Penney's and Sears, receive over 90 percent of their orders via telephone. It is expected that within the next two to three years, a majority of direct marketers will exceed 75 percent telephone orders. Most direct marketers use the toll-free WATS 800 number; others have found that it is not cost-effective because of product complexity or low-dollar order size. Fax is becoming a sizable order source for business-to-business catalogers.

Telephone orders are usually entered directly into the computer as received. This streamlines the processing steps and enables customers to learn whether the products ordered are in stock. Because of mailing time and extra handling, mail orders can add as much as three days to the delivery time.

2. Credit Approval and Check Verification

Provision of credit has been a major factor in the growth of direct marketing. Some direct marketers offer their own time-payment or open-account programs, but the majority utilize the services of the bank or travel and entertainment credit cards. The cost of the latter can range from 2–5 percent of sales. Credit approval is obtained by:

Checking internal credit records

Calling the card company to obtain an authorization number

Keying the order into a special authorization terminal

Using credit checking services such as Dun & Bradstreet, TRW, or the special direct marketing oriented credit services of the Direct Marketing Guaranty Trust or Litle and Company.

To avoid bounced checks, companies follow one or more of the following routines: (a) they refuse checks with low check numbers or without printed names and addresses; (b) they call the bank to verify checks over a given amount, (usually starting at $75); or (c) they use a check-guarantee service.

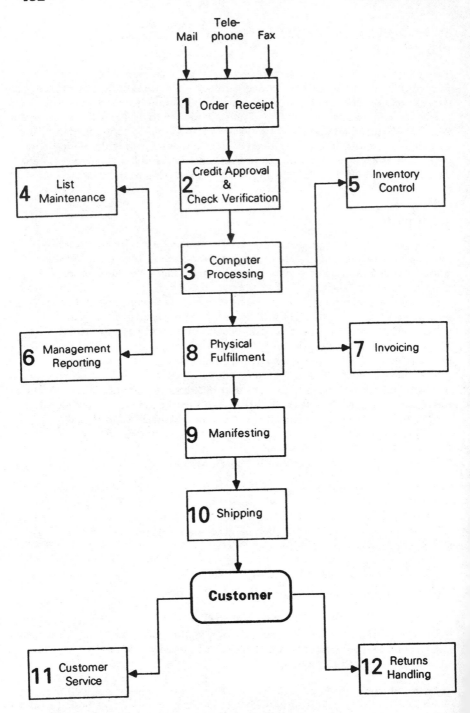

Figure 31-1. The twelve steps in the fulfillment cycle.

3. Computer Processing

Except in the smallest of enterprises, direct marketers employ a computer. Data processing can either be performed on the company's own computer or through the use of an outside data processing service contractor to handle all or part of the functions described in steps 4 through 7.

The availability of low-cost microcomputers and specialized direct marketing software packages on a wide variety of hardware platforms has made internal data processing practical for even small ventures. In the case of start-up operations, however, many have opted to use contractors for all their processing or for specialized segments, such as list maintenance, inventory control, or marketing analysis work.

4. List Maintenance

The quality and applicability of customer and prospect lists and the way they are employed determines the success or failure of a direct marketing venture. Therefore, the accumulation, maintenance, and control of lists is an important by-product of the fulfillment process. Accurate, up-to-date lists and their inherent data are essential for:

Selecting and mailing catalogs and promotions

Creating package or subscription labels

Initiating telephone sales calls

Accumulating marketing information and customer purchasing history

Although they possess large internal computer systems, many of the major direct marketers often contract out the task of list maintenance to firms with sophisticated list maintenance programs. This relieves in-house operators of the task of processing list rental requests and frequently results in lower costs because equipment and personnel are shared with others.

5. Inventory Management

To avoid back orders and overstocks, a computerized perpetual inventory system is essential. With the availability of microcomputers and inventory-management software packages, manual inventory control systems that use visual cards or multi-ring notebooks should be avoided. Computerized stock status reports are regularly prepared showing stock on hand and on order, recent and comparable items' sale experience, and, if appropriate, minimum stock levels.

There is a growing trend in larger companies to use statistical forecasting techniques, such as exponential smoothing, to determine inventory requirements and economical order quantities. The result has been lower inventory investment, reduced back orders, and less warehouse storage space.

6. Management Reporting

A well-run direct marketing business relies on the computer to produce meaningful and timely reports to assist in making marketing and merchandising decisions and to maintain adequate financial and operating controls. There are four types of information and representative data to be reported:

- **Marketing.** Customer profiles by demographic and psychographic factors, profitability of mailings, test results of selective mailings and list rentals
- **Merchandising.** Sales and profit results by promotion vehicle, or by product classification and price point
- **Financial.** Sales tax and accounts receivable analyses, shipping and handling and list-rental income, and operating results by profit centers
- **Operations.** Summarized output and labor productivity, work backlogs, reasons for customer complaints and returns, average service times, and quality measurements

One of the characteristics of direct marketing is that it is measurable in all of its aspects, which preponderates the depth and scope of the computer reporting.

7. Invoicing

This step involves the billing of the customer directly or through a credit card agency. Customers can be either prebilled or postbilled. In prebilling, the invoice is prepared before the merchandise is shipped. In this instance the computer establishes whether the merchandise is in stock and includes a predetermined shipping and handling charge. In the postbilling system the invoice is created after the package has been shipped. The customer is billed for products shipped and the actual cost of shipment.

The production of a shipping directive, a packing list, and shipping labels is usually part of the invoice processing step. Products to be picked and packed are sequenced for efficient picking by item number or warehouse location.

8. Physical Fulfillment

This function includes the receiving, checking, quality examination, storage, picking, assembly, and packing of the merchandise for each order. Order picking and packing are often labor-intensive and frequently represent the largest part of the fulfillment effort and costs. Depending upon the products involved and the number of orders to be processed, picking and packing can range from a completely manual effort to the use of bar-coded product identification, automated and computer-controlled merchandise stacking and retrieval and merchandise packaging systems.

Based on the physical fulfillment advances already achieved in the European direct marketing community, substantial upgrading of merchandise handling tasks can be expected in the United States during the 1990s. The result should be less direct labor and considerable cost savings.

9. Manifesting

The classic weighing-and-metering system that employs a scale and a postage meter has largely been supplanted by computerized manifesting systems. Order number, package weight, and shipping charge are transferred to the computer by one of several methods: operator keying, hand-held scanning of the shipping label; or bar-code reading by a fixed scanner as the package moves across the scale. The end products are a computer printed manifest of parcels shipped and a positive confirmation in the customer's record of the date the package was shipped.

Manifesting also provides a number of labor saving and expense reduction benefits. It

Eliminates hand-written shipping logs and the filing of shipping copies

Abolishes the labor needed to apply meter tapes

Does away with monthly meter-rental expense

Simplifies and expedites the initiating of tracers and claims

Reduces supply costs

Improves the accuracy of shipping records

10. Shipping

From 85 to 90 percent of direct marketing packages are shipped by United Parcel Service. The U.S. Postal Service is principally used in cases where delivery is to a post office box or in cases where lower rates are available (such as books and parcels under one pound). Because customers want to receive merchandise quickly, the use of expedited shipping methods, such as Federal Express, is increasing rapidly, a trend expected to continue.

Constantly increasing shipping costs have motivated direct marketers to seek ways to reduce this expense factor. Here are four of the most common approaches to solving the problem:

- Reduce the weight of the package by eliminating overpacking, changing to lighter dunnage, and substituting bags for boxes.
- Use mixed U.S.P.S. third class bulk for packages under one pound.
- "Zone-skip" (use a contract carrier to transport premetered parcels to distant UPS distribution centers).
- Employ alternative delivery systems that offer lower rates than UPS.

11. Customer Service

What comprises customer service? It is answering customer telephone and mail inquiries, responding to complaints, and effecting adjustments for disappointed customers. There is a strong correlation between successful direct marketers and those providing superior customer service. Studies have repeatedly shown that customers whose problems are satisfactorily resolved report the strongest company loyalty and are more likely to buy again than noncomplainers or those whose complaints were not satisfactorily resolved.

Service-oriented companies encourage customers to use the telephone to resolve problems. Telephone customer-service contacts are both easier and more economical to handle than customer mail. A separate customer service telephone number is listed in the catalog, in the instructions, and on the packing list. Specially trained personnel are then able to handle customer service problems effectively. Should the number be toll free? That is largely a marketing decision. Although a toll-free 800 number will increase total contacts (mail and telephone) by over 40 percent, it does improve customer relations. Notwithstanding, many prestigious catalogs do not provide a toll-free customer service number, although they do offer an 800 ordering number.

12. Returns Handling

Depending upon the type of merchandise involved, a typical direct marketing venture can expect customer returns of 4–25 percent. Businesses that market high-fashion women's apparel and shoes could experience returns as high as 35 percent. The usual reasons for returns are the use of an inadequate address, incorrect merchandise, damage, poor quality, wrong size or color, late arrival, change of mind, and dissatisfaction.

Customers who return merchandise are disappointed with the transaction. Therefore, it is important to stay current in this operation in order not to frustrate the customer further. Some companies send the customer a computerized acknowledgement indicating that the goods have been received. This reassures the customer that the transaction is in process and forestalls subsequent customer service inquiries. If the company is at fault, the customer is reimbursed for the returned shipping expense. Otherwise the customer is expected to pay. Some firms will reimburse if the customer requests, regardless of the reason for returning. Original shipping and handling expenses are rarely refunded.

FULFILLMENT PLANNING

Because of the specialized requirements and large investment that needs to be made in facilities, in computer hardware and software, in materials-handling equipment, and in experienced personnel, management should carefully consider various available fulfillment alternatives. This applies to start-up ventures. It also applies to mature businesses facing the problems of expanding their product offerings, diversifying through additional catalogs or acquisition, or fulfilling a growing number of orders.

An early decision should be made as to whether the additional "power" required will be developed internally or whether an outside contractor will be used to handle all or a selected segment of the fulfillment function. Among the factors to be considered are the capital or borrowing ability available; management know-how; and the time required to become totally operational. Another is the need to free the executive team from day-to-day fulfillment, thereby enabling it to concentrate on marketing, merchandising, catalog production, circulation development, and inventory management.

There are a number of service organizations that can provide assistance ranging from total catalog fulfillment to specialized services such as telephone order-taking, continuity order-processing, and list maintenance. The magazine industry relies heavily on the use of outside contractors. Only the largest publishers perform subscription fulfillment internally. Reliance on contractors has enabled the majority of magazine publishers to concentrate on editorial work, advertisement selling, and circulation building, leaving fulfillment to professionals.

Fulfillment Options

There is no pat formula to determine whether a company should use outside services. Each situation has to be individually studied. Here are some of the available options and the benefits of each:

Contract Out the Total Fulfillment Task. This alternative begins with receiving orders by mail and telephone and continues through warehousing and shipping, including handling returns and responding to customer service contacts. The advantage can be cost savings because of sharing equipment and services with others and the availability of trained personnel to meet seasonal demands.

Employ a Data Processing Contractor. In this case a contractor is used to input orders, obtain credit approval, produce warehouse picking directives, maintain perpetual inventory records, and produce the management reports previously discussed. The direct marketer handles the physical fulfillment, customer service, and returns functions. This approach eliminates the need to acquire computer hardware and software and data processing technicians.

Utilize a Physical Fulfillment Contractor. This option assumes that the direct marketer would perform its own computer processing and customer service functions. This eliminates the requirement to buy, build, lease, expand, and equip and staff a distribution center.

Use a Telephone Contractor. This system provides that orders be received by a contractor and transmitted to the company. Because outside services are charged on a per-call basis, the cost is usually less than for a small internal function that requires overhead, personnel training, and equipment costs to handle varying volume levels. On the other hand, inside functions usually offer a more personal and responsive service to customers due to the availability of the database and the more intensive training that is provided.

Establish the Company's Fulfillment Function. This is the most prevalent practice, although the use of outside contractors has been increasing in recent years. With the availability of low-cost computers and computer packages, an effective system can be developed on a limited budget. Experienced fulfillment management is the keystone of an effective and economical internal system, and executives with the necessary skills are in short supply.

Using Fulfillment Contractors

There are two basic approaches to having fulfillment services provided by an outside organization. First is the use of contractors that offer a basically standard package. This could involve direct marketers who have developed and employ a comprehensive fulfillment system in their own operation and have decided to process other companies' orders on the same system. Similarly, a service company could offer their standard service to direct marketers. This approach is economical, but it raises concerns about privacy and security. Also, it limits the amount of customizing that can be provided to meet the company's special requirements.

The second approach is called facilities management. Here the company has a custom fulfillment system developed for its own application and its fulfillment is performed by a contractor in space dedicated solely to its own use. In summary, this enables a company to have its own system and facilities, while retaining a facility manager to run the function for a fee.

CONVENIENCE AND SERVICE PERFORMANCE LEVELS

The performance levels listed below are achieved by most of the major direct marketers who comprise almost two-thirds of the revenue of the direct marketing business.

Turnaround time on orders. The package should be received by the customer within 2 calendar weeks of mailing the order; the time should be less for telephone orders and for customers near the distribution center. As was mentioned earlier, it is a proven axiom in mail-order operations that the faster the order is fulfilled, the lower the unit-fulfillment cost. Therefore, quick service makes good sense from the standpoint of both customer relations and the bottom line.

Customer service response cycle. An answer should be received by the customer in the calendar week following the mailing of the letter. Considering incoming and outgoing mailing time and nonworking weekends, that leaves 2 or 3 working days to read, research, and respond.

In-Stock condition. Where merchandise is repeated in a following catalog or staple products are involved, less than 5 percent of the orders should be shipped incomplete. In the case of new products or fashion merchandise, not more than 15 percent of the orders should involve a back order.

Ratio of customer service contacts to orders. Only 4–6 percent of the shipped orders should result in an inquiry or adjustment. In the fashion business, the ratio increases to about 10 percent.

Returns. The number of returns is greatly affected by the clarity of the promotion, the fulfillment cycle, and the extent of merchandise inspection. Returns should be less than 8 percent unless it is a fashion business with size and color offerings. In the latter case, returns of 15–25 percent can be expected. In business-to-business sales, returns are in the 3–5 percent range. Approximately one-quarter of the returns will probably involve an exchange and re-shipment.

Answering telephone calls.   Both incoming orders and service calls should be answered 90 percent of the time without a holding delay. Seventy-five percent of customers' inquiries or problems should be resolved while customers are on the line. The abandon-call rate should be under 3 percent.

Serious complaints.   Less than 2 percent of the complaints should be consumer advocate letters, mail from governmental agencies, communications addressed to company officers, or letters indicating that the customer has written before and has not received an answer.

Work backlogs.   Orders in process should not exceed 1 day's shipments; in peak period, this can increase to 3 days.

Personnel turnover.   Fewer than 15 percent of the regular fulfillment employees should have less than 6 months' service.

Housekeeping.   The order-handling offices, the data center, and the warehouse should look neat and well organized. There should be a place for everything, and everything should be in its place. If the operation does not look well organized, it probably isn't.

MERCHANDISING RETURNS: A LOOMING AND CRITICAL PROBLEM

Merchandise returns have become a serious fulfillment problem that is permeating the entire direct marketing business. It impacts all products in different degrees, and all areas from product selection and ordering to fulfillment and customer service. Merchandise returns appear to be affecting direct marketing in three ways. First, returns impede the growth of buying direct. Research and focus groups report that returns are one of the most frustrating aspects of buying direct. Many nonbuyers indicate they do not order direct because of the fear of not getting what they ordered and therefore having to return it. Second, returns impact customer satisfaction. If the customer has to, or decides to, return a purchase, he or she has become a disappointed customer. Third, returns increase costs. Included in these expenses are such elements as the cost of original order handling, the loss of gross margin, and the cost of merchandise disposition/liquidation and refurbishing. In addition, there is the cost of the whole returns-handling process, from package opening and customer service to shipping-charge reimbursement, issuance of refunds, and the handling of exchanges.

Why have returns increased? The principal reasons are that

Customers are becoming more demanding and want better quality.

The practice of ordering multiple sizes or colors and keeping only one item is increasing.

Merchandise quality has deteriorated in some companies.

Fashion trends tend to make style and size selection difficult.

Catalog copy is unclear and frequently misleading.

Impulse telephone orders are multiplying and often result in a change of mind.

Back orders are increasing.

What can be done to combat the returns problem? Here are ten actions taken by those who have been most affected:

1. Make company personnel at all levels "returns conscious."
2. Establish returns reduction as a corporate goal.
3. Curtail mailing to chronic returners.
4. Cancel back orders after 45–60 days.
5. Limit the return period.
6. Intensify in-house quality inspection.
7. Train telephone personnel in giving proper-fit guidance and handling customers contemplating a return.
8. Include meaningful reason codes on the packing list and summarize what the customer has indicated.
9. Upgrade size-guidance in the catalog.
10. Provide meaningful and clear product installation and operating manuals.

THE 12 STEPS TO SUCCESSFUL FULFILLMENT

By following these 12 proven steps, a direct marketer can be assured that its fulfillment operation will deliver the superior level of service, quality, and profitability vital to its growth.

1. Establish Realistic and Attainable Objectives

Experience has shown that high service and low cost fulfillment are attainable goals for any company that sets its mind to it. Yet there are organizations, both well established or new to direct marketing, that frequently suffer from a different and regrettable mind set. They are either complacent with respect to service or they believe that high performance isn't attainable in their organization.

Management should not be satisfied with its operation until it is achieving the realistic performance objectives identified previously. Further, these positive intentions should be communicated to the entire organization. Experience has shown that this strategy in itself can immediately change attitudes and upgrade performance.

2. Acquire Professional Management

The specialized operating and control requirements inherent in direct marketing fulfillment require managers who have a proven track record of training, motivating, scheduling, and controlling the large numbers of clerical, data processing, and materials-handling workers involved in high-volume, rapid-order throughput. Further, individual managers must possess the systems and engineering skills appropriate to their specialty.

Fulfillment management experience need not necessarily be obtained from a catalog company. Data-processing and distribution background in book publishing, direct selling, general merchandise, drug, office supply, electronic wholesalers, and, even retailers, is often just as appropriate.

3. Develop a Part-Time Work Force

Those operating executives who have experienced the processing peaks and valleys common in direct marketing feel that a part-time work force is the most important element in maintaining service and controlling costs. The use of part-time employees is widespread throughout general industry and, in particular, in direct marketing. Employment data shows that 25 percent of the total workers in the United States work less than a full week. Part-time employment provides flexibility for both employees and employers.

Studies have shown that part-time workers are at least as productive as full-timers, and that in many cases they are more cost-effective because they don't usually receive fringe benefits and can be sent home when the work runs out. Part-timers can be used effectively in such operations as mail opening and sorting, taking telephone orders, order picking and packing, receiving merchandise, and responding to correspondence.

4. Obtain Adequate Space

A company can't operate efficiently, either in the office or in the warehouse, if it does not have adequate space and reasonably pleasant working conditions. Today, employees expect a good working environment. You can't keep a good work force in substandard conditions. Personnel will become less productive and will eventually move on.

Space impacts more than personnel morale. It also affects introduction of new equipment, workflow, supervision, security and pilferage, employee productivity, and housekeeping. It is frequently said that space is the cheapest element in the fulfillment cost structure.

5. Have Systems in Place Before Expansion

In the marketing process, fulfillment is the key element in achieving customer satisfaction. For this reason, it is critical that all the essential elements be in place before the new catalog is launched or a new promotion initiated. If merchandise is not on hand or orders cannot be handled properly, customers will be disappointed and reorders—the lifeblood of direct marketing—will not be forthcoming.

What good is business that cannot be handled? It will only result in bad customer relations and hurt the company's image. It could also result in no profits and a series of operating headaches.

6. Practice Quality Assurance

Quality is one of the most powerful ways a direct marketing company can differentiate its business from its competition. James D. Robinson III, chairman of American Express, is frequently quoted as saying his company's success is dependent on four factors: quality, quality, quality, and quality. Quality improvement starts with management's commitment to raise quality. Quality is then assigned as a specific responsibility for a senior operating executive, and a program is undertaken to make all employees quality-conscious.

A total quality program should involve these five elements:

- Internal quality control—reviewing work performed in a particular department and reporting the audit results
- External quality control—continually initiating test orders and returns
- Merchandise quality examination—inspecting all or a representative sampling of incoming products
- Questionnaires—enclosed in packages or performed on the telephone to determine the satisfaction level of customers
- Statistical reports—summarizing problems encountered with customers, adjustments made, and reasons for returns

7. Produce Operations Control Reports

A direct marketing company must establish meaningful and timely operations-control reports to manage order turnaround, direct labor expenses, and high-quality service. These reports are the fulfillment equivalent of navigation aides to a pilot or a profit-and-loss statement to a company CEO.

Data to be reported should include: output, in terms of orders processed, returns handled, and adjustments made; personnel hours; labor costs; and service control indices (benchmarks or budgets against which performance is compared). Depending upon the data, reports should be issued either daily or weekly. Weekly reports should be distributed to all top executives, not just to fulfillment management.

8. Install Productivity Improvement Programs

All of the large and efficient direct marketing companies have productivity programs in place. Their experience is that labor costs are 20–30 percent higher if they do not use work measurement techniques. In addition to cost savings, they promote improved methods and procedures, better supervisory control, and higher employee morale, as well as making it easier to forecast workforce requirements, carry out personnel evaluations, and standardize costs.

Installing productivity improvements involves these five basic steps:

- Establishing productivity as a company goal
- Assigning staff
- Installing a productivity information system
- Establishing basic standards
- Recognizing performance that exceeds standards

9. Utilize Telephone Monitoring

Telephone order taking and problem resolution represent the only personal contact a direct marketing company has with its customers. Therefore, it is essential that this contact be personal, friendly, courteous, attentive, and empathetic. The practice of call monitoring can assure that the desired level of service is being provided to your customers. With call monitoring, a third party (a monitor) listens to conversations between customers and telephone representatives. A full-time monitor is assigned when there are between 15 and 20 representatives.

Monitoring has proved to be very effective in:

Keeping telephone personnel on their toes

Identifying personnel who need further training

Isolating policies, procedures, and merchandise information that need clarification

Providing training case-examples

Protecting the company's image

10. Commit to Work Standardization

One of the basic operating characteristics present in an efficient fulfillment operation is work standardization. This refers to production disciplines and organization that assure that work is performed in the method that has been determined to be the most efficient. Workers involved in similar tasks perform them in an almost identical manner. With minor exceptions, personnel are encouraged not to vary from the basic practices.

To further support the benefits of work standardization, individual work stations are standardized, arranged, and equipped to make it easy and pleasant for the worker. Further, there is no interruption in production time to obtain work and supplies or to deliver completed work to the next station. Where practical, this is accomplished with fixed transportation systems, such as conveyors, or by service personnel.

11. Impress Personnel with the Importance of the Customer

One of the prime responsibilities of management is to focus all employees on satisfying and developing customer loyalty. The principal people responsible· for this process are fulfillment personnel, because they are the ones who are fulfilling the promises made to the customer in the catalog or promotion.

When workers are motivated to think of themselves as the most important link to customers, they develop a self-respect and a sense of responsibility. Many companies give lip service to this concept, but where the importance of the customer has been emphasized, it can be readily discerned in the care exercised at each step in the fulfillment process.

12. Maintain Near-Zero Backlogs

Efficient fulfillment functions operate according to the principle that keeping current on a daily basis is mandatory. This means that, except for the small amount of work carried over from the previous day, which is used to get the operation started in the morning, there is no work in a unit other than processing or filling the orders that came in today.

Experience has shown that when near-zero backlog is adhered to, productivity increases by as much as 40 percent. In the near-zero backlog technique, an office or warehouse runs without the security of a work backlog. Management and employees are forced to give a high level of service, or they are faced with no service at all.

CONCLUSION

What has been emphasized in this chapter is that fulfillment *service* and *quality* are vital to the growth of the direct marketing channel of distribution. If both are improved, using some of the suggestions offered in this and subsequent chapters, more consumers and businesses will order from their homes and offices and the individual direct marketing companies that serve them will prosper.

32

Lead Management Systems

Suti Prakash

The Direct Marketing Group, Inc.
New York, N.Y.

This chapter addresses lead management systems: what such systems are, their benefits, and the characteristics of effective systems.

A lead management system consists of a systematic and organized process for receiving, recording, qualifying, distributing, and tracking leads for a product or service. Its purpose is to enhance the effectiveness of a lead generation program by helping to assure that all leads are followed up and managed properly. For a lead management system to be successful, it should be timely, clear, consistent, and complete. It should also make the sales force a partner in the process.

LEAD GENERATION AND LEAD MANAGEMENT

Direct marketers use lead generation programs for products and services that require a multistep sale; because the product is too expensive to sell off the page, it requires a demonstration, a visit, or a corporate purchase order. Such programs are discussed in Chapter 43, Lead Generation: An Overview.

What is important to note here is that the leads generated by these programs are the starting point, the input, of a lead management system. Thus, lead management is a continuation and should be an integral part of the lead generation program. Basically, this requires that all fulfillment activities and materials must be consistent with the initial communication.

Fulfillment activities include all contacts with the prospect that stem from the ad or mailing that produced the lead; these may range from a telephone inquiry, to any information that may be sent to the prospect, to the meeting with a sales-person. If the materials sent to the prospect are of a lower quality than the communication that generated the lead, not only will a less favorable image of the business be conveyed, but the sale may be jeopardized.

A lead management system will also provide the feedback that will help to fine-tune the lead generation programs. This feedback is both quantitative (the response percentage, for example) and qualitative (prospect/customer input regarding follow-up to their inquiry, for example). It is not an exaggeration to say that a well-designed, well-run lead management system is critical to the ultimate success of a lead generation program.

A LEAD MANAGEMENT SYSTEM

A lead management system is a process that takes a prospect from his/her initial inquiry about a product or service through the various stages necessary to make the sale. Such a system must track and monitor the inquiry from its initial receipt all the way through to its final disposition, whether this means that a sale was made, that the prospect requires follow-up at a later time, or that the prospect is not interested. However, since it is salespeople who make the actual sale, the system should be designed and operated to support the sales force. A lead management system assures that all leads are followed up, and it monitors the quality and effectiveness of the follow-up actions.

THE LEAD MANAGEMENT PROCESS

Traditionally, the process has meant generating leads, fulfilling them with literature, and then referring the leads to the sales force. But all too often, the leads are never contacted, or the contact is made long after the inquiry is received. In either case, the sale is often lost—and, more important, the prospect may be lost. While this traditional process is basically correct, the challenge is not just to fulfill inquiries with literature, but also to qualify, track, and monitor the lead; not just to refer the lead to the sales force, but to involve the sales force in the lead generation and qualification process by obtaining their input during program planning.

An important step that should be added to this process is that of capturing lead data and analyzing results. An effective lead management system is a closed-loop system, one that uses the feedback provided by the system to improve the system itself. For example, sales data is used to evaluate and, if appropriate, change lead generation programs. Such data, combined with research, can be used to fine-tune the lead generation program, the fulfillment literature, or the lead qualification criteria.

Effective lead management systems include the following activities:

1. Lead receipt
2. Lead recording

3. Lead qualification

4. Literature fulfillment

5. Lead distribution to sales force

6. Follow-up on lead disposition

7. Updating of database

8. Lead analysis

9. Reporting of lead data

Some programs may not require all these steps. For example, if all leads are to be followed up by the sales force, the lead qualification step may not be necessary. Similarly, there may be no need for literature fulfillment if "send information" is not an option offered to prospects. But such programs are likely to be infrequent, so consideration should be given to building these nine steps into any lead management system. It is simple to factor all these steps into the system, and a comprehensively designed system will have a long-term utility.

It should be noted that while a manual lead management system can be set up, a computerized system will be more efficient and useful. A personal computer with hard disk memory and a few software programs—such as a database management program, a spreadsheet, and a word processing program—are all that is necessary to run a sophisticated lead management system. (Alternatively, lead management software is available, eliminating the need to develop it from scratch.)

1. Lead Receipt

Leads are generally received over the telephone, via the mail, and increasingly by fax. Sometimes leads may be received "in person." For example, prospects may hand their business card to a salesperson at a trade show or drop their card at the exhibit.

A second consideration in lead receipt management is whether the leads are to be processed at a central location or at branch offices. While the receipt of leads may appear to be automatic, it requires planning. Planning for lead receipt should include the following steps:

- Telephone line(s) and post office box(es) should be set up as appropriate.

- Telephone representatives should be trained to handle inquiries. The reps should be knowledgeable about the product and should be able to answer basic questions about it. If leads are to be qualified, then the reps need to be trained to conduct the qualification and be provided with a qualification script.

- The system should be able to handle the anticipated volume. This can be a major issue, if, for example, the commercial is on prime-time TV, when a very large number of calls may be received within minutes or hours after the commercial runs. This will cause peaks and valleys in staffing needs.

- If the leads are going to be handled at branches or other decentralized locations, then these locations' ability and capacity to receive and track leads must be evaluated. As the number of locations increases, quality control and good tracking become difficult. Ideally, leads should be received and processed at a central location. If the leads need to be pursued immediately, they can be phoned or faxed to the branches. Branch personnel should, nevertheless, be in the loop of a lead generation program. Often, customers may respond to an ad or mailing by bypassing the response system and calling their salesperson directly. So the sales force should know what was communicated that generated the lead.

2. Lead Recording

Recording the leads received is a critical element of any lead management system, since the information recorded is the foundation of a database. What data is recorded depends upon what was requested on the response form or on the phone. Ideally, all the data available on the response form should be recorded. This presumes that if the data was not useful, it would not have been requested.

The data elements most frequently recorded are:

1. Name, including title of respect (Mr., Mrs., Ms., Miss)

2. Corporate title

3. Company and division

4. Address, including department or mail-drop number

5. Telephone number, including the extension

6. Fax number

7. Whether the inquirer is a customer or prospect

8. Customer account number and/or the customer's sales rep's name

9. Product or service of interest

10. Lead source information, including the medium, the specific ad or creative execution, the offer, and the date of the ad

11. Response medium (mail, phone, fax, trade show, etc.)

12. Date of lead receipt

This is a typical list, neither complete nor exhaustive. The list should be based on what the lead is for and what actions will take place after the lead is received. Obviously, corporate title and company are not necessary for consumer programs. Similarly, if the program is a mailing to prospects and the customer list has been merged with and purged from the prospect list, it isn't necessary to ask for a customer account number or sales rep's name.

Alternatively, in a customer mailing, filling in such information in advance should be considered. Previously known information, such as the customer's account number and sales rep's name, can be imbedded in a code to save space on the order form and speed up lead recording. However, to update the database, the information should be printed out so that customers can easily make changes in it.

Another category of information that is generally coded relates to the ad or mailing itself. The medium, the ad, the product, the offer, and the date of the ad or mailing can be coded. (Such codes are called source codes.) Even broadcast ads can be source coded, simply by assigning a different telephone number or extension to each variation of the ad.

However, no matter how it is done, it's very likely that there will be some inquiries in which the prospects cannot remember where or when they saw or heard the message. It must be decided how such "no-source-code" leads will be recorded. A common way is to proportionately allocate these leads across different ads, or else to maintain a no-source-code category.

There are many programs that ask for much more information than has been specified above. Examples of such programs are credit card solicitations that ask for detailed financial data about the prospect, or travel solicitations that ask about destination, class of service, number in the party, etc. In such instances, it must be decided what data is needed from the prospect. Of course, sometimes this data can be obtained during lead qualification, rather than during lead generation, thereby enhancing initial response rates.

3. Lead Qualification

Lead qualification is a matter of definition. What is considered to be a "qualified" lead? The reason for qualifying leads is to determine how much effort and expense should be put against different leads, based on an assessment of the likelihood of a sale. A working definition of a qualified lead is that it is an inquiry that has a high potential for a sale (and potential is a matter of degree).

In lead qualification it is axiomatic that:

- There is no perfect lead, since it can't be known how good a lead is until it is pursued and concluded, whether or not it results in a sale.
- All leads have some qualification already built in, by the very nature of the way they are generated. For example, the media that are used will reach only certain people, and the offer that is made will interest only some of the people reached.
- The more that leads are qualified during the lead generation process, the fewer the number of leads that will be generated.

The basic objective of lead qualification is to determine the prospect's degree of interest and the timing of the need for the product or service. The challenge is to manage the qualification process so that the quantity of leads is balanced with their quality. In developing the criteria for qualification, input should be obtained from the sales force. Nothing can kill a lead generation program faster than the sales reps' lack of interest in the leads. They become disinterested if the leads are of poor quality. At the very least, the sales reps' involvement at this stage will make them more receptive to pursuing the leads.

The criteria selected should be regularly tested to determine how effective they are. This means testing not only whether too little or too much information is requested, but also whether it's the appropriate or useful information to request.

Leads can be qualified before or after they are received. However, most often it is more efficient and cost-effective to qualify them at both stages. The initial screening is done through the data requested on the reply form and through the response options provided. For example, if the sole response option is "have a sales rep call," with no provision for "send literature," then only the more interested prospects are likely to inquire.

Telephone follow-up is the preferred way to qualify leads, although mail surveys are occasionally used. Telephone qualification is preferred because it is timelier and it is easier for the prospect than filling out a form. Mail should be used when phone contact cannot be made and when lead volume precludes 100 percent phone qualification.

Information that is elicited for lead qualification may include:

- Planned purchase timing
- Current product/service provider and length of that relationship
- Purchase criteria
- Prospect's role in purchase (influencer, user, decision maker)
- Reason for need (new function, expansion, replacement)
- Best time for sales rep to call

4. Literature Fulfillment

Literature fulfillment can be an automatic step in the lead management process, or it can be an option based on how qualified the lead is. In a multistep program, the first communication may be designed only to pique interest, with the next step being to send the information necessary for the prospect to make a decision. Examples of such programs include investment products where the prospectus needs to be sent to inquirers, and travel products where the prospects request specific information. In such programs, literature fulfillment becomes a necessity.

In programs where a sales visit or product demonstration is a possible response to an inquiry, literature may be sent to prospects who do not meet the qualification criteria.

In all instances, fulfillment materials can impact the company's image in the prospect's mind and thereby affect the potential for a sale. Some guidelines are:

- Literature should be fulfilled on a timely basis—ideally within 3 days of receipt of inquiry. The oft-repeated truism that a cold lead is a dead lead applies just as much to literature fulfillment as it does to sales rep follow-up.
- The materials sent should be consistent in their tonality and quality with the ad or mailing that generated the lead.
- The literature should be complete; it must provide the information that was offered.
- Either an order should be requested, or the prospect should be advised of the next step(s).
- It is often more appropriate to include qualification questions in the literature

fulfillment package than in the initial ad. The questions can be included on the response form or in a separate survey.

- For tracking and monitoring purposes, the prospect database should be tagged to indicate what materials were sent to whom, and when.

5. Lead Distribution

Once leads have been qualified, they must be distributed to the sales force for follow-up. The three things to consider are: (a) allocation of leads; (b) method or medium of lead distribution; and (c) the information to be distributed with the lead.

Leads are generally allocated based on the sales reps' geographic proximity to the prospects, since this facilitates sales visits. However, if special product knowledge is required, then the leads may be allocated to specialists without consideration of the prospects' geography.

Allocation depends upon how the sales force is organized: by product, by geography, or both. The other consideration in lead allocation is capacity: can the branch handle the volume of leads in a timely fashion? If not, a change in the distribution of such overflow volume must be considered. It may also be possible to control lead generation programs to regulate lead flow to a manageable volume.

The methods or media used to distribute leads are as varied as the available media. Commonly used media are: phone, fax, computer-to-computer, courier services, or the U.S. Postal Service. Each of these has advantages which must be weighed against its costs.

Distribution by phone, fax, or computer-to-computer is the quickest way to distribute leads. However, phone communication (other than voice mail) is rarely advisable, since it is difficult to convey detailed information and have the sales reps or their support personnel accurately record the necessary information about the prospect and the nature of the inquiry. Fax and computer transmissions avoid this problem, as does the mail option. Mail is obviously slower and should be avoided so that the leads are "aged" as little as possible.

The sales force needs information about the leads that are distributed to them. Some of this information, including the relevant details of the lead generation program—the target audience, medium, offer, etc.—should be distributed before the sales reps begin to receive leads. This is necessary so that the reps know exactly what the prospect is inquiring about. While such materials can be faxed or sent via computer, mail distribution will show the ad materials better and more economically. When communicating such information, care should be taken to explain any special offers or marketing tests that impact the sale, such as a special price, trade-in, or value-added offer.

With each lead that is distributed, the basic information about the prospect (name, title, company, etc.) should be provided, as should the qualification information (degree of interest, role in product purchase, purchase timing, etc.). Other data to be included are items such as when the lead was received, the medium that the prospect used to respond, and whether any literature was sent. (Additionally, if a central location is making appointments for sales reps, then the appointment information must be conveyed.)

The leads should be communicated in clear language without using codes to convey information. While sales reps may be expected to know product numbers and other product details, they should not be required to know source codes.

The final necessity is to distribute leads on a timely basis. As noted earlier, the longer the time period between the receipt of a lead and the follow-up action, the less likely it is that a sale will result from the inquiry.

6. Lead Disposition

A lead management system must close the loop by getting input on the final action on a lead. The purpose of ascertaining lead disposition is to evaluate the effectiveness of the lead generation program as well as of the lead management process. The purpose should not be to follow up on the sales force.

However, sales reps are notoriously reluctant to do any paperwork, and lead disposition data tends to rank very low in priority for them. Therefore, the challenge is both to convince the sales reps of the usefulness of their input on lead disposition, and to make it as easy as possible for them to provide the data.

The sales reps benefit from providing such data because with it, the lead generation program or the lead qualification criteria can be modified to improve lead quantity and quality. Good leads make for sales successes.

Making it easy for the reps to provide input is a matter of not asking them to do any more than is absolutely necessary. Only data that is actionable and readily available should be requested, so that the sales reps spend minimal time providing the information.

A simple yet effective format is based on distributing one lead per sheet with an attached copy or perforated response form. The basic lead disposition data required for analysis are:

- Was the lead sold or not?
- If it was sold, what was the product and dollar amount?
- If it was not sold, what follow-up, if any, is planned?
- Any comments, such as, why not sold?

Other information about the lead, such as the source code, the response medium, etc., should be precoded on the form to facilitate updating the prospect database.

There are two other ways to obtain at least partial lead disposition information. One is to match the prospect file against the customer file after waiting an appropriate time for the lead to be followed up. The limitations to this approach are that: (a) only sales made during the elapsed time period will be identified, without any data on deferred purchases or future potential; and (b) the records may not match, either because the final buyer is different from the original prospect or because the company/division name is spelled differently. The accuracy of company name matches depends upon the sophistication of the match code system.

The second way of obtaining lead disposition data is to follow up directly with the prospects. When this approach is used, it is generally positioned as a helpful inquiry to the prospect, with questions such as: was the requested literature received, does the product meet needs, etc. The limitations are that: (a) the response rate to such a survey is likely to be low, and (b) a different person from the original prospect may have concluded the sale. However, prospect surveys are useful even if not necessary to determine lead disposition, because such surveys provide input on the timeliness, completeness, and quality of lead follow-up.

7. Updating the Database

When data is received on lead disposition, the database must be updated to reflect the disposition. Updating is necessary so that the leads can be properly tracked and evaluated.

Updating generally means that sale/no-sale data, including the dollar amount, should be appended to the prospect records. Additionally, records should be flagged when a later follow-up is indicated. Such flagging will enable the lead management system to serve as a "tickler" file for future actions. If a second call by a sales rep is not warranted, the effectiveness of a mail or phone follow-up to the prospect at a later date should be tested. The timing of this communication will depend upon the prospect's level of interest and on the sales cycle for the product.

8. Lead Analysis

While lead analysis is noted as the next step, it is an ongoing process that starts when the leads are recorded. At that time, a preliminary analysis on lead volume can be made, though more conclusive lead value analysis requires lead disposition data.

What can be analyzed depends upon the data that is captured about the lead. A good overall measure of lead generation programs is the cost per lead and cost per sale. Other overall measures include the response rate or percentage and rate of conversion to sales. These measurements are relatively easy to calculate, and all of them should be analyzed. Lead analysis is also done to evaluate the impact of different elements on the success of the program. These elements are both program-related and prospect-related.

Program-related elements are those that are the same for a given prospect segment and are controllable, including:

Media used

Creative execution and format

Product or offer

Timing and seasonality

Alternative fulfillment materials

Response medium

This means that the relative effectiveness of variations in these elements can be determined. For example, if media and offer are being tested, lead analysis will provide the cost per sale of each medium and offer variation.

Prospect-related elements are those that vary by prospect or prospect subsegments. These elements can be controlled only to the extent that the message or offer can be targeted, including:

Prospects' SIC grouping

Company size and geography

Title/function of prospects

Trade-in or upgrade offer

With lead analysis, a direct marketing program's effectiveness can be improved by determining:

- What title/function at what kind of company (SIC, size, geography) is the best prospect for the product?
- What offer, with which creative execution and format, should be made in which media, and when, to generate the best prospects?

It should be noted that in addition to production and media costs, lead expenses can include the costs of lead receipt (the cost of business reply mail or 800-number calls), the qualification process, and fulfillment materials. What cost factors are included depends upon individual company needs. Also, since lead disposition data is rarely complete, projections may have to be made based on the disposition data about an adequate sampling of leads received.

9. Reporting of Lead Data

Three types of lead data are generally reported to management: (a) lead distribution and control; (b) lead status; and (c) lead analysis. All lead reports may be segmented; that is, selective elements may be included for specific audiences. For example, while branch management needs to know individual lead details, marketing management may need only summary reports about lead distribution. The format, content, frequency, and distribution of lead data are a matter of individual company needs: there are no universals.

Lead data reporting begins with the distribution of leads. (Lead distribution is described in step 5 above.) Lead control reports are used to provide summary data. For example, a report that summarizes which leads were assigned to a particular branch will be helpful to the branch manager. Such a report should include the prospect's name, company, address, product interest, and date of assignment. It does not need to include all the known details about the prospect or the lead source, since such information is made available with the lead when it is distributed. The report for regional or corporate sales management may show only the number of leads, by product, assigned to a branch, and omit all information about individual leads. As with much reporting, the reports for senior management present more aggregate than individual data.

Lead status reports are used to report on the status of outstanding leads. Again, as with the lead assignment report described above, the basic status reports show which leads are open and which have been closed. A useful status report is one that summarizes how many leads have been assigned and closed, by current period and cumulatively; how many were sold; and how old the open leads are.

The last category of lead reports deals with lead analysis, discussed in step 8 above. Again, various audiences will be interested in different analyses. For example, branch management probably cannot benefit from promotional analysis, but will want lead closure analysis.

An audience that is often forgotten in reporting data is the sales force. Sharing data with them not only keeps the sales force informed and in the lead management loop, it also reinforces the quality of the leads that are referred to the sales reps by showing the sales generated from the leads. Since the sales force is critical to the ultimate success of any lead generation program, it is very important to have their involvement in and commitment to these programs and to following up and closing the leads.

SUMMARY

A lead management system is vital to the success of any lead generation program because such a system will increase sales potential. An effective lead management system involves both a disciplined process and the cooperation of the people involved in the entire process, including marketing and sales staffs. Such systems work best if the process and the activities are planned in conjunction with the planning of lead generation programs. The sales staff should be involved in the planning to assure that they will be interested in following up on leads and reporting on lead closure.

A good lead management system has the following characteristics:

- It responds to inquiries on a timely basis, on the proven principle that a cold lead is a dead lead.

- It utilizes fulfillment materials that are complete and consistent with the marketing approaches and the image conveyed in advertising.

- It qualifies leads so that the sales reps want to pursue the leads and not ignore them.

The system should be set up to record and track only actionable data, and not just to collect information because it is available. The process should seek to complete the information loop so as to determine not only how many leads were generated, but also how good the leads were. The system should be flexible enough to accommodate the needs of different lead generation programs, and be able to provide information relevant and useful to diverse audiences (marketing, sales, finance). To assure that the system continues to perform, it should be monitored regularly.

A well-designed and well-operated lead management system is a necessary investment to optimize the return on sales and marketing activities.

33
Catalog Fulfillment

Jeff Coopersmith

DIRECTEL, Inc.
Columbus, Ohio

INTRODUCTION

Generally speaking, the people who run catalogs are marketers, merchandisers, creative people. Yet their ability to succeed is dependent on efficient and effective fulfillment. Too often in this business, entrepreneurs become captives of their own creative ideas. They concentrate on the marketing strategies, believing that the operations side will take care of itself.

Certainly a beautifully produced catalog sets the stage for your relationship with the customer, but remember that you must depend on the fulfillment function to complete your promises. Catalog fulfillment is a highly specialized, complex, intensely managed integration of people and systems and service. No matter how well conceived your marketing plan, if it can't get the merchandise to the customer quickly, efficiently, and accurately, you're likely to fail. Either operational inefficiency will prove too costly, or poor service will drive your customers away.

If you are new to direct marketing, one of the first things you need to do is plan and organize your fulfillment operation. If, on the other hand, you are an old hand in the business, you'll be on the lookout for a few new fulfillment tricks.

Although every catalog operation is unique, this chapter offers a general overview to guide you through the fulfillment process so that you may better manage this complex and critically important function. Before we delve into the basics, let's set the stage with some background information.

Fulfillment Standards

In determining your company standards you should consider both your operating budget and catalog customer expectations. The following list defines the standard fulfillment expectation levels in the catalog industry:

- Orders for in-stock merchandise shipped within 48 hours
- Returns processed within 72 hours of receipt
- Customer service issues handled within 48 hours of receipt
- 85 percent of all phone calls answered within 20 seconds, with an average wait time of less than 30 seconds and an abandon rate of less than 3 percent

Key Areas

Catalogers divide the fulfillment function into two key areas of function and responsibility:

In the Warehouse	In the Office
Receiving	Telemarketing
Quality Assurance	Customer Service
Returns Processing	Caging
Inventory Control	Order Entry
Picking and Packing	Computer System
Shipping	Telephone System

SETTING PARAMETERS

This planning phase involves a series of exercises aimed at understanding your business. The exercises involve the building of financial, operational, and organizational models based on revenue forecasts and anticipated characteristics. The characteristics, known as *parameters,* represent the building blocks of the operation. Below is a list of parameters that affect the key areas of the fulfillment process.

Order Volume. The availability of capital usually dictates your catalog circulation. In turn, order volume depends on circulation. The entire fulfillment operation — size, components, maybe even location — is dependent on projected order volume. Once you know your circulation size, you must anticipate response rates in your market and forecast volume. For instance, if you have a circulation of 500,000 catalogs and can expect a 1.5 percent response rate, your projected order volume is 7,500 orders.

Hours of Operation. Many of the expenses you will incur, including those for overhead and personnel, are influenced by the hours you choose to be open for business. You can limit your costs by having phone representatives during normal waking hours only, replacing them with a phone message system and/or transfer calls to a telemarketing firm at night.

Order Methods. The manner in which your orders come to you—via 800 lines, toll lines, mail, or facsimile (fax) machine—influences your personnel and equipment requirements. Determine which options you're going to provide for your customers and build the operation procedures associated with each. Don't forget to include customer service calls and catalog-request volume in your consideration of personnel and phone lines.

Merchandise Information. The number of stock-keeping units (SKUs), line items, sets, inventory turns per year, peak inventory volume, assembly requirements, and the size, stackability, and type (hanging or folded, soft goods or hard goods) of your product greatly influence your warehouse space requirements. The computer software system you select dictates your ability to manage the merchandise in the system and in the warehouse.

Order Characteristics. Knowing the percentage of orders that are drop-shipped from manufacturers, the percentage of back orders, and the average number of units per order affects warehouse space needs, labor requirements, and demands on your computer system. As you might expect, drop-shipped items eliminate the need for space in your warehouse. Back orders put added stress on data processing and productivity. The system must generate 30-day, 60-day, and 90-day Federal Trade Commission notices for back orders. Split shipments, in particular, require duplicated effort in picking and packing time and extra shipping costs. One 2-pound box, for instance, obviously costs less to ship than two 1-pound boxes.

Special Services. Offering gift boxes, cards, and wrap requires additional packing time and, depending on the volumes, additional personnel. Customization procedures such as engraving and monogramming require extra space and special skills. Before offering a special service in your catalog, you must determine how it will be handled in your operation.

Forecasting fulfillment parameters is probably one of the most frustrating number games you'll ever play. It is extremely important, however, to establish each projection carefully, because every aspect of your operation is developed from these parameters.

ORGANIZATION AND FUNCTION

Executives

Although most catalog company hierarchies are represented at the executive level by finance, operations, marketing, and merchandising, there is a trend to include an executive management information systems (MIS) position as well.

Given the impact of technology on the direct marketing industry in general and on operations specifically, this should come as no great surprise. MIS represents the "system": all the hardware, software, and ancillary equipment that a company relies on to make the organization (i.e., people, equipment, and all resources) efficient and productive. As the functional requirements of your company evolve and change, so does the system and, as a direct result, the operation. The capabilities of your computer and related systems are the backbone of efficient and effective fulfillment.

Management

Typically, the fulfillment operation relies heavily on the office operations manager operating in complement with the warehouse operations manager. Depending on order volume, these divisions can be supported by many other management positions. In today's technologically rich environment, each management position requires a working knowledge of fulfillment techniques and an understanding of the data processing (DP) support system to be truly effective.

But besides performing the day-to-day functions, managers must have an eye on the future as well. They must watch the industry trends, set and revise associate performance standards, and constantly look for new and better ways to operate within their area. As you may surmise, this forces most managers in fulfillment to wear at least three hats: the "then," the "now," and the "what if"! In addition, and just as important, the manager must work in concert with MIS to match operational requirements with new and existing DP technologies that can enhance the fulfillment process.

The fulfillment function is supported by two operations areas: the *office* and the *warehouse*. In most operations *administration* supports both the office and the warehouse. It is charged with the handling of all accounting, communication, supplies management, budgeting, and personnel. While the following two groups interface directly or indirectly with the catalog customer, it is the charter of administration to provide the framework and materials necessary to make the other office areas fail-safe.

Office Operations

Order processing receives and enters all new orders by phone or by mail/fax. Phone operator activity is monitored via the report capabilities of the automatic call distributor (ACD). In the mail/fax order area, the caging and phone order entry functions, as well as other clerical activities, must be tracked to measure efficiency and establish productivity standards.

Customer service handles pending orders and other inquiries as well as complaints. Good customer service is absolutely necessary. While these associates should aspire to efficiency, their prime motivation must be to resolve customer problems and save the sale if possible.

There is some debate as to whether order entry and customer service should be supported by the same telephone number. The need to maintain the two areas separately is determined by your order volume as well as by operator pro-

ductivity issues. As your call volume grows, it becomes increasingly difficult to
manage the two functions as one. You will quickly determine that the productivity of order entry operators is very different from that of customer service
operators. So creating performance standards for one individual handling both
is tricky at best.

A final word on the office associates. Depending on your order volume, it is
possible for all three functions (order entry, mail and phone, and customer service) to be handled by the same associate. Systems tools, such as order entry
screens designed to up-sell and cross-sell, prompt generic answers to product
and policy inquiries, and detect input mistakes, are expediting the order handling process and reducing the cost of office labor overall.

Warehouse Operations

The simplest breakdown of the warehouse functions must include: *receiving*
and *quality assurance* checks of new merchandise; *returns processing* of customer merchandise; *inventory control*; and *shipping* of parcels to customers.
The warehouse staff is charged with maintaining the merchandise so that the
orders may be processed accurately and efficiently.

STAFFING FOR SUCCESS

Hiring Associates

A successful fulfillment operation depends on finding and keeping the right people. Since people are the backbone of a catalog business, don't underestimate the
amount of time the hiring process requires. By spending more time interviewing in
advance of actually hiring, you can dramatically reduce associate turnover.

Pre-employment Screening Techniques

In addition to completing a company-specific employment application and personal interview, consider using other pre-employment screening techniques,
such as written integrity tests, before hiring an associate. For example, there are
multiple choice questionnaires designed to assess an individual's character.
These tests can tell you if a person is prone to violent behavior, dishonesty, or
otherwise unsuitable for certain types of employment. Medically supervised
physicals and drug screenings are recommended.

It's also advisable to have the office manager call and voice-test prospective
phone representatives, because a pleasing voice creates a pleasant buying experience for your customer. Make every effort to match the personalities of your
customer service representatives with those of your customer base. Studies show
that the phone representative and the customer are more comfortable if they
share common interests.

Start-up Personnel

For a smooth start-up (new business or new catalog), plan to have most of your
personnel in place 2 to 4 weeks prior to mailing the catalog. New employees can

assist in setting up the office and warehouse facilities if you are just staring out. In either case, always plan an adequate amount of time for the all-important training effort.

Flexible Associates

Since it is unrealistic to expect a work force that processes 20 orders per day in June to process 100 orders per day in November and December, you'll need more associates during the peak season. Consider building an organization of permanent part-time associates. These people should be skilled, well-trained, *and* available year round to complement your full-time work force. You can keep a flexible staff loyal to your company by offering competitive hourly rates with increases, accrued vacation pay, and medical benefits.

The profile of the ideal permanent part-timer is an individual who is not interested in working full-time, but is seeking supplemental income. Look for flexible people who require little notice to work extended hours—college students, housewives, disabled persons, and retired people, to name a few.

Lastly, if you can afford to work with a reputable employment firm, do it. This will reduce the initial time required to screen for certain positions.

Associate Work Areas

The selection of work stations for *all* of your associates deserves time and thought. To perform the functions of his/her job effectively and efficiently, each associate needs to have sufficient space, a clean environment, and the necessary tools.

TRAINING

Every associate, from CSRs and support staff to pickers and packers, needs to know his/her job. If this sounds simple, be forewarned: it isn't. Fulfillment is a complex series of functions systematically linked for efficiency.

Procedures

To assure good customer service, *every* associate must be familiar with the company policies and procedures, as well as receiving job-specific training relative to his/her job function. In addition, some associates require special training and a license to operate equipment such as forklifts. Last but not least, be sure to build outside training needs, such as software classes, into the process and the budget.

Training takes anywhere from 3 days to 2 weeks for most entry-level associates such as mail handlers, receiving and returns clerks, and other associates who are cross-trained to support another job function. Preparing a person for a management position takes substantially more time.

Customer Service Representatives

For CSRs supporting a simple and easy-to-understand product line, a 3-day training agenda might consist of a half day reviewing the products, policies, and procedures, and 2½ days of working on the phone and CRT with an accomplished associate. More complex products, such as computer peripherals and business equipment, usually require more training and hands-on experience.

A catalog product manual is a great reference guide for phone representatives and an absolute necessity for good customer service. Create your own product manual by removing the binding of your catalog and putting the sheets in a three-ring binder. Behind each catalog page provide the detail necessary to support each item displayed; for example, dimensions, true color, weight, or other features not easily seen in the catalog photograph. Also, sophisticated systems allow you to enter SKU-specific reference information directly into the system. As a result, CSRs can access this on-line data during the order-entry process. Your vendors can be very useful in helping you compile this data for your CSRs. Remember, a well-prepared phone representative can sell more and, in the process, facilitate greater customer satisfaction.

Management Programs

Although many catalogers recruit at colleges, many associates begin their careers as part-timers while pursuing their degrees in a variety of subject areas. Some companies offer intern positions as well. Extensive experience and/or inherent ability should be highly regarded, and associates without degrees may be selected and encouraged by management to participate in career development programs.

Since there is no formal fulfillment education available, a requisite skills management training program in complement with on-the-job training and mentoring is quite effective. The classroom should emphasize: 1) the marketing side of DM; 2) finance; 3) controlling and measuring fulfillment; 4) working with hourly associates; and 5) developing and improving productivity standards. Lateral moves are encouraged, so that management trainees will have a broad-based working knowledge of the fulfillment environment.

Recognition

A key to guiding your associates toward achieving their peak efficiencies is to train your managers to recognize good performance. Encourage them to get to know their people, be active in the mentoring process, and provide incentives whenever possible.

CALCULATING ASSOCIATE PRODUCTIVITY

To find out how well your associates are performing their jobs, you need to gather and evaluate statistical data on productivity. To calculate productivity, first identify each labor task as a measurable unit. By dividing the total units of output by the total labor hours associated with the activity, you have a current performance statistic for a given task.

A reverse of this process is to set performance standards and calculate their associated labor costs. Eventually, after accumulating output and cost data on each task, you can summarize the information into the total labor cost per unit of output for the fulfillment operation.

You may initially need to make well-educated guesses (for example, the number of units your pickers and packers will move in an hour). Since efficiencies will vary by product type, every statistic should, of course, improve with experience.

Communicate the productivity standard for each task to your associates and measure individual performance against it. As a result of this monitoring activity, each associate can measure his/her performance against the standard and the performance of their peers. Also, if an associate falls short in accomplishing the standards, you can quickly intercede to find out why.

While each associate must know his or her function, it is up to the manager to determine how these processes mesh together. By calculating standards and measuring results, you can determine what processes should be combined for higher productivity and lower labor expense. Lastly, it is always to your advantage to motivate and involve your associates by encouraging them to constantly seek out and report their ideas for efficiency and improving performance.

INVENTORY CONTROL

Your computer system handles repetitive inventory tasks such as counting merchandise and compiling the day's demand. A good system updates inventory records instantly so that the merchandise is immediately available and orders can be filled expediently. As a result of the process, you have a perpetually current listing of what and how much merchandise is in your warehouse. This data can be used effectively throughout your organization.

Order Entry/Customer Service

The ability to access inventory records as an on-line resource enhances your level of customer service. The CSR can advise the customer if the merchandise is in stock; or, if a back-order situation exists, when the next shipment is due. When an item is significantly back-ordered or unavailable, the system must be able to offer the most likely cross-sell opportunity from existing inventory.

Orders Out, Ship Confirmations

Some catalogers live by the credo that once the order is in the warehouse, their system considers the merchandise "out the door." Working on this principle, credit cards are charged before goods are actually shipped, and the cataloger maintains a position of "crossed fingers" in regard to fulfillment. But system-controlled inventory in conjunction with bar-code technology and a manifest system can make guessing when the order actually shipped a thing of the past.

Product Vendors

Since each SKU originates with a purchase order and a vendor, you should maintain a complete history of all product-related transactions with your suppliers. Your system should keep track of goods from the time you forward a purchase order until the merchandise is delivered to and accepted by your customer.

To simplify the receiving process, instruct your vendors to mark inbound shipments with a purchase order (PO) number(s). This PO triggers the system to call up the vendor record, a listing of all pending transactions. Your receiver may then compare the details of the goods received with the PO and note any discrepancies.

Receiving

When new merchandise is received, the system assigns an SKU number and selects an appropriate prime or bulk storage location, taking into account such product specifics as size, weight, storage requirements, and sales forecast. Depending on demand, replenishment goods go directly to a prime location. Back-ordered merchandise should bypass storage and be sent directly to the packing area so that pending orders may be immediately expedited.

Since the SKU is an internal tracking number, the system must automatically cross-reference each SKU to one or more merchandise catalog numbers. This facilitates test marketing of the prices and position of the goods in the catalog while maintaining a single warehouse location.

To further assist inventory control, some systems generate identification stickers with a product description and SKU imprinted both alphanumerically and in a bar code. These may be bulk- or item-specific and are affixed to the goods prior to storing. The product descriptions assist the materials handlers, pickers, and packers; the bar code facilitates the speed and accuracy of cycle counts (random physical counts of select SKUs in the warehouse) and annual physical inventories.

Stock Status

Some systems reconcile inventory against all SKU activity from a beginning position, weekly, monthly, or cumulative to a time fixed by the cataloger. To get the most out of this inventory report, the system must list every transaction that affects your inventory status—by SKU *and* reason code. Your sorting parameters should include specific activity categories such as receivables, returns, damaged, defective, outbound orders, and goods returned to vendors. You may further define your stock activity in adjunct reports by volume (SKUs with the most activity listed first) and/or revenue (SKUs with the highest dollar value).

Ancillary Costs

Inventory costs include inputs above and beyond the price of purchased goods. Besides handling costs, there are holding costs such as taxes, insurance, and storage space. With better inventory control techniques, you can reduce these ancillary costs relatively.

Impact on Nonwarehouse Functions

The data associated with an inventory control system provide accurate trend and point-in-time information on stock availability to *marketing* and *merchandising*. As a result, demand and product reception in the marketplace can be analyzed daily as well as over time to assure more accurate and timely purchasing and forecasting decisions.

The system updates the cataloger's book inventory to subtract goods/orders shipped and add receipts and returns for the day. In addition, the daily system reconciliation process includes back orders, held orders by reason, and in-the-warehouse (packed and labeled but not shipped) packages. Not all the monies have been received in *accounting* nor have all the goods been shipped, but as a direct result of the inventory control process the system provides an audit trail to accurately represent a day's revenue activity.

FULFILLMENT TECHNOLOGY

While labor-intensive by tradition, technology is making a great many of the fulfillment functions easier and nearly mistake-proof. Bar coding, computerized inventory control, electronic purchase orders, and system-generated pick lists and customer packing slips are just the fringe of the technological tools making their way into the fulfillment operation.

The shipping process has been expedited significantly through the use of *bar codes*. When the packing label displaying the bar code is wanded at the shipping dock, several things happen simultaneously in the system: the customer record is updated to show that the merchandise has shipped; the physical inventory and book inventory are revised; an electronic data transfer (EDT) advises the credit processing company of the transaction so that the proper payment is issued to the cataloger; and the shipping manifest is printed automatically. So five tasks are expedited immediately by merely wanding the bar code on the outbound packages.

With the new technologies, the associate time and related expense to perform warehouse functions is reduced significantly, thus reducing the actual number of people required to perform the activity. Just as important, the customer's order can be accommodated more quickly and accurately. As you must by now surmise, the selection of a core software system is one of the most important decisions you will make. Determining your catalog policies and fulfillment procedures will be infinitely easier with an understanding of the system's capabilities.

SYSTEMS SUPPORT

Evaluating fulfillment software systems is a topic that warrants a chapter in itself, and in fact, much has already been written on the subject. The key point is, do your homework, including talking to current users of your final software options.

The same recommendation applies to the selection of an automatic call distributor (ACD) telephone system. Check around to determine the telecommunication package that is right for you; ideally, your telephone system should interface with your computer software. Both decisions carry heavy price tags and long lead times for implementation, so take the time to make your final decisions with confidence.

SPACE REQUIREMENTS

Once you know your projected order volume, the number of SKUs, the average number of items per order, the peak inventory level, the number of phone-versus-mail orders, and the type and size of your products, you are on your way to determining your facility's space requirements. In other words, if you have defined your parameters as we discussed earlier, you're halfway there.

Order Entry/Customer Service

In the office you need space for caging, telemarketing, order processing, customer service and supervision, clerical support, and management. Since the size of telephones, computers, and desks is easily measurable, office space requirements may be determined by allowing an average of 85–100 sq ft for every workstation. Although these stations do not generally exceed 85 sq ft, the extra space allows for common areas such as aisles, restrooms, and break rooms.

CSRs are your direct line to the customer. Make each CSR workstation a self-contained selling unit. Most catalogers have found that individual cubicles work best for CSRs. In addition to acting as a sound barrier, the fabric-covered partitions come in handy for posting up-sell, cross-sell, and other pertinent information. These personal bulletin boards keep your CSRs informed at all times.

Merchandise Storage and Handling

The storing of merchandise in bulk, display, and other specialized areas such as high-value, represent up to 70 percent of your total warehouse space requirements. In general, there are two objectives of a catalog warehouse storage plan:

1. To maximize the use of available space to accomplish safe, efficient merchandise storage
2. To maximize labor productivity by minimizing the distance a product travels within the warehouse and minimizing the number of times the merchandise is handled from receipt to shipping

Variables such as racking, products and their stackability, back-order percentage, drop-ship items, return figures, and the number of inventory turns per year, all influence warehouse space needs as well. Your racking vendor will supply you with exact dimensions of the racks to calculate your storage space requirements, but don't stop there.

You still need to consider more space for the receiving, returns-processing, picking, packing, and shipping areas. But remember, the amount of space required for these key merchandise handling areas depends on the characteristics of the product and your anticipated sales volume. For instance, handling furniture requires a much different work space and storage configuration than handling jewelry would.

In addition to allocating specific work areas, you should also allocate appropriate space for computers, telephone equipment, management offices, associate training, and any other special customer services your catalog offers, such as engraving or alterations.

BUILDING SUPPLIER RELATIONSHIPS

Credit Authorization

Since the majority of catalog customers place orders using credit card numbers, you should develop a solid relationship with an authorization company. Today's systems communicate electronically, so be sure your computer system is able to transmit information back and forth to the authorization company. Smooth communication between systems ensures the proper flow of funds from the customer's account into yours.

Check Verification

The remainder of your orders will probably be by check. Consider an outside service here as well. It is quite costly to have every check verified, but you can perform a cost/risk analysis to determine what procedures are appropriate for your business. Consult with a few check-verification companies to make sure your specific needs are being met.

Transportation

Shipping companies are obviously a necessity for catalogers. The most commonly used carriers for outbound shipments to customers are UPS and the U.S. Postal Service. Whichever carrier you choose, develop a computerized manifest system to track the shipment of each order. Perform a cost analysis to forecast your shipping costs per year. For example, if you don't know the average weight per package shipped, calculate the cost to send 2-lb, 5-lb, and 10-lb packages from your facility to major cities around the country. From this data you can compare delivery times and estimate the average cost per shipment. This will help you decide how much to charge your customers for shipping and handling.

Look to your inbound transportation effort for savings opportunities as well. While it may seem easier to let merchandise vendors arrange for transportation of the product, don't yield to laziness. Your vendors aren't interested in saving you money. Instead, you should calculate your annual shipping requirements and, based on these compilations, negotiate volume discounts with no less than three carriers. The potential for an immediate savings of as much as 20 percent is well worth your effort.

Consultants

If you need help with your fulfillment operation, seek out a consultant who is familiar with the direct marketing industry and the characteristics of your particular catalog segment. A good consultant can provide estimates on key operating parameters, such as the percentage of back orders, returns, and mail-versus-phone orders, based on the customers you're targeting and the product you're marketing. For example, soft goods (clothing items) usually generate a higher returns percentage than hard goods because of sizing and color variations. An experienced consultant should help take some of the uncertainties out of your forecasting decisions. In addition, a consultant can provide information on the systems and suppliers that are applicable to your operational requirements.

THIRD-PARTY FULFILLMENT

Every cataloger knows that an innovative telecommunications and computerized fulfillment operation provides a competitive edge in the drive for customer satisfaction and repeat business. But keeping up with the latest technology is expensive, so more and more companies are considering third-party fulfillment as a viable alternative to their in-house operation.

The economies of scale realized by third-party operations enable them to provide quality service below the cost of an in-house operation. Simply put, the client companies share major expenses, such as real estate, computers, and telephone systems, and, as a result of combined client volume, pay lower prices for transportation, supplies, and printed materials.

FULFILLING YOUR PROMISES

A thorough understanding of the importance of fulfillment in your company goes a long way toward defining or redefining your policies and critical customer service. Make sure your operations people are prepared to effectively and efficiently deliver your catalog's promises. In today's competitive catalog arena, your very survival depends on it.

34

Magazine Subscription Fulfillment

Jane Imber

Neodata Services, Inc.
Boulder, Colo.

FULFILLMENT OVERVIEW

Fulfillment is a function within the magazine or newsletter organization that includes the receipt, servicing, and tracking of subscription orders. Fulfillment is the least understood aspect of magazine publishing because on the surface it seems quite simple: you put an order in and labels come out. In practice however, fulfillment is a highly complex, constantly evolving group of functions that are heavily reliant upon both state-of-the-art computer technology and a well-managed, flexible clerical work force.

Fulfillment has tremendous leverage to make or break the success of a subscription-driven magazine. It is the primary liaison between the magazine and its subscribers, its printers, the U.S. Postal Service, list rental brokers and buyers, and, through circulation audits, the advertising community. Fulfillment represents the magazine to the market in many ways and provides invaluable feedback from the market to the magazine.

The Fulfillment Functions

Fulfillment receives new orders, renewal orders, gift orders, address changes, file inquiries, payments, and subscriber complaints. Fulfillment produces an up-to-date subscriber file, responses to subscriber inquiries and complaints, magazine address labels, statistical reports, list rental orders, subscription invoices, and renewal notices. Fulfillment also deposits money into the magazine's bank account, answers telephone inquiries, and inserts, meters, and mails bills and renewals.

Levels of Service

There are different levels of fulfillment service, ranging from that which provides just the basics, to those that create a marketing partnership with the publisher. The functions at the most basic level include opening the mail, depositing money, entering orders, applying payments, changing addresses, printing and presorting labels, mailing bills and renewals, and printing statistical reports. When all of this is done reasonably quickly and accurately, the publisher rarely notices it. But if any of it falls behind or falls apart, the publisher is in immediate pain. Subscribers are angry, renewals drop off, there is less money to pay other vendors, and a fortune is spent mailing unnecessary bills, renewals, and copies of the magazine.

The next level of service is not within the capabilities of every fulfillment organization, but represents a level of sophistication that most publishers need in order to meet their customer service and marketing objectives. This level includes scan entry, electronic credit card authorization and funds transfer, gift subscription processing, mechanical presorting, 800-number service, continuous auditing, and PC-based statistical reporting.

The highest level of fulfillment service meets the unique and rapidly evolving marketing needs of each user while testing the economic constraints of the fulfillment organization. Special services may include automatic renewal, installment billing, laser printing of customized bills and renewals, circulation modeling, combination order processing, zip+4 bar coding, alternate delivery, and so forth. What best distinguishes the highest level of service is its capacity for collecting and presenting marketing information in multiple formats for varying uses. How the information is presented is often as important as what information is presented. Report formats range from hard copy standard reports, to hard copy custom reports, to downloaded reports, to downloaded data, to ad hoc on-line data access and circulation modeling.

Future Directions

The subscription file itself takes on a new dimension and greater value if it can incorporate more than one magazine or product into a single customer record. The state-of-the-art fulfillment system (which few have attained today but which all must attain in the future) employs interactive database technology. This enables the publisher (aka the "marketer") to know the history of every purchase transaction made by Joe Green at 123 Main Street—whether it be a magazine subscription, a book purchase, or a donation—in terms of recency, frequency, and monetary value. Insight into a customer's purchase history and preferences is a powerful tool in the marketer's hands. In fact, in this time of rising postage expense, anything that enables the marketer to mail fewer promotion pieces without reducing sales volume is invaluable. Interactive database technology will also enable the publisher to select lists and reports directly from the subscriber file while sitting at a remote terminal in an office and without paying programming fees or waiting for the next update.

IN-HOUSE VERSUS OUTSIDE FULFILLMENT

Fulfillment may be handled in-house, by an outside service, or with a combination of the two. For small or start-up magazines with cash-only offers, no gift business, and few requirements beyond the basics, an in-house fulfillment system may make sense. Some large publishers with deep pockets and complex or unique needs have also opted for in-house fulfillment. They believe that direct contact with their subscribers gives them an advantage, in terms of market feedback and customer service, that is worth the extra expense and management time. However, as outside services increase their flexibility, and as the cost of in-house fulfillment skyrockets relative to outside service pricing, the trend for magazines of all sizes and levels of complexity is toward outside or partially outside fulfillment.

Control over, and access to, the subscriber file is another one of the more frequently stated reasons for retaining in-house fulfillment. However, the advent of personal computers and on-line access to service bureau mainframes has made this reasoning obsolete. In one of the more popular combination configurations, customer service is handled by the publisher utilizing an on-line system that accesses the mainframe, and all other functions are handled by the service bureau. This gives the publisher the best of both worlds and an added advantage no in-house publisher has: the ability to change service bureaus as needs change.

The most important benefit of outside fulfillment comes from the influence of multiple users. These users, with their multitude of needs, have contributed to stretching the limits of the system. As a result, a huge variety of pretested, off-the-shelf programs, reports, and sources of expertise are available for use whenever the need arises. If an in-house publisher wants to try something new, he or she must wait until it is designed, programmed, and debugged, before the new idea can be tested. Then, if that new idea doesn't pan out, the publisher has incurred those research and development expenses to little benefit. For some applications, the necessary expertise or equipment doesn't exist in-house.

THE FULFILLMENT ORGANIZATION

Fulfillment organizations are structured by function.

Mail Receiving and Distribution

This department handles the receipt, sortation, and opening of the mail as well as bank deposits and distribution of the media for further processing. All media is sorted into batches according to the type of processing required. For example, orders are separated from complaints. Media received with money (cash media) must be marked to indicate the amount received. Once the cash media has been separated from the checks or currency, good controls must be in place to ensure that all the money deposited is balanced against the cash value of the media processed. All the money received should be deposited within 24 hours.

Data Entry

This division keys, scans, and tape-enters transactions to the system. Most handwritten media is key-entered. Most renewals and payments are printed on scannable forms and can be scan-entered. Cold mail orders can sometimes be scanned if a finder number is used. A finder number is a code which identifies a record on the promotion list. Orders received from large-volume subscription agents are usually submitted on tape. Tape entry is the fastest and most accurate mode of entry. Key entry is the slowest and least accurate.

Data Processing

This group programs and runs the computer, processing the various inputs and instructions to the system and creating the desired outputs. In an on-line system, this is a continuous process. In a batch system, the application of transactions to the subscriber file in order to produce a new file happens periodically and on a set schedule. This process is commonly referred to as an "update" or a "file reorganization." Most of the day-to-day communication between the publisher and the fulfillment department centers around planning and coordinating the processes that must take place during an update.

Mailing Services or the Lettershop

This department prints labels, bills, and renewals and prepares them for mailing.

Customer Service

The members of this department respond to and resolve all subscriber inquiries and complaints. Customer service has grown significantly in importance as the value of the subscriber to the publisher has increased. The total annual volume of customer complaints should not exceed a number equal to 5 percent of the active subscriber list. However, some types of magazines, such as computer magazines, get a higher volume of complaints from their subscribers.

Information Services

This is the department that designs and creates statistical reports and information services, such as PC downloads and circulation models.

Client Service

This is the department that handles liaison between the publisher and all the other departments of the fulfillment operation. (Regardless of whether it is an in-house or an outside service, there should be such a department.) The client service manager must understand both the fulfillment function and the circulation function so that he or she can be an active participant in planning and controlling all activities. A good account manager can make a mediocre service look great. A bad manager can turn a good service into a disaster. One of the most important decisions a fulfillment buyer makes in choosing a service bureau is the selection of his or her account manager.

SUBSCRIBER FILES

The Mainfile

The mainfile consists of all current subscriber records, some expired records, and other types of records such as donor controls (used to bill and renew gift orders) and change-of-address ghosts (used to link records after an address change). Mainfile records are either active (eligible to receive a magazine) or inactive (suspended for nonpayment or expired). The subscriber record contains all the information pertaining to a single subscriber, such as name, address, telephone number, credit card number, original order date, times renewed, total issues to go, last copy sent, and original source.

Trailer Records

The record also includes segments, sometimes called "trailers," which contain information pertinent to each order received from that subscriber: one order per trailer. There may be an expired trailer from a previous subscription, an active trailer representing the current subscription, an underlying service trailer representing a renewal order which hasn't yet been activated, and one or more trailers pertaining to gift subscriptions that the subscriber has purchased for other people. Trailers contain information such as order term and amount, payment status, record type (gift, regular), and record status (active, suspended, canceled, expired).

The Matchcode

Within the record is a code, either a matchcode or an account number, which uniquely identifies each subscriber. Matchcodes are constructed using elements of the subscriber's name and address and are, therefore, subject to change. An account number is a sequential number which stays with the subscriber regardless of any changes made to name or address. The matchcode or account number is printed on labels and reply documents such as bills and renewals to facilitate matching those documents to a record on the file. When a payment or renewal is received from the subscriber, fulfillment enters the matchcode, or an expanded variation of it called a "keyline." During update, the system uses the entered keyline to identify a record and mark it paid or renewed. It is much faster and more accurate to enter a keyline than to enter a complete subscriber name and address.

ANCILLARY FILES

Dead Expire

Expired records are periodically removed from the mainfile and placed in archive storage. This file is called the "dead expire" file. Expires are usually not moved to the dead expire file until several months after expire, in case the record is reinstated. Some publishers find the dead expire file to be a good promotion list. Older records must be deleted from this file periodically because the accuracy of the address information declines over time.

Bad Pay

Records that have been canceled for nonpayment may be accumulated on a "bad pay" or "kill" file. This is used as a purge file against cold mail promotion lists. Bad-pay names may also be maintained on the subscriber file for a period of time to block the processing of additional credit subscription orders from the same people.

LIST RENTAL

Some publishers have list rental selections performed by a service other than their subscription fulfillment service. Copies of the mainfile must periodically be created and shipped to the list rental service bureau. This creates a disadvantage for the publisher if the list rental file is not updated as often as the mainfile, because the age of the file may preclude hot line rentals. There is also a security risk in shipping a copy of the file to a second location.

Multi-title publishers sometimes maintain a list rental file containing all the subscribers to all their titles on a single file. This type of file is also used for cross-promotion.

FULFILLMENT MANAGEMENT AND CONTROL

The Update

In the update, file maintenance activities take place. Among these are the application of payments or renewals, the addition of new orders, the inactivation of expired orders, and the cancellation of unpaid or voluntarily canceled orders. Addresses are changed and any other transaction affecting the record is recorded. For example, each time an issue is served, the issues-to-go number in the record is decremented by one. It is usually during the update that all outputs from the system are selected. Among these are labels, bills, renewals, and list rental orders.

Master Schedule

A master schedule is prepared jointly by the circulation department and fulfillment. It provides an overview of what is to be done in each update over the next 12 months. It shows when donor or cash order acknowledgements are to be mailed, when end-of-month or end-of-year reports are to be issued, and when issue labels are to be selected and printed. It indicates whether an issue is ABC/BPA audited, when subscribers with open credit orders are to be sent each billing effort, when they are to be suspended or canceled, when they are to be sent each renewal effort, and with what issue new subscribers will start. It also includes a schedule of regular weekly or monthly selections, such as reports, galleys, or premium labels.

Update Instructions

Detailed instructions must also be prepared for each update. Two of the most important functions controlled by the update instructions are billing and renewal promotion. The update instructions indicate how new subscribers should be assigned to groups that are billed and renewed together. These groups are called billkeys and expire groups. Subsets of these groupings may be defined on the basis of source, sourcekey, state code, or times renewed as well as other record characteristics. The key is to create a unique identifier for each group of subscribers according to how the publisher wants to invoice, promote renewals, and track the results.

In addition to defining how subscribers will be assigned to the various billing or renewal groups, the update instructions indicate which of the groups should be selected from this particular update for each bill and renewal effort. The instructions will list, by effort and subscriber group, the stock items (letter, form, outer envelope, reply envelope) that are to be sent to each group, as well as an alternate selection to be substituted if one of the stock items is out of stock. An estimated count of the subscribers to be selected is included in the instructions for each group. The number of credit subscribers in a mailing group can be estimated using credit order production reports or the counts from previous billing efforts. The number of subscribers in a renewal mailing can be estimated using an expire inventory report or previous renewal effort counts. After update, the actual selection counts must be checked against the estimated counts before printing or mailing the efforts.

The update instructions indicate the type and class of postage to be used (meter, permit, stamp) on bills and renewals and the desired mail date. Bills always mail first class, as required by the U.S. Postal Service. Renewals usually mail third class. Both bills and renewals are sometimes mailed along with the magazine. This is called "attached mail."

The update instructions may also include a special message that is to be printed on the forms, such as a renewal-at-birth message. In addition to bill and renewal instructions, all other selections from the mainfile are defined. Among these are address label edition splits, presort levels and dispatch schemes, list rental selections, and report selections.

BILLING

Billkeys

A bill group consists of all of the credit orders that came in during a particular 1- or 2-week period. The bill group code, or "billkey," controls the billing, suspension, cancellation, and statistical tracking of a group of credit subscribers. Billkeys go through a life cycle of billing, suspension, and cancellation that usually includes 5–9 billing efforts. Unless the subscriber pays, claims to pay, or voluntarily cancels his order, suspension of service occurs after two or three billing efforts. Mass cancellation occurs at the end of the billing series when all attempts to collect payment have failed. All of the unpaid subscribers in the billkey are then either deleted from the file or changed to a bad-pay status.

Who Receives Bills

Bills are sent to all unpaid records (regular and donor), with a mailable address, except for subscription gift recipients. If a bill is returned to the publisher by the U.S. Postal Service marked "undeliverable as addressed," the record is placed in a suspended status called "stop and hold." Nothing can be mailed to the subscriber until a corrected address is received. Returned bills should be recorded promptly so that money is not wasted sending additional bills or magazine copies to a bad address. Bills may also be sent to salt names.

Billing Efforts

Each invoice tells the subscriber that his or her credit order has been received, the term of the subscription ordered, and the amount of money due. First-effort bills, or credit acknowledgements, use very soft copy to remind the subscriber of his or her debt. As the series progresses, each effort is more strongly worded from "perhaps you've forgotten" to what is humorously referred to as a "pay up or die" message. On average, five to six efforts are sent. Some industry experts believe that the billing copy has much less impact on pay-up rates than the timing of the bills. They believe that a bill is more likely to be paid if it is received almost immediately after the order was sent. It may be advantageous to send first-effort bills daily instead of waiting for a weekly update.

Billing Formats

Bills may be mailed in a package that includes a form, letter, reply envelope, and outer envelope, or they may be attached to the magazine itself or generated on tape to a collection agency. When attached billing is used, it is important to remember that donors and credit-suspended records do not receive a magazine and must be billed separately. Other complications arise in attached billing, and not every fulfillment system can handle it. Programs which select, address, and track bills were not created to select, print, and track issue labels. The functions of these two systems must be merged. This ensures that the billing keyline (a code which identifies the order) is printed on the address carrier, and that everyone who should get a bill or a magazine, does get it.

The update instructions for bills indicate:

- Which billkeys are to be selected
- When each billkey should receive the first effort
- How many efforts are to be sent
- How often each effort should be sent
- Which subscribers are in the billkey
- Which stock components should be used
- What kind of postage should be used on the bills
- What messages should go on the form
- What the renewal-at-birth term and amount is
- Which efforts are handled by a collection agent

Billing Reports

Statistical reports show the rate of response to each bill by billkey, billing effort, order sourcekey, and billing package, broken out by control and test packages. Reports are also needed to show outstanding, paid, suspended, request-cancel, mass-cancel, and claims-paid counts by billkey. In addition, reports are needed to show the aging of outstanding accounts receivable. Using these reports, publishers can determine which sources of subscribers generate the greatest proportion of paid orders and which billing packages or techniques generate the greatest pay-up.

Testing

Tests are conducted in order to find the most efficient means of inducing pay-up on credit orders. Tests are made of timing, copy, package, and even mode of billing, such as installment billing. Fulfillment provides the tools needed to randomly select test groups and to evaluate the results of the tests. Random samples can be selected for testing, using an insignificant character in the record such as a matchcode check digit. Samples should not be based on a demographic characteristic or any other field in the record which may skew the results of the test. (Among these might be a state code, zip code, or order date.) An A-B test sample is sometimes created by assigning every other record to the test or control group. Unique codes are assigned to each package so that the results can be broken out by package in the statistical reports.

Collection Agents

Magazine collection agencies provide additional collection efforts after the publisher's last collection effort. They may also replace one or more of the publisher's own efforts within the billing series. If done properly, a third-party invoice will give a subscriber the added jolt necessary to persuade him to pay. Third-party billing letters often lead the subscriber to infer that the subscriber's credit rating is at stake. However, some experts believe that subscribers who pay in response to a high-pressure third-party invoice are not likely to renew. Collection agents are usually compensated by the publisher on a contingency basis.

Renewals-at-Birth

A renewal-at-birth (RAB) is a renewal of a credit subscription received with the subscriber's payment, in response to an offer sent with or on the invoice. In most cases, it represents the least expensive source of renewals but can be relied upon to generate only a small quantity of renewals. An RAB usually offers a steep discount on an additional year of service.

RENEWALS

Expire Groups

Subscribers are most often grouped by common expire issue for renewal promotion. To simplify renewal promotion and tracking, weekly publications often accumulate all subscribers expiring during a particular month into one expire group. Subsets of expire group may be created based on source or type of promotion. For example, agency-sold orders are sometimes sent a different renewal series than direct-to-publisher sold orders. Publishers often use a renewal sweepstakes or premium offer to renew orders previously generated by a sweepstakes or premium offer. There is a widely held belief that using a premium or sweepstakes offer locks you into using it forever. However, a strong renewal package and a strong editorial product will generate renewals regardless.

Who Receives Renewals

Renewals are sent to all paid subscribers with mailable addresses. Gift subscriptions are renewed by sending one to three renewal notices to the donor, followed by one or more notices to any unrenewed recipients. A great deal of time and attention is often paid to planning and implementing the annual renewal of Christmas and Hannukah gift subscriptions. All gift orders received during the months prior to Christmas and Hannukah are assigned a common start date and expire date so that they can be renewed together using a promotion written explicitly for holiday gifts. Some subscribers are excluded from renewal promotion if they have requested that no renewals be sent. Salt names are usually included on all renewal promotion lists.

Renewal Efforts

A publisher may send as many as 15 renewal efforts, but most send 7 efforts. The renewal series is scheduled to begin at some point prior to expire, such as 7 months before expire, and may continue to be sent beyond the expire date. However, some renewal series begin as soon as the first issue is received. As long as the value of the returns received on each effort exceeds the cost of that effort, the publisher will continue to promote. There may also be one or more advance renewal efforts sent prior to the first effort of the regular renewal series.

Renewal Formats

Most renewal notices are sent in a mailing package which includes a renewal form, letter, reply envelope, and outer envelope. A telephone effort may be scheduled after all the mailed efforts or in between mailed efforts; sometimes an attached renewal is used. When attached renewals are sent, it is important to remember that gift subscription donors do not receive a magazine and must be renewed separately. Other complications arise in attached renewal, and not every fulfillment system can handle it. Programs which select, address, and track renewals are not created to select, print, and track issue labels. The functions of these two systems must be merged. This ensures that the renewal keyline (a code which identifies the subscriber) is printed on the address carrier, and that everyone who should get a renewal or a magazine, does get it. Despite the complexity, this is a very cost-effective means of renewal promotion.

The update instructions for renewals indicate:

- Which expires should be promoted
- When the first effort is scheduled for selection
- How many efforts will be selected
- How often the efforts should be sent
- Which subscribers should be selected
- What output format is to be produced
- Which stock components should be used or substituted
- What kind of postage will be used to mail renewals
- Which messages should be printed

Renewal Reports

The renewal rate of an expire group is measured in terms of advance and regular renewals as well as identified and unidentified renewals. Identified renewals are generated by promotions created for the express purpose of soliciting a renewal. They are called "identified" renewals because a renewal keyline is printed on the promotion form to identify the subscriber record. Unidentified renewals are all the other means used by a subscriber to renew a subscription, including subscription agency promotions, insert cards, space ads, and requests written on the subscriber's own stationery.

Renewals are also tracked by prior source and sourcekey, source-to-source migration, promotion package, and effort as well as by the number of times a subscriber has renewed. The first renewal is a "conversion renewal." Subsequent renewals are considered "pure renewals" or, depending upon the sophistication of the reporting system, a "renewal of a conversion" and a "renewal of a renewal."

Another popular mode of measuring renewal response is a "horse race" report. This looks at the timing of renewals in terms of percent renewed by expire group relative to expire month.

Renewal Percentage

There are different ways of calculating a renewal percentage, depending upon what you consider to be the "total expire" count. Some publishers base the renewal percentage calculation on the number of unrenewed subscriptions in an expire group at the time the first renewal effort is mailed. This gives them a feel for the relative effectiveness of the promotion series. Others count all the subscriptions that would have expired with that particular issue, including those that renewed in advance of the first effort, renewals-at-birth, and short-term orders that came in after the first effort mailed. If a renewal percentage is reported on the ABC or BPA audit statement, the total expire quantity used must include all advance renewals. There are additional ABC and BPA audit requirements related to the calculation of renewal percent. Both ABC and BPA allow renewals to be counted up to 6 months after expire, but for ABC only, renewal cancels must be deducted.

Renewal Testing

Renewal testing is a never-ending search for the optimum number of efforts, the best time to initiate a renewal series, and the most enticing stock package, offer, and copy. Random samples can be selected for testing using an insignificant character in the record such as a matchcode check digit. Samples should not be based on a demographic characteristic or any other field in the record which may skew the results of the test, such as a state code, zip code, or order date. An A-B test sample is sometimes created by assigning every other record to the test or control group. Unique codes are assigned to each package so the results can be broken out by package in the statistical reports. A unique code should be assigned to each package, offer, and effort so the results can be tracked.

STOCK AND FORMS DESIGN

When designing and ordering stock, it is important to consider the current postal regulations as well as warehouse stock numbering systems. For example, bill and renewal outers must meet certain specifications in order to be processed on a mechanical presorter. What must also be considered is how the forms will be handled once they are returned by the subscriber to the fulfillment operation. Scannable documents will always get through the system faster and more accurately than key-entered documents.

Scannability is determined by the type font, print quality and alignment, ink, and paper stock. Some promotion techniques (stamps, stickers, tokens, oversize dimensions, or round edges) can interfere with feeding the documents into a high-speed scanner. Address labels are also usually incompatible with high-speed scanners because label placement can vary from one label to the next. Hand-held wand scanners don't have feed or label float problems, but process many fewer documents per hour. A good high-speed scanner can read up to 18,000 documents per hour.

CUSTOMER SERVICE

Customer service has grown in importance in recent years as the value of the subscriber to the publisher has grown. Customer service is an extremely challenging task because it requires a combination of speed, accuracy, literacy, and diplomacy as well as an ability to understand a subscriber whose communication skills may be below par. Some publishers find it helpful to send a brochure to new subscribers telling them how to complain. For example, a brochure can instruct the subscriber to send both his old and new address when he submits a change of address request.

Of course, customer service begins long before a complaint arises by providing a service that meets the subscriber's expectations. Unfortunately, there is no such thing as perfect fulfillment and there is no subscriber as dissatisfied and less likely to renew as one who gets no response, or the wrong response, to his complaint. The good news is that subscribers who complain and are satisfied with the publisher's response are among the most loyal subscribers from that point on.

Customer complaints and inquiries should be responded to promptly (within 1–5 days) and in nontechnical language that the subscriber can understand. Consumers today expect an 800 number to be available to them, and the benefits in terms of customer satisfaction and improved communication far exceed the cost. All calls should be answered within the first three rings.

GETTING THE MOST FROM A FULFILLMENT SERVICE

Nothing has a greater impact on the quality of a fulfillment service than the quality of the information provided by the users. The publisher should tell the fulfillment service not only what is needed, and when, but also why it's needed. It is the publisher's job to define the objective and it is fulfillment's job to figure out the best way to accomplish that objective. Circulation plans should be communicated as soon as they are made. More errors are made as a result of inadequate time or incomplete information than for any other reason. Last-minute changes are another big factor contributing to problems. The best fulfillment services are those utilized by demanding publishers. Most of the improvements made to fulfillment systems are the direct result of user requests.

35

Continuity and Negative Option Fulfillment

Henry W. Rossi

Eastern Credit Corporation
Bohemia, N.Y.

INTRODUCTION

The basic goal of any direct marketing business—of any business, for that matter—is to acquire a large number of good customers who are loyal, repeat buyers. The "club" concept was devised as a means of manufacturing profitable customers by preprogramming the repeat-buying habit. The two basic approaches to club marketing, continuity and negative option, are explained in the following pages. Both represent rather unique forms of direct marketing, with equally unique promotion and fulfillment challenges.

The implementation of club marketing is very complex and expensive due to the substantial up-front investment in product, market testing, and sophisticated computer systems that are required before the first order can be processed. Why do so many companies use this form of promotion to sell their products? Simply because, for those with the right product, marketing approach, and computer systems, the rewards can be substantial. Due to the significant start-up investment, there is somewhat less competition than is prevalent in other areas of direct marketing.

Typical continuity or negative option clubs will entice the prospect to join by means of very exciting introductory offers, designed specifically for that purpose. Once the individual is a member, the product will sell itself to generate profitable repeat sales.

The secret to customer retention is good product and a superior fulfillment system, in terms of both people and computer hardware and software. Also critical is the process of comprehensive long-term attrition analysis which enables the marketing group to properly target the offer within the prospecting universe.

Continuity and negative option marketing usually fall into one of two areas:

- Large, general-interest clubs, such as Book-of-the-Month Club, the Columbia House Record and Tape Club, and the Walt Disney Book Club. These companies rely on hot titles that will interest large segments of their membership.

- Small specialty clubs, such as the Mystery Book Club and the History Book Club, which sell to a specific audience. These clubs seek out titles of special interest to their membership that may not be readily available to the general public. The smaller clubs rely on the fact that their customers will accept a greater proportion of the specialized product that is offered.

For the most part, specialty clubs will have higher average shipments per member than the general-interest clubs.

CONTINUITY CONCEPTS

As the term implies, continuity marketing involves an ongoing purchasing process in which the customer agrees to buy a series of products, usually sharing a theme. There are two popular types of programs that require repetitive sales technology:

- The standard book program, in which customers sign up for a series of titles to be shipped at a predetermined interval (usually 4–8 weeks).

- The annual program, in which the customer agrees to receive an update of the product on a yearly basis. Calendars and desk diaries are examples of products that are naturals for this type of marketing.

Another example of continuity marketing is an offer for specialized woodworking projects. The customer is unlikely to want all of the individual projects, but over the life of the program will purchase many of them. On average, a continuity program becomes profitable when a customer purchases four shipments, and it is not uncommon to see seven or eight paid purchases per starter in specialty areas.

A home improvement encyclopedia is yet another typical example. The marketing approach for this product revolves around selling the customer the concept of purchasing an entire set. (Of course an alphabetically organized set is incomplete with one letter or volume missing.) The product is designed to be impressive on a bookshelf, which also encourages completion. In this context, the continuity program offers a means to sell a high-ticket product in installments, reducing the amount the customer must pay at one time.

CONTINUITY PROMOTION

Frequently the first item in a series is offered free or at a very low price. For example, the first volume of a set may be priced at $1.95 plus postage and handling, with the rest of the set priced at $9.98 per volume. Some continuity programs offer bulk shipments of an entire set, followed by installment payments after the fact. The concept here is to place the full product in the home before the customer has a chance to decide against it and cancel. This may also be more attractive to the customer for those products that are most useful when complete (e.g., a how-to encyclopedia). Generally, customers who have paid for several individual shipments can be trusted with bulk shipments and installment payments.

As distinct from negative option, continuity customers are either in the program all the way through to completion, or drop out at some point along the way. Usually there is no "contract" or minimum-purchase agreement, as is frequently the case with negative option.

The Different Types of Promotion

In establishing continuity systems and fulfillment operations, it makes sense to plan on providing capability for several types of promotions. There are at least seven different types:

Volume 1 or Initial Shipment Free.   The customer receives the initial shipment free of charge and additional shipments are sent on a predetermined schedule. In some instances, the shipping pattern is not established until the customer makes the first payment.

Volume 1 Free, Combined with First Charge Shipment.   The customer receives the initial combination shipment in one package with an invoice. This technique achieves immediate cash flow by billing the customer for the first charge shipment. However, this technique may produce higher initial returns.

Free Examination.   The customer receives the initial product for a free examination in the home. The customer is billed for the product, but may return it for full credit within a specified time period. This technique is used when it is undesirable to "give away" the first volume for whatever reason.

A Series of Titles or Products for One Low Price as an Inducement to Join the Club.   The customer can select a series of titles or products from a list presented in the initial promotion piece. The idea is to position a bargain, or loss-leader, up front and set the price for later shipments at higher margins, where the actual profit generation occurs.

An Introductory Shipment for a Low Price.   This promotional method dictates a system that is capable of accepting payment with the first order. The up-front payment requirement is a form of credit-screening and audience-targeting vehicle, because only those sincerely interested in the product will send the initial payment.

An Initial Shipment for a Shipping and Handling Charge. This technique is a favorite of the calendar people, who will sell the first calendar for a shipping and handling charge only, provided that the customer agrees to accept and inspect next year's calendar when it becomes available. This technique can generate and retain sufficient customers to support extremely lucrative programs.

Bulk Shipment Programs. Often categorized as one of the most successful approaches to continuity promotion, bulk shipment permits a customer to review several individual shipments as part of the process of credit qualification, requiring one or two payments. The customer's action in making the initial payments indicates product acceptance. The company then takes the credit risk of sending the balance of the program in one big bulk shipment or in a series of minibulks. The theory is to place as much product as possible in the customer's hands, while still continuing to bill on a monthly basis. Many studies confirm that the right product shipped in a bulk fashion to the right credit-qualified customer will produce the maximum net-paid sale per new enrollment.

All the above promotional techniques are based on attracting a sufficient number of customers who will like the product enough to remain in the program. The key difference between continuity and negative option programs is the automatic shipment feature around which continuity revolves. All products are shipped automatically with full return privileges, and many sales are based on the inertia of the club members. Product arrives on a regular basis, and the customer accepts and pays for it.

CONTINUITY FUNCTIONS

The Steps in a Continuity System

The process by which a thriving membership is built, serviced, and maintained involves a series of crucial steps. Efficiently implemented, these steps will take a continuity club program smoothly all the way from promotion through to payment.

New-Member Promotions. New members are generated via prospect mailings of list rental names, print ads, TV, and various cross-promotion sources.

Order Entry. This is the point at which the new member is first entered into the system. Name, address, ID code or source key, etc. comprise the entry.

Credit Screening. Various criteria are applied to screen out any poor-credit-risk enrollees. Credit screening usually consists of two types of processing:

- **Matching to in-house and purchased/shared (if any) bad-debt files.** These should be consolidated among the various club and subscriber sources.

- **Applying specific credit criteria.** Poor-credit-risk prospects can be eliminated on the basis of failure to supply phone number, invalid address, hit against bad-debt list, bad-debt ZIP, or combinations of these criteria. While the credit exposure on the introductory offer is low, it becomes much higher with the first selection. Use of payment on the introductory ("intro") shipment, while applicable, is not adequate. (A fair number of poor-credit-risk people will pay the low intro amount to gain access to the balance of the shipments).

Credit Acceptance. After meeting the various credit criteria, the prospect is enrolled as a new member in the club file.

Introductory Shipment. This takes place upon enrollment. The invoice for the introductory shipment is generally enclosed with the shipment itself. The processing of introductory shipments involves:

- Completion of entry into the file
- Generation of shipping labels and bills
- Deduction from inventory
- Preparation of shipping manifests
- Flow-through to affected reporting subsystems

Billing. This commences at a set point in time following the initial shipment. The new member might pay on the initial bill (enclosed with the shipment) or on any one of n bills mailed. After the nth bill, a third-party letter (or two) is sent. If the customer fails to pay or return the shipment, he or she will be turned over to a collection agency and placed in a permanent bad-debt file.

Payments. Customers' payments are processed as they arrive. Payment for the intro shipment is generally required before further automatic shipments go out.

Automatic Shipments. These are made on a cyclical basis. Several individual shipments are made (with invoices enclosed) prior to the application of any bulk shipments.

Bulk Shipments. These can be made to members who are in good standing after payment has been received for several prior shipments. This process helps qualify them as good credit risks. A bulk shipment may consist of a portion of the set, or the entire balance of an encyclopedia-type product.

Cancellations. These are received along the way as part of what is often called an "attrition curve." They may come in the form of:

- **Cancellations with payment.** In these cases, the member pays for the last shipment and requests that no more be sent.

- **Returns.** In these cases, the member returns the last shipment(s) and indicates a desire to cancel.

Exchanges. These occur when the member is not cancelling but merely returning defective merchandise.

Regular Returns. These usually occur in cases where the product is not in the form of a contiguous set and the customer simply does not want the item, but is not cancelling membership at the same time.

Refurbishing. This is the continuous process of unpacking, checking, and repacking returned merchandise so it can be reused.

Changes of Address. Information about customers' change of address needs high-priority processing to avoid shipment to outdated addresses and the resulting loss of merchandise that may occur.

Attrition

The initial promotion produces a large volume of "starters" who respond to the free or low-priced introductory shipment. The sharpest drop-off generally comes with the second, and possibly the third, shipment. Many will either pay and cancel, or return the item. Attrition after this stage tends to be more gradual, with the initial with-pay credit cutoff resulting in the second major drop-off.

The first shipment, frequently priced as a loss-leader, is usually purchased by more than 50 percent of the customers. There is generally a sharp drop-off at, or just after, the second full-price shipment. Customers who continue in the program and pay for subsequent shipments buy enough to offset all promotional and fulfillment costs. An important key to successful continuity programs is comprehensive attrition reporting to fully support the marketing effort.

Returns

High volumes of returns are a fact of life with continuity businesses. The return rates are higher with new customers and diminish as the accounts mature. Because shipments are continuously generated, many with a previous balance, rapid returns-processing becomes a critical issue. A general guideline is that returns received must be processed and credited to customer accounts within 48 hours. As a general rule, returns for replacement are very few, unless clothing items are involved or special problems are experienced with the product.

It is also important to accurately forecast attrition curves and plan returns as part of inventory. Sophisticated continuity programs include the ability to have variable return/cancellation criteria (e.g., two consecutive returns may automatically cancel an account).

Bulking

While the basic proposition is "24 volumes over 24 months," or something similar, bulking is often applied after the third or fourth shipment. In some extreme instances, this is done on the payment for Volume 1 in the series. As previously mentioned, bulking refers to the practice of shipping customers the entire balance of the set at one time. However, they may be billed on the original basis.

Bulk shipments may also be made in groups of two or three items at a time, partly to save on shipping costs, but also to support purchasing momentum. While customers are billed on the original basis, they may feel more inclined or obligated to stay with the program.

The timing of bulk shipments is the subject of regular testing. The idea is to position them sometime after the initial attrition "cliff." At that point, the remaining customers are qualified buyers.

Premiums

Continuity systems use premiums in various ways to maintain customer interest. The premiums are issued at strategic times:

- With introductory shipments
- At various shipping levels (e.g., a free binder at a particular shipment level)
- At completion

An important front-end variable is the initial cost, which is constantly subject to testing. There are many ways to present it: no cost, postage and handling only, registration fees, a low introductory price plus postage and handling, and so forth. The higher the cost, the fewer starters, and the lower the attrition. The key is to find the right balance.

FULFILLMENT/INVENTORY REQUIREMENTS

Fulfillment

Continuity programs are generally fulfilled on a "wheel": a preset sequence or title-of-the-month of automatic shipments. This is affected by the nature of the product. A sequentially numbered set of books calls for a strict sequence. Where there are no volume numbers per se, there is more flexibility. The challenge is that new customers are starting up all the time, so different start groups are at different stages in the program. The fulfillment system must track these start groups.

One basic requirement is that a customer's automatic shipment be new, not a selection already purchased. This is logically simpler where there is a preordained product sequence. When a variety of selections is possible, the system must keep track of each customer's previous selections. This can get complicated with more than a handful of products.

A program may be based on monthly shipment cycles, but the frequency of updates has to be higher so that customers aren't kept waiting excessively. At a minimum, there will be backup cycles between the major ones. These serve to reactivate and ship to customers who are late with their payments to the extent of missing an update. Payment patterns have an impact on the complexity of fulfillment.

Inventory management requires: (1) a good projection system; and (2) a perpetual inventory system. These must take into account the following:

Starter volume

Attrition factors

Refurbishable and nonrefurbishable returns

Lead time for resupply

Bulking combinations

Premiums (along with shipments or at preset payment levels)

While it depends on the product, a large proportion of returns are generally reusable. However, some degree of refurbishing is usually needed, even if only to the extent of replacement of packaging materials and inserts.

Inventory

Continuity systems maintain inventory in several different ways, based on marketing/shipping concepts:

Title of the Month.   Shipping projections are critical with this method and companies are forced to overorder to guarantee that all eligible customers are served with the monthly title. Returns and overstocks are eliminated with a backup cycle that follows the original cycle by a preset number of days (e.g., 60). This approach depends on having either brand-new product every month or product that is new to the membership.

The Wheel Concept.   The "wheel" refers to a predetermined hierarchy of product delivery. An inventory amount for each product or title is keyed into the system before a shipping run within a ranking sequence. The update logic assigns product, starting with the highest ranked item and working down the list as the inventory counts are depleted. The system checks customers' records to make sure that they do not already have the item. Essentially, customers are assigned the highest-ranked in-stock item that they have not already received.

Prenumbered Titles.   This applies to products such as encyclopedias, numbered book sets, and correspondence courses, which must be delivered in a preset sequence to the consumer. Inventory needs are forecast based on response projections for promotions. Historical attrition curves and other factors are used to project product need by month or week. In this environment, projection accuracy is critical, as there is no option to substitute product.

BILLING AND COLLECTION
FOR CONTINUITY CLUBS

A simplified form of account-based billing is used for each club. Shipping invoices are either enclosed with the merchandise, attached to the shipping carton, or sent separately, timed to arrive just after the product does. With each update, the customer's account is charged for another shipment (if due) and credited for any payments that have arrived.

A simpler form of handling the billing is the tip-on approach. Invoices are generated for a full cycle of members at one time. They are separately streamed (i.e., list-split) and possibly also keyed to indicate which package (volume/item number/bulk pack) the customer is to receive. The invoices are tipped to the prepacked items and shipped out. (A mail-sort-bag or UPS manifest system is used for high-volume shippers.)

Credit Screening

As already discussed, offers can vary widely. In some cases, the first selection is free or is at a very low introductory rate. For some continuity programs, the offer is promoted as "subject to credit approval." This is more prevalent when print ads are used to generate new members. Credit screening may be accomplished through reply devices (requesting a phone number on the order form, etc.) or by matching against internal and external sources. One internal source usually consists of a "do not promote" of bad-debt and low-profitability names accumulated to screen direct mail campaigns. Space-, television-, or insert-generated names may be screened according to history by zip code or census tract as well.

Credit Holds

Parameters are set to stop automatic shipments once a customer is late in paying. Frequently, this is expressed in the form of "one or two shipments for no-pay accounts" and "two or three shipments for with-pay accounts." More aggressive marketers, with the ability to apply sophisticated segmentation methods, are finding that it is profitable to allow as many as five open shipments before credit cutoff.

Once on credit hold, customers typically receive a collection/reactivation billing series, which flows out of the same updates. These are separately identified and separated to mail first, however.

Payments

Timely payment processing is critical to a continuity program, because failure to credit customers' accounts means the loss of shipments and transfer of customers into a billing process. Many companies have used the latest technology to post payments within 24 hours of receipt.

Reactivation

When customers reactivate, they resume with the next numbered shipment in the series or the current title of the month. The "backup cycles" between major updates, or file maintenance runs, serve to expedite the process. Systems can vary. In some cases the backup cycle represents a temporary situation, and the customer is returned to the regular shipment/billing cycle thereafter. This means that at one point, they will be getting a shipment one or two weeks after the prior one, rather than a full month. In other systems, customers remain with the new cycle they join and receive shipments according to the new pattern.

Billing

Credit and collection billing categories can be viewed in terms of gradations from no-pay, to part-pay, to full-pay. The credit-hold parameters can vary depending upon how many payments have been made to date. Zip and original list source are often part of the formula used to place a customer in a credit group.

Customers can become delinquent, owing for various numbers of shipments. The amount outstanding may also be used to tune billing pulse and write-off factors. Early bills are written primarily to reinforce and resell the club and to encourage early payment. Later bills stress payment and/or return unpaid items.

Whether or not the customer has canceled is yet another important factor channeling the billing process. People can cancel while still having an open balance for prior shipments. A separate billing series asks for return of the unpaid shipments or complete payment.

Typically, there will be a large number of people who have paid for the introductory shipment and nothing since. They may represent as many as three unpaid shipments. This category usually calls for a separate, relatively firm collection series.

In a continuity program, credit and collection activity is closely meshed with promotional and shipment plans. It anticipates the special conditions that this type of promotion forces into existence, and is tuned to stem attrition or limit exposure. The name of the game is to find the right mix to maximize profit.

NEGATIVE OPTION CONCEPTS

Among the various direct marketing configurations, negative option programs are the most complex to operate from a systems point of view and the most expensive from a fulfillment point of view. The complexity comes about as the promotional concept requires continuous, closely timed communications with the customer to maintain the involvement in the purchasing phase of the business. This is accomplished through a series of announcements offering the latest selections.

Key to the negative option program is the mailing of announcements that tell customers about the next selection that will be shipped to them. They are given the option of: (1) accepting the main or automatic selection (which is usually a new bestseller) by taking no action; (2) skipping the current selection; or (3) requesting an alternate selection. Each announcement mailing usually carries a

whole series of offers. The announcement package is additionally used to increase sales for each month by offering something that will attract attention. It
is also a convenient vehicle to unload excess inventory at discount prices.

Introductory offers are the rule, and they are generally part of a "contract" in
which the customer agrees to purchase a certain number of items over some
period of time. In recent years, we've seen a form of this with no purchase requirement — simply the agreement to receive periodic announcement mailings.
More typically, however, the customer agrees to purchase two to four selections
over a one or two year period.

The introductory offers are frequently substantial (a $35-book for $1.98, or
"11 records or tapes for $1.98"). As a general rule, the greater the value of the
introductory shipment, the greater the obligation to purchase additional product at "regular club prices." As with the record clubs, the new member is often
given the opportunity to buy the first regular selection at a deep discount when
it is ordered with the introductory package. In addition, special discounted offers are presented during membership, and/or a bonus system is used. A simple
form of this might be: "Get one selection at half price for each selection you've
purchased at regular club prices."

The negative option method introduces a major category of customer: those
who take the introductory shipment, pay or don't pay for it, and never live up to
their obligation to complete the contract. There is a much larger degree of exposure with each new member; therefore, credit screening is critical.

The obligation concept runs throughout billing and reselling efforts. Many
customers pay for the initial shipment and one or two regular ones, and then
drop off. The obligation theme is used in copy to reactivate them. While the
membership is in the format of a "contract," this is not necessarily binding in the
legal sense — or at least it's not practical for the marketer to view it that way. A
customer who has not purchased the minimum number of regular shipments
over the contract period is not really delinquent in the usual sense of the word
and can be in fully paid status.

Negative option marketers do a great deal of front-end testing involving a
wide variety of propositions. Prepayment may or may not be required for the
introductory offer. The amount may range from 1 cent plus postage and handling, to a few dollars. Offers are usually pegged to list sources, with less exposure risked on the poorer sources.

There is a dynamic parallel to that which occurs with "free-home-trial" promotions. The more liberal and attractive the up-front offer, the greater the response, but — on the downside — the greater the attrition and bad debt. Once
again, the trick is to find the right balance.

NEGATIVE OPTION PROMOTION

Announcements of selections of the month are equivalent to prescheduled promotion mailings. The flow of responses from them — rejects and requests for alternates and additional selections — are part of the ordering process. As a general rule, bills are not combined with these, but mailed separately.

Negative option marketing typically involves several elements:

- An introductory offer at a very attractive price (in some cases at no cost).
- A commitment on the part of the customer to purchase a specific number of items over a set period (e.g., 1 or 2 years).
- Periodic mailing to the customers announcing an automatic selection which will be shipped if they do not respond. They may return a postcard indicating an alternate or additional selection or that no selection is desired.

The last item is key to negative option programs. Recently, some programs have been introduced that require no customer commitment for a minimum number of purchases.

A typical form of negative option starts with an introductory offer, such as a book presented as a $29.95 value for $1.95 plus postage and handling. The customer agrees to purchase two more selections at special club prices. Every 4 weeks, a bulletin is mailed announcing the special selection. If the customer wants to receive it, he or she need do nothing; it will be shipped on a free-trial basis. If the customer wants an alternative book, or none that month, he or she can so indicate on the reply card.

The Intro

Frequently, the introductory item is offered free or at a very low price—often below cost. For example, the intro selection may be priced at $1.95 plus postage and handling as above, with regular monthly selections priced between $12.95 and $29.95.

Typically, but not always, a commitment, or "contract" is involved, wherein the customer agrees to purchase additional items. Often, a time period of 1–3 years is imposed, during which the customer must complete the commitment.

In setting up systems and fulfillment for negative option programs, one must plan capability for several types of promotions. Two of these are: (1) free examination; and (2) a series of titles or products for one low price.

Free Examination. As with continuity programs, the customer receives the initial product for a free examination for 10 or 15 days. The customer is billed for the product, but may return it for full credit. Often, the same policy also applies to all purchases, not just to the introductory one.

A Series of Titles or Products for One Low Price. The customer can select an assortment of offered titles or products from a brochure included in the introductory offer, at an extremely low price (e.g., seven CDs or tapes for 1 cent plus postage and handling). Generally, the larger the number of items in the intro, the greater the commitment (e.g., eight purchases at regular club prices during the next 3 years). Fulfillment of multiple-intro orders is somewhat more complex than is fulfillment of solo-intro orders, especially when the items are of different sizes and weights. The capability needed is similar to that for catalog fulfillment. Other forms of introductory offers are similar to those described for continuity clubs, such as introductory offers based on an initial small prepayment, and free offers, usually requiring payment for postage and handling only.

Repeat Sales

All the various promotional techniques are based on attracting customers who will like the product and remain in the program at least long enough to purchase the minimum number of items at regular prices. The key difference between continuity and negative option programs is the latter's announcement package, which alerts customers to what is coming and provides a vehicle for purchasing more than the monthly selection alone, or rejecting the entire offer.

Announcements

Negative option programs require an announcement bulletin or news mailing to precede the actual shipment. Members may skip many shipments while still remaining in the club. This is not so with continuity programs, in which the shipments are part of a series.

As with continuity programs, negative option works through momentum. The customer basically agrees to receive promotion materials and to be shipped to on an automatic basis. In most negative option programs there is a contract element: an obligation to purchase additional merchandise. While there are limits on enforcement, the marketer can use the obligation as a device to urge repeat sales on members who may not be purchasing or those who attempt to cancel membership prematurely. Customers are reminded that they agreed to purchase additional items when they joined and accepted the introductory offer.

Many repeat sales flow in as customers fail to send rejection replies. Many will also neglect to take advantage of return/credit privileges when the shipment arrives. Of course, there are a number of customers in this group who also neglect to pay promptly.

The basic business concept of negative option, as with continuity, combines a very attractive loss-leader promotion with several profitable sales. Often the combination of the intro sale with the minimum required purchases is set to break even or net a small profit. The real profit comes from those good customers who continue to buy after the commitment is reached.

Attrition/Acceptance Rates

The whole key to the successful operation of a negative option club lies with the selection of titles that will appeal to members of the club. Proper audience targeting will result in more members choosing to accept one of the titles offered during the period. Providing marketing with the proper title analysis is key to any well-run negative option club.

Premiums

Negative option programs may use premiums at various levels to maintain customer interest. Common premium approaches are:

Bonus points that are accumulated for a number of items purchased. They can be applied as credits on future purchases.

Warehouse clearance sales.

An offer that enables the customer to buy the monthly selection and get another item at ½ price.

Returns

The negative option process—which requires that the customer take action to decline a shipment—results in the automatic shipment of unwanted titles regardless of the effort applied to prevent it. The arrival of a shipment triggers a reaction in some customers reminding them that they failed to send in the card. Some customers will keep and pay for the shipment, while others will send it back with a note. Others simply write "refused" on the shipment and send it back. This interaction generates many returns. They should be processed within 48 hours of receipt to prevent unnecessary billing.

NEGATIVE OPTION FUNCTIONS

Phases Unique to Negative Option Processing

The functional flow for negative option fulfillment is basically the same as the process for continuity clubs, up to a point. The common elements include new member promotions, order entry, credit screening, introductory shipments, billing, and cancellations. The following describe those phases unique to negative option processing.

On-Arrival Payment Processing.   Negative option programs generally permit credit up to a certain dollar limit, usually a multiple of the amount of payments made.

Regular Announcement/Bulletin Mailings.   These include an automatic selection which, in a simple system, may be the same for every member. The mailing also contains a list or brochure of alternate selections and a reply card. Maintaining statistics on the rejection responses and reading curves is critical. A shipping run cannot be done until it is certain that a majority of rejection cards have been processed.

Announcement Response Processing.   For those members who exercise their refusal or alternate options, reply cards must be processed into an update that controls the shipments. A cutoff date is applied that allows the member a number of days to reply.

Cyclic Semi-automatic Shipments.   These are subject to announcement responses which form four basic shipment groups: automatic selection; alternate selection; additional selection; and skip selection. (In addition, there are credit holds, reships, ship immediately, and other categories formed by other conditions.)

BILLING AND COLLECTION
FOR NEGATIVE OPTION

Negative option generally requires account-based billing. Shipping invoices are either enclosed with the merchandise, tipped onto the package, or sent separately, timed to arrive just after the product. With each monthly shipment, the customer's account is incremented for another shipment and credited for any payments that have come in. A descriptive billing system, similar to MasterCharge or Visa, is important to this process.

When the title-of-the-month approach is used, it results in a very large group of members who will be receiving the same product. In this case, it is usually more cost-effective to tip the invoices onto the prepacked items. (A mail-sort-bag or UPS manifest system is used for high-volume shipments.)

When introductory offers involve a selection of multiple items by the new member, a form of catalog fulfillment is employed. However, the billing is simpler for the introductory selection, as all are billed at the same (low) total price.

Another treatment frequently employed in negative option billing is a reminder about remaining obligations. This can be a promotion letter advising customers that they have not purchased in a while and reminding them of their obligation. This special treatment is often handled in sophisticated, segmented billing systems in which targeted copy is directed toward the major source and status groups within the club.

Credit Screening

For some negative option programs, the offer is promoted as "subject to credit approval." This is more prevalent when print ads are used to generate new members. Credit screening may be accomplished through reply devices (such as requesting a phone number on the order form), or by matching against internal and external bad-debt sources. Space-generated names may be screened using history by zip. In addition, negative option screening should be designed to identify those members who repeatedly apply for the intro offer, and those past members who did not complete their obligation.

Credit Holds

Parameters for negative option credit-holds are usually defined in terms of dollars rather than number of shipments, as used in continuity programs. This is due to the greater variety of ordering patterns that occur among negative option club members. Frequently, the credit-hold criteria are expressed in the form of a mathematical formula based on the dollars paid by the customer. For example, if a customer pays $10, he or she receives a $30-credit line; a payment of $20 opens the credit limit to $60; and so on, up to a top limit of $200.

Once on credit-hold, customers typically receive a collection/reactivation billing series which flows out of the update system; these are specially keyed and mailed first. Critical to a good credit-hold system is proper analysis of a customer's paying habits. Knowing how much credit to extend to slow-paying customers is a science that must constantly be studied.

Payments

Timely payment processing is as critical to a negative option program as it is for continuity programs. Failure to credit customers' accounts means the loss of shipments and the transfer of customers into a billing process.

Reactivation

When customers reactivate, they resume with the next announcement or bulletin mailing. The backup cycles between major updates serve to expedite this. Systems vary: in some cases the backup cycle represents a temporary situation and the customer is returned to the regular cycle thereafter. The kinds of questions to address in reactivation programs include: How many selections were ordered when the customer was in credit-hold? And how many should we ship when the customer comes off credit-hold?

Billing

Credit and collection billing categories can be viewed in terms of gradations from no-pay to part-pay, premium-pay (e.g., intro only), to some total-paid dollar level, or full-pay. The credit-hold parameters can vary depending upon the dollar total of payments made to date. Zip and original list source can also be part of the formula used to place a customer in a credit quality group.

As with continuity clubs, some customers become delinquent, owing for various numbers of shipments. The amount outstanding also can be used to tune billing pulse and write-off factors. Early bills are written primarily to reinforce and resell the club in the process of obtaining payment. Later bills stress payment and/or return for unpaid items.

Whether or not the customer has canceled is yet another important factor channeling the billing process. People can cancel while still owing for shipments. A separate billing series asks for return of the shipments not paid for, or if a commitment has not been completed, the total balance due.

A typically large group consists of those who took the introductory shipment and have taken nothing since. This category usually calls for a separate, firm series. Others will pay for the introductory shipment, but will reject everything else.

Another factor which can be useful in billing segmentation is announcement response. Members who have rejected shipments and are late in paying for one or two, represent one type. Those who have accepted all shipments and have paid for nothing since the intro shipment, represent a difficult-to-collect-from group.

As with a continuity program, credit and collection activity is closely coordinated with the promotional and shipment plan. It anticipates the special conditions that this type of promotion forces into existence, and is tuned to stem attrition or limit exposure.

The name of the game is to find the right mix which maximizes profit. The more alluring the introductory offer, the larger the initial response. However, there are trade-offs. If regular selections are not sufficiently attractive, response drops off more sharply. The less the new member has to pay for the intro, the less well qualified he or she is in terms of credit risk.

A big credit bonus is the offering of a major blockbuster title. When people want this title they will pay the complete balance to obtain it. The collection department will occasionally establish a tighter credit-hold just before shipment of a major title and then use a personalized letter advising that a copy has been reserved in the customer's name, but held because of the balance still due. This stimulates pay-up.

INVENTORY REQUIREMENTS

Negative option programs require sophisticated inventory management in two areas:

1. Announcement package components driven off the active members being mailed to
2. Available quantities of the main and alternate selections being offered

Payment patterns have an impact on the complexity of fulfillment.

As in the case of continuity programs, inventory management requires a good projection system and perpetual inventory system. These must take into account the following:

- Starter volume
- Components of announcement packages to be mailed to the active membership
- Purchase history of the main selection and alternates
- Refurbishable and nonrefurbishable returns
- Lead time for resupply
- Bonus books (with shipments or at predetermined payment levels)

While it depends on the product, a large proportion of returns is generally reusable after some degree of refurbishing. Here the process is almost identical to that of continuity programs.

IN CONCLUSION

Club marketing represents one of the most complex forms of direct marketing, as a great deal of activity—bulletin mailings, automatic shipments, etc.—is preordained by the original offer. The combination of so many details calls for sophisticated fulfillment and reporting systems. However, given the right formula, club marketing has been known to produce very stable and profitable businesses. Those long-famous book and record clubs attest to that.

PART 7

Financial and Tactical Planning

36

Financial Planning: An Overview

David D. Shepard
David Shepard Associates, Inc.
Dix Hills, N.Y.

This chapter* will deal entirely with the economics of traditional direct marketing. We will begin with a review of the major business issues associated with:

- Solo promotions
- Multistep promotions
- Catalogs
- Continuities
- Clubs
- Newsletters
- Magazines

This review will initially focus attention on the economic trade-offs that direct marketers deal with on a day-to-day basis. After a general discussion of each business form, we will return to analyze each business in terms of the relationship between acquiring new customers, which direct marketers refer to as *front-end analysis*, and the profitability that results from transactions that occur after the customer is acquired, called *back-end analysis*.

Long before databases were fashionable, direct marketers understood that

---

*The material in this chapter is reproduced by permission of David D. Shepard from *The New Direct Marketing: How to Implement a Profit-Driven Database Marketing Strategy* (Chicago: Business One Irwin, 1990).

long-term growth and profitability depended primarily on the direct marketer's ability to manage the equation that balances expenditures on new-customer acquisition with the flow of sales and profits that come back over the economic life of the acquired customer. Of course, it's a lot simpler to measure the immediate costs of acquiring a new customer than it is to measure the value of an acquired customer, particularly when that value may take years to fully materialize. And, as we'll see shortly, in an increasing number of direct marketing situations, the long-term value of an acquired customer is not simply a value waiting to be discovered; the long-term value of a customer is directly related to the way in which the customer is served by the direct marketing company. So we have a kind of a chicken-and-egg problem that we'll try to solve after we've established some of the basic economic ground rules.

SOLO PROMOTIONS

The simplest form of direct marketing is the solo, or single-shot, promotion. Assume for the moment that the marketer has no other use for the name of the customer acquired. The only economic reason for the promotion is to make an immediate profit on this one mailing. In this situation, the marketer must design, produce, and mail promotion pieces to enough potential buyers to generate a response that will cover the cost of the promotion and yield an acceptable level of profit.

Single-shot promotions are relatively simple but the seller must still answer many questions in the course of the promotion process. Should the promotion piece be a classical, direct-response, full-mailing package, including an outer envelope, letter, brochure, business reply card, and return envelope? Or should the seller use a less expensive mailing piece? If the classical full-mailing package is used, should the latter be two pages or four pages, and should the flier be black and white or in full color? Should the seller offer credit or require cash with the order? Should credit cards be used? Should the seller offer an inexpensive premium to hype sales or as a reward for cash with order? Should the mailing use third-class postage or would the extra costs of first-class postage somehow result in extra sales and thereby pay for itself? Should an 800 number be used? How strong should the guarantee be? Should the outer envelope contain copy and an illustration of the product, or just inviting copy, or no copy at all?

The list of legitimate questions that can be raised about even the simplest form of direct marketing is extensive, and answers to these questions will affect the economics of the promotion. Many of these questions have to do with economic trade-offs. Does it pay to spend more on the promotion piece, to offer a premium, to offer credit, to mail first class, and so on? These questions raised with regard to a solo promotion apply to all types of direct-response businesses and will be raised again and again throughout this chapter.

MULTISTEP PROMOTIONS
LEADING TO A DIRECT SALE

Frequently, it is possible to identify the potential market for a product in terms of the circulation of one or more magazines while at the same time it is not profitable or legally possible to sell the product "off the page" in those magazines regardless of the unit of space employed. In some situations, the price of the product is exceptionally high, and closing the sale requires the power of a more expensive direct-mail package with full-color illustrations and sufficient copy to define all the features and benefits of the product. Or, in the case of financial services, it may be neither economically feasible nor legally possible to attempt to directly consummate a sale. In these instances, magazine space often is used to generate leads or inquiries, which are followed up by one or a series of direct-mail pieces. In some cases, the initial leads are followed up by a combination of mail and phone. Products sold in this fashion include, in addition to financial services, encyclopedias, expensive exercise equipment, office equipment, and many business-to-business services. The "bingo cards" found in trade magazines and airline magazines are prime examples of this kind of direct-response marketing.

The economics of multistep marketing differs from the economics of single-shot promotions in that the total costs of both the initial effort and all of the follow-up efforts must be tracked carefully and balanced against the sales and gross margin resulting from the total effort.

CATALOG SALES

A catalog may be thought of as a very expensive solo mailing, selling anywhere from a few dozen to hundreds or even thousands of products. It is also possible, as in the case of the solo mailing, to compare the total gross margin resulting form a catalog mailing with the total costs of the mailing, but the analogy between a catalog business and a business based on solo mailings cannot be taken much further.

The success of a catalog business is related directly to a catalog manager's ability to efficiently develop and manage a company's database of past buyers, or its *house list,* as it still referred to by many in the industry. In very general terms, the response of an outside rented list to a catalog mailing may range anywhere from .5 percent to 2 or 3 percent, depending on the quality of the rented names and their predisposition to the products being offered in the catalog. By way of comparison, the response of past buyers to another catalog offering may range from 5 to 20 percent or even higher.

Naturally, a new catalog company cannot open its doors with a list of past buyers. However, catalog operators have developed a number of techniques for developing house lists. One technique is to develop a relatively inexpensive "prospecting" catalog that can be mailed to names that have been rented from outside list owners. Respondents to these prospect mailings then are entered on the catalog company's prospect list. Of course, it is possible to mail a company's complete catalog to an outside rented list, and the limiting or deciding factor in this decision often is the catalog company's willingness and ability to sustain a large negative cash position while building its house file. Large companies wishing to enter the direct marketing business often are in a position to finance this development period, provided that they are convinced the eventual returns will justify the initial cash investment.

Smaller entrepreneurs generally attempt to exhaust all the other more conservative ways of building prospecting lists that can be converted eventually into buyers lists. Other techniques for building house lists include advertising the catalog free or for a token price in targeted-space media, using the same space to sell the most popular items in the catalog, and sending out solo mailings of individual popular products to names on rented lists. In general, regardless of the techniques used, it is common for a catalog operation to be in a net loss position with regard to new names added to the house list. As the mix between new names that result from cold prospect mailings, space advertising, and catalog buyer names changes in favor of the buyers, the profitability of the catalog operation will increase.

However, even after the initial start-up period is behind the cataloger, this issue of allocating the amount spent on new-customer acquisition versus the amount spent on mailing catalogs to customers will remain. In fact, this decision is one of the most crucial decisions a cataloger must make.

Ironically, advances in database marketing techniques have made this decision even more difficult. In predatabase days, most catalogers had a limited number of catalogs, which were mailed to all of the customers on their buyers file. In many cases, the entire customer mailing strategy could be summed up in a sentence: "We mail four general catalogs a year to all customers on our file who have made a purchase within the last two years."

Now, given the ability to segment a file not only in terms of how frequently different customer segments should be mailed, but also in terms of which customers might respond better to specialized as opposed to general catalogs, the decision-making process has become infinitely more complex. Because of the importance of this subject, not only to catalogers but to all direct marketers that have implied as opposed to contractual relationships with their customers, let's spend some more time on the issue.

To the extent that a cataloger spends promotion dollars on acquiring new customers, the potential size of the business will grow. However, as we have seen, the response rate on new-customer acquisition mailings is significantly less than the response rate to mailings to the customer file. So in any one year, a dollar spent on new-customer acquisition, as opposed to customer mailings, will reduce both sales and profits. On the other hand, if year after year, decreasing amounts are spend on new-customer acquisition, the potential of the business will diminish and eventually the actual size of the business will shrink as the customer file fatigues. Therefore, there has to be a strategy for managing both potential growth and annual profits.

In the simpler times referred to above, a cataloger could estimate the sales and profits expected from mailing a single catalog to the house file, say, three or four times a year. After allowing for overheads and desired profits, the cataloger could calculate the amount available for new-customer acquisition, and that would be that. The first complication was the discovery that not all customers need be or should be mailed the same number of catalogs each year. Relatively simple RFM models were developed by catalogers that allowed them to segment a file into dozens of segments or cells based on recency of purchase, frequency of purchase, and the various measures of the dollar value of past purchases. The basic conclusion drawn from RFM cell segmentation was that individuals within the highest performing cells should be mailed more frequently than individuals within the poorest performing cells. So even if a cataloger still only produced four general catalogs a year, the best-performing customers might receive those four catalogs 8 to 12 times a year (perhaps with a cover change), the poorest-performing customers might receive only one catalog a year, and some customers would in fact be dropped from the file of active buyers.

The introduction of more sophisticated forms of predictive modeling (regression, logistic, discriminant analyses) did nothing to change the basic finding that some customers should be mailed more frequently than others. However, the introduction of these techniques and the introduction of models that predict falloff from mailing to mailing have improved the efficiency of the modeling process.

What did make a fundamental difference for some catalogers was the not surprising discovery that not all buyers bought the same mix of products, and that segmentation techniques could be extended to include the kinds of products purchased as well as the quantity of products purchased. Now the decision-making process also had to be extended to include consideration of the creation and distribution of specialty catalogs. It is obviously a more difficult problem to decide who shall get what mix of catalogs with what frequency than it is to simply decide how many general catalogs any one individual should receive.

Unfortunately, while predictive models are good at scoring customers in terms of their probability of responding to a promotion similar to one received in the past, the complications discussed above do not lend themselves easily to statistical modeling solutions of the regression variety. To answer these kinds of economic trade-off questions we must rely on computer models that simulate an entire business structure and that are capable of answering "what if" questions. The good news is that such models are relatively easy to build using spreadsheet programs such as Lotus 1-2-3; the bad news is that the output of the models is only as good as the input assumptions. The model will tell you, for example, what the fiscal impact will be if you create a specialty catalog that will increase response for 30 percent of the file by 20 percent, but only old-fashioned direct marketing testing will tell you if the 20 percent number is correct.

Finally, no discussion of the catalog business would be complete without mention of the extraordinary problems of inventory control and fulfillment that are inherent in the catalog business. Success in mail order requires almost immediate fulfillment of orders as they are received and, with high interest rates, the costs of carrying excess inventory can be as disastrous as the cost of being out of stock. Again, the ability of the catalog manager to perform advanced statistical analyses comes into play. Not only must catalog managers be able to forecast the expected level of overall response to a catalog mailing, they must be able to forecast the mix of products purchased so as to be in a position to manage inventories correctly.

CONTINUITY PROGRAMS

Continuity programs represent an important segment of the traditional direct marketing business. The continuity formula involves the periodic delivery of a product or service against periodic payments from the customer. The Time-Life Books series, the various Cooking Card programs, and the books and collectibles sold by the Franklin Mint are prime examples of products that are marketed this way. Because of the contractual nature of continuity programs, the management of a continuity operation is in many ways much less complicated than the management of a catalog operation. Given the product, such as a series of books, cards, or coins, the marketing problem is relatively straightforward. Options are severely limited relative to our catalog example.

New members or subscribers are acquired through the classical direct marketing channels: direct mail, magazine advertisements, newspaper preprints, broadcast (generally spot TV), and package inserts. In most cases, the first item in the continuity program is offered free or at a substantial discount. The subscriber then receives periodic shipments of the remaining items in the program until all the items have been shipped or until the subscriber notifies the seller to stop shipping the product.

From the subscriber's point of view, continuity programs are simple and easy to understand. From the seller's viewpoint, a number of key questions must be answered before the program can become operational. How should the items in the series be priced? Should the items be priced relatively high and therefore targeted against the upper end of the potential market, or should a lower-price, higher-volume strategy be attempted? How generous should the initial offer be? Should the first item in the series be given away free, or for $1, or at no discount at all? Should the interval between shipments be 4 weeks, 6 weeks, or 8 weeks? How much open credit should be granted? Does it make sense to ship the third item in a series if payment has not been received for the first item? How does the credit decision depend on the interval between shipments? Should the program be open ended with no limit on the number of items in the series, or should the series be limited to a fixed number of items, and if so, what is that number?

Clearly, the answers to these questions will have an important impact on the economics of the continuity program. Again, we are faced with a question of trade-offs. The more generous the offer and credit policy, the larger the program in terms of subscribers and sales volume. But what will be the effect on returns, bad debts, and profits?

Finally, let us briefly discuss the concept of a continuity load-up. The continuity programs we have described rely on periodic shipment of a product until cancellation or completion of the program. In continuity load-ups, the subscriber is informed that after he or she receives three or four single shipments, the balance of the items in the program will be shipped in a single load-up shipment. The load-up plan is an effective device for increasing the total number of items shipped to the average subscriber but again, there are economic trade-offs to consider. Federal trade regulations require that the load-up provision be defined clearly in all promotional messages, and this can reduce the total number of respondents to any given promotion. Second, most load-up programs follow a policy of reminding subscribers that the load-up shipment is about to be mailed unless the subscriber notifies the company not to proceed with the shipment and to cancel membership in the program. This reminder will cause some subscribers to cancel their membership faster than they might have done in an open-ended continuity program. Finally, there is the problem of credit collections. A load-up program is based on the assumption that after the subscriber receives the full load-up shipment, he or she will pay for the shipment on a monthly or bimonthly basis. Of course, some percentage of the load-up ship-ment will not be paid for and eventually will have to be written off as a bad debt.

On balance, only testing the load-up concept against the open-ended, or "till forbid," continuity plan will determine which plan is best for any given product.

NEGATIVE OPTION CLUBS

We have discussed negative option clubs before and they are indeed efficient vehicles for the distribution of books and records. The Book of the Month Club and the Columbia Record Club are well-known examples of this type of direct marketing business. There are some similarities between continuity operations and negative option clubs. Most important, both employ contractual relation-ships with their members, thereby limiting service options. Both vehicles often are used as a means of distributing books, and both use the same media and direct marketing techniques for acquiring new members. But after the new member is acquired, the similarity from an operations or fulfillment point of view ends.

Negative option clubs constantly must ask their subscribers whether they wish to receive the coming selection, receive an alternative selection, or receive no product at all from the current catalog offering. If the member fails to respond, the shipment of the month is sent automatically. The fulfillment systems needed to handle a negative option club are much more complicated than those needed for a continuity program. In addition, the Federal Trade Commission has placed stringent restrictions on negative option clubs to ensure that mem-bers have sufficient time to return the negative option card should they not wish to receive the automatic shipment of the month.

Despite the differences in operating characteristics between negative option clubs and continuity programs, the economics of both types of businesses are remarkably similar. In both operations, new members are always acquired at a loss. The $1 or even the $4.95 that is often charged for the introductory ship-ment (the first book in a continuity series or the four books chosen from a book club's lead list) is never enough to cover the costs of promotion plus the cost of the introductory shipment. Therefore, continuity programs and negative op-tion clubs are always in an investment position. The return on investment stems from future sales to the continuity subscriber or club member. In the case of continuity programs, future sales are simply a function of the price of the items in the program and the number of periods a subscriber chooses to stay in the program. In a negative option club, the member need not buy from every cat-alog offering, and therefore sales are more dependent on the perceived quality of the merchandise offered and the effectiveness of the ongoing marketing ef-fort. In both continuity and negative option, the final measure of profitability is the relationship between the cost of acquiring new members and the sales and payments those members yield over their economic life in the club or program. Later in this chapter, we will develop the techniques used to measure and fore-cast these statistics.

As mentioned previously, up until quite recently, nearly all negative option clubs operated on the principle that all members would receive the same set of promotional materials. The notable exception was the record clubs, which have always asked their members to place themselves within listening preference segments. But within the book clubs, equality of treatment among all members was the general rule. Recently, the larger clubs have begun experimenting with customizing the negative option book selection to individuals based on the demonstrated reading preferences of the individuals. And clearly in a major book club that offers a wide range of both fiction and nonfiction, it makes sense to do so. This is particularly true in data-processing environments in which this kind of decision making can be handled efficiently. Of course, there are production costs to pay for not treating all members the same but these costs are offset by higher acceptance and lower returns of the negative option selection, increased purchase of alternate selections, and a longer member life as club members receive more and more selections that match their reading preferences.

NEWSLETTERS

Newsletters can be very profitable vehicles for distributing information to highly targeted markets. The most profitable newsletters often are aimed at small professional or business markets. Newsletters that are editorially able to provide critically needed information to a business audience that has both the need to know and the ability to pay (often referred to as "company money") have the greatest chance for success. This does not mean that more broadly based, lower-priced, mass-market newsletters can't be profitable, as witnessed by the continued success of the *Kiplinger Washington Newsletter* and the popularity of a number of consumer health newsletters such as the *Harvard Medical Letter* and the *Mayo Clinic Letter,* to name just two.

The economics of newsletters centers on four key variables: pricing, new-order acquisition, conversion or pay rates, and renewal rates. Pricing is the most controllable of all the variables and perhaps the most important. Newsletters targeted at business markets can be priced anywhere from $9.95 to $495. Generally, it is not difficult to determine whether the value of the information is worth closer to $10 than to $500, but it is often next to impossible to tell without testing whether a given newsletter should be priced at $37, $49, or even $97.

Clearly, pricing can make an enormous difference in profitability. Price testing is therefore almost always a necessity when one starts out in the newsletter business, particularly if the newsletter has little or no perceived competition.

Newsletters are almost always marketed solely by direct mail; therefore, it is critical that, before starting out in the newsletter business, the publisher be assured of continued access to the target market. If access to the market depends on the cooperation of a trade association, provisions should be made with the association to guarantee a continuous supply of names.

Properly priced newsletters can be successful with a relatively small response to initial new-subscriber promotions. Profits can be achieved with initial response rates as low as 5 to 10 orders per thousand names mailed because renewal rates are usually high.

However, before a newsletter can be considered a proven success, it must demonstrate the merits of the editorial material. The first test of the quality of the editorial material is the pay rate or conversion rate on new orders. Most newsletter promotions allow for payment (and cancellation) after one or more issues have been sampled by the reader. A high pay rate (over 70 percent) will be indicative of a high future renewal rate. Products that demonstrate a high cancellation rate should not count on a high renewal rate to ensure the profits of the newsletter venture.

MAGAZINES

Magazines are, of course, much like newsletters in that they depend on direct mail for much of their new-subscriber marketing and are highly sensitive to fluctuations in pay rates and renewal rates. The obvious differences between newsletters and magazines are that magazines are much more costly to produce and have two additional revenue streams: newsstand sales and advertising revenues. But even in the subscription circulation area, where one finds the greatest similarity to newsletters, there are important differences.

Magazine subscriptions are sold in many more ways than newsletter subscriptions. There are door-to-door sales, telephone sales, and sweepstakes-sold subscriptions from companies such as Publishers Clearing House. In addition, a magazine company's direct-mail efforts may be dependent on preview or premium offers to an extent not often found in newsletter circulation. Each of these promotional channels and devices runs the risk of producing subscriptions with relatively low pay and renewal rates. Therefore, the evaluation and management of a magazine's circulation list is considerably more complicated and subject to greater risk than the evaluation and management of a newsletter.

FRONT-END PERFORMANCE

Front-end performance and *front-end analysis* are terms used by direct marketers to describe the process of measuring the initial costs of and response to a direct marketing promotion. The economic analysis of the process that takes place after an initial response is received is referred to as back-end analysis or back-end performance.

Measuring Promotion Expense

The first step in the process of measuring front-end performance is the measurement of the total expense attributable to a promotion. The only difficulty associated with this task is deciding which expenses will be included in the analysis and which expenses, if any, will be excluded.

Later we shall see how direct marketers generally approach this problem, but for now, let's assume we agree that it costs exactly $19,000 to mail 50,000 pieces of direct mail. The first statistic to be calculated is cost per thousand pieces mailed, more simply referred to as cost per thousand (CPM).

$$\text{CPM} = \frac{\text{Total promotion expense}}{\text{Number of pieces mailed}} \times 1000$$

In our example:

$$CPM = \frac{\$19,000}{50,000} \times 1000$$

$$CPM = \$380$$

The CPM concept applies to space advertising as well as to direct mail. In space advertising, CPM is calculated by dividing total media costs plus the costs of printing any special insert material by the circulation of the magazine.

$$Space\ CPM = \frac{Media\ costs + insert\ costs}{Circulation} \times 1000$$

For example, consider a magazine with a circulation of 1 million and ad or media costs of $40,000 running an insert card that cost $20 per thousand to print.

$$Space\ CPM = \frac{\$40,000 + (20 \times 1000)}{1,000,000} \times 1000$$

$$Space\ CPM = \$60$$

In both direct mail and space advertising, the question always arises whether the fixed creative fees paid to an agency or a free-lancer and the fixed mechanical preparation and art expenses should be included in the calculation of CPM. Opinion is divided on this subject. Some direct-response marketers insist on including all costs in the calculation of CPM to ensure that their profitability analyses will include consideration of all costs associated with the promotion. Other direct marketers argue that creative material and mechanicals are intended for use in multiple promotions. These marketers either allocate a portion of the fixed creative expenses to each use of the material or maintain separate budgets and controls for creative expenses. They do not include consideration of fixed nonrecurring costs in the analysis of promotion results. This latter approach, which is more oriented to decision making, is favored by most large mailers who are concerned more with the decision to remail a promotion or repeat a space insertion than with the recording of historical costs. For decision-making purposes, the direct marketer wants to know the incremental costs of repeating a promotion that has been used in the past, regardless of such costs.

Calculating CPM for Different Direct-Response Media

Direct Mail. There are three major types of direct-mail promotion pieces, excluding catalogs, that are used by direct marketers to generate new orders or new leads: the full-package solo mailing, the less expensive self-mailer, and the insert piece.

Full-Package Solo Mailings. Table 36-1 shows the components of a standard direct-mail package, including a four-page letter and color brochure. The

Table 36-1. Calculating CPM for a Typical Direct-Mail
Promotion at Two Mailing Quantities

Package Element	Quantity	
	50,000	250,000
Outer envelope	$ 30	$ 22
Four-page letter	38	28
Four-color brochure	90	65
Reply card	23	15
Return envelope	22	17
Total printing cost	$203	$147
Outside list rental	75	75
Lettershop	23	20
Merge-purge	6	6
Postage	132	132
Total CPM	$439	$380

CPM of the full package is shown at two mailing quantities: 50,000 and 250,000. Printing costs per thousand are shown to vary with the quantity printed as the fixed printing preparation expenses (which must be incurred at each print run) are amortized over the number of pieces to be mailed. These fixed printing preparation expenses should not be confused with creative fees and mechanical costs, which are truly one-time costs and do not vary with the quantity mailed or the number of print runs.

The example shown in Table 36-1 is typical of a consumer mailing of the kind used by book and record clubs, continuity programs, and magazines. In these situations, a color brochure generally is required to display the product fully, and third-class postage almost always is employed.

On the other end of the direct-response spectrum, a high-priced newsletter aimed at top corporate management may not use a full-color brochure but may be mailed first class to create a more businesslike impression in order to get past the secretary. In this case, the cost of the promotion will be reduced because the flier has been removed but increased because of the use of first-class postage.

Therefore, there is no hard and fast rule to determine the correct cost of direct-mail promotion. Costs are a function of the components of the mailing package. Direct-mail package costs can vary from $300 to $1000 per thousand. The real question is what mailing package will be most profitable for the product or service being offered.

Self-Mailers. One sure way to reduce mailing costs is to use a self-mailer, which is a promotion piece that does not contain multiple loose components. The most common format is the two- or three-panel 8½ by 11-inch card stock format. A self-mailer eliminates the need for an outer envelope, reduces lettershop expense, and combines the selling message of the letter and the brochure in one format. There is also no need for a separate business reply card and business reply envelope. The self-mailer is a perforated form, one portion of which is a business reply card, and the respondent is instructed to tear off this card and return it to the mailer. With the use of a self-mailer, promotion costs can be reduced significantly, but again the question arises as to what will happen to response. Will the self-mailer turn out to be more or less profitable than a full-mailing package? As usual in direct response, only testing can provide the answer.

Inserts or Enclosures.   Another very inexpensive but cost-effective mailing format is the insert piece or enclosure promotion. An insert or enclosure is any promotion piece that is mailed at no additional postage expense inside an invoice, statement, merchandise shipment, or other primary mailing piece. Insert pieces that are mailed along with first-class mailings such as bills or statements must be small so that they do not increase postage expenses. Enclosures in third-class mailings and merchandise shipments are not weight-restricted.

In general, insert pieces pull a much lower response than direct-mail packages or self-mailers. However, because of the lower cost, which can be as low as $20 per thousand, response does not have to be very great in order to generate a profit.

Space Advertising.   The cost per thousand for space advertising is considerably lower than the CPM for direct mail. A typical magazine page may cost from $5 to $75 per thousand circulation, as compared with direct mail, which ranges between $300 and $1000 per thousand pieces mailed. Of course, the response to a space advertisement will be less than the response to a direct-mail promotion. In direct mail, a 3 percent response (30 orders per thousand) to a promotion costing $600 per thousand will result in a cost per response of $20, and is not atypical. In space advertising, a $20 cost per response is likely to be the result of a response rate of .1 percent in a medium with a CPM of $20.

As small as these numbers seem, they nevertheless result in very significant absolute numbers. For example, consider a mass-market magazine with a circulation of 3 million. The cost of a single black-and-white page is likely to be around $24,000 for a CPM of $8. If an ad in that magazine pulls at a rate of just .05 percent, or a rate of .5 orders per thousand circulation, the ad will generate 1500 responses at an average cost of $16 per response. (See Table 36-2.)

The actual CPM for an ad in any magazine will vary greatly, depending on a number of factors. For example, cover positions cost more than inside-the-book positions, color costs more than black and white, advertising in the direct-mail section frequently costs less than advertising in the general editorial section, and discounts are available for multiple usage. Regional editions may be purchased, generally increasing the CPM but lowering the total dollar expenditure, and so

Table 36-2. Calculating Front-End Space Results

Total circulation	3,000,000
Cost per single black-and-white page	$24,000
Total response	1,500
CPM	$8
Percent response: (1,500/3 million) × 100	.05%
Orders per thousand circulation (OPM): (1500/3000)	.50
Cost per response (CPR): CPM/OPM = $8/.50	$16

on. The point is that buying space advertising is not simply a matter of placing an ad in a magazine. As always, the key decision is whether the more expensive ad format will result in a significantly greater response and increased profitability or, conversely, whether the less expensive format will result in fewer responses and lower profits.

Broadcast. Broadcast is an increasingly important direct-response vehicle, and the emergence of cable TV with its highly targeted audiences has increased the significance of this medium.

TV broadcast advertising generally is purchased in one of two ways. In the first instance, an advertiser will purchase a certain amount of time from a local station or national network at an agreed-on price. The exact times the commercial is to be aired and the number of spots or showings are agreed upon in advance. This procedure is similar to placing an ad in a magazine. Before the running of the ad or the showing of the commercial, the total investment in the medium is known. The cost per response will depend on the number of responses in the form of telephone calls to the local station or to an 800 number or on the number of responses received in the mail.

The second method of purchase is per inquiry (PI). Very often, a broadcast station will agree with an advertiser to run a given commercial at times chosen by the station. In exchange for this airtime, the advertiser will pay the station an amount based on the number of responses received. This method of payment also is referred to as PO (per order). In these situations, the initial response usually is directed to the local station and sent from there to the advertiser. PI or PO arrangements also are frequently available in space advertising.

When broadcast is used either to consummate a final sale or to generate leads, the key economic considerations are the length and frequency of the spot. Traditionally, direct-response spots ran for 90 or 120 seconds, the argument for this length being the 20 seconds or so necessary for the tag line and the time it takes to establish the product and the offer in the viewer's mind. From the very outset, buying a two-minute spot on network TV was expensive and very often not available. Thus, direct marketers turned to local spot TV with its larger inventory of late-night or non-prime-time spots. The advent of cable TV opened up a whole new inventory of available times, and the cable networks were more than happy to sell 90-second and two-minute spots to direct-response advertisers. However, as cable's popularity grew, the inventory of two-minute spots decreased and direct marketers are once again trying to make 30- and 60-second spots pay for themselves. Closely aligned with the issue of the length of a direct-response ad is the issue of frequency. How frequently should the spot appear on any one station? In any one market? Conceptually, there is a buildup period, a time in which response may be low but building, and then there is the falloff period after response has peaked. Obviously, the profits of a successful flight can be erased if airtime is purchased in significant quantity after the spot has peaked.

Thus, the economics of broadcast TV depend heavily on one's ability to forecast response patterns and to tightly control spending decisions.

A second important use of broadcast is in support of a major direct-mail, newspaper-insert, or magazine promotion. It is intuitive that broadcast spots urging the viewer to look in the paper, mailbox, or TV guide will increase response, but the economic question is how much airtime is enough and how much is too much? Up to a certain point or media weight, the broadcast advertising will not be able to make a significant impact and the support money will be wasted; on the other hand, too many spots can be equally unproductive. The answer, of course, is testing to determine the appropriate mix of broadcast support.

Finally, on the subject of broadcast, TV is not the only broadcast medium; we shouldn't forget radio. Radio, particularly drive-time radio with its upscale commuting audience, has always been a great captive market. But until the advent of the cellular car phone it has not been a great direct-response medium. Of course, all that is changing rapidly as car phones move from luxury to necessity status among the most desirable market segments. So we see a great future for direct-response radio, and when that happens, the same issues of time and frequency that affect broadcast TV will have to be addressed for radio.

Telemarketing.   Outbound telemarketing is apparently here to stay, certainly for magazine renewals as well as for cold solicitations offering a one-issue trial examination offer. The phone also is used with great success in business-to-business direct response, in which the goal is to generate a lead or qualify a lead generated from a space ad or a direct-mail offer.

Independent telephone operations currently sell their services at rates of approximately $30 to $40 per hour. Within this time period, a qualified phone operator can make between 6 and 20 contacts. The contact rate will vary depending on the time of day, the day of the week, and whether the call is to a consumer at home or to a business executive or professional at the place of work. Because of its ability to operate low-cost trial subscriptions or leads, the telephone must be used with care. A low conversion rate can transform a very low cost per lead into a very high cost per order, as we'll see a little later on in this chapter.

MEASURING RESPONSE

One-Step Promotions

The response to a direct-mail promotion is expressed as a percentage of the quantity mailed or stated in terms of the number of responses per thousand pieces mailed (RPM). If the response is an order, the term *orders per thousand* (OPM) is used.

$$\text{Percentage response} = \frac{\text{Total response}}{\text{Quantity mailed}} \times 100$$

$$\text{RPM} = \frac{\text{Total response}}{\text{Quantity mailed}/1000}$$

$$\text{OPM} = \frac{\text{Total orders}}{\text{Quantity mailed}/1000}$$

Because the response to a direct-mail promotion often is less than 1 percent, many direct marketers prefer to use the RPM or OPM terminology rather than express results in terms of a fraction of a percent. This is particularly true with regard to space advertising in which a response of one order per thousand or even less is not uncommon.

Two-Step Promotions

As discussed above, not all direct-response promotions are one-step promotions. Often, the initial response to a direct-response promotion is only the first step in a two-step or even a multistep promotion process. A magazine promoted by direct mail, using an offer that allows the potential subscriber to cancel after previewing one issue, is an example of a two-step promotion.

Consider a direct-mail promotion of a magazine through a preview offer. Assume that 500,000 pieces are mailed and that 10,000 responses are received. The initial RPM is equal to:

$$\text{RPM} = \frac{10,000}{500,000/1000}$$

$$\text{RPM} = 20$$

If only 40 percent of the respondents to the preview offer convert to paid subscriptions, the final paid orders per thousand pieces mailed will be equal to:

$$\text{OPM} = 20 \text{ RPM} \times 40\%$$

$$\text{OPM} = 8$$

CALCULATING COST PER RESPONSE

One-Step Promotions

In a one-step promotion, the cost per response can be calculated by dividing the total number of responses into the total cost of the promotion. A quicker way that is preferred by many direct marketers is to divide the cost per thousand of the promotion by the number of responses per thousand to arrive at the cost per response (CPR):

$$\text{CPR} = \frac{\text{CPM}}{\text{RPM}}$$

Referring back to our magazine example, assume that the cost of the mailing was $350 per thousand. The initial cost per response would be:

$$\text{CPR} = \frac{\$350}{20} = \$17.50$$

Two-Step Promotions

In two-step promotions, the promotion portion of the total cost per order is equal to the promotion cost per response divided by the conversion rate. In our magazine example, the cost per response is $17.50 and the conversion rate is 40 percent. Therefore, the promotion cost per order is equal to:

$$\text{Promotion CPO} = \frac{\text{Initial CPR}}{\text{Conversion rate}}$$

$$\text{Promotion CPO} = \frac{\$17.50}{.40} = \$43.75$$

However, dividing the promotion cost per response by the conversion rate understates the cost of acquiring a new magazine subscriber.

Assume that in the process of converting preview subscribers into paid subscribers, those potential subscribers who eventually will cancel will receive three issues of the magazine and five invoices. Let's also assume that those who decide to subscribe will receive an average of three invoices before paying. The costs of this conversion process can be added legitimately to the cost of acquiring the average paid subscription.

The calculations would be as follows. If the cost of one issue of the magazine on an incremental basis is $.75, and the cost of one invoice, including first-class postage, computer expense, and printing, is $.55, the amount spent on each eventual nonsubscriber or "cancel" is equal to:

$$3 \text{ issues} \times \$.75 \text{ per issue} = \$2.25$$

$$+ 5 \text{ invoices} \times \$.55 \text{ per invoice} = \$2.75$$

$$\text{Total cost per cancel} = \$5.00$$

Since only 40 percent of the initial respondents will subscribe, the cost of attempting to convert the eventual cancels or nonsubscribers must be allocated over those who do subscribe. The equation for this calculation is as follows:

$$\begin{matrix}\text{Conversion expense per} \\ \text{subscriber because of} \\ \text{cancellations}\end{matrix} = \frac{\text{Cost per cancel} \times (1 - \text{Pay rate})}{\text{Pay rate}}$$

$$\text{Conversion expense per subscriber} = \frac{\$5.00 \times (1 - .40)}{.40}$$

$$\text{Conversion expense per subscriber} = \$7.50$$

In addition, the cost of billing the respondents who eventually will pay will be equal to 3 × $.55, or $1.65. Therefore, the total conversion expense is equal to $7.50 plus $1.65, or $9.15 per paid order.

The total cost per new subscriber, including both promotion expense and conversion expense, is equal to the total new-subscriber acquisition expense:

Promotion expense + Conversion expense = Total acquisition expense
$43.75   + $9.15   = $52.90

The lesson to be remembered from this example is that the initial CPR may be only a small part of the total cost per final order in a multistep promotion. The costs of converting initial responses or leads can be particularly expensive when the conversion process requires expensive sales literature or requires a sales call.

TRACKING BACK-END PERFORMANCE

In the section on front-end performance, we discussed the techniques used to measure the costs of acquiring leads, buyers, or subscribers. In each case, costs were expressed not in terms of the total dollars spent but rather in terms of the amount spent to acquire the average customer from a particular media investment. By defining costs in terms of the average cost per customer, it is possible for us to compare alternative media without regard to their size.

This same approach will be followed in the discussion of back-end performance. In general, back-end performance refers to the purchase behavior of a group of respondents from the time their names are entered on the customer file. More specifically, we shall define back-end performance as the sales, contribution, and profits resulting from a group of respondents acquired from a particular advertising medium.

In order to measure, or track, back-end performance, it is necessary to maintain a system in which each individual customer is identified as coming from a specific advertising medium: a list, a space insertion, or a broadcast spot. When this is done, it is possible to accumulate the behavior of all customers from the same initial source medium and calculate average contribution, or profits.

For this reason, direct marketing advertisers include a key code on every coupon in every space ad and print a key code on the return card or label of every direct-mail promotion. The key code identifies the advertising medium and becomes a permanent part of the responding customer's record, along with name, address, and purchase history.

Direct marketers have proved over and over that for a given order, back-end performance will vary significantly from one advertising medium to another. In general, direct marketers have discovered that buyers acquired from direct mail behave better than buyers acquired from space and magazine advertisements and that buyers acquired from direct mail or space will perform better than buyers acquired from broadcast promotions. However, there are wide variations in performance within the same media category. The best customers acquired from space media will perform better than the worst customers acquired from direct mail, and so on.

The critical concept to remember is that back-end performance will vary from medium to medium and that the only way to operate a profitable direct-response business is to be able to track the performance of customers in terms of the original source group so that the decision to reinvest promotion dollars can be made on the basis of proven performance.

At this point, it will pay to remind the reader that what is being described is classical direct marketing theory. Concern is with the performance of the average customer, and what is being measured and about to be evaluated is the relationship between back-end performance and front-end or acquisition expense.

Back-end performance in this classical approach is assumed to be the same for every individual acquired from a given source code. In practice, when direct marketers set out to influence back-end performance, they do so using a natural extension of the source group concept. For example, if a classical direct marketer thought that it might be better in a continuity situation to ship books every six weeks instead of the usual 4-week shipment cycle, the procedure most likely to be followed would be to run an A/B split in one or more important media sources disclosing the 6-week shipment cycle to the A group and a 4-week shipment cycle to the B group. The marketer could then measure if there was any immediate difference in up-front response and begin the process of waiting to see if back-end performance was better or worse for either group. More on influencing back-end response, through classical as well as database methods, later. First, let's finish the discussion of how back-end performance is measured.

Measuring Back-End Performance

Single-Shot Mailing. The measurement of back-end performance for a solo, or single-shot, mailing is simply the statement of profit or loss for the promotion. Table 36-3 lists the assumptions that would be typical of a solo mailing of a product with a sales price of $60. The profit-and-loss statement that follows Table 36-4 is based on the assumptions defined in Table 36-3.

Clubs and Continuity Programs. In clubs and continuity programs, the statistic that measures back-end performance is the contribution to promotion, overhead, and profit. If this contribution for a group of new orders or starters is greater than the cost of acquiring the starting group, the investment in the starting group can be considered to be at least marginally profitable.

This contribution statistic sometimes is referred to as the *order margin*, the *allowable*, or the *breakeven*. Each term implies a comparison to the cost per order expended to bring the starters into the business.

The contribution statistic excludes consideration of all fixed costs and overhead. Contribution is calculated by subtracting all direct expenses from the net sales of a group of starters and then dividing the result by the number of starters in the group.

In a club or continuity program, sales accumulate over the economic life of the starting group, and that life often can extend over a number of years. Therefore, in clubs or programs with an exceptionally long member life, the contribution from each monthly cycle should be discounted by some amount, generally the seller's cost of capital or opportunity cost, to take the time value of money into consideration.

The ability to forecast final sales and payments from individual starting

Table 36-3. Assumptions for a Single-Shot Promotion

Selling price	$65.00
Shipping and handling charge	$3.00
Return rate (percent of gross sales)	10.0 %
Percentage of returns reusable	90.0 %
Cost of product per unit	$15.00
Order processing:	
Reply postage per gross response	$.25
Order processing and setup per gross response	$2.00
Percentage of gross orders using:	
Credit cards	75.0 %
Checks	25.0 %
Credit card expense	3.0 %
Percentage of charge orders with bad checks	5.0 %
Shipping and handling per gross response	$3.00
Return processing:	
Return postage per return	$1.50
Handling per gross return	$.50
Refurbishing costs per usable return	$2.00
Premium expense per gross response	$6.00
Promotion CPM	$350.00
Quantity mailed	100,000
Percent response	2.0 %
Overhead factor as a percent of net sales	10.0 %

groups on the basis of early performance data is critical in clubs and continuity programs. In these businesses, as in most direct-response businesses, the key marketing decision is the decision to reinvest in media that have already been tested. Because of the long economic life of a club or continuity member, the decision to reinvest must be made on the basis of forecasted behavior. For example, if a new list is mailed in the winter and pulls as well as most other lists used by the club, the marketer may wish to remail the same names or test a larger segment of the list universe in the summer or fall campaign. However, by that time only a few cycles of actual data will be available for analysis. The decision, therefore, must be made on the basis of expected final contribution per starter. The forecast itself is based on the actual data accumulated to date.

In both clubs and continuity programs, one of the most important forecasting variables is the *attrition rate*. This is the term used to measure the rate at which members in a club or program either cancel their memberships or are canceled because of failure to pay for previously shipped items.

In negative option clubs, the attrition pattern measures the percentage of original starters eligible to receive the periodic advance announcements that advertise the negative option selection of the cycle and the alternative selections. In addition to being able to forecast the attrition pattern, it is also necessary to be able to forecast the acceptance rate of the featured negative option selection and the acceptance of the alternative selections as well as the average price of each category of sale.

Table 36-5 shows a simplified negative option club model that forecasts and accumulates average gross sales per starting member. As was mentioned before,

Table 36-4. Profit and Loss Statement for a Single-Shot Promotion

	Units	Amount	Percent
Gross sales	2,000	$130,000	
Shipping and handling	2,000	6,000	
Total revenue	2,000	136,000	111.1%
Returns	200	13,600	11.1
Net sales	1,800	$122,400	100.0%
Cost of sales:			
Product:			
Net shipments	1,800	$ 27,000	22.1%
Nonreusable units	20	300	.2
Order processing:			
Reply postage	2,000	500	.4
Setup costs	2,000	4,000	3.3
Credit card costs	1,500	3,060	2.5
Bad check expense	25	1,700	1.4
Shipping and handling	2,000	6,000	4.9
Return processing:			
Postage	200	300	.2
Handling	200	100	.1
Refurbishing	180	360	.3
Premium	2,000	12,000	9.8
Total cost of sales		$ 55,320	45.2%
Operating gross margin		$ 67,080	54.8%
Promotion expense		35,000	28.6
Contribution to overhead and profit		$ 32,080	26.2%
Overhead allocation		12,240	10.0
Profit		$ 19,840	16.2%

in an actual club operation, the forecast would include separate estimates for the negative option selection and the alternative selections.

According to the model shown in Table 36-5, the average sale per starter will be $48.19. Assuming that direct costs, excluding all promotion and premium costs, are equal to 35 percent of gross sales, the contribution to promotion, overhead, and profit from this group of starters would be $31.32. It is this number minus premium costs that would be compared with promotion costs to determine the profitability of the starting group.

In continuity programs, there are two attrition patterns to be concerned with. The first pattern measures the percentage of starters who initially receive each shipment level at the earliest possible date. This attrition pattern reflects the payment behavior of starters who pay for each shipment on time and continue in the program. The second pattern represents the percentage of original starters who eventually receive each shipment level by the end of the economic life of the starting group. The difference in the two patterns is due to starters who fall behind in their payments and are suspended temporarily from receiving further shipments. As these starters eventually pay, the percentage of starters receiving each shipment level gradually increases.

In order to forecast sales properly, it is necessary to be able to forecast both

Table 36-5. Average Sales Accumulated over Time in a Negative Option Club

		Percent		Sales per Starting Member	
Cycle	Still Active	Buying Product	Average Price	Incremental	Cumulative
		Actual Data			
1	97.0%	51%	$12	$5.94	$ 5.94
2	95.0	47	12	5.36	11.29
3	83.0	42	12	4.18	15.48
4	75.0	38	12	3.42	18.90
5	70.0	33	12	2.77	21.67
		Forecast Data			
6	65.1	32	12	2.50	24.17
7	60.5	31	12	2.25	26.42
8	56.3	31	12	2.09	28.52
9	52.4	30	12	1.89	30.40
10	48.7	30	12	1.75	32.15
11	45.3	30	12	1.63	33.78
12	42.1	30	12	1.52	35.30
13	39.2	30	12	1.41	36.71
14	36.4	30	12	1.31	38.02
15	33.9	30	12	1.22	39.24
16	31.5	30	12	1.13	40.38
17	29.3	30	12	1.05	41.43
18	27.3	30	12	.98	42.41
19	25.3	30	12	.91	43.32
20	23.6	30	12	.85	44.17
21	21.9	30	12	.79	44.96
22	20.4	30	12	.73	45.70
23	19.0	30	12	.68	46.38
24	17.6	30	12	.63	47.01
25	16.4	30	12	.59	47.60
26	15.2	30	12	.55	48.15
27	14.2	30	12	.51	48.66
28	13.2	30	12	.47	49.14
29	12.3	30	12	.44	49.58
30	11.4	30	12	.41	49.99
31	10.6	30	12	.38	50.37
32	9.9	30	12	.36	50.73
33	9.2	30	12	.33	51.06
34	8.5	30	12	.31	51.36
35	7.9	30	12	.29	51.65
36	7.4	30	12	.27	51.92
37	6.9	30	12	.25	52.16
38	6.4	30	12	.23	52.39
39	5.9	30	12	.21	52.61
40	5.5	30	12	.20	52.81

attrition patterns. A forecast using only the first attrition pattern will understate eventual sales. A forecast using just the second pattern will forecast final sales correctly but will not be able to forecast when those sales will occur. Table 36-6 provides an example of continuity attrition and the growth of the average number of units shipped over time to a group of starters in a continuity program in which one item is shipped per month.

Table 36-6. Attrition Patterns in a Continuity Program

Shipment Number	Attrition Pattern Start	Attrition Pattern End	By End of Cycle	Average Units Shipped	By End of Week	Average Units Shipped
1	100%	100 %	1	1.00	40	5.09
2	92	92	2	1.00	41	5.23
3	85	85	3	1.00	42	5.25
4	50	60	4	1.00	43	5.26
5	35	45	5	1.92	44	5.27
6	30	40	6	1.92	45	5.39
7	20	28	7	1.92	46	5.40
8	18	25	8	1.92	47	5.41
9	16	23	9	2.77	48	5.42
10	15	20	10	2.77	49	5.54
11	13	18	11	2.77	50	5.55
12	12	17	12	2.77	51	5.56
13	11	15	13	3.29	52	5.56
14	10	13	14	3.30	53	5.67
15	9	12	15	3.32	54	5.68
Total		5.94%	16	3.34	55	5.69
			17	3.70	56	5.69
			18	3.74	57	5.79
			19	3.75	58	5.80
			20	3.77	59	5.80
			21	4.10	60	5.81
			22	4.14	61	5.83
			23	4.17	62	5.83
			24	4.19	63	5.84
			25	4.40	64	5.85
			26	4.43	65	5.86
			27	4.45	66	5.86
			28	4.46	67	5.87
			29	4.65	68	5.88
			30	4.67	69	5.88
			31	4.69	70	5.89
			32	4.70	71	5.89
			33	4.88	72	5.90
			34	4.89	73	5.91
			35	4.90	74	5.91
			36	4.91	75	5.92
			37	5.00	76	5.92
			38	5.07	77	5.93
			39	5.08	78	5.94

Newsletters and Magazines. The key economic variables that determine the profitability of a newsletter are (1) price, (2) the initial pay or conversion rate, (3) renewal rates, and (4) the response rate to direct-mail promotions at different levels of promotion expense.

As was mentioned earlier in this chapter, many newsletters and magazines are successful in attracting trial subscribers through the use of preview offers that allow the potential subscriber to cancel without paying after examining one or a few sample issues. In these situations, the initial pay rate or conversion rate is the single most important variable affecting the ultimate success of the venture. However, even a relatively high initial pay rate can be offset by a poor renewal rate. Only after both conversion rates and renewal rates have been tested can one be sure of the potential profits of a newsletter. Table 36-7 shows the range of profits after 2 years from a direct-mail investment of $3000 that resulted in 200 responses. In this situation, the $3000 investment is recovered in the first year if the conversion rate is 60 percent or greater. The investment is profitable within two years if the initial conversion rate is 40 percent or more and the first renewal rate is 50 percent or better.

The profits that can be generated from a newsletter are related directly to the price charged for the newsletter, since editorial costs and printing costs are not affected by the price of the service. Thus, it is very important that price testing be employed at the outset to determine the best and most profitable price for the service. Tables 36-8 and 36-9 show the effect of a $10 increase or decrease in price on the newsletter described in Table 36-7.

The economics of magazines is similar to the economics of newsletters but with a number of critical differences. First, magazines rely heavily on newsstand sales and advertising to supplement the revenue stream provided by subscription income. Second, because of competition and because magazines are targeted to reach circulation levels measured in the hundreds of thousands rather than just thousands, as is the case with most newsletters, there is much less price-setting flexibility. However, just as in newsletters, the response rate to direct mail, the conversion rate, and the renewal rates are the key economic variables that eventually will determine the success or lack of success of the magazine venture.

Catalogs. The term *back-end analysis* in a catalog operation can have multiple meanings. We may use the term with regard to the analysis of past media selections in much the same way as we analyze media performance in a club or continuity situation. Or we may be concerned with the profitability of an individual catalog mailing, that is, did the catalog make a profit, which items sold well, which didn't, and so on. Or we may be referring to the decision-making process in which we attempt to decide which customers should be mailed which catalogs and with what frequency in the future.

The first decision deals with the evaluation of individual media sources, and we act as if all customers acquired behave in exactly the same way by looking at the average performance of all customers acquired from the media source. Again, this is the classical direct marketing approach, as opposed to the database approach, which focuses its attention on the performance of individual customers across media sources. The reason we need two approaches is that two dif-

Table 36-7. The Economics of Newsletter Direct-Mail Marketing

		Initial Pay or Conversion Rate				
		30 Percent	40 Percent	50 Percent	60 Percent	70 Percent
First-Year Results						
Subscribers		60	80	100	120	140
Revenues		$2,820	$3,,760	$4,700	$5,640	$6,580
Fulfillment and re-newal costs		750	850	950	1,050	1,150
Promotion costs		3,000	3,000	3,000	3,000	3,000
First-year profits		$ (930)	$ (90)	$ 750	$1,590	$2,430
Second-Year Profits*						
If renewal rates are:	40.00%	$ 864	$ 1,152	$1,440	$1,728	$2,018
	50.00	1,118	1,490	1,863	2,235	2,608
	60.00	1,371	1,828	2,285	2,742	3,199
	70.00	1,625	2,166	2,708	3,249	3,790
Cumulative Second-Year Profits						
If renewal rates are:	40.00%	$ (66)	$ 1,062	$2,190	$3,318	$4,446
	50.00	188	1,400	2,613	3,825	5,038
	60.00	441	1,738	3,035	4,332	5,629
	70.00	695	2,076	3,458	4,839	6,221
Assumptions						
The price of the newsletter						$47.00
The cost of fulfilling a paying subscriber						6.00
The cost of fulfilling a canceling subscriber						2.25
The cost of renewing a subscriber per starting subscriber						1.25
The cost of fulfilling a subscriber who fails to renew						2.50
Range of possible conversion rates from trial to paid subscriber						30% to 70%
Range of possible first renewal rates						40% to 70%
Mailing quantity						10,000
Mailing costs						$3,000
Percent response						2.00%
Results						
Number of gross orders (.02 × 10,000)						200

*Second-year profits if renewal rate is 70 percent and conversion rate is 70 percent:
Subscribers: (10,000 × .02 × .7 × .7) = 98
Revenue = 98 subscribers × $35 = $3,430
Fulfillment and renewal costs: 98 subscribers × (6 + 1.25) = $710.50
Issues to nonrenewals: 42 × 2.50 = 105
Second-year profits: $3,430 − $710.50 − $105 = $2,614.50

ferent decisions are involved. When evaluating a media source, we are asking, "Is this media source profitable?" and "Should we invest in it again?" What counts is the total or the average performance of all customers expected to be acquired from a future investment when compared with the cost of the investment. And we use past performance as a guide to future performance.

Table 36-8. Cumulative Second-Year Profits if Price Is Reduced to $27

Renewal Rates	Conversion Rate				
	30 Percent	40 Percent	50 Percent	60 Percent	70 Percent
40%	$(1,746)	$(1,178)	$(610)	$ (42)	$ 526
50	(1,613)	(1,000)	(388)	225	838
60	(1,479)	(822)	(165)	492	1,149
70	(1,346)	(644)	58	759	1,460

Table 36-9. Cumulative Second-Year Profits if Price Is Increased to $47

Renewal Rates	Conversion Rate				
	30 Percent	40 Percent	50 Percent	60 Percent	70 Percent
40%	$ (66)	$1,062	$2,190	$3,318	$4,446
50	188	1,400	2,613	3,825	5,038
60	441	1,738	3,035	4,332	5,629
70	695	2,076	3,458	4,839	6,221

In a noncontractual relationship, after a customer is acquired from any media source, the decision to promote that customer is an independent decision. This decision should be based on the expected future performance of the individual, regardless of the source from which he or she was acquired, even though the original media source may be, as we'll see later, an important variable in making a prediction of future performance.

The mechanics of media source evaluation in a catalog or in any noncontractual relationship requires computer systems that track performance by original source code. Again, as always, the key question is, Will the eventual contribution from the customers acquired be greater than the cost of acquiring those customers, and if so, by how much?

In practice, the same media source will have been used many times in the past, and an evaluation of each use will reveal that profitability will vary from use to use. Not only will the prediction of eventual contribution vary but the cost of acquiring new customers, as measured by the cost per order, will vary from promotion to promotion. Therefore, the prediction of future performance, both front-end CPO and back-end contribution, must be based on a forecasting procedure that takes this variability into account. Time-series analysis, taking such factors as trend and seasonality into account, may be employed if the data is suitable, or the analyst may use simpler averaging techniques giving greater weight to more recent occurrences. In practice, this becomes much more of an art than a science, and to imply that there are highly reliable standard procedures for this process would be misleading.

Financial Services. The provider of financial services is, in theory, in a nearly identical position to the traditional catalog marketer with respect to the noncontractual nature of the relationship between the company and the customer. However, in practice, we've found financial service providers to be more concerned with individual level database marketing decisions than with the classical direct marketing issue of relating back-end performance to initial cost per acquired customer. There are a variety of reasons for this, none of which justifies current practices but which go a long way toward explaining why things are the way they are.

To begin with, many financial services providers using direct marketing methods are not traditional self-contained direct marketing companies whose only contact with the customer is through direct marketing media. Therefore, since it is difficult if not impossible to attribute response to a single ad or direct-mail promotion, little attempt is made to do so. More significant, we suspect, is the fact that many direct marketing operations within financial services firms are developed in an ad hoc manner. Someone at a high level within the firm, perhaps because of exposure to competitive direct marketing offers, decided that direct mail or direct marketing should be done within the firm, and set out to do so using the existing computer support systems, which were not designed for direct marketing purposes but were, in all likelihood, designed to support a sales force network.

In an information or database environment, where decision making is based on knowledge about the individual customer, one might argue that knowledge about the average behavior of all customers acquired from the same media source is unimportant. This argument, while it seems reasonable, is wrong for two reasons. The first reason is that the original media source is an important piece of individual information. The second reason is that it confuses the need to make decisions about customers with the need to make decisions about where one shall prospect for customers. Again and again, direct marketers must make trade-off decisions about how much to spend on current-customer marketing and how much to spend on new-customer marketing. This is true for any company using direct marketing methods, be they a traditional direct marketing firm or one of the newer nontraditional users of direct marketing.

The Return of the Chicken-or-the-Egg Problem

By now, the reader who has been paying close attention should have realized that we're back to the chicken-or-the-egg problem raised earlier in this chapter. This argument goes as follows. We wish to compare the lifetime performance or behavior of customers acquired from a media source with the cost of acquiring those customers. However, their performance will be a function of what we send them and how often we promote them. If our promotion decisions are faulty, if we mail too often or too infrequently, or if we mail the wrong products, the contribution of the group of customers will be less than it would have been if our decisions had been better. Fortunately, the only practical way to treat this problem is to ignore it, and that's OK if all media source groups have been treated in the same way, however good or bad that way was, and if all we're trying to do is rank media sources in terms of relative performance in order to decide how to allocate future media acquisition dollars. On the other hand, we always have to guard against self-fulfilling prophecies. If, for example, customers from a particular media source are always mailed less frequently because their performance is expected to be less than average, then we shouldn't be surprised to find that indeed sales from these customers always turn out to be less than sales from customers acquired from other sources. The solution to this problem, if the problem is thought to exist, is to create and track test groups across all media sources that are always treated in the same fashion.

Let's assume that we can agree on an acceptable way to estimate the lifetime performance of customers acquired from individual media sources, and that we can even agree on the expected CPO and the expected lifetime contribution of customers to be acquired in the future. How do we use this information in decision making?

MEASURING PROFITABILITY: COMBINING FRONT-END AND BACK-END STATISTICS

In the previous discussion, it was implied that if the contribution to promotion, overhead, and profit for a given media investment was greater than the cost per order, the investment could be considered to be at least marginally profitable. We shall now continue to develop the relationship between front-end and back-end statistics.

Many direct marketers, particularly those engaged in club and continuity programs, prefer to use the concept of return on promotion to measure the relationship between front-end and back-end performance. Return on promotion (ROP) is defined as the ratio of the contribution to promotion, overhead, and profit minus the cost per order divided by the cost per order times 100.

$$ROP = \frac{[Contribution - Cost\ per\ order]}{Cost\ per\ order} \times 100$$

Conceptually, the ROP approach treats the decision to run a space ad or mail a list as an investment against which some financial return is expected. The return is measured by the difference between the contribution that results from all the purchases that occur after the order enters the house and the cost of acquiring the order.

For example, in the discussion on clubs and continuities, we showed how a group of starters with average sales of $52.81 might generate a contribution per starter of $34.21. Let's assume that the cost of acquiring this group of starters was $20 per starter. In this case, the ROP would be:

$$ROP = \frac{[\$34.32 - \$20.00]}{\$20.00} \times 100 = 71.6\%$$

The ROP statistic can be used in a variety of ways by direct marketers. One important use of this statistic is to evaluate alternative offers. The decision rule to be followed is that if the media investment required to implement both offers is the same, the offer with the highest ROP is the best offer.

Consider the examples described in Table 36-10. In this example, the deci-

Table 36-10. Using Incremental ROP to Evaluate New Offers
(from 20 to 25 OPM)

	Case 1	Case 2	Incremental Results
	Assumptions		
Quantity mailed	50,000	50,000	
Orders per thousand	20	25	
Average revenue per starter	$70.00	$70.00	
Direct costs excluding premium expense	$30.00	$30.00	
Contribution	$40.00	$40.00	
Advertising CPM	$350.00	$350.00	
Advertising expense	$17,500.00	$17,500.00	
Advertising CPO	$17.50	$14.00	
Premium expense	$6.00	$9.00	
	Results		
Orders	1,000	1,250	250
Sales	$70,000	$87,500	$17,500
Costs	$30,000	$37,500	$7,500
Contributions	$40,000	$50,000	$10,000
Advertising	$17,500	$17,500	$0
Premium	$6,000	$11,250	$5,250
Total contribution to overhead and profit	$16,500	$21,250	$4,750
Per starter	$16.50	$17.00	$.50
ROP	94.3 %	121.4 %	0

sion concerns whether to use a premium costing $6 per starter or a premium costing $9 per starter. The assumption is made that the average sales resulting from the use of either premium offer will be the same and will be equal to $70 per starter.

Naturally, increasing premium expense will reduce profits unless the premium offer results in an increased response. Thus, the question is, What increase in response is necessary to justify the use of a $9 premium? One way to answer this question is to assume a response rate to the $6 premium offer and then search by trial and error for a response rate to the $9 offer that would result in the same profit and loss as the profit and loss resulting from the $6 offer.

Under the Results column for Case 1 in Table 36-10, we see the profit and loss resulting from the $6 premium if a response rate of 20 OPM is assumed. For Case 2, at a response rate of 25 OPM, which is assumed to result from the use of the $9 premium, contribution to overhead and profit would be increased by a total of $4,750. The ROP for each case is shown at the bottom of Table 36-10. The ROP for Case 2 is 121.4 percent, which is greater than the ROP of 94.3 percent for Case 1. As long as the media investment is the same—in this case, the $17,500 required to mail 50,000 pieces at a CPM of $350—the alternative with the higher ROP will be the most profitable.

Therefore, it is possible to use the ROP equation directly to determine the response rate that would cause the ROP on the $9 premium offer to equal the ROP on the $6 premium offer:

$$ROP = \frac{\text{Contribution} - \text{premium} - \text{CPO}}{\text{CPO}}$$

$$\text{Old ROP} = .943 = \frac{\$40 - \$6 - \$17.50}{\$17.50}$$

$$\text{New ROP} = .943 = \frac{\$40 - \$9 - \text{New CPO}}{\text{New CPO}}$$

$$\text{New CPO} = \$15.95$$

$$\text{New OPM} = \frac{\text{CPM}}{\text{New CPO}} = \frac{\$350}{\$15.95} = 21.94$$

The required new response rate is 21.94 orders per thousand.

When the initial media investment is not the same, the ROP analysis must be applied to the incremental investment in order to result in the correct decision. In this situation, if the incremental ROP is greater than zero, there will be an increase in the contribution to overhead and profit.

Refer to Table 36-11. In this example, the decision is whether to increase the quality of the mailing package in order to increase response. Costs are expected to increase from $350 per thousand to $400 per thousand, and the response

Table 36-11. Using Incremental ROP to Evaluate New Offers (from 20 to 22 OPM)

	Case 1	Case 2	Incremental Results
	Assumptions		
Quantity mailed	50,000	50,000	
Orders per thousand	20	22	
Average revenue per starter	$70.00	$70.00	
Direct costs excluding premium expense	$30.00	$30.00	
Contribution	$40.00	$40.00	
Advertising CPM	$350.00	$400.00	
Advertising expense	$17,500.00	$20,000.00	
Advertising CPO	$17.50	$18.18	
Premium expense	$5.00	$5.00	
	Results		
Orders	1,000	1,100	100
Sales	$70,000	$77,000	$7,000
Costs	$30,000	$33,000	$3,000
Contributions	$40,000	$44,000	$4,000
Advertising	$17,500	$20,000	$2,500
Premium	$5,000	$5,500	$500
Total contribution to overhead and profit	$17,500	$18,500	$1,000
Per starter	$17.50	$16.82	$.68
ROP	100.0 %	92.5 %	0
Incremental ROP	100.0 %	92.5 %	40.0 %

rate is expected to increase from 20 OPM to 22 OPM. In Table 36-11, we see that if the more expensive mailing package was chosen, the average ROP would decline from 100 to 92.5 percent, but the incremental ROP would be 40 percent and total dollar contribution would increase by $1000.

However, if the response rate increased to only 21 OPM, as shown in Table 36-12, the incremental ROP would be negative, and contribution would decline.

The decision to invest funds up to the point at which the incremental ROP is zero is a management decision. Generally, the cutoff rate is substantially higher, around 30 percent, to reflect other factors such as risk, the company's cost of capital, and opportunity costs resulting from competing uses of funds from other investments.

Another important use of the return on promotion statistic is to rank alternative investment opportunities for budget allocations. We have already seen that if the size of the investment is held constant, the investment alternative with the highest ROP is the most profitable.

In planning annual media budgets, a good first step is to begin by calculating the expected ROP for each independent media opportunity and then to rank all such opportunities in terms of descending order of ROP. Conceptually, as the size of the media budget increases, the average ROP generated by the budget decreases, but for any given budget total, a media budget constructed in such a fashion will always yield the highest possible ROP.

Table 36-12. Using Incremental ROP to Evaluate New Offers (from 20 to 21 OPM)

	Case 1	Case 2	Incremental Results
	Assumptions		
Quantity mailed	50,000	50,000	
Orders per thousand	20	21	
Average revenue per starter	$70.00	$70.00	
Direct costs excluding premium expense	$30.00	$30.00	
Contribution	$40.00	$40.00	
Advertising CPM	$350.00	$400.00	
Advertising expense	$17,500.00	$20,000.00	
Advertising CPO	$17.50	$19.05	
Premium expense	$5.00	$5.00	
	Results		
Orders	1,000	1,050	50
Sales	$70,000	$73,500	$3,500
Costs	$30,000	$31,500	$1,500
Contributions	$40,000	$42,000	$2,000
Advertising	$17,500	$20,000	$2,500
Premium	$5,000	$5,250	$250
Total contribution to overhead and profit	$17,500	$16,750	$(750)
Per starter	$17.50	$15.95	$(1.55)
ROP	100.0 %	83.8 %	0
Incremental ROP			−30.0 %

One caution in the use of ROP in budget planning: The ROP statistic is an economic measure and does not take fiscal-year profit-and-loss considerations into account. An investment with a 50 percent ROP and a first-of-the-year expense date is considered to be the same in an ROP ranking scheme as an investment with a 50 percent ROP with an end-of-the-fiscal year expense date. From a financial accounting point of view, the investment made on the first of the year will result in sales from new members in that same fiscal year. The investment made at the end of the fiscal year will result only in expense; the corresponding sales will come in the next fiscal year.

This problem is alleviated to some extent by accounting procedures that allow new-member acquisition expense to be amortized over the economic life of the acquired new members or subscribers. For example, assuming an economic life of 12 months, only one-twelfth of the expense of a promotion that was released in the last fiscal month would be charged to the current fiscal year.

ROP AND THE INFAMOUS 2 PERCENT RESPONSE RATE

It is customary for direct marketers to be accused of settling for low response rates. The implicit assumption is that through better targeting, response rates will increase to a rate higher than 2 percent—2 percent in this case being used as a kind of shorthand for a breakeven level of response. Of course, adoption of the ROP principle suggests that direct marketers should, if funds are available and fiscal budget restraints are not an issue, always continue investing promotion dollars until the marginal rate of return on promotion approaches the cost of capital, and if that happens at a 2 percent response level, so be it. The goal of targeting should therefore not be to increase the marginal cutoff rate from 2 percent to some higher number; the goal of targeting should be to find more names that can be mailed with a response rate of 2 percent (that is, the breakeven level) or better, and in this way to increase the size of one's business. Of course, if promotion funds are limited, then the effect of targeting will be to increase the average response rate over its current level, in turn increasing the average return on promotion.

37
Product Development

John T. White

GRI Corporation, World of Beauty Division
Chicago, Ill.

WHAT WILL YOU SELL YOUR CUSTOMERS NEXT?

It is perhaps the most important question facing direct marketers today: What are you going to sell to your customers next? That is the focus of this discussion. It assumes you already have a direct-mail business and a database of customers. This will provide you a general framework for approaching product development, with:

1. Suggestions for *generating* new product ideas
2. Analytical techniques for *evaluating* new product ideas
3. Suggestions for *hedging* risks of new product introduction

SUCCESSFUL PRODUCT DEVELOPMENT: THE MARRIAGE OF ENTREPRENEURIAL INSTINCTS AND ANALYTICAL TECHNIQUES

The Odds Are Stacked Against You

Product development involves risk taking, creativity, and entrepreneurial instinct — the stuff that was second nature to the pioneers in our industry. But the odds of a new product succeeding are only about one out of four or five. Product development is expensive and virtually always represents a *major* investment of time and money. How can you approach product development to improve the odds for success?

Know Your Customer, Listen to Your Gut

Product development is largely about learning how to see through your customer's eyes. It starts with knowing your customer better than anyone else. The early entrepreneurs in our business had a hands-on, "gut" knowledge of who their customers were and what they wanted. They were personally involved in the business: opening mail, reading correspondence, typing letters, filling orders. They knew what customers wanted because they were having a personal dialogue with them on a day-to-day basis.

Today, direct marketers in many companies have become too isolated from the customer. Some of our managers in the largest and most sophisticated mail-order companies are highly myopic and overly specialized. They *only* analyze results or *only* buy media or *only* manage the database, because that's what they do in the company. What we see is often reminiscent of an idiot savant—they perform their one special task expertly but have little or no understanding of *why* they do it or how if fits into the bigger picture. Tragically, that intimate knowledge of the customer has too often been lost. Now hear this: You cannot succeed at product development without it!

Listen to the Numbers

But good gut instincts and knowledge of the customer alone are not enough. For ultimately, it is the marketplace that will vote on your work and determine whether a new product is a success or failure. The scary part about new product development is trying to predict in advance how the marketplace will use their dollars to "vote" on your product.

Potentially, we can do an even better job of product development today than the old entrepreneurs did with their instincts alone. We have an arsenal of sophisticated analytical tools at our disposal. By developing a fundamental, intimate knowledge of the customer and marrying it to modern analytical and research techniques that were unavailable or unknown to the pioneers, anyone can be a pro at product development.

GENERATING IDEAS: WHAT DO YOUR CUSTOMERS TELL YOU THEY WANT?

If you listen, your customers will tell you what they want. Customers are the best sources of new product ideas—the best new products and services are those that your own customers want but can't find. Here are some ways to generate ideas from your customers.

Develop a Customer Monitoring Program

Talk to Some Customers.   Go to your customer service department and listen in on calls for 2 to 4 hours twice a month. Make it a habit and a standing commitment on your calendar. Try fielding some incoming calls and talking firsthand to your customers. Have your data systems department randomly select 100 customer names with phone numbers each month and spend 2 to 4 hours calling a couple dozen customers to solicit their ideas and get feedback about your products and services.

Scour the White Mail.   Insist on seeing a random sample of white mail (incoming customer correspondence) each week, read it carefully, and then think about what is being said. This is one of the best ways to develop new product ideas. Your customers will tell you what they are looking for, often in amazing detail. But it may take some imagination to dream up new products that address the needs you are hearing. Approach customer correspondence monitoring with the attitude that anything can be done—then figure out how to do it. You are looking for a major point of differentiation from your competition. Force yourself in the process to continually ask "why not?"

For example, many years ago in the apparel-by-mail business, a marketer learned from customers that the only way to successfully sell ready-to-wear fashions through the mail without trying them on for size was to have an extremely liberal return policy. Someone asked the fundamental question, Why not allow the customer to try it on at home with no risk? The idea of an unconditional, unquestioned, easy-return policy at no cost to the customer, with items picked up right at the door by UPS, must have been a scary idea. The financial people must have hated it—there was certainly no rational, logical, money-saving reason for doing it. Yet someone had the courage to try this revolutionary approach and opened up a whole new way of doing business by mail.

Years ago, Garden Way asked why not sell 300-pound rototillers through the mail—perhaps the most unlikely products ever to be sold via mail order. There were a million very good reasons why it couldn't be done. But Garden Way set about systematically overcoming each of the individual objections to selling rototillers by mail—and in the process arrived at a completely unique position in the market. And that is exactly how you need to approach product development in your company.

Conduct Customer Service Roundtable Discussions.   Set up periodic informal roundtable discussions with your customer services operators. Pick two to three groups of no more than six each and choose a slow time of the week to avoid interfering with business. Ask several very general questions and then spend 99 percent of the time listening and taking notes. Try to get each person in the group to participate. Here are some ideas for questions:

1. Have you noticed any unusual trends in customer suggestions or complaints lately?
2. Have you heard any interesting ideas or suggestion about new products or services from our customers lately?

3. What is your most common complaint?

4. How do you think we could improve our product line or service?

5. What, more than anything else, do our customers tell you they want but can't find?

Remember, a new product idea often starts with a weakness or problem. The product itself is only a solution to the problem. The more impossible or unsolvable the problem seems, the more unique your competitive edge will be when you finally solve it.

Develop a Market Monitoring System

Get on Other Mailing Lists.   Get on the mailing list for every direct competitor in your business. Subscribe to every magazine that your competition advertises in. Be very liberal in how you define your competition. Get other people in your office or department to clip interesting offers and bring in all interesting direct-mail packages they receive at home.

Order Competitive Products.   Routinely order products from your competition. Test their customer service, measure their response times, read their personalized and computer-generated customer letters and notifications. Don't pay the bill for the product for a while and see how they handle it. Just as chickens will peck a weak and bleeding member of the brood to death for survival, you are looking here for *any* sign of weakness or opportunity that would give your company a competitive edge and prompt a new product idea.

Carefully Evaluate Competitive Products and Services.   Look at the competitor's products. Are they what you expected from the advertising? How would you improve them if you could start all over? Do you see evidence that they have tested and are now rolling out in direct mail, magazines, or other media? If so, do you think the product is successful? What is it that makes the product successful? Is there some common element that seems to underlie the success that is a hot button and could be ripped off in another form? How can you piece the clues together into a new product idea?

Generalization

Generalization is when an elemental thread of learning gained from one experience is applied to a new and different experience. In marketing, I think the masters of generalization are the networks who spin off new television shows. You've seen it done a dozen times. Perhaps the best example is "All in the Family"—one of the most successful series of all time. The network plucked George Jefferson out of this series and transplanted him into a new show, "The Jeffersons." It worked.

And it works in mail order too. You can figure out ahead of your competition what the central, underlying success to a product line or program is and transplant it in a different setting ahead of them. You can also go to school on your own company's history of most notable successes. What was the underlying thread that made each of those products or programs so very successful? How can you do some window dressing to transplant that central theme or idea into a new spin-off? This is a hotbed for new-product ideation, and perhaps some of the best spawning ground for truly successful new products.

Customer Focus Groups

Another technique is to organize consumer panels of six to eight customers and get them to spend 2 hours talking about your products in a moderated discussion. Focus groups are subjective and only provide directional information, but they are invaluable for seeing how customers describe your products, what they like and don't like, and for generating ideas for new products, service improvements, and new ways to sell. Have the groups review four or five of your products and comment on them. Ask probing, discussion-stimulating questions about motivations for buying, satisfaction with service, and other general topics that will help you get a feel for who you are selling to, why they buy, and what else they want.

Consumer Surveys

The best way to really find out a lot about your customers is to field a consumer research survey. It is incredibly easy to do and need not be terribly expensive if done right. You already have names and addresses of customers, so you can pull a random sample of names from your mailing list. Consider sending the survey out in your outbound shipments at a much lower cost.

In developing a questionnaire, consider what critical information would be most helpful to you in understanding why people are buying, what else you could sell to them, and where you could find more people like them. If a question doesn't help you hone in on one of these areas, you probably shouldn't ask it. In my opinion, it is best for you as a marketer to take the first shot at drafting the questionnaire—no one understands your business better than you do. Then get an outside research vendor to help polish the questionnaire. Talk to several different vendors. Here are a few questions you should certainly ask in your survey to help you in new product development:

Which magazines do you subscribe to, which magazines do you regularly read, which magazines have you bought from?   If you find several magazines that skew heavily toward your customers, subscribe to those and see what other products are being sold by mail—it may be a clue for a possible new direction. But you have to be careful here: results of magazine readership on your survey may be biased by where you have previously spent a lot of money advertising and prospecting for customers.

What are your leisure-time hobbies?   This question is a key guidepost to finding new products. Suppose you are selling nursery products and bulbs through the mail and find that 45 percent of your list also enjoys camping, as compared to 12 percent of the national population. You may have a clue to a possible new spin-off catalog business. In my experience, it is not at all uncommon to find unusual skews in questions like this that can be very helpful in finding new direction for your business.

What major organizations do you belong to?   This question can be invaluable for pointing to useful third-party endorsements and rented-list opportunities. I have used this question as the basis for some very lucrative deals. Suppose a direct marketer of porcelain collector's plates asks this question on a survey and discovers that nearly 35 percent of its customer base also belongs to the American Audubon Art Print Society, a nonprofit organization. The marketer strikes a deal with the organization to use reproductions of original Audubon sketches on a series of plates, to market them under the club's name as an official collection, and to offer the collection to the club's extensive mailing list of 750,000 names that would have otherwise been unavailable for rental, all in exchange for a percentage of the sales. The possibilities for these kinds of deals are real and as limitless as the imagination.

What other mail-order catalogs or companies do you buy from regularly?   This question can point out new areas of strong product interest that may not have been apparent to you before. For example, you find as a marketer of gourmet coffee that an unusual percentage of your customers have also bought from the Horchow catalog. You would never have suspected this otherwise. You test the list and find it to be highly responsive. What clues might this give for spin-off lines? How about for media selection?

A complete demographic battery of questions.   This will help you profile your customers. This is particularly important as you break out groups of customers by hobby, product interest, or other critical variables, to see how they vary by age, sex, income, education, and other key variables.

Usage of and interest in other key product areas that you are considering offering in the future.   To probe about lifestyles, motivations, and product interest, don't just ask yes or no questions. Develop strong opinion statements that make a stand in one direction or another and ask for a level of agreement or disagreement with the statements. For example, a mail-order marketer of gourmet steaks is considering a new exotic fish catalog business. He might develop a line of questioning on a survey as follows:

"Our family rarely eats beef any more."

"We simply can't find fresh fish that we can trust where we live."

"I try exotic types of fish in restaurants but can never find them at the store."

Each of these statements is followed with an agreement scale: strongly agree, somewhat agree, neither agree or disagree, somewhat disagree, or strongly disagree. This line of questioning is invaluable in really honing in on your customer's lifestyles, beliefs, and product preferences. A good research vendor can do all the tabulating and statistical analysis of results for you. But as a tip, if you get outside help, strongly consider *not* having them do a written analysis of the research. Just have them deliver the raw statistical tabulations and do the analysis yourself. In my experience, outside analyses are worthless—vendors simply don't know your business well enough to draw the proper conclusions and you are probably going to get (and pay for) several hundred pages of drivel.

If you are in a hurry for information, conduct research via phone survey. It is more expensive, and you can't ask as much information over the phone, but you can get answers within 7 to 10 days if you push it. If you are looking for information outside your mailing list on a national basis, a big list compiler and manager such as Metro Mail can do a random pull of names with valid phone numbers from their list at a reasonable charge.

In summary, consumer research is an invaluable tool to new product development and separates the pioneers from the modern new-product rainmakers. You need to read more about research elsewhere in this and other books.

Plug into the Media—Watch Trends

Sometimes your customers can be heard by listening to the general media. Subscribe to and read at least two news weeklies, read the paper once a day, read *The Wall Street Journal*, watch the news. There are also several very good marketing journals available that project consumer trends and report on new consumer developments. Subscribe to them. Keep your finger on the pulse of the market. Be aware of things that play into your position or that suggest you should be looking for a new position. The health craze, concern about cholesterol, the environmental movement, the push for recyclable products, the infatuation with the Simpsons and Ninja Turtles—all can have a critical impact on new-product development and the survival of your company. If you are first with products that are well timed, you are going to succeed.

Event Marketing

As part of plugging into the media, be aware of major events that will be emotional and monumental to Americans. Critical events can lead to excellent marketing opportunities and may lend a free windfall of publicity to a campaign. Nothing, but nothing, is more likely to help a product succeed than free publicity and national emotional fervor. Have someone responsible for doing a 3- to 5-year sweep of critical upcoming anniversaries against which products could be marketed or campaigns launched. This of course is most applicable to those who sell commemorative products.

But take as an example Earth Day 1990. Millions of Americans were buying and planting trees. The publicity was staggering. The whole world was watching. An astute marketer of trees and nursery products could have launched a carefully orchestrated marketing blitz centered on the buildup and culmination of this event, possibly involving endorsements, and if timed precisely, riding on the coattails of millions of dollars worth of free media exposure. Linkups like this have the potential of being the most unprecedented successes, if managed perfectly, with precision timing and guts of steel (it can be very risky).

List Rental and Package Insert Patterns

Does your company rent its mailing list? Does it sell space in its outbound product shipments to other companies for drop-in inserts? If yes, then you should analyze very carefully who has used your list or insert program. It will give you great clues as to what else your customers are buying and from whom.

To do a good job, go back 3 to 5 years. Look at who has rented your list, how much they tested, how much they rolled out, and how long they have been rolling out over the years. Study the list selection instructions. Look for sex sorts, age sorts, recency and frequency sorts, and any other clues. See how select instructions changed over time as users got more experience. Find the sample mailing pieces provided and read them carefully so you can add to your analysis the price of products marketed. This will help you build a range of customer price sensitivity and product interest for your list. You may be on to valuable new-product opportunities.

Database Analysis

Use your internal data systems department or hire a vendor to do a systematic analysis of your database. Most direct marketers fail to realize that they have a virtual wealth of information right at their fingertips hidden in their mailing list. Your list can potentially be very simply segmented into groups by product category or interest, by dollar volume, by sex (from the title code on the mailing address), or by the original media source of the name. But this is only the start. There are many excellent companies that can enhance your list with appended geodemographic variables and then analyze the list.

For new-product development, start by asking some very basic questions, like, What are the characteristics of my very best customers? Are there certain segments of my list that are more responsive and profitable than others? How do customers generated through mail differ from those generated by other media? Where do my customers live and what are their lifestyles and spending patterns?

You need to know the answers to these basic questions in order to understand where to go with new products. There are many wonderful canned programs that can be run against your list for a charge, such as Claritas.

Claritas is a zip code–based model that has simply divided all the zip codes in America into 40 lifestyle and income buckets, each with wonderful descriptions. It assumes that the people in a specific lifestyle group exhibit the same basic characteristics and lifestyle patterns regardless of whether their zip is in Arizona or Kansas. If plotted on a map, any one of the 40 groups might look like a shotgun spray on a target. Of course, your mailing list is made up of zip codes, and an analysis of your list can tell you if your customers tend to cluster into one or more of the 40 zip code–based lifestyle buckets. Then by reading about the lifestyles associated with the zip code buckets where your customers are located, you can discover valuable information about them. This can help you determine what else to sell.

You need to get far more into database analysis than this discussion can provide here. Understanding these techniques can help you understand your customer base and help you hypothesize about what else your customers will buy. There are many fine products on the market, and the cost need not be prohibitive.

Database Profiling

Some companies are starting to ask their customers basic questions about product preference and lifestyles in questionnaires and then adding the information to the customer's record as a permanent part of the database. I have seen L. L. Bean utilize a reply postcard in outbound shipments to solicit answers to a half-dozen product preference questions. This was undoubtedly being stored on the customer's record to guide targeted mailing of specialty catalogs and targeted offers in the future.

Some companies, like GRI, have been asking a battery of profile questions as part of the enrollment form to their continuity clubs for years. This information on product preference, consumer habits, age of children, and other important data is stored as part of the customer's record. It was originally gathered to help profile future product shipments, but has become an important tool in analyzing and segmenting the database and in making the mailing list more marketable.

Gathering profile data via reply postcards in outbound product shipments is relatively inexpensive. You have to be sure there is the file room and capability to capture and store the information when it returns from the customer. Also, if information is collected by survey *after* enrollment, you can be sure that your response is going to be some factor less than 100 percent, so that the profile data will only be available on a portion of your customer records (those who choose to respond). But if your list is big enough and you don't ask too many questions (splitting the list into too many segments), database profiling may be worthwhile to you and may lead to list segments that are large enough to be of interest for marketing new products.

Group Brainstorming and Ideation Sessions

Another idea-generating technique is the group brainstorming or ideation session. Gather one or more groups of four to six creative free thinkers from your company, set a specified well-defined objective, develop a discussion outline, and establish some ground rules. A group session can generate lots of quality ideas.

First, select people who will be comfortable being openly creative in public—this is no place for wallflowers, even with strong rules of engagement. Select people who are in tune with the marketplace and who know your customer. There is no one who knows your customer better than you, so help the participants out well in advance by providing them with videotapes of consumer focus groups to watch, a research overview, a good customer profile, a 5-year analysis of the top performing products, and any other critically relevant materials you have about your customer and business.

Send out a well-prepared discussion outline well in advance. Decide on two or three topics at the most, and make it very clear what the objective of the session is. A continuity series book marketer's discussion objective might be: to arrive at a list of three new book series capable of generating at least 50,000 subscribers each for marketing next year.

Establish strict ground rules at the beginning of the session. Split the discussion into two segments: brainstorming and evaluation. Make it clear that criticism and evaluation are not allowed in the brainstorming segment and that there is no such thing as a bad idea or suggestion. You want to encourage a phenomenon called "hitchhiking" in the brainstorming session. This is when one idea prompts someone else to take off with an improvement on it or to think of a better idea—this is where the value of group dynamics really pays dividends.

Then reserve an hour at the end of the session to evaluate the ideas. Get the group to participate and encourage members to use their knowledge of the customer and the marketplace to rank the ideas for development. This can be done gently so as not to crush anyone's pet idea—remember, you need not throw out *any* of the ideas here, simply give the less interesting ones a lower priority for development.

EVALUATING IDEAS: DECIDING WHERE TO PLACE YOUR MONEY

Now that you have some good new-product ideas, you need to evaluate them for their likelihood of success. The outcome of your decision will lead to the outlay of enormous resources in the form of valuable time and money. Here are suggestions for narrowing the field on a winner.

Concept Testing

You are a continuity book series marketer and have narrowed the field of ideas down to five new book series. You can only market the strongest two. How do you choose? One valuable technique is concept testing.

Concept testing will *not* generally help you predict consumer response to a new product. What it will do is help separate the winners from the turkeys. It costs some money to do, but can save a fortune, especially if the fixed development costs of launching a new product are very high. (If they are not high, then you are probably better off to proceed directly to a direct marketing test without concept testing.)

You need to establish benchmarks for measurement. If you are the book series marketer described above, you would want to pick a couple of successful series offered in the past several years. Make sure the benchmark programs were not tied to a one-time event that has now lost relevance, for example, a book series on the topic of the American Revolution offered in 1975–1976.

Prepare a very good sales description of each of the five new book series and the two benchmark series in your best sales copy—about one paragraph—with the offer and terms of sale. Prepare photographic dummies and show a color illustration of the product concepts. The treatment should be equal in size and length for each of the concepts. The materials are then prepared in a full-color printed brochure, with appropriate questions after each concept soliciting consumer reaction to the series and intent to buy. Get some help from a research vendor on this. The preparation of dummies and printing in small quantities can be expensive, but must be done well and should only be undertaken, again, if the fixed development costs are high.

The concept test is then mailed to a preselected consumer panel of your customers or inserted in outbound product shipments. The results are analyzed and measured against the two benchmark products. You then try to gauge the relative strength of each new concept by how its marks stack up against the benchmark products.

Focus Research

If you have locked in on a strong idea, you can get help evaluating it through additional consumer focus research. Write a tight position statement and description of the product and service, develop some product dummies or prototypes, and then conduct a discussion on the concept. Be careful about directly asking if there is interest in buying the product through the mail. I'm convinced there is no way to find this information short of a live test. People are fickle and dubious about admitting they buy through the mail. Even if you have screened your participants about past mail-order purchase and know that they shop by mail, you may be disappointed and end up throwing out a valid idea if you're not careful here.

Stick to probing for reaction to the concept itself, the price value perceptions, and the level of interest in the goods or service. This is a chance to see if your product solves a legitimate consumer problem. Be sure to run three or four groups, and don't hesitate to modify the script between sessions if you see an opportunity to clear up confusion or tighten the positioning.

Mall Intercepts

One way to get some quick gut reaction to a new-product concept is through mall intercepts. This needs to be organized through a research vendor. This is especially useful for getting feedback on price-value relationships and for doing advertising communication research. The latter is described below. Mall intercepts are directional and not statistically valid. To work best, you should do a couple at different locations across the country. The cost depends on how tightly you prescreen your test subjects and how extensive your interview is. The smaller your interest group and the more questions, the more expensive.

Basic Economic Analysis

Nothing can replace an old-fashioned, over-the-thumb economic analysis of the likelihood of success for a new product. Does going into this line of products lead the company anywhere in the long term or is this just a high-risk, one-shot gamble? Can you sell the product for enough money to deliver it and make traditional margins? As a rule, you probably have to get $25 to $30 an order nowadays with the cost of postage just to break even on most products.

But be very careful. I have made enormous profits and added millions of new names to the list on several occasions with products priced from $1 to $5. If the timing is right, the multimedia support is extensive, and there is an incentive to buy multiple units, anything can happen and there are no rules — you have to consider all these factors. Traditionally, you will need a four to five times markup over the raw cost of goods to make money. But put all the variables together — your multiple-order assumptions, your response assumptions, your cost assumptions, the lift from supporting media, your delivery cost assumptions — and be conservative.

Secondary Research

One of the best sources of information is actually free. You can gather a lot of information about your new-product idea simply by reading what other people have researched on the subject. One of the best sources of free information is through research conducted by magazines. Magazines spend a fair amount of money conducting research to gain a better knowledge of their subscribers in order to attract advertisers. Chances are, the key books that you and your competition advertise in have done some very good consumer research on their subscriber bases to find out what their readers are buying and why.

For example, I was recently trying to find out information on how cosmetics consumption varied by age group. I was also trying to find out how cosmetics consumption patterns would vary over the next 20 years as demographics and lifestyles changed in the United States. I found two invaluable landmark studies on these subjects that would have cost a small fortune to field. They were commissioned by *Self* and *Cosmopolitan* magazines. The information was critical to my project and cost me nothing.

Newspaper and trade journal articles can also be very helpful when evaluating a new product. If you use an ad agency, they probably have a library of key article clippings organized by company and topic and can pull information at your request. If not, there are companies that can do searches for information for you and write reports on key subjects at reasonable costs. You can also get a graduate student to do a literature search for you at a small cost if there is a university nearby.

Communications Research

When you are testing a new-product concept with high risks, it may pay to conduct some communications research on your advertising concepts. A good media test in magazines can cost a lot of money — find out how well your ad is communicating before you place it. Prepare tight comprehensive color layouts for the various creative executions being considered, with a tight draft of copy.

Get a research company to help develop a questionnaire. Respondents look at and read the ad concepts and evaluate them across several dimensions. Was the message clear? Can you recall the offer and terms of sale? Was anything confusing? Did any of the words seem odd or hard to understand? Would you purchase this product? In the evaluation mode, this technique can help you weed out the field of product ideas and to choose between alternative creative executions. This procedure can be a good disaster check prior to spending a lot of money, to be sure that you are communicating effectively with your target audience.

HEDGING RISKS: HOW TO GET EXPERIENCE WITHOUT BETTING THE FARM

Now that you have decided to proceed with a new-product launch, here are some ideas on how to test your proposition without exposing the company to unnecessary financial risk.

Developing a Tight Marketing Plan

When you have locked into a new product idea and the concept has been thoroughly evaluated, you owe it to yourself to prepare a rigorous marketing plan. A marketing plan helps you communicate to the rest of the organization what will be required of them to help launch the product, and it serves as a record for future reference. But the main reason for preparing a marketing plan is to help you, the marketing manager, to think things through in detail and address all the critical details involved in a new-product launch.

Your plan should lay out all the strategies, the financial projections, the cost estimates, the basis for your response projections, the offer and terms of sale, the testing plan, the media plan, and the critical next steps for project completion. If you force yourself to do a very thorough and rigorous job on the marketing plan, chances are that you will change your mind on a few things during the course of preparing it, and when you get done and are still convinced you have a winner, it probably is.

Prioritize Media Testing

In approaching a new-product test, you need to be prudent in how you select your media, especially if the company has limited financial resources. Use some common sense to build a media-testing hierarchy. For example, common sense tells you that the best mailing list you have is your own list. If a new product aimed at your existing customers won't work on your own list, then how could it possibly work on rented lists? Therefore, you may decide that in the initial test, you will experiment first with segments of your own mailing list and then try rented lists in the next continuation.

Similarly, it is hard to imagine that a product could be sold successfully on television without also working in mass publications like *Parade* or *TV Guide.* The penetration of these two publications approaches that of a national television network. But it could cost you a minimum of $50,000 or more in produc tion costs alone to develop a television commercial, while you can test a million circulation in *Parade* or *TV Guide* for a fraction of the cost. And if you can't make your offer work in a mass publication, what would lead you to believe it would work in television? In this case, it might be better to hold off on TV and get some experience in a more limited way in a mass publication first.

These are just two examples. Try to develop a plan for your launch that will provide you with some good learning and some good roll-out experience, but that will not expose you to too much financial risk up front when you are not even sure that the product is a success.

Test in Inserts

One of the easiest and least risky methods of getting some experience on how a new product will be received is to try it out in your own package-insert program to your own customers. Depending on the size of your outbound shipments, the size of your advertising test piece is limited only by the size of your smallest shipper. Chances are, you can design a test package that inserts in an envelope and looks like a mailing, but rides along for free in your outbound shipments. You have just saved the biggest expense of a direct mailing—the postage! This is a very good way to get some experience. A statistical analysis can help you identify which segments of the list were most responsive and profitable if the test is set up right.

For example, a continuity club marketer of recipe cards wanted to start selling low-end jewelry and fashion items via catalog to its female customer base. The marketer started by experimenting with a folded brochure positioned as a catalog supplement with a fair range of products, but produced much more economically than a bound catalog. The flyer was inserted in outbound shipments for one week, and the sorted output tape from the billings was carefully preserved so that response could be tied back to the universe inserted.

Overall, the results of this insert were only fair—a little above breakeven. But after a thorough statistical modeling analysis, the marketer found that about 40 percent of the list had actually performed well above traditional margins on this test. This segment was identified through demographic variables appended to the list on age and income and through internal variables on number of continuity shipments paid for and media source. Since the company had about 2 million names, this 40 percent subsegment of the list presented a nice start on a mailing list for a jewelry and fashion accessory catalog business. The marketer successfully mailed an 800,000 piece mailing with a full 32-page stitched catalog the next fall while simultaneously testing segments of former subscribers to the recipe club and several rented lists.

Category Testing

When planning a test campaign for a new-product introduction, you should put a good deal of thought into the media plan. In selecting rented lists and magazines for the test, it is helpful to categorize the opportunities in various groups. Then test only one or two lists or titles in each group.

For example, you might have a print category called "Women's Service Magazines." You may decide that while there are a half-dozen possibilities in the category, you will test only in *Ladies Home Journal,* which seems to be the best fit for your product. If this test works, you can then test three or four other titles in that category at the time of the *Ladies Home Journal* roll-out.

Categorize your rented lists and package-insert tests in a similar fashion. In new-product testing, I believe it is better to test *more* rented lists in *smaller* quantities that to test fewer lists in larger quantities—you are after direction and experience, and if a list is marginal, you can always retest it in a larger quantity the next time out. If you are looking for circulation, load up your test in the most logical, promising categories and then test very gingerly in the more "iffy" categories with only one or two lists and no more than one magazine in each.

Limited Capital Investment

When launching a new product, regardless of how cash-rich your company might be, try to hold off investing in major equipment, software, or resources during the test phase. For example, if you are a continuity marketer and experimenting in a catalog venture that is new and not supported by your data system, consider using a reputable outside order processor rather than spending to develop or purchase a pick-and-pack software system. Try to tough it out with existing personnel during the test mode if you can. Then, if the project is a success, go and hire the people the business needs to run on an ongoing basis.

Remember, there is already enormous inherent risk in the marketplace with a new-product test: you don't even know how the marketplace is going to vote on your product yet. Chances are it could be a flop. Why add to the high market risk with flamboyant investments in personnel and equipment until you get a sense for what the market will do? When launching a new product or program, try to be frugal and save the extravagance for when you know how the market is going to react.

Dry Testing

Sometimes it is necessary to use dry testing—actually fielding an ad for a product that has not even been fully developed or produced with the understanding that if it flops, a letter and gift will have to be sent to everyone who responded telling them that the program will not be fulfilled. This is a potentially dangerous method and can get a company into trouble if not executed properly. At best, the company stands to lose customer goodwill. With all the other techniques available to marketers, this one should be used only when absolutely necessary and very cautiously.

Staged Media

To hedge the risk of a new test, consider staging your media test. For example, you may do an initial test in direct mail to your own list as the first stage, followed by a test 2 months later in rented lists and package inserts, followed 2 months later by a test in magazines. What this allows you to do is to pull the plug on the later media if the initial stage is an unmitigated disaster. This technique is especially useful if you as a company have historic information on how different media perform against each other side by side and you can project based on a direct-mail test response what the likely response range is going to be in print and in inserts.

Staged Inventory Buildup

Like staging the media to hedge risks, it is also sometimes possible to stage product acquisition in two or more orders so that if you are wrong on your initial projections, there is still a chance for pulling the test off without losing money. You as a marketing manager should look for ways to structure your inventory buys on tests so that this is possible. In my experience, you have to be firm and patient with your vendors and educate them about direct mail and testing.

I have found that if you will take the time to explain about doing testing and not wanting to overcommit until the test is complete, you can get special deals that were normally not available. Lay out your testing plan and roll-out plans to your vendors. Tell them that you want them to be part of the long-term business. Then ask them to let you order smaller quantities up front for the test and tantalize them with the potential of the roll-out. Tell them you want to pay the lower roll-out price for the product needed for the test with the understanding that you will order from them for the roll-out if the test is successful.

This has seldom failed to work in my experience—you just have to ask for it. This strategy is particularly easy to implement if you have also staged your media. Your orders and demand for product will already be staggered and will permit you to respond accordingly. On the other hand, there is nothing quite as tragic as a manager who has been caught up in optimism and committed the company to a ton of inventory in advance of a risky test that ends up flopping. It is in your best interest to work out deals on inventory and delivery. Many vendors will also consider consignment arrangements for certain products.

CONCLUSION

In conclusion, putting it all together to successfully develop products is a tricky but manageable process. You can be a successful rainmaker for your company if you go about product development in a systematic fashion, put together all the steps, don't try to take shortcuts, and use a little common sense and discipline. Look for multiple signals along the way, listen to what your customers are saying, and don't be afraid to take advice from those you trust. Good luck!

38
Analytic Methods

Behram J. Hansotia
Kestnbaum & Company
Chicago, Ill.

INTRODUCTION

Testing offers excellent opportunities for direct marketers to fine-tune their product offerings, based on actual behavior rather than "purchase intention." The approach described in this paper draws heavily from the area of conjoint analysis. However, instead of modeling purchase intention or preference as a function of product attributes, we discuss how tests can be structured to model response rates as a function of product attributes.

The chapter briefly delves into the area of experimental design and discusses full factorial, fractional factorial, and central composite designs which can be employed to systematically capture behavioral information. The presentation is pedagogical and shows how these designs can be constructed. The casual reader who is not interested in such details can skip the sections on fractional factorial and central composite designs and move directly to the examples.

Experimental design has been used extensively by clinical psychologists as well as quality control and chemical engineers to capture system response behavior when attributes affecting the response are systematically varied *simultaneously*. For example, this author used a central composite design to capture the effects of "speed, feed, and depth of cut" on tool life in machining tests while working as an internal management science consultant at a major manufacturer.

Logistic regression is next discussed in the paper and recommended as the tool for analyzing the data. An example showing a fractional factorial design, the fitted logistic regression model, and how to use the results of the analysis is finally presented in the paper.

TRADITIONAL APPROACHES

Direct marketers have long used testing in an attempt to identify the best offer. Generally, different offers are mailed to prospects or customers and the offer that returns the best results (highest net profits) is deemed the best. On roll-out, however, the marketer is often surprised with lower-than-expected results, and much has been written about why roll-outs do not perform as well as tests. The key reason is regression toward the mean. The high value observed by the marketer was probably an aberration, caused by sampling variance. Since several offers were tested simultaneously, the marketer basically increased the likelihood of observing a high value by chance. An analogy can be drawn to rolling a die; the more times a die is rolled, the greater is the likelihood of observing a 6 by chance. Here we know, however, that all numbers, 1 through 6, have the same likelihood of appearing. With the test there could be a similar situation; all the offers, in reality, may have very similar profitability. The marketer may have observed a very high value, one from the tail end of the distribution, by chance.

One way out of this dilemma is the use of larger test samples so that the sampling variance can be reduced. Better up-front planning with sample size decisions guided by the statistical methods of "multiple comparisons" and "order statistics" can be used to address this problem. However, the required sample sizes will generally be very large.

Most elementary statistics books describe sample size calculations for a single or two-sample test. These formulas have been well documented in direct marketing textbooks. If the objective, however, is the determination of the *best* offer, when more than two offers are tested simultaneously, these standard formulas are not valid. The appropriate formula is based on Bechhofer's method.[1] This is discussed next and a simple example illustrates the calculations.

BECHHOFER'S METHOD FOR IDENTIFYING THE BEST OFFER

Bechhofer has developed a table which allows the decision maker to determine the necessary sample size for the following situation: The decision maker wishes to determine, to a certain confidence level, that the test (sample) offer with the best results is indeed the true (population) best offer. To apply Bechhofer's method, the decision maker needs to specify:

$(1 - \alpha)$ The confidence level

σ The population standard deviation

λ The tolerance, or the smallest difference between the best and the second best result which should be recognized

r The number of offers tested

Though Bechhofer's approach was originally developed to calculate sample sizes for sample means, the method can be approximated for response rates.

The population standard deviation σ of all tested offers is assumed to be the same. This is a common assumption in all T and F tests. The value of σ, of course, is generally u?known but can be estimated by $\sqrt{R(1 - R)}$, where R is the common, assumed response rate of all the tested offers.

Bechhofer's method assumes that *equal* sample sizes are to be employed for all test samples. This sample size n can be calculated by:

$$n = B^2(r,1 - \alpha) * R(1 - R)/\lambda^2$$

where $B(r, 1 - \alpha)$ is a number that can be looked up from Bechhofer's table.[2] Note that this formula is very similar to the single sample size formula, substituting Bechhofer's B value for the standard normal Z value. An example will help illustrate the use of this formula.

Suppose a marketer is considering testing eight different offers. Past experience indicates that the response rates are generally around 1 percent. If he wishes to recognize a difference of 0.1 percent between the best and the second best offer and be 90 percent confident that he had chosen the right test offer as the "true" best offer, how large should the test sample sizes be? From Bechhofer's table we know that $r = 8$, $1 - \alpha = 0.90$, $R = 0.01$, $\lambda = 0.001$, and $B(8, 0.90) = 2.8691$. Hence,

$$n = B^2(8, 0.90) * \frac{R(1 - R)}{\lambda^2}$$

$$= (2.8691)^2 * 0.01 * \frac{0.99}{(0.001)^2}$$

$$= 81,494$$

Hence, the marketer would need eight samples, each approximately 82,000 in size. As discussed earlier, if the marketer wishes to truly control for the multiple-comparisons effect, rather large sample sizes are required to reach the right decision.

In the above example, no information was provided on what the eight offers were, or how they differed from one another. Even if the marketer had a budget for mailing the required 656,000 pieces, beyond identifying the best offer, the test would not reveal directly the contribution of different offer attributes. The marketer may attempt to make additional pair-wise comparisons with the test results (there will be a total of 28 such pair-wise comparisons), but this test was not set up for that. To be 90 percent confident about the *family* of 28 comparisons, the marketer will need even larger sample sizes. The Bonferroni and Tukey's methods[3] can be used to calculate the appropriate sample sizes for the family of comparisons.

The key message we wish to leave the reader with is this: To identify the appropriate sample size, not only do we need prior estimates of response rates (so that the standard deviation of response rates can be calculated) and assumptions about tolerance (maximum allowable difference in value) and probability of type 1 error (1 minus the confidence level), but we also need a precise definition about the purpose of the test. For example, is the decision maker interested in *all* pair-wise comparisons or a subset of pair-wise comparisons (perhaps against the control), or is she interested in ensuring that the sample with the best results is, in fact, the true best?

The appropriate sample size depends on the purpose of the test, since different hypotheses are implied in each case. In general, if a test involves multiple samples (more than two), the required sample sizes, for the same tolerance and confidence level, will be larger than for the two-sample case. Also, all pair-wise comparisons will *require* larger samples than ensuring that the sample with the best results is, in fact, the true best. Data snooping after test results are in requires substantially larger differences for results to be significant than if the specific comparisons to be made were stated explicitly before the tests are run.

A FULL FACTORIAL TEST FOR
MEASURING RESPONSE

Rather than discuss the different multiple-comparisons methods, all of which generally require rather large impractical sample sizes, we would like to discuss a different approach to the analysis. The method we recommend views products, offers, and creatives as bundles of attributes. An attribute may assume just two values, on-off, or a few discrete values, or it may take on any value, perhaps within a given range of values. In the first instance we would term the attribute *binary*; in the second *discrete*; and in the third, *continuous*.

As an example, suppose an offer can be defined by payment terms (monthly, annual), premium (present, absent), fast-response incentive (present, absent), and discount (present, absent), then a total of 16 possible offers can be constructed. Each attribute can be represented by a dummy coded variable which can assume two values, 0 and 1. An offer can thus be represented by an array, or vector, of four such numbers. Table 38-1 displays the coding of the attributes using variables X_1 through X_4, to represent the four attributes. A monthly offer with a premium and a fast-response incentive but no discount, can thus be represented as

$$X_1 = 1 \quad X_2 = 1 \quad X_3 = 1 \quad X_4 = 0$$

or by the array (1, 1, 1, 0). The experimental design that employs all 16 offers is a 2^4 full factorial design and is shown in Table 38-2. In this design, 16 panels, or random samples, generally of equal size, are selected and members of each panel mailed one of the offers. The standard sample size formula based on a

Table 38-1. Coding attributes

Attribute	Variable	Attribute value	Variable value
Payment terms	X_1	Monthly	1
		Annual	0
Premium	X_2	Present	1
		Absent	0
Fast-response incentive	X_3	Present	1
		Absent	0
Discount	X_4	Present	1
		Absent	0

Table 38-2. 2^4 Full Factorial Design

PANEL	X_1	X_2	X_3	X_4
1	1	1	1	1
2	1	1	1	0
3	1	1	0	1
4	1	0	1	1
5	0	1	1	1
6	1	1	0	0
7	1	0	1	0
8	1	0	0	1
9	0	1	1	0
10	0	1	0	1
11	0	0	1	1
12	1	0	0	0
13	0	1	0	0
14	0	0	1	0
15	0	0	0	1
16	0	0	0	0

single sample and "two tails" assumptions can be used to set the size of each panel. For example, if we think response rates are around 1 percent, a tolerance of ±0.15 percent and a 90 percent confidence level would imply panels of roughly 12,000.

The key property of the full factorial design is that the effect of changing one variable can be assessed independently of the others. In a factorial experiment, all factors are varied simultaneously, whereas the somewhat simpler one-factor-at-a-time procedure would involve, as the name implies, varying the levels of one factor at a time. This practice to this day is very popular with direct marketers, even though the factorial approach has some significant advantages, namely,

- It lends itself to assessing the joint effect of two or more variables through the use of interaction terms.

- It results in effects estimated with greater precision. That is, when models are built using the design data (as discussed below) the model coefficients have smaller variance.

- It results in model coefficients that are *uncorrelated* with one another; hence, the effect of changing one variable can be assessed independently of the others.

MODELING RESPONSE

Once the response rates are available, the information is used to construct a model to predict response rates as a function of the four dummy variables. If $\hat{R}$ is the predicted response rate, a saturated model can be written as:

$$\hat{R} = B_o + \sum_i B_i X_i + \sum_i \sum_{i>j} B_{ij} X_i X_j + \sum_i \sum_{j>i} \sum_{k>j} B_{ijk} X_i X_j X_k + B X_1 X_2 X_3 X_4 \qquad (1)$$

Note that this model will fit the data exactly, since 16 parameters (B) are being estimated from 16 observations; hence the term *saturated model,* since no degrees of freedom are left for estimating the mean squared error.

If we decide to ignore the third and fourth order interaction terms (since their contribution is often negligible), we would have a model that requires estimating 11 coefficients: the intercept B_o, 4 fixed effects coefficients, B_i, and six second-order interaction effects, B_{ij}, as follows:

$$\hat{R} = B_0 + \sum_i B_i X_i + \sum_i \sum_{j>i} B_{ij} X_i X_j \tag{2}$$

In this instance, the fit of the model can be evaluated, since five degrees of freedom (observations) are available to compute the mean squared error. The above models are often called linear probability models, and there are at least two statistical problems in using them to estimate response rates. First, the predicted response rate is not constrained to lie between 0 and 1; hence, it is quite conceivable that the model may produce results that lie outside this range. Second, since the variance of response rate, $R(1 - R)$, is a function of the response rate R, the variances of the offers will *not* be constant; a fundamental requirement (homoscedasticity) of regression analysis.

Fortunately, there are methods to help us overcome these problems. If, for example, the sample response rates all fell between 0.2 and 0.8, weighted least squares can be employed to overcome the problem of unequal variances. In this case, the weights would be the reciprocals of the variances of the expected response rates. If W_j denotes the weight for the jth panel (offer) and R_j the observed response rate, then W_j is given by:

$$W_j = \frac{N_j}{R_j(1 - R_j)} \tag{3}$$

In the above approach, the observed response rates should preferably be between 0.2 and 0.8 for the predicted response rates to fall within the (0, 1) range. However, such as assumption is rarely met in direct marketing, where response rates below 5 percent are the norm. We can ensure that the predicted response rates do fall between 0 and 1 by modeling a function of the response rates such that the predicted response rates can never be outside the (0, 1) range. One such function is the logistic function. Hence, instead of predicting the response rate directly by Equation (2), we predict the logit or the logistic function of response rates. The logistic function is basically the natural logarithm of the odds of the response rate: $R/(1 - R)$. Equation (4) below shows this model:

$$\hat{R}' = \ln\left[\frac{\hat{R}}{(1 - \hat{R})}\right] = B_0 + \sum_i B_i X_i + \sum_i \sum_{j>i} B_{ij} X_i X_j \tag{4}$$

Several statistical routines are available to fit the above model to sample data. In the example discussed later we have used the logistic regression procedure in SPSS.[4] Equation (4) can be rewritten so that the predicted response rates can be calculated directly:

$$\hat{R} = \frac{\exp\left(B_0 + \sum_i B_i X_i + \sum_i \sum_{j>i} B_{ij} X_i X_j\right)}{1 + \exp\left(B_0 + \sum_i B_i X_i + \sum_i \sum_{j>i} B_{ij} X_i X_j\right)} \tag{5}$$

where, $\exp(.) = e^{(.)}$ and e is approximately equal to 2.72.

If we denote the terms in parentheses in Equation (5) by y, it can be shown that $\hat{R}$ is an increasing S-shaped function of y with range (0, 1). Another transformation of R which results in a very similar model is the inverse standard normal distribution, or the probit function. Note, since an inverse probability distribution is the transformation here, R must be between 0 and 1.

ONE-HALF FRACTIONAL FACTORIAL DESIGNS

If the number of attributes is large, even if each attribute can assume only two values, a full factorial design often results in too many panels. In the four-attribute case, a full factorial model is needed only if we think all six two-way interaction terms are significant and must be explicitly modeled, or if the total variability (pure error) in the data is high. If prior research leads us to believe that the interaction terms are insignificant, we would be interested in capturing only the "fixed (or main) effects"; that is, the four partial regression coefficients B_i, plus the intercept, shown in Equation (4). Since only five parameters must now be estimated, we should be able to accomplish that with fewer panels. For example, a one-half fractional factorial design consisting of eight panels can be used to develop such a fixed-effects model.

A one-half fractional factorial design, often written as 2^{4-1} fractional factorial, consists of eight of the sixteen possible total panels. A large number of such designs can obviously be created. A good design, however, will enable the fixed effects to be estimated accurately. Assuming that all two-way and higher-order interactions are insignificant, it would not do any harm if a fixed effect was aliased, or confounded, with a third-order interaction term. By aliased here we mean that B_i, instead of being an estimate of just the effect of the ith variable, will be estimating the joint effect of both the ith variable and a specific third-order interaction term. In no case would we want two fixed effects to be aliased with each other.

The key concept in generating a fractional factorial with the appropriate aliasing is the defining relation or defining contrast, I. To develop a 2^{4-1} fractional factorial we start with a 2^3 full factorial design. However, instead of using the (0, 1) dummy variables scheme, we will use $(-1, +1)$ values to generate this design. The logistic regression model, with only fixed effects, can then be estimated using either schemes. The interpretation of the model coefficients will, however, be different. This is discussed later.

Table 38-3 shows a 2^3 full factorial design. The "1" following each sign has been omitted, as is the normal custom.[5] The columns which are often referred to as contrasts are now labeled 1, 2, and 3 instead of X_1, X_2, and X_3. Note that each column has four minus signs and four plus signs. This is a common property of all factorial designs. Also note that the three variables X_1, X_2, and X_3 are

Table 38-3. A 2^3 design using ($\pm$) notation

Panel	Factor 1	2	3
1	−	−	−
2	+	−	−
3	−	+	−
4	+	+	−
5	−	−	+
6	+	−	+
7	−	+	+
8	+	+	+

independent, or orthogonal, to each other. (We can validate this by multiplying the vector X_1 with either X_2 or X_3 and noting that both products equal 0. Also, in carrying out the vector multiplications we would, of course, add a 1 after each sign in the columns in Table 38-3.)

The fourth factor, X_4, can be now generated by multiplying the entries in each row, using standard algebraic sign conventions. This is shown in Table 38-4. Note that X_4 is also independent of X_1, X_2, and X_3. Hence, the four main effects will not be confounded with each other.

To identify which effects are confounded (or aliased), we turn next to the defining relation or defining contrast, I. *A defining contrast is a column generated by multiplying two or more of the columns (contrasts) of a design such that the resulting column has only plus signs in it.* Note: $1^2 = 2^2 = 3^2 = 4^2 = I$. Writing one of the 4s in 4^2 as 123, we get the defining contrast $I = 1234$. Also, I times any contrast is the contrast itself; that is, $1*I = 1$, $2*I = 2$, etc. We thus note:

$$
\begin{aligned}
1*I = 1 \ &= 1*1234 = 1^2234 = I*234 = 234 \\
2*I = 2 \ &= 2*1234 = 12^234 = I*134 = 134 \\
3*I = 3 \ &= 3*1234 = 123^24 = I*124 = 124 \\
4*I = 4 \ &= 4*1234 = 1234^2 = I*123 = 123 \\
12*I = 12 \ &= 12*1234 = 1^22^234 = I^2*34 = 34 \\
13*I = 13 \ &= 13*1234 = 1^223^24 = I^2*24 = 24 \\
14*I = 14 \ &= 14*1234 = 1^2234^2 = I^2*23 = 23 \\
23*I = 23 \ &= 23*1234 = 12^23^24 = I^2*14 = 14 \\
24*I = 24 \ &= 24*1234 = 12^234^2 = I^2*13 = 13 \\
34*I = 34 \ &= 34*1234 = 123^24^2 = I^2*12 = 12
\end{aligned}
$$

Hence, effect 1 is aliased with 234, effect 2 with 134, etc. Table 38-5 lists the effects which are aliased with one another. Since effect 1 is aliased with effect 234, in a fixed effects model, B_1 is actually estimating $B_1 + B_{234}$, but since B_{234} as well as all third-order interaction effects are assumed to be 0, the one-half fractional factorial design can be used to provide good estimates for the fixed effects B_1, B_2, B_3, and B_4. Note that the remaining eight panels of the full factorial design also comprises a 2^{4-1} factorial design. This is shown in Table 38-6.

Table 38-4. A 2^{4-1} Fractional Factorial Design

Panel	Factor			
	1	2	3	4 = 1*2*3
1	−	−	−	−
2	+	−	−	+
3	−	+	−	+
4	+	+	−	−
5	−	−	+	+
6	+	−	+	−
7	−	+	+	−
8	+	+	+	+

Table 38-5. Aliased Effects

Effect of variable	Aliased with effect of variable
X_1	$X_2X_3X_4$
X_2	$X_1X_3X_4$
X_3	$X_1X_2X_4$
X_4	$X_1X_2X_3$
X_1X_2	X_3X_4
X_1X_3	X_2X_4
X_1X_4	X_2X_3
X_2X_3	X_1X_4
X_2X_4	X_1X_3
X_3X_4	X_1X_2
$X_1X_2X_3$	X_4
$X_1X_2X_4$	X_3
$X_1X_3X_4$	X_2
$X_2X_3X_4$	X_1

Table 38-6. Another 2^{4-1} Fractional Factorial Design

Panel	Factor			
	1	2	3	4
1	+	+	+	−
2	+	+	−	+
3	+	−	+	+
4	−	+	+	+
5	+	−	−	−
6	−	+	−	−
7	−	−	+	−
8	−	−	−	+

INTERPRETATION OF MODEL COEFFICIENTS

In the dummy variable (0, 1) coding scheme, the model coefficient, B_i, represents the incremental impact of the ith variable on the response. In the $(-1, +1)$ coding scheme, the B_i are contrasts and for the fixed-effects model represent half the incremental impact of the ith variable at the $+1$ level over the -1 level. Figure 38-1 demonstrates this. When interaction terms are present, the (0, 1) coding scheme results in interaction term coefficients which have a straightforward interpretation. This, however, is not true for $(-1, +1)$ scheme. This author therefore prefers to use the (0, 1) scheme whenever possible.

OTHER DESIGNS FOR METRIC VARIABLES

In the designs discussed above, the variables were assumed to be nonmetric. Coding them as (0, 1) or $(-1, +1)$ allowed us to model their impact on response rates. The logistic regression models discussed, moreover, were all linear models. These designs are still appropriate, even if the variables affecting response are metric (continuous), provided that the linear model is still appropriate. If the variables are metric and the linearity assumption is valid over the domain of interest, each metric variable can still be binary with values at its minimum and maximum. Generally, the smaller the domain of interest in the predictor variables, or factors (product attributes), the better will be the linearity assumption about the model.

Examples of discrete variables that may be modeled as continuous predictor variables for product attributes are price, amount of discount, number of benefits, number of free transactions, etc. Examples of continuous predictor variables for "creatives" are length of letter, reading difficulty score, envelope size, etc. When predictor variables are continuous and the domain of interest of one or more of those variables is relatively large, it may be worthwhile to consider models with quadratic or other higher-level terms. Several designs exist for metric variables, with each design having different properties.[6] We will discuss

X $\quad = (0, 1)$		$X \quad = (-1, +1)$	
$\hat{y} \quad = B_0 + B_1 X$		$\hat{y} \quad = B_0 + B_1 X$	
For: $X \quad = 0, \; \hat{y} = \hat{y}_0 = B_0$		For: $X \quad = -1, \; \hat{y} = \hat{y}_{-1} = B_0 - B_1$	
$X \quad = 1, \; \hat{y} = \hat{y}_1 = B_0 + B_1$		$X \quad = +1, \; \hat{y} = \hat{y}_{+1} = B_0 + B_1$	
and $B_1 \quad = \hat{y}_1 - \hat{y}_0$		and $B_1 \quad = (\hat{y}_{+1} - \hat{y}_{-1})/2$	
Hence, B_1 = incremental impact of X on response		Hence, B_1 = contrast, or ½ incremental impact of X on response	

Figure 38-1. Interpretation of model coefficients under two coding schemes

below one of the more versatile designs — the central composite designs which can be used to estimate the quadratic function:

$$\hat{R}' = B_0 + \sum_i B_i X_i + \sum_i \sum_j B_{ij} X_i X_j \tag{6}$$

Note that the term $X_i X_j$ represents the quadratic term when i equals j.

To estimate a quadratic-response function, each factor must be observed at at least three levels. A full factorial design with each factor at three levels — the two extremes $(-1, +1)$ and the center (0) — will thus require 3^k panels or treatments, where k is the number of factors or variables. For example, for $k = 3$, the full factorial design would require 27 panels, which would enable us to estimate all 11 coefficients in Equation (6). The central composite design, however, enables us to estimate a quadratic-response function using fewer panels.

CENTRAL COMPOSITE DESIGNS

The central composite designs are basically factorial or fractional factorial designs augmented by additional "axial" and center points to allow the estimation of the coefficients of a second-order response function. Table 38-7 shows the general central composite design for three factors. Note that the total number of panels or treatments is 15 and each factor is measured at five levels: The two axial points $(-a$ and $+a)$, the two corner points $(-1$ and $+1)$, and the center of the design (0). In three dimensions, this can be thought of as the eight corner points of a unit cube, consisting of combinations of -1 and $+1$, a point in the center of the cube, and six axial points on axes perpendicular to the six faces of the cube and at a distance of a units on either side of the center.

Depending on the number of center points used and the values that are set

Table 38-7. General central composite design for three factors

Panel	1	2	3	
1	-1	-1	-1	
2	$+1$	-1	-1	
3	-1	$+1$	-1	
4	$+1$	$+1$	-1	2^3 factorial design
5	-1	-1	$+1$	
6	$+1$	-1	$+1$	
7	-1	$+1$	$+1$	
8	$+1$	$+1$	$+1$	
9	0	0	0	Center point
10	$-a$	0	0	
11	a	0	0	
12	0	$-a$	0	2×3 axial points
13	0	a	0	
14	0	0	$-a$	
15	0	0	a	

(Factors are columns 1, 2, 3.)

for a, central composite designs with different properties can be developed. We have already seen that the factorial designs are orthogonal, and this is an important property for accurately estimating the model coefficients. Two other properties we will discuss briefly are rotatability and uniform precision.

A design is rotatable when the variance of the estimated response is the same for two points that are equidistant from the design center; hence, the quality of the response estimator $\hat{R}'$ in Equation (6) will be the same for all points lying on a sphere (circle in two dimensions), with the design center as its center.

A uniform precision design extends the concept of rotatability in that the variance of the estimator $\hat{R}'$ is the same within the unit sphere. Hence, the quality of $\hat{R}'$ is the same for all points within a unit distance from the center. For points beyond the unit distance, the variance of R also starts increasing.

By selecting appropriate values for a and the number of center points, near-uniform precision and orthogonal rotatable central composite designs can be generated. Table 38-8 shows the appropriate values for $k = 3$.[7] The axial points at $\pm a$ for $k = 3$ are located at ± 1.682. Note that both designs require fewer than the 27 panels required by the 3^3 full factorial design. Even though the above near-uniform precision design is not orthogonal, the correlation among the factors is relatively small. Hence, little precision is lost if this design is used. We illustrate next the usage of a 2^{5-1} fractional factorial design in modeling response rates using logistic regression.

Example

In marketing a continuity product via a direct-mail solo offer, management is interested in understanding the impact of the following five attributes or factors on response rates.

- Digital watch premium.
- Fast response incentive (first 50 responses receive a free cellular telephone).
- Payment terms (annual versus monthly dues).
- Discount (first 3 months free versus first month free).
- Temporary plastic membership card.

Table 38-8. Near-Uniform Precision and Orthogonal Rotatable Central Composite Designs for Three Factors

		Number of panels	
Panel type	Value of factor levels	Near-uniform precision	Orthogonal rotatable
Factorial points	± 1	8	8
Center points	0	6	9
Axial points	± 1.682	6	6
Total		20	23

Because of budgetary constraints and some prior research, the company's research department recommended a one-half fractional factorial design consisting of 16 panels. Prior research had shown only two interactions of any consequence to be present: between the digital-watch premium and the fast-response incentive (Interaction 12) and between the digital-watch premium and discount (Interaction 14). The research department thus wanted a design where these two interactions would not be confounded with each other or other main effects.

The 2^{5-1} factorial design is constructed by first writing down the 2^4 factorial design and then defining the factor 5 column as the product of the first four columns. The meaning of the signs is reported in Table 38-9 and the design is shown in Table 38-10. Note how the 2^4 factorial design is constructed. In the first factor the signs alternate; in the second factor the signs alternate in pairs; in the third factor the signs alternate for sets of four panels; and in the fourth factor the first eight panels have a negative sign and the last eight panels, a positive sign.

Table 38-9. Interpretation of Factor Signs in Design

Factor	+	−
1	Premium present	Premium absent
2	Fast-response incentive present	Fast-response incentive absent
3	Monthly dues	Annual dues
4	First 3 months free	First month free
5	Plastic card present	Plastic card absent

Table 38-10. 2^{5-1} Fractional Factorial Design

			Factors		
Panel	1	2	3	4	5 = 1*2*3*4*
1	−	−	−	−	+
2	+	−	−	−	−
3	−	+	−	−	−
4	+	+	−	−	+
5	−	−	+	−	−
6	+	−	+	−	+
7	−	+	+	−	+
8	+	+	+	−	−
9	−	−	−	+	−
10	+	−	−	+	+
11	−	+	−	+	+
12	+	+	−	+	−
13	−	−	+	+	+
14	+	−	+	+	−
15	−	+	+	+	−
16	+	+	+	+	+

Table 38-11. Aliases of Main and Two Key Interaction Effects for Defining Contrast $I = 12345$

Effects	Factor	Aliased with
Main	1	2345
	2	1345
	3	1245
	4	1235
	5	1234
Interaction	12	345
	14	235

Since the defining contrast I is factor 5, that is, $I = 12345$, the main effects and the two interaction effects 12 and 14 are aliased as shown in Table 38-11. Note that the main effects are aliased with fourth-order interaction terms and the two second-order interaction effects are aliased with third-order effects. Assuming that the third and higher order effects are zero, or negligible, the response model developed from the 2^{5-1} fractional factorial design should estimate the key effects as accurately as the data will allow. Table 38-12 shows the observed response rates for the 16 panels.

The $(+1, -1)$ coding as well as the $(0, 1)$ coding was used to fit the model; the "minus" in Table 38-10 was set to 0 for the $(0, 1)$ coding. The $(0, 1)$ coding does cause the effects of the interaction terms to be correlated to their respective main effects, resulting in higher standard errors for the model coefficients, but it does not affect the values of the estimated coefficients. This was validated using the approach shown in Fig. 38-1. Since model coefficients have a more in-

Table 38-12. Test Response Rates

Panel	Observed response rate*
1	1.10
2	1.18
3	1.25
4	1.82
5	1.05
6	1.30
7	1.42
8	1.58
9	1.14
10	1.82
11	1.48
12	1.88
13	1.23
14	1.55
15	1.53
16	2.10

*All panels of equal size = 15,000.

tuitive interpretation when (0, 1) dummy variables are used, only those results are presented in this paper. Using X_i to define the level of the ith factor, the following model was fitted to the data:

$$\hat{R}' = B_0 + B_1X_1 + B_2X_2 + B_3X_3 + B_4X_4 + B_5X_5 + B_{12}X_1X_2 + B_{14}X_1X_4 \quad (7)$$

where $\hat{R}' = \ln$ (response odds) and response odds = Probability of response/ probability of nonresponse.

Table 38-13 shows the fitted model. The model chi square is very similar to the model F of multiple linear regression and, if significant, implies that all partial logistic regression coefficients are not equal to zero. The Wald statistic is similar to the F statistic for partial regression coefficients and, if significant, implies that the variable has a statistically significant relationship with the criterion variable after accounting for the effect of the variables in the model. The R statistic is very similar to the partial correlation coefficient. Hence, the ordering of the Wald and R statistics should be identical.

Since X_3, payment terms, and X_1X_2, the interaction of the digital-watch premium and the fast-response incentive, are insignificant, the model was rerun after dropping these variables. The results are shown in Table 38-14.

Since the criterion variable is log (odds), the coefficient of X_1, 0.2015 represents the amount by which ln (odds) would change if the premium was present. The right-most column, exp (B), represents the factor by which the response odds would change if the ith variable was present. Hence, the factor by which the response odds would change if the digital-watch premium was present is 1.2232. This information is very valuable since it allows one to predict response rates for any offer, even if a different creative is used. This is discussed next.

Example

Suppose a new creative consisting of a fast-response incentive and first 3 months free, but no plastic card or premium, results in a response rate of 1.95

Table 38-13. Logistic Regression Model Key Statistics (Full Model)*

Variable	B†	Standard Error	Wald	df	Sig	R	exp (B)‡
X_1	0.1988	0.0634	9.8123	1	0.0017	0.0146	1.2199
X_2	0.2313	0.0518	19.9482	1	0.0000	0.0221	1.2603
X_3	0.0074	0.0340	0.0474	1	0.8277	0.0000	1.0074
X_4	0.1114	0.0515	4.6675	1	0.0307	0.0085	1.1178
X_5	0.0962	0.0340	7.9965	1	0.0047	0.0128	1.1010
X_1X_2	0.0049	0.0690	0.0051	1	0.9433	0.0000	1.0049
X_1X_4	0.1155	0.0688	2.8211	1	0.0930	0.0047	1.1225
Constant	−4.5816	0.0533	7388.357	1	0.0000		

*Model chi square = 144.65, df = 7, sig = 0.0000.
†Partial logistic regression coefficient.
‡exp $(B) = e^B$, where e is base of natural logarithm.

Table 38-14. Logistic Regression Model Key Statistics (Reduced Model)*

Variable	B	Standard Error	Wald	df	Sig	R	exp (B)
X_1	0.2015	0.0505	15.9082	1	0.0001	0.0195	1.2232
X_2	0.2341	0.0342	46.8152	1	0.0000	0.0350	1.2638
X_4	0.1114	0.0515	4.6645	1	0.0308	0.0085	1.1177
X_5	0.0963	0.0340	8.0017	1	0.0047	0.0128	1.1011
X_1X_4	0.1156	0.0688	2.8248	1	0.0928	0.0047	1.1226
Constant	−4.5795	0.0456	10079.20	1	0.0000		

*Model chi square = 144.60, df = 5, sig = 0.0000.

percent. Using the information in Table 38-14 you can predict the response rates for the following offers:

- A: Premium, fast-response incentive, first 3 months free, but no plastic card
- B: Only premium and fast-response incentive present
- C: All four factors (premium, fast-response incentive, first 3 months free, and plastic card) present

We again use X_i (0, 1) to represent the presence of a factor where premium = X_1, fast-response incentive = X_2, first three months free = X_4, and plastic card = X_5.

The response rate of the new creative is

$$r(X_1 = 0, X_2 = 1, X_4 = 1, X_5 = 0) = 1.95\%$$

The response odds of this creative are given by:

$$\text{Response odds } (X_1 = 0, X_2 = 1, X_4 = 1, X_5 = 0) = \frac{1.95}{98.05} = 0.0199$$

The predicted response odds of offer A can now be calculated by multiplying 0.0199 by 1.2232 and 1.1226, the odds effect factors for X_1 and X_1X_4. Hence,

$$\frac{r}{(1 - r)} = \text{response odds } (X_1 = 1, X_2 = 1, X_4 = 1, X_5 = 0)$$

$$= 0.0199*1.2232*1.1226$$

$$= 0.0273$$

Thus, r = 2.66 percent

Predicted response odds of offer B:

Response odds $(X_1 = 1, X_2 = 1, X_4 = 0, X_5 = 0)$

$$= \text{response odds } (X_1 = 0, X_2 = 1, X_4 = 1, X_5 = 0)$$

$$*(\text{odds effect for } X_1/\text{odds effect for } X_4)$$

$$= 0.0199*(1.2232/1.1177)$$

$$= 0.0218$$

Thus, $r = 2.13$ percent

Note that in comparing the response odds for offer B we divided by 1.1177, the response odds effect for factor 4, since offer B did not have "first 3 months free."

Predicted response odds of offer C:

Response odds $(X_1 = 1, X_2 = 1, X_4 = 1, X_5 = 1)$

$$= \text{response odds } (X_1 = 0, X_2 = 1, X_4 = 1, X_5 = 0)$$

$$*(\text{odds effect for } X_1)*(\text{odds effect for } X_1 X_4)$$

$$*(\text{odds effect for } X_5)$$

$$= 0.0199*1.2232*1.1226*1.1011$$

$$= 0.0301$$

Thus, $r = 2.92$ percent

SUMMARY

This paper discussed a response surface modeling approach to understanding the effects of offer attributes on response rates. To obtain reliable estimates of the effects, we recommended collecting data using factorial, fractional factorial, and central composite designs. An example was shown where a 2^{5-1} fractional factorial design was used and the response rates modeled using logistic regression. In a second example we showed how the model results could be used to estimate response rates for three different offers when test results were available for only a specific offer.

Models similar to those discussed above, along with segmentation models (using customer behavior data) and financial information if stored in databases, can form the building blocks of knowledge-based systems. These can be used by marketers to help them with circulation planning and other critical marketing decisions.

NOTES

1. R. E. Bechhofer, "A Single-Sample Multiple Decision Procedure for Ranking Means of Normal Populations with Known Variances," *Annals of Mathematical Statistics*, **25**: 16–39 (1954).

2. J. Neter and W. Wasserman, *Applied Linear Statistical Models,* Homewood, Ill.: Irwin, 1974.

3. Ibid.

4. M. J. Norusis, *SPSS Advanced Statistics User's Guide,* Chicago: SPSS, Inc., 1990.

5. G. E. Box and N. R. Draper, *Empirical Model-Building and Response Surfaces,* New York: Wiley, 1987.

6. See, for example, Box and Draper, op. cit., and R. H. Myers, *Response Surface Methodology*, 1976.

7. For other values of k, see G. E. Box and J. S. Hunter, or Myers, op. cit. "Multifactor Experimental Designs for Exploring Response Surfaces," *Annals of Mathematical Statistics,* **28**:195–241 (1957).

39
Quantitative Database Methods

Robert D. Kestnbaum

Kestnbaum & Company
Chicago, Ill.

Of all the techniques available to marketers, those employed in database marketing are the most amenable to quantification and analysis. This is true because this form of marketing has a particular characteristic. *There is a closed loop of information:* Every action that the marketer takes can be quantified in terms of volume and cost. More important, responses or reactions can be determined with some accuracy and can be specifically related to the original actions. Since a cause-and-effect relationship can be established, it becomes possible to evaluate the initial action in terms of its results: the responses received, the purchases made, or other measures.

The ability to quantify results and relate them to initial marketing efforts has been one of the major appeals and strengths of direct marketing. The methods available for quantitative analysis have become much more sophisticated. This has been made possible in part by development of increasingly sophisticated computer-based techniques for both statistical and financial analysis. In addition, computers have made possible analysis of tens and even hundreds of thousands of transactions or customer records. This has led to the development of new techniques and new guidelines for application of familiar statistical methods that were designed initially to analyze a few thousand cases at most. The result has been an ability to obtain insights of great marketing power even though the actions of only a relatively small number of persons can be accurately predicted.

With the development of analytical methods, the goals of analysis have also changed. In this chapter, we will discuss the development of quantitative analysis and its transition across six major areas:

- Customer circulation planning
- New customer acquisition
- "Back-end" or customer performance analysis
- Multidimensional segmentation
- Relationship building and investment optimization

CUSTOMER CIRCULATION PLANNING

The earliest of modern mail-order practitioners recognized the value of their closed loop of information and the importance of relating marketing actions to subsequent customer performance. Records show that in 1902, Richard Sears decided to send his catalogs to customers who had purchased more than a specified amount in the prior season. He was using terms that later became known as *recency* and *amount* to set circulation policy. He observed empirically that customers who bought more recently and in greater amounts were likely to buy more in the future.

What Richard Sears was doing, knowingly or not, was applying what has become a fundamental premise in all quantitative analysis of marketing actions: Human beings tend to repeat earlier behavior and maintain fairly consistent product preferences, at least over a short time period. If we can successfully group together relatively large numbers of customers who have similar action patterns and preferences, we can begin to predict the amount of purchase or other activity we will obtain from that entire group. We may not be right about each individual in the group, but we can be quite accurate about predicting activity of the group as a whole.

In the depression of the 1930s, there was great pressure on the major mail-order companies to save money and obtain a high level of marketing efficiency. Without the benefit of modern computers, analysts began to study in more depth the relationships between recency, amount, and frequency of prior purchases as predictors of purchase in the next season. These studies were codified by one of the analytical pioneers, George Cullinan, who worked for a mail-order company named Aldens. Cullinan's rules defining relationships between *recency*, *frequency*, and *monetary* value of purchases (RFM) provided the basis for segmenting mail-order buyer lists for years to come. Many mail-order companies divide their customer files into cells based on combinations of recency, frequency, and monetary activity, and continue to use these divisions as the primary methods for circulation planning today.

RFM cells were not an effective answer for every company that wanted to segment its customer file. In fact, RFM analysis probably does not provide the best ranking for anyone. This is true for some basic reasons.

First, a great many subdivisions of recency, frequency, and monetary value are possible. Each of these components could readily be broken into many bands. If eight were used for each of the three measures, the resulting scheme would have 512 cells. This is a great many to contend with for decision making. Moreover, the population of many of the cells will be too small to yield statistically reliable results. Marketers will then try to group cells together or try to find other ways to rank cells.

Second, cell boundaries often were determined arbitrarily or with little analysis.

- In the beginning, recency was defined by many marketers in terms of annual or semiannual periods. Later, three-month quarters became useful. For some companies, perhaps one-month periods are significant. For other activities like television shopping, weeks, days, or even hours may become significant.

- Frequency can also have many aspects. Is it important to know how many times a customer has bought during his or her active life as a customer? Is it more important to know how many times a customer has bought during the last season or during each season? Has the frequency of purchase within a period changed from period to period?

- Similar questions arise in connection with amount of purchase. Is it more important to know the lifetime purchase amount or the amount purchased during each period? What is the significance of changes in purchase amount over time?

Third, each of the terms recency, frequency, and monetary value can be defined as a continuous scale rather than as having discrete bands. It would require many small breaks and consequently a huge number of cells to discern the relationships that exist between each of these terms and ultimate purchase.

This raises yet another problem. Cell definitions weight each of the components equally. In fact, hundreds of analyses have shown that one can be almost certain that recency, frequency, and monetary value should not be equally weighted in order to give the best prediction of future purchase.

Finally, there is another factor that marketers recognized intuitively but were very slow to inject into the analytical process. *What* customers have bought in the past makes a great deal of difference. When marketers are trying to direct their messages to a group of people who are more likely to purchase a product or service, it is always with a specific product or service in mind. The premise stated before that people tend to repeat earlier behavior also applies to the kind of product or service they will buy. This is a fourth aspect that must be taken into account when analyzing marketing data: the *category* of product or service that was purchased in the past and that is being offered now.

Recognition of this factor prompted me in the 1970s to coin the acronym FRAC (frequency, recency, amount, and *category* of product). The "C" highlights the requirement to group what people have bought before into bundles that have meaning in predicting future customer behavior. This calls for some imagination and invention.

When we are analyzing a large or complex product mix, it has been very helpful to think about products or services in terms of *attributes*. A series of attributes or dimensions can be defined and each product or service offered can be categorized according to each of its attributes or dimensions. Here is an example of a set of attributes defined for a catalog of home decorative and entertainment products:

- Function or use: wall display, tabletop display, food service, container, etc.
- Material: porcelain, ceramic, wood, brass, gold, leather, etc.

- Room in which used: kitchen, bathroom, living room, etc.
- Region of the world in which manufactured
- Design: high-tech, contemporary, traditional, Asian, Middle Eastern, etc.

A list of product attributes can go on almost indefinitely, but analysis can determine which attributes are most useful and significant for grouping products and services that the company sells or might offer in the future, and more important, which attributes predict future customer purchases. This set of issues has spawned a special kind of analysis focused on defining product affinities. If product attributes are defined in an insightful way, then various forms of affinity analysis will prove extremely helpful in providing guidance for product development and innovative combination or bundling of products.

NEW CUSTOMER ACQUISITION

At this point we need to follow a second important strand in the development of database-marketing analysis. Acquisition of new customers by direct-response advertising has been the driving force behind growth at many of the largest organizations that use direct marketing as a primary sales method. Many such companies actually will spend more money to acquire new customers than they will spend contacting old customers to get them to buy again.

Originally in the United States, and still today in most countries outside North America, advertisements in magazines and newspapers were the primary medium used to attract new customers to a direct marketing business. Although it is possible in many cases to buy portions of the publication audience that are targeted along demographic or occupational lines, the amount of analysis that these activities would support and the opportunity to vary marketing activity according to the results of such analysis are very limited.

Starting in the 1950s in the United States and Canada, and growing at a rapid pace since then, the availability of large numbers of rented lists and compiled name-and-address databases from which data elements could be extracted has radically changed the opportunity to apply analytical methods to improve customer acquisition promotions.

Direct marketers were quick to apply the lessons learned from analysis of customer activity. If one's own customers who bought most recently, most frequently, and in greatest amounts were the most likely to purchase again, the best RFM cells of other lists would hold the best prospects to buy one's own products.

In many ways, persons selecting lists for customer acquisition purposes were quicker to recognize the important fourth dimension, *product category*. If you were selling cookbooks, you looked for people who had already bought cookbooks, or other items related to cooking, or other product categories such as gardening that seemed to have close affinity to cooking.

A hierarchy of preferences developed. People who had taken specific *actions* were the best prospects. Of those who had acted, recency and amount of purchase appeared to be the best discriminators. For some unaccountable reason, although frequency is a powerful discriminator it often was not made available or was ignored for rental list selections.

When information describing prior activity was scarce or unavailable, marketers turned to demographics. Although these are less powerful, they do provide some additional ability to pick better prospects.

Most recently, carefully screened information derived from questionnaire respondent and other databases has been found useful for identifying better new prospects.

CUSTOMER PERFORMANCE ANALYSIS

Marketers have long recognized that some customers are more valuable than others. Mail-order sellers, benefiting from their closed-loop marketing information systems, used RFM or FRAC cells or multivariate analysis to identify customers who were more likely to purchase in the next period and then tracked ongoing purchases of people in each group. It was not hard to relate the actual amount of subsequent purchase to these predictions. A logical next step was to build models that defined how much product customers might buy, or even how profitable customers might be over the next 6 months to 1 year. Many direct marketers now make their customer acquisition or customer circulation decisions on the basis of the expected profit that will be derived over a 6- to 12-month period or over a longer term.

In some businesses, one could not develop an adequate estimate of customer profitability simply by looking at promotion expense and resulting sales. Product lines carry different profit margins. Customers have differing likelihoods of purchasing product categories. Some customers were more likely to return their product, to stop buying, or to not pay for products they had purchased. Different combinations of these factors yield varying profitability, period by period. And then there is the question: For how many periods will the customer continue to buy? The long-term value of a customer has become a critical marketing estimate.

Although the concept of customer lifetime or long-term value was advanced early in the 1980s, the complexity of executing this analysis with reasonable accuracy for small groups of customers has deterred most database marketers from making effective use of such estimates. Although there are variations in methodology, the best approaches to estimating long-term customer value establish different probabilities of action and then follow each line of action through its subsequent probabilities until each terminal group has minimal or no activity. For discrete periods of time, the money spent on promotional activity is summed along with resulting revenue and contribution to overhead and profit. Cash flows are computed for each time period and resulting profits or contribution to overhead and profit are discounted to compute the present value of the future profits. This present value is the long-term value of a customer.

If marketers can estimate the long-term value of customers obtained from different offers or media or in connection with different products, they will be in a position to set appropriate targets for the allowable cost to acquire customers in each of these ways.

Equally important, if marketers have a good way to estimate the long-term value of customers, they can evaluate ongoing programs to existing customers in terms of the changes wrought in the long-term value of those customers. As we will see later, this will turn out to be a much more effective way to evaluate the success of marketing campaigns.

MULTIDIMENSIONAL SEGMENTATION

Multivariate Analysis

The threads of customer circulation planning and customer acquisition came together around the same set of issues. There are many types of data available for consideration. Some of these data have continuous or scalar values. Others are inherently categorical or can be conveniently sorted into meaningful groups. Somehow these data must be combined and weighted and then used to group people to identify those most likely to purchase.

Fortunately, the development of various forms of computerized multivariate analysis held out answers to these needs. Other chapters in this book deal with list segmentation in depth, so the methodology will not be discussed in detail here. Instead, we will now divert to pick up the fourth strand important to quantitative analysis.

Defining Segmentation Criteria

Building on the history of customer circulation planning and customer acquisition, direct marketers have tended to segment their audience primarily in terms of ranking on likelihood of future purchase. Sophistication has taken the form of building better models to rank the probability of purchase and, to a lesser extent, to identify *what* customers might buy. Where customer action involves a substantial extension of credit, marketers have devoted considerable attention to developing credit-scoring models that identify persons who are not likely to pay their bills. With few exceptions, this is the state of the art today in direct marketing.

Mass marketers, on the other hand, have taken a much broader view toward market segmentation. They have worried about attitudes, perceptions, and lifestyles of their customers and prospects. They have experimented with positioning their products in order to attract the most suitable audience. They have expanded their markets by creating new desires or new needs among consumers where none existed before.

Mass marketers have developed these capabilities by conducting intensive research among relatively small but representative groups of customers and prospects. From such research, they have been able to define overall market segments both demographically and psychographically. Then they develop advertisements to appeal to the particular segments of the market that they are targeting.

The problem that mass marketers have faced is that they cannot determine in which market segment to place any particular person who has not been specifically researched. Mass marketers know that their prospects can be divided into very well-defined segments, but they do not know the names and addresses of specific persons in each segment.

Modern analytical methods now are closing the gap between the kind of segmentation historically performed by direct marketers and that performed by mass marketers. It is the closing of this gap and the tremendous extension in the ability to use data to guide marketing efforts that have prompted this author to use the term database marketing.

We learned years ago that we could use multivariate models to rank prospects and customers according to their probability of purchase. It was not much of an extension to build models that rank customers according to *how much* they might purchase, *how long* they might continue to purchase, *when* they might make the next purchase, whether they would *return* the goods, what *combinations of products* they might buy, and other specific issues relating to potential customer profitability.

More recently, when an organization's internal data are rich enough and appropriate enough, it has become possible to build models that estimate demographics such as age, family structure, income, or assets and key psychographic factors or attitudes relating to the product category in question, using only the internal data available about all customers.

Modern database marketers, therefore, are confronted on one hand with the opportunity to understand their customers and prospects in many dimensions and on the other hand with the problem of developing practical methods and decision tools to combine the outputs of many models into a single actionable picture of an individual customer and the multidimensional segment to which he or she belongs. Work is progressing rapidly to solve this problem, but it remains today one of the most important frontiers in database marketing.

Timing and Patterns of Activity

Another important analytical issue that is just beginning to receive appropriate attention is the timing and pattern of customer activity. Every marketer has recognized that timing is an important matter. Every prospect and customer is not ready to buy at every moment.

The general rule that the customer who has bought most recently is most likely to purchase again certainly does not hold in many product categories. For consumers, the more expensive the product is, the less likely most people are to buy again immediately. Purchase of a home, an automobile, a major appliance, or a suite of living room furniture takes the typical consumer out of the market for a repeat purchase for quite some time.

On the other hand, we know there are events in life such as getting married, having a new baby, moving house, getting promoted, or receiving a large sum of money that cause quick changes in historic purchase patterns. An alert marketer would detect such changes as quickly as possible and move aggressively to exploit them.

Database marketers have been relatively slow to develop models that detect such important changes and generate appropriate actions. Certainly there are companies that regularly promote persons they can identify as new movers, new mothers, or newly promoted, but most organizations using database-marketing techniques have not built into their everyday marketing fabric a set of techniques that will quickly identify and respond to customers who are *changing* their historic patterns of activity. This is another area where insightful analysis of data available to many companies can do much to identify significant new marketing opportunities.

RELATIONSHIP BUILDING AND MARKETING OPTIMIZATION

State-of-the-art quantitative analysis guided by sophisticated marketers is poised to lead marketing into an extraordinary future of greater understanding of customers and their needs, faster ability to respond to those needs and wants, and better planning and control of the entire process.

Greater Customer Insight

We have passed over an important threshold in developing the ability to understand large numbers of individual customers in terms of many dimensions or attributes. Looking at it one way, we seek to return much of marketing to its status at the turn of the last century. In those days, most products were bought from a retailer who knew you and your family, knew your preferences, knew what you had purchased recently, knew important events in your life, and knew just what would suit your needs and tastes today. With the advent of mass marketing, most customers have lost this sense of relationship to the seller. Today when we encounter a seller of any kind who knows us this well, we consider it remarkable, and we tend to respond with fervor noting the special service that is being rendered.

While I do not think that we will be able to use database marketing methods to recreate all of the earlier capability, many marketers who collect and use the appropriate data about their customer behavior will be in a position to have much of this insight for most of their customers. Clearly they will be in a better position to offer the right product or service to the right customer at the right time.

Responsiveness and Timing

As database marketers focus new attention on the issue of timing, we will make great strides in adjusting marketing efforts quickly to react to changes in customer circumstances. The old divisions of recency, frequency, and amount of activity will not be sufficient. We will need to know how much activity to expect from each customer during the next marketing period. We will need to determine as early as possible in that period whether actual customer activity is substantially more or less than the expected range. We will want to respond quickly to customers who are out of range to take corrective action, adjust our marketing expenditure, and learn how we can serve them better.

Perhaps we will use neural networks and artificial intelligence to detect, diagnose, and respond to changes in activity patterns. Perhaps we will further develop the often referred to, but essentially undeveloped, capability of database marketing to undertake two-way dialogue with customers to stimulate them to tell us quickly about impending changes or new developments. Through some combination of methods, the best database marketers will develop real understanding of their customers and ability to respond effectively. These marketers will fulfill the ultimate goal of marketing, which is to build and maintain strong relationships with customers.

Contact Management and Control

If we are entering an era where quantitative analysis will help database marketers to better understand their customers and be more responsive to changes that are affecting customers and their needs, we are also entering an era where the factors that guide planning and management of marketing activities will change.

Direct marketers typically have used their closed loop of information to focus on the immediate results of their marketing actions. They plan mailings or campaigns to produce enough response or revenue to be profitable. The primary decision in planning a campaign is to determine who should be contacted and who should not.

Mass marketers, who do not know the ongoing behavior of their individual customers, content themselves by measuring the results of campaigns in terms of new trials, product movement, and market-share changes.

Database marketers, who understand their customers in multiple dimensions and can formulate expected ranges of activity and long-term customer value, will soon adopt a different planning point of view. If we want to enhance relationships with customers and increase customer long-term value, we must develop a *longitudinal* plan for our communications with customers.

Our firm has adopted the term *contact strategy* to denote this aspect of database marketing. To develop a contact strategy, marketers will define groups of customers and prospects with relatively homogeneous characteristics and activity patterns. Marketers will then want to plan a long-term sequence of communications to each segment such that the frequency, media mix, message, tone, offer, and indeed the cost of the communications stream are carefully adjusted to the group of customers and the revenue that those customers are expected to yield. Simulations and other kinds of analytical techniques will be used to develop these kinds of longitudinal contact strategies. The measurement will move from immediate revenue generated to one of long-term return on long-term marketing investment. This kind of understanding may even help shift the focus of corporate management to longer-term strategies.

Up to now, it has been difficult for corporate management to assess the long-term impact of short-term marketing decisions. Database marketing analysts are likely to lead a thrust toward better understanding of the long-term implications of what heretofore were viewed as short-term marketing decisions. Good database marketing analysts already have learned that there is no such thing as a short-term marketing decision. All marketing decisions have long-term implications that can be assessed when the right data are available and the right methods are used.

If quantitative analytical methods do achieve the promise that they appear to hold out, marketing activities in many kinds of companies will acquire a new dimension of measurement, accountability, efficiency, and sophistication. Marketers in possession of the kinds of data that will support such analysis are likely to have real competitive advantage. The more interaction a company has with its customers, the richer the flow of data will be, and the more benefit can be obtained from applying the analytical approaches discussed here.

Who are the marketers with the most customer interaction? For the most part, they are not today's mail-order companies. They are financial service marketers; they are supermarket, convenience, fast-food, and drug retailers; they are telecommunications companies; they are airlines, hotels, and car rental companies; they are organizations selling their products repeatedly to the same businesses. In short, they are companies with the intelligence, resources, and capability to assemble the large amount of data about their customers and apply a broad range of analytical techniques to drive their marketing actions.

40

Accounting Considerations

James B. Kobak

James B. Kobak and Company
Darien, Conn.

Why on earth does accounting exist? There is only one reason — to help you run your business better. If you don't care about that, you shouldn't bother doing accounting. Just get a desk with a large drawer. When the money comes in, stuff it in the drawer. When you have to pay bills, take some of it out. No sense keeping all those ledgers and journals and other records.

There are two other major purposes of accounting which should not, however, be overlooked. A good accounting system must be designed to safeguard the funds of the business — control spending, to make sure that collections are made, discounts are taken, bills are reviewed and paid only if proper, and the like. The accounting system must also provide the necessary data to meet various governmental requirements such as income, sales, and other taxes.

We are going to approach this subject in a number of ways:

1. By explaining some of the principles of good accounting — and showing how these should be applied to the very specialized business of direct marketing.

2. By outlining the accounting records that are most useful in the direct marketing business and explaining what each account contains.

3. By explaining the statistical information that is helpful in supplementing the basic accounting records.

4. By giving examples of periodic reports that are most useful in analyzing what is going on — and how to use them.

SOME BASIC ACCOUNTING PRINCIPLES

Accounting principles can seem (and can be) as complex as the tax laws. For the purpose of developing helpful information for a direct marketing business, it is important to understand only a handful of them.

Organization of the Accounting System

The accounting system must be set up to follow the way the business is organized and operated and not for the convenience of the accountants. In the magazine business, for instance, you generally have several sources of income — subscription, single copy, advertising, and other (list rental, etc.). There are five major departments in a magazine — production (including paper, printing, and postage), editorial, advertising sales, circulation sales and fulfillment, and administrative. The accounting system for a magazine should be organized in the same way. So a brief operating statement would look like this:

Income		
Subscription	$1,406,000	
Single Copy	395,000	
Advertising	2,224,000	
Other	63,000	
	4,088,000	
Expenses		
Production	1,690,000	
Editorial	436,000	
Advertising	478,000	
Circulation	812,000	
Administrative	436,000	
	3,852,000	
Income (loss)	$ 236,000	

It doesn't necessarily have to be that way, however. If you have a marketing department which sells both advertising and circulation, your statements would be changed to reflect that.

You will also note that the statement for a magazine does not contain two items which are on the operating statement of most other businesses — Cost of Goods Sold and Gross Profit. If the figures were shown that way, interpretation would be difficult because a magazine is unusual. It is one product with several interdependent revenue streams. The advertising rate, for instance, depends on the amount of circulation. But the profit depends not only on the advertising rate but also on the cost of obtaining circulation and the price you can get for it. So you cannot consider them separately.

In most direct marketing businesses the Cost of Sales and Gross Profit approach is used because you are selling products with only one revenue stream. An example of a book publisher who does this is shown later.

Accrual Versus Cash Basis

There are two basic methods of doing accounting: accrual and cash. Cash is just what it says. You record transactions as the money changes hands—when you receive dollars from a customer and when you actually pay a bill.

In the accrual basis you record transactions when they take place—when you ship an order to a customer but will not be paid until later, when you incur an expense, even though you might not pay for it right away.

Most of us keep our personal records on the cash basis. In running a business, however, it is vital to record things as they happen, not at the time the money changes hands—or you will really not know what is going on. And the 1986 Tax Reform Act denies the vast majority of businesses the use of the cash basis for tax purposes.

This does not mean, however, that the cash flow aspects can be ignored. You still want to know how much money you have and when the cash comes in and goes out.

Match Income with Applicable Expenses

In order to get an accurate picture of what is going on in a business, it is essential to measure things that happen together at the same time or the figures will be distorted. In a magazine, for instance, advertising income is recorded at the time the issue is published. At the same time you must record the cost of paper, printing, and postage, as well as the salespeople's commissions and other expenses which apply to that issue.

Allocations of Expenses

In every company there are people who have jobs which overlap in two or more areas. For instance, you may have an advertising promotion director who works for two magazines. When this happens, in order to get the most accurate picture of the expenses applicable to each of the magazines, an allocation of the promotion director's salary and other applicable costs is made between the two magazines as accurately as the situation warrants.

Also allocation of other costs is often made—telephone, rent, overhead, and any other items where an allocation would be meaningful.

Practicality

The tendency of many accountants is to try to do everything in as detailed and as precise a way as possible. Very often the cost and trouble of doing this is not worth the reward. An element of practicality is needed. In the allocation of the promotion director's salary, for instance, an estimate of the time he or she spends on each magazine is sufficient. Time records are not needed, although they probably are for production workers where you must know the precise cost of each item made.

In the same way, while an editor works on the June issue of a magazine in April—and one of our principles is that we must match income and expense—it is not worth the trouble of accruing the April salary and applying it to June, because the editor's salary is the same in both periods.

ACCOUNTING STATEMENTS

There are only four types of accounting statements used in any business, although subsets and details of these may be quite extensive:

1. *The operating statement* tells what has happened during a given period on the accrual basis.

2. *The cash-flow statement* tells what has happened during a given period on the cash basis.

3. *The balance sheet* tells the condition of a company at one point in time. It shows the assets, liabilities, and owners' equity at that time.

4. *The source and application of funds* shows what has happened to the assets and liabilities during a given period.

Of enormous value, in addition to the accounting statements, are certain statistics which measure the most important features of the business. These will, of course, vary from one field to another. Such things as cost to obtain a customer, size of the average order, and renewal rate are of great help in the direct marketing business. We will discuss some of these later.

After the form of the accounting statements has been determined, a chart of accounts is developed. This is simply a list of the accounts in the accounting system with a definition of what should be in each so that there is uniformity in handling items. A number code is usually assigned to each account so that bills and other items can easily be marked and applied where they belong.

It is useful to organize the financial and other information so that you can look at a company's operations in a number of different dimensions. Interpretation becomes more meaningful when the major items can be viewed in various ways—and can be related to one another where it is helpful. This involves not only looking at the bare dollar figures but also comparing them with the budget and prior periods, developing percentage relationships, and then supplementing these with statistical data.

DESIGNING A SYSTEM

To design an accounting system, start by determining what figures will be most helpful in running the company, and then let the financial people figure out how best to get them. It is helpful to keep all the information regularly developed on just two pages: an operating statement and a statistical statement. Otherwise, interpretation becomes difficult. (Examples of both are shown with this chapter.)

Figure 40-1 shows a form of operating statement for a book publishing company. This form is similar to those used by many other direct marketing businesses. Of course the company in the exhibit sells books in many ways other than through direct marketing.

Various dimensions of viewing operations are available on this one sheet:

- Actual operations for the 7 months through July

- Actual operations for July alone

- The percentage each item is of net sales for each of these periods

- Comparison of data for this year against that for the prior year for the same period

- Comparison of percentages of net sales for the same periods versus the prior year

- Comparison of data for this year against the previously developed budget

- Comparison of percentages of net sales for the same periods versus the budget

Figure 40-2 adds a number of statistical dimensions to the picture. And it is probable that further details would be developed to show results of different marketing methods.

ACCOUNTING FOR DIRECT MARKETING OPERATIONS

We have been talking so far about principles which apply to any business. Let's now get into specifics for direct marketing operations.

We first must recognize that, while some companies are completely devoted to direct marketing, for most it is just one method of selling products and services. It is not an industry by itself such as steel making or real estate is. For that reason there is no universal method for presenting accounting statements.

We have already seen the approach taken for magazines and book publishers. In each field the presentation methods will be those which fit it best. Mail-order companies follow retail accounting systems (and may use the retail inventory method); fund-raisers, fund-raising systems; insurance companies, insurance systems; and so forth.

There are, however, common factors and methods to be considered in accounting for the direct marketing portion even though some aspects may be handled differently.

Summary Operating Statement, July 1991 (in thousands)

	Current Month					Seven Months to Date					
	Year	Budget		This Year		This Year		Budget		Last Year	
	%	$	%	$	%	$	%	$	%	$	%
Gross sales						$31,999	109.2%				
Less: Returns and allowances						2,697	9.2				
Net sales	100%		100%		100%	29,302	100.0		100%		100%
Cost of sales											
Manufacturing						5,963	20.4				
Royalty						955	3.3				
						6,918	23.7				
Gross profit						22,384	76.3				
Subsidiary rights income						256	.9				
						22,640	77.2				
Operating Expense											
Editorial											
Salaries						1,209	4.1				
Outside editorial fees						222	.8				
Other						413	1.4				
						1,844	6.3				
Selling											
Salaries & commissions						548	1.9				
Travel & entertainment						124	.4				
Other						203	.7				
						875	3.0				

Figure 40-1. Sample of a summary operating statement for a publishing company

Summary Operating Statement,
July 1991 (in thousands)

	Current Month						Seven Months to Date					
	Year	Budget		This Year			This Year		Budget		Last Year	
	%	$	%	$	%		$	%	$	%	$	%
Promotion												
Salaries							374	1.3				
Advertising							2,113	7.2				
Direct mail, catalogs							8,327	28.4				
Other							227	.8				
							11,041	37.7				
Fulfillment												
Order processing—salaries							1,247	4.3				
Order processing—other							918	3.1				
Shipping & warehousing							1,514	5.1				
Other							2,284	7.8				
							5,963	20.3				
Administrative												
Salaries							655	2.2				
Travel & entertainment							122	.4				
Employee benefits, taxes							73	.2				
Occupancy							325	1.1				
Office costs							474	1.6				
Taxes							133	.5				
Professional fees							106	.4				
Other							145	.5				
							2,033	6.9				
Total expenses							21,756	74.2				
Publishing income							884	3.0				
Less: Cost of money							2,461	8.4				

Statistics, July 1991 (in thousands)

	Current month						Seven months to date					
	Last Year		Budget		This Year		This Year		Budget		Last Year	
	$	%	$	%	$	%	$	%	$	%	$	%
Sales by type of customer												
Bookstores							$2,504	8.5%				
Wholesalers							429	1.5				
Libraries and institutions							173	.6				
Mass market outlets							145	.5				
Direct to customer							25,869	88.3				
Special sales							182	.6				
		100%		100%		100%	$29,302	100.0%				
Units sold												
Hardcover							2,224					
Softcover							527					
Net sales per unit												
Hardcover							$11.92					
Softcover							5.30					
Production cost per unit												
Hardcover							$2.37					
Softcover							1.31					
Number of invoices							1,932					
Average sale per invoice							$15.17					
Fulfillment cost per unit							$2.17					
Inventory turnover							1.8 times					
Accounts receivable							$9,728					
Percentage of net sales							33.2%					
Average collection period							101 days					
Aging of receivables												
Current							50.4%					
1–30 days overdue							22.7					
31–60							11.2					
61 and over							15.7					
Employees							137					
Employees per $1,000,000 of sales							4.7					

Figure 40-2. A number of statistical dimensions have been added to the operating statement

Direct Marketing Is a Statistical Business

Probably more than any other business, direct marketing is based on the sophisticated massaging and understanding of numbers. Creativity is required in developing or finding products or services which people want and in developing sales techniques and programs. But just as much creativity is needed in developing, understanding, and interpreting data after the results are in.

Because of this, whether you like it or not, the development of accurate data—sometimes in excruciating detail—is essential. Also essential, however, is to know what is most important. Otherwise you can become drowned in a sea of figures.

The Promotion Effort

In direct marketing everything starts with the promotion effort. Accounting begins with careful recording of the results of each effort from each source, whether it is to new or old customers—and whether it is a test or a roll-out. The data to be collected for *each* direct-mail effort, for instance, are:

- Number of pieces mailed
- Cost per thousand pieces
- Gross response
- Gross-response percentage
- Gross income per average order (including shipping-and-handling charge)
- Returns
- Return percentage
- Percentage cash, credit, credit card
- Bad debts
- Bad debt percentage
- Net response
- Net response percentage
- Net income per average order
- Cost of premium
- Average cost of goods sold (manufacturing, royalty, etc.)
- Percent cost of sales is of net income
- Fulfillment cost
- Fulfillment cost per order
- Cost of handling returns

These items all apply specifically to the direct income and direct costs of a particular mailing.

With all this data in hand, it is useful, too, to develop an entire operating statement for each source and each separate effort. Allocations of indirect cost such as promotion, administrative costs, and any others which come into play should be included so that you reach an operating profit figure.

With operating statements of this kind, comparisons can be made of the relative profitability of different products, prices and offers, mailing pieces, lists, and other variables. Naturally, a budget will have been made previously with which results can be compared.

While the figures above are designed for direct-mail efforts, similar data should also be developed for each other source.

Tying Data into Accounting Reports

In a marketing business the people doing the marketing are physically separate from accounting. Marketers have a tendency to develop their own forms and methods of tabulating and analyzing results. Seemingly, this makes sense because they understand their end of the business and know what they are trying to accomplish. On the other hand, it almost invariably leads to erroneous figures because they lack the discipline, essential in any good accounting system, of having to make everything balance. I have found too often that companies that thought they had made good profits after looking at the informal marketing department's figures, find later that important items were missing and they really suffered a loss.

With the ubiquitous computer to handle the storing of information and the calculation of results, there is no reason why the basic correct data cannot be made available for both areas. Accounting statements for the operation as a whole should be developed by adding the data from all the promotion efforts together, using the same basic information. Then there will be no surprises—or misconceptions.

HANDLING DIFFERENT DIRECT MARKETING SALES TECHNIQUES

The promotion effort is the base from which all knowledge starts. The information required from its results are pretty much the same, no matter what sales technique is used. A number of other factors, however, are needed in judging the success of some methods.

The techniques which cover the vast majority of selling efforts are:

- Sale of single items
- Catalog sales
- Clubs
- Continuity series
- Subscriptions

Each has a set of special factors to be weighed in conjunction with one another and with the basics to determine results—and, more important, to develop future plans.

Sale of Single Items

The simplest direct marketing method involves selling one item (or set of items) to one customer at a time. Prices and costs are relatively uniform. Interpretation is simpler than in some of the other methods. The operating statement and statistics would be very much like those in Figures 40-1 and 40-2.

Catalog Sales

While the operating statement for catalog sales may not be very different from that of the single-item sale, interpreting results becomes a high art. Statistics are needed about such things as:

- Which catalog
- Number of items purchased
- Price of items purchased
- Total value of the order
- Sales of each item and class of item in the catalog
- Returns in same categories
- Pages in the catalog from which the items were purchased
- Area of the page of the purchased items

The current practice of taking outside advertising in catalogs (magalogs) and selling copies in bookstores and other places requires operating figures much like those for magazines.

Clubs

The cost of obtaining members to clubs is very high. Profits are only achieved if a member stays long enough and buys enough items. The following information is vital:

- Result of each effort. This includes each member bulletin, which may include 13 or more cycles per year. This data is normally kept by entry class (the time first becoming a member) and by source.
- Cost to obtain a member
- Number of selections taken before ceasing to be a member
- Price of books taken — reduced price or full price
- Price per unit
- Cost per unit
- Prime selections versus alternates
- Percentage of members taking prime selection
- Returns

- Cost of returns
- Bad debts

The operating statement for a club reflects the importance of the type of selection taken by members and of the cost of acquiring them. As you can see in Figure 40-3, the cost of acquiring a new member is considered an operating expense because of the very small amount of income normally received. Because it will be some time before a member is profitable, the calculation of the cost of money is particularly important.

Gross sales		
Regular	$2,531,000	
Reduced price	91,000	
	2,622,000	
Less: Returns & allowances	533,000	
	2,089,000	
Less: Bad debts	154,000	
Net Sales	1,935,000	
Cost of Sales		
Manufacturing	511,000	
Royalties	99,000	
	610,000	
Gross Profit	1,325,000	
Operating expense		
Advertising & promotion		
New member offers		
Cost of books	150,000	
Space advertising	127,000	
Direct mail	131,000	
Other	42,000	
	450,000	
Less: Income from offers	24,000	
	426,000	
Promotion to members	143,000	
Salaries, other costs	102,000	
	671,000	
Fulfillment (net of recoveries)	241,000	
Administrative	223,000	
Total expenses	1,135,000	
Marketing income	190,000	
Less: Cost of money	203,000	
Operating income (loss)	$ (13,000)	

Figure 40-3. This operating statement for a club shows that the cost of acquiring a new member is considered an operating expense.

Continuity Series

While continuity series operate somewhat differently from clubs, the idea is the same: If a buyer stays with the series long enough, it can be profitable. If not, it can be a disaster.

The items to be measured are the same as with clubs, but the mix which brings profit may be very different. Operating statements usually are very much like those of clubs.

Subscriptions

By their nature magazine, newsletter, and other subscriptions result in repeated exposure to the product—and with it a familiarity which brings higher repeat purchases than other direct marketing methods. The key factor to be added to our basic list is renewal rates, which should be tracked through the first, second, third, etc. renewals as well as by the original source of the subscription and the renewal effort to which a subscriber responded.

IMPORTANCE OF REPEAT SALES

It is very difficult to make money on one-shots. The whole function of clubs, continuity series, and subscriptions is to develop repeat sales. While the sale of single items or catalog sales seemingly are one-time events, the real goal should be to develop loyal customers. For that reason, those who sell in these ways should keep just as detailed records about the behavior of their buyers as do magazine publishers and record clubs. They need lifetime histories of customers:

- When did they buy
- What did they buy
- Size of orders
- Did they buy by cash, credit, or credit card
- Return and bad-debt history

VALUE OF A CUSTOMER

This leads to the next point: To get the most out of customers, you must think of them buying not just what they started out with but other products in other ways. After all, Time-Life and Readers' Digest book and record operations grew from magazine buyers. And oil company mailings arose from gas station buyers.

The most sophisticated direct marketers think far beyond the initial sale. They plan in terms which are very long term. They expect to acquire a customer today and may not expect to make any profits for two or three years

Through careful record keeping and analysis they can determine the customer's interests and the type of product he or she might buy in the future. It becomes a terribly complex calculation, but you can determine the eventual value of different types of customers—and then figure out how much you can afford to pay to acquire each new one.

COMBINATION OF SOURCES

We have been talking about keeping track of each individual effort in detail. Let's not forget that a combination of different sources of new orders can make a project profitable where it could not work by using just one.

A magazine, for instance, may not be able to develop sufficient circulation just through direct mail. But, by adding subscriptions obtained through exchange advertising, insert cards, and agent-sold (or other) business, plus single-copy sales, you may be able to have a winner. In the same way, a book publisher may be able to develop enough volume for a title by selling it as a one-shot, through a book club, and in bookstores to make it profitable, where any one of those sources alone would not work.

IMPORTANCE OF CASH FLOW

We concluded earlier that the accrual method of accounting gives more accurate results than the cash method. In planning, however, cash flow is terribly important, particularly in direct marketing. Many direct marketing efforts call for large up-front payments for promotion and inventory, and customer responses and payments may lag for some time. If you have not planned for the required amount of cash, you may find that you cannot carry out the program you want to do.

INVENTORY WRITE-OFFS

Frequently the cost of sales is determined without taking into account the fact that, no matter how well the business is run, a sizable part of the inventory of virtually any item will have to be written off or sold at a depressed price because either you bought too much or the product is obsolete. If allowance is not made for that in the regular cost-of-sales calculation, you may find that you have a disaster when you thought you were making profits.

COST OF MONEY

I have carefully put in a line at the bottom of each sample operating statement for the cost of money. Too many companies ignore this—or think about it only once a year or so. In all direct marketing operations except magazines, the cost of money is very important and should be included every time you try to determine what profits might be. Inventories and accounts receivable represent cash which might better be used in other ways. In addition, if you have calculated the value of a customer where profits will not come for a long time, the calculation is incomplete without the cost of carrying that customer during that period.

USE OF COMPUTER MODELS

Direct marketing is a statistical business, but it must be apparent by now that it is much more complex than that. Because it is long-term, you cannot really be successful without careful planning.

Some very powerful tools have been developed to assist with that planning process. For instance, the Magazine Publishing Model and Direct Marketing Model were developed by Kobak Business models (now Media Services Group) to help in the process. They have been used by more than 1000 magazines and other direct marketers in various parts of the world.

These models enable a company to play "what if" games to determine the optimum plans over a period of 5 or more years. They help you determine accrual and cash basis profits based on various assumptions which you can control, as well as to find circulation levels and other statistical information during the period. These are calculations which you could theoretically do by hand, but which the models enable you to do much faster and more accurately, as well as giving the opportunity to examine many variations.

THE DANGERS OF COMMON DEPARTMENTS

In a company with more than one profit center, it is common for employees to spend their time on more than one activity. If the situation is as simple as this, allocating their salaries and other costs (payroll taxes, fringes, etc.) based on an estimate of the time spent is usually adequate.

Larger companies tend to set up departments to handle functions that are common to all the activities. It is the norm to see such departments covering production, promotion, and circulation.

Other departments are sometimes set up that are, in essence, suppliers to the magazines. Examples are composition, photography, art, direct mail, and subscription fulfillment. Every multipublication house also has general and administrative costs that apply to the overall operation rather than any one magazine. These include executive, accounting, maintenance, office services, and corporate.

In addition, some very large companies tend to have staff functions that do not directly serve any one activity. These would include such titles as group president, director of manufacturing, marketing director, and advertising director, together with their related housing and other costs.

It is important to make very careful allocations of the costs of these groups to the various activities. Because they normally do not have direct responsibility for the profits of any one profit center, their costs tend to become soft and unrelated to specifics. And because they are working for a department rather than for any single activity, their loyalties often lie with their departments rather than with any specific profit center.

I deplore this type of organization. I believe in organizations where each activity is an independent unit with all its people working together for that activity and nothing else. There may have to be some centralized services, of course, but the fewer, the better.

I recognize, however, that not all the world agrees with me about this organizational situation. So we do often have all the different types of departments above (and probably some others). The question, from an accounting standpoint, is how to keep track of them and how to be sure that they are contributing value for what they cost. I think each has to be handled in a different way.

- *Service departments:*   The costs are accumulated and allocated on some logical basis. For instance, production costs should be allocated according to number of issues, number of pages, and total production costs. Promotion costs depend on total promotion spending for each activity.

- *Supplier departments:*   The best way to allocate these costs is through charges based on an actual price list, just as you would if you were dealing with outside companies. In this way, equitable charges are made, comparisons can be made with outside firms, and the departmental costs are not allowed to grow at an uncontrolled rate. Some companies with departments of this kind give the individual profit centers the option of buying either from the in-house departments or from outside firms. This gives some control over both cost and quality.

- *General and administrative costs:*   There are some costs that cannot be allocated on any very logical basis. But still, they should be applied to the individual magazines in order to allow you to get an idea of the real profitability of each. Some sort of formula is generally used. Common ones are total sales, total sales plus total expenses, and number of people.

  Some companies do not apply administrative costs to start-up operations. The old argument is that you would not be able to reduce the overhead costs if you didn't have the new operation. In my mind, this is simply a ploy to make the losses on the new property look smaller. I think the costs should be applied to every operation, start-up or not.

CONTRIBUTION TO ADMINISTRATIVE COSTS AND PROFIT

A number of companies have adopted the misguided approach of developing for each activity a bottom-line result called "contribution to administrative costs and profit." They arrive at this figure by charging all direct expenses against each profit center, but not making any provision for administrative costs (that's overhead, of course). A composite statement for the company might look something like this:

	Sales	Expenses	Contribution	% of sales
Activity A	$ 2,000	$ 1,600	$ 400	20.0%
Activity B	5,000	4,500	500	10.0
Activity C	7,000	6,000	1,000	14.3
Total	$14,000	$12,000	$1,900	13.6
Administrative costs			1,400	10.0
Net profit			$ 500	3.6%

As you can see, the company as a whole earned only 3.6 percent, yet the operators of each activity had the feeling that they were running an operation making 10 to 20 percent of sales. But had we allocated the administrative costs to the individual activities on any reasonable basis, it would be apparent that one of them is not profitable—and that even the best is not making much. For instance, suppose we allocate based only on sales. The result would be:

	Profit	%
Activity A	$200	10.0%
Activity B	—	—
Activity C	300	4.3
Total	$500	3.6%

Hardly a superior performance.

Aside from resulting in the development of misleading numbers, this approach brings about a thinking by the managers of the operations that automatically depresses overall profits. "Hey," they say, "I made a nifty 30 percent contribution!" But all they really did was make 20 percent profit when they should be aiming at 30 percent or more.

NATURAL CLASSIFICATIONS

It is useful every so often—maybe once a year or so—to take a look at the expenses for a company according to their natural classifications. By that I mean accumulating all the costs of a single type to find whether in total they are growing and whether in the abstract they seem reasonable.

For instance, if you total all the salaries, or travel, or office, or any other cost category, you sometimes end up saying to yourself, "That just sounds like too much money for our size operation."

The Floating Breakeven Point

I don't remember who introduced me to the concept of the floating breakeven point. It had to be someone from one of the larger publishing houses that had had lots of experience starting new magazines. It works something like this:

1. You carefully project the expected results for the new magazine for 5 years. You anticipate that it will break even in the third year when there is 250,000 circulation and 400 advertising pages.

2. After publishing for 1 year, you project that the magazine will break even in the fourth year when there is 350,000 circulation and 600 advertising pages.

3. After 2 years' experience, you know that it will break even in the fifth year with 450,000 circulation and 800 advertising pages.

4. After 3 years, you are certain that it will break even someday.

Budgeting

Budgeting: the very idea is frightening to many people. They think in terms of the federal or family budget that will end up with money unspent at year's end: Both are obviously impossible exercises.

It is too bad the word *budget* is applied to business activities. The budget for a business is nothing more than a plan. It does not have the rigidity that a government budget must have nor the personal application needed in a family budget. When perceived correctly, budgeting for a business can be the most useful exercise any company can engage in. The negative connotations almost always arise either because of a poor budgeting process or because the purposes and processes of good budgeting are not understood.

As I said, a budget is a plan for a business. That's all! Usually, it is for a relatively short time, most likely a year. It covers all the income, expense, and profit items involved in an operation. It is expressed in terms of dollars because that is the unit we use to quantify just about everything we do in business. But parts of it can also be expressed through other types of statistics and in narrative form.

Budgeting fulfills many purposes:

1. It develops a blueprint for operations. Any business works better if it is planned ahead.

2. It forces key people in an organization to think through what they are doing. All of us have trouble thinking hard and in detail about our future plans. Budgeting forces us to do this.

3. It coordinates activities in various areas of the company.

4. It examines alternative strategies and tactics. During the budgeting exercise, calculations can be made to determine what different prices might mean to the bottom line, what increased promotion might cost, and what benefits might be derived.

5. It involves key people in major decisions and develops their interaction with one another. Most people tend to become immersed in their own day-to-day activi-

ties and to forget the whole. The budgeting process involves many people in an organization in the important decisions and forces them to work with those in other departments, people whom they normally might rarely contact.

6. It enables evaluation of performance against a plan. As the year goes on, evaluation of reality versus the plan becomes automatic. Trends are spotted easily and changes can be made quickly when deviations occur.

7. It controls operations. It is very easy for expenses to get out of control if you do not have a way to measure what they ought to be. With a budget, you can spot differences when they first occur and take corrective action.

8. It ensures that the key people know what the overall plan is and what each must do to make it work.

Types of Budgets.   Budgets can be made for any economic activity. They will vary with the nature of that activity, the success of the enterprise, the state of the economy, and, most important, the people involved.

In business there should be, at the very least, an operating budget, a cash-flow budget, and a balance sheet budget. Some people, those who dislike the word budget, may call them projections or pro formas. In a capital-intensive business there will be a capital budget. In a people-intensive business there will be a people or payroll budget. Sometimes there are project budgets.

Some companies develop only one budget a year. Others have several, such as high, low, and expected. When company or economic conditions warrant, contingency or "disaster" budgets are prepared so that action can be taken quickly if sales decline precipitously.

Periods for budgeting coincide with accounting periods so that comparisons with actual results can be made easily.

In some companies the budget is dictated by the boss. The most effective budgeting, however, is known as a "ground up" budget. This means that every person who has responsibility for any part of the business does his or her own budget for his or her own area. The overall budget is the result of putting all the pieces together in a coordinated way.

There are several reasons for this approach. First, and most important, you cannot expect as good compliance with a dictated budget as you can with one that the individuals involved helped create. Second, you want to take advantage of all the thinking and planning that you can get in a company. Third, the more people who are involved and feel that they are part of the team, the better. Fourth, the lower on the ladder you go, the more detailed knowledge there is of a function and its costs, so the more realistic the budget will be.

Steps in Preparing the Budget.   When done right, budget preparation takes a long time. Planning has to be done on many levels. The individual budgets then have to be fitted together to yield a coherent, workable whole. This calls for lots of give and take, studies of various alternatives, and, usually, compromises.

Normally, several months before the end of a company's fiscal year the financial department sets the budget process in motion by giving each of those involved some background material designed to be helpful in developing next year's budget. The treasurer or controller is generally in charge of pulling the budget together and monitoring it.

It is helpful if the president sets the overall tone of what is expected by describing the state of the economy and the state of the field served, and then making a general statement about what is expected from a profit standpoint. Then all the others involved will have a feeling for the overall direction desired.

The type of information given varies by department, but would include the following:

- This year's budget and actual figures so far this year and projections for the period of the year not yet completed.
- Statistics for these periods
- Competitive information
- Industry norms

Each department head passes the first budget try to the level above, where it is discussed and eventually merged into one document for the company as a whole. The boss reviews the entire budget, consults with others as necessary, and sends the material back down the line with suggestions that will result in an overall budget that will be satisfactory. This process continues until agreement is reached on the best plan. This can take many meetings and the study of countless major and minor alternatives. Eventually, the final budget is adopted and becomes the plan for the year.

But a good budget is not just developed, adopted, and put on the shelf. It must be a real working document used throughout the year. At the end of each accounting period, the financial department issues reports comparing actual results with the budget. These reports go to everyone who prepared a budget for an area.

If there are deviations of any significance, either better or worse, the financial department investigates the causes and indicates what they are. It is then up to each superior — and eventually the boss — to judge the real significance of each, to determine whether a trend is appearing, and to take whatever action might be necessary. With a good budgeting procedure, surprises of any kind should become very rare.

Remember that a business budget is just a plan; it is not fixed in concrete. If major changes take place during the year, rebudgeting must be done. In doing this, however, the original budget should not be lost or abandoned; otherwise, it will appear that you are always on budget, no matter what changes take place. It is good to continue to compare the original budget, in addition to the new plan, with the actual results.

Some companies rebudget automatically every quarter or twice a year. Others run a revolving budget, planning 12 months ahead every quarter. This probably is not good for everyone because it can be very time-consuming and can easily lead to a mere updating rather than a real review in depth once a year.

Fixing Profits

This is a wild one: Our operating statements are upside down. Our operating statements carry profit as the last item on the page. It seems to be only the result of what is left over from sales after we have paid everybody else. And we talk about looking at the "bottom line." Why not make it the "top line"?

Similarly, the owners' equity on our balance sheet, which should be the most important item, is way down in the lower right-hand corner—and, in logical sequence, at least, is the last item to be read. Our British friends know better than this: Their balance sheets are backward and upside down to ours, but owners' equity is at the top left, where it is the first thing you see. I know how we got this way. It's us accountants. We're better at subtracting expenses from sales than the other way around. But in this age of computers, we should be able to do it either way.

Please view this idea as more than a simple exercise in logic. Thinking that puts profit at the bottom of the column is warped. It does not give enough importance to the reason we are in business. Even worse are those people—and there are lots of them—who set up their statements this way:

- Expenses
- Income
- Profit or loss

The minute I see figures set up in this sequence I know that I have a loser who doesn't have a profit motive.

Profit should be a fixed item—and the first fixed item. If we cannot make the rest of the figures fit, then something else should be changed or the method of doing business should be radically altered. This is a whole new way of thinking for most of us, but it puts the emphasis where it belongs: on what we are trying to achieve. This very simple change in concept can have a radical influence on how we conduct ourselves.

But there is more to it than simply developing the concept that profit is fixed. A change in the manner of making operating statements is needed because a whole new mindset is involved. The table below shows one approach to a new form of operating statement:

Profits	
Fixed	$ 500
Additional	200
	$ 700
Net sales	
Advertising	2400
Subscription	2500
Newsstand	500
Other	100
	$5500
Costs	
Mechanical	$2200
Advertising	500
Editorial	400
Circulation	1300
Administrative	400
	$4800

We have accomplished a rather remarkable thing. The first item is the most important one!

What is strange is that the normal way is completely contrary to the way we do just about everything else. I don't know of any football team that consciously says, "We'll give the other guys 24 points—and if we can score more, we'll win." But that is the approach our normal financial statements take.

The same approach can be applied to a number of the other familiar tools used in business. For instance, the "breakeven approach." I don't ever want to break even. I want to make money. Why not call it the "minimum acceptable profit approach"? Not a very catchy title, but it does get the point across.

About now you should be asking, "What, specifically, have we accomplished besides establishing a different state of mind—one that is focused on profits rather than on thinking of profit as that which is left over after everybody else has had his or her take? Look at the possibilities:

- The focus is on profits—not sales or costs.
- If the fixed profits do not look as if they can be achieved, then something else must change—but not that particular number. If this means a change in the way of operating, so be it.
- If there is no way of achieving the fixed profit, then let's get out of the business. This may make us stop some of those efforts which go on year after year—with good results to be obtained next year, every year.
- In new business, if the fixed profits can never be achieved—or take too long—let's not even get started.
- Management time, the most precious commodity we have, is not wasted in fruitless pursuits.

The concept is simple: Profits are a fixed item, and the first and only fixed item. Anything else must be changed to achieve it.

41

Predictive Modeling

John Banslaben

Applied Regression Technology
Centerport, N.Y.

Sherlock Holmes, the fictitious world-famous detective, was well known for his ability to ferret out countless details that missed the ordinary observer's eye and solve the mystery at hand with wondrous logic. Selecting profitable names for direct-mail promotions has at times been a bit of a mystery, too. Fortunately, there exists now a quantitative methodology known as *predictive modeling* which applies scientific systems of logic to marketing databases and, much like Sherlock Holmes, solves the mystery of who will respond to the next promotion.

RFM VERSUS REGRESSION

This chapter is about a specific form of predictive modeling known as regression modeling, or regression analysis, and covers how regression models are created and applied. A model is a set of response predictions used for all direct-mail name-selection decisions such as omitting or selecting names in a mailing. These decisions are based on features of the customer's history. Historically, the most common form of response prediction used in direct-mail name selection is the recency, frequency, and monetary value (RFM) model. In RFM name selection, these are the only three variables from the customer's history that are used (see Table 41-1). No Sherlock Holmes is necessary when a handful of variables or customer characteristics are evaluated and a rudimentary manual name-selection formula is employed, such as RFM.

While this method of name selection was an evolutionary improvement over mailing to the whole file, today's competitive marketplace demands more. Di-

Table 41-1. Sample RFM Cell Definitions

Recency of last order	Frequency of order	Cumulative monetary value
0–6 months	2 or more	$200 plus
0–6 months	2 or more	$100–$200
0–6 months	2 or more	$50–$75
0–6 months	2 or more	$25–$50
0–6 months	2 or more	$1–$25
0–6 months	1	$200 plus
0–6 months	1	$100–$200
0–6 months	1	$50–$75
0–6 months	1	$25–$50
0–6 months	1	$1–$25
6–12 months	2 or more	$200 plus
6–12 months	2 or more	$100–$200
6–12 months	2 or more	$50–$75
6–12 months	2 or more	$25–$50
6–12 months	2 or more	$1–$25
6–12 months	1	$200 plus
6–12 months	1	$100–$200
6–12 months	1	$50–$75
6–12 months	1	$25–$50
6–12 months	1	$1–$25
.	.	.
.	.	.
.	.	.

rect marketing has, more than ever, become the complex business of managing details about the customer's and prospect's characteristics in order to select the best names. In recent years there have been advances in both computer technology and quantitative analysis methodologies that have enabled the level of name selection decisions to rise to a high art form. Owing to these innovations, regression-type predictive models can utilize infinitely larger numbers of variables and can discriminate response with the variables utilized in much finer focus for more precise targeting. The reasons for this are simple and few: There are inherent limits to the amount of information beyond RFM that can be used in a manual or RFM-like method; and there are unlimited variables on the customer's history that can be utilized in a regression model, unlike RFM.

Statistically speaking, the major difference between RFM and regression models is that regression draws response predictions from many variables beyond RFM in a statistically efficient manner. The regression models are defined as a set of coefficients or weights that are assigned to individuals depending on their many characteristics, including RFM. These weights are added or summed to produce a single score for each customer record. This final score is then used for all name-selection decisions.

According to the DMA's *Direct Marketing Practices and Trends Survey,* most direct marketers expect to increase their planned usage of statistical analysis over

70 percent. Regression modeling is at the vanguard of quantitative methodologies that will dramatically alter and improve the direct marketing landscape.

A caveat: It is the author's goal to provide the layperson with a basic understanding of what is needed to create a regression model. The topic is sophisticated, complex, and replete with mathematical and statistical assumptions and terms. The reader's forbearance is requested: Not all technical concepts can be reduced to a palatable level without a loss of correctness. The creation of a true high-performance model involves numerous steps and considerable time and effort. The increased profit potential, however, makes the investment worthwhile.

The article will take the reader through five basic levels of instruction:

1. Identifying which promotions would benefit from regression modeling
2. Deciding what database elements should be included in the model
3. First-level data analysis: univariate
4. Second-level data analysis: multivariate
5. Integrating regression models into a marketing plan

These five steps are followed by an overview of possible developments in regression modeling. The majority of the examples and illustrations in this chapter focus on regression models that predict response rate for customer mailings. Regression models can also be used to predict other performance data, such as dollar sales per thousand, and sales success on noncustomer files, such as rental lists.

HOW TO IDENTIFY PROMOTIONS BEST SUITED FOR REGRESSION MODELING

The first step in creating a regression model is to identify which direct marketing promotions will significantly benefit from this type of quantitative analysis. In order to produce a regression model which will generate a high cost-benefit ratio the mailing should (1) meet a minimum sample-size criteria, (2) have a whole-list response rate that is relatively near to the breakeven response rate, (3) have a "suitable snapshot" of the customer record available, and (4) have significant roll-out potential.

Minimum Sample Size Criteria

In order to produce consistent results, the mailing should contain a large enough number of names and a response rate that generates at least 1000 orders or responses. For example, an offer with a 4 percent response rate would require a test mailing of 25,000 names. In contrast, an offer with a 0.10 percent response rate would need 1 million names to generate 1000 responders. Although successful regression models have been developed with fewer names, samples that meet this criteria have generally been proved to produce more reliable results.

Whole-List Response Rate to Breakeven Response Rate

A second requirement for the test mailing is that the total response rate—dollars per thousand ($/M)—for the whole list should be relatively near the breakeven response rate ($/M). Regression modeling will not usually improve an already highly successful promotion or list; nor will it magically improve an extremely nonresponsive list or an unappealing offer. It is therefore important to carefully consider the relationship between the whole-list response rate and the breakeven response rate. Since regression models typically produce gains near the 50 percent level when selecting half of the list, it is suggested that the target mailing selected for analysis have a breakeven response rate that is 50 percent higher or 50 percent lower than the whole-list response rate. For example, a promotion with a 4 percent response rate would be a good candidate for regression modeling if the breakeven response rate was between 2 and 6 percent.

Suitable Snapshot

A third requirement for selecting the optimum sample is to save a "snapshot" of the customer's marketing database record as it looked at the time of the current promotion and "marry" the responses to this promotion later, just as in a typical RFM analysis. It may therefore be necessary for the marketer to make plans to save this information from a future test mailing if it is not available from previous test promotions. It may also be possible to analyze a past mailing for which responses have already been received.

Have Significant Roll-Out Potential

The marketer must next consider whether a test mailing has roll-out potential in sufficient quantities to justify development costs of a regression model. Alternatively, if a single mailing does not possess roll-out potential, a generic model could be developed by selecting one or more test mailings which are representative of future mailings. A generic model is a model which is applicable to a class of promotions whose responders possess similar discriminating characteristics.

To form an analysis sample for developing a generic model it is necessary to first combine several promotions that are representative of the several products that define the generic group. Each individual product promotion will need to meet the minimum sample size requirement set forth in step 1, above. This requirement may be somewhat relaxed if the products defining the generic group are closely related in terms of their respective buyer profiles based on previous knowledge. A response grouping of products based on the customer's characteristics is optimally developed using the statistical procedures known as factor or cluster analysis to conduct what is known as a product purchasing affinity study. Care should be taken in evaluating the applicability of the resulting regression model by determining that the profiles of the high responders from the test sample match those of the high responders in the roll-out promotion.

DECIDING WHAT DATABASE ELEMENTS SHOULD BE INCLUDED IN A MODEL

The clues to determining which customer will respond to a future promotion are contained in the wealth of information about that customer on what is called the marketing database. The value of the data elements on the marketing database comes into play when segmenting the high responders from the low responders. Virtually any piece of information available on the database about a customer is a candidate for inclusion in a regression-modeling analysis.

In general, RFM information about the customer's previous purchases, have the highest discriminatory value in segmenting the best customers from the worst. Next in order of significance are other individual characteristics, including promotional history and individual demographics. This would be followed in order of priority by the in-house demographics, such as the customer penetration rate by zip code, and finally, zip code level demographics. However, the discriminatory value of the data will vary not only by the product offer but also by the list segment being analyzed.

The RFM information plays a much less significant role in identifying customers in the one-time-buyer list segment than in the multibuyer list segment. The reason is that the multibuyer list segment, which is defined as the list of customers that have purchased at least twice, contains more of the important historic information on previous customer purchases than does the one-time-buyer list. The predictors of response that are more significant than RFM for the one-time-buyer list segment include the original source of the name; individual and area demographic enhancements, especially age, income, sex, and single- versus multiple-family dwelling unit; and survey questionnaire responses and in-house demographics.

The question that often arises is, What additional value to the mailing will regression models contribute over and above RFM selection? Regression's contribution over RFM is, for the most part, determined by the availability of regression variables that discriminate response beyond the RFM variables and the reduction of variability in the RFM response estimate due to data analysis methods employed by using regression modeling.

The marketing database contains data elements in addition to RFM which significantly predict response as determined by the statistical technique known as response cross-tab (discussed in greater detail under the section on univariate analysis). A regression model will outperform RFM by an amount that is proportional to the unique contribution of these additional data elements. The marketing database may include well over 100 data elements that have the potential to segment, beyond RFM, the best- from the poorest-performing names and may include information from the following data classes:

- *Previous product purchasing history:* Names in the same RFM cell that have already purchased product A may be more likely to purchase product B. The response relationships between two products at a time are studied in a response cross-tab report, while more than two products are best studied in a product-purchasing analysis using the statistical methods known as factor and cluster analysis.

- *Prior promotional history:* number of promotions since last order, average number of orders per promotion, etc. The better prospects have fewer promotions since their last order and also a higher average number of orders per promotion.

- *Survey questionnaire response data:* responses to product-related preferences and demographic information such as age and income may indicate high responsiveness to a specific promotion.

- *Sweepstakes response data:* Both yes and no responses indicate a degree of direct-mail responsiveness and may add to the discriminatory value of the regression model.

- *Address data:* title (relates to sex and lifestyle), date of last address change and number of address changes (relates to mail responsiveness and deliverability), address type (relates to urban versus rural and dwelling type).

- *Date and source:* acquisition date (date entered on the database) and original list source of the first order.

- *In-house demographics:* These include customer penetration and response rates by zip code. These variables become more reliable and valuable as the absolute number of customers in a zip code increases, and also as the number of names that were exposed to the promotion in the zip code increases.

- *Individual and area demographics:* zip code, census-tract and census-block level, age, income, sex, education, magazine penetration, etc. The census-tract and census-block level data define a finer level of geographic detail and may have a greater amount of variability in their response estimates. These finer levels are consequently used to augment, not replace, the zip-code level demographics.

- *Geographic location:* This is important especially for climatically seasonal products. Examples include state, average temperature, rainfall, and latitude and longitude.

- *Method of previous orders:* cash or charge (related to income), telephone or mail (related to presence of children).

The contribution in value of regression modeling over traditional RFM name selection is also a result of the methods used to analyze the data. Traditional RFM analysts must make a trade-off between using smaller RFM cells with fewer names and greater discrimination in response to larger RFM cells with a greater number of names and less discrimination in response. This trade-off is illustrated by considering the RFM cell that contains 1000 names that have ordered in the past 6 months and responded to the current promotion at a 3 percent response rate (30 orders). A higher level of discrimination is attained by redefining the RFM cell into six separate RFM cells containing those names that had recency values of 1, 2, 3, 4, 5, and 6 months, respectively. However, the six new RFM cells now contain fewer names, and therefore the response rate for each new RFM cell is less reliable than the original RFM cell definition.

Regression-based modeling addresses this problem by looking at each of the new RFM cell definitions at the finest, most detailed level simultaneously, and modeling the trends from this data, extracting the maximum segmentation power in the most reliable manner.

UNIVARIATE ANALYSIS

Response Cross-Tab Report

A response cross-tab report is a univariate (one-variable-at-a-time) analysis of the elements on the customer database. Response cross-tab analyses are the fundamental means for reviewing the detailed relationships between the performance variables such as response, and the predictor variables, including RFM, to determine which variables should be inputted into the regression variable selection program. Response cross-tabs also provide marketing managers with a detailed understanding of the characteristics that differentiate their best and poorest customers. They are used in developing optimum marketing strategies.

Like a profile analysis (where counts are given but not response rates for each group of names), response cross-tabs include recoding the data so that each reporting cell contains a fixed number of names. For example, if each reporting cell or row contained 5 percent of the sample, then the response cross-tabs would include 20 rows, plus a row for totals. Response cross-tabs go beyond the standard profile analysis in that they illustrate, for each variable, the response, sales, and other performance information as well as the mean for key variables such as RFM, age, and income for each reporting cell (see Table 41-2).

Plotting response and other performance data versus each regression variable helps the marketer to easily understand the output. These plots may also include various transformations of the data, such as the log of the response rate, in order to evaluate the benefits of using these transformations later in the regression modeling.

Prior to developing the response cross-tab analysis, it is very important that the statistical analyst conduct a thorough audit of the test sample to ensure that the sample was properly composed. A review of a sample of customer records along with a comparison of means for all database elements and response rates for known list codes is essential.

Table 41-2. Sample Response Cross-Tab Report

Number of pro- motions since last order	Mail quantity	Orders	Re- sponse rate (%)	Re- sponse index	Pull ($/M)	Pull index	Pay (%)	Pay inde
0	10,000	500	5.0	167	$1250	192	95	11
1	10,000	400	4.0	133	$ 900	138	90	10
2	10,000	300	3.0	100	$ 600	92	85	10
3–5	10,000	200	2.0	67	$ 350	53	80	9
6+	10,000	100	1.0	33	$ 150	23	75	8
Total	50,000	1500	3.0	100	$ 650	100	85	10

The marketing manager and the statistician review the response cross-tab report and the data graphs in order to identify which variables should be candidates for inclusion in a regression model. The variables are grouped as follows: (1) variables whose response rate is as predicted from previous experience, (2) variables with either no response relationship or one that is contrary to previous experience, and (3) new variables with new previously unknown response relationships.

The first group contains those variables whose response relationship shows the expected response relationship in the response cross-tabs (as per the marketing manager's previous knowledge). This might include RFM, related products purchased, survey questions checked, and the basic age, sex, and income demographic variables with which the marketer has extensive experience.

The second group is composed of those variables that show either no relationship to response or are not consistent with known response relationships. These variables are dropped from this particular analysis.

The third group contains the remaining variables which may contribute significantly to the regression model's ability to segment the file's best from poorest responders. However, their response relationships are not well known to the marketing manager. Depending on the marketer's strategy, a conservative approach is to set these variables aside until additional corroborative evidence is available from response cross-tab analysis on other test samples in order to maintain a maximum reliability for the model's application to future promotions.

Variable Interactions

An interaction between two variables is a relationship that affects response. When it occurs needs to be incorporated into the regression model with special coding. For example, a product might generate a high response in both older men and younger women and a low response in both younger men and older women. This example would result in a flat response relationship between older and younger people in general and between males and females in general. Thus the response relationship would exist only in the interaction of age and sex. An interaction may also exist when the individual variables (age and sex) have response relationships.

There are several ways to identify these interactions, including two-dimensional response cross-tabs and chaid analysis. Chaid is an acronym for

Sales	Sales per order	Average recency (months)	Average number of orders	Average monetary value	Average age (years)	Average income
2,500	$25.0	4	5	$50	50	$100,000
9,000	$22.5	9	4	$40	40	$ 75,000
6,000	$20.0	12	3	$30	35	$ 40,000
3,500	$17.5	15	2	$20	30	$ 35,000
1,500	$15.0	20	1	$10	20	$ 25,000
2,500	$21.7	12	3	$30	35	$ 55,000

"chi square automatic interaction detector." It is a process whereby names are successively split into subgroups based on the available data such as age, income, and gender, forming a so-called tree from the variables used to form the subgroups. Chaid analysis is an extension of the RFM name selection technique in that RFM-type cells are defined using other data in addition to RFM. Although chaid is useful for identifying interactions, it does not by itself produce the optimal modeling results of a regression methodology. Once the interactions have been identified, their effects are then included into the regression model by, for example, creating new variables that are the product of the original variables.

Variable Recoding

The response cross-tabs contain plots or graphs which illustrate the relationships between the customer's characteristics such as RFM and the response rate as described in the response cross-tabs section above. These relationships are used to determine how to recode or transform the data in each record.

After selecting the individual database elements that predict response in the response cross-tabs, the next step is to develop the best recoding program for the data prior to regression modeling. For each variable, the response cross-tabs with response plots will indicate either (1) a group of names with equal response rates that should be combined (for example, age groups ranging from 20 to 25 and 26 to 30), (2) linear response rate relationships (for example, low-responding low-income versus high-responding high-income groups) and/or (3) nonlinear or curved response rate relationships. The subsequent recoding is of a more technical nature.

Equal Response Rates. The first method of recoding is to create a new dummy or indicator variable for each value of the variable that has shown a significant response difference in the cross-tabs. For example, if the response rates of customers with one, two, or three or more previous purchases was 2, 3, and 3 percent, respectively, then the two and three-plus groups would be combined and a dummy variable would be created that had a value of 1 if the customer had only one previous purchase and a value of 0 otherwise. A second dummy variable would be created that had a value of 1 if the customer had two or three or more previous purchases and a value of 0 otherwise. The effect of the dummy variables is to model very closely the subgroup response rates. Dummy variables, like RFM cells, are defined so as to strike a balance between defining a large subgroup which reduces the variables' power to discriminate high responders from low responders versus defining a small subgroup which maximizes discriminatory power but increases variability and hence reduces reliability.

A minimum is established for the number of names to be allowed to define the smallest dummy variable subgroup by empirically analyzing the relationship between response and cell size. A plot of the response rates by sample size across all variables will indicate a sample size at which the reliability of the data is maximized. This is the point where the variability of the response rates stabilizes for larger samples but increases for smaller sample sizes.

Linear Response Rates. The second method of recoding is to identify in the response cross-tabs those variables that exhibit two or more strictly linear response relationships—for example, an inverted V-shaped response curve (low- and high-income groups are low responders, middle-income groups are high responders). These variables should be split into two or more splines (lines or curves) or separate variables for input into the regression-modeling algorithm.

Nonlinear Response Rates. The final group of transformations attempts to create a linear response relationship from a nonlinear one. This class of transformations includes using several mathematical operations on either the independent predictor variables or dependent response variables. This may give rise to new forms of analyses such as a log-linear type logit modeling. A typical example of variables that may, upon applying such a log transformation, become linear are the strongly curved relationships between the response rate and the RFM variables.

The main area of caution in using these types of transformations is that the nonlinear response relationship needs to be very consistent from mailing to mailing and therefore several response cross-tab reports need to be compared across several promotions in order to avoid bias.

MULTIVARIATE REGRESSION CLASS ANALYSES

Regression analysis selects the best set of variables and creates a set of coefficients or weights which are multiplied by the value of the respective regression variables. The resultant products are then totaled to produce a single score for each customer which predicts the response rate or whatever performance variable is being modeled. This regression score is the basis for selecting names from the customer database for future mailings.

Simply stated, regression analysis reviews the complete record of each individual customer and combs the data to select the best names for each promotion. The final resulting regression model may be viewed as a scorecard where each important piece of information is assigned a weight or score which reflects its importance in predicting response. Table 41-3 shows a two-variable scorecard. From it we can calculate a customer's score. For example, if customer A has received one promotion since her last order 5 months ago, her score would be computed as follows:

$$\text{Score} = \text{Recency} + \text{number of promotions}$$

$$= 390 + 435$$

$$= 825$$

Stepwise Regression

The regression coefficients or weights are computed by a stepwise method which looks at the correlations between all of the recoded predictor variables

Table 41-3. A Simplified Two-Variable Scorecard with File Distribution

Variable name	Level	Regres-sion score	4/89 Test sample distrib. of names (%)	4/90 Master file distrib. of names (%)	Increase or differ-ence (%)
Recency	0–3 months	500	20	22	+2
	4–6 months	390	15	18	+3
	7–9 months	290	15	16	+1
	10–12 months	180	10	10	0
	13–15 months	125	15	15	0
	16–18 months	95	10	8	−2
	19–24 months	75	5	4	−1
	25+ months	25	10	7	−3
Number of promotions since last order	0	500	15	25	+10
	1	435	15	20	+5
	2	330	30	30	0
	3–5	200	20	15	−5
	6+	25	25	10	−10

and the dependent response variables. The stepwise regression algorithm begins by selecting the variable that has the highest correlation with response. Next, it "subtracts out" of the response rate the predictive value of the first variable and selects the second most important variable having the highest correlation with the adjusted response rate. This continues on until a predetermined level of significance—called the alpha level, which measures the statistical significance of the new weights being nonzero—is no longer attained.

The precise meaning of the term "subtracts out" used in the previous paragraph is defined as follows. In effect, at each step in stepwise regression a predicted response is generated and subtracted from the actual response rate to form an adjusted response rate. In each subsequent step the variable that is chosen next is the one with the highest correlation with this adjusted response variable.

If only a single predictor such as frequency were being used to predict the response rate then the resultant regression model would be akin to fitting a straight line using a ruler on a piece of paper. A better fit using our ruler model would be attained using a logarithmic transformation of the frequency variable, since this latter form has a linear relationship with the response variable.

The final regression model is next reviewed for statistical reliability and to be certain that the weights for the variables follow a logical consistency with past experiences. If the sign of the coefficient is negative but should be positive (as the number of previous products purchased increases so does the response rate and therefore a positive coefficient is expected), the usual reason is that two or more predictors are highly correlated, in which case the statistician will consider dropping one of these codependent variables from the model.

There are several variations of regression methodology: discriminant analysis, latent root regression, ridge regression, logistic regression, probit regression, and arc-sine regression. The main attribute of the latter three is that they all constrain the predicted value to have a value between 0 and 1. This has significance when either fewer than 25 percent of the list or more than 75 percent of the list are being selected; otherwise the difference in segmentation is minimal.

Breakeven Regression

A new regression procedure which is called *breakeven regression* is a method to improve the accuracy of predicting the response rate of the customers that are near the breakeven response rate level. Increased sensitivity in the regression model is most beneficial at this point because the names that respond at a rate significantly above breakeven are going to be mailed whether they score a little higher or lower, and conversely, the names that respond at a rate significantly below breakeven will not be selected for promotions even if their score changes a little.

The breakeven regression method is a two-stage regression methodology. The first stage is to develop the regression model as described in the previous section. The next step is to determine the regression score level at which the customers respond at a rate equal to breakeven. The gains chart, which is described in the next section, is used to determine this score level.

The difference between the regression score level that corresponds to the group of customers that are responding at a breakeven rate, say, 0.04, and the original regression score SCORE is then computed for each individual customer. A second regression model is then developed using a weighted least-squares algorithm where the weights are inversely proportional to the distance from breakeven. An example would be to weight each customer by 1/(SCORE − 0.04).

Thus the customers that are near breakeven will make a much greater contribution to the regression weights than the names that are significantly above or below breakeven. However, the names not near breakeven will still contribute, although to a diminishing degree. This results in a regression model that is most accurate in predicting the customer's response rate near the breakeven level and therefore selects the group of customers with the greatest overall response rate.

The Gains Chart Report

The regression model's performance is measured by the increased response rate, or gains, achieved over the whole list pull when selecting the top scoring names (see Table 41-4). The gains chart is similar to a response cross-tab of the resultant regression model score.

The sample, which now contains a score from the regression model, is sorted by score from high to low and divided into buckets, or groups, with an equal number of names in each bucket. The response data are computed for each bucket. As in the response cross-tabs, a plot of the response rates by high to low regression score is very instructive in showing the amount of segmentation achieved in the results.

The gains chart is used to examine several customer characteristics of each

Table 41-4. Sample Gains Chart Report

Regression score range	Mail quan- tity	Or- ders	Re- sponse rate (%)	Re- sponse index	Pull ($/M)	Pull index	Pay (%)	Pay index
0.050–Max.	10,000	500	5.00	182	$1,250	207	95	112
0.045–0.049	10,000	450	4.00	164	$1,080	179	95	112
0.040–0.044	10,000	400	4.00	145	$ 920	152	90	106
0.035–0.039	10,000	350	3.00	127	$ 770	127	90	106
0.030–0.034	10,000	300	3.00	109	$ 630	104	85	100
0.025–0.029	10,000	250	2.00	91	$ 500	83	85	100
0.020–0.024	10,000	200	2.00	73	$ 380	63	80	94
0.015–0.019	10,000	150	1.00	55	$ 270	45	80	94
0.010–0.014	10,000	100	1.00	36	$ 170	28	75	88
Min.–0.009	10,000	50	0.50	18	$ 80	13	75	88
Total	100,000	2,750	2.75	100	$ 605	100	85	100

group of names as defined by subsequent regression score ranges. As in the response cross-tabs, in addition to mail quantity, number of orders, response rate, response index, total dollars, dollars per thousand mailed, or pull, pull index, average dollars per orders, and other response characteristics, the gains chart report also contains the average RFM values and any other available descriptive statistics such as age, sex, and income. This cell-profiling information is very useful both to corroborate that the best names are being selected in an RFM, age, sex, and income sense and to illustrate to the marketing manager the profile of the customers that are being selected.

The marketing manager uses the gains chart report to determine the cutoff level or the score level above which names will be selected. The production scoring program will produce a report of how many names fall into each score group. A second report will monitor the occurrences of any distributional shifts in the customer database for the key regression variables that might cause an upward or downward shift in the scoring of these names.

HOW TO INTEGRATE REGRESSION MODELS INTO A MARKETING PLAN

After the regression model has been developed the next step is to integrate it into the marketing plan. The goal is to establish a smooth transition between the current name-selection technique, usually an RFM-based selection, and name selection using regression models. By using the regression models to successively add and suppress names in the RFM selects, the marketing manager can lead up to a total replacement of RFM with regression models in a controlled manner.

Initially, the marketing manager will begin with a standard RFM selection of names for a particular promotion and key the names according to their respec-

Sales	Sales per order	Average recency (months)	Average frequency (#orders)	Average monetary value	Average age (years)	Average income
$12,500	$25	4	8.0	$25.0	50	$100,000
$10,800	$24	5	7.0	$23.0	50	$ 90,000
$ 9,200	$23	9	6.0	$22.0	40	$ 75,000
$ 7,700	$22	10	5.0	$21.0	40	$ 50,000
$ 6,300	$21	12	5.0	$20.0	35	$ 40,000
$ 5,000	$20	13	4.0	$19.0	35	$ 40,000
$ 3,800	$19	15	4.0	$18.0	30	$ 35,000
$ 2,700	$18	18	3.0	$17.0	30	$ 35,000
$ 1,700	$17	20	2.0	$16.0	20	$ 25,000
$ 800	$16	24	1.0	$15.0	20	$ 25,000
$60,500	$22	13	4.5	$19.6	35	$ 50,771

tive RFM cell definitions, as was done in the past. Next, the regression model is applied to the names that fail the selection via RFM. The highest-scoring names (using regression) in this group that are above the breakeven score level are added to the mailing; keyed according to regression model score ranges, from best to worst; and sent more promotions. The marketing manager then applies the regression model to the names that were initially selected using RFM (passes). The lowest-scoring names in this group that are below the breakeven score level are deleted from the mailing in question.

This method allows the marketing manager to fully specify the quantity of names to be added and suppressed via the regression model and monitor the results in a manner that allows a comparison with those from previous mailings. This method will allow the marketing manager to make a smooth transition from the RFM analysis, for which results are available from many past mailings, to the ultimate goal, which is to select names by using the regression models exclusively.

Checks and Controls

It is important to establish a set of checks and controls to ensure the quality of the names selected using any name selection methodology, including regression models. The checks-and-controls system for regression models is used both to ensure the reliable application of scoring the model and to monitor any changes or shifts in customer characteristics that could affect the name selection.

The scoring of the regression model is usually accomplished in the main production program that selects the names for mailing. The program is usually written in a computer language such as Cobol. To ensure that the recode definitions and model coefficients are correctly applied, a comparison needs to be made between the Cobol program and the original code that was used to develop the model—for example, Statistical Analysis System (SAS). A sample (for example, 10 percent) of names are selected from the master file, usually from the previous month's selection tapes, and are scored using both the Cobol and SAS programs. First, 200 or so names are compared name by name to identify any inconsistencies and correct them. Next, the total sample is scored and distributed or grouped into 20 buckets based on predetermined regression score levels. Then the counts between the Cobol and SAS program are compared. Any discrepancies between these counts are completely reconciled by a comparison of the values for each variable in the model using the Cobol and SAS programs.

Once the Cobol scoring program has been validated as described above, the next step is to evaluate if the characteristics of the customer file have significantly shifted from the time that the names were selected for the test promotion that was used to develop the model to the time that the names were selected for the current promotion. The most important customer characteristics to compare for this purpose are those that are included in the regression model. The Means Report (Table 41-3), which is generated for this comparison, contains the following information for each variable that has been included in the model or set of models:

1. The variable name—for example, customers whose most recent purchase was in the past 3 months
2. The number and percentage of people that have this particular characteristic at the time that the names were selected for the test promotion that was used to develop the model
3. The number and percentage of people that have this particular characteristic at the time that the names were selected for the promotion that is currently being scored
4. The coefficients or weights that are being applied to customers with each respective characteristic

The marketing manager uses this means report to identify any distributional shifts of the customer's characteristics and the degree to which they may impact the name-selection process. The variables that have larger coefficients and larger distributional shift will have the largest impact on how the names score.

A monthly house census report, which includes counts and percentages for the most important variables on the house file, enables the marketing manager to understand the long-term distributional shifts on the customer file.

WHAT'S NEW ON THE HORIZON

New Methodology

Typically, the best customer models are able to achieve gains equal to 200 percent above breakeven for the best 10 percent of the file and 50 percent above breakeven for the best half of the file. The theoretical maximum gain for selecting the best 10 percent is 900 percent above breakeven versus a theoretical maximum of 100 percent above breakeven for the best half of the list. It is therefore obvious that much more improvement is theoretically possible in selecting names. The newer statistical methodologies which will improve the gains in response rate for the best names include (1) improved use of ordinal variables, (2) a better weighting function for the breakeven regression, and (3) advances in artificial intelligence.

Ordinal Variables. Variables are classified as either nominal, ordinal, or interval. Nominal variables are simply labels of different categories, such as male versus female. Ordinal variables also allow an ordering into higher and lower groups, such as social classes. Interval variables give a measure of the distance between categories such as age or income.

Current regression-modeling algorithms accommodate nominal and interval variables very well, but ordinal variables must be adapted to a nominal or interval form, resulting in a loss of information. A statistical modeling procedure which accommodates all three types of variables (known as alternating least squares) is now available in an SAS procedure called PROC TRANSREG and should result in a significant increase in segmentation potential.

Improved Breakeven Regression. Empirical research as to the optimal parametric form of the weighting function in the breakeven regression will further enhance its performance. The weighting function determines the degree to which each name contributes to the final model. For example, should names near breakeven contribute two, three, or four times as much as the names that are twice as far from breakeven?

Artificial Intelligence. Advances in the area of artificial intelligence do not equate with improvements in statistical modeling methodologies. However, they will simplify the modeling process and allow for industrywide quality standards to be implemented, although this is an ambitious goal.

New Applications

The application of regression models may be extended from selecting the highest-responding names to selecting the most deliverable, highest dollars per order, highest pay, lowest returning, lowest bad-debting names — and ultimately the highest lifetime-value names. Regression models developed for predicting deliverability, pay, returns, and bad debts tend to be very generic, that is, independent of the product being promoted. Therefore, new response model scores may be combined with standard, generic deliverability, pay, return, and bad debt scores to form an expected-profit score for name selection. In general, it is possible to identify the best names using (1) deliverability models, (2) bad-debt models, (3) rejector models, and (4) zip-code models.

1. *Deliverability model:* Identify up to 15 percent of the list that is twice as undeliverable as the whole list.

2. *Bad-debt model:*   identify up to 10 percent of list bad-debting four times the average.

3. *Returns model:*   identify up to 25 percent of list returning three times the average.

4. *Zip code modeling:*   identify up to 10 percent of a rented list that pulls 80 percent above average using zip code and/or census tract and census block demographic models.

Additional applications that are proving successful for regression models include predicting how many bills to mail before sending the account to a collection agency, projecting final reserves from as early as second bill, and projecting final intake from as little as 2 weeks of intake.

SUMMARY

The benefits and rewards of learning how to use regression models are well worth the effort. Regression models are proving again and again to be not only more accurate than RFM but also more manageable by providing the marketing manager with a single ranking of all names from the best to the worst performers along with a high level of detail on their characteristics. The key to establishing a solid regression-modeling program is selecting the right promotion, developing a good model, and rolling out with the appropriate checks and controls.

Regression modeling begins with the appropriate definition of the analysis sample. It is essential to save a "snapshot" of the customer file as it looks at the time that names are selected for the promotion in order to develop the best models. The targeted sample should also meet certain sample-size and response-rate level considerations in order to ensure maximum success.

The subsequent steps toward developing and successfully implementing regression models—whether using mainframe computers, minicomputers, or personal computers—are well defined. A growing number of marketing managers are able to understand even the advanced statistical methods.

Like Sherlock Holmes, we too are detectives seeking the clues in our marketing database as to who will respond to the next promotion. With our advanced twenty-first-century statistical tools and high-speed computers, perhaps we now have the advantage over Mr. Holmes.

42

Credit and Collection

Robert Graham

Retrieval Masters Creditors Bureau, Inc.
New York, N.Y.

James J. Carey

The Carey Group
Chicago, Ill.

WHY CREDIT AND COLLECTION MANAGEMENT IS IMPORTANT

In direct marketing, offering credit to your customers and prospects is critical to your success. When you fulfill an order from a "bill me" offer, c.o.d. shipment, installment payment plan, or continuity program, you have created credit.

The effective use of credit can dramatically boost your response. An effective collections management policy can prevent a "bill me" offer from becoming an inadvertent free offer. (Remember, it's not a sale until it's paid for.) Together, credit and collections can have a major impact on the success of your marketing strategies—and ultimately your profits.

Given a choice, most businesses would operate on a cash basis. Any offer that allows the consumer to use your product or service in advance of payment runs the risk of nonpayment. We all know that any bad debt at all is too much, right? Wrong! Avoidance of bad debt may cause you to miss significant profit opportunities.

CREDIT AS A MARKETING TOOL

As a marketer, you have several leverage points to make your sale. Most important is the audience: If you don't reach the right person, it doesn't matter what you say.

Second in importance is the offer: the combination of product, price, promotional incentive, and credit terms that is irresistible (you hope) to your audience.

However, many direct marketers overlook credit policies as an integral component of the offer. Credit policy making is left to the "bean counters" in finance. That's a mistake. *Credit is too important to the consumer.*

A good credit and collections policy can stimulate qualified response, reduce your promotion costs, and protect you from nonessential write-offs. Mail-order buyers expect the extension of credit. Marketers use credit to help overcome consumer resistance to buying through the mail, in the same way that these marketers use comprehensive product descriptions, strong guarantees, and great customer service.

The extension of credit—and the subsequent risk of bad debt—should be considered a variable cost of doing business. Credit policies should be evaluated based upon how they contribute to reaching your growth and profit objectives. But a too-tight credit policy restricts growth. A too-loose policy will reduce profits. Therefore, your task is to develop *both* a credit policy and a collections policy. Your mission is to "loosen" the front-end credit policy to optimize sales, while "tightening" the back-end collections system to minimize bad debt.

CREDIT AS A FINANCIAL TOOL

Which set of credit and collection policies is right for your business? Your first consideration should be to bring your policies in line with your business and marketing objectives. A business objective of aggressive growth will drive different policies from those driven by a goal of maximizing profit. Figure 42-1 shows the effect of a range of credit policies on the sales and profits of a hypothetical company.

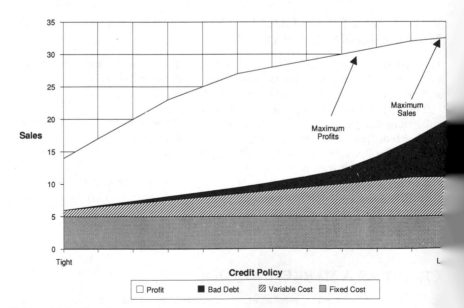

Figure 42-1. The effect of credit policy on sales and profits.

Your company's "personality" will further reduce your credit policy options. A cataloguer with high customer lifetime values must operate differently from a one-shot direct-response television marketer. A charity can't act like a publisher, and *Good Housekeeping* shouldn't sound like *Playboy*.

Other factors to consider include:

- The billing amount
- Your cost of goods
- The timeliness of your product (like a magazine's cover date)
- The variable fulfillment, delivery, and billing charges
- The payment history of the market segment
- Long-term customer values
- The payment history of similar credit programs
- Competitive practices in your market
- The cost of account screening and recovery versus the cost of order fulfillment

Figure 42-2 illustrates how response relates to bad debt risk for the most-used credit policies.

ELEVEN SMART PRACTICES FOR EVERY DIRECT MARKETER

Here are eleven practices you should implement to improve your existing credit and collections policies:

1. **Screen mailing lists for promotions for high-priced products.** This will reduce the chance of fulfilling a high-risk order. Credit-reporting agencies can provide this service and can also correct bad addresses, suppress addresses such as prisons, and eliminate individuals with a history of credit fraud.

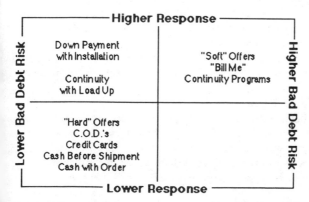

Figure 42-2. How response relates to bad debt risk for the most-used credit policies.

2. **Create an internal bad-debt file.** Screen your responses against this file to avoid shipment to individuals who have already taken advantage of you.

3. **Prequalify orders with a down payment.** Marketers of higher-priced products (such as collectibles) often use partial prepayment to screen out credit fraud. Often this first payment covers the cost of goods shipped. Even though this practice depresses response, it can reduce your bad-debt write-off in excess of lost sales. Test several different down-payment amounts: a higher down payment will lower your bad debt, but it will also reduce your responses.

4. **Be careful with COD.** Cash on delivery shipping to high-risk market segments can cost you money. Cod can increase your response rate and reduce your nonpayment exposure. Postal and freight carriers will not leave your product without a check or cash.

   However, only 20 to 40 percent of shipments will be accepted. The shipper can be charged more than $3 per shipment up front, regardless of whether the product is accepted, so the effective cost to you can be up to $15 per accepted delivery. In addition, bad checks are more common among COD users. These costs can only be justified by high-margin, higher-priced products, or by billing the consumer for the extra shipping and handling charges.

5. **Take precautions to prevent bad checks.** Hold all check orders for funds to clear before shipping the product. Arrange with your bank to automatically redeposit checks returned for nonpayment. Submit larger-balance bad checks to the originating bank for collection. If asked, most banks will hold a check for funds for up to 2 weeks. (You will usually be charged by the bank for these services.) Don't be afraid to notify the consumer of the situation. Ask for payment to cover both the bad check and the bank charges.

6. **Credit cards can reduce your risk—at a price.** Every credit card purchase is subject to a "discount rate" charge from your clearinghouse bank. This can range from 1 to 8 percent of the sale price. Your bank will determine the discount rate from a variety of factors, including your sales volume and business history, and the bank's experience with your product or market.

7. **Reduce your credit card chargebacks.** All companies that accept credit cards experience chargebacks (the reversal of credit by the bank for a variety of reasons, including customers' complaints). However, direct marketers have chargebacks five times greater than in-store retailers, ranging up to 5 percent of their total credit card sales. These procedures can reduce your chargebacks significantly:
   - Authorize *every* transaction.
   - Reauthorize every back order. Then, ship the product before submitting the charge voucher for deposit. This procedure ensures that the customer will receive the product before the bill.
   - Handle refund requests and customer complains promptly and courteously.
   - Run a "clean shop" and respect your customers—they'll respect you.

8. **Recognize the value of long-term customers.** Successful direct marketers are good at promoting long-term relationships with their customers. Your

billing series should nurture that relationship. The billing series can be an opportunity to sell. Magazines often offer new subscribers extended subscriptions in the bill, creating an opportunity for "renewal at birth."

"Pay history" customers—those who have paid you before and are a good risk—present a special opportunity. You can build sales by extending credit to them in three forms:

- Negative option shipments—automatic shipment of product until told to stop
- Load-up shipments—shipping several orders at once and billing for one shipment each month
- Higher credit limits—allowing more products to be shipped before additional payments are received

9. **Review pay history before suspending shipment.** Magazine and continuity programs must decide when to suspend shipments for nonpayment. You must limit your risk, while allowing the consumer the opportunity to evaluate your product.

When testing to establish the appropriate cutoff point, consider:

- The cost to fulfill the next shipment versus the potential value of the relationship
- The time sensitivity of the product (like the cover date of a magazine)
- The time elapsed since the last shipment and/or invoice
- Problems that the customer has voiced about the product

Your cutoff policies should be more tolerant of "pay history" customers than of "no pay history" customers, as Figure 42-3 indicates. "Pay history" customers of the continuity program receive an additional product shipment (a higher credit limit) before they are cut off. Customers without a payment history are kept on a lower credit limit. It is important to note the timing in this example. Product shipment does *not* coincide with your billing cycle. You may contact the customer up to six times with your internal billing series and third-party letters before the account is referred to a contingency collection service.

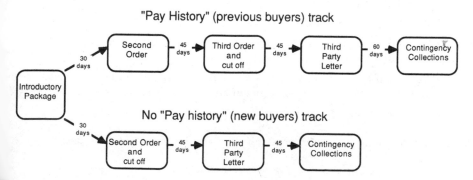

Figure 42-3. Sample credit and collections policy for a continuity program.

10. **Test reinstatement policies.** Historically, 85 percent of "pay history" customers eventually pay their bills. These individuals can be an important source of sales. Upon payment, consider repromoting to them, offering reinstatement in your program, and shipping new product (although with a more conservative credit limit).

11. **Bring in a collection agency early.** A good direct marketing collection agency will offer you a variety of recovery programs that will be a natural extension of your in-house effort. An agency can net you more cash earlier, without offending your customers.

COLLECTIONS POLICY TESTING

By now, you're convinced of the value of testing your credit and collections policies, and understand the opportunities that may be yielded from different approaches. But direct marketers know that an interesting hunch isn't a great idea until it passes the acid test of the marketplace.

Your first step should be to redefine your back-end collections policy. There are four reasons:

- You should fix your profit "leaks" before adding more volume to the program.
- You can use the existing pool of nonpaid responders to test—and any incremental collections drop straight to the bottom line.
- Testing collections policies is cheaper to execute and has less down-side exposure than testing credit policies.
- Finance will insist on it.

Set up your matrix as you would any test. Define matched samples of nonpaid responders and test new policies against your existing control system. Variables include the timing of communications, the tone and manner of your letters, and the actions you will take if payment is not made. But be patient—it will take several efforts and many months to mature.

Your internal billing series should always:

- Thank the customer for the order.
- Resell the features of the product or service.
- Remind the customer of any discounts for paying early or increasing the original order (i.e., "renewal at birth").
- Let the customer know what will happen next. (It should be coordinated with your credit policy—such as shipment cutoff or referral to a collection agency).
- Set a deadline.

In addition, you may want to test the following proven techniques:

- Vary the billing cycle, text, letterhead, and external envelope.
- Promote the shipment of any premium as soon as payment is received.

- Offer a second premium for rapid payment.
- Test an in-package premium in early billing efforts.
- Test different payment options: credit cards, installments, etc.
- Insert a customer service questionnaire with the first bill to new customers.

A final proven winner is the substitution of a third-party collection letter as part of the billing series at key points, such as when product shipments are suspended. This letter is from an external firm—not the marketer—and is often the final attempt to convert the slow-paying account into a good customer.

The letter can be in the form of a customer questionnaire, a verification of product delivery, or a very mild dunning letter. It can create a greater sense of obligation on the part of the consumer, encouraging him or her to pay or respond. Savings from the elimination of additional internal billing cycles can more than offset the incremental cost of using an outside vendor.

You may need different collections policies depending on the media source of the account. For instance, television and sweepstakes offers usually have a higher bad-pay rate than direct mail.

As receivables age, they become less responsive. Direct marketers typically capture 65 to 90 percent of outstanding accounts over 180 days with a series of five or six billing efforts. However, each effort becomes less responsive, as shown in Figure 42-4. "Pay history" files will typically pull twice as many paid responses as files without pay histories. And almost 50 percent of your cash recoveries can occur before the third dunning level. Given the diminishing return on additional mailings, alternative strategies should be considered.

Among your options is testing in-house billing systems against outside collec-

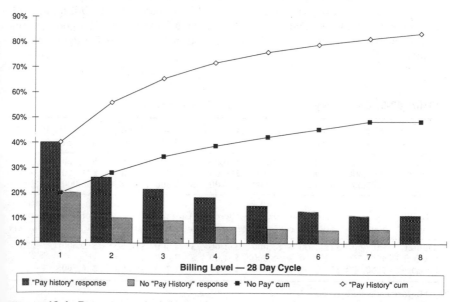

Figure 42-4. Recovery rate by billing cycle.

tions specialists. Give the vendor a representative sample of your open delinquent accounts, and set up an A/B test against your in-house system. When evaluating test results, track both the gross amount collected and the net recoveries after collections costs. You can use this formula to measure the results:

$$\frac{\text{Gross recoveries} - \text{collection expenses}}{\text{Original amount placed with the agency}} = \text{Net recovery rate}$$

Keep in mind the financing cost of your funds—the most profitable system may cost more in direct expense, but yield faster results.

CREDIT POLICY TESTING

When you see progress in tightening up your back-end collections policy—"plugging the leaks"—you're ready to begin front-end testing of credit policies.

As with collections strategies, you may need· different credit strategies for each media and audience segment. Structure credit tests as you would with any other variable, with one exception. You will need more extensive testing of the credit policy. This is because of the sizable down-side risk of a too-loose credit policy, and because the purpose of these tests is to analyze pay-up variations among responders on the back end—a small pool of the total responders.

Work with your finance department to develop specific test objectives and to define scenarios for success for each of the credit policies.

Having established your new collections policies, you can integrate both credit and collections variables into a pro forma such as is shown in Figure 42-5. In this case, the most profitable choice (as shown in boldface) is a looser credit policy compared with the control, combined—as always—with a tight collections policy. This is true even after factoring in a higher bad-pay rate and higher collection costs. In addition, you will have created an incremental 525 good-paying customers, or 11 percent more (5200 net customers versus 4675) than with the control policies.

Figure 42-5. Credit policy pro forma for a hypothetical marketer

Credit policy	Mailing quantity	Response rate	Re-sponders	Average sale	Gross sales	Pay-up rate	Write-off amount	Paid-up customers
Tighter	500,000	0.90%	4,500	$50.00	$225,000	90%	$22,500	4,050
Control	500,000	1.10%	5,500	$50.00	$275,000	85%	$41,250	4,675
Looser	500,000	1.30%	6,500	$50.00	$325,000	80%	$65,000	5,200

Credit policy	Net sales	Gross costs*	Profit before collection	Collection $/account	Cost of collection	Net profit	Profit im-plication	Incre-mental customers
Tighter	$202,500	$121,500	$ 81,000	$ 1.00	$ 4,500	$76,500	($ 9,300)	−625
Control	$233,750	$140,250	$ 93,500	$ 1.40	$ 7,700	$85,800	—	—
Looser	$260,000	$156,000	$104,000	$ 1.80	$ 11,700	$92,300	**$ 6,500**	**525**

*Before collections costs.

THE ROLE OF OUTSIDE VENDORS

The billing and collection of high-volume, small-dollar-balance receivables is typically handled by fulfillment houses and computerized collection agencies. Each type of organization has a specific role in the account recovery process. A full-service fulfillment house offers a broad range of services. It will take orders, ship product, send the initial bill, cashier the account, track performance on open accounts, and handle customer service. In addition, it may use outbound telemarketing to reinstate customers. A collection agency specializes in just one function—the recovery of outstanding receivables.

Typically, the fulfillment house acts as your in-house operation, using your stationery to handle normal operations. It is often referred to as "internal billing." *To the consumer, the fulfillment house is you.* Usually, the role of the fulfillment house in the collections process is to handle the bulk of the receivables with a multiple-stage billing cycle.

A collection agency is brought in when returns from the normal billing cycle are unsatisfactory and a third-party specialist is needed. A collection agency is not "you" in the consumer's eyes, and that is the agency's strength.

A relationship with a fulfillment house is usually at least a 2-year commitment. There are no such structural barriers with collections agencies. In fact, often more than one agency is used at a time. A fulfillment house is rarely selected based exclusively on its ability to manage a billing cycle, but the same criteria used to evaluate a collections agency can be applied to fulfillment house operations.

HOW TO CHOOSE A COLLECTION AGENCY

Full-service collection agencies offer two different types of programs—third-party mailing efforts and contingency collections (see Table 42-1).

Put simply, an outside collection agency should be an extension of your marketing effort. When choosing between collection agencies, think of them as a direct marketing agency whose call to action is always "pay this bill." As such, you should evaluate them as a direct marketing resource:

- How many collection efforts does the agency send? Many agencies give up after two or three efforts, which may be too early. Try to get an agency that pursues more than the "easy" receivables.

- What creative techniques does the agency use to enhance response? A good agency will vary its dunning cycle and the text, size, and color of its mailings, and use teaser copy on the envelope. Experience has shown that a change in letterhead will lift response *every* time. All these things will keep the mailing "fresh" to the consumer.

- Does the agency use other proven direct marketing techniques? A good agency will test the timing and frequency of efforts, use database segmentation, and retain customers by working with them to resolve the obligation.

Table 42.1. Third Party vs. Contingency Collection Plans

	Third-party efforts	Contingency collections
Tone and manner	Mild: attempts to save the relationship	Stronger: demands payment
Letterhead	Generic, nonoffensive	Says "collection agency"
Cost	$450–$550 per thousand	40 to 50 percent of funds collected
Payment method	Agency paid for each letter mailed	Agency paid from funds collected
Investment	Up-front mailing costs	None
Strengths	Greater profit with a high recovery rate Predictable cost	No loss if recovery rates are low No budget expense
Risk to marketer	Moderate	Lowest possible

- Do you have approval of letter copy? Review all letters and question any language that you find inappropriate. The tone of the letters should be consistent with your company's philosophy and personality. But be sure to listen to the agency's recommendation: they will tell you which letters have been their best producers.

- Does the agency have telecollections capacity? Advances in computer technology have revolutionized small-balance phone collections. The use of automated call processing, predictive phone dialing, digital call management, and proven telemarketing practices has given collection agencies and their clients new profit opportunities. But be careful: As Table 42-2 shows, a telecollection is not as controllable as a direct-mail dunning effort, and you can't predict how the consumer will react to your call.

  Note that the Fair Debt Collection Practices Act requires that the first contact from a third party be in writing, disclosing the consumer's rights to dispute the bill (see Figure 42-6).

Table 42-2. Tips on Telecollections

1. The purpose of the call is to inquire to find out why the bill hasn't been paid, *not* to coerce and badger the customer over the phone.
2. Tone and manner of the telecollection script should be similar to your other direct marketing efforts.
3. Be sure to review every script before calls are made.
4. Telecollections is about three times as expensive as direct-mail dunning efforts. Telecollections will usually yield a higher gross recovery rate than mail. However, this is not always enough to offset the higher cost. It works best with large-balance customers ($50+).
5. The higher the dollar balance, the earlier in the cycle telecollections should be started.

The Fair Debt Collection Practices Act affects *every* third-party contact with a consumer. A disclosure of the consumer's rights must be included with all third-party or contingency dunning letters.

The law protects the rights of consumers with collection agencies and other third-party vendors. It is wise to adhere to this law in internal billing procedures also.

The disclosure copy follows:

This is an attempt to collect a debt. Any information obtained will be used for that purpose.

This debt will be assumed to be valid by the collector unless the consumer, within thirty days of this notice, disputes the validity of the debt or any portion thereof.

If the consumer notifies the collector in writing within the thirty-day period that the debt, or any portion thereof, is disputed, the collector will obtain verification of the debt against the consumer and a copy of such verification will be mailed to the consumer by the collector.

Upon written request within the thirty-day period, the collector will provide the consumer with the name and address of the original creditor, if different from the current creditor.

Figure 42-6. Collections and the law

In addition to technical questions, you should also evaluate the agencies as business partners.

- Do they have significant experience (at least 5 years) in large-volume, small-dollar-balance billings typical of direct marketing?
- Is the agency bonded?
- Are their policies consistent with your corporate administrative, accounting, and legal policies?
- Is their data-processing system compatible with yours?
- What do current clients say about the agency?
- Do they have a track record of success?
- Are they easy to work with?
- Is the agency a member of the Direct Marketing Association (most are not), American Collectors Association, or the American Commercial Collectors?

When you have narrowed your search to two finalists, there is no better selection technique than to test them against each other. Give each agency a sample of your uncollected file to see how it performs in the real world. Make sure the samples are large enough to have significance. If you complete your in-house billing series on over 1000 accounts per month, you can A/B the file. If you have fewer accounts, give each agency the entire file in alternate months. Evaluate both the results of the test, and the service you receive. The test will give you results rather than promises and allow you to evaluate each agency as a potential long-term partner.

An external collections cycle proceeds quickly, with only 2 or 4 weeks between efforts. The agencies should provide you with easy-to-read reports on a timely basis, including this information:

- The number of accounts referred to the agency
- The average dollar balance per account
- Payments made to the agency, the fulfillment house, and the client (giving details of full and partial payments and reflecting total funds recovered in dollars and as percentages of the original uncollected amount)
- Dunning status of each group of accounts
- The number and percentage of bad addresses ("nixies")
- Credits and adjustments
- The amount remaining to be resolved

Agency fees, of course, are important. But beware—the least expensive agency may cost more if it doesn't perform. Similarly, the agency generating the highest gross recovery may not generate the greatest amounts of funds. Your goal is to find the agency generating the highest net recovery rate.

To locate an agency specializing in direct marketing collections, contact the Direct Marketing Association, the American Collectors Association, or the American Commercial Collectors Association. Also, many leading agencies regularly advertise in the direct marketing press.

SUMMARY

The proper use of credit can dramatically increase your response rate. With the proper controls, it can add incremental profits even while generating more bad debt.

A good billing series will allow you to keep a higher credit limit with your customers—a higher risk profile—and still maintain a more profitable program.

It is critical to carefully monitor how changes in your credit and collections policies affect the results of your program, making sure that a balance is achieved between your growth and profit objectives.

PART 8

Applications

43

Lead Generation

Eugene D. Sollo

Carlyle Marketing Corporation
Chicago, Ill.

This chapter has been written for readers who may be investigating the field of lead generation for the first time as well as for experienced marketers attempting to gain a new perspective or, at the very least, shake up habitual patterns of activity.

DEFINITION

It is important to define the exact nature of the lead you wish to develop. To paraphrase an old saying, "A flower that smells as sweet is *not* always a rose." Regardless of how you define your lead, it should be defined. In general, a lead is an invisible arrow leading to a person or business with a variable amount of interest in your product or services. This definition applies to every business, but it is probably not specific enough for your needs.

The best source for developing your definition lies within your own sales force. Salespeople are universally interested in leads that result directly in sales. While management would certainly not mind getting a sale for every lead, they are faced with the problem of costs and obtaining market penetration. Only a limited number of leads can be obtained when you are looking for a 1-to-1 closing ratio.

The salespeople at IBM want to know the size of the businesses that they are calling on, the type of equipment they have, and the problems the businesses have with their current equipment. For IBM salespeople, a lead that does not include this kind of information in its definition would not be considered very good. The salespeople at *Encyclopaedia Britannica* are interested in leads where the family has requested information on how to buy the encyclopaedia; they also want to know what other encyclopaedia materials this consumer has or had used and who in the family would use the encyclopaedia.

As you can readily see, there is not one easy definition of a lead that applies to all business and situations. It is vital that you not only define your leads properly, but that you continue to assess that definition in light of the constantly changing business environment.

SOURCE OF LEADS

There are many different sources which can be developed. Some of these sources will be dealt with in-depth in other chapters, but to establish a proper context, I will mention them at this time. Traditional lead sources include newspapers and magazines, direct mail, telemarketing, trade shows, referrals from customers or prospects, past inquiries for the same or different products or services, inactive customers, and current customers. Some of the more esoteric sources include grocery cart and bag inserts, "take one" racks, advertising on public transportation vehicles, or even signs on your personal automobile with a phone number and coupons for passersby. Lead sources can include any method that gives you access to your market.

I am sure that you can probably add any number of sources to this list, but as you can see there are some time-tested traditional methods and some that are excellent lead sources, but very individualistic. The question is, How do you decide which sources to select? Let's see if your definition gives us any clues. The IBM salesperson wants leads from small businesses, between 10 to 50 employees, and from certain Standard Industrial Classification (SIC) codes, such as manufacturing and distribution companies. You can buy media and mailing lists with most of these special characteristics.

Most successful lead programs today combine two or more sources for optimum results. An example of multimedia lead development is direct mail containing mail-back response card, a phone number for people to call you, and a follow-up to the nonresponse portion of your direct mail with telemarketing: direct-mail response card, inbound phone, outbound telemarketing—several different sources to achieve your maximum potential.

If I were trying to develop leads for the first time and could only afford one method, I would use telemarketing. Telemarketing is the most accessible and controllable source available. Almost everyone has a telephone, and since you make only one call at a time, you can react to what you hear and adjust your lead program instantly. Just follow some basic guidelines: Select a group of names to call from your current customers or inactive customers. Write yourself a script continuing your offer, no matter how well you know the subject. Make your calls to determine the effectiveness of your approach. Finally, keep a record of the results.

TYPES OF LEADS

Previously we discussed sources of leads, and as you have read, they are rather diverse and numerous. The types of leads that can be placed in these sources is equally diverse and numerous. To name just a few, there are coupons in publication advertising; television and radio card inserts, either bound or loose;

third-party promotions; direct-mail self-mailers; direct-mail packaged with countless variations; and telemarketing which is both a source and a type of lead. Again, the selection of the type of lead depends upon the source that you are using, whether you are addressing a consumer or business audience, and the cost considerations.

QUALITY COPY

Now that we have decided to use telemarketing to test our defined lead and we have further determined that we will be calling current customers (everyone's best prospect), and that we will be offering a new product that costs $200, we have decided what we are going to say in order to obtain our lead. First, we must consider the definition we have obtained from our sales force as well as management so that we produce a quality lead that everyone will agree is worth working with.

We could decide to use a copy format offering a free drawing for a new Mercedes Benz. I would anticipate that we would get a very large response, but that the primary reason for the response would be the free automobile, not my product. This is just the opposite of the 1-to-1 conversion definition of the sales force. This approach would result in a very low cost per lead, but would require so many leads to get a sale that the ultimate cost would be very expensive. And if the salespeople had to make too many sales calls to get the sale, they might not work the leads at all. You can't get too far away from the 1-to-1 conversion principle.

The other side of the coin is writing copy that says, "If you want to *buy* this product, we will be happy to send a salesperson to take your order and if you are not sure, don't waste my time." You may feel that this is a somewhat ludicrous approach, but keep in mind that this copy approach is *every* sales person's definition of a quality lead. It would be very difficult to get very many of these leads, and, frankly, if they were that qualified you probably don't need a sales force to follow them up and get the order.

You may find it interesting that I have used both of these approaches with success, because the definitions I had written called for these copy and quality approaches. Most of us, however, will find our definition requires a solution that would be somewhere in between these two extremes.

The two basic components to every sales presentation, whether it is a written or verbal presentation, are "need" and "deal." If your prospect hasn't a perceived or latent need for your product or service it will be extremely difficult, if not impossible, to convince that prospect to buy, regardless of how good the "deal" is. For example, I have a brand new diesel locomotive for sale. It normally sells for $10 million, but today's "special" is only $5000. The deal is great, but unless you own a railroad, you don't need a diesel locomotive.

On the other hand, if you have a perceived or latent need for a product or service and the "deal" isn't compatible with your ability to pay, you probably won't buy. Again, I need an automobile. I like the new Mercedes. The price is $90,000 and I can buy it for $64,000. My need for an automobile is definite. The Mercedes is an automobile. The price for the Mercedes is excellent but the "deal" isn't compatible with my ability to pay.

How much should you say. Copy should be as long as it is necessary to tell the whole story and no longer. You should be able to tell the essence of your message by just reading the headline, subheads, and postscript.

COSTS

The definition of your lead should include the maximum amount of money that you are willing to pay for the lead and for the sale or what are termed "front-end" and "back-end" costs. Let's assume in my development of a sample lead program that my product will cost $100 and that I can afford to spend $20 (20 percent) to get the order. What this means is that I can create a $1 lead that closes at 1 to 20 or a $20 lead that closes at 1 to 1 — or something in between such as a $5 lead that closes at 1 to 4 — and still end up with a $20 cost per sale. One of the most frequent errors in the development of lead promotions is the failure to properly consider the implications of the front-end costs as well as the ultimate back-end costs. The front-end cost is controlled by source of media, type of lead, and copy. The back-end cost is controlled by the sales force's conversion of that lead into a sale.

A perfect example is an incident that occurred when I was executive vice president of *Encyclopaedia Britannica*. One of the sales executives decided to develop a lead that was in the 1-to-20 category, completely disregarding the convertibility as demonstrated by the sales force during the initial testing. They were convinced it was a quality lead. The *Encyclopaedia Britannica* sales force was convinced it was a poor quality lead. They refused to work these leads and as a result this program created financial havoc and a tremendous morale problem that lasted many months. Failure to consider the sales force's desires and ability to convert the lead will result in a disaster regardless of how good the front-end development seems to be.

LISTS

When you select a source of leads you are also selecting the source of the names you will be soliciting. The people who read the publications you choose have as a group demographic characteristics, such as age, income, sex, and so forth, which should be a part of your lead definition. Direct mail can be sent to your house lists of customers or prospects, but you can also purchase outside lists that contain the names of people or businesses that are not contained in your house lists. If you are using telemarketing, the lists are the prime consideration. When you obtain leads at a trade show, the people who will be attending are your list, and when you use some of the esoteric methods such as grocery bag inserts, the people buying in the stores you are using become your list.

Regardless of which list you choose the definable characteristics should be a part of your lead definition. Your lists should be as up-to-date as possible and every business, regardless of size, should incorporate their lists into a formal computer database. In order to do this you require a PC and one of the many software packages that are available to organize your database and obtain its maximum potential.

SEGMENTATION

Segmenting your lists simply means identifying the parts of that list that fit your economic definition of a lead. In other words, what you can afford to pay front-end and back-end. In over 40 years of promotional experience, I have never found a list of over 5000 names that was totally viable economically and, frankly, most of the lists under 5000 were not either. Therefore, you must identify as a part of your lead definition the segments of your list. We will find out which segments work when we do our test.

RESULTS

How much will it cost? How many people will respond? How many sales will be consummated? These questions and many others will be going through your mind as you begin to risk dollars and reputation on your lead effort. How then can we anticipate these results before we commit ourselves to expense. The answer is a promotional pro forma, which predetermines the answers to all of your questions based on a variety of expectations. It should be possible to predetermine the viability of a lead program by committing some time rather than money to prepare a proper pro forma. This pro forma outline can be used to determine the viability of your promotion.

The pro forma breakeven formula is as follows:

$$N \times SP = N \times C - A$$

where N = Number of orders needed to break even
     SP = Selling price (average order cost)
      C = Total cost of product (to company) includes all costs, even overhead
      A = Advertising cost

TEST, TEST, TEST

There is a school of thought that says every time you do a lead promotion you should be testing something. If you have developed a successful direct-mail package or a successful lead-producing advertisement that you should be trying to improve the results with every opportunity. I agree with this completely. Define a small amount of your budget for testing and maintain your original lead format as a control for the major portion of your budget. Under no circumstances, regardless of outside pressures, change the control without adequate front-end and back-end testing that supports that conclusion.

Test formats, test lists, test offers, test color versus black and white, test size, test publications, test anything that you consider to be worth evaluating, but only test on a proper split-test basis. A split test is simply alternating your test idea or ideas so that your control goes out to the first person on the list and your new idea goes out to the second person and the control goes to the third person, etc. Every source you select does not provide true split testing. Only use sources for testing with true split-testing capabilities.

The following case histories demonstrate the use of telemarketing to develop definitions and strategies for big-ticket lead programs.

CASE HISTORY 1

Situation

Our client is in the medical construction management business. While it was relatively simple for management to *identify* potential prospects, the problem was to find out when—and if—these prospects would be planning new facilities, expanding, or renovating and how much money would be spent on building plans.

Objectives

1. Qualify the institution called as to building plans, if any
2. Determine dollars budgeted for building, renovating, or expanding
3. Determine when the plans are to be put into effect
4. Find out if the institution has a need for an architect or construction manager

Strategy and Tactics

The institutions called were selected on the basis of a minimum number of beds. The script was designed in a "questionnaire" format and sectionalized by the answers received to key questions; that is, depending upon the responses to certain questions, other questions were (or were not) asked.

Questions were positioned to determine "hot" prospects—those planning on building within 6 months—as well as to qualify others who were planning to build, expand, or remodel in the more distant future.

Results

Approximately 8 percent of the calls resulted in hot prospects, because they were planning to build within 6 months and had not yet contracted for an architect or construction management company. In addition, nearly 60 percent more of those called were qualified by varying degrees, depending upon when building was planned to begin. Only 9 percent of the executives contacted did not choose to answer the questions.

Within just 90 days of the calling, a multimillion-dollar project was contracted for as a result of the program.

Conclusion

Telemarketing is a very effective way to reach decision makers and qualify sizable institutions as to their building plans and needs.

CASE STUDY 2

Situation

A manufacturer and supplier of chemical products found that the inquiries coming in for samples and information were not being qualified or consistently followed up by the company's field sales force or independent representatives.

In addition, a number of companies who bought small quantities of the competition's products were never contacted by a company representative.

Furthermore, companies who were contacted and accepted product samples to test were frequently not followed up to be sure the testing had, in fact, taken place; nor were further selling procedures carried out.

Objectives

1. To determine the impact of direct marketing methods—list selection, segmentation, and telemarketing—on market penetration and product sales
2. To develop total lead programs, identifying best prospects, decision makers, product need, and receptiveness to a visit by a sales representative

Strategy and Tactics

Five industries which were considered best prospects for the company's products were selected, as well as companies that had requested samples within the past 12 months. The first challenge was to reach the proper decision maker; thereafter, the decision maker would be asked a series of qualifying questions as to interest, need, and usage of the products. Finally, the contact would be asked for permission to have a company representative call, thereby paving the way for a personal contact.

The second tier of the calling portion of the program involved a follow-up call to companies that accepted a product sample to test. The purpose of this call was to encourage and remind people to perform the test and provide test status feedback to the reps for further sales development.

Results

Nearly 33 percent of *all* people called gave approval for a representative to call on them to present product information. A little over 18 percent already used the product(s), and 38 percent had no need for them. Only 4 percent refused to answer the qualifying questions.

Employee size made a significant difference in companies already using the products versus those not using them.

Conclusion

Upper-level decision makers can be reached and used to prequalify. Prequalifying prospects in the chemical business can be quickly and successfully accomplished by phone. Appointment setting—and conversion—is appreciably higher when companies are properly qualified.

44
Continuity Marketing

Eric Nussbaum
Nash/Wakeman/deForrest
New York, N.Y.

Since the introduction of Book-of-the-Month Club in 1926, club and continuity marketing have come to embrace not only books but records, tapes, compact discs, videotapes, recipe cards, cosmetics, foods, fruits, coffees, and more.

Clubs originated as an alternative means of distribution that made certain products available, generally at a discounted price, to consumers who resided outside the range of traditional retail outlets. While advances in transportation, increased concentration of the population in urban centers, and the proliferation of both specialty stores and discount chains have all caused a certain degree of erosion in various clubs' bases, they remain an important source of products for many consumers.

Today, clubs represent a means of distribution that supplements traditional retail. Clubs enable publishers, record companies, and others to reach segments of the total market that are not well served by such retail outlets. Selection of a particular title by a book club also serves a function for the publisher's publicity and sales efforts as it is interpreted as an endorsement of that title.

The people joining clubs now are seeking, in addition to an attractive invitational offer, the guidance a club provides by sifting through all the products available in a particular category and singling out the best. Those joining continuities are looking for products they can identify as unique or authentic.

As a result of business and societal changes, many of the older clubs have had to change the very way they conduct business. They have had to adapt to, and serve, a customer base potentially served by many diverse sources. In order to counter erosion from these other sources, club offers have, of necessity, become more aggressive — that is, more generous — while commitments have become less and less stringent.

This chapter will focus on membership acquisition efforts for clubs and continuities. After defining and comparing the different club structures, it will cover new-member offers, testing strategies, media selection, analysis, back-end marketing, and the future of clubs as a marketing mechanism.

CLUBS VERSUS CONTINUITIES

Clubs typically offer a particular category of merchandise, for instance, records or books. They have traditionally been defined by the presence of a generous introductory offer, such as several units of the club's product for a small charge plus shipping and handling, and an obligation or commitment on the member's part to buy a certain number of units within a specific period of time.

Clubs generally operate with one of two structures: negative option or positive option.

Under the *negative option structure*, members receive on a regular, cyclical basis a catalog offering the club's latest selection, along with a variety of alternate choices. The selection (sometimes called the main selection) will be shipped automatically unless the member indicates on the reply form that he or she does not want it and returns that form to the company by a specified date.

If the reply form is not returned, the club assumes that the member wishes to receive that cycle's selection and it is shipped. Other options include ordering alternative selections or nothing at all for that cycle.

Under the *positive option structure*, members receive only the products that they have specifically ordered. There are no automatic shipments. This is offered as an option to members who live overseas or in areas to which shipment within the required 30 days may be prohibitively expensive. Some clubs offer positive option memberships to "expires" (that is, members who have resigned from the club) as an alternative to regular negative option membership. Generally, this is offered only to those members who had exhibited high buying rates during their memberships. While response to such an offer is usually quite strong, back-end is bound to suffer since it is so much easier, under a positive option membership, to turn down a selection.

It is important to recognize the "inertia factor" in club marketing. A certain number of members simply get used to receiving, and paying for, the selection. Others are too lazy to return a book they didn't really want. These members, along with the core of truly interested active members, often make up the bulk of sales in a club.

Continuities differ from clubs in that they offer a series of related products: books by a particular author (for example, Louis L'Amour or Agatha Christie) or on a particular subject (Time-Life Books' *Mysteries of the Unknown*), recordings of certain types of music, or collectibles such as the Franklin Mint's figurines.

More so than negative option clubs, membership in a continuity series is representative of an individual's lifestyle. People who subscribe tend to be immersed in the subject, whether it's the American West, paranormal phenomena, or porcelain figurine collecting.

UP-FRONT AND BACK-END

Club and continuity marketing can basically be put into two related categories: *up-front,* which is the initial offer that attracts a prospective member, and *back-end,* which is the effort made to sell to your current club members.

In a continuity program, the initial offer is usually the program's most popular product, offered at a reduced price, sometimes accompanied by an additional premium. The variables in a continuity offer are:

- The initial offering: What is the actual unit offered?
- Pricing: How much does the first unit cost? How much will subsequent units cost?
- Frequency of shipment: How often will the member receive shipments? Every 3 weeks? Every 6 weeks?

Each of these variables can be altered depending on the medium or type of list being used to generate members.

In a club there are three basic offer components:

- The offer itself: for example, four books for $2 plus shipping and handling.
- The premium: an additional incentive to join. Often it is merchandise sent with the initial shipment. In general, customers are allowed to keep the premium even if they choose not to stay in the club.
- The commitment or obligation: an agreement by the member to make a certain number of purchases within a specified time frame, for example, purchase four books in 2 years.

TYPES OF OFFER

In a *one-step offer* the customer joins straight from the ad or direct-mail piece. Application for membership is essentially a contractual agreement in which the member agrees to specific terms, such as taking four books for $2 plus shipping and handling, returning the reply form each cycle, and buying a certain number of books within a specified time period. The club's obligation is to send appropriate materials on a timely basis, respond to the customer's wishes, and accept (at no charge to the customer) returned, unopened shipments received by, but not ordered by, the customer.

In a *two-step offer* a customer is invited to make a purchase. After making a purchase, usually with the initial shipment, the customer will be offered actual membership. The offering price here may actually yield a profit, but it should at least be designed as self-liquidating.

A two-step offer is often appropriate for media which do not lend themselves well to the explanation of the "compliance copy," that is, the copy which explains the obligations of the club and the customer. As an example, on television you may have 2 minutes or less to get your message across and make people pick up the phone to order. This is a very short time if you are trying to fit in all the information the FTC requires. By positioning your offer as a one-shot you can close the sale while soliciting actual membership via a bounceback in the shipment or with a separate mailing or through the telemarketing operators handling the in-bound calls.

UP-FRONT RESPONSE VERSUS BACK-END PERFORMANCE

Success in clubs and continuities comes from finding the equilibrium point between up-front response and back-end performance. Unfortunately, it seems to be a pretty good rule of thumb that as up-front response goes up for a list or a publication, back-end performance declines.

Mailing to lists of other club members will often generate terrific response. But for a number of possible reasons, they typically are very poor performers. This could be because there is a limit to how many clubs people can handle before they lose track of which reply form they've sent back and which they haven't. It could also be that these people know the ins and outs of club membership and are "premium shopping," that is, taking the introductory offer and then merely fulfilling the minimum requirements of membership (or not even doing that). Either way, these are lists you should be wary of.

NEW-MEMBER ACQUISITION

Direct Mail

Generally, direct mail is the best source of members in terms of both volume and quality. It is also the medium that allows for the greatest degree of testing, including list testing, creative approaches, offers, commitments, premiums, and so on.

There are a number of different kinds of lists. These include:

Subscribers.   These can be readers of magazines that work for your offers in space advertising as well as magazines that deliver an audience with a similar demographic and psychographic profile as your current member file. In general, direct-mail–sold magazine subscribers outperform all others, especially TV-sold subscribers, who are usually the weakest performers of all. Whenever possible, you should "select out" TV- and agent-sold subscribers from your mailing lists.

Hot lines.   These are people who have displayed some sort of recent activity, such as new subscribers, new credit card holders, people who have ordered by mail within the last 6 months, and so on. These active customers are often much more likely to respond to your offer. List owners usually charge a premium for hot-line names. The response lift they deliver must be sufficient to cover this increase to your mailing cost.

Renewals.   Magazine subscribers, for example, who have chosen to renew their subscriptions, represent very strong prospects. Their decision to renew

represents a financial commitment and ability and offers proof of their satisfaction with the product or service.

Changes of address.   New movers are often prime candidates since they are
ready to fill up their new homes with new possessions. With a new home often
comes new furniture, such as bookcases which need to be filled, or a new stereo, and so on.

Expires.   People who have stopped subscribing to a publication may be looking for something new. Since these names are generally cheaper than regular
subscribers, a lower response rate can still make them profitable.

House lists.   If your company owns other mailing lists and you can test them
for free, or for just the price of running charges, by all means do so. By eliminating the list cost from your total mailing cost, you lower your required response rate.

Compiled lists.   These are lists of people with similar demographic and
psychographic profiles, gathered from a variety of sources, including phone
books, census data, and automobile registration lists. Additional name sources
for compiled lists include survey respondents and lists of people who have
redeemed coupons or sent back requests for rebates. While these are not usually the strongest respondents, in many instances they have answered questions about product usage or their lifestyles. Thus, they can be segmented
into a number of different lists.

Space Advertising

Not as strong as direct mail and more subject to fluctuation, space advertising
can be broken into three broad categories: special-interest publications, general-
interest publications, and mass-audience publications.

Special-interest publications are most appropriate for specialty clubs or for
continuities. By advertising in such publications, you are targeting an audience
already predisposed toward your product. Some examples of special-interest
magazines would be *The Magazine of Fantasy and Science Fiction*, *Ellery
Queen's Mystery Magazine,* and *Soldier of Fortune,* which cater to the science
fiction, mystery, and military categories, respectively.

General-interest publications cater to a broader audience of readers. They can
range from women's magazines such as *Ladies Home Journal* or *Cosmopolitan* to
extremely upscale publications such as *Architectural Digest* or *Connoisseur.*

Mass-audience publications such as *Parade* or *TV Guide* offer very high circulations and are excellent if your goal is to bring in high numbers of members.
However, because the audience covered is so broad, the back-end performance
of members brought in from these publications is often very weak. It usually
takes clubs a good deal of testing to find the offer-and-commitment configuration that works profitably in this category. In general, you have to be ready to
sacrifice up-front response in favor of stronger back-end performance from
these members. These are some of the methods used: requiring payment with
order instead of billing later; and asking screening questions on the order form
(answers received can be tabulated and used to develop member acquisition
models).

Screening questions are another method of qualifying respondents. Even questions such as, Do you have a phone? or Do you own a VCR? can help identify both likely customers and likely bad prospects.

People who go to the trouble to answer the questions tend to be better members than those who don't. The appearance of questions on the order form can often be enough to scare away likely bad members. A more sophisticated use of such questions would be to key the responses and score new members based on their answers and their performance (that is, their sales activity). Later, once you have compiled some history for these members, you can use the results as a means for determining whether to accept respondents who provide specific combinations of answers.

Publication Selection. Seek out publications with audiences that match the profile of your membership. In general, look for publications with paid circulations, rather than controlled, nonpaid circulation. As a rule, publications with a high percentage of direct-mail–derived subscribers as well as a high newsstand price will perform best, while publications with a high percentage of television- or agent-sold subscribers often do not perform very well.

Timing. Generally, as in direct mail, first and third quarters are the best times to run space advertising. Results tend to slacken in the spring and as you enter the Thanksgiving and Christmas period.

Position. Direct-response advertising in general benefits dramatically if the ad runs in the first third of the publication. Of course, if specific editorial adjacency is required, such as near book or record reviews or near a feature story, then the ad will benefit from such positioning.

Right-hand page placement is usually preferred. Generally, the coupon should run in the lower outside corner.

Business reply cards (BRCs) bound into magazines usually double the media cost but generate tremendous lifts in response. However, this usually is accompanied by an equally tremendous depression in back-end performance. When the BRC is postage-paid, response will be highest and back-end will be lowest. Non-postage-paid cards can be used as a "qualifier" to screen out potential bad customers. The shortfall in response is usually compensated for many times over by better overall performance.

Supplied Inserts. These are single or multipage inserts bound into magazines. They are often printed on heavy stock in order to accommodate a tear-off BRC.

In order to run cash with order offers, many clubs have recently used an insert printed on lighter stock that can perforated, folded, and sealed to form an envelope in which up-front payment can be sent.

Free-Standing Inserts. Free-standing inserts (FSIs) run loose, usually in newspapers (most often in Saturday or Sunday editions). This larger format allows you to display more product and provide more information. FSIs are an excellent means for testing since you can provide specific quantities (with unique keys) to newspapers. They provide a quick read of results and are often used in advance of full-space roll-out or to support efforts in other media, such as television.

Member-Get-Member Leads. Member-get-member (MGM) leads are an extremely cheap means of acquiring new members. In this approach you use your current members to refer friends to the club by offering them an incentive. In general, your members will respond better if the incentive is the club's actual product rather than some sort of merchandise. Ideally, if you could induce referrals with other merchandise, you would avoid eating into your sales.

It is important to pay careful attention to response and profitability by different member segments in order to determine optimal cutoff points. MGMs should only be sent to your better members—those who have at least paid for their premium shipment and perhaps one additional purchase.

Expires. Mail to your best *expires,* or former members, again keeping careful track of results of expire segments in order to determine appropriate return-on-promotion (ROP) cutoffs.

Cross-clubs. *Members of other clubs* run by your company can be solicited for membership through insertions in actual product shipments or in the envelope carrying the cycle news.

TELEVISION

Television is perhaps the most difficult medium to make work for clubs and continuities. In addition to generating actual memberships, television can be used in support of other promotions such as print advertising and direct mail. Advertisers can use short-format TV to announce upcoming mailings and ad appearances.

Television is limited in that usually you have a maximum of 2 minutes to get your message across. Given the amount of required legal copy that appears in club offers, advertisers have often been forced to work around this time constraint.

Because of this, using a one-step offer on TV may prove challenging, since the information concerning commitments must be provided to the new member. This alone could eat up half your television time. There are several ways around this problem. The first is to make a no-commitment offer. By eliminating the obligation, you are certain to boost response; but, equally certain, the back-end performance from these members will be extremely weak.

A second approach is to have the commitment copy read to the customer by the telemarketing operator. The risks here are that these operators are usually answering the phones for several different offers currently on the air, and this level of dialogue with the customer will take up a lot of time and cost you a lot of money.

A third approach is the two-step offer. Bring the customer in with what appears to be a one-shot, e.g., one book for $4.99. Then promote to this person via an in-pack in his shipment or through a separate direct-mail piece.

Cable Television

Unlike regular network television, cable television provides a highly qualified audience since these viewers have paid for the service they are watching. In particular, cable networks such as Arts & Entertainment, CNN, and Discovery provide upscale audiences not previously available through broadcast.

While direct-response advertisers helped build the cable industry, general advertisers have moved into the medium in large numbers, taking advantage of lower rates than network and a more upscale audience. As a result, direct-response advertisers are faced with lower clearance rates as time inventories shrink.

"Infomercials." In the early days of television, 15-minute commercials were the norm as stations sought whatever they could get their hands on in the way of programming to fill air time. As more and more advertisers started to understand the value of the medium and began competing for time, networks started breaking commercial time into smaller and smaller segments.

With 2-minute spots harder and harder to secure, many advertisers have begun producing longer-format commercials. These "infomercials," running from 15 to 30 minutes in length, often resemble actual programming and can be produced to wrap around shorter format spots.

The long format is reemerging as a solution to the time constraint problem usually associated with promoting clubs on television. However, it should be noted that infomercials can be costly to produce, and, at this writing, they are coming under close scrutiny by legislators.

Telemarketing. Inbound telemarketing is used in conjunction with television efforts. Outbound, however, has been applied with some success in promoting clubs, especially to expires. It has also been used to activate slow-buying members or members who are about to be automatically canceled.

Clubs have been understandably reluctant to introduce 800 number "no buying" for fear of making it too easy for customers to turn down selections.

Alternative Media

Co-ops. These are mailings featuring a variety of offers—usually noncompetitive—geared to specific demographic and psychographic groups of consumers. This medium tends to skew too downscale for most clubs and continuities, although recently an effort has been made to reach upper-income segments via specially designed co-ops featuring higher-ticket products.

Third-Party Inserts. There are two approaches used here:

- **Package inserts.** Promotion pieces enclosed in product shipments from other mail-order companies (for example, a book club offer in a Lillian Vernon shipment).

- **Statement inserts.** Promotion pieces enclosed in billing envelopes from other companies. These could be invoices from other clubs, mail-order merchandise companies, magazines, and so on.

Third-party inserts take advantage of affinity purchases by consumers in a variety of categories and often represent the only way to approach consumers of a particular demographic or psychographic profile who may not be accessible through other direct marketing media.

Take-Ones. Rarely effective for clubs and continuities, takes-ones—for instance, promotion pieces displayed in supermarkets—tend to attract lower-quality members. This sort of medium would require careful attention to the offer-commitment configuration since the audience is so untargeted. A cash-with-order offer and a strict purchase commitment would be called for here.

Payment Plans

Bill Later. Customers pay upon receipt—and acceptance—of their initial shipment. This is the most common plan and usually generates the highest response rate.

Credit Card. In general, for lower-ticket offers, credit card payment options will depress response, although when offered as an alternative to bill later, will generally result in better back-end performance.

Cash with Order. This is virtually guaranteed to depress response but it can play an important role in certain instances. Use it as a means for screening and "qualifying" new members derived from traditionally weak media (such as mass publications or TV). By requiring cash with order you weed out potential premium shoppers and poor performing members.

TESTING

For a club to stay profitable and competitive, and to meet the changing needs and wants of its market, it is imperative that it commit itself to regular, planned testing, not only of new-member acquisition efforts but also of sales approaches used to existing members.

Dry testing is a means for testing new club concepts. In these tests, a company can determine whether the interest level is sufficient to merit actually producing the products. It is important to note that FTC regulations require that promotional materials state that the product has not yet been manufactured.

In new-member efforts, there are three primary variables that are usually tested:

- More versus less generous giveaways
- Merchandise premium versus no premium

- Different product and price combinations: four books for $1 versus one book free when you take three for $1, or four books for $2 versus four books for $1 each, etc.

You can test stricter or looser commitments by varying either the length of time the member has to meet the obligation to the club or the number of units he or she must purchase.

Headlines, body copy, format, features, and graphics are all important. If you tend to use generic ads regardless of media, try segmenting your media and creating ads that cater to the specific types of audiences provided by the different types of publications you use.

Two-, three-, and four-way splitting is available in most larger circulation publications. Mass publications such as *Parade* and *TV Guide* offer regional splits which enable you to test new products or offers in a much more covert and economical manner before taking them to a national roll-out.

Take your largest and strongest lists and isolate control and test quantities in direct proportion to the percentage of the total mailing quantity that each of these lists represents.

Here are some other factors to be aware of when you test:

Seasonality and timing of tests.   If you have been mailing successfully in January and July, you might want to consider dates in between these two periods, say, April or September. Different seasons often exhibit different response patterns. By testing you can determine the threshold of how many times in a year you can mail profitably. Similarly, timing tests help you determine optimal mailing dates. These tests are especially helpful in figuring out when to mail around critical dates such as Christmas, New Year's, Fourth of July, and so on.

Paper stock.   Determine whether a more expensive paper provides a response lift or, conversely, a lower-priced paper does not depress response. In the first instance, your response lift must cover the increase in your mailing cost. In the second instance, you are attempting to lower your in-the-mail cost to see whether it is accompanied by a lower, but still profitable, response rate.

Size and format.   Will your response be hurt if you convert your package from a "jumbo" format to a "mini"? Can you generate a sufficient lift by moving from a 6 × 9 format to a 9 × 12?

Postage.   Is mailing first class versus third class a viable option for your product? If your club operates in a crowded field and you feel speedy delivery is important to your success, this might be a direction to take.

Color.   Even color changes can sometimes help breathe new life into a fatiguing control package by making it appear new. This approach can work if you promote to a small universe, such as a special-interest book club.

Selection.   Test specific categories of product to specific segments of your audience (split selections), or test two selections at a special combination price (dual selection).

Pricing. Can you (profitably) lift selection acceptance by offering it at a lower price?

Whatever you test, the most important thing to remember is to test only one variable at a time in each test cell. Otherwise, you will end up with unreadable results and be unable to make a judgment as to which factor caused your test to turn out the way it did.

BACK-END MARKETING

Back-end, or postacquisition, marketing is taking on a greater and greater importance in the club and continuity environment today. Many marketers are adopting an umbrella strategy which links the messages presented in up-front efforts and those presented in back-end materials. By tying together these messages, you help insure the perception that membership in your club meets the expectations generated through your advertising.

Bonus or dividend plans are incentive programs in which members accumulate points through their purchases which can be redeemed either for specially selected products which are offered on occasion or for the regular product.

Offering membership in other clubs to your better members (as opposed to "premium shoppers") can be a very cheap way of acquiring qualified new members. There is a limit to how deep you can "fish" for members from your own family of clubs before you start to risk cannibalization and an overall drop in profitability.

ANALYSIS

Basically, clubs analyze their efforts on two fronts: up-front, that is their membership acquisition efforts; and back-end, the postacquisition sales generated by members.

Most companies have unique, often elaborate formulas for evaluating members by source key, that is, the individual ad or mailing piece to which they initially responded. Ultimately, financial success comes from acquiring members whose back-end purchases generate income in excess of the costs associated with bringing them in.

In general, clubs and continuities use a return-on-promotion approach, which takes average sales per member for a specific time period (this could be months, years, or cycles of membership), subtracts out the cost of acquisition (media plus the "gift" cost of the product offered in the initial ad or mail piece less what the member paid), and then divides the difference by the acquisition cost. The sales figure should have bad debt, returns, cyclical servicing costs, overhead, and so on, worked into it.

Every club or continuity has what it considers an acceptable ROP level. This varies not only by medium but by category within medium. It can also change depending on a company's policies at any given time. For instance, a club may tolerate a lower ROP from mass publications when there is a corporate call for more "bodies" in the club.

THE FUTURE

While clubs have had their ups and downs over the past 60 years, their future appears dependent upon managers' learning to promote "smarter" by mailing or advertising more efficiently. Below are three approaches.

Premail modeling. Profiling prospect lists and comparing them to your current members (as well as to your past rejects and cancels) can enable you to skim profitable segments from mailing lists and eliminate those names that are likely to generate unacceptably low ROPs.

Regressions. Use regression analysis to isolate profitable segments from lists that are, overall, unprofitable. This "creaming" approach helps you make use of these marginal lists that traditional ROP analysis might dictate be left out of your mailing.

Enhanced communication with members. On the back-end, clubs should encourage member involvement, perhaps by publishing a letters column in the cyclical news or by conducting contests.

Challenges to Clubs

In addition to some of the challenges mentioned at the beginning of this chapter, clubs today face two additional obstacles to success.

Club managers should be on the lookout for *members who fail to purchase*. As a rule, if a member has not been active during the first three or four cycles of the membership, he or she probably will never buy from the club.

Clubs may want to consider special programs designed to get these dormant members buying. There is a good chance that once you get a customer into a buying mode, he or she will continue to be an active member. Inactive members should be canceled.

Again, the media that bring in such members should be reevaluated and precautions, such as cash-with-order offers, or credit-screener questions on the response device, considered.

Chronic returns can be indicative of a number of problems. Returns of positive option purchases (normally a low percentage of a club's returns) could indicate that members are not satisfied with the content of the club's product. Returns of negative option purchases could mean that shipments and member reply forms are crossing in the mail. This is certain to alienate members and is often heard as a complaint about the club mechanism.

Members who return with great frequency should be monitored carefully and, assuming they have fulfilled their commitments to the club, should be canceled. Club managers should look for patterns in lists or publications that generate members who return in large numbers and should adjust media schedules accordingly.

New Media Opportunities

On-line services such as Prodigy and Compuserve represent a way of reaching highly qualified prospects via personal computers in their homes or offices.

These services allow potential customers to receive a great deal of information in one sitting and to place an order immediately through the computer.

While television is hardly a new medium, with the emergence of highly specialized cable stations that meet the needs of unique audience segments (fans of westerns, science fiction, or classical music), clubs and continuities can target their messages to a more receptive television audience and avoid the risk of bringing in poor-quality members usually associated with direct-response television.

Telemarketing, especially via 900 numbers, which serve as a qualifier since the caller pays, could represent a new opportunity. The ability to let prospects hear targeted messages by using their telephone keypads could help steer new members into clubs. This is a medium that could have tremendous potential if tied into other media efforts such as space advertising, television, and perhaps even radio, a medium normally dismissed for direct response.

As we enter the 1990s, clubs and continuities must position themselves at the forefront of a new era of relationship marketing. Membership offers that induce premium shopping and one-shot trial will no longer be acceptable. The clubs that survive and thrive will be those that establish long-term relationships with their members.

Club success will be judged not only by measures of profitability but also by member satisfaction which will be gauged by member life, returns, and so forth.

By always improving club member communication, by "rewarding" better members, by eliminating lower-quality members, and by continuously striving to enhance and build upon the product offered to members, clubs will be better poised to meet the challenges that today's—and tomorrow's—market presents.

45

Subscription Marketing

Eliot DeY. Schein

Schein/Blattstein Advertising, Inc.
New York, N.Y.

The generation and retention of subscribers to both paid and unpaid circulation magazines has become a science in itself. Without question, some of the basic rules of all direct marketing have been developed, defined, and diversified through the testing and resulting information produced by the discipline of subscription marketing.

In recent years the circulation departments of paid subscription publications have moved from the ramshackle basement quarters which housed noisy Addressograph machines, cinder block partitions, and tedious work to where they now reside on the upper executive levels of virtually every publishing company. The prime mover of the cause of this remarkable upward mobilization was the success of direct marketing, which made circulation income surpass advertising income for those publications for the first time. In fact, sticking to paid subscription publications, it is expected that sometime well before the turn of the century circulation revenues will more than double that of advertising sales revenues.

The simple formula is that subscriptions plus single-copy sales equal circulation; and even in this competition the subscription area has been gently pulling ahead on all fronts. Just what does it take to develop a subscriber? What is a good subscriber compared to a bad one? Let's look at some of the methodologies used "from scratch" by publishers in the know. But before we do this let us bear in mind one of the soundest principles of direct marketing: Regardless of which rules you follow there will always be an exception, and some publisher or marketer is going to come up with a program you think can't possibly succeed which outperforms everyone's wildest expectations.

THERE WILL ALWAYS BE AN EXCEPTION

Don't let these deviations from the norm get you down. At best they occur rarely. In fact, without taking credit away from the braintrust at Doyle, Dane, Bernbach in the 1960s, just about any advertising agency in the world could have sold hundreds of thousands of Volkswagens—it was the right car at the right time at the right price. The advertising techniques employed to sell these cars weren't nearly as important as the combination of "rights"! Sometimes a publication is too good, and any amount of testing of price and offer will be lost in the shuffle of stemming the tide of an unbelievable demand.

And, as in every other business activity, when things are going well there's no need to try and discover how to make them better. "If it ain't broke, don't fix it," tends to be the prevailing mentality. So most of what we hear as dramatic success comes from either a launch or new issue of a publication or a remarkable change in strategy and tactic following a weakness or failure.

RENEWABILITY IS CRUCIAL

The best subscriber for any publication is one who will pay the highest possible price for a subscription to that publication and continue to pay it over and over and over again. The renewability of a subscription is crucial and the renewability potential of a subscriber begins with the very first contact he or she has with the publication and its marketing.

The main traditional medium for generating new subscribers to publications is direct mail. Assume a market potential for subscriptions of one-tenth of the market available. This is a guideline which basically reflects the fact that only 1 in 10 of the people interested in a particular special interest are interested enough to want to pay for a publication to read about that interest. There is a large market from which to draw an audience—a market which permits a significant amount of testing of mailing lists, prices, and creative approaches. Naturally, the larger the potential market, the greater the opportunity for large-scale testing. But basically most publishers of large-scale publications (100,000 circulation or more) rely on a test sample of 5000 names. The projectability after testing of the results of a 5000 name test comes dangerously close to 100 percent. The fewer the names mailed to, the less reliable the results and the more shaky or roughhewn is the projection accuracy. In a normal (if any can be called normal) launch of a new publication a minimum of 100,000 direct-mail pieces are put in the mail on the very same day to no fewer than 20 groups of people. The 20 groups can be broken down in a variety of ways. Let's say two prices, two different creative approaches, and five different mailing lists. This would result in a perfect crosshatch test in that 5000 of each variable would be tested. The results would be counted based on the key numbers on the order form or response document or some other code on an 800 number response or fax response. And a "winner" in each category will be chosen.

There will be a winning price. Now this price can either be the higher price or the price that brings the greatest potential income. For example, if you test $25 a year against $10 a year and $25 pulls half as well in percentage points, the $25 price will project out to bring in more income for the publication for the same effort. In this case the $10 price would have to do two and a half times as well as the $25 price even to come close. Understand this, if you realize an income of $25 by sending out one copy per month of a publication or two and a half copies per month per year of a publication it is certainly more efficient only to send one. On the other hand, if the number of subscribers is essential for advertising sales purposes, the $10 price in this scenario could easily be the winner. So the result and its interpretation are usually based on the needs of the publication's business plan and personality.

THE "WINNER" WILL BE DECLARED

The creative approach that becomes the "winner" is the one that will be declared the control package and one which will continue to be used exactly as it originally went out until such time as a package testing against it beats it on a confirmed and continuous basis.

With mailing lists the situation is significantly different. There is no winner or loser. There are only values. The best mailing list may not have a great amount of roll-out potential. In fact, very often smaller, sharply focused lists will pull a high percentage response but leave significant desirability in terms of their roll-out potential. This book would not be complete without the following example of how this can be all too painful a realization after the fact. More than 10 years ago, a well-known professional sportswoman and her businessman husband decided to start a magazine about participation sports, targeted specifically to women. They went to a company which they believed was a crack direct marketing firm. The company mailed the requisite 100,000 pieces of direct mail with various price and copy testing and when the flash counts had settled down the result was a remarkable 7 percent success. Ecstatic, the now "publishing" couple went back to their "expert" and said, "Okay, here's the money, mail 2 million." The "expert" responded with a question which would cause instant ulcers in even the most uninitiated practitioner of direct marketing. "Who would you like us to mail to this time? The last (and only) 100,000 were to the 100,000 members of the women's Amateur Athletic Union."

For every success story there is a horror story, and sadly enough the couple went back to the proverbial square one and started testing lists as well as price and offer. So, when evaluating lists, evaluate them based on their roll-out potential. In addition, it is quite common to choose a cutoff percentage and all lists above the cutoff will be rolled out and all below will not. Therefore, there is no single clear winner in mailing lists.

OVERCOMING PREVIOUS OBJECTIONS

But what really sets subscription marketing apart from all other kinds of direct marketing? There are several factors that can make a major difference. A special problem faced with new magazines is difficulty of selling a product that your potential customer has never seen, cannot hold at the point of sales development, and must be described in words and pictures. In the case of an existing publication with widespread acceptance and recognition by the consuming public, overcoming previous objections to the magazine may strain the talents of the copywriter and creative people. But the most crucial aspect of subscription marketing can be summed up in one word: renewability. For regardless of how well your pricing and list selection and creative material produce the desired effect of paid and unpaid orders for the publication, if the resultant subscriber does not renew his or her subscription, you have just designed a blueprint for bankruptcy. The renewal is where the money is, and without the renewal no publication can last very long.

BE FAITHFUL TO YOUR PRODUCT

Fortunately, there are some interesting techniques to provide renewability and we will examine some of those. The first rule in developing promotion that results in renewable subs is to be faithful to your product. One of the longstanding analogies vis-à-vis this renewability problem concerns a hypothetical publication that promises in its promotion that every subscriber will be treated to a visit at home by a famous star, who will not only deliver the magazine on a regular basis but sit down and have a cup of coffee with the family or subscriber. Naturally subscribers will not be happy once they discover that the awaited celebrity does not show up and the magazine arrives by normal mail. This is an example of how to overpromise or oversell a publication. Another example often noted is the now infamous *Time* magazine computer package that offered a fill-in for the city or town of the recipient. For example, a package might be addressed to Eliot Schein, 420 Madison Avenue, New York, New York 10017. The copy would read in part, "And *Time* magazine will deal with all the news events the world over with special emphasis on what's happening in New York." This is a fine approach and a good use to some degree of computer programming capabilities. However, if the recipient lives in Hilo, Hawaii, or Elk City, Oklahoma, that subscriber is going to be less than excited about *Time* magazine at renewal time because *Time* probably hasn't covered very many major stories on Hilo or Elk City. Therefore, the Hilo subscriber who subscribed saying to himself, "Wow, they're really going to put Hilo on the map" in his moment of provincial pleasure sets himself up as a nonrenewer.

If a publication is printed and produced in black and white and a promotion piece is four-color, fidelity has been set aside in an effort to get high up-front response. This again contributes to a failure to renew.

Most of the prime direct-mail copywriters are aware of the fact that a magazine or other publication is in fact a "continuity series"—one that has to be renewed. A one-time sale of a Rolls Royce could feature marketing misrepresenting some of the advantages or failing to mention some of the disadvantages of ownership of that premier automobile. However, with magazines, most customers get 12 opportunities to decide whether or not they like what they receive.

Unfortunately, some copywriters being well aware of the problems of renewability fail to treat this important aspect of their craft and push solely for high front-end response. Getting high front-end response does not necessarily produce the best result. In fact, the more unfaithful the promotion is to the actual publication, the higher the front-end response could be — with the lowest back-end benefit possible. And further trouble emerges down the line because there are still (believe it or not) some publishers that don't even go through a promotion analysis system to attempt to determine the actual pay-up and renewal value of each variable they test. Renewability is fiscally critical, and there are some less than totally scrupulous writers out there who are taking advantage of a lazy marketplace.

This is the right moment to discuss the soft offer. The soft offer is a conditional opportunity for a new subscriber to sample the publication being offered. These promotions are usually put in the following terms:

> Your first issue is free for you to examine and hold and keep whether or not you pay the bill that we will send you or write "cancel" across it. If you believe that our publication is everything we say it is, or more, then just pay the bill. If for any reason you don't agree with us 100 percent, simply write "cancel" across the invoice, the first issue is a gift from us and that's the end of everything.

Soft offers have become the rule in recent years in subscription direct marketing. The soft offer has emerged as the number-one offer used by most publications. The renewability of soft-offer-generated subscriptions is predicated in part, of course, on the pay-up of those soft offers. Since most new subscribers request the "bill me later" option on the order form when subscribing, more than 90 percent of all soft offers come in initially unpaid. It is not uncommon for a soft offer promotion to generate a pay-up rate of well under 50 percent. Yet there are ways to make soft offers work better.

One technique is to offer a premium that will be sent as a free bonus "upon receipt of payment." This helps to generate the payment, especially if the premium is perceived by the subscriber as something valuable and/or worthwhile. Of course, it would be better to have a control promotion prevailing that does not rely on soft offers and would have a hard offer, which generally results in a much higher pay-up rate.

MAKE SURE YOUR
PUBLICATION IS WORTH
SUBSCRIBING TO

But barring your publication's ability to develop and generate anything other than a significant number of soft offer subscriptions, there is one hard and fast rule that deserves your attention: Make sure your publication is worth subscribing to.

Here's where a strange anomaly in publishing comes in. For those publications carrying advertising, the months of January and February (as well as the summer months) usually have the least amount of advertising and as a result are the thinnest and thus appear less tangibly valuable than any other issues of the publication. What a shame that two of the best mail dates for direct-mail subscription promotion of the year are the last day of December and the last day of June. This unfortunate situation requires that publishers send as the first issue of a new subscription (and obviously the one upon which the soft offer's performance is going to hinge) with one of the skinniest, least appealing issues of the year.

In the formative stages of a publication it might be a good idea to rig the thickness of that publication, especially for those issues which will be used for the most part to serve the incoming legions of soft offer subscribers, those who are sampling their first issue of the magazine. Some techniques for increasing the heft of these issues include using heavier paper stock, adding more inserts even if they are inserts bound in to sell additional subscriptions to the magazine. One of the most effective methods of swelling the size of a publication is to provide advertisers with combination schedules which will feature a February issue, for example (that's the one that comes out in January), as a bonus or half-price issue for advertisers who also advertise in two issues in the previous year. This technique forces or pushes the issues which are most pivotal in producing soft offer payments and is well worth the time and effort.

But let's come back to this story about premiums. During the 1970s and early 1980s there seems to have been a derby especially among the weekly news publications to see who could give away the premium with the highest perceived value in the shortest period of time. *Newsweek* was giving away telephones, *Sports Illustrated* was giving out colorful videotapes a mile a minute, and *Time* magazine was using everything from a waterproof radio, mirrored dental-floss-dispensing telephone perpetual-calendar item with built-in digital clock in order to generate greater action from their direct-mail investment. The fact is, many consumers perceived that the actual value of the premium, be it a camera or pair of binoculars or what have you, was greater than the cost of the entire subscription. If the premium was juicy enough the "subscriber" would in effect buy the premium. The magazine would come as the real bonus.

Here's where we must pause for a moment and talk about Audit Bureau of Circulations (ABC) rules and regulations for magazine subscriptions. The Audit Bureau demands that the publisher receive no less than 50 percent of the "regular subscription price" *including* the value of the premium. For example, if the retail or perceived value of the premium is $10 and the regular subscription price is $60 the publisher must collect no less than $40—that is, 50 percent of the regular subscription price ($30) plus the value of the premium, which adds the other $10 to the amount of money the publisher must receive.

Some astute publications get away with giving premiums that have no real cash value. These are usually reprints about specific subject matters that have already appeared in that publication. These reprints, while they do involve some cost for production and typesetting and other costs, are not considered to be dollar value premiums in most cases by the ABC. Therefore, a publisher can still give these premiums while charging half-price for a subscription.

NEWSWEEK WOULD BE WISE TO MAIL TO *TIME*'S SUBSCRIBERS

The selection of mailing lists is in itself an important science when it comes to subscription solicitation. Every professional understands the best mailing list that can be used to develop subscribers for any publication is that of its major competitor.

For example, *Newsweek* would be wise to mail to *Time*'s subscribers. That's the good news. The bad news is, and it only takes a cursory look through any of the major directories of mailing lists, that "competitive offers are not accepted for rentals." Certainly *Newsweek* and *Time* have competitive offers, so the chances are the best list for your publication's mailing will not be available to you.

But here's where astute thinking and the chance to be a hero come into play. Every marketer should be aware that the competition offers one of the best arenas for information and learning. In the case of this hypothetical *Newsweek/Time* situation the circulator at *Newsweek* should be a subscriber to the competitive publication. Now don't worry that *Newsweek* is wasting its money subscribing to its competitor. In fact, the *Newsweek* circulation people should have at least three subscriptions not only to *Time* but to *US News and World Report, Insight,* and probably some other weekly publications that they find to be of similar price and demographic. The reason for three? Very simple. One subscription is always kept renewed and current so it is possible to monitor the mailing list usage of the active subscriber file. Simply by specially keying the name or address used for the subscription the people at *Newsweek* can identify which subscription is *Time, US News,* etc. This monitoring of the competition's mailing list rentals can produce great benefits. More about that in a moment.

The other two subscription orders should be used as follows: one which never gets paid so that the unpaid subscriber can collect the billing or invoice direct-mail series that the competition is using. This can open a lot of eyes and provide great insight into how the competition is doing. The third subscription should be paid for but never renewed. This will yield, much to the delight of the subscribing competitor, the total direct-mail and telephone (if any) renewal series that is being currently used or tested by the other company.

Now back to the mailers that are using the competitor's list. Even if the competitor will not allow you direct access to their list, it is possible over a period of not much more than a year to see which mailers "continue" to use the competition's mailing list. You may assume that those who continue to use the list on a regular basis are realizing decent performance from that list and that single fact means that names from the competitive file are being promoted and captured as new names on the mailer's file. In fact, this attraction can in some cases result in a significant number of your competitor's names being on the file of a noncompetitive mailer.

Now, after monitoring your competitor's list and seeing what kind of offers you get in the mail (with that specific spelling of your name or other coding device to identify it as your competitor's mailing list being used) you should test-mail all of the regular mailers who utilize the competitor's list. Naturally, if something is totally off the wall and so far afield from what you are after that you can't believe it can possibly work for you, you might want to make an exception. But generally speaking, those companies that continually use your competitor's mailing lists have mailing lists of their own that you can and should rent at least for test purposes which will yield very well for you. This is just one way to get around the noncompete kind of approach that many publications have when their competitors try to rent their names.

But choosing mailing lists besides that of the competition doesn't have to be that tricky, although there is one basic problem when launching a new publication that should be mentioned here. In the formative stages of a new publication most practitioners, if not all, will recommend a small (50,000- or 100,000-piece) mail test. Assuming the average rental cost of a mailing list is $80 per thousand (expressed in the industry as $80/M) a 100,000-piece mailing will have a cost of $8,000 for mailing list rentals alone.

The list broker's commission is 20 percent, which means the broker can hope to realize $1600 for the privilege of recommending and doing all the paper work to generate those lists for you to mail. The unfortunate aspect of these statistics is that $1600 is not (in today's day and age) a great deal of money, and as a result the high-priced top talent in the direct marketing list business is not going to spend the required number of hours to pick, choose, and research the appropriate lists for you for such a small payoff. Chances are the launching of a publication (which is the most critical moment in a publication's life, to be sure) is met with the lowest level of expertise in the mailing-list research business. There are some consultants who, for a fee, will be willing to research mailing lists for you and if you are at all serious about the launch you might want to consider that path. One publication with which your author has a more than passing relationship regularly retains a mailing-list "expert" for $1000 a project just to be an additional recommender of mailing lists to test. Of course, when it comes to the roll-out of 1 or 2 million names, the stakes are multiplied by 10 or 20 and list brokers come out of the woodwork with high-profile recommendations. By then the die is mostly cast, and the broker that helped you most in the beginning is the one that you should probably stay with.

As previously discussed, when putting together a direct-mail test promotion for subscription generation most professionals rely upon the results of a 5000-piece minimum test per variable. In some cases 5000 is not sufficient owing to the fact that a response for a daily publication that costs upwards of $400 or $500 a year for a subscription can be as low as two-tenths or three-tenths of 1 percent. In order to be statistically valid a minimum of 10,000 or 15,000 in some cases is required to produce a reliably projectable result.

The use of corollary lists allows for even greater projectability in this case. If a perfect list can be located and much to everyone's disappointment is not large enough to provide a reasonable roll-out, there may be a saving grace in the use of corollaries. For example, attendees of DMA seminars is a small but valid mailing list for a publisher such as *Direct Marketing* magazine to use. However, the roll-out potential of that list may not be sufficient to cause jubilation at *Direct Marketing* magazine. Fortunately, there are some corollaries. The attendees of Direct Marketing to Business (DMB) national conferences, when added to other such conventions' or conferences' attendees lists, can provide a larger universe than meets the eye.

This is the kind of bonanza that comes from hard work and careful research. There is also a very major element of common sense incorporated into most of your list selection.

FAVORED MAILING LISTS

Some lists, however, may not project out year after year after year. For ongoing publications there is usually a set of favored mailing lists that are used on a regular basis. In these cases a caveat is required. Mailing lists can change, and if you are used to rolling out, let's say, all the new subscribers of the past 12 months from one of your pet mailing lists year after year, it is your responsibility to make sure that that list has stayed consistent through the most recent period. If an important change was made in the way the list was generated it may have an equally important effect either positive or negative on your promotion. Here's an example: *New York* magazine subscribers is a favored mailing list of a good number of publications seeking subscribers. For years, *New York* magazine used a hard (unconditional) offer to generate its subscribers. Suddenly the emphasis of its direct-mail marketing changed and *New York* magazine marketed with a sweepstakes which featured in the beginning a Mercedes Benz convertible as the grand prize. The list of new subscribers for the first year of the sweepstakes promotion was significantly different from the list available for the new subscribers for the previous year. What *New York* magazine was now renting for the first time was "sweepstakes sold subs." However, no announcement appeared in any of the listings or trade journals reminding subscription marketers that *New York* magazine's list had now changed to a great degree. Pity the poor practitioner who, unaware of *New York* magazine's change of marketing premise, rolled out the names as a knee-jerk reaction to what worked well in the past. The list would not work anywhere nearly as well. The astute marketer would have done one of two things: either reduced the use of *New York* magazine's list to a mere test quantity to confirm (or refute) that it would not work as well, or develop a sweepstakes of its own (not a recommended strategy), which of course would work very well to sweepstakes-sold subs. A situation such as this once again outlines the requirement of assiduous attention when it comes to list selection.

LISTS THAT WORK WELL

Very often lists that work well in testing do not work as well when they are rolled out. There are reasons for this which are not at all encouraging. The basic reason that there is usually some fall-off between an initial test quantity of names and a roll-out defies definition. Technically speaking, as often as not the roll-out should be better than the test, but this does not seem to be the case. The anomaly is impossible to explain unless of course you are willing to delve into an area of unscrupulous practice by some list managers. Fortunately, they are the exceptions and not the rules. There are ways to augment or amplify a mailing list. For example, most direct marketers know that a "hot-line" mailing list will work better than the general list from which the hot-line is drawn. *Hot-line* means simply recent additions to the list. Clearly someone who is recently active and has just accomplished a participation in a direct marketing purchase or inquiry has a more up-to-date address, is usually interested in the subject matter, is someplace close to the peak of that interest, and in a psychographical mode of buying or responding. If a list manager provides hot-line names for a test quantity without telling the mailer that an augmented version of the list has been delivered, the mailer will no doubt assume that the entire list is projectable for roll-out from the quantity being tested. Unfortunately, most mailers learn this lesson the hard way and at the risk of censure, experience dictates that somewhere close to 10 percent of all lists ordered come in much higher in testing than they do in roll-out.

TESTING IS CRUCIAL

This is just one other reason why testing is so crucial. But testing just the mailing list is only the beginning. As said before, in today's world of subscription marketing the soft offer (or conditional offer) is responsible for more than 60 percent of all consumer publication subscription orders. The soft offer is described simply as the one that offers the potential subscriber a free examination copy and the opportunity to write "cancel" across the invoice if the publication is not up to expectations. This free issue or soft offer program is not complete in its effectiveness until such time as the billing goes out, the cancels come in, are subtracted from the total, more billing goes out, and each variable cell is evaluated based on its pay-up percentage as well as its initial yield-of-order percentage. Some lists will work very well for the soft offer in terms of resulting in high percentage response and fail miserably when the back-end result is factored in. So testing in the case of soft offer utilization through the net pay-up period can change a good response from the list to one which is more trouble than it's worth.

THEY HAVE SIGNALED
CERTAIN CHARACTERISTICS

The basic rule of selecting a mailing list to generate subscriptions for paid publications is very simple. Here it is: Wherever possible use lists that are lists of paid subscribers of magazines. If you want to generate paid subscribers you must mail to lists that are of paid subscribers. These people are not only familiar with what it's like to pay for a subscription to a magazine but they have signaled certain other characteristics about themselves. One, they have an address where a subscription can be sent. Two, they're interested in reading a publication. Three, they have the wherewithal (either credit card or check in almost every case) to pay for the publication. It is a known fact that subscribers to any publication are demographically superior to newsstand or single-copy buyers of that same publication. It is only fair to assume as well that the higher the demographic break, the better the response and result in pay-up.

THE LIST BUSINESS IS TRICKY

The list business is tricky for sure. One that is fraught with an incredible number of hurdles and possibilities that can end only in disappointment. But the thrill of seeing your selections work and produce positive results is the kind of business excitement most people would do anything to achieve.

After package and list, the third component of good direct marketing is offer. The offer is the specific term (period of time or number or issues) and pric and additional bonus, if any, and guarantee that are used in an effort to generate a sale. During the 1980s the best price for the standard 12 issues a year special-interest publication was $9.97. As 1990 came around, $11.97 became easier and easier to generate; $14.97 will probably be the right price for the mid-1990s, and $17.97 will probably be the turn-of-the-century benchmark. While this is pure theory, there is something to be said for ending all of these prices with an odd number. Technically, the more difficult it is to determine exactly how much a subscription costs per issue of the publication when compared to the single-copy price, the more it keeps a potential subscriber from a mental evaluation process of how much his or her money is worth. Additionally, all you need do is go to your local supermarket (and unless you are buying a quantity of 10 of one item) most assuredly the price of every individual item ends in 9. Certainly, we all at one time or another have a tendency to round off to the *lower* dollar value, whatever the number of cents are on a price.

NUMBER OF SUBSCRIPTIONS HAS GONE UP

Here's another theory about offer that proves once again why it's important for a book such as this to be updated and revised every so often. Now, while it's only a theory, understand that the number of subscribers to magazines as individuals has gone down in the past decade. The number of subscriptions has gone up. This must mean that each subscriber is subscribing to more publications than ever before. This being the case, the prediction can only be that lesser frequency than 12 times a year is going to be easier to sell than ever before. Just reducing the number of issues of a magazine which at one time was the kiss of death for any upstanding publication may now make it more attractive to a target consumer, who is already deluged with more than he or she can possibly read in one short period of time. This same theory would begin to suggest that nonnewsweekly weekly magazines could currently be in serious jeopardy. This in discussion with many people in the publishing business appears to have some validity.

In generating subscriptions, a guarantee of delivery and satisfaction is sometimes wise. Many years ago two Italian-American magazines, *I-AM* and *Identity*, were launched by two separate organizations. They both folded, leaving an excruciating (for the industry) couple of subscriber lists with unfulfilled subscription liability that was never made good. Since both events occurred within 6 months of each other, it could easily be said that the paid subscriber files of both of those publications represented the center of the bull's-eye of the best of the potential subscribers to such a publication, and now they were all soured because they were ripped off. Along came Jeno Palucci, the gentleman originally most noted for selling Chung King foods for more than a small fortune and starting a company you now know as Jeno's, which makes pizza rolls and pizza. Mr. Palucci wanted to start an Italian-American magazine to prove that the two failures were not indicative of the Italian-American community's lack of desire to read about Italian-American subjects. But he had a rough row to hoe because the major part of his constituency, his prime target market, had already been poisoned by people who failed to keep a publishing promise. Palucci had his accounting firm produce a guarantee which was backed up with Palucci's personal wealth that assured every subscriber to the new magazine (called *Attenzioni*) would be fulfilled for the entire period subscribed for like clockwork or cash would be returned to the subscriber.

This was the right move at the right time. In fact, it is incumbent upon every publisher who sells subscriptions to be willing to return a pro rata amount representing the unfulfilled or unserved portion of a subscription whenever any subscriber requests it. Sometimes making this statement as a guarantee will help serve the subscription effort. It is usually worded as follows: "If at any time during the course of your subscription to this magazine you desire to cancel your subscription, we guarantee to refund the amount represented by the as-yet-unmailed number of issues left on your subscription." Since by being a publisher, at least in the United States, you are just about forced to honor this commitment anyway, it might make sense for you to consider using it to add if not credentials, at least a safe feeling in the mind of your potential new subscriber.

CABLE TELEVISION IS BECOMING A STRONG MEDIUM

Those who are in subscription marketing are proud of what they do. Even though at cocktail parties they are constantly being accused of being "the person who puts those little cards in the magazine that fall out on the bathroom floor." Well, in subscription direct marketing it is worth saying that those shake-out cards continue to be the most efficient way of generating new subscribers. It would be wise to respond to the accusatory person at the cocktail party that you will take the shake-out cards out of your magazine as soon as they stop working and bringing in the least expensive subscriptions to that publication. There are other channels (no pun intended) of subscription generation. Cable television is becoming a strong medium for many types of publications, especially those that are sports-, business-, and music-oriented. Those that give premiums for subscriptions (especially videotapes) seem to be doing really well using inexpensive cable television spots.

Radio is a good medium to use for occasional emergencies to meet instantly rate base guarantees for city and regional publications especially. Since subscription circulation is up and provides the lion's share of income for paid publications, outstripping in many cases even the combination of newsstand or single-copy sales and advertising sales dollars, special emphasis and special pains should be taken to continue to streamline and make more efficient the subscription-generating process in every publication. Strangely enough, one of the biggest errors circulation professionals sometimes can make is by going with the tried and true and not experimenting with what is new.

46

Financial Services Marketing

James R. Rosenfield

Rosenfield & Associates
San Diego, Calif.

Rosenfield/Dentino, Inc.
Jersey City, N.J.

INTRODUCTION

Definitions, Problems, and Opportunities

During the 1980s, financial services direct marketing more than came into its own. It became one of the predominant modes of marketing for financial institutions throughout North America, Europe, and Australasia.

The popularity of direct marketing, though, has not necessarily been mirrored by a true understanding of its dimensions and implications. More often than not, financial services marketers confuse direct marketing with a medium (direct mail), with a distribution channel (mail-order distribution), or with a methodology (database marketing).

Direct marketing is none of the above. It's an approach to marketing, a way of looking at marketing that involves:

- Knowing who your customers are
- Knowing who they aren't
- Communicating with them relevantly
- Enhancing and refining the relevance of the communication

Based on information, direct marketing is a natural for financial institutions, which—unlike packaged-goods firms, for example—possess specific data about their customers. Importantly, by the end of the 1980s, cheaper and more effective data processing methods enabled even the smallest financial services firms to turn their customer information files into marketing-friendly databases.

At the same time, though, that direct marketing technologies have achieved new levels of sophistication, marketing financial services has become more difficult than ever before. The difficulties revolve around a complex array of factors:

- In an early deregulated environment, there's what amounts to a pent-up demand for products and services. The pent-up demand has long since been satisfied in North America, meaning that products now have to be *sold*, rather than merely bought.

- As geographical and institutional lines blur among different financial services firms, financial services themselves take on more and more of a commodity nature. The bank across the street can offer anything that the bank down the street offers; and the insurance firm and brokerage firm across the block can probably offer pretty much the same thing. You can get a credit card from Prudential; you can buy insurance from Citicorp; and you can get just about anything from American Express.

- Media clutter and saturation have reached an all-time high. Americans now get over 60 billion direct-mail solicitations a year, 4.3 pieces per household per mailing day. But the saturation is even worse for financial services marketers, because their target market—people with money—gets much more than the average amount of direct mail.

- An aging, changing America creates less demand for certain financial services (for example, mortgages), and more demand for others (for example, long-term care insurance). An increasingly bilingual America creates new and unprecedented marketing challenges (California will be majority Spanish-speaking within a few years). An increasingly fragmented America makes target marketing a continually changing endeavor.

- The complex technology underlying financial services has become a mixed blessing from a consumer perception standpoint. What facilitates convenience (automatic teller machines, for example) can also create frustration and even panic (how do people feel when an ATM system crashes?). The ease of using a credit card can turn into a nightmare when people become overextended.

- As the 1990s began, consumer confidence in U.S. financial institutions was at its lowest ebb since the Great Depression. The stock market crash of October 1987 had a demoralizing effect, but was generally accepted as a necessary correction—something of a balancing act of nature. The Savings and Loan debacle, though, which will ultimately cost every American man, woman, and child several thousands of dollars, has given rise to a national cynicism that will affect consumer attitudes for some years to come.

That's reality. And the reality of financial services marketing is challenging, and getting more challenging, as we move into the final years of the twentieth century. Smart financial marketers who are also smart direct marketers can turn the problems into opportunities. One of the best ways to do this is to get away from the product.

No One Wants Financial Products: A Word on Organizational Structure

People aren't interested in checking accounts, home equity credit lines, term insurance policies, or mutual funds. They're interested in doing smart things with their money.

Financial services marketers who think they're in the banking, insurance, or investment business are making a profound mistake. In reality, they're in the information business and/or the gratification business and/or the peace-of-mind business.

Unfortunately, though, a product-focused attitude has been institutionalized in financial services marketing organizational structures through the product management style of organization.

Borrowed from packaged-goods firms, product management is an ideal structure for a demand-driven marketplace. Its heyday was in post–World War II America, where pent-up demand made manufacturing and distribution the key business issues. Similarly, product management worked well in the early days of deregulation, when pent-up demand prevailed.

Now that things have changed, though, organizational structure should change also. Product managers should be replaced on the line by market sector managers, who are responsible for deepening and broadening customer relationships and augmenting the customer base with new customers The product manager should play a staff role, supplying appropriate product to the appropriate market segment manager.

The best way to manage a market segment is through a marketing database. This suggests that the most effective financial services marketing managers of the future will be managers of databases, in other words, direct marketers.

Because so many financial services people confuse direct marketing with direct distribution, the idea of a direct marketer running marketing is anathema to a traditional agent-driven insurance firm or a traditional broker-driven investment firm. But direct marketing, as pointed out above, has nothing to do with direct distribution. In fact, one of direct marketing's most effective uses is to drive customers and prospects into existing brick-and-mortar distribution centers, in which many companies have a substantial financial and psychological investment.

THE STRUCTURE OF A DIRECT MARKETING PROGRAM

Overview

You can't implement a direct marketing program without media and creative execution. Given a marketable product, the direct marketing task is to determine the right medium or mix of media; the right offer; and the right way to articulate the message.

Traditional direct marketers often quantify the relative importance of these components. A familiar formulation is the 40/40/20 rule, which says that 40 percent of the direct marketing program is the medium, 40 percent the offer, and 20 percent creative execution.

In today's world, though, it's more helpful to look at a direct marketing program as a whole system, organically intertwined. In the case of direct mail and telemarketing, for example, the database should produce the target segment, which in turn should suggest the right offer and execution.

Media: Uses and Changes

Here is a basic rule of thumb for the use of media in financial services marketing: The more complex and more expensive the product, the greater the number of media involved.

For example, one-step direct mail can sell a simple credit card or term-life insurance policy. A home equity credit line, on the other hand, may require direct mail for lead generating; further direct mail for fulfillment; and telemarketing follow-up to help prospects fill in the application.

One of the most common and fundamental mistakes financial services marketers make is to truncate the number of steps necessary to sell a product. For example, a mutual funds firm in the eastern United States recently mailed out 100,000 unsolicited prospectuses. Result: zero dollars invested!

Following is a review of media that lend themselves to financial services direct marketing, with emphasis on current and anticipated changes.

Visionary Media: The Future May Not Be Now.   Visionary media include personal computer–based communications and videotex. As of the writing of this chapter, the most important experiment of this sort in the United States is Prodigy, the joint-venture of Sears and IBM.

Prodigy is committed to gaining a hold in American households and can potentially breathe new life into at-home banking. And the ability to interact via Prodigy facilitates its potential use as a direct-response advertising medium.

Prodigy can be attractive for financial services marketers. Its users are affluent, highly educated, and upwardly mobile—an appealing market segment.

As the 1990s began, Prodigy had yet to take over the world. Indeed, its time may be in the future. By the end of the 1990s, Prodigy and similar videotex–personal computer technologies may emerge as critically important media for financial services marketers. Two factors make this likely: An entire generation of computer-literate children will be in a life-cycle stage where they'll need a variety of financial services. And by the end of the decade computers themselves may be as easy to use as telephones, a necessity for the convenience-craving American consumer.

Radio: Hot Medium for the 1990s?   Radio should appeal to financial services direct marketers, because of its targetability. The local classical station, for example, delivers an identifiable audience, totally different from the local country and western station.

Radio has a limitation, though, as a direct-response medium. The best time to buy radio advertising is during drive time. That's when people actively listen rather than merely use the radio for background. The problem is, how do they respond?

The solution: cellular car phones, which are becoming more common all the time. It's quite possible that in the next few years, car phones will be omnipresent, at least in the affluent professional-managerial market segment that provides the most important financial services customer.

Another factor: the driving environment. Traffic steadily gets worse, nationwide and worldwide, creating long periods of motionlessness. It's a frustrating environment that creates a psychological need for action and interaction (such as dialing a phone). It also provides more than enough nondriving time in which to dial the phone.

There's another even larger reason why radio may emerge in the next few years as a key direct marketing medium: demographics. American society is getting lonelier—25 percent of American households now consist of one person, living alone. Lonely people listen to the radio.

Inbound Telemarketing: The Medium That Changes Other Media.
American society is also getting older. As people get older, they sleep less and less well and are increasingly inclined to dial the phone at any hour of the day or night. That's why it's smart for financial institutions—particularly investment firms—to have 24-hour 800 numbers. And that's one of the many phenomena behind the growth of the 800 number, perhaps the single most important marketing technique of the late twentieth century.

It took a few years, but by the mid-1980s Americans had become astonishingly conditioned to dial 800 numbers. This has huge implications for the use of other media, which will be discussed below. What's unique about the 800 number is that it's the medium that has the power to transform other media—and the transformation, of course, is into direct-response media.

American Express, for example, has transformed its celebrity image ad campaign ("Neil Simon. Cardmember since 1974.") into an inquiry-generating campaign merely by placing 1-800-THE CARD below a picture of the plastic. Outdoor billboards have been transformed into direct-response media as a result of the 800 number. And direct-response television commercials can now be shorter—and therefore cheaper—as a result of the 800 number.

Television: Shorter Commercials, More Targeted Stations.
Direct-response television has been used for years by financial services firms to generate inquiries. Charles Schwab, for example, has used television consistently for some time. National Liberty's homey, slice-of-life, celebrity-spokesperson insurance commercials have long been a staple of daytime TV.

As referenced above, a change is taking place in direct-response television. The willingness of Americans to call 800 numbers has shifted the information burden from the initial medium (in this case, television) to the 800 number itself. This means that the TV commercial merely has to stimulate interest, rather than tell the story. The implication: In the future, a 30-second spot may be able to accomplish what a 90-second spot historically did. Another implication: The 800 number may facilitate the merging of image-building commercials with direct-response commercials.

Cheaper (because they're shorter), harder-working (melding image with re-sponse) TV commercials may emerge as one of the bread-and-butter lead-generating vehicles for a wide variety of financial services firms in the 1990s.

The increasing fragmentation of television into numerous stations, most of them cable-accessed, facilitates target-marketing, one of the basic tenets of the direct marketing approach. The Financial News Network, Cable News Network, and ESPN—for just a few examples—deliver demographics attractive to any financial services marketer.

Print: A Quiet Revolution.   The 800 number is beginning to change direct response television advertising. It has already dramatically changed direct-response print advertising.

Look at *The Wall Street Journal*, the mainstay of financial services direct-response print advertising. On any given Tuesday, page C2—the second page of the "Money & Investment" section—will have a stack of direct-response print ads in its far left column. The advertisers, typically, are Charles Schwab, Fidelity, T. Rowe Price, and Quick & Reilly. None of the ads has coupons, just 800 numbers. And all of the ads are in the traditional worst position for direct response: the far left side of a left-hand page.

What has happened, quietly and without fanfare, amounts to a radical transformation in direct-response print ads. The power of the 800 number has eliminated the coupon. The elimination of the coupon liberates the advertiser from paying a premium for the right-hand page. It also enables the advertiser to take a smaller ad. Net effect: cheaper, more cost-effective direct-response print advertising. And it's all the result of the transformational power of the 800 number.

In the world of magazine advertising, selective binding is a recent development that can potentially revolutionize customer-acquisition direct marketing. Several magazines—among them *Time*—can now bind in personalized communications. Targeted demographically and ultimately psychographically, these personalized communications may enable financial services marketers to talk individually to individual prospects in a less ephemeral environment than direct mail. In contrast to direct mail, people don't throw out *Time* magazine until they read it.

Outbound Telemarketing: A Double-Edged Sword.   Outbound tele-marketing is the most obtrusive, potentially the most powerful, and certainly the most controversial of all media. Virtually all marketing-oriented financial services firms use outbound telemarketing to some degree. Certain firms use it as a mainstay: Core States Bank, for example, reportedly uses outbound telemarketing as its sole medium for credit card acquisition.

Outbound telemarketing is at its most effective when used in combination with other media (for example, following up a direct-mail program); when used judiciously to deepen relationships with current customers; and when used to fulfill a request for further information.

Like any powerful tool, outbound telemarketing has its dangers. The biggest danger is that the American consumer has gotten tired of interruptions in the middle of dinner. A financial institution that persists in this kind of interruption is in danger of eroding its image in the marketplace, the long-term damage of which can outweigh any short-term results the telemarketing itself generates.

The solution: Use telemarketing carefully, if possible avoiding cold calls into the consumer household. Business-to-business telemarketing is a less delicate issue, since people spend so much of their business day on the telephone anyway.

Direct Mail: Meeting the Marketing Imperatives of the 1990s. Direct mail is the core financial services direct marketing medium, the most essential tool when it comes to communicating with a customer base.

The critical marketing imperatives of the 1990s — the preservation of market share and the maximizing of profits from current customers — can be most effectively attained through the intelligent use of direct mail.

Direct mail, though, is the most unusual and trickiest of all media. It's the only medium that has an intense tactile dimension, for example. It's the only medium that's not surrounded by other messages. And it's the only medium that requires a total manufacturing process.

DIRECT MAIL: THE CORE FINANCIAL SERVICES DIRECT MARKETING MEDIUM

Mailing Lists and Databases

Mailing lists can be categorized three ways:

1. Internal lists (a financial institution's customer information file)
2. Outside response lists
3. Outside compiled lists

Internal Lists. These usually are far more responsive than outside lists. The reason: There's an existing relationship with the financial institution. Financial services firms historically have problems manipulating and accessing data from their customer information files, though. CIFs were originally put together for operations and finance, not for marketing purposes. Therefore, extraneous data are likely to be tied into the name and address (for example, "ITF Mrs. John Smith"). Even worse, file entries are likely to be by product, rather than household, meaning that a customer with a three-product relationship will get three copies of a solicitation.

Cleaning up a customer information file and making it functional for marketing purposes is no longer a Herculean task. A number of companies throughout North America specialize in this kind of activity, which is fundamental for using direct mail effectively.

Internal lists — as well as outside lists — can be enhanced in a number of ways. The most popular modes of enhancement are *regression analysis* and *geodemographic modeling*.

Regression analysis takes a look at customer behavior and attempts to isolate variables that underlie direct-mail response. If skillfully done, regression analysis can hone in on variables that serve as predictors of future direct-mail behavior, refining marketers' ability to segment a customer base.

Regression analysis is based on actual behavior. Geodemographic modeling is based on a sociological hypothesis: "You are where you live, and you are similar to your neighbor." Geodemographic modeling systems, which are marketed by a number of firms, typically cluster the American population into about 48 groups, each group with a certain demographic and psychographic profile.

Geodemographic modeling, which was first developed as a tool for retail site location, is more precise in aggregate than in individual information, not unexpectedly in the heterogeneous United States. For example, two neighbors on West 73rd Street in Manhattan may be of different races, educational levels, and socioeconomic status. On the other hand, the geodemographic profile of West 73rd as a total environment is likely to be quite accurate.

Geodemographic modeling can be extremely helpful in analyzing a customer base and suggesting like prospects to seek out as new customers. More than one finance company, for example, has been surprised to learn through geodemographic modeling that its customer base was less blue-collar, more professional-managerial, than it had ever expected.

Outside Response Lists.   These are composed of people with a behavioral track record of responding to direct-mail solicitations. This is important because approximately half the U.S. population responds to direct mail and half doesn't. A good response list theoretically eliminates nonrespondents. (This dynamic, incidentally, changes for a customer list: Even usual nonrespondents will frequently respond to solicitations from financial institutions with which they have a preexisting relationship.)

Money magazine, for instance, generates its subscribers through direct mail. Therefore, the people on its list are likely to be mail-responsive, and also likely to be curious and informed about financial matters. Not unexpectedly, *Money* magazine's list frequently works very well for financial direct mail.

Response lists have advantages and disadvantages. The key advantage is the theoretical elimination of nonrespondents and the attendant increase in response rates. Disadvantages involve cost and quality. Response lists are expensive, and becoming more so all the time. The expense, though, is usually justified if the list is a good one. That's the tricky part, though. Mailing lists, unlike magazines or newspapers, are not audited by a third party. And with over 20 percent of the American population moving each year, a mailing list is a perishable commodity indeed. Unless kept scrupulously up-to-date, a list goes sour in a hurry. Many of the response lists on the market aren't worth the labels they're printed on. So it's *caveat emptor* all the way. For protection against low-quality lists, as well as for informed advice, it's always best to order lists through a recognized, reputable list broker.

Compiled Lists.   These are put together from a variety of public sources: telephone books, motor vehicle registrations, census bureau data. Compiled lists are the only way to get saturation coverage, for example, in bank branch radius mailings. Compiled lists are cheaper than response lists, but tend to generate fewer responses, since nonrespondents are on the lists. In recent years, though, through a variety of modeling and scoring methods, compiled lists have become more responsive than in the past.

What's the difference between a mailing list and a database? Current terminology is a bit fluid, but a mailing list begins to turn into a database as soon as information other than name and address is added. When a customer file has random access capabilities, it becomes a database, since financial institutions have far more information than merely the name and address.

Therefore, financial services direct marketers, as long as they have a viable customer information file, are in the business of database marketing. And in database marketing, the market segment—targeted and extracted through database management—becomes the focal point for creative execution.

Creative Execution

There is one general rule for financial services direct-mail creative: the more complex the product, the simpler the creative execution.

And in fact simplification, tangibilization, and humanization are the three imperatives that make financial services direct-mail creative different from other direct-mail categories.

- **Simplification** is a recognition of the fact that most financial products are complicated and hard to understand—even for intelligent, well-educated consumers. Enumeration and question-and-answer sequences are two commonly used simplification techniques, particularly powerful when tied together: "Eleven Answers to Critical Questions about Our New Overseas Equity Fund."

- **Tangibilization** recognizes the fact that financial products are abstract and intangible. People are uncomfortable with abstraction. Tangibilization is an attempt to give the benefits of a financial product a physical reality: picturing home improvements in a home equity credit line mailing, for example.

- **Humanization** is another way of dealing with abstraction. Pictures of people enjoying the benefits of a financial product help to warm up the direct-mail package.

There's one more vital imperative that financial services direct-mail shares with other direct mail: tactile involvement. Direct mail is the only medium that involves the hand, and there is a strong positive correlation between hand involvement and response. By getting the hand involved, the marketer causes the prospect to spend more time with the package. And by getting the hand involved, the direct-mail transaction—filling out a coupon, making a phone call, or carrying a voucher into an office—is subliminally suggested.

One of the most brilliant innovations in the history of financial services direct mail has been the personalized plastic card, so prevalent in insurance mailings. The card creates tactile involvement, tangibilizes the product, and creates legitimacy through the personalization.

Personalization, though, as a technique may be wearing out, victim to the sheer quantity of direct mail at present. The consumer is on to the tricks, and the problem with personalization is that when it goes wrong—for example, if the name is misspelled—it can create a negative image. Intelligent financial services direct marketers should use personalization carefully and in a limited way: in the salutation of the letter, for example, and on the response device or application, but not in the body copy of the letter.

As the twentieth century draws to a close, copy seems to be getting shorter, and graphics seem to be getting more important. People are busier than ever before, and less literate, so it stands to reason that a shorter, more graphic creative approach will become increasingly effective.

Also as the twentieth century draws to a close, offers need to become more authentic. Consumers are sensitive to empty hype. The traditional—and still important—function of the offer is to create action: through time limits, discounts, bonuses, and premiums. A newer and more subtle function of the offer is to promote a credible and trustworthy image to a skeptical and saturated marketplace.

Credibility and trust underlie a new and important use of direct mail: as a nonpromotional way to build relationships with current customers. American Express, for example, sends its members periodic "love letters," which also serve as subtle premailers for an upcoming renewal solicitation.

CONCLUSION: WHO'S ON THE LEADING EDGE?

Although a number of companies do excellent direct marketing work, the most consistently superior financial services direct marketers are American Express, Fidelity, Citicorp, and USAA.

American Express has a superb database, which, importantly, is combined with superb customer service. "High-tech, high-touch"—a cliché of the 1980s—has to become a reality in the 1990s, and American Express is in the forefront of making this happen. Among its many interesting activities, American Express is quietly pioneering the advertising of the future through its subtle combination of image advertising and direct response via its 1-800-THE CARD number.

Fidelity is the master of the 800 number. Their telemarketers are highly trained, intelligent, and responsive, to a degree far beyond that attained by most other marketers. Fidelity also has quietly used media—particularly print media—in innovative ways, by dropping the coupons from their ads, and by using *The Wall Street Journal* as a customer communication medium. It's reported that most of Fidelity's *Journal* inquiries are from current customers. These inquiries are generated, of course, at a fraction of the cost of direct-mail–generated inquiries.

Citicorp is less centralized than the other companies on this short list, and the quality of its direct marketing ranges from superb to pedestrian. But Citicorp is one of the largest mail-order companies in the world, through its huge bankcard base, and is one of the most aggressive and visionary companies anywhere. John Reed, Citicorp's CEO, has stated that he wants to turn Citicorp into a worldwide brand, à la American Express. Citicorp has the firepower to make this happen, through its superb technology and through its commitment to information-based marketing.

USAA (United Services Automobile Association) is the least known of the elite financial services direct marketers, but probably the best of them all. Located in San Antonio, Texas, USAA, which began as an automobile insurer, offers a comprehensive array of financial services to a large affinity group: U.S. military officers, ex-officers, and their dependents. Service and simplicity—two things that the financial services consumer craves—are bywords at USAA, backed up by some of the most sophisticated telecommunications and data processing technology available anywhere. By combining high-tech and high-touch with an almost ferocious intensity, USAA has engendered high loyalty among its members, and serves as a model for financial services direct marketers, for now and for the future.

47
Fund-Raising

Bruce R. McBrearty

TransAmerica Marketing Services
Washington, D.C.

Fund-raising is thought by many to be the most difficult form of direct marketing because it deals with the intangible, emotional act of making a contribution. The challenge of motivating people to take an action and write a check, simply because it will make them feel better, involves the greatest of creative and copy-writing skills.

Because of this challenge, and the ever-increasing competition for the "fund-raising dollar," fund raisers must stay on the cutting edge of new ideas. They are constantly breaking new ground, primarily through direct mail, but also with telemarketing, space advertising, television, and electronic banking.

In this chapter I will briefly highlight many of these skills. It has been compiled with the help of many fund-raising experts. Our goal is to provide a brief overview and share with you enough information to further investigate areas of interest to the reader.

OUTLOOK FOR THE 1990s

Bill Olcott, editor of *Fund-Raising Management,* the industry's oldest independent magazine, reports that fund-raising has enjoyed its greatest growth during the 1980s. Total giving rose from $48.7 billion in 1980 to the current figure of $114.7 billion—an astounding increase of 135 percent in that decade alone. And it is entirely possible that giving will double again by the year 2000.

In fact, fund-raising, and specifically direct-response fund-raising, appears to be poised on the brink of a golden age. The signs all point to it. First, there's the increased professionalism in the field; second, fund-raisers are learning to harness the new computer and communications technologies; and third, demographics are leaning heavily toward philanthropy.

694

Olcott suggests that we look at the signs. Since the cutbacks on federal grants to charities in 1981, we have seen an ever-widening gap between needs and resources. But those cutbacks did something else — they forced fund-raisers to become more professional. With the government slashing programs, fund-raisers had to go out and do it themselves. And, they have done it with a vengeance. An increase in the amount of money raised is proof enough, demonstrating that fund-raisers have learned to master the arts of direct mail, telemarketing, planned giving, and special events.

Additionally, demographics are leaning heavily toward philanthropy. There are four major demographic movements. One is the baby-boom generation — 76 million Americans born between 1946 and 1964; the second is the explosive growth of minorities; the third is the aging of America; and the fourth is the number of working women, who now account for 53 percent of the labor force.

All of these demographic changes will impact fund-raising in a different way. The baby-boomers, by their sheer numbers, are such a powerful force that they can do anything they want, any way they want. They're destabilizing the process. Clearly fund-raising is changing because of them.

Consider the profile of a baby-boomer: They're highly educated. They're doing well financially and stand to inherit the wealth of the richest elderly in history. They're very demanding — they want more information — they're not influenced by negatively framed fund-raising the way their parents were. And they're less deferential to authority or experts, perhaps because of the breakdown in respect for government, school, and church in the 1960s.

During the Vietnam war, the chant was, "Hell no, we won't go." Now they say the same thing about aging. To prevent the onset of aging, they take better care of themselves. Look at the growth of exercise clubs, health spas, and plastic surgery.

The rapid growth of minorities presents fund-raisers with an additional problem. Minorities must be approached in a different way, with consideration for their backgrounds and traditions. Fund-raisers have no choice but to think in multilingual as well as multicultural terms, despite their given field — be it education, health care, or human services.

The over-65 age group is the fastest growing segment of our population, numbering more than 30 million persons. The over-65 age group gives most of the money, and with individuals living longer these days, it bodes well for fund-raising.

Olcott adds one caveat here. As the life span of individuals grows longer, from the 70s into the 80s and beyond, fund-raisers are discovering that the elderly reach a point where they begin to fear they will run out of money. This could have a negative impact on their giving.

DIRECT MAIL

However, even the most generous people in the world still need to be asked before they can give. And, the primary method of reaching these individuals has been and will continue to be through the mail.

David Bufkin and Shelley Gentile, both of Stephen Winchell & Associates, had some observations about direct mail. They observed that even though direct-mail fund-raisers have faced some critical challenges in the late 1980s, direct mail has remained the backbone of charitable fund-raising and nonprofit membership development.

The new realities for the 1990s in direct-mail fund-raising include increased printing and postage costs, increased list costs, fewer proven charitable donors on the market, and an increasing demand for accountability among American "charitable consumers."

In 1980, the average prospect direct-mail package cost 25 cents or less. Today, this same package costs 40 cents or more. Increased costs have forced today's direct-mail fund-raisers to "de-massify" fund-raising direct-mail efforts. While in the past direct-mail fund-raisers depended on large volume, low-cost prospecting for a constant influx of new names and revenue, today's successful nonprofits are making much bigger investments in keeping and upgrading current donors.

More and more, fund-raisers are combining multimedia fund-raising techniques such as outbound and inbound telemarketing, direct-response television, and print with traditional direct-mail efforts. They're mailing to fewer, more selective universes and creating monthly donor and exclusive high-dollar programs. And they're testing demographic overlays and other list enhancement technology to open new universes of potential donors and improve the performance of existing lists.

One new development making an impact in nonprofit direct mail is predictive modeling. Predictive modeling is a way to compare those who respond to a mailing—or other direct marketing efforts—with those who do not, taking into account hundreds of variables and their interrelationships.

The immediate result of this process is the segmentation of all prospective recruitment candidates into "declines," which are ranked by likelihood of response. These rankings are stored with each prospect's name and address and become the basis of determining the occurrence or frequency of subsequent promotional efforts. The net result of this type of targeted marketing is a higher total response from a smaller total mailing quantity.

But high-tech marketing wizardry hasn't been the only change in direct-mail fund-raising. Take a look in your mailbox. Chances are you won't find a stack of drab standard number 10 corner card packages.

Savvy direct-mail fund-raisers have discovered the response-lifting ability of color; the drama and excitement of graphic design; and the checkbook-opening power of involvement devices like stickers, tokens, and scratch-off panels. The average creative quality of direct mail produced today at leading agencies that have survived the industry shakeout of the 1980s is far superior to yesterday's product.

Another major trend in direct-mail fund-raising is the ever-increasing reliance on premiums—gifts or tokens designed to entice a contribution. From elegant enameled lapel pins, to wisecracking bumper stickers, charities and nonprofit organizations are now enhancing the satisfaction of giving with a wide range of tangible symbols of a donor's support.

Bufkin and Gentile agree that, in addition, organizations that don't want to limit their possibilities to traditional premiums are using photographs, original art, or graphics to create their own custom notecards or calendars. Specially developed programs that use these kinds of cost-effective premiums are especially successful in boosting contributions during slow times of the year. An appropriate gift or premium also serves as a year-long goodwill reminder of the charity or organization.

Finally, financial products such as credit cards and insurance are also making their presence felt in today's fund-raising.

DIRECT-MAIL PREMIUMS*

Direct mail has changed dramatically in the last decade and will continue to change; those nonprofit organizations that stay on the edge will continue to prosper.

One of the organizations that has continued to prosper in the mail, and one that places a great deal of emphasis on the use of premiums, is the Disabled American Veterans (DAV).

To find out the secrets of the DAV's success, I asked Max L. Hart, their director of direct mail. Hart provided me with both an overview and some tips on how to use premiums more effectively. Premiums have long been one of the most powerful incentives used by nonprofits to increase their results, whether it's a front-end or back-end offer.

Front-end premiums are inserted in the mailing package, and it is not necessary to respond to obtain the premium. In the case of a back-end offer, respondents have to make a minimum contribution to receive the premium.

Because many nonprofit organizations do not have the pulling power to succeed in their fund-raising effort through a straight appeal (letter, reply form, brochure, and reply envelope), they must turn to such promotional techniques as sweepstakes, matching-check programs, or premiums.

Here are Hart's basic rules for premiums:

- Use premiums that have a logical tie-in with your organization. For example, disease-prevention pamphlets for health agencies, endangered-species seals for wildlife, and patriotic premiums for veterans' organizations.

- Use premiums with the highest perceived value at the lowest cost. This usually occurs with printed items such as seals, greeting cards, return-address labels, pamphlets, certificates, etc.

- Feature the premium in the copy. Copy should be developed around the premium, particularly if there is a logical association between the agency and the premium.

- Use premiums that require periodic replacement. Consumable items, such as greeting cards or name stickers, accomplish this. You can also build in a need for replacement by using a year of membership on a card or certificate.

- Provide quality premiums. A good print job generally costs little or no more than a poor print job. However, a poor-quality premium may have a negative effect on your response rate.

- Use premiums only when cost-effective. Make sure your return on investment

---

*This section reprinted with permission of *DM News*. Copyright Mill Hollow Corporation.

is cost-effective and justifies the additional expense. Do not use a premium because you think it is a clever strategy and will help your return.

- Finally, it's a good idea to state in your copy that the premium is "a gift" and there is no obligation to contribute. This prevents the premium from being considered unordered merchandise by consumers and regulatory agencies.

The proof is in the results and Hart reports that these tips do work. DAV's premium appeal produces three times the number of returns on acquisition mailings as its no-premium appeal.

Premiums can and will provide a lift to an organization's bottom line; however, the prudent fund-raiser would only move into new ground, whether it's a new premium or a new appeal, after careful testing. Again, the DAV is successful because the organization is cautious in testing new ideas before implementation.

Testing is imperative to determine the most productive appeals, whether it is copy or the appropriate premiums for your organization. Testing is the lifeblood of any fund-raising organization. After a proven winner is written, smart fund-raisers begin to look for a direct-mail package that can produce even better results.

Hart sums up his feelings in seven rules for testing:

- First of all, test either a single element or a completely different approach: Totally different approaches are used when launching a new program and will tell you which package or approach does best. Single-element testing usually occurs after a program matures and will allow you to know which specific change accounted for the results.

- Make sure tests are statistically valid. Use a large enough sampling to ensure that continuations will achieve the same relative results.

- Mail all tests at the same time. If part of the test is mailed one week, and the balance another week, you completely destroy the integrity of the test. Some weeks are better than others, some months are better. Changes in news events, weather and economic conditions can result in major differences in test results.

- Test the big things. Important gains are realized in testing meaningful variables, such as lists, offer, copy, format and design.

- Test against your control. Try new approaches against your winner. You should never change a winner until you find something that beats it.

- Analyze results carefully. Unique codes should be assigned to each test to make sure that data can be properly credited, measured, and analyzed. Since quantities, costs, average contribution, response rates, and net income can vary, it is important to account for each variable in an orderly, clear, and accurate reporting system.

- Finally, retest past winners. Test results do not last forever. Market and economic conditions change, family socioeconomic and lifestyles change. That's why you have to retest regularly.

I have found that Hart's seven rules will work for all direct marketing whether it's direct mail, telemarketing, space, or direct-response television.

CONTINUITY PROGRAMS

Certainly, the culmination of any successful direct-mail campaign is the conversion of one-time donors into multiple, monthly donors.

Rodney A. Smith, a direct marketing consultant, observes that continuity programs can take many forms as long as they somehow relate to the overall conceptual framework of the parent organization. Continuity programs can be targeted at large or small donors. However, it is vitally important that each program have its own identity, theme, benefits, and unique method of promotion and packaging. It is the blending of all these factors that give each program a unique personality. And it is just this unique personality that ultimately makes or breaks every newly created continuity program.

When creating a continuity program, keep in mind that it must have the right image because it is this image that ultimately does 90 percent of the persuading.

Smith feels the National Republican Senatorial Committee in Washington, D.C., is an excellent example of a fund-raising organization that has conceived four very successful continuity programs. Here is a quick overview of the four continuity programs set up by the NRSC:

- *The Republican Senatorial Trust:* membership $10,000 per year. This is a very prestigious major donor group where membership is strictly limited to 200 members. All trust members are annually invited to a number of private briefings in Washington, D.C., that are held in various conference rooms in the United States Senate, followed by a cocktail party and dinner at the homes of various Republican dignitaries and U.S. Senators.

- *The Republican Senatorial Business Advisory Board:* membership $2500 per year. This program is specifically targeted at businesspeople who run small and medium-sized businesses. Members are periodically invited to Washington, D.C., to participate in round-table discussions which specifically focus on current problems facing American small business. These discussions are followed by an intimate dinner at a good local restaurant with political VIPs who are especially concerned about the problems of small business.

- *The Republican Senatorial Inner Circle:* membership $1000 per year. This program is specifically targeted at Republican major donor activists. All money donated to the Inner Circle goes directly into a special escrow fund that can only be used to support Republican senatorial challenger candidates. All Inner Circle members are invited to Washington, D.C., twice a year for a day-and-a-half long conference at a local hotel that includes dinner and regional breakfast with a Republican VIP.

- *The Republican Presidential Task Force:* membership $10 per month or $120 per year. This is a small-donor program founded by President Ronald Reagan. Each person who agrees to join former President Reagan's special task force is given a Presidential Medal of Merit; a Presidential Medal of Merit lapel pin; a full-size ceremonial American flag specifically dedicated for the donor at a ceremony in the rotunda of the United States Capitol. Members also have their names permanently inscribed in President Reagan's special Task Force Honor Roll and receive other more usual kinds of small-donor benefits.

Smith points out that the cost of admission can range from $10 to $10,000. And, each of these programs was primarily "sold" through direct mail. Packages for the highest dollar programs were centered around a personal "engraved" invitation from a senator followed up by a letter. The lower-dollar names received a series of direct-mail pieces. All programs used telemarketing as part of their overall strategy.

LIST RENTALS

Somebody once said that over 50 percent of the success of a direct-mail campaign can be attributed to the list that is being mailed. That makes the role of the list broker critical to the success of any fund-raising program.

Don Kuhn, of Walter Karl, Inc., and a pioneer in direct response for nonprofit organizations, shared with me his thoughts on the ins and outs of list rental.

Prospecting for new donors to add to your donor file is a *fundamental* need. Your first goal should be to acquire more new donors during the year than you are losing through deletions. Your second goal should be to do so at the least cost per new dollar raised, or if not the least, the cost that produces new donors that best fits your long-term needs. Popular causes can sometimes raise replacement donors and dollars for better than the cost of the mailings. However, if your organization is like most, your donor acquisition program will have a cost per dollar raised of $1 to $2 or more.

Kuhn thinks you should view prospecting as an investment in gaining future income. Some studies have shown that if you gross $100,000 from a prospect mailing, you can expect more than $50,000 per year in renewal income over the next 10 years. A growing donor file is like a growing savings account. Its benefits compound through renewal mailings, sustained response rates, higher gift accounts, and bequests.

To acquire new donors, most organizations must rely on renting outside lists. These lists fall into two categories: *compiled lists* (telephone or automobile ownership, for instance) with demographic overlays, rented from compilers (and brokers); and *donor and customer house files*, rented and exchanged through brokers. Both kinds can achieve desired results. Compiled lists are less expensive, but require as much as 70 percent more mail quantity to achieve results equal to that of rented house lists. Rented house lists cost four or five times that of compiled lists, but require far fewer mailings. Exchanges reduce your costs.

Use the following guide as a rule of thumb for general order of list effectiveness:

- Donor lists similar to yours
- Other donor lists
- Mail-order buyer lists
- Subscriber lists, direct mail sold
- Compiled list, enhanced psychographically and demographically (mail responder, income, sex, etc.)

- Compiled list, demographically selected (income, sex, zip code, etc.)
- Compiled list, occupant, demographically selected

Marginally performing lists can sometimes be improved by overlaying the lists with additional information for selections, such as exact age, and characteristics derived from multivariate analyses of donors from previous prospect efforts — at additional costs.

There are a couple of other things that Kuhn suggests direct marketers take note of:

- When you rent house lists (the first four categories above), realize that the cost of each list is set by the list owner, not the broker.

- The minimum order is usually 5000 names and sometimes 10,000. Generally, your course of action will be to test a number of lists at minimum volume, and cautiously retest the winners with larger volumes. The process never ends.

- When you begin using large numbers of lists with larger quantities, a computer merge-purge is recommended to eliminate duplicates between all lists and your house file. The duplicate elimination will pay for itself through savings in materials, postage, and communications with donors.

- Also, with brokered lists you pay for what you order, and not for what you mail. Your broker may negotiate reduced charges for names not used, for example, some duplicates from the merge-purge.

- And finally, you are entitled to a one-time usage of names from each list. Donors received from mailings are yours to maintain and promote.

OUTBOUND TELEMARKETING

One of my favorite telemarketing quotes was in *MaxiMarketing* by Stan Rapp and Tom Collins. They state:

> While you were looking the other way, the telephone became the nation's third largest advertising medium, surpassing direct mail in 1984 to take its place in the big three with television and newspapers.
> If you are not maximizing the use of the telephone in marketing the product, service, or business you are promoting, you are in danger of being left behind.

As fund-raisers, we have known this for years. Over the last 10 years, telemarketing has moved from the back room to the boardroom of the nation's largest and smallest nonprofit organizations.

As postage, printing, and other mailing costs continue to go up, successful fund-raisers have begun using telemarketing more and more to renew lapsed donors, solicit additional gifts from current donors, turn one-time donors into multiple donors, and recruit new donors.

Without question, telemarketing is still expensive, but the improvements in computer technology, the ever-lowering long-distance rates, and the better utilization of lists, make telemarketing a very manageable and affordable alternative.

In any telemarketing effort, there are four key ingredients to your success:

- The database
- The telemarketing script
- The telemarketer who makes the calls
- The follow-up direct-mail package

Each of these can contribute dramatically to your success or failure.

The Database

First of all, you should be concerned about phone numbers—and with the increased incidence of unlisted numbers, this is becoming more and more difficult.

Telephone numbers can be appended to your file in two ways. First, files can be electronically matched against databases of existing phone numbers, or second, numbers can be looked up manually. The most cost-effective method for appending phone numbers is computer-matching. However, you will probably only match 50 to 60 percent of your file.

Many sophisticated marketers are adding phone numbers to the database when contributions are received, simply by requesting the information on the response device.

Keep in mind that telemarketing is a two-way communication vehicle, and the phone call itself can be an excellent means to gather additional information on your donors. At the same time you are asking for contributions, your donors will be giving you clues about themselves: indications of age, income levels, and specific areas of interest. Capturing this information at the point of the call can be useful in future telemarketing and direct-mail campaigns.

The Telemarketing Script

Unlike any other direct-response medium, telemarketing allows only a very few words to gain attention, arouse interest, and motivate a donor into action. And what is said in these very few words will make or break the program.

Critical to your success are:

- **The introduction.**   You must be calling from an organization that is immediately recognized by the donor or on behalf of an individual whose name is well known.
- **The offer.**   The offer should be structured to quickly and persuasively explain the need and the benefits of giving. Telemarketing will allow you to not only upgrade the donation by 20 to 30 percent but also negotiate lower amounts if necessary.

- **The resell.**   For those who hesitate, additional benefits are necessary.
- **The close.**   In closing, the telemarketer must not only thank the donors for their support, but also reconfirm the amount of the contribution and the address and reemphasize the importance of making the gift immediately.

The Telemarketer

My own research has indicated that the decision to make a contribution is going to be based on your organization, and the validity of the request, not the individual making the call. However, a bad communicator can destroy a call and a relationship which otherwise might have ended in a contribution.

Communicators must be thoroughly educated about the organization, how the donor's contribution will be used, the type of responses or questions they can expect from the donor, and, most importantly, the type of individual they're calling.

The Follow-up Direct-Mail Package

After the lists are selected, telemarketing scripts developed, and communicators trained, only one step remains — collecting the pledge. Research has shown time and time again, that a pledge given over the phone is felt to be "a promise" to make a contribution. Generally, the donors feel strongly about that commitment and will do everything possible to fulfill it. Your job is to make the fulfillment process easier.

To begin with, the telephone pledge is an impulse decision. You must follow up that decision immediately before buyer's remorse sets in. Your follow-up should be in the mail within 24 hours of the call. Our experience has shown that there is a fall-off of 10 percent for each day that the mail is held up after the phone call.

The follow-up fulfillment package should stand out among the many other letters being received. Colorful envelopes, "urgent-gram" formats, phones on the carrier, and handwritten teaser copy are just a few ideas for the outside carrier. Once inside, the copy should reference the phone call, remind the donor of the amount that was pledged on the phone, and, naturally, thank them for their contribution.

Within 10 to 20 days after the first letter is mailed you should send a second reminder to those who have not responded to your first letter. This second reminder will generate an additional 30 to 50 percent over the response to the first mailing. For example, if the first mailing received a 40 percent response, the second reminder should bring in another 20 percent (50 percent of the first mailing), bringing the total response to 60 percent.

Telemarketing works! It is a personal fund-raising approach which will allow you to raise new money from your existing and lapsed donors. Most importantly, it will not detract from your existing fund-raising program, but rather add to and strengthen it.

DIRECT-RESPONSE TELEVISION AND SPACE ADVERTISING

One of the very few new direct-response mediums that has been discovered in the last decade is the use of direct-response space advertising and television.

Keith Jespersen, president of the Russ Reid Company, shared with me that for years the strengths of traditional telethons were considered to be their entertainment value and their ability to draw an audience with a loose, informal format that gave it a "live" feel. Over a period of hours, a snowballing response effect was built as the viewers were urged to meet a goal at the conclusion of a 12- to 24-hour period.

The advertising time was donated by stations or substantially discounted. Usually the organization sponsoring the telethon also had a strong involvement in the community through local promotions and events.

With two or three exceptions, these telethons have fallen by the wayside from high costs of production, loss of free air time, and lack of viewer response. The few remaining "winners" have been kept alive by their ability to solicit past television donors and bring large corporate gifts into the annual television event.

A newer television fund-raising strategy comes from half-hour and one-hour specials incorporating all of the disciplines of good direct-mail fund-raising. In fact, it is likely that an organization that is not successful in the mail will also not do well in television.

A direct-response rationale says that even though you are broadcasting to the masses you still must speak to one person at a time. Television fund-raising works best when the cause is a life-and-death issue, when it can be related directly to one needy person. This creates a sense of urgency and empathy necessary for viewer response.

For instance, if the program is about cancer research, it should show and tell the stories of people who have benefited from that research or hear from the families of those who have died because it wasn't available. A tour of the research facility or hospital talking to doctors and administrators is just talking heads and makes for very bad television.

A television fund-raising special must frequently remind the viewer to call and the appeal must be clear and specific. It is important to suggest a specific gift amount and to show the viewer how that amount will help people.

It is hard to make television work as a stand-alone fund-raising vehicle unless you are asking for monthly pledges—usually $15 to $20 a month. Asking for monthly pledges can raise the average viewer response from a single gift of $20 to $30 to a pledge promise of $150 to $200 a year. Fulfillment on these pledges with a strong monthly follow-up program can vary from 50 to 75 percent.

Television is an expensive proposition which must be carefully thought through before the risk of producing and buying air time is undertaken.

Discussing Russ Reid's strategy on direct-response space advertising, Jespersen stated that, in general, fund-raising for new donors is a difficult challenge in magazines and newspapers. It normally requires a two-step process to generate leads from space ads and then convert and follow-up these leads with a strong direct mail program. This requires an average gift or donor lifetime value expectancy which can justify the high expense of deficit prospect acquisition.

There are some exceptions to this general experience. Magazines which feature a special issue on hunger or homelessness or some specific societal problem can sometimes result in a lift in response for ads placed in that particular issue. Some magazines have also begun featuring major articles on a problem and then giving free space ads to a selected charity and tying into the article a request for a contribution. This is an arrangement which must be negotiated between the magazine and an individual charity.

And finally, some organizations involved in local emergency feeding and shelter programs have made small, inexpensive ads work on a seasonal holiday basis. Also, crisis ads around emergencies such as earthquakes, tornadoes, and the like, have also made local newspaper fund-raising work close to the event itself. This response tends to fall off dramatically within 2 weeks of the crisis.

Jespersen concludes that both mediums, television and space, can work. However, both are very expensive and should not be undertaken without a thorough investigation of the cost and potential return.

ELECTRONIC BANKING

In an environment where fractions of response rates are critical, every nonprofit is looking for a magic wand to generate donor dollars.

To discover whether electronic banking, with the automatic transferring of funds from the donor's account to the nonprofit's account, is such a magic wand, I spoke with Willit H. Sawyer, whose company, EFT Corporation, has been on the forefront of electronically transferred donations. Sawyer feels that if we substitute "competitive edge" for "magic wand," expectations are not only clearer but achievable. Electronic funds transfers (EFT) can facilitate higher contributions, guaranteed fulfillment, automatic pledge renewal, reduced solicitation costs, and predictable cash flow. Even when a monthly pledge program is cost-prohibitive, it's possible to derive dramatic contribution increases with electronically transferred donations.

Programs already in place show that contributors pledge higher, fulfill more regularly, and remain on your file longer than other donors; $25 annual donors can suddenly become $96 contributors year after year.

Donors are asked to make a single support decision with monthly payments made automatically thereafter. This automatic withdraw system provides a 97 percent fulfillment rate. And donors are committed, showing annual losses of less than 10 percent. This decrease in file "churn and spin" allows you to redirect time, money, and the energy spent recapturing donors through donor acquisition programs.

A brochure and authorization form explaining the benefits of electronic donations should be sent with *every* regular solicitation and reminder mailing, with a letter asking donors to convert to "checkless" giving. The brochure should link the donor with a program name geared to the "why" of the pledge, not the "how" of payment. United Negro College Fund has their Dollars for Scholars program, the Sierra Club has its Wilderness Guardians, and Help Hospitalized Veterans has the Patriot Pledge.

To enroll, donors need only sign an authorization form to effect transfer. This form is an agreement between donors and their banks that contains the disclosure statements as required by federal law. Most nonprofits combine the explanatory brochure with the authorization form.

Donor data is then transmitted through the National Automated Clearing House Association (NACHA) network to effect transfers each month automatically. You will need a service bureau or bank to assist with these electronic transactions.

Sawyer concluded by stating that "EFT isn't a 'magic wand' but the advantages are enormous and exemplify EFT as the fund-raising vehicle to provide a true competitive edge in an arena of limited donor dollars."

CONCLUSION

Fund-raising is constantly changing. The demographics of our audience change, the costs change, new lists become available, and new techniques are still being discovered. And the techniques that worked last year may not work this year but may be successful again next year.

It's difficult to stay abreast, but if you monitor the marketplace by reading the industry publications and the many books that are written on the subject, you can keep a good feel for the trends of the industry.

Equally important is to watch what others in the industry are doing because if it's working for the country's largest nonprofits, it is probably worth testing for your organization.

NOTE

1. Stan Rapp and Thomas L. Collins, *MaxiMarketing* (New York: McGraw-Hill, 1987).

48

Third-Party Endorsements

Marge Landrau

Landrau's Hispanic Concepts
Yonkers, N.Y.

Third-party endorsements combine elements of convenience and necessity. Often called syndications, they are direct-response campaigns combining all the strategies of direct marketing; in the background there usually is a party known as a merchandise syndicator, manufacturer's representative, or broker.

In third-party endorsements, most of the risk is taken by the syndicator, who assumes the risk of maintaining the merchandise inventory. The manufacturer provides the merchandise. Another party to this type of endorsement is an endorser who owns a list and can extend credit to its customers, usually as part of its primary business.

Third-party endorsements originated shortly after World War II with retail credit jewelers and credit furniture stores. They took off early in the 1960s when a major oil company decided to enhance the value of its credit card by allowing its use for the purchase of nonrelated merchandise. Since then, third-party endorsements have been growing at a rapid pace.

Currently, they are offered to customers of large book publishers of encyclopedias and card members of oil companies, banks, and airlines as well as to travel and entertainment credit card members. Our credit-oriented society has enabled this business to continue its growth at a rapid pace.

Third-party endorsements started as billing inserts and expanded into catalogs and solo direct-mail pieces. Package inserts and bouncebacks also are being used. The newest medium is cable television. Third-party endorsements will continue to grow, especially if electronic funds transfers become a national or worldwide reality. Wherever there is credit available, there will be third-party endorsements.

The most common type of third-party endorsement involves a manufacturer, a merchandise syndicator, and the endorser who has a customer list. Each of these parties brings assets and liabilities into the marriage. For reasons which will be covered later, neither can or wants to promote products and services via direct-response vehicles without the other two parties.

MANUFACTURER

A manufacturer is usually only in the business of manufacturing. It can develop products for mass marketing and can wholesale them to retailers and others. Its resources are concentrated in the manufacturing and product development processes. Its mass-media advertising is geared toward overall customer acceptance and the selling of its products to wholesalers and retailers.

It is not economically feasible for a large manufacturer to spend advertising dollars in selling directly to the consumer. Its primary asset is the product and its primary liability is the lack of direct-response know-how and the economics of drop-shipping individual pieces of merchandise.

MERCHANDISE SYNDICATOR

A syndicator is like a jobber, buying in bulk and reselling in units. It arranges to buy the merchandise in bulk from the manufacturer. It warehouses the merchandise and, in some instances, repacks it into individual shippable units.

A syndicator is also very knowledgeable in the direct marketing field. It can put a complete direct marketing package together, drop-ship merchandise, bill the endorser's customer, and handle customer returns as well as most customer service inquiries and problems relating to the merchandise.

Its expertise in the field and the ability to do mass distribution of its mailing piece or campaign are its primary assets. Its primary liability is the need for constant financing because it pays in advance not only for the merchandise but also for the development, printing, and mailing of the advertising campaign as well as the warehousing of its merchandise inventory.

ENDORSER

The endorser is the third party to the arrangement and usually is in a different (nondirect marketing) business, such as a bank whose primary business is banking services (checking accounts, loans, etc.). The endorser does direct mail because it is a profitable business to be in. It does not want to take title to the merchandise, and, in fact, may be prevented by law or management policy from doing so.

Endorsers do not warehouse or handle drop-shipments of merchandise. There are retailers who do such endorsements without warehousing and treat them as they would concessions within a store and share in the profits.

The endorser's primary assets are its customers' files and credit facility (prescreened credit customers). Its liability has to do with lack of knowledge in the product purchase, pricing, warehousing, and drop-shipment, mainly because as a result of being in a different primary business it does not want to get involved in another business. The endorser's name is also an asset because the customers trust it and will continue to buy from it. It may be capable of preparing the campaign or may require a special direct-mail campaign developed to maintain the image it would like to project.

As a result of the unwillingness of the manufacturer to sell directly to the consumer and the endorser's inability to do so, the syndicator came into being. There was a need for someone to put all the pieces together to promote the products of major manufacturers successfully. Subsequently, syndicators also got into the import business to further increase their margins and expose the public to products which many Americans couldn't get unless they did extensive traveling overseas. Major syndicators are now also able to get products developed for a specific audience. This is possible because of the substantial involvement with the manufacturer, who is willing to give the syndicator a direct-mail exclusive.

TYPES OF THIRD-PARTY ENDORSEMENTS

Syndications

Syndicated endorsements are the most common of the third-party endorsements and the most advantageous to the endorser.

The syndicator makes an agreement with a manufacturer to become the exclusive direct-mail representative of the manufacturer. The syndicator has very good credit terms with the manufacturer, which may go to the extent of carrying "paper," or the cost of money.

The syndicator selects merchandise with mass appeal that can be taken to many different types of endorsers (credit card companies, oil companies, airline catalogs, retailers, etc.). Currently, mass-appeal merchandise is found primarily in the electronics area, with products such as calculators, stereo systems, and videocassette recorders. This category, however, traditionally has low profit margins. Therefore, a syndicator must be able to sell thousands of units in order to make a profit.

The syndicator develops an insert or other direct-mail piece with general appeal. Usually, with just a plate change, it can print the same piece for several endorsers, thereby reducing its cost over a much larger print run than would be possible if it had to print for just one company.

Wholesaling

Wholesaling works almost like syndication and is very advantageous to the syndicator. The differences are as follows.

1. The endorser shares in the cost of developing the direct-mail campaign but restricts the use of the campaign to its own audience.

2. The endorser pays the syndicator net 30 days and carries the receivables. Therefore, there is no cost of money on the part of the syndicator.

3. The remuneration to the endorser is a much larger percentage of the sale, allowing the endorser to cover the cost of money and also making a substantial profit. The percentage is usually double the amount of the syndication remuneration.

In this situation, the endorser assumes the risks, but the syndicator still warehouses and drop-ships the merchandise.

HOW THIRD-PARTY ENDORSEMENTS WORK

To illustrate how third-party endorsements work, here is a hypothetical case:

The XYZ Company is a very big manufacturer of stereo components. It advertises heavily on television and is well known. XYZ has up to now sold stereos to jobbers and retailers at 55 percent off the suggested list price, minus 10 percent, net 30 days. The basic units are shipped in lots of 20, and speakers in lots of 40. The jobbers usually break down the shipments into more manageable lots and individual sets into four cartons. XYZ's latest stereo is state-of-the-art. The company has put together a specially matched component system which will not be available at retail as a package. XYZ is approached by ML Company, a merchandise syndicator interested in an exclusive arrangement, to sell the product through direct-response advertising.

ML Company makes a contractual agreement with the manufacturer. The system will retail for a minimum of $1000. ML agrees to warehouse, and the manufacturer will pack the system in four individual cartons. ML's cost is based on the same jobber terms (55 percent/10 percent, net 30). ML gives XYZ a letter of credit and asks XYZ to ship five units immediately (four to ML's warehouse and one unit to SOL Company). ML has been in business for 10 years and has complete warehousing, drop-shipping, and customer service capabilities. It services 10 major clients, including SOL Company (a third-party endorser).

ML meets with the direct marketing people of SOL. ML tells SOL that it believes SOL's customers would be receptive to a unique stereo system. SOL's customers are in the upper-income bracket; 90 percent own homes with an average market value of $170,000. They are college-educated, busy executives who do not have time to shop. They are also used to reasonable credit terms and are allowed to take up to 10 months to pay for any merchandise that sells for at least $250.

The stereo system is the best money can buy. It has been packaged in such a manner that it would take months of shopping to be able to put it together at its special price. The stereo will be shipped by truck after the trucking firm makes an appointment with the customer. Returns will be handled in the same manner; the trucker will pick up the system from the customer. This process will give the customer confidence since there will be no hassles should the customer decide to return the stereo.

SOL agrees to promote the stereo system. For its participation, it will get a commission equal to 20 percent of the gross amount of the sale. However, it may retain 12 percent of the sale as a reserve against future credits for returned merchandise. The participation includes the endorsement, carrying the receivables on installments, and guaranteeing the sale to ML. SOL gives

ML a few pointers on the way it sees the promotional piece developed to fit its image with its customers. It asks ML to develop a basic composition of the mailing piece and advertising copy. It gives ML a contract to sign which is subject to approval of the advertising material and an independent testing laboratory's confirmation of all the claims made in the advertising.

ML asks its advertising agency to develop the basic layout, theme, and copy. It takes it to SOL, which will ask for changes until it is satisfied with the presentation. SOL works very closely with ML in the development of the mailing piece, including the photographs to be used in it.

It is decided that they will go with a self-mailer format. The cover will be a very modernistic and futuristic shot of the components floating out of the sky. As you open the self-mailer, the first page will have a letter of endorsement signed by the president of SOL, introducing the stereo system and leading into the basic features and advantages of owning the system. The latter is one of the most important parts of an endorsed promotion. Not only should it be a merchandising letter, it also should bring out the relationship between the customers and the endorser. It should emphasize the convenient monthly terms and the ease of shopping by mail for the merchandise endorsed by the company. The consumer trusts the endorser, and this point must be reinforced constantly so that the customer believes that the endorser is giving its seal of approval (see Figure 48-1).

The next two spreads of the self-mailer contain a full-blown shot of the entire system with callouts pointing to the best features. (Don't be afraid to get technical when describing a stereo system. Consumers are better-educated now. Lack of information about the product may cause you to lose a sale.)

The last inside panel is devoted to the order form and the special purchase terms. (While there are certain legal requirements on installment sales, don't let the order form become a legalistic document. If there is a warranty, don't just bring out the specific legal requirements but also bring out the uniqueness of the warranty in a positive manner. Let it be the last thing the customer reads on the order form. Sometimes this can clinch the sale.)

The outside panel includes individual photographs of all the components, with subparagraphs outlining the state-of-the-art of each component.

ML is given the go-ahead to print and mail. SOL supplies the mailing list in segments mutually agreed on by the parties, and the test is mailed. The orders in this case go to ML's address for the sake of expediency in fulfillment. (In other instances, the orders would go to the endorser mainly for control purposes. Or if you prefer, have an independent service bureau do the order processing. The cost should be charged to the syndicator. You will have better control and better financial reporting.)

ML obtains credit approval from SOL for every order before the merchandise is shipped. This is a guarantee that ML will be paid for the merchandise whether or not SOL gets paid by its customers. It also gives SOL a chance to double-check its customers' prior payment history.

ML computerizes the order and generates shipping labels, which are then forwarded to its warehouse with a manifest. ML's warehouse arranges with the trucking firm to ship the stereo to SOL's customers and sends the appropriate shipping documents with a copy of the manifest back to ML's headquarters. ML prepares the billing on magnetic tape for SOL to bill its customers and code its files with the lastest purchase information and forwards the magnetic tape with its own invoice to SOL.

SOL bills its customers in installments and pays ML according to the terms mutually agreed on. In this case, ML gets 80 percent of the amount billed and charged by SOL's customers. The difference between the 45 percent ML paid the manufacturer (XYZ) and the 80 percent it gets from the third party

The Sol Company
100 Main Street
Anytown, U.S.A.

Dear Sol Member:

Selecting the right stereo system no longer has to be a time-consuming task. As part of our continuing service to you, we have asked XYZ, one of the most respected names in audio equipment, to create a stereo system exclusively for our members. The result is the XYZ Special Stereo System which is being made available to you through this advanced private invitation.

The XYZ Special Stereo System has all the sophisticated features you need to produce truly outstanding stereo sound. It incorporates the latest technology available with perfectly matched speakers to give you the sound you only heard while seated in the best seat at a concert hall. And the system is ready and waiting for you to try it in the privacy of your own home with no obligation to buy.

Selecting the proper components is the difficult part of acquiring a truly outstanding stereo system. The selection of the components has been made by XYZ's audio engineers, the best qualified people to make such a selection. Now, all you have to do is listen to the Special Stereo System in the comfort of your home with no obligation to buy. If you're not completely satisfied with the performance and quality of this stereo system, it will be picked up directly from your home at no cost to you.

If you decide to keep the XYZ Special Stereo System, you can take up to 12 months to pay. To acquire your exclusive stereo for a 30-day risk-free trial, simply fill out and mail the enclosed postage-paid order form today!

Sincerely,

Marge Landrau
President

ML:cd
P.S. For the details of this exclusive stereo, I suggest you review the enclosed brochure now.

Figure 48-1. Sample letter of endorsement.

is its margin. Its 35 percent margin must cover ML's promotional expense, warehousing, drop-shipping, and the cost of handling returns and refurbishing, as well as its profit.

SOL's 20 percent margin basically covers the cost of billing its customers, the cost of carrying the receivables until it receives payment in full from its customers, and any losses for accounts which may go bad during the length of the installment payment plan. SOL has developed a fairly good credit history file on each of its customers. As a result, less than 0.5 percent of the receivables are never paid for.

Merchandise returned for credit or refund is received at ML's warehouse. Depending on the condition of the merchandise, it may be returned to the manufacturer (XYZ), which in turn will refurbish the merchandise. XYZ may charge a refurbishing charge between $30 and $50 per unit to ML. If the merchandise cannot be refurbished, ML may have to sell it at cost to a discounter who may get rid of it through a warehouse sale. ML sometimes also runs its own warehouse sale to sell returned merchandise for slightly above its cost in order to recover the cost as well as make a very small profit. In some instances, the syndicator and the endorser will share refurbishing costs; in other instances, the endorser pays the refurbishing costs and auctions off the returned merchandise.

This hypothetical case applies to almost any advertising medium. The only differences would be in the cost of printing and mailing. In the case of a billing insert (bill stuffer), the endorser pays for the cost of placing the insert into its statement envelope; the syndicator pays for the cost of printing the insert. This also applies to other types of inserts such as package inserts and bouncebacks.

Service-type offers such as insurance policies and credit card registration services are promoted in this matter. However, the traditional syndicator may be replaced by a broker or agent. They also can become two-party endorsements, as in the case of some insurance offers in which the marketing arm of the insurance company, which usually is a division of the company, or an underwriter replaces the syndicator. The basic concept remains the same.

Large mail-order catalog firms use endorsed promotions as an additional benefit for their customers. Promotions are usually for services but are also for unique merchandise offers such as a negative option monogrammed glassware offer in which one glass is shipped each month. Merchandise offers are noncompetitive and are used for merchandise which is not economically feasible for the catalog firm to warehouse and drop-ship.

Banks use third-party endorsements because banking laws and regulations prohibit them from being the legal seller of the merchandise. The syndicator therefore plays a more important role and is the legal seller of the merchandise. Oil companies also are restricted in the selling of nonrelated merchandise. For these endorsers, the syndicator also assumes the state sales tax liability. The endorser collects the sales taxes, but the syndicator remits them to the appropriate states. In some instances, taxes are collected only in states in which the syndicator has a physical presence; in other instances, the endorser collects taxes in states in which it is liable for sales tax collection, but the syndicator still is responsible for remitting to the states.

BENEFITS

There are benefits to all parties involved in endorsements.

Manufacturers gain an additional distribution outlet for their products. They can diversify into other products with minimal risk. Tests of new gadgetry can be done at a much lower cost than if the manufacturer had to expose it to the mass market. The manufacturer's representatives can serve syndicators without the need for staff expansion. The manufacturer can devote time to the primary business: developing and manufacturing products. And finally, there is no need to expand and train staff in the direct marketing field.

A syndicator can mass-market products at substantially lower cost as a result of being able to develop one direct-response campaign for many endorsers. As a result of getting guaranteed orders from the endorser, the risk of collection and extension of credit is eliminated. Syndicators can become self-employed by subcontracting all the work to established firms. The syndicator does not need to establish itself with customers because the endorser has already done this. Therefore, there is no need to develop a customer list. It takes a free ride on the endorser's image and the customers' trust. A syndicator can be one person or a very small operation that subcontracts all its administrative needs.

Endorsers generate profits by using their customers' lists. They add benefits of a nonrelated nature to their credit facility, therefore making their primary business more attractive to their customers. They save on payroll because they do not have to have in-house merchandising talent.

The endorser turns its major asset (its customers' list) into a major profit center. It does not assume unknown risks such as may occur in the warehousing of merchandise. And it has an automatic customer activation program. Card members who may not use their credit cards frequently for regular purchases will be tempted to use them for the purchase of merchandise on installments. If a card member is in the middle of an installment payment plan, the card member is most likely to renew the membership in order not to have to pay for the remaining installments all at once.

Third-party endorsements are easy to implement. All you have to do is find a reputable syndicator who will work with you. However, third-party endorsements are not for everyone. If your list size is under 200,000, most syndicators will not want to work with you unless you can give them an exclusive contract which includes not only all your billing inserts but also all your direct-mail merchandise campaigns for at least 1 year.

You could, however, offer other services such as insurance and credit card registry without the need of a syndicator. When in doubt, ask the experts for advice. They will help you protect one of your most valuable assets: your customers' list.

49
Catalog Marketing

Jo-Von Tucker

*JVT Direct Marketing
and Clambake Celebrations
Orleans, Cape Cod, Mass.*

Prior to 1971 and the Kenton Collection, there were a handful of high-ticket catalogs around, primarily department and specialty store projects. Most notable were the sophisticated books produced at Christmastime by Neiman-Marcus featuring expensive and bizarre "his and hers" specials that were used more to achieve publicity than to reflect sales.

Most department store mail order was used simply to generate store traffic. Very few store catalogs even contained an order form, much less a toll-free number. Tracing sales from mail order in the stores was not deemed worthwhile, and so the retailers never knew for sure how much their floor sales were affected by their direct marketing promotions.

Within the space of a few years, many catalogs directed to both upscale and midscale audiences appeared. An educational process evolved for the mail-order customer. The well-presented, obviously expensively produced catalogs that were suddenly appearing in mailboxes did not fit the "junk mail" syndrome that was prevalent at the time. These books reflected credibility to the consumer, implying by touch and glance a trustworthiness on the part of the owner or company. The customer began to order high-ticket items (porcelain, silk, crystal), with confidence that each would arrive intact and that they would be pleased with the purchase. Credibility was gained through realistic portrayal of the merchandise as well as a certain standardizing of the key elements that go into the physical presentation, such as coated paper stocks and plus-covers. Additionally, customers learned to accept catalog shorthand techniques such as the placement of postage and handling charges in parentheses following the item price.

THE TARGET AUDIENCE

Marketing Research for Customer Identification

The most successful catalog firms have learned the importance of identifying the customer. Through selected and intensive marketing research we have access to information that tells us who our customers are, where they live, their leisure activities, their available discretionary income, and many other pertinent facts. Application of this resource helps direct our promotional efforts to best appeal to these customers' needs and interests.

Methods of Marketing Research for Catalogers

Four basic categories are used to obtain customer profiles and reaction. The first—requesting information on the catalog order form—is the most obvious opportunity yet the least frequently used. The catalog serves as a free carrier for a survey to help define customer demographics and psychographics. In asking for the customer's time to relay this information, the cataloger should consider extending the courtesy of prepaying the postage on the envelope. A sound system for compiling the research information from the order form should be planned carefully before you consider using this technique. Valuable data have been lost because of oversights in programming.

Shopping Center Intercepts.   When planned and conducted by a professional research team, these have proved to be valid information-gathering projects. The first rule for shopping center intercepts is to qualify the prospective interviewee as a mail-order customer. An opportunity then exists for a one-on-one reaction measurement. Consumers typically are quizzed on their response to existing catalogs within the market (usually competitive in nature with the firm conducting the study), desirability of merchandise offerings, reaction to graphics and presentation, and even likes and dislikes regarding prospective names or titles for proposed catalogs.

Focus Studies.   These are used extensively by many catalogers. A small group of customers is brought together to give reactions to new format proposals, for examination of actual merchandise, and for comparison studies of competitive books. As with shopping center intercepts, established, experienced marketing help should be used to conduct these sessions. Results can be heavily weighted by the interviewer's technique, and so a distaff direction is important in this process.

Telephone Survey of Customers.   This is an economical measurement that produces immediate input. The format for such calls is flexible, but it is wise to keep such interviews short in order to avoid taking too much of the customer's time. Questions may be structured to provide data on a recently received catalog mailing.

MARKETING CONCLUSIONS

Compiled information from these and other research methods has painted a portrait of the upscale catalog customer. Here is a composite of the customer profile.

1. *Age bracket:* 35 to 55 years.

2. *Sex:* Eighty-five percent of responders are women, with the exception of house lists for firms like American Express and The Sharper Image.

3. *Marital status:* Fifty percent of the female customers are married, and 50 percent are unmarried (single, divorced, or widowed).

4. *Employment status:* Seventy percent of responders are employed outside the home.

5. *Combined family income:* $50,000 annually.

6. *Discretionary income:* Sixty percent of customers represent a two-income family.

7. *Property status:* Sixty-five percent are homeowners.

8. *Charge account holders:* Average 3.2 per customer (excluding gasoline credit cards). Most prominent are MasterCard, Visa, American Express, and department or specialty store accounts.

9. *Mail-order frequency:* 5.1 times per year per customer. Expressed positive response when queried about desirability of ordering through the mail more frequently.

10. *Average dollar order:* $60 to $100.

11. *Education:* Average 3.2 years of college or university. The married customer reflects a lower educational level than the unmarried.

Narrative Vignette of the Upscale Catalog Customer

Since 85 percent of the responders were women, this narrative is worded to reflect that definition of sex. The upscale mail-order customer is referred to in the feminine gender here, with no reverse chauvinism intended.

A busy, involved lifestyle is a key factor in the generic appeal of mail order for this customer. Convenience is listed most often as the primary motivating factor in making a mail-order purchase. Secondarily, desirability of merchandise (including exclusivity) prompts action to order. Other determining factors which lead to customer conversion are

1. Credibility of catalog name

2. Catalog presentation (graphics and quality reproduction)

3. Succinct, informative copy

4. Psychological use of color

5. Timing of mailing (seasonality)

6. Previous mail-order fulfillment experience

Price of goods is rarely the determining factor. The customer has a small amount of leisure time and prefers other activities to fill that time than journeying to a store to make a purchase.

Typical leisure activities for the customer are entertaining at home; attending social functions; movies; reading; sports participation (tennis, golf, racquetball, skiing, swimming); sports attendance (professional and college football games, tennis matches); volunteer work for hospitals, charities, and sororities; travel (for business and for recreation or holiday); community and civic involvement (Scouts, schools, PTA, political party affiliation); family outings; exercise and dance classes; and educational courses (foreign languages, gourmet cooking, Yoga, creative writing, etc.).

The customer is brand-aware and has a closet filled with ready-to-wear garments bearing names like Blass, Klein, and Beene. Additionally, a representation of higher couture names will be there. She avoids fabric blends in her wardrobe in favor of pure contents like silk, wool, and cotton. She carries leather bags and wears leather shoes; vinyl and polyester do not figure in her wardrobe or her vocabulary.

The look of her home is important to her. She wants pretty things surrounding her and will select such merchandise impulsively, without planned purchase action. This tendency reflects one of the major reasons for the success of high-ticket catalogs.

The typical mail-order customer buys items for gift-giving occasions an average of eight times per year exclusive of Christmas shopping. These occasions include birthdays, anniversaries, weddings, graduations, baby showers, Valentine's Day, Mother's Day, Father's Day, Easter, Halloween, etc. One out of two mail-order purchases from high-ticket catalogs is a gift selection. The convenience factor of catalog shopping figures prominently in gift purchases.

Listen to Your Customer

In a recent focus study, mail-order customers reflected an amazing level of sophistication in terms of appreciation for quality catalog format and presentation. They were harshly critical of cheaper papers and expressed dislike of low-quality separations and printing. They demonstrated a preference for catalogs with plus-covers as opposed to self-covers and recognized changes in format, fashion trends, and new directions. Subtle deviations from established catalog companies were noticed and commented on.

LIST SELECTION

Reaching the potential customer ranks high on the priority list of catalog objectives. While a house list produces many percentage points better for any mailer, most catalogers must rely on rented lists to get the total mailing quantity high enough to amortize creative and production costs.

With the marketing research information previously covered, list selections for cold tests should be made by incorporating these data along with mail-order buying history. Lists segmented according to previous mail-order purchasing generally tend to produce better for catalog firms. Further segmentation can be achieved by targeting according to dollar select (average dollar order) or by recency and frequency of mail-order purchases. List companies provide information cards for each representation which contain marketing statistics and history of performance. Demographics, geographics, psychographics, and lifestyle segmentation are all criteria for selection. The overall universe (total number of names available) may help determine both the size of the test and its roll-out potential.

It is important to be able to track the performance of each test list. The code listed on the mailing label will key the sales information to the correct test list, and proper computer programming will record pertinent response data. Control or house information should be monitored and evaluated continually, particularly as decisions are made to retest a list.

Experience within a market segment should be factored when you select a list broker or list management firm. A solid working knowledge of the upscale market is a prerequisite for high-ticket catalog responsibility. It is suggested that credentials and track record be checked thoroughly before you assign list selection or list management to any firm. Do not hesitate to place calls to existing and former clients to verify credentials. Professional list companies should have no qualms about presenting references.

Building a house list requires a vast investment of both time and money, and catalogers must guard carefully against overexposure. Competition in the mailbox is fierce with the recent explosion of mail-order catalogs, and unfortunately, catalogers are using the same available rental lists over and over again. The average upscale mail-order customer now receives seven catalogs per week in the mailbox. A policy decision to rent a house list only to noncompetitive catalogs therefore seems wise. Exchange of lists is a common practice among noncompeting catalogers, but it is highly recommended that the merge-purge technique be applied to clean all mailings and avoid duplicate names.

DEVELOPING A NICHE IN THE MARKETPLACE

A catalog needs a strong reason for being considered above its competition. The more unique the merchandise offering and the more outstanding the physical presentation, the better the reception by the customer. Credibility and desirability must be instantaneous on receipt and perusal.

The Ultimate Concern of Catalogers

Establishing a niche in the marketplace of catalogs can be accomplished best by answering the needs and requirements of prospective customers. The philosophy to guide all formative and directive decisions toward this objective is one of overall consideration of the consumer. A catalog should be produced with the customer in mind at every step, from point-of-view concept through print production. Bottom-line sales will reflect whether all considerations are working, but interim guidelines can be used as checkpoints along the way.

Exclusivity of Merchandise

An important way to stimulate a customer's interest is to offer merchandise that is not available in local department stores or other catalogs. Frequently this can be achieved through packaging (a unique combination of items). Changing a color or fabric can give an old product new life, and personalizing or monogramming can set an item apart from competitive offerings.

Working with vendors and manufacturers to provide exclusives on products will help establish an identity for a catalog. It is difficult to get a vendor's attention in this matter unless catalog quantities are large enough to promise large orders. To begin with, newer catalogs will be forced to seek out cooperative manufacturers for the development of exclusive items. As success builds and reputation grows, unusual products will be submitted for consideration, and catalog exclusives will be offered. Be patient in building a rapport with vendors, and in the meantime, devote more time to seeking out new items in showrooms and markets. Look for merchandise that hasn't appeared in other catalogs and check to be sure that the projected quantity is available.

A Unique Catalog Presentation

As the customer's level of sophistication regarding catalogs has risen, so has consumer demand for quality presentation. On any given day, multiple catalogs may appear in the mailbox of a mail-order customer. The overall image projected by the book in the hand will determine which catalog gets the attention. Format, physical size, color reproduction, and quality-feel figure prominently in the impact or first credibility impression. Name awareness and merchandise desirability complete the motivation to purchase.

Credibility of Image

Gain the customer's trust by presenting one face: quality. To be perceived as reputable, a catalog must be presented factually, with an emphasis on color fidelity. Merchandise match is imperative, with the colors shown in the book totally representative of the products. It is unacceptable to the customer to receive an item in a color different from the color that was selected from a catalog depiction.

Ultimate consideration of the customer should guide descriptive copy technique as well. It is unwise to use abstract words to describe colors and fabrics. Primary colors are easily understood, but subtle deviations of shades or pastels should be tagged as specifically as possible. For instance, "mauve" is more difficult to visualize than "dusty lavender"; "heather" can range from pinks to greens and includes any shade in between.

BUILDING A PAPER STORE

A catalog is a paper store, a measurable medium for advertising items for sale on a one-to-one direct-response level. Careful consideration should be given to the direction of building this paper store, emphasizing to the customer the service, choices, and quality offered. The effect is even more concentrated and intensive than that of a retail display center. It has less time to work and therefore must be effective at first glance.

Merchandise Selection

The paper store, or catalog, is created around the products that will be offered for sale. Certain parameters should be used to qualify merchandise for inclusion. Each cataloger should develop a personalized checklist that reflects the desired niche. A general set of guidelines could include the following questions.

1. Is the item unique by description of features?
2. Is the basic design good?
3. Does it fill a need or desire?
4. Is the price point fair and competitive?
5. Will returns be high? If so, avoid grief and pass to another product.
6. Are there inherent fit problems? If the answer is yes, pass it.
7. Can the items be shown effectively by photography?
8. Has this merchandise been around too much in other catalogs?
9. Would it probably be received well as a gift?
10. Would I buy it for myself or for someone in my family or circle of friends?

Developing Exclusive Packaging

It is strongly recommended that exclusivity be sought as much as possible when you select items for a catalog. This provides the customer with an additional reason to buy through the mail. Merchandise that is readily available through retail stores has less reason to appear in a catalog.

Packaging can be defined in two ways: the physical presentation of a product (i.e., the gift box or wrap), and the method of combining two or more products into a unique set or offering. Personalized stationery can be expanded from the basic letter set to all correspondence needs. The customer will appreciate note cards, postal cards, formal thank you notes, invitations, RSVP cards, and tablets with envelopes all in the same graphic format with personalization—a complete line of stationery needs that presents one personal image or statement.

Distaff Editing

Most catalog merchants, or buyers, are too emotionally involved in their own selection of products to be wholly trusted with the responsibility of final editing.

Rather than make a decisive choice between two similar items, buyers tend to want both pieces in the catalog.

Stanley Marcus, chairman emeritus of Neiman-Marcus, has been quoted as saying that mail order works because it is a preedited selection of merchandise. Much of the decision factor has been removed, making a purchase decision easier on the customer. There are no racks of dresses for a customer to flip through, requiring the elimination of perhaps fifty to get down to a choice of one or two. In a catalog, that preliminary editing has been done already.

Too many choices within a single category may confuse the customer and remove the motivation to buy. If a customer wants a set of coffee mugs, it is usually sufficient to offer one set or at most two within the catalog. If the set you show makes a statement about your buying selectivity and authority, if it meets the criteria of good design, fair price, uniqueness, etc., the prospect will feel comfortable selecting from your offering.

When merchandise is edited thoughtfully, it enhances your positioning as an authority. It also gives the people charged with production of the catalog a better opportunity for dramatic display. In a typical high-ticket catalog of 32 pages plus cover, an ideal maximum number of products would be 120 to 140. Higher density would require too many small depictions, eliminating the marketing flexibility of showing the merchandise to its best advantage.

If mail-order experience is well represented within the creative staff or freelance catalog production, final decisions on merchandise selection can be guided by their input. While a buyer may be emotionally close to the products being considered, the creative staff does not have that built-in bias. At merchandise presentation, reactions by these people should be heeded. If they stress the strong desirability of one item or their intense dislike (or even apathetic response) toward another, it is highly likely that your customers may react the same way. Don't take up valuable selling space in your catalog just to present merchandise that may be considered less than great.

Increasing the Average Order

In addition to the exclusivity factor, packaging can increase the average catalog order. Adding a special wicker carrier for a product will enhance the offering as a gift and bring the price up. Putting together a wire whisk with a special cookbook on sauces combines two inexpensive items into one nice sale.

These are logical offerings to the customer and should make the merchandise more attractive while adding to the bottom line of your catalog sales. A set of table napkins is an ordinary kind of gift selection; combined with a hard-to-find table runner that matches, it becomes an outstanding gift, even for oneself.

Another method for increasing the average order is to fill the catalog pages on either side of the order form with impulse items. Products with relatively low price points can stand alone as interesting offers. These items tend to be considered as "add-ons." As an order form is being filled out, a product from one of the facing pages also may be picked up.

The order form itself provides another opportunity for displaying impulse items. The products selected to appear on the order form should be unusual or, at the other extreme, very basic. Be sure that they can be understood easily in black and white if your order form is in one color and that the rougher textured paper generally used will not hurt the reproduction. Contents such as stainless steel, silver, plastic, and ceramic are well suited to black-and-white depiction.

Conceptualizing the Catalog

A successful catalog must have a point of view, a personality statement made by the selection of merchandise, the physical presentation of the book, and the quality and service offered. It requires up-front thinking time to define that direction and to establish point of view in presentation. Allow ample thinking time to idealize the objective and visualize the various solutions.

To begin the process, review all the available marketing information about the customer. Familiarize yourself thoroughly with the consumer's needs, lifestyle, and mail-order shopping habits. Review your competitors and learn their point of view. Then study the merchandise to be offered, seeking a common level of quality and depth of categories of products.

After a level of comfort has been attained with each of the foundation steps listed above, begin by writing notes on a legal pad or tablet. List organizational notes at first and then ideas.

Ideas tend to grow and to feed on each other. A creative approach to an objective can result in the generation of a wealth of thoughts. These thoughts become ideas, and then they can be fleshed out or added to.

As the ideas and thoughts crystallize on paper, begin to think in terms of rough thumbnail sketches. It is not necessary to be an artist to translate ideas successfully into small rough sketches. Notes written beside the thumbnails will help to capture random details of thought that may add a strong dimension to the idea.

Themes

If you are conceptualizing a lingerie catalog, you may see the entire merchandise offering shown out of context (that is, out of the bedroom or dressing room). Perhaps you visualize it photographed in a beach setting at sundown. Jot your ideas down and rough in your thumbnail sketch of the physical format. Flesh out your thumbnails with additional details, such as using very soft filtration in photography to stress the softness of the subject matter. If you are thinking of sunset colors reflecting on water as a background, note it on your pad.

You'll find that the process of conceptualizing a catalog becomes easier if you allow your mind to open up to new thoughts. Be receptive to imagination and let creative ideas flow to your paper. The pen on paper at this point is there merely to translate thoughts into a more comprehensive way of storing and building. If you are more comfortable with words than with sketches, confine yourself to notes instead of rough drawings. Do not try to design the catalog unless you are an accomplished graphic designer. Just capture your thoughts and build them into ideas. When you are satisfied with your collection of ideas, turn them over to the catalog designer. Communicate your wishes for direction and give input to establish your point of view.

Themes can give a logic to the presentation of merchandise and can be used to establish your own catalog identity. A lingerie catalog photographed out of context on a beach is a theme in itself. An unexpected treatment of expected merchandise usually is received very well by the customer and is a way of marketing the merchandise and adding an element of entertainment.

Seasonal themes are used widely both for holiday presentation and for time of the year offerings. Some Christmas catalogs drop in late August and early September in order to allow a long enough life span. Since that is early in the year to ask customers to think of Christmas shopping, it is important that a strong holiday theme be emphasized in presentation. Psychologically, we would like the customer to pull our catalog out of the mailbox and hear Christmas chimes and smell roasted turkey. Chances are that there are no chestnuts roasting over a crackling fire; more likely, when the book is received, there are hot dogs roasting in the backyard. Christmas shopping is hard to consider when the sounds you hear are not sleigh bells but splashing from the swimming pool.

While the late summer heat lingers on, attempt to create a feeling of crisp, cool holiday atmosphere. A Christmas theme can grow from studio-created snow sets, fireplaces, Christmas trees, candy canes, and candlelight. Saint Nick can backdrop his way through 60 pages or more, and ornaments can twinkle and glitter to set off your merchandise as if it were displayed in a beautifully wrapped package.

Entertainment for the Customer.   A theme should never detract from the presentation of the merchandise but should enhance it. There is a certain amount of the child in all of us, including our customers. That childlike appreciation of being entertained and charmed can be appealed to by the catalog presentation. Customers enjoy using their imagination and should be given the opportunity to do so. This is why items shown out of context are found to be entertaining.

Random examples of subtle entertainment from some previously produced catalogs include a gold and diamond ring photographed on an antique cannonball; ruby earrings shown in closeup on a giant elephant ear leaf; a brass ashtray in the shape of a foot, shot in the sand; a pearl necklace photographed draped on the foot of a Greek statue; a crystal candlestick placed in a field of bluebonnets; a man's necktie draped over a nude woman's shoulder (close-cropped, of course); and a diamond goldfish pin shot in a glass of champagne.

It is not necessary to entertain totally out of context. Amusing and charming themes can be developed within the context of the product. For example, a tiny brass sculptured frog, a miniature collectible, was photographed on a real lily pad on a pond; a crystal apple paperweight was shot on a bed of shiny, red Delicious apples; an ivory hand-painted strawberry necklace was placed on a solid field of dewy fresh strawberries; coffee mugs were placed on piles of coffee beans, etc.

Merchandise presented for the customer's consideration in an interesting way, stimulating imagination and making the products more desirable, represents entertainment through a catalog. It requires thought and concept and consideration of the customer. It demands innovation and is limited only by your creative resources. Your customers will appreciate the creativity and thoughtfulness behind the presentation.

Marketing the Merchandise. The primary objective of any mail-order catalog is to sell merchandise. In conceptualizing the most effective way to present the merchandise to the customer, let common sense be your guide. Catalogs are a pictorial medium for selling, and interest must be obtained on behalf of the product by the photographic depiction. Entertainment, themes, setting, and backdrops must frame the item, not compete with it.

Pagination. The planning process of assigning each item of merchandise to a spread in the catalog is called pagination. Sometimes pagination is done by the buying staff. But more frequently and usually more effectively, it is assigned to the creative team, who have more of a distaff view of the merchandise and are less attached emotionally.

Pagination can be used to group items by special-interest category, tie in a theme, or logically place one product beside another. Many times the buying staff makes their merchandise selection with a specific theme in mind. However, there are times when you are confronted with over 100 separate items presented for inclusion in a catalog with no definitive direction for their grouping. In these cases, the process of pagination begins when the merchandise is viewed by the creative staff, a time in the overall production schedule called merchandise presentation or line closing.

Products may be grouped by seasonality, color of the merchandise, category, or logic of use. It is important to remember in paginating as well as in design that the customer views catalogs spread by spread, with a facing two-page spread standing alone as a visual unit. The only exception to this rule would be pages that are separated by the order form. They should be presented as single-page concepts since they are set apart physically by the bound-in order form.

If a theme such as home entertainment is formulated for a spread, it should be explained to the customer with a headline, and the pagination should include logical products. Buffet organizers, patio dresses, brightly colored plastic dishes, garden candles, pool umbrellas, and serving dishes are naturals for informal entertaining. This kind of pagination presents items in an interesting way and also suggests actual uses.

Realization and Catalog Production

Mail-order catalogs are an expensive medium for advertising and must be cost-effective. Adherence to a production schedule and budget will prevent costly extras on the bottom line, and submitting accurate specifications to production suppliers is imperative in establishing the schedule and budget.

Preparation of Specifications. In order to obtain realistic bids for catalog printing and color separations, a set of specific requirements on the job must be submitted to suppliers. These specifications always should be in written form, preferably typed, never verbal instructions by telephone. When layouts for the catalog have been approved, photocopies should be sent to the separator for confirmation of the bid. It is possible to have more or fewer random focus enlargements in a book than originally anticipated, and this factor can alter the job estimate drastically.

Specifications for the printer should include the following:

1. Date of submission
2. Date of requested estimate to be received
3. Name of client
4. Title of catalog
5. Requested press date
6. Begin mail drop date and complete mail drop date
7. Date of remail drop if required
8. Quantity, including acceptable over and under run
9. Bind-in order form information
10. Furnished film information
11. Press configuration requested (sixteen- or thirty-two-page form)
12. Request for press imposition running dummy
13. Trim size of catalog
14. Number of pages (indicate plus cover when required)
15. Request breakout of charges separately
16. Mailing and label information (cost per request qualified quantity estimate; type of label)
17. Ink coverage and expected density maximum
18. Paper specifications by text and cover categories; specify weight and brand; if equivalent paper is acceptable, so state
19. Special requirements, e.g., use of fifth unit for color or varnish
20. Whether final set of chromalins is required
21. A copy of a previous issue

On approval of the completed layout, submit a photocopied set to the printing representative to avoid costly surprises.

Working closely with the representatives from the separator and printer will facilitate the production of the catalog. Frequently, this results in time-and money-saving ideas that add up to a better finished product.

A good policy is to submit your specifications to three printers and two separators. Comparative bid study is healthy and educational, although it is not recommended that you assign a contract strictly on the basis of the lowest estimate. Be sure that you are comparing apples to apples and place a critical eye on previous samples for quality.

The Production Schedule. About 120 days are required to produce a top-quality 36-page catalog. While this type of schedule is somewhat formulated, it does allow sufficient but not excessive time for each of the vital elements in catalog production.

Day 1	Merchandise presentation to creative
Day 2	Pagination
Day 3	Pagination approval
Day 4	Begin layouts
Day 18	Layout approval
Day 19	Production meeting with photography studio
Day 20	Begin photography and copy
Day 50	Photography and copy approval
Day 51	Begin mechanical art
Day 62	Mechanical art approval
Day 65	Final mechanical art changes incorporated
Day 66	Turnover to color separator
Day 96	Press proofs (ink on paper)
Day 105	Final cromalin proofs
Day 114	Film to printer
Day 120	Press make-ready

The Budget. To study a catalog budget is to take a look at harsh reality. Talent is expensive, and paper and printing are equally costly. The monies allocated for catalog production never should be spent lightly. Rely on support people with a proven track record of experience in catalog marketing. Do your delegating to professionals who will watch after the job as if it were their own money being spent.

The budget for catalog and order form production should include estimates for the following, each broken out:

1. Creative design and photo art direction
2. Copywriting
3. Photography
   a. Still life
   b. Fashion
   c. Film and processing
   d. Stylist, hair and makeup, and presser
   e. Props and rentals
   f. Models
4. Photo retouching
5. Typography and positioning of photostats
6. Stripped assemblies
7. Illustration
8. Mechanical art

9. Supervision of color separations
10. Press make-ready supervision
11. Freight and deliveries
12. Air fare and per diem
13. Miscellaneous (phone calls and photocopies)
14. Color separations and proofing
15. Order form printing and paper
16. Printing of catalogs
17. Paper stock for catalogs
18. Mailing charges
19. Postage
20. List rental (including merge and purge)
21. Label charges and lettershop
22. Binding of order form

TESTING

Concepts may be tested, products can be tried out, and graphic techniques can be pitted one against another. However, this is an expensive educational process. In order to change a four-color process image, you must be prepared to spend additional dollars. Simple copy changes are less expensive unless you make changes in an area of reverse copy, and this involves all four plates being remade.

Good graphics sell better than bad graphics. Why not put your best foot forward and present the merchandise up front in the most effective way. Even low-end catalogs should strive to improve their presentation.

Testing has proved that remails to the house list work effectively in spurring response, particularly at the Christmas mailing time. A new cover will help, and the amortized cost of production is reasonable.

Through tests we also have learned that an outside mailing wrap around the cover of a catalog is not well received by the upscale customer. While mailing wraps are acceptable for lower-end books, a high-ticket catalog loses credibility when a wrapper is used. This is true even of wraps that are well designed and tasteful in appearance. Don't waste your money on a technique that already has been discarded by many knowledgeable upscale catalog marketers.

CREATIVE TECHNIQUES

You'll find the most flexibility at your disposal in this segment of the total production. Don't copy someone else's format or techniques. Innovate in order to achieve your own image; imaginate to establish your catalog's credibility. Although catalogers work in a two-dimension medium, there are ways to set each catalog apart. Technique almost becomes a signature; presentation of your paper store is yours to develop, polish, and refine until it shines like a jewel and makes the right statement to the customer.

Innovation and imagination are the keys to producing a unique catalog presentation. The look and feel of the book will state your point of view and establish your image and credibility in the customer's mind. A catalog that obviously looks as if time, attention, and caring were devoted to producing it infers that the customer's order will be treated the same way. The perception of being a trustworthy mail-order firm results in sales and repeat customers. The orders must be fulfilled promptly and accurately, and the products should be received exactly as they are depicted in the catalog. Customer service must be professional, reliable, and consistently good.

Special techniques to set your catalog apart require creativity and vision and a lot of up-front work. You are entitled to your own look, your catalog's identity. Insist on it from your creative sources, whether they are in-house, freelance, or an outside studio. Do not accept a graphic format that is merely the signature of a certain catalog designer or a knock-off of someone else's image. When you contract for catalog design, you are paying for creativity; be sure that you get it.

Catalog Design and Formats

While it is not necessary to reinvent the wheel each time a catalog is produced, it is highly recommended that catalogers be aware of the fact that design can be updated and improved on. There is no state of the art that remains consistent for catalog design, which is continually changing and becoming more dramatic. Among the flood of catalogs currently being received by the mail-order customer, more and more of these books look alike.

The Two-Page Visual Spread. As was mentioned before, a customer perceives a catalog in two-page visual units. A spread should be designed with this in mind. The best way to approach it is to visualize the two pages as one complete unit, almost like a blank canvas in front of a painter. You also can think of the spread as space in a display case or window, since a store window is seen as a whole rather than in small sections.

Consider the merchandise to be marketed as single elements that must work together on the spread. Each must be given its proper positioning and best display opportunity. Think of the products and their use rather than zeroing in on an item because it has an interesting shape.

Combining the elements on the spread in layout form begins the process of establishing the format. The design format should not be so rigid that every spread looks exactly the same. Allow for some flexibility or you risk having your catalog look boring.

Pacing. By varying the spreads with design format, you can control to a degree the physical speed with which a customer goes through your book. Achieving this control is called pacing, and it can be used to encourage the consumer to linger in certain areas of your catalog presentation. If the book is essentially light in feeling with lots of white space and light background colors, try varying the presentation by placing two or more spreads through the catalog to achieve a heavy visual impact. They can be bleed photos (running off the page top, bottom, and sides) or high-density backgrounds that depict a richness in color saturation.

Another design technique to achieve pacing involves using the entire spread for one shot of merchandise. You must be sure that nothing will get lost in a group shot if this idea is considered. A basic rule is to have merchandise for the grouping that is of a similar size scale.

A crossover (or full-bleed spread) shot must be controlled carefully for quality reproduction at press make-ready. Be sure that the pages, even if run on different forms, are lined up next to each other before you approve a sheet for color. An imbalance of ink on one side can result in an obvious break between the pages, destroying the objective of drama and the believability of the catalog. There is enough control on the press to be able to balance the crossovers effectively. But it is unwise to design a crossover that breaks an intricate pattern in the middle or one that splits the picture down the middle of a model's face because of slight variability in binding.

Eye Movement Direction. The eyes of the customer can be led gently around the visual spread by the design of the elements and directional use of the merchandise or models. Since the left-hand page is weaker on first impact than the right-hand page, it is important to make that page work harder. A large photograph on the extreme left side will gain the customer's attention. If the depiction is a fashion shot, the model's physical attitude or pose can direct the customer from this shot into the adjacent one. The model's eyes should be looking back into the spread, not off the page.

Placement of the other elements on the spread should nudge the customer's eyes gently from one to the next so that everything is perceived at a glance. Further impact can be obtained with dramatic lighting or display to slow the physical act of leaving the spread and moving on to the following one.

The Use of White Space. A portrait is seen better when framed, and a merchandise depiction is cleaner and more understandable when framed by white space. In addition to adding to the impact of a color shot, white space should be used generously to tie together all the diverse elements in a spread. White space provides a relief to the customer's eye, a respite from the richness of multiple items shown on strong backgrounds. Don't hesitate to give your customer this break.

Many merchants object to leaving white space on a spread; they assume that valuable selling space is being lost. There are no definite results that lend authenticity to their theory, and so you must choose your own direction on the basis of your philosophy of catalog marketing. Before you opt for a crammed, busy format, examine the success of catalogs whose look is more open and clean.

The Use of Themes. Entertainment is an important ingredient in catalog marketing. A theme can be woven throughout the book by combining your merchandise with interesting photographic backgrounds and appropriate props and accessories. Themes can serve to humanize a catalog as well as to entertain.

In the G. Willikers 1981 toy catalog for the Singer Corporation, a new star made her debut. She was a small, black, fuzzy kitten with charming white whiskers and startled golden eyes. We promptly named her Eartha Kitty, and her pictures are found throughout the catalog, scaling a set of building blocks here, napping beside a pajama bag there. She peeps from a magic hat and plays chess with a little boy. Eartha was added to the book to soften the hard sell of toys, and the customers loved her. While the kitten was well received as an entertaining element of this catalog, we had to abandon plans to use her talent in subsequent books. She grew up too quickly and became a big, ordinary cat without the appeal of her previous stage.

Positioning.   Positioning the catalog to the customer can help in determining a theme. If your catalog is aimed at active sports enthusiasts, your positioning should be perceived as that of an authority on sporting activities and related merchandise. It is better to photograph on tennis courts and golf courses, showing the models involved and having fun, than to stand the figures like fashion sticks in front of a no-seam. Be sure to check the details, such as how the model holds a tennis racket. If you are shooting a chess game as a still life, have a knowledgeable chess player set up the board.

Editorial Content within a Catalog.   The use of some editorial copy content can achieve several points. It can help establish you as an authority on the merchandise. Editorials also can be entertaining and educational for the customer. Used discriminately, editorials can enhance the desirability of the products.

Bill Nicolai's Early Winters Catalog celebrated its tenth anniversary in 1982 with an issue that contained 32 pages (of a 132-page catalog) of editorial content on nature, the animal world, and exotic places such as Africa and the Himalayas. Well-presented editorial copy enforced this catalog's authenticity. The content was intensely interesting and almost like a present. While this issue of Early Winters was created especially to celebrate an anniversary, the ambience of nature and the outdoors became entwined with positioning for merchandising authority.

The 100 pages of merchandise offerings further support the credibility of this outdoor equipment catalog. The products are shown in believable outdoor locations, and the models are people who look like they spend their leisure time hiking, camping out, trekking, participating in white water trips, etc.

Designing with Typography, Borders, and Silhouettes.   A careful and tasteful use of available graphic elements can add further identity to a catalog as well as tie a spread together. Borders (straight ruled lines of any desired thickness) and decorative borders frequently are used to enclose photos individually or all the way across a spread, uniting the whole presentation of copy and photography. They also can be designed to work physically as a unit with headline treatments. Most catalogs have so many items that the use of borders becomes one element too many. Unless a limited number of products are shown, it is better to present them in the most straightforward manner graphically, forgoing the use of decorative borders or other visual gimmicks.

Borders never should be added after the fact. If they are to be considered at all, they should be a basic part of the design concept. Borders that will be run in color should be simplified as much as possible, avoiding any registration problems that may occur in printing. A clean, thin black rule can crisp up a photo with a very light background, but rules of this kind should be used consistently if at all.

Typographic treatment is another vital design element, one that should be planned as the catalog layout is created. Since copy and type are a sustaining part of the overall format, it is wise to limit the number of typefaces within a catalog. The headline treatment should be one size and face, and the body copy should be specified in one size and face. It is acceptable to vary the body copy with boldface or italic for lead-ins or price points, but these should be within the same typeface selected for the body copy. Too many different typefaces and sizes will present a jumbled appearance and draw the customer's attention away from the primary selling tool: the photograph.

If headlines are considered, they should explain the presentation. If they are not necessary, eliminate them to simplify the spread. The typographic treatment of headlines should be consistent throughout, whether you opt for serif, sans serif, all caps, boldface, italic, script, or calligraphy. Headlines are like an announcement. Keep them informative and entertaining in both content and presentation.

In addition to the use of silhouettes, photos may be shown in circles to vary the design, or they may be partially silhouetted. A photograph can be square-finished on three sides, for instance, and have the item outlined just at the bottom. Or the color-butting-color technique can be considered, where a color shot fits directly into another color shot. Both silhouettes and color-butting-color techniques are interesting design options, but they increase the cost of your already expensive color separation process. Have your engraver give you a laundry list of extra charges for these requirements so that you'll know what additional charges may be incurred.

Mechanical Tints.   These represent the most misused application of color in catalog design. By definition, they involve the use of a tint of color created by combining screens of the process colors. Found usually in the lower-end catalogs, they appear in upscale books as well. The use or misuse of mechanical tints in catalog design tends to cheapen the overall perception and presentation. The reason is simple: The eye functions like the lens of a camera. When color is seen, all four of the color process spectra are perceived in varying degrees of density. In mechanical tints, an even screen of one or more colors is applied. In other words, mechanical tints are colors created falsely, not naturally to the eye, and are perceived as unbelievable. The whiteness of the paper should be considered as the cleanest frame available for copy and photography.

A Nondemocratic Merchandise Display.   The most interesting way to present items to the customer is to vary the sizes of depiction. Little square boxes of equal size presented all the way through a catalog are boring.

Do not be afraid to make a statement about a product by giving it more space Tell the customer that it is unique, exclusive, a fabulous design, or a great value by showing it importantly. Let it work for you by slowing the readers' action as they go through the book. Use it as a punctuation mark on your visual display: a comma at the very least, or more desirably, a semicolon or exclamation mark.

There is no established rule that says you must be democratic in the treatment of graphic display. Merchants and buyers always express a wish for everything to be large on the page, but it is difficult to accomplish this with multiple items and lots of descriptive copy to work with. Something must give. Working creatively with layout to determine space allocation will give you the flexibility needed to come up with a solution, making some items a feature or minifeature and giving smaller space to others that don't require as much space to sell.

Grid Design.   Many catalogs present a format by grid design. As the name implies, the layout is accomplished by taking the page or spread and dividing it equally on a mathematical basis for merchandise display. It is as democratic and uncreative as you can get with graphic design. As a matter of fact, grid design could be done equally well by a draftsperson; you don't really need a designer to set out equal square boxes. A computer can produce your catalog layouts in grid design, but you'll have a book that just lies there instead of one that is emotional and persuasive.

Design to Avoid Problems on Press.   Ask your printer to provide you with a press imposition dummy and be sure that your designer has this information before beginning the layout. Technical problems can be avoided by knowing the page sequence on press. Large, heavy blocks of density followed by a light use of ink may result in a condition called ghosting. The heavy requirement of ink on press in a strategic area will not give the press a chance to recover and equalize quickly enough for smooth ink application immediately behind it. The imposition dummy will show your designer where to avoid these situations. Very few surprises in catalog production turn out to be good ones. Usually they are disappointments that cost a lot of money.

Physical Format Sizes.   Economically, catalog sizes are dictated by press requirements. Most people elect to produce a catalog that best fits the presses, realizing the maximum efficiency of manufacturing for both printing and paper. Traditionally, the most economical catalog size for web printing has been 8⅜ inches wide by 10⅞ inches deep, with 32 pages. Pages should be planned in 8-page increments.

The variations are many. You can add a plus-cover form, which is usually on heavier paper stock, to present a more important feel to the book. A 16-page body form can be combined with a 4-page cover form to produce a 20-page catalog. Digest, or half-size, catalogs are extremely economical but present less space for display. Williams-Sonoma, the Catalog for Cooks, is well known for its digest format.

Your printing representative will make you aware of special features that are available on particular press equipment, such as 32-page forms, fifth units, inline binding, etc. If you are deviating from the standard press cutoffs, be prepared to waste paper. To some catalogers this wasted paper is worth the effect of looking different in the mailbox.

The Cover

The first and most important impression of your catalog must be obtained by the cover. From the time a catalog is retrieved from the mailbox, it has exactly 3½ seconds to gain the customer's attention. This means that the cover of a catalog must work effectively to communicate your message. It must say hello, remind the customers that they have met before, promise that tantalizing merchandise is shown in the contents, and assure the credibility and reliability of the catalog company—all within the 3½ seconds allotted by the customer for a first impression.

There are essentially three current theories of catalog cover concepts: a merchandised presentation; an editorial approach, nonmerchandised; and a combination cover showing merchandise treated editorially. Each technique has its own merits and potential for capturing attention, but since the cover can be the number one selling space, a merchandised cover usually is used.

On catalogs whose cover approach involves combining an item with an esoteric or editorial technique, the back cover may be used to show the same product more within a practical context and for the selling copy. American Express's Expressly Yours Catalog has presented several issues this way, always incorporating the American Express credit card editorially.

Bachrach's covers are merchandised, showing men's wear on a model, but at the same time they depict an atmosphere that creates image and ambience. Williams-Sonoma covers also are merchandised, and the product is enhanced by a wonderful gourmet concoction.

Establishing a cover format is a good idea so that the customer will build an awareness of your catalog company each time a new issue is received. Flexibility with an established format hinges on the amount of creative thinking invested. It should be limitless.

Encourage your designer to be idealistic about the cover concept. Communicate your point of view so that the artist can interpret it into a graphic approach. Think of your customers and how best to approach them. Emphasis should be placed on dramatic treatment for the cover. This can be achieved through lighting in photography, which provides a way to set a mood or establish a feeling. Dark, rich colors of heavy density portray a luxurious image. On the other hand, a technique of light, high key colors can create a subtle understatement of elegance. Lighting and use of color should be considered creatively for maximum beauty and drama.

If the cover is merchandised, select an item that is representative of the product mix inside the book. Judge your selection for uniqueness, exclusivity, and potential for dramatic portrayal. More drama can be obtained by zeroing in on one special item than by showing a collage of merchandise, and so it is generally best to pick one product for your cover feature. An item that is somewhat ordinary by description can become extraordinary in portrayal if you find a new way to illustrate its use. For example, a tall glass vase becomes a cover possibility when shown as a receptacle for a matchbook collection. Or depict it with colorful layers of jelly beans. Or fill it with water and float a candle in it. Let your imagination run free. Anybody can show a vase with pretty flowers in it. It takes creativity to market a product in an askance, or out of context, way.

Analyze the Effectiveness of Your Own Covers. Be honest with yourself and allow your eyes and mind to see that cover as your customer would. Does it capture your attention in 3½ seconds? Does it pique your interest and make you wonder what is inside? Do you want to open up the book to see? Do you recognize the logo as an old friend? Do you anticipate finding an interesting mix of merchandise inside? Do you understand what is being offered? Do you perceive the company as reliable and professional? Does the book have a quality look and a good tactile feeling? Would you like to receive it in *your* mailbox?

The answers to all these harshly judgmental questions should be *yes* if your cover is working effectively for you. If you had to answer *no* to any of them, review the reasons for a negative response. Work on that aspect for your next cover and try to improve. Chances are that if you answered negatively, your customer would also. Remind yourself that in mail-order catalogs, a book certainly can be judged by its cover.

PHOTOGRAPHY

The single most important graphic element in catalogs is photography. Catalogs are a pictorial medium. The customer's attention is obtained first by the photography. Descriptive copy may close the sale, but the photograph must generate interest.

Photography generally is chosen over illustration for catalogs because customers find it easier to relate to and seem to accord more credibility to it as an advertising medium.

Essentially, catalog photography can be broken down into two major categories:

Still Life or Table Top Shots

These are photographs of inanimate products presented for the customer's consideration. They can be executed in the studio or on location.

Fashion Shots

These are clothing shots, shown on a model to illustrate fit and features. They also can be photographed in a studio or on location.

Studio Still Life Shots. These usually are shot to size for actual size reproduction on view camera equipment of 4 by 5 inches, 5 by 7 inches, or 8- by 10-inch film size. Shooting to size eliminates the need for random focus enlargement or reduction and is the most economical way to turn over photography to the color separator.

The photographer should shoot to fit the layout; normally, an acetate tracing of the actual space depiction is used to line up the shot. A Polaroid test shot before exposure on the view camera can be used to check composition and lighting.

Bracketed exposures (at least one f-stop up and one stop down) should be made for a choice of densities. While film and processing is expensive, it is less costly to bracket than to reshoot. If you are in doubt as to which exposure is best for color and density, let your separator guide you in making a final choice.

Lighting Techniques.   These contribute heavily to the success of any shot. Dramatic lighting will portray the products best, allowing for emphasis on special features. One style of studio lighting that has worked well for many catalogs involves darkening the background of the sweep for drop-off lighting to the foreground. This provides a spotlight effect for the product, framing dramatically. A shot with a wide scale of density has more dimension and is more interesting than flat lighting that appears to have no sparkle or life.

If an art director is not available on the set, the photographer should be allowed some creative license to turn an item slightly for a better view or add a minispot to pick up a detail.

Still-Life Location Shots.   When a fashion book is planned as a location shooting, it is wise to incorporate some of the still-life shots on location too. This gives the catalog a look of continuity and can be entertaining for the customer. Even if you cannot plan each still-life shot in advance for precise location, you know which products can be transported easily. A natural, complimentary setting can be decided on at the scene.

Location Shots

These can firmly establish a theme for a book and allow us to take advantage of nature's perfect lighting. (We can never truly simulate outdoor lighting in a studio.) There are three areas of difficulty in location shooting: It must be planned well in advance; there can be problems with the logistics of moving merchandise, crew, models, and equipment from place to place; and bad weather may occur.

Foreign Location Shoots.   Through an exchange of promotional services, it may prove more economical to shoot in a foreign country halfway around the world than to shoot in a local studio. By working with an airline and the tourist organization of the country to be visited, a catalog company with a large distribution to the right demographic market can offer a page for promotion of travel to that part of the world. The exchange is usually for all airline travel expenses, hotel accommodations, ground transportation, guides, and sometimes food.

Deals can be struck with the models for less than their usual day rate and excluding travel time. The same is true for the stylist, art director, and photographer's assistant.

Communications to plan and execute a trip like this are detailed and should be done at least 6 months in advance of the shoot. Here is a checklist for procedure when considering a foreign location:

1. Establish contact with the sponsoring airline.
2. Establish contact (usually through the airline) with the tourist organization representative.

3. Get the agreement on exchange of promotional services in writing and signed by all parties.

4. Plan the dates for the actual shooting, allowing 3 or 4 days longer than necessary in the event of bad weather.

5. If possible, make an advance scouting trip to the country to select possible shooting sites.

6. Go to the library and check out books for research on the country. Familiarize yourself with geographic and cultural points of interest. Learn about the customs. Your crew will be guests in a foreign country. Never take the risk of offending the local residents as a result of lack of knowledge about their customs.

7. Get advance clearance for the shipment of merchandise and camera equipment in writing from the airline (including no overweight charge), from the tourist organization, and from U.S. Customs.

8. List and tag all merchandise and camera equipment.

9. Be sure that all members of the crew understand their job responsibilities. Brief them on customs, passport information, required vaccines, drinking water and food, and expected behavior.

10. Finalize all ground arrangements, e.g., rental of van, services of an interpreter, etc.

11. Go back over the entire list again.

Details should not be overlooked because they can make the difference between breezing into a country to start right to work and having your merchandise or camera equipment confiscated at the point of entry.

Familiarizing yourself with the customs of a foreign country is a courtesy you should be willing to extend. It can help avoid embarrassing incidents and will assure a welcome for a repeat visit. Seemingly small things can be important. You and your crew should conduct yourselves professionally and with studied courtesy.

In China and Nepal, it is forbidden for women to wear short shorts that expose their legs. In Thailand, it is an insult to the person in front of you if you cross your legs, and you should never step over someone's extended legs or feet in that country. In most African countries, it is an insult if the voice is raised. In French Polynesia, the natives would be embarrassed if you offered them a tip. In all countries, including your own, it is unacceptable to leave a location site less clean than you found it. Always inquire politely for permission before you take anyone's photograph. The Masai tribe in Africa believes that if you snap their pictures without permission, you are stealing their souls. You may run the risk of having your camera snatched away and stamped into the earth.

If you choose tight cropping, eliminating any feeling of location, you should be shooting in a studio in the first place. Don't make the mistake of shooting in a wonderfully interesting place and then cropping out all the atmosphere. Most catalogers who shoot on location commit this grievous error. It infuriates the sponsoring airline and country and makes it very difficult for the other catalogers to arrange anything with a country that considers itself to have been betrayed by tightly cropped photographs.

Imaginative, Organized Art Direction

On all photographic shoots, this will ensure the best possible end results. The art director is ultimately responsible for showing the merchandise to its maximum advantage. An art director with marketing ability will recognize optimum shooting potential, whether in a studio or on location. Shapes, colors, textures, lighting, and contrast will be received by an art director almost with a tactile sense. Opportunity becomes more than a challenge for this talented person; it becomes excitement.

The art director becomes the orchestrator on a shoot, pulling the best efforts from the support crew, which consists of the photographer, stylist, hair and makeup person, photographic assistant, and models. Rapport must be established for a smooth shooting; respect must be given and received. Communication is the key to achieving this objective.

In a typical fashion shoot, the crew functions as a team, each with his or her own role responsibility and high degree of professionalism. The art director and photographer select the location or backdrop together, based on theme, contrast, interest, and lighting. The hair and makeup person prepares the model, and the stylist pulls the clothing and accessories. The assistant loads the cameras and sets up reflectors or strobes. When the shoot begins, the art director is stationed directly behind the photographer, watching the composition of the shot. The stylist should be closely attendant for details such as wrinkles, buttons, threads, etc. The model takes direction from both the photographer and the art director.

If clients are on the set, their input should go through the creative team, not directly to the model. Too many voices shouting instructions will destroy the ambience. A client should make wishes known through the art director, who will convey the information to the model or to the photographer or stylist. Most clients have a tendency to step into the set to straighten a tie or tug on a hem. That responsibility belongs to the stylist and should stay there.

Model Selection.   This should be done with your customer in mind. Choose models who fit your marketing input on your customer profile as closely as possible. Of course, they should look prettier or more handsome, because *a catalog is a wish book*, and all people wish to look more attractive than they do in reality.

Propping and Accessorizing.   A decision to prop a still-life item should be based on whether the product needs to be scaled for size or explained for use. There is a tendency in current catalogs to overprop. Use props to show how an item is to be used or to suggest an alternative use if the usual one is readily understood.

Props also are used to show immediate scaling for size. For instance, a child's bank is both explained as a bank and scaled by showing coins in the shot.

Overuse of props will clutter a book and detract from the merchandise. Use props only when they will help the customer understand the product better. A clean, straightforward graphic presentation is still the best. You have the sellin copy with which to answer all the anticipated questions. Don't attempt to do it all in photography.

Shot Composition.   This refers to the arrangement of merchandise within the designated display space. The items should be arranged in an interesting composition, incorporating any required props artistically. The cropping of the photograph can enhance the composition, making it even more appealing. Angle of the product becomes important in composing before the camera and should be determined by the merchandise itself.

Before photography begins, a layout qualification meeting should be held for the entire creative team. Schedule it to take place a day or two before you start photography. Invite the art director, photographers, and assistants assigned to the project; the stylist; the scheduler or traffic manager; and the copywriter.

Qualifying the Layouts.   This involves explaining every shot that will be required of the team. Communicate the theme, mood, or concept of the whole catalog. Describe backdrops required, sets to be built, accessories and props to be obtained, models to be booked, and whether you want coffee shown in the mugs. Discuss drop shadows for silhouette shots, acrylic versus no-seam or painted backgrounds, and desired special effects such as lighting, color, or use of slight filtration.

Use this qualification meeting as a well-organized planning session. It will save time, money, and frustration in the long run. An informed team will function more efficiently, and pride of authorship will be reflected in the finished catalog.

Photo Retouching.   This should be kept to a minimum. With the advent of supersensitive scanners for color separation, retouching tends to show through. Use it sparingly to correct minor flaws in the merchandise. Do not attempt to change the color of a product completely by retouching. Get another sample in the correct color and reshoot the photograph. Don't try to cover up bad photography with retouching.

COPY

Catalog copy is the informational mode that augments the primary selling tool of photography. Like the other graphic elements, it should be considerate of the customer.

Since most of the selling space is allotted to pictorial depiction, copywriters must be intensely disciplined in their use of words for catalog copy.

Basic Rules of Catalog Copy

1. Be as concise as possible.
2. Be informative and descriptive.
   a. Give size and weight where applicable.

    b. List contents.

    c. Suggest the use or an alternative use.

    d. List the unit number, price, and postage.

    e. Give a shortened, descriptive tag or lead-in.

3. Avoid clichés and slang usage.

4. Write to fit the layout.

The client should provide the copywriter with filled-in merchandise information sheets (MIS) and with access to the products for touching and seeing. The MIS should contain all the available information about each item, including fabric content, country of origin, exclusivity, measurements and weight, etc.

Inclusion of Personalization

Some catalogs have descriptive copy written in first-person form for style. If a strong personality is associated with the book, this approach seems well received by the customer. Perhaps in these days of impersonal service in retailing, this touch of personalization is appreciated in mail order. At the very least, it is suggested that an opening letter of greeting or introduction be used in catalogs, ideally signed by the president of the company. An identity that the customer can relate to is an important consideration for all catalogs.

Merchandise That Requires Longer Copy

Some items need more descriptive copy than others. The layout artist should be made aware of those products in order to allow more space for copy. Electronic items need more words to explain technical features. Expensive stereo sets must be described by outlining all the components and special parts. To sell a cruise around the world with a price point of several thousand dollars requires a profusion of pretty words and exotic-sounding names. Common sense should be used to determine which items need longer copy.

THE PSYCHOLOGY OF COLOR

The use of color is an important motivational factor in presenting merchandise for sale in a catalog. Recent research has proved that people react emotionally to colors. Some colors soothe, and others excite. One color will suppress, and another will initiate. Since color is one of the primary selling tools in catalog marketing, we should educate ourselves about the effects and emotions colors are capable of evoking.

Male customers respond best to earth tones, or colors of nature, such as warm browns, rusts, grays, greens, and blues. Women are partial to softer, more pastel colors and to rich, glossy blacks and pristine whites. Red is an action-oriented color and serves to motivate. Very soft pink is a soothing tone but does not promote movement or activity. Harsh, magenta-type pinks are irritating colors and cause a customer to *turn the page* to avoid the color.

Colors of the sky, blues of all shades, are acceptable to both sexes, as are greens in all shades. Ivory, when used as a fashion backdrop color, makes flesh tones appear more "peachy" and pleasing. Yellows are sunshine colors and are received well as backgrounds. Warm gray is better for framing merchandise than cool gray; beige is another shade that is most effective toward the warm scale. Silver is restful to the eye, and gold tones are rich colors. Orange should be avoided as it is a violent color and detracts from almost any other color around or in front of it.

Just as the eye will follow any light, the mind reacts to color without thought or deliberation. Out of consideration to the customer, use of colors within catalogs should be pleasing as opposed to displeasing. Contemplative colors invite longer perusal of photographs. With a palette of nature's colors at our disposal, we should be able to create catalogs that promote ease on behalf of our customers and frame our merchandise considerately.

CAMERA-READY ART

This refers to the preparation of catalog material to be turned over for separations. Camera-ready art should be prepared professionally and accurately. Mechanical artboards are flats done to size with photostats of the photographs trimmed, cropped, and mounted in position. All type, including headlines, body copy, and photo keys, is set and pasted up in position on the boards. Each flat is covered with a tissue overlay that is marked with special instructions such as reverse copy blocks, color borders, silhouette with drop shadows, etc.

THE ORDER FORM

Most catalog mailers have chosen the preformed order form to be bound into the book. A few still are using the die-cut flat order form that must be folded by the customer. The copy style should be brief and to the point. A complicated order form can be overwhelming, causing a prospective customer to abandon any thought of ordering. If you keep the design clean and understandable and structure the copy in a simple, instructive way, the customer won't be discouraged at first glance. For customers who prefer to order by phone, the toll-free number should be displayed prominently on the order form as well as throughout the catalog.

The order form may be planned to run in one color or in two or more colors. Four-color-process order forms are more expensive to produce than one- or two-color ones, and it is doubtful that enough additional sales will come in to justify the expense.

THE BIRTH OF THE BOOK

After all the caring that has been invested in the building of a catalog from the merchandising and creative end, it is natural to be a little nervous when the finish approaches. The birth of the book is imminent whenever you get to the color separation stage. All the labor pains will have been worth it when the catalog is born.

Color Separations

Separations are done by scanner or by conventional camera, and some correction work usually is required. When the color proofs are submitted with type in position, it requires a full day of marking up the press sheets or chromalins for an average catalog job. At this point in the schedule, you or your print production manager should go over each transparency again, comparing it with the proof. If you don't have the technical expertise to tell the separator how to correct, simply point out how it looks to you and let the separator interpret the move.

Final press proofs or chromalin proofs usually are provided to show the corrections that were made. Minor changes may be made at this stage if time has been allowed before the film is due at the printer.

The Press Run

It is an exciting feeling to walk into a pressroom and get your first whiff of ink and hear the presses roaring. The books come off the finishing line at an incredible speed, and a blink of the eye will cause you to miss several hundred impressions as the signatures are folded and trimmed.

The press make-ready is the startup time before signatures are saved, when the registration is fine-tuned and the color is balanced. Web printing does provide for some flexibility on press for minor color adjustments. But if you are doing the make-ready okay yourself, know what you are asking for and be aware of the compromises that must be made on press. Radical alterations at this point are not advisable.

Very few press okays run strictly on schedule; be prepared to be patient if you are waiting in the customer lounge for your invitation to the pressroom. If the printing salesperson suggests a game of gin or a tour of the plant, relax; it won't take too long. But if the suggestion is for dinner and a tour of the city, it's going to take quite a while. A general rule of thumb is to add 2 more hours to any estimated time given. A printing press is a complex, multifaceted piece of technology, and it can be complicated getting the job running. Give them the time they need to make it right for you.

Once the balancing of colors and adjustments has been done, you are ready to sign the press sheet. Don't forget to be courteous to the press crew. A smile and a thank you will help them feel that their efforts were appreciated.

As you cradle the new catalog on your way out of the plant, you'll start to think about the next issue: ways to make it better, things you've learned from this one, how you can improve the cover concept, or maybe even a new format approach.

EPILOGUE

As the number of catalogs in the mailbox grows, so does the level of sophistication of the customer. The demands grow on our ingenuity, innovativeness, and imagination to make smarter-looking, better catalogs. Our customers want to see more, and they want to be entertained and sweet-talked. While you're at it, show them something new and different.

The emphasis in this chapter has been on marketing, merchandising, and creative graphics. This is not meant to imply that this combination alone will produce a successful catalog company. All our suggestions have been tested and proved and will produce a successful catalog when they are applied effectively. But to build a sound catalog business you must apply equal parts of good management, order fulfillment, and customer service in addition to outstanding catalog marketing pieces.

Catalog marketing has become a science, appealing to the senses and desires of the mail-order customer. What has created this phenomenon in advertising? Remember the days of your childhood when the long-awaited Captain Marvel secret signal code ring arrived in your mailbox? Consuming all those boxes of cereal to accumulate enough box tops became worth it with the excitement of opening that package. Our Captain Marvel rings now come in boxes labeled Horchow, American Express, Sharper Image, Neiman-Marcus, Lilian Vernon, L. L. Bean, and Saks Fifth Avenue. The mystique of the mailbox lives on.

50

Business-to-Business Marketing

Richard Bloch
Manus Direct Response Marketing
Seattle, Wash.

The phrase "business-to-business direct marketing" is difficult to pin down because it does not lend itself to an easy, concise definition. Because it can mean so many things to so many different marketing professionals, business-to-business direct marketing can span a wide range of direct marketing strategies and techniques.

For example, consider these scenarios:

- A marketer of office supplies may use catalog selling and/or inbound telemarketing.
- A publisher of a newsletter or magazine uses a variety of subscription marketing techniques.
- A book publisher or distributor might make good use of direct-response space ads or postcard decks.
- A sales manager may use any number of media to generate sales leads for further follow-up by a sales force.

Indeed, the direct marketing that I am exposed to in my role as a businessperson is as wide and varied as the consumer direct marketing I am exposed to in my role at home.

It is not as important to understand the actual definition of business-to-business direct marketing. It is more important to understand its benefits and the strategic considerations necessary to prepare a successful direct marketing program for business-to-business marketing. Strategies which encompass direct mail, telemarketing, and catalogs can eliminate or reduce the need for large outside sales forces. And when outside sales forces are necessary, direct marketing can be used to generate qualified sales leads — eliminating the need for cold sales calls. Because cold calls are a very inefficient use of a salesperson's time, it is easy to see how direct marketing can provide a measurable, response-oriented system to make the best use of sales time.

Even businesses which do not control their own distribution channels can make good use of direct marketing. Businesses which use distributors or manufacturer's representatives can set up direct marketing programs to benefit their distributors (and ultimately, themselves). Distributors themselves can set up a direct marketing program and allow them to function independently of the manufacturer's marketing program.

It should be clear at this point that there are many business-to-business uses for direct marketing. I am pleased to see that more and more businesses are giving these response-oriented techniques a try. I also know, however, that direct marketing suffers from an image problem in the minds of some business owners because they consider the direct mail they receive at home as encompassing all of direct marketing.

Many widely read books on direct marketing do leave us with the impression — a mistaken one — that direct marketing is only the use of massive mailings to consumers. We are left with the idea that direct marketing is the mailing of millions of sweepstakes entries or selling millions of knives on television. True, direct marketing is an excellent way to sell to mass audiences, but the business-to-business applications are plentiful as well.

Too often, however, business-to-business direct marketing is given little attention in these books which extol the uses of large mailing lists. It is either not covered or tossed into a little chapter in the back of the book. This does nothing but leave us the impression that when audiences are extremely limited (that is, as little as a few thousand names), direct marketing is not possible. Indeed, I believe the opposite to be true: that direct marketing is an even more important thing to consider when there is a very limited audience for a message.

It is interesting to note, however, that some of the books on direct marketing treat business-to-business marketing as being a very different discipline — almost the *opposite* of consumer-oriented direct marketing. Here we are left with the impression that someone with an intensive knowledge of the consumer end of direct marketing would be totally lost in the world of business-to-business direct marketing.

In other books, business-to-business direct marketing is treated as being very much the *same* as consumer-oriented direct marketing. The tone here is that once you understand consumer techniques, all you need do is change some mailing lists and begin marketing to businesses.

Who is right? Is business-to-business the same as consumer-oriented marketing or different? Really, both are right, and to understand some of the important strategic issues which are critical to successful business-to-business direct marketing, it is important to look at the picture from both perspectives.

Business-to-business direct marketers need to understand *all* of the important strategic issues of direct marketing planning, independent of consumer or business orientation. These include general-offer strategy, list and media strategy, creative strategy, and the back-end implications of all of these issues. These are the *same* planning issues faced by our colleagues on the consumer end of the business.

Yet, there are critical differences. There are a whole host of organizational and psychological issues in business-to-business marketing which are important to the process of planning a business-to-business program.

To get an accurate picture of business-to-business direct marketing and to explore the critical strategic issues, we should look at the subject from *both* of these perspectives. First, I will make the case that business-to-business direct marketing is the same as consumer direct marketing. Then I will make the case that these are very different from each other. Once this is done, we can explore some specific strategic issues.

BUSINESS-TO-BUSINESS IS SIMILAR

Many professionals treat business-to-business as if it existed in an entirely different universe from other forms of direct marketing. You could, however, make the argument that business-to-business is a lot more similar to consumer direct marketing than many practitioners would have us believe. How similar? Consider these factors:

Offer Strategy Controls Response Rate and Commitment Level

As in every other area of direct marketing, the offer can make or break the success of a program. Creating the right offer is the key to generating the right kinds of sales and leads for optimum back-end performance. All too often, whether at home or at the office, I receive mail which has *no offer at all*—an astonishing occurrence when one considers that the mailer may have spent a dollar or more to write me and effectively tells me there is no incentive at all for me to respond.

We may make different kinds of offers to businesspeople than to consumers, but it still boils down to the same principle—our offer controls our response rate and the level of qualification of the response. High response rates mean nothing if commitment levels are so low that there is little chance for back-end conversion and follow-up purchases. Conversely, low response rates may be excellent if the conversion rate is high. This is simple direct marketing mathematics at work. It is the same math whether applied to consumer or business-to-business applications.

People Are People

Many professionals make the assumption that we are communicating with other businesses when we engage in business-to-business direct marketing. That is wrong. We are communicating with *people*—as in every other form of direct marketing. These people just happen to own (or work in) businesses, and we are reaching them in that role. These are the same people you might meet at conventions, in restaurants, or on the street on the way to work. They are like you and me with needs, hopes, and fears which need to be addressed. Their motivations do not suddenly and miraculously transform once they leave the home and enter the office. We need to communicate with them while keeping this in mind. Perhaps this chapter should be called "Business*person*-to-Business*person* Marketing."

Because people are people, business-to-business direct marketers need to follow some of the same principles which hold for all forms of direct marketing, especially in terms of creative strategy and motivational analysis. Many direct marketers totally miss the mark in these key areas because they have not carefully considered some of the basic human needs which influence response.

Whether we are communicating with a corporate vice president or a lower-level administrator, we must examine motivations. Does a businessperson purchase an office copier because of speed, efficiency, dependability, and the all-important benefit of money saved? In part, yes. But there are other factors at work. Our prospect wants many things. These include looking good in front of the boss, gaining status and prestige, fulfilling a sense of duty to shareholders, and many more. We don't necessarily spell these out when selling a copy machine to a businessperson. We do, however, need to make sure that our creative strategy is developed with these considerations in mind. Companies like Federal Express, AT&T, and IBM have all been very successful at capitalizing on these approaches.

People may think you are crazy to read a textbook on *consumer* behavior (instead of one on organizational behavior) when formulating strategies for business-to-business direct marketing, but what you learn about reference groups, cultures, attitudes, perceptions, and motivations will round out your organizational behavior knowledge. After all, businesspeople are consumers, too.

The Decision-Making Spectrum

The decision-making processes within a household are almost always considered very differently than the decision-making processes within an organization. One falls into the domain of consumer behavior, the other into the domain of organizational behavior. True, there are some general organizational differences which may influence our strategy, but the psychology is very similar.

In a consumer application, we need to be concerned with how our product fits into the decision-making spectrum. On one end of this spectrum is highly routinized or habitual decision making. On the other end are decisions which require extensive problem solving and cognition. For example, the purchase of toothpaste or produce probably fits on the habitual end of the spectrum. After all, people do not spend a lot of time thinking hard about these purchases. They are made out of habit. They *do*, however, think a lot about what house or car to buy. These purchases are on the extensive problem-solving end of the spectrum. And there are purchases that fit in the middle of the spectrum. These are purchases which have some elements of habit and some elements of problem solving within the framework of the decision. These might include such decisions as where a car is to be serviced or what restaurant to dine at.

In businesses, there is a similar spectrum. Routine decisions like what paperclips to buy or where to buy copier paper are approached much differently than where a manufacturing plant will be located or what computer system to buy. There may also be decisions that fit in the middle of the spectrum. Examples of purchases here might be office furniture or fairly inexpensive equipment like typewriters.

Decision making in the organization has always been treated differently than decision making in the home. An interesting study in the *Journal of Marketing*, however, concludes that there is much more of a variation in the *way* people approach decisions than in whether the decision is made in the home or office.[1]

In other words, for direct marketing purposes, we need to be primarily concerned about whether the decision to buy a product or service is habitual, requires cognitive problem solving, or fits in the middle of the spectrum. This means we can make some key strategic decisions in the same framework, whether the application is consumer or business-to-business.

If the decision is a habitual one, such as may be the case for the purchase of routine office supplies, we know the decision is likely made at a relatively low level in the organization, perhaps by a secretary or in the purchasing department. Therefore, we can choose strategies that mesh with this conclusion.

If the decision is likely to require extended problem solving, we may use direct marketing as a lead generation tool with more personal follow-up by phone or in person. Executives do not make major purchases through a one-step offer in the mail. Instead, leads need to be generated for follow-up. The entire sales cycle can take several years.

Building a Database

Whether it is in the consumer or business-to-business area of direct marketing, many people misdirect their resources by focusing on the securing of rental lists for direct mail and telemarketing or on the purchase of space in advertising media. These should only be viewed as tools, however, toward the more important goal of building an internal database. This house list is of critical importance because it is the basis of determining how well back-end marketing will work. For lead generation, this means conversion to sales. For mail order, it means repeat purchases. For subscriptions, it means renewals. In general, back-end performance is more important than front-end performance.

In both consumer and business-to-business direct marketing, these outside media are not just limited to direct mail. Telemarketing, print advertising cooperative mailings—even broadcast media in certain circumstances—are efficient and effective ways to reach target audiences. Yet understanding the relationship of these media in terms of the goal of building and segmenting the internal database is as important to consumer direct marketing as it is to business-to-business direct marketing.

BUSINESS-TO-BUSINESS IS DIFFERENT

Our perspective on business-to-business direct marketing would be incomplete unless we understood that there *are* some critical areas which tend to differentiate business-to-business from consumer direct marketing. If there weren't such differences, there would really be very little need to consider business-to-business as a separate discipline. How does business-to-business differ from consumer direct marketing? Let's examine these criteria:

Large Number of Decision Makers

We have already seen that one critical marketing consideration relates to where our product fits into the spectrum of "routine-to-extended" problem solving. In both consumer and business-to-business direct marketing, an understanding of how decisions are made (whether in a mode of habit or of careful consideration) is important to shaping strategy.

The difference, however, between business-to-business and consumer direct marketing is that in the business-to-business arena, there are often many *more* decision makers—sometimes dozens of them. And the title of the person who makes a decision about your product or service can vary from company to company. This can make it very difficult to identify the key players you need to communicate with.

In addition, we need to be concerned with the many other people who contribute to the process of decision making in companies. An analysis from the *Journal of Marketing* which offers a good perspective on the subject explores the various roles people occupy in making decisions in companies.[2]

These roles include *users,* who actually make use of the product but may or may not have any influence at all in the actual decision to purchase; *influencers,* who can affect a decision in a variety of different ways by providing information or criteria for purchases; and *gatekeepers,* who screen information and control the flow of it to decision makers. It should be noted that these roles may be shared to some extent. A gatekeeper may also serve as an influencer. The existence of these roles, however, means direct marketers need to be concerned with understanding all of the roles of people who may have the slightest influence on the decision to purchase our product, or seek more information about it. One thing many people don't understand about direct marketing is that we can use it to *obtain* information as well as disseminate it. We can use surveys and questions on response devices to find out which people occupy which roles. Once this information is added to our internal database, we can make later use of it.

A Fast-Changing Environment

The business environment is constantly changing. People are constantly moving up (and down) the corporate ladder, making the business environment more dynamic than the home environment. Certainly those concerned with consumer applications need to be concerned with changes in that environment, including aging and divorce, but the family unit does not change as fast as the corporate one. People may change jobs many times throughout their careers. Because of this constantly changing structure, our database of prospects and customer names can become out of date very quickly—a lot more quickly than a consumer list would.

Does this mean that the investment of time and resources into establishing a relationship with people in a company is often wasted? Certainly not. Today's so-so prospect at company ABC can literally be tomorrow's hot prospect at company XYZ. Perhaps this person moved into a new job where more power to make a decision in your favor has been granted. If you have established a relationship and dialogue with this person through direct marketing channels, your investment may pay off. This process also works within companies through job promotions. Today's user, influencer, or gatekeeper can be tomorrow's decision maker. Use this changing environment to your advantage.

Smaller Universes

Often, the total pool of potential buyers is much smaller in business-to-business direct marketing than in consumer applications. In some cases—perhaps a company that sells sophisticated software in a certain specific industry—the total universe of potential buyers may be as small as a few thousand or a few hundred names. This is a far different situation than in the consumer end of the business where universes may be measured in the millions of names.

Smaller universes generally mean that we can afford to spend more resources on each company than would be the case if there were millions of names on the list. However, it also means that the consumer direct-mail–oriented concept of running a split-run test with a few thousand names and then rolling out to the entire list won't work because the test will have used up the entire universe.

Instead, when dealing with smaller universes, it is useful to view them as a prospect list and create a communications dialogue. This includes both obtaining information and disseminating it. The general process is to look for ways to find out which prospects are hot leads and then spend more time and resources on these names.

Admittedly, there are many cases where the universe will be large. This is often the case for horizontal markets where a product or service might be purchased by virtually any company. Products such as office supplies or computer equipment may fall into this category. In this case, we should look toward segmenting these lists into smaller ones by industry so that we can focus marketing efforts in a specific way to these subuniverses.

We achieve greater success with this technique because businesspeople see themselves in certain industries and often look toward your experience in their field and may expect certain industry-specific product and service benefits. Direct marketing offers us the perfect opportunity to communicate different messages by industry segment.

DIRECT MARKETING STRATEGIES

There are four major areas of strategic importance when planning business-to-business direct marketing programs. These include offer strategy, list strategy, media strategy, and creative-format strategy. Each element must be carefully planned to work in harmony with all of the others.

Offer Strategy

It is no secret that offer controls response rate. What is often forgotten, however, is that offer controls commitment level, too. The more appealing you make the offer, the more you will raise your response rate. However, commitment level for those respondents will be relatively lower. There are many types of offers which can be made in business-to-business direct marketing. They range from "buy now" (certainly a high commitment offer) to free information (a rather low commitment offer). Selecting the right offer depends upon overall direct marketing strategy, staffing, inventory, and resources available to follow up responses.

The important thing to remember about offer strategy is that it can be finely tuned to your specific back-end goals. In lead generation, you may want to ask questions on your response devices to help qualify responses, or ask the telephone numbers of key decision makers. These techniques tend to depress response rates but heighten qualification level.

In his book *Successful Direct Marketing Methods,* Robert Stone describes these techniques as falling into the areas of *appeals* and *conditions.*[3] Adding appeals (guarantees, free trials, discounts, premiums, etc.) to an offer will raise response and dampen commitment level. Adding conditions (more questions, long-term commitment, financial qualification, etc.) will lower response and heighten commitment levels. Appeals and conditions, therefore, are the fine-tune controls of direct marketing offer strategy.

List Strategy

The choice of mailing lists is endless. As in consumer direct marketing, we are faced with a choice between two basic types of mailing lists—compiled lists and response lists.

Compiled lists are created from scratch. They are compiled from directories, membership rosters, etc. They tend to be rather exhaustive lists but contain names of people who are not mail-responsive.

Response lists, however, are not created from scratch. They are the lists of people who have responded to someone else's offer. Response lists tend to be less exhaustive than compiled lists but usually perform better because the names on these lists have responded to something—and may respond to your offer.

Standard Rates and Data Service's *Direct Mail List Rates and Data* offers many choices in selecting a list.[4] Trade magazine lists, directories, trade show and seminar attendees, and professional and association lists are all various ways to approach the problem of securing good lists.

Whether you use a compiled or response list, you need to think carefully about how to address your piece. We are often given two choices—name addressing and title addressing. Each has advantages and disadvantages.

In name addressing, we address mail to specific people, as in "John Doe, Marketing Manager, ABC Corp." It is obviously more personal but in a business-to-business application, it can create problems in the corporate mailroom. Remember, the business environment changes rapidly. There is a good chance that John Doe has left the company. What happens then? Does it go to John Doe's replacement? Does the mailroom discard it? Does the mailroom forward it on to John Doe's new company?

Title addressing, though less personal, can reduce this effect and may be useful if you are interested in writing to whoever may happen to occupy the position of marketing director at ABC Corp. In many lead-getting applications, this may be the method of choice. A decision must be made as to whether the personal look or the mail-forwarding problem takes precedence.

When using self-mailers (in which we are not usually trying to make a piece look personal), a good hybrid approach may be to *tell* the mailroom where you want the piece to go. A line like "Attention mailroom: Please deliver to the person in your company in charge of marketing" may be useful.

Try to use merging and purging to achieve the goal of little duplication, especially if you are after a personal look. The appearance of one name on several lists may signal greater interest—and may be worth more frequent mailing, but at different times. Nothing more clearly signals "unimportant" to a secretary who screens mail than receiving several duplicate pieces on the same day.

Media Strategy

Direct mail is certainly an important media for business-to-business direct marketing, but there are other media at our disposal.

Telemarketing suffers from an image problem in the consumer area of direct marketing when cold calls are made, but is an accepted way to approach business-to-business direct marketing. It offers immediate feedback, a much higher level of interpersonal communication, and flexibility. If you have not reached your decision maker, for example, you have the flexibility to inquire as to who that might be. Some problems may be encountered, however, unless you choose personnel or service bureau very carefully. You may not be able to control the accuracy and consistency of your presentation. Further, telemarketing is more expensive than other media and may be best reserved for follow-up and requalification situations.

Cooperative mailings in the business-to-business area usually take the form of postcard decks. Your offer appears on a 3½- by 5½-inch card packaged with other offers geared toward the same audience. Because your offer competes with many others, you have a few seconds—if that—to convey your offer and benefits on a small surface. This is difficult to achieve, especially when you consider the production and creative limitations of such a card. But because per piece costs are low, it may offer many opportunities in mail order and lead generation applications.

Print advertising in business-to-business applications often means choosing between two types of publications: paid circulation and controlled circulation publications. Paid circulation publications are received by businesspeople who pay for it; therefore, it may be better read and more people may pay attention to your direct-response ad. Because they are paid for, however, they may not achieve as high a penetration in your target audience. Controlled circulation publications do achieve high penetration because they are mailed free to nearly everyone who meets the publication's criteria; because they are free, however, they may be unread or merely scanned.

Whether paid or controlled, you may wish to purchase space in publications which cater to a vertical market, a horizontal market, or both. Selling computer equipment to hospitals may work with ads in vertical publications reaching people in hospitals only, or in horizontal publications reaching people interested in computer equipment.

Broadcast advertising is not often thought of as a business-to-business media, but it is changing rapidly, especially as more narrowly targeted cable networks emerge. Networks such as Financial News Network may offer excellent ways to sell to horizontal business markets.

Creative-Format Strategy

In business-to-business direct-mail marketing, it is critical to make sure our mail gets to the right person. We achieve this through list and addressing methods, but it is important to consider the role of the secretary who may screen mail for an employer.

A study by the Richmark Group, a Chicago-based consulting firm specializing in distribution channel marketing, identified the decision-making parameters and processes secretaries use to screen mail.[5] Issues of credibility, relevance, and whether the mail appears to be personal correspondence emerged as criteria in the decision about whether to discard mail, reread it, or forward it on to the boss.

When our mail actually reaches the decision maker, the copy approach we have taken may be critical. Business-to-business direct mail often tends to have different copy strategies than the mail addressed to consumers at home. Why? Simply that the desires, needs, and motivations of people are different in the office than at home. We must carefully consider the motivations of our audience when creating packages.

These motivations can be related to making more money, being successful, career advancement, and status. Each audience for the same product may have different motivational considerations. In selling office copiers, for example, we may write a piece that addresses the benefits of lowering costs and saving money. However, we make subtle changes in tone to address differing motivations. In writing to business owners, we should be mindful of financial motivations. In writing to office managers, we should be mindful of the motivation to achieve status and promotion and looking good in front of the boss. We don't state these things overtly, but address them through subtle changes in creative execution.

LEAD GENERATION

As we have seen, business-to-business direct marketing is a wide and varied field, but one important and highly useful application seems to be in the area of sales lead generation. Because this area requires cooperation between sales and marketing managers, it is useful to consider it in some more detail.

To create a strategy which meets overall marketing objectives, we need to ask some questions about how the leads will fit our goals. The questions which should be addressed include these.

How Many Leads Do We Want?

We need to decide the quantity of leads to be generated. Before you answer "as many as possible," consider that a large number of leads may be less qualified than a smaller quantity and that the sales staff may not be able to follow up all those leads effectively in a short time. This may defeat the purpose of the whole endeavor. It is easy to calculate the number of leads needed by setting a time frame and dividing by the response rate to deliver optimum mailing quantities.

For example, if we have 10 sales people who each need 10 leads per month, that is 100 leads needed per month. If we assume a 2 percent response rate, we need to mail 5000 pieces per month (100 divided by 2 percent).

What Is Our Lead Schedule?

An optimum approach, no matter how many leads are needed in the aggregate, would be to have leads flow on a continuous basis—some every day. Planning mailings to achieve this goal, however, is problematic, as the best cost efficiencies are obtained in mailing in large quantities. This results in more of a batch flow than a line flow.

We need a happy medium here. Pay a bit more for more frequent smaller mailings which will provide a more continuous flow of leads, but don't mail so frequently as to drive the cost per piece too high. In addition, you may find that there are some unique seasonal issues in your specific industry which may necessitate altering the schedule at various times of the year.

Finally, lead flow may be adjusted if we determine that we are getting too many or too few leads in a given time.

What Kind of Leads Do We Want?

Do we want few leads which are highly qualified—or many leads which are less qualified? This is certainly related to the question of the number of leads we want, but has commitment level implications, too. For example, if our resources are such that we can only follow up a few leads in a given time period, then we want to generate as highly qualified leads as possible. This means using a rather high commitment offer.

What Kinds of People Should Be Leads?

As we have seen, the roles of decision making are important to the business decision-making process and need to be considered. To whom should we address our offer? The answer is that we do not always know. It is, however, no crime to solicit inquiries from a variety of titles in a company to determine the actual decision-making processes in an organization. Later, we can use telemarketing and personal selling as follow-up tools to the right people.

What Media Should We Use?

Direct mail is probably one of the most common media for sales lead generation, but it is also possible to achieve lead generation goals through print advertising and cooperative postcard decks. This approach may generate a lower cost per lead, but we do not have as great a control over who responds to our offer. Telemarketing may offer greater flexibility, but costs more than other media.

LEAD FOLLOW-UP

Lead generation is only one part of the problem. Proper management of leads is another area of concern. Much has been written about generating leads, but little about what to do with the leads once they are obtained. What do we do with them? Turn them over to the sales staff and let them work their magic? To a certain extent, yes. But the sales staff has a natural tendency to begin to work on new leads and let older leads sit around.

We must be sure that leads are followed up in a systematic manner. In most business-to-business situations, the cost per lead or cost per new customer achieved can be rather high, allowing us to devote significant resources to the follow-up of leads.

Lead follow-up is often thought of as a pipeline. Leads enter the pipeline; are followed up through further mail, telemarketing, and personal selling; and exit from the pipeline as sales. It does not always work this way, however. There may be many on-again, off-again cycles in the purchase decision. Can we track these cycles with direct marketing? Certainly—if we view the model as one of a "ladder" rather than a pipeline.

I choose the ladder analogy because I believe it more accurately reflects the picture of our lead base. This ladder is occupied by our prospects. Some occupy positions at the top of the ladder because they are almost ready to buy. Some occupy positions at the bottom of the ladder because they are certainly not ready to buy yet. But the business environment is a dynamic one. It is constantly changing. A hot prospect may have a sudden budget reduction and move down the ladder. A recently hired executive may reinitiate a decision-making process and move up the ladder. Companies may go through cycles of moving up and down the ladder many times before they buy. Leads should not be assessed at a commitment level and remain there. We need to constantly monitor this ladder.

To make the best use of our salespeople's time we need an accurate picture of where prospects are at any given moment. That way, they can spend their valuable sales time working the hot leads while colder leads can be worked through telemarketing and direct-mail follow-up. It is wasteful to have a salesperson call everybody. Many offers can be made through direct mail and telemarketing, which "poll" our database to see if they would like to move up the ladder.

Offers of helpful information are ways to see if prospects at the lowest rungs of the ladder are ready to move up. Offers of newsletters or sales literature (which tend to have higher commitment levels) can be used to see if prospects would like to move up another notch. Offers of consultations and seminars (which have still higher commitment levels) are ways to see if prospects are ready to move to the highest rungs of the ladder.

If at any point, our response to an offer is no (a nonresponse), that's fine, because we can approach them again later and use direct marketing offers to attempt to reinitiate dialogue. Direct marketing, therefore, is useful not only in generating our leads but in monitoring follow-up strategies.

Does the process end once the sale is made? Of course not. We begin all over again trying to find out when it is time to buy again, upgrade, purchase a service contract — even get referrals.

SUMMARY

This chapter has discussed some key areas including the nature of business-to-business direct marketing, offer strategy, list strategy, media strategy, creative-format strategy, and lead generation. These issues have been addressed specifically as they relate to business-to-business direct marketing. Yet, to fully understand some of these strategies, you may wish to read other chapters of this book which cover these specific issues in further detail.

NOTES

1. Edward Fern and James R. Brown, "The Industrial/Consumer Marketing Dichotomy: A Case of Insufficient Justification," *Journal of Marketing*, vol. 48, Spring 1984, pp. 68–77.

2. Frederick E. Webster, Jr., and Yoram Wind, "A General Model for Understanding Organizational Buying Behavior," vol. 32, April 1972, pp. 12–19.

3. Robert Stone, *Successful Direct Marketing Methods* (Chicago: Crain Books, 1984), 43–45.

4. Standard Rates and Data Service, *Direct Mail List Rates and Data* (Wilmette, Ill.: Standard Rates and Data Service, published bimonthly).

5. Richmark Kerndt, "Getting Past the Secretary," *Direct Marketing*, January 1989, 46–51.

51

Conquest Marketing

Joshua Moritz

Lowe Direct
New York, N.Y.

Mark Heller

Marketing Alternatives
Mamaroneck, N.Y.

INTRODUCTION

The term *conquest marketing* was probably invented by the U.S. auto industry. It is used to describe the way companies build sales and market share at the expense of the competition. The auto industry coined the phrase in recognition of the fact that their U.S. markets had ceased to grow, and that an individual company's success would be driven by how successfully they could increase (or maintain) volume in a flat or declining market. The auto makers discovered that direct marketing techniques were highly effective, both in maintaining brand loyalty, and in driving a significant portion of repairs to factory-authorized dealers, who in turn purchased manufacturer's parts for repairs. Today, when you buy a car, your dealers' cost often includes a fee for a manufacturer-run direct marketing program. This relationship-marketing program typically consists of a manufacturer's magazine, discount repair offers, and a program to build brand and dealer loyalty.

In this chapter, we'll describe when and how to use conquest marketing and the direct marketing techniques that are key to a successful conquesting campaign. We'll look at:

- The characteristics of a conquest market

- Five market types in which conquesting has been used successfully and the direct marketing techniques that worked

- Key steps in designing an effective conquesting strategy
- How to find your competitor's customers and prospects
- How to defend against conquest marketing
- Case studies illustrating successful conquest marketers who use direct marketing techniques

We will use examples from our case studies throughout this chapter. The case studies appear at the end of the chapter. They are:

AT&T Universal Card. AT&T successfully launched a new bank credit card and acquired over three million cardholders in the first year in a market where the average cardholder already carries five to seven competitive products. While the jury is still out on when (or whether) the resulting credit portfolio will prove profitable to AT&T, the initial market conquest has been highly successful.

New Pig Corporation. Take a nonglamorous product that's up against dirt, a funny name, and a distributor who couldn't sell the product. Add innovation and a conquest strategy, and you have New Pig Corporation—which sells over $20 million in pigs a year. (Not the squealing kind, but the kind that sop up oil and other spills from around industrial equipment.)

Borland Software and Quattro Pro. How do you compete with a market leader whose products define a category, a leader that's the software equivalent of IBM as the safe choice in the spreadsheet market? Borland found the answer in conquest direct marketing.

Perkin Elmer. This industrial and electronic equipment manufacturer had left the supply of consumables and other supplies for its extensive line of products to aftermarket suppliers. Perkin Elmer used conquest marketing to recapture a significant share of this lucrative market.

Stride-Rite Shoes. In the market for childrens' shoes, where the parents' first purchase usually determines the brand they buy for their children for years to come, Stride-Rite used a conquest campaign to become the shoe manufacturer of choice for many new parents.

BASF. The floppy diskette market is a highly competitive one, in which consumers often see no difference between brands. BASF successfully penetrated the corporate bulk-purchase market with conquest direct marketing techniques.

CONQUEST MARKETING: A DEFINITION

Acquiring market share and sales at the expense of your competitors with a marketing strategy that targets users or prospective users of a competitive product.

THE CHARACTERISTICS OF A CONQUEST MARKET

A market must have at least one of the following characteristics to be a candidate for conquesting:

Slow or No Growth in Total Units or Total Dollars (Adjusted for Inflation) Purchased

If a market is rapidly growing, other strategies are generally more appropriate than a conquest strategy. In a growing, dynamic market with relatively low product penetration and no customer affiliation, you have an opportunity to build sales from a large potential base of noncategory users. Stealing share from a competitor is not as important. Examples of slow/no growth markets include:

The automobile industry, in which the total units sold in the United States has remained relatively flat

The credit card industry, in which each household has an average of five to seven cards, and in which most bank card marketing is focused on getting greater "share of wallet"

A Few Players in Control of the Market

In a market with many players, a conquest strategy is much more difficult. A successful conquest strategy generally targets customers of a specific competitor with a focused marketing effort. Examples of this type of market include:

Long-distance carriers (AT&T, MCI, US Sprint)

Spreadsheets (Lotus, Microsoft, Borland)

A Generic, Noninnovative Product

A product category with a generic product is ripe for conquesting if the conquestor can introduce a significant innovation in product or distribution. Examples of this type of market include:

Industrial cleaners

Office supplies

Personal computers (IBM clones)

Consumers with Some Brand Loyalty

In markets or product categories where consumers show no reluctance to switch or no brand loyalty, conquest marketing is generally not appropriate. While a conquest campaign could cause a consumer to switch brands, the consumer will show no loyalty to the conquestor. The casino industry would appear to be a conquest market, and meets most of the above criteria. However, consumers show little loyalty to a particular casino, and are quick to switch to a competitor whenever they feel their luck at a particular casino has run out. In casino marketing, much of the emphasis is on influencing consumers to start their evening at a particular casino. *An exception can occur if the conquestor can bring a significant innovation to the market that will change the consumer's buying behavior.*

WHAT CONQUEST MARKETING IS NOT

Most marketers feel that their markets are highly competitive, and that they and their competitors are all chasing after a limited universe. It is important to understand the boundaries between conquest marketing and other marketing strategies. The following examples are not considered conquest marketing, even though they might be used alongside conquest marketing as part of a company's marketing plan:

Increasing Sales Through Purchase Stimulation to Existing Customers

Once you have a customer, you no longer have to "conquest them." *Retention, usage stimulation, cross-selling,* and *reactivation* are all "internally" directed, whereas conquesting is directed at noncustomers.

Creating New Uses or Markets for Existing Products

This could be an appropriate strategy for companies whose primary markets exhibit the characteristics that make them suitable for conquesting. If it was appropriate, a company could use a conquesting strategy to enter the new market but creating new uses for an existing product is not, in itself, conquest marketing.

Creating New Markets Through New Distribution Channels

Establishing a new distribution channel is often a good way to create a new market. It can also be used in conquest marketing. For example, Dell Computers successfully established mail order as a distribution channel for high-quality, low-priced personal computers. Dell offered high-quality technical support via telephone, extensive customer service, and low prices. Dell was successful in conquesting the existing business market, where they gained significant share, *and* in encouraging new customers to enter the market. Dell was able to support two strategies with the same tactic.

It is important to note that a conquest marketing strategy can use all the same direct-response tactics used by other strategies. It is not the tactics that are unique, but the strategy, which focuses on gaining share from competitors.

FIVE MARKET SITUATIONS IN WHICH CONQUEST MARKETING WORKS

1. A Replacement Market

This is a market in which a majority of the purchases each year are from customers replacing or upgrading existing products. If the existing product served the customer well, and if the manufacturer has updated the product, the purchaser will be predisposed to replace it with the same brand.

A conquest marketing plan for this market might include:

- A positioning that offers a discount or promotion for upgrading from the customer's current brand to your brand
- Building a database of current product owners
- A survey to this database collecting information on purchase plans
- Purchase of demographics and lifestyle information on prospects
- Modelling to predict which current product owners are most likely to purchase your product and when they might do it
- Direct marketing campaigns timed to coincide with their purchase cycle
- Special offers and promotions that reference the product they currently own

In the auto industry, for example, manufacturers can purchase information about the models, their age, and the length of ownership of all the cars registered to an individual. Combined with demographic and lifestyle information, this can be the backbone of a very powerful direct marketing program.

2. A Brand-Loyal, Repeat-Purchase Market

This market is one in which the customer is constantly purchasing additional units of the product, and would continue to buy the same brand without significant intervention. This is also a market in which there are barriers to change.

The corporate PC software market is a good example of a brand-loyal market. Most companies try to standardize one or two products for each software category to maximize their employees' ability to share files and work on each other's projects. This also minimizes training and software support issues for the company. Once a certain software package is established as the standard in that company, most future purchases of that category will be the same product. (The children's shoe market shares the same repeat-purchase pattern.)

One way to conquest this type of market is to identify the people who influence the purchase decision, and target them for the conquest effort. For example, Borland recognized that it would have to break Lotus' stranglehold of the corporate market for spreadsheets, and targeted existing Lotus users for their marketing efforts. One main goal was to generate good word-of-mouth within a company and to get Quattro Pro placed on a company's approved title list.

Another example of a brand-loyal, repeat-purchase market is the infant formula market. Infant formula manufacturers target pediatricians and hospitals, who in turn influence (and often specify) the brand of infant formula that new parents should buy for their infants. Recently some manufacturers have attempted to market directly to parents. Their efforts have met with strong medical-community objections, and the jury is still out at the time of this writing on the programs' effectiveness.

3. A Geographically Defined Market

This type of market is often a retail market, in which stores carrying similar products compete for a limited number of customers within a specific trading area. It can also be a market in which sales territories are geographically defined.

A number of companies offer innovative products to help marketers working with geographically defined markets. Products useful in conquesting campaigns include Donnelley Conquest, Lotus Marketplace, Spectra, and their equivalents. Citicorp POS Information Business also offers innovative help in conquest marketing for package-goods manufacturers who work with markets defined by a supermarket chain's trading area.

Manufacturer-sponsored programs for lead generation and retail traffic stimulation are often used in conquesting a geographic market. The manufacturer identifies appropriate prospects and executes specific campaigns that motivate the prospect to visit or contact a specific retail outlet. Retailers often develop databases of prospects who work or live in their trading area and segment these databases using lifestyle and demographic characteristics to target their direct marketing efforts. These efforts can be general traffic builders, or be centered around specific products. Retail chains that have a catalog program often use the catalog to generate traffic at their retail outlets. The Stride-Rite case study at the end of this chapter is an example of conquesting a geographically defined market.

4. A Transient Market

This is a market in which the total number of users is not growing, and in which the population using the product category is constantly in transition because individual users need the product for only a limited period of time.

In conquesting a transient market, efforts should generally be spent on identifying prospects about to enter the market. Unless a consumer makes a large number of repeat purchases in the category, efforts made to switch users often cannot be cost-justified.

Procter and Gamble, for example, makes extensive efforts to identify expectant mothers, and even offers a free parents' magazine as an incentive. Their goal: to make a mother's first purchase of diapers a P&G brand, and to lock in brand loyalty early on. This is followed by constant promotion and discount couponing to continue promoting brand loyalty. (Similarly, colleges and trade schools regularly target high school juniors and seniors for their marketing efforts.)

5. An Inertia Market

In this market, customers make repeat purchases and generally use the same brand out of inertia, but have no strong brand loyalty and will change suppliers with appropriate innovation or promotion.

Inertia markets must be approached carefully in determining whether a conquest campaign will be successful. Because there is little brand loyalty, a conquest campaign must have a short-term pay-back, since consumers may have no more brand loyalty to the conquesting company than they did before. Conquest marketing campaigns for inertia markets often have a very short pay-back or are not executed at all. Some companies use a conquest campaign to switch a competitor's customers to their brand and link that to a campaign to immediately build brand loyalty.

Bank credit cards (MasterCard or Visa) are an excellent example of an inertia market. Most U.S. households have around 5–7 bank credit cards. Banks regularly wage conquesting campaigns to capture "share of wallet" and to ensure that their card is the one consumers use. Once they select their primary card, consumers will often continue to use it out of habit, although they might have selected it initially for a specific interest rate, affinity, or added service benefit.

Citibank is one of the nation's most effective bank-card marketers. They wage an annual conquest campaign to capture share of market during the 5 months before Christmas when consumers make the majority of their purchases. Citibank runs a free-gift program with rewards ranging from waiving of fee to free airline tickets, VCRs, and TVs to motivate the consumer to switch all their purchases to their Citibank card during the busiest charge season. The payoff to Citibank is two-fold: increased interest and merchant interchange fees during the promotion because of the higher charge volume, and a residual effect in which their card remains the primary card in the consumer's wallet even after the promotion.

Implication: *Understanding which of these market types applies to your product will determine the appropriate direct-response tactics to include in a conquest marketing plan. Many markets will exhibit characteristics of more than one market type, which increases the variety of tactics that could be used in a successful conquest campaign.*

FIVE KEY STEPS IN DEVELOPING A SUCCESSFUL CONQUEST MARKETING PLAN

Developing a successful conquest marketing strategy is similar to developing any successful marketing strategy. However, the steps outlined below deserve special emphasis in conquesting. They are the ones successful conquestors credit most with being key to their success.

1. Identify Competitive Weaknesses and Market Opportunities

One common characteristic of successful conquest marketing campaigns is that they exploit a temporary or permanent weakness in a competitor.
Questions you might ask:

Who are your major competitors?

What are their strengths?

How are your products better than theirs?

Do any competitors have a significant weakness, whether real or perceived by the market?

Are there substitutes for your product outside your traditional competitors?

How is the market, and mix of competitors, changing?

You are looking for a significant window of opportunity opened by your competitor.

MCI and US Sprint recognized that AT&T's pricing policies and delays in introducing technology into the telecommunications services marketplace had created a significant opportunity for an innovative competitor.

Toddler University, a children's shoe manufacturer, saw that the children's shoe market basically had no fashion and technological innovation, and created an overnight success by bringing innovative design (and a premium price) to children's shoes.

Borland Software recognized that Lotus' long delay in providing a significant upgrade to its basic spreadsheet product, and its customers' growing dissatisfaction presented a conquesting opportunity.

2. Understand Your Customers and How They Buy

Understanding your customers' and prospects' purchase patterns, hot buttons, and loyalties is critical to designing a successful conquesting campaign and choosing the correct direct-response techniques. Areas to consider include:

Frequency of purchase

Typical volume of purchase

Duration of purchase patterns (lifetime, during limited period, one time)

Importance of brand in purchase

Importance of price in purchase

Source of information in making purchase decision

Need for convenient distribution

Likelihood that customer will switch brands

Is the purchaser the decision maker?

Other people influencing the purchase decision

How the purchase decision is made

Analyzing these factors will help you determine who to target for your conquest: the end user, the influencer, the specifier, the distribution channel or other intermediary

The timing of your campaign

The offer and promotion

New Pig Corporation, the maker of a product that absorbs industrial spills and oils from the manufacturing floor, recognized that the buyers of their product, companies' purchasing agents, bought on the basis of price. They realized that the end user of the product, the maintenance staff, had very different concerns: effectiveness, how frequently they had to replace the product, and ease of use. By focusing their conquesting efforts on the end user, New Pig was able to build a $25-million business.

3. Look for Opportunities Among the Existing Distribution Channels for Your Product Category

Many marketers overlook the existing distribution channels in planning a conquest strategy, and miss significant opportunities. Two possible approaches along these lines include:

- Designing a conquest campaign for the distribution channels to generate support and sales efforts for your product
- Developing a new distribution channel through catalogs or direct to end-user sales efforts

If you have a sales force or retail store, make sure they are part of your conquest effort. Communicate effectively, early, and frequently. Promote the purpose of the program and the likelihood that your direct-mail effort will likely drive more sales to the retail store or sales force. A poor communications effort can result in chaos. Retail stores can decide to withdraw brand support, feeling that direct mail is in competition with them. The field sales force can become discouraged and leave, or not bother selling that particular product. Without the underlying understanding, a critical gap in your marketing efforts will occur.

4. Innovate

A common theme of most successful conquest campaigns is innovation. Whether in distribution, product, pricing, promotion, marketing, or service, innovation can mean the difference between success and failure in conquesting. The customer needs a reason to switch.

5. Deliver on Your Promise

In many markets, your competitors will launch a win-back campaign to counter your successful conquesting efforts. A key part of a conquesting strategy must be to ensure that your company delivers on its promises; otherwise, your new customer will be a transient one.

SEVEN CONQUESTING TACTICS (OR HOW TO LEGALLY REACH YOUR COMPETITORS' CUSTOMERS)

Generally speaking, your competitors won't rent you their customer lists, although it never hurts to check with a list broker or the *Standard Rate and Data Service Directory* on their availability. If your competitors are uncooperative, there are a number of other ways to find and reach their prospects.

1. Analyze Your Database

Your database is the first place you should look when trying to identify potential prospects. It is likely that a simple city, state, and zip analysis correlated with product sales information can help you determine the geographic skews for each of your products, as well as rough spending patterns. Once analyzed, try to deduce why those patterns exist. They could come from the demographics of the media or lists which you used to market your product, or represent the natural profile of people likely to use your product. Census demographics are an inexpensive way to start. Other ways include:

Information Overlays.   Most computer service bureaus have the ability to append demographic and psychographic information to a customer file. The file is then analyzed to determine which characteristics are predominant. Once the dominant traits are identified, list rental, media, and marketing test plans can be designed which focus on prospects with similar traits.

Cluster Analysis.   Like information overlays, cluster analysis helps identify broad customer-characteristic groups. The difference lies in the way the information is collated. Rather than just identifying the dominant characteristics, several discriminate factors are used to group together consumers who generally share similar product preferences and purchase behavior patterns. Each individual on a database is assigned to one of the clusters. The clusters generally have descriptive names that provide an image of the individuals in the cluster. For example, Claritas, a company that specializes in cluster analysis, has created over 40 cluster groups with names like "Shotguns and Pickups." Similar products are offered by CACI, Donnelley, and others.

In cluster analysis, the names on your database are analyzed to determine which clusters your existing customers fall into most frequently. Once the most promising clusters are identified, names with similar characteristics can be purchased from numerous list sources, including the major compilers. The analysis can be refined to target prospects down to a census block group.

Implication: *Your own list provides the best guide to who your prospects are and what they are likely to buy in the future.*

2. Ask Prospects and Customers for Their Opinions

Unless your company has been highly pro-active at the time of sale, you probably have not captured lifestyle, income, or general demographic information for the database. By using a statistically significant number of surveys aimed at people already on your database, you can determine prospect needs, wants and desires, the types of media they read, and the types of products they use. Questionnaires can be used to identify seemingly irrelevant information. For example, one such questionnaire asked about leisure-time activities, successfully identifying gardeners as potential prospects in a category that had nothing to do with gardening.

Also examine people who have purchased in the past but are no longer customers. These "trial resistors" could provide useful insights into why people with the same profile might not want to buy your product.

Implication: *If there are information holes in your database, don't fret. Use questionnaires, information overlays, or even cluster analysis to help determine the best ways to reach your audience.*

3. Look for Affinity-Product Ownership

Even if your direct competitor won't rent its list, companies selling affinity products to prospects will rent theirs. For example, Borland wanted to reach users of Lotus 1-2-3. Not surprisingly, Lotus wouldn't rent its list. Instead, Borland rented lists of people responding to other direct-mail offers for Lotus enhancement products, such as "Sideways," a spreadsheet printing program. Based on information from the list manager, Borland knew that this particular list contained over half a million names of Lotus users who purchased aftermarket products via the mail; that they lived in households generating over $70,000 per year in income; and that 80 percent were males. These represented good targets for Borland.

Also consider compiled or mass lists provided by credit bureaus such as TRW and Equifax, and compilers such as R. L. Polk, Donnelley, and Metromail. For an additional fee, these companies will provide a number of enhancements based on public record, demographic, and lifestyle information. These providers will develop models or screens that select names from their databases with characteristics similar to your existing customers. Unfortunately, compiled lists don't necessarily indicate whether a person is a direct-mail buyer or not. Therefore, response is likely to be less from these lists than from known direct-mail-responsive lists.

Implication: *When blocked, look for lists in which there is a high probability that users of the competitive product use another product that indicates a predisposition to buy your product. If necessary, consider the use of compiled lists, but recognize their weaknesses.*

4. Identify Customers Based on Geographic/Lifestyle Changes

There are numerous services that can identify potential customers based on geographic data combined with demographic and psychographic information. These services will advise you about which geographic areas offer the best opportunities. You can then rent geographically selected lists that match the resulting market profile.

Donnelley Conquest. This is a series of computer programs based on matching geographic boundaries, addresses of existing customers, and demographics. Conquest offers a number of useful tools. Of particular interest is its support of conquest direct marketing for retail- and sales-territory-based markets. In a typical application, you first define the boundaries of your market, trading area, or sales territory. Conquest then maps your existing customers within those geographic boundaries. It can access most of the D&B and Donnelley business and consumer databases to develop various profiles of your existing customers and of your market, based on demographics and other data. Using these profiles, you can then select names off the Donnelley and D&B databases which both match the profile, and which reside within the appropriate geography. The geography boundaries do not have to follow existing boundaries like zip codes, but can be almost any shape.

Lotus Marketplace. This is a new product that allows marketers to select names to mail from a database provided on CD ROM using their personal computer. Names come with some basic demographics, and users can select by demographics or geography. They pay a fee in advance which entitles them to download a fixed number of names from the CD ROM. They can purchase access to more names via telephone from Lotus. This brings conquest direct marketing to the desktop, and makes it possible for small organizations to become conquestors.

Spectra. Package-goods companies have been trying for years to utilize direct marketing techniques to sell more product against their prospect base. Most of these programs have been discontinued due to the high cost of execution, low product margins, and questionable sales results. However, there are some modeling techniques that are direct marketing derived and that may be of help to package marketers. One promising conquesting tool is called Spectra Advantage.

A database product, the Spectra premise is that lifestyle alone is not an ade quate predictor of consumer behavior. Rather, the presence of children and household age must be overlayed against specific lifestyle segments.

Spectra differs from other cluster analytical techniques in that household diary panel data is included in their model. This consumption data is generated by NPD Nielsen and/or IRI, a check-out scanner system located in several markets throughout the United States. Since more households are tracked by IRI, regional panel projections can be created to reflect geographic differences. This information is then mathematically projected to 92 million U.S. households resulting in grocery volume per household at the brand and category level. This information is organized by six age/children breaks subsegmented by nine lifestyle segments. The result is a 54-cell analytical matrix used to rank order category buyers by type of brand used, based on purchase behavior, lifestyle, and lifestage. As in other cluster techniques, the resulting analysis can be used to drive the selection of names for a targeted conquest campaign.

Implication: *Enhancements have the potential to make your campaign more efficient by minimizing unproductive names and lower-than-average geographic response areas.*

5. Get Your Competitors' Customers to Call You

Prospects are like grammar-school children. They'll voluntarily raise their hands to indicate an interest in a product or service. Sometimes the prospect will even pay the way, either through phone calls or by responding to an inexpensive self-liquidating offer.

Lead generation programs require a means for interaction between the customer and the company. Methods include phone numbers (toll-free and paid), mailed-in orders from advertising, fax numbers, computers, coupon redemption, etc.

Utilize effective media, such as print ads, television direct-response commercials, on-line databases (like Prodigy and CompuServe), radio, free standing inserts, co-op mailings, Sunday supplements, and outdoor advertising. You should also consider piggyback promotions with affinity products through package-insert programs, bouncebacks stuffed in retail boxes, and joint marketing programs.

A recent development in lead generation is the use of partially or completely self-liquidating lead generation promotions based on 900 numbers. When a consumer dials a 900 number, he or she is charged a fee for the call, which is split between the telephone company and the program sponsor. The sponsor can use his or her share to fund part of the promotion.

Implication: *Lead generation programs help you go outside the limiting rental list universe. As a result, offers can be targeted directly at competitive users. Importantly, since the customers have "raised their hands," they have indicated an interest in buying your product or service. Therefore, they have prequalified themselves, making these prospects better purchase candidates.*

6. Draft Help from an Intermediary

Use direct mail to convince an intermediary to support your product. This is an approach used frequently in medical marketing. The intermediary can be an influencer, the end user or the specifier in organizations where purchases are made by purchasing departments, or links in the distribution chain who can act as your sales force.

Infant formula manufacturers, for example, target most of their direct response and promotion to intermediaries: pediatricians, nurses, and OB/GYNs, along with an extensive in-hospital free sampling program, because mothers rely heavily on the recommendation of their pediatricians in choosing their brand of infant formula. The pediatrician, not the parent, generally makes the formula brand decision.

Formula companies, including Gerber, with its new product introduction, are starting to target parents directly via direct response, but have met with extensive resistance from the medical profession. But to date, direct-to-consumer programs are still uncommon.

Implication: *Word-of-mouth is a powerful tool. It can be made more effective when the intermediary receives the necessary information to become your expert on the subject.*

7. Check-It Out at Supermarkets

The introduction of scanner technology in supermarkets and other retailers has opened up a whole new world of conquesting techniques, as well as new forms of direct response. Citicorp POS Information Business, for example, sponsors a number of programs in which it tracks the purchases of individual households. This information is used for frequent-buyer programs and to enable package-goods manufacturers to launch direct marketing conquest campaigns, targeted at households that purchase competitive products. Other companies offer point-of-sale programs in which coupons are issued at the cash register based on the purchases the consumer has made.

Implication: *New scanner technology offers interesting opportunities for package-goods marketers to identify heavy users of competitive brands. This information can then be used to develop programs that encourage change in buying behavior.*

NINE WAYS TO DEFEND AGAINST A CONQUEST MARKETING SITUATION

The best way to defend against conquest marketing is to make sure it can't happen to you. Consider implementing the following steps:

1. Determine Who the Real Customer Is

The purchaser may not be the user or the key influencer. After you identify the key people, allocate the necessary marketing dollars to let them know about your product and improvements.

Airline travel programs recognized long ago that their customer was not the corporate travel department, but the business traveler. By targeting the ticket holder with incentives to specify particular airlines, the travel department became merely the agent, not the decision maker.

2. Listen to Your Customers

Use primary research techniques like interviews, focus groups, and analysis of white mail to keep track of customer needs, wants, and desires. Track customer complaints and compliments that come in via inbound telemarketing, with orders, or from unsolicited letters. Look at the information frequently, at least weekly, so that you can respond quickly to the problems and needs your customers have.

Lands' End is well known for listening to its customers. Weekly, the company tracks customer complaints, product returns, and the reasons why products are returned. Information is compiled from telemarketing operators and letters describing product problems. As a result of tracking this information several years ago, Lands' End discovered that its rugby shirt shrank after only one washing. Product improvements were subsequently made that made the rugby shirt a popular item.

3. Innovate, Innovate, Innovate

Improvements in your products, customer service, marketing techniques, and offers should be tested and implemented on an ongoing basis. Make sure to communicate these improvements to your existing customers as well as to your prospects.

Sometimes innovative improvements are as simple as taking advantage of readily available direct marketing techniques. For instance, 800-FLOWERS began selling flowers and gift baskets via an 800 number several years ago. Unlike FTD, 800-FLOWERS maintains a database of about 250,000 active customers, utilizing it to keep current customers happy and loyal. For example, customers will receive a dozen roses free after 12 orders. There are also special automatic-reminder and shipment programs that remind you about special occasions. According to *Direct* magazine, these innovative methods have enabled the company to grow to four telemarketing centers with over 200 operators and a network of 10,000 florists.

4. Expand Your Product's Competitive Horizon

Is your market too narrow to defend? Can it be broadened, not only as a way to build share and sales, but also as a defensive measure against unexpected competitive marketing programs?

For example, Nintendo is not just competing in the video game market. It is competing in the leisure market for its share of 7-to-12-year-old attention. Several direct marketing programs are utilized to build product awareness and generate retail traffic, including *Nintendo* magazine. Sent to over 10 million paid subscribers, the magazine highlights new products and provides advice and hints on how to play various games. As a result of these efforts, Nintendo is not just generating retail traffic for its products but is also redefining how children spend their time.

5. Show Your Customers You Love Them

Customers love acknowledgment. Send thank-you notes, information updates, order confirmations, fast and continual apologies for back orders, and even holiday greetings. Even while you are resolving a problem, you can be strengthening your relationship with your customer.

One of the best direct-mail "love you" programs is probably the American Express newsletter. Every month, the newsletter provides American Express members with travel tips, new product information, and articles on a variety of subjects. Although any credit card could be used to purchase products reviewed in the newsletter, this form of relationship direct marketing creates a strong association between the product being reviewed and the American Express company.

6. Provide Tangible Incentives That Generate Customer Loyalty

Incentive programs, if structured correctly, provide an excellent way to retain customers at minimal cost. A good example is the REI camping gear catalog. For a minimal fee, you can become a lifetime member of the REI co-op. Using inbound telemarketing operators and catalog sell copy to help sell memberships, the program is designed to build customer loyalty over the long term. The incentive to join, and reorder from the catalog, is that a certain percentage of excess REI profits are rebated to co-op members at the end of the year. This yearly rebate helps to reinforce customer loyalty.

7. Provide Excellent Customer Service

Nothing beats an unlimited, unconditional guarantee or well-trained, knowledgeable and friendly telemarketing personnel. Or a customer service department that responds quickly to questions.

Eddie Bauer is a good example. A friend once bought an Eddie Bauer down coat through the mail. Several years after the purchase, the coat had lost a lot of its down feathers. An Eddie Bauer telephone operator informed the customer that the coat would be repaired for cost plus shipping and handling. The coat was sent out to Bauer. A return notice came back about a week later asking the customer if they would like the coat to be repaired for about $10. Since a replacement coat was $200, the customer took advantage of the offer.

Nothing was left to chance. The operator was well trained, the repair offer was excellent, and the company asked for authorization to spend the customer' money. The result is a loyal customer.

8. Anticipate Demographic and Lifestyle Changes

Build a database model that recognizes that your customer is a changing, dynamic creature given to lifestyle and attitude changes that impact purchase behavior. Predict likely purchase behavior based on age, household income, number of family members living at home, and other demographic and lifestyle data. Determine which categories your customers fall into when they first become purchasers. As they and their families get older, try to identify changing product needs. For example, a family with a 1-year-old will probably buy clothing, but as the child reaches kindergarten, parents may shift their buying patterns to continuity children's book clubs and away from direct-mail clothing purchases. As children get older, parents may also decide that it's time to trade in the subcompact for a station wagon. A well-designed database that tracks this maturing customer could be preprogrammed to send out a direct-mail piece, or a telemarketing call, to try to convince the prospect that now is the time for a larger car.

9. Never Lose an Opportunity to Sell

Use cross-sell and upsell techniques within your mailings and telemarketing operations to upgrade purchases or sell affinity products.

The Swan Tussey Computer company uses upselling and cross-selling techniques to increase the average order. Operators are trained, and motivated, to ask first-time computer purchasers if they need additional software, accessories, memory upgrades, and extended warranty protection.

By recognizing that first-time computer buyers have need for additional items, the company is able to capture a larger share of their overall category purchases and establish a stronger relationship with the first-time buyer.

CONQUESTING CASE STUDIES

The following case studies illustrate a wide variety of circumstances in which conquest direct marketing has worked.

Borland Software: Changing the Way PC Software Is Marketed

Background. The purchase of personal computer software is driven by product reviews, word-of-mouth, compatibility with current products, and office standards. Most corporate users of a particular category purchase the product already being used in their offices in order to be compatible with their coworkers. Once an initial base of users is established within a company, it is very difficult to switch.

Within this marketplace, Lotus is the dominant force in the spreadsheet arena, with close to 70 percent of the existing market. Other major competitors include Borland's Quattro Pro and Microsoft's Excel. The total spreadsheet market is valued at nearly $1 billion.

Borland Software introduced Quattro Pro in October of 1989. Not surprisingly, Borland identified Lotus 1-2-3 as its main competitor. While new users continued to purchase spreadsheets, the installed base of Lotus users offered a market with more potential than did trying to win a greater share of new spreadsheet purchases. In addition, in understanding market dynamics, Borland determined that new purchases of spreadsheets were driven primarily by word-of-mouth, and by what products were currently in use in the workplace. (Importantly, once people have become used to a particular product, getting them to switch is a very tough sell.)

Borland also recognized an opportunity to conquest Lotus' user base since Lotus had failed to release a significant Lotus 1-2-3 upgrade for almost two years. In addition to including most of the new features Lotus users had been requesting, Borland designed Quattro Pro to be 100 percent information-compatible with current Lotus software, overcoming a significant barrier to usage.

Aside from an innovative product, Borland introduced the "Competitive Upgrade," by which Lotus users could upgrade to Quattro Pro for $99, about one-third of the normal retail selling price. Competitive owners had only to bring a copy of the title page from a competitor's manual to get the discount. This is now a standard way to market software.

Borland's Program Objective: To build significant sales and share from the largest installed base of spreadsheet users.

Strategy and Tactics. Borland's strategy was to introduce a new and improved product ahead of the competition that was highly information-compatible with the competitor's installed base. Users were motivated to switch by means of a strong financial incentive; the normal selling price was maintained for repeat purchases.

Borland's tactics were as follows:

1. To develop direct-response print and mail programs targeting the installed Lotus user base that also supported the retail trade

2. To create a dealer-locator program to drive traffic to the retailers

3. To provide competitive users with a hard-to-refuse incentive, i.e., the ability to purchase Quattro Pro at about one-third the normal selling price

4. To identify the installed user-base via affinity lists that indicated competitive product ownership

Results: While specifics were not available, Borland has been able to capture a large number of Lotus users through a deep discount program, while maintaining a normal selling price for repeat purchases.

Implication: *If the margins are there, offer innovative products at a deep discount that makes it hard to refuse. Use direct marketing operations to support the retail channels of distribution to maintain their support of your sales efforts.*

AT&T Universal Card: The Best Defense Is a Good Offense

Background. Long-distance telephone growth is maturing. Currently, the three major competitors, Sprint, AT&T, and MCI, are battling each other for sales and share at the expense of one another. Given the size of the market (over $40 billion per year) each company is seeking to offer more innovative service offerings than the others as a way to build business.

One of the most successful efforts has been phone cards. Patterned after the AT&T calling card, MCI and Sprint cards have enabled callers to charge their phone usage from pay phones and phones not hooked up to their long-distance carrier. This has enabled people on the road to take advantage of discounts that MCI and Sprint offered relative to AT&T. These efforts, among others, have reduced AT&T's market share to under 70 percent.

In early 1990, AT&T launched the Universal charge card in conjunction with Universal Bank. The card, available as a Visa card or MasterCard, was offered with a guarantee of no fee for the life of the holder. Additional benefits included a 10 percent discount on all long-distance calls, instant credit on disputed charges, free collision coverage on rental cars, and a slightly lower than average interest rate. The card generated over 4.5 million signups by the end of 1990. It is estimated that mailings generated more than a 5 percent response.

It is thought that AT&T entered the market not only as a way to reinforce customer loyalty, but also to develop a new source of income to offset their share declines in the long-distance arena.

Not surprisingly, research indicates that the card not only replaced at least one calling card, it also eliminated at least one other credit card. Given that each qualified American adult has access to more than one Visa and MasterCard, AT&T is actually running a conquest effort against competing credit card issuers. Conversely, AT&T is running a defensive, loyalty building program against its own customer base.

AT&T's Program Objective: To generate new source of income and revenue and reinforce the advantages of using AT&T.

Strategy and Tactics. AT&T's strategy was to undercut the competition and eliminate its tactical advantage.

AT&T's tactics were as follows:

1. To utilize in-house database to target customers, all of whom might be using more than one carrier, or might be likely to switch to another product sometime in the future

2. To deliver the primary offer via direct mail, but utilize 800 number within print ads (TV was a support medium for mail in that it did not provide for a response mechanism)

3. To make the AT&T long-distance operators part of the marketing mix by having operators automatically switch request-for-information calls to an inbound telemarketing group

Implication: *Defensive marketing doesn't have to be defensive. Identify the ways you can leverage your customer base into other, profitable areas.*

New Pig Corporation: Changing Old Habits

Background.   Companies spend in excess of $150 million annually to clean up oil and other machinery-fluid drippings on factory floors. A dirty and mature business, most of the sales are made by distributor sales representatives calling directly on factory managers. As a result, if a new product doesn't catch on quickly, or provide a significant profit margin for the distributor, it does not sell.

The market is currently dominated by clay-type products that are loosely spread on floors around machinery, much the same way salt is spread on snowy and icy road surfaces. An alternative is to use a socklike product, called a pig, named after the New Pig company that developed it. Containing absorption materials stuffed inside it, the product is just picked up when it can no longer absorb any more oil.

Generally, these pigs are more expensive on a pound-per-pound basis. However, many claim that these socks are easier to handle and can absorb much greater amounts of oil than loose clay.

Currently doing in excess of $20 million in sales, New Pig first distributed its products via distributors. But although the distributors were initially intrigued by the product, their customers were not, and the distributors eventually returned most of the inventory to New Pig. The problem was that the pig was almost five times as expensive as loose clay and that distributors were selling to purchasing managers, not to the facilities managers. New Pig owner Don Beaver discovered that purchasing agents focus on costs, not innovation. The people the distributors did not speak to, facilities managers, on the other hand, were the real market. To help push sales, New Pig told prospects that if they didn't like the pigs, they didn't have to pay for them.

By accident, the company discovered that direct mail was the most effective means to reach its prospects. In an effort to circumvent the distributors, New Pig created its own outside sales force and supported its efforts by direct mail to prospects, i.e., facility managers. To the company's amazement, in one month alone, 3000 mailers produced 100 responses and $10,000 in sales in 1 month.

New Pig's Program Objective: To build sales and share at the expense of the competition.

Strategy and Tactics.   New Pig's strategy was to convince end users of other products that pigs are a better way to absorb oil than loose clay products, and to have the end users purchase directly or influence the purchasing agents to order.

New Pig's tactics were as follows:

1. To utilize direct mail, catalogs, and solo mailings targeted at facilities managers, and to provide a response device for direct ordering.

2. To use humor to sell. (For example, New Pig is located at 1 Pork Plaza and has a toll-free number that spells out HOT-HOGS.)

Results: During the last five years, New Pig Corporation sales have gone from $0 to $20 million, all due to direct mail.

Implication: *Conquesting requires innovative thinking. Utilize resources to bypass roadblocks. Find the key influencers, the people who actually use the product, in order to convince the decision maker to buy the product. Humor can help.*

BASF: The Trial Strategy

Background. The highly competitive computer diskette market has many entries, including major players such as Sony, Fuji, Kodak, Dysan, and Precision. Private-label discounters, from companies such as Quill Business Supplies and MEI Micro Center, provide equivalent product at nearly 25 to 50 percent of the cost of branded product. Research indicates that most users perceive little product differentiation, and for branded products, little difference in quality.

BASF is a major player in the computer diskette marketplace. In 1987, BASF 5.25-in diskettes were rated the best in the "Floppy Disk Quality Report" appearing in *Computer Reseller News.*

BASF's Program Objective: To convince volume corporate purchasers to consider it as a source for their purchases and to call a sales representative for an appointment.

Strategy and Tactics. BASF's strategy was to prove the superiority of BASF diskettes with a free giveaway.

BASF's tactics were as follows:

1. To obtain rental lists containing 12,018 prospects identified as heavy-volume purchasers

2. To offer a free test of three diskettes with a brochure that looked like a diskette (with a reply slip included in the actual diskette sleeve)

3. To emphasize in the brochure the fact that BASF was named the best brand by *Computer Reseller News,* a well-known publication among the prospect audience

Results: The campaign generated a 14 percent response rate. Of those responding, over 30 percent asked to see a sales representative. Actual sales were 40 percent over projections.[1]

Implication: *Within a unique marketplace, strong offers are a powerful conquesting tool. Outside substantiation also provides the impartial expertise to support the offer. Unique creative execution helps to cut through the clutter, further enhancing this conquesting vehicle.*

Perkin Elmer: Listening to Customers and Giving Them What They Want

Background. Ranging from $500 lamps that could pass for small halogen bulbs, to metal columns, the aftermarket for chemical, biological, and optical analytical supplies is estimated to gross over a billion dollars a year. These products are primarily sold via mail order for a variety of instruments manufactured by different companies. The products are generic and interchangeable. The hardware lasts for years, but supplies integral to the workings of the instruments are used up quickly. Replacement parts and supplies not on hand are needed quickly to keep expensive instruments running.

Major growth comes from price increases, not from an expanding market. Prospects tend to be highly educated scientists, technicians, and purchasing agents. Frequently the people using a particular instrument are also the ones placing the order.

Due to a superior customer-service strategy that allowed for easy ordering and delivery, competitive aftermarket suppliers had reduced Perkin Elmer's market share significantly by the late 1980s. Also, while Perkin Elmer instrument sales representatives could take supply orders, they did so only as a customer courtesy. (Primary commissions are generated from instrument sales, not supply sales.)

Given this situation and research that indicated that more Perkin Elmer instrument owners would prefer to buy Perkin Elmer branded aftermarket products, the company decided to aggressively pursue this potentially profitable segment in 1988. (Note: it is common to find competitive aftermarket products in use on Perkin Elmer machines.)

Perkin Elmer's Program Objective: To regain lost aftermarket sales and share among the installed Perkin Elmer customer base.

Strategy and Tactics.   Perkin Elmer's strategy in the aftermarkets area was to position itself as a company that provided excellent customer service and quick and easy access to instrument products.

The technical nature of its products required extensive copy and illustrations to portray its offerings accurately, so Perkin Elmer decided that a well-focused catalog program offered the best opportunity to build its aftermarket business. Specifically, its tactics were as follows:

1. To target the installed base of 110,000 Perkin Elmer users (chemists, laboratory managers, and lab purchasing agents), building lists from warranty cards and sales force hardware leads, and to confirm names via outbound telemarketing

2. To create a series of catalogs addressing the different segments within the analytical supplies area

3. To provide toll-free telephone ordering and technical assistance as well as a number for faxing orders

4. To offer an unconditional guarantee

5. To minimize back orders with high in-stock on all items

6. To ship products within 24 hours and offer emergency overnight delivery via Federal Express or UPS

7. To reinforce customer service within catalogs via illustrations, copy, and photographs of customer service representatives

8. To make the catalog user-friendly by including a table of contents, clear page

headings, a comprehensive product index, and blow-apart diagrams that show how to order the correct part

9. To utilize lead generation techniques, such as 800 numbers in trade publications, blow-in cards in catalogs, and qualifying questionnaires to ensure that the company has sent the correct catalog to a prospect within a particular specialty

Results: Nonproprietary information indicates that in a little over a year, program revenue more than doubled, with an average order of over \$500. Since the instrument market is stagnant, it is assumed that orders are coming in at the expense of the competition.

Implication: *Regaining share in a mature market against an installed user base is possible if a company is willing to commit the necessary resources to customer service.*

Stride-Rite Shoes: Retail Conquest Marketing

Background. The retail shoe market is highly competitive, and consumers usually have the choice of more than one retail outlet. On the Upper West Side of Manhattan, for example, prospects can choose a shop among dozens of stores within easy walking distance of their homes. The number of potential customers is finite and their disposable income is limited. The retail shoe market is not a dynamic segment. Therefore customer acquisition programs for both the retailer and the manufacturer are a necessity.

After examining the way parents purchase shoes for their children, Stride-Rite identified the following characteristics in their consumers:

- Once they bought their first pair of shoes, they were fairly brand loyal and hard to switch.
- Convenience of purchase was important.
- Purchase at retail was the primary distribution channel.
- While they were only somewhat price-sensitive, they would respond to price as an incentive.

Stride-Rite developed a campaign to make a parent's first shoe purchase a Stride-Rite purchase, by using direct mail to establish Stride-Rite, along with a selected local retailer, as an expert provider of children's shoes. Stride-Rite targeted parents with 4-month-old babies living within a retail store's trading area. The program was designed to introduce Stride-Rite's progressive fitting process, a continuity-like retail program that provides for new shoes for growing children on a periodic basis (every few months).

Names are gathered from birth certificate files. When a child reached the age of 4 months, its address was matched with the nearest local retailer and a mailing went out to the child's parents. The retail store had the option of selecting one of two standard Stride-Rite offers as the incentive offered in the mailing.

Stride-Rite's Program Objective: To introduce new parents to Stride-Rite shoes while developing a long-term relationship with local retailers.

Tactics.   Stride-Rite's tactics were as follows:

1. To rent the names of parents whose children were about to need their first pair of shoes
2. To match the parents with a local retailer and offer an incentive in the mailing to motivate them to visit the retailer

   Results: Although specific numbers were not available, a retailer participating in the program reported that it has been very effective in generating traffic, and that customers who have purchased through the program have generally become loyal customers of the retailer.

   Implication: *Even relatively small businesses can benefit from the use of fairly inexpensive publicly available records to conquest on a local basis. All you need to know is who your prospects are and where they live.*

NOTE

1. Source: Direct Marketing Association Echo awards submission, 1988.

52

Customer Loyalty Programs

Karen Hochman
Jordan, McGrath, Case and Taylor/Direct

INTRODUCTION

An investment banker takes an early morning flight to a late afternoon meeting. She could have spent the morning at her desk, but elects to make two extra stops en route to earn double frequent-flyer miles...

A corporate vice president attending a conference eschews the fine hotel where it is held and stays at one several miles away, so he can get a complimentary upgrade to a suite, plus points toward free gifts...

A couple furnishing a million-dollar home charge all their household effects to a credit card that offers a cash rebate. Because their expenditures far exceed their card's $15,000 limit, each *week* they mail in a payment check to free up their credit line for the next week's charges...

A celebrity crisscrossing the country on a media tour elects not to have the PR firm pay directly for his extensive travel reservations. He charges them to his own credit cards and floats the money, tracking and tallying a plethora of receipts just to earn the bonus points...

The people in these four examples are hot in pursuit of rewards from customer loyalty programs, a decade-old marketing phenomenon. Contemporary programs go far beyond the promotions of the 1950s, where retailers and manufacturers courted the brand loyalty of housewives with trading stamps, glassware, and towels. The real-life examples above demonstrate what marketers a couple of decades ago would not have believed: how even the busiest and most affluent individuals will go out of their way to get something for nothing...and become brand-loyal in the process.

The precursor of today's nationally publicized programs was the frequent-flyer program launched in 1981 by American Airlines. Conceived as a strategy to capture market share in a recently deregulated industry, their AAdvantage® program was quickly imitated by competitors, and frequent-flyer programs became a permanent industry fixture. Today every commercial carrier has one.

Loyalty programs — interchangeably known as frequent-user programs — have provided a windfall to many: to the companies sponsoring them, who have realized incremental revenues...to the consumers who participate in them and acquire free products and services...and to direct marketing professionals who have been hired to develop and manage these sophisticated database marketing programs. They have shown mass marketers, many of whom had not previously been able to identify their best customers, how to use direct marketing both to build relationships and to increase short- and long-term profitability.

The original airline programs awarded free or upgraded travel by providing available airplane seats in exchange for points earned through paid travel. The awards were highly valued by the recipient and cost the carrier virtually nothing. In fact, such programs actually *increase* consumer spending, since participants will take an extra flight, purchase more impulsively, and even deliberately buy more than they need in order to reach a certain reward level. While there is no doubt that the programs appeal to an underlying greed motive, the gamesmanship of "playing to win" adds an undeniable element of excitement and fun to the purchasing process. And, because they let others know how much one has charged to a credit card or how much traveling one has done, an individual's importance can be measured by the frequent-user award levels he's achieved. In a sense, frequent-user programs have entered the ranks of sociological phenomena.

Certainly they have entered the ranks of *marketing* phenomena. You don't need to conduct market research to know that your customers will enthusiastically respond to a frequent-user program. And how else can you convince customers that buying more from you is more lucrative, more fun, and more prestigious?

Loyalty programs have a down side, of course. They're expensive to start up and maintain, and they're highly visible, so back-end failures can be harmful. But many companies who have instituted programs claim they are their most successful marketing technique. And although many programs are cost centers, others turn a tidy profit.

This chapter will help you decide if your business should have a loyalty program, and how to begin to make the many decisions required to start one. While the information relayed is drawn from the experience of the largest and most sophisticated programs, most of the points covered are relevant even to the smallest businesses. Even simple, nonautomated programs have proved their ability to increase profitability by cultivating frequent users.

WHAT A LOYALTY PROGRAM IS AND ISN'T

A loyalty program is a long-term marketing tactic to secure the brand loyalty of a company's most profitable customers. It is based on the 80/20 rule, that 80 percent of one's business comes from 20 percent of one's customers. For marketers, a loyalty program identifies that 20 percent through customer enrollment, and (in sophisticated programs) uses database marketing to activate and maintain the relationship. For customers, a loyalty program is a *commitment* from the marketer that their behavior will be rewarded on an ongoing basis.

Although certain short-term sales promotions can pass as loyalty programs, it is critical to understand the differing *objectives* between the two. For example, on the surface it may be difficult to distinguish between the periodic free-gifts program offered by Citibank's VISA® and MasterCard®—a sales promotion technique—and the free-gifts program of Diners Club, an ongoing loyalty program. Both programs award points for each dollar charged to the card, which are redeemed for valuable gifts.

While the *strategies* behind the programs are the same—they both provide an incentive for customers to use only that card—the *objectives* differ in a subtle but key way. Citibank's is to encourage increased spending during key periods of the year (sales promotion). Diners Club's is to differentiate itself through an integral product (i.e., goods and services) benefit that generates long-term preference (brand loyalty). Otherwise stated, if you offer a customer a 10 percent rebate to boost sales during a particular time of the year, that's sales promotion. If the rebate is an ongoing feature of your product or service offer, that's a loyalty program.

Although a loyalty program is *not* a limited-time offer, it certainly can begin as one. American AAdvantage evolved from a short-term program in which coupons distributed on board were accumulated for free flights. Citibank has considered making its successful free gifts program a year-round feature, but thus far has chosen to allocate its resources among a variety of preference-generating programs.

For many marketers, loyalty programs have evolved into built-in product benefits, integral differentiators that engender the customer's "faithful adherence" (the dictionary definition of *loyalty*). How important are they? Some managers say that it would be "marketing suicide" to discontinue them.

WHEN TO CONSIDER A LOYALTY PROGRAM

Frequent-user programs aren't appropriate for every business. They are most effective when all of the following factors are in play:

1. A product that is *purchased frequently,* enabling the customer to work actively toward a level of reward
2. A product whose *margin* enables you to support the program

These first two features are critical. A product may have a high margin (an automobile, e.g.) but if consumers don't need to purchase it on a continual basis, the program cannot generate either the awareness and interest or the volume of purchase activity that rewards loyalty. Correlatively, gasoline is purchased frequently, but it doesn't have the margin to support the promotion.

If your product passes these two checkpoints, there are five more criteria to consider:

3. A *parity item* that makes it is just as sensible and convenient for your customer to purchase your competitor's product as yours.
4. A product with a history of *brand switching*.
5. A company that can *commit all the resources*—dollars, plus marketing, systems, and service-staff support—required to sustain the program over the long term.
6. A company with a *service culture* in which concern about the customer is integral to the business. (It's important to distinguish here that not all companies are customer-driven. A company that can compete on a service basis is the right company to undertake a service-intensive loyalty program.)
7. A company that has an aggressive *commitment to excellence*.

It takes great energy and conscientiousness to run a successful loyalty program. The program must be a priority, not an afterthought. Me-too programs that have started up without the enthusiasm of management and staff generally are not successful.

Next we'll take a look at a sample of companies whose loyalty programs give customers the incentive to buy from them again and again.

WHO OFFERS LOYALTY PROGRAMS

Loyalty programs are used by all kinds of businesses: large national companies and local concerns, product vendors and service providers, niche marketers and mass merchandisers. The following examples are just a few of the fine programs in existence.

Airlines

A review of loyalty programs must logically begin with the frequent-flyer plans, whose concept is to award one "bonus mile" for every air mile flown. Generally, with 10,000 bonus miles, a customer can receive a free upgrade to first class; higher award levels include deep discounts and free tickets for domestic and international travel. The major carriers enhanced their programs by signing up "partners"—foreign and regional carriers, hotels, and car rental companies—enabling members to earn points wherever and however they journey.

Principally targeted to the business traveler who provides the industry's most powerful economic base, some programs are reaching for a second tier of traveler, which includes senior citizens, college students, athletic teams, and others who travel at a much higher incidence than the average consumer. Initially a few carriers charged annual membership fees but, with the increase in competition, dropped them.

Just under 20 million Americans have signed up for 70 million frequent-flyer program memberships. The number of programs and partners has grown so large, the reward structures within each program so extensive, and the changes so constant, that they have engendered an independent newsletter, *Frequent*, that enables members (and all the competitors) to keep on top of them, as well as a glossy features-oriented magazine, *Frequent Flyer*.

Hotels

Frequent-guest programs award points for dollars spent, which can be traded for room upgrades (e.g., a suite), free stays and other travel awards, plus express check-in and check-out. Hotel loyalty programs followed fast on the heels of the airline programs. In 1983 Marriott transformed its existing service program, Club Marquis, into Marriott Honored Guest Award$®; Holiday Inn initiated a loyalty program, and every other chain then geared up to follow. Except one. This eminent hotelier felt it didn't need a loyalty program because its name and properties were valued so highly by its customers. When it started to lose market share and conducted market research, it learned that its customers in fact preferred the "something for nothing" frequent-user programs to the hotelier's fine properties.

Insight: *If you think your position is so preeminent that you don't need to match your competitor's loyalty program, do some research.*

Marriott Honored Guests are guaranteed room availability and can cash checks whether or not they are registered at the hotel. Other perks include room upgrades, express check-in and check-out, and special check-in gifts. Awards are largely travel-based, although limited merchandise offerings that are complementary with members' demographics (e.g., custom-made golf clubs) have been successful. Marriott provides free enrollment, as do most programs.

Sheraton and Holiday Inn have successfully charged annual fees since their programs' inception. Members of Sheraton Club International^{sm} pay $25 and receive special benefits regardless of point level: unlimited room upgrades on a space-available basis, guaranteed late check-out until 4 p.m., a morning newspaper, and points that are redeemable not only for travel awards but for more than 200 items from tennis rackets to a BMW convertible. They also can be traded for gift certificates at quality stores and catalogs like Sharper Image; or for any kind of travel arrangements desired by the member. If members are short some points, they can pay the difference in cash. Members also earn one point per dollar charged on Sheraton's affinity MasterCard—and many members have become cardholders. For $10 a year, Holiday Inn provides similar benefits.

Car Rentals

The major car rental companies have frequent-user programs, but the innovator among them appears to be National Car Rental's Emerald Club®. They deliver what frequent renters want most—no forms, no waiting in line. In 40 seconds members can rent or return a vehicle.

The club's basic benefit, the Emerald Aisle®, is unique in the industry. Other companies assign vehicles; at the Emerald Aisle, members can select from any vehicle in stock, depending on what they feel like driving that day. Recognizing that frequent renters are a very upscale group and don't drive moderate-priced cars at home, the Emerald Aisle provides Cadillacs and other premium cars at the midsize rental rate (an equivalent to a triple upgrade).

After selecting their car, customers receive their rental contract and keys through the industry equivalent of banking's automated teller machines. Members simply drive to the exit booth, where SmartKey®, a completely automated system, reads the magnetic strip on their membership card. The profile obtained on the club application has already captured information like credit card number and frequent-flyer memberships, so points are credited automatically. The member simply drives away.

Free weekend rentals and free upgrade certificates are part of the membership package, as are discounted business and leisure rates and membership in a vacation travel club. Points are redeemable not only toward car upgrades and travel awards, but for the merchandise awards that are unique to National in the industry. After $25,000 in car rentals the top reward is free use of a luxury car, convertible, minivan, or four-wheel drive for one year; *plus* a complete home entertainment system or a fur coat. During the first three years of the program, a significant number of members earned the top award!

National Car Rental's Emerald Club® charges a $60 annual membership fee and enjoys a high rate of renewal.

Insight: *A membership fee is no deterrent when innovation and quality are the heart of the offer. (See page 791 for a discussion of free versus fee.)*

Cruise Lines

At first glance, leisure cruises may not seem to meet the loyalty program criterion of frequency of purchase. But frequent cruisers take two or more trips a year and thus are frequently in a decision mode. To win customer loyalty, many cruise lines automatically enroll their past passengers in loyalty programs, mailing quarterly newsletters that highlight upcoming destinations and include special discount offers, stand-alone special-offer mailings, and relationship-building letters and postcards from the captain of the ship.

Holland America Line, whose fleet includes the *Rotterdam* and *Nieuw Amsterdam,* has had a loyalty program for almost 20 years. All passengers are awarded memberships in the Society of Honorary Mariners, and are offered exclusive discounts on selected cruises as enticements to rebook. Back on board, they are treated to a special cocktail reception with the captain. Special certificates are bestowed after three, five, and ten cruises. But the greatest form of recognition—a silver or gold medallion worn on board with great distinction—is achieved after 40,000 miles (115 cruise days) and 100,000 miles (285 cruise days) respectively.

Those who have sailed the *QE2, Sagafjord,* and other Cunard Line ships are enrolled automatically in the Cunard World Club, and enjoy each subsequent cruise with a $25 shipboard credit for bar bills and sundries, an exclusive check-in counter, invitations to special events on shore and at sea, and toll-free access to the Cunard World Club Desk, where special service representatives provide information and handle special requests.

Depending on the ship, as many as 50 percent of Cunard's past passengers prove their loyalty by rebooking within a year. Holland America says that some of its cruises are totally sold out by returning passengers.

Credit Cards

Americans carry more than 800 million credit cards; the average cardholder has eight of them, from national credit cards like American Express, MasterCard, and VISA to proprietary gasoline and department store cards. Since all plastic performs the same function, how does a card issuer convince the customer to use its card instead of the other seven? Here are two programs that have generated a large return on investment in terms of card usage.

When Sears decided to enter the competitive (but lucrative) credit card market, they knew they needed a critical differentiator. So, in addition to offering the Discover Card with no annual fee, they created the Cashback Bonus loyalty program, offering cardholders rebates of up to 1 percent of their annual purchases. The rebate structure encourages usage consolidation through four tiers: .25 percent back on the first $1,000, .50 percent on the second $1,000, .75 percent on the third $1,000, and 1 percent back on any amount over $3,000. The amount of rebate earned is reported on monthly statements; on the card's anniversary date a check is mailed to the cardholder.

The smallest of the national card issuers, Diners Club also recognized the need to distinguish its product to attract cardholders. They created the industry's only gift-based loyalty program, Club Rewards®. Cardholders receive one point for each dollar charged to the card; the annual gift catalog offers hundreds of items, from a waiver of the annual fee to computers, vacations, and diamonds. Special short-term promotions within the overall program help the business to achieve specific marketing goals (e.g., increase spending among marginal users, increase card usage at restaurants) by offering members double or triple points.

Retailers

One prestigious department store that sells high-end merchandise to very affluent customers has discovered that only 2 percent of its credit card holders spend more than $5,000 a year at the store. Clearly, these customers are spending a large portion of their large discretionary income elsewhere. The situation is similar for all retailers, and others could learn a lesson from Neiman-Marcus, which tackled the problem in 1984 with its In-Circle® Program.

Enrollment is automatic; customers receive one point for every dollar charged to the store card, and points are reflected on the store card's monthly billing statements. Points are earned during the calendar year and cannot be carried over. The lowest level of gift award is 7,500 points, the highest 500,000. (These have grown considerably from the program's initial 3,000–12,000 ranges.)

But the In-Circle Program goes beyond gifts: it provides service and recognition amenities as well. At 3,000 points, customers receive a coveted gold In-Circle charge card to replace the standard store card. (The gold cards, like the points, expire at year-end.) They also can choose a year's free subscription to magazines like *Art & Antiques* and *European Travel & Life*, free gift-wrap, and a host of other services. The most interesting of these is the "Date Reminder" service: customers register birthdays and special occasions; Neiman-Marcus reminds them two weeks prior to the event and makes it easy for them to send a gift. Finally, quarterly newsletters take customers "behind the scenes" and make them feel part of the Neiman-Marcus "family."

Given the economic polarization in the industry—predictions are that retail will become an industry of discounters and specialty stores with the middle squeezed out—we may see a proliferation of upscale retailer loyalty programs in the future. Several retailers who have watched the success of the In-Circle Program commented that their only barrier to initiating a similar program is the cost. However, it may become just another cost of doing business. Sears, which only recently repositioned itself at the discount end, has just adapted the Cashback Bonus from its Discover Card as an extra incentive to cultivate store customers.

Telecommunications

While selecting a long-distance telephone carrier may not be a day-to-day decision like choosing a credit card or deciding which department store to patronize, the carriers' need to cultivate loyalty is equally important. Long-distance telephone customers receive frequent incentives, including free hook-ups and usage credits to jump to the competition. Accounts are especially vulnerable when a customer moves.

Customer-retention was the rationale behind U.S. Sprint's Callers' Plus[sm] program. Subscribers to the service earn points corresponding to the amount of their phone bill, and can redeem awards for free interstate long-distance calling, plus travel and merchandise awards.

Callers' Plus targets both consumers and small businesses, and its awards selection (comprising not only free long-distance calling but travel awards and gift merchandise) reflects items of interest to both. If the account is canceled, the points are forfeited. Since any customer with a moderate amount of long-distance calling can earn free usage and more, Callers' Plus is an excellent tactic to neutralize competitors' promotions.

Book Clubs

The major book clubs have loyalty programs targeted to keeping members in the program and buying more. At Book-of-the-Month Club, the Book Dividends® program began back in the 1930s. (Stocks weren't paying any dividends then, so BOMC decided to reward its members by paying "book dividends.") Members receive a dividend credit (point) with each book purchased, and can combine their credits with cash to purchase an extensive selection of designated books at 50–80 percent off the publisher's price. (Normal BOMC discounts are 10–30 percent off publisher's price.)

At BOMC's Quality Paperback Book Club and History Book Club, members receive one credit for every book purchased. The credits can be redeemed for any of the club's selection, and every book has two prices: the cash price and the credit price. Other programs use variations on the theme. At Doubleday's Literary Guild, for example, members can buy any book with two credits; every third book is half-price.

Smaller Companies

You don't have to be a large corporation with millions of customers on your database to operate a successful loyalty program. Midsize and smaller chains, regional marketers, and small local businesses have them, making consumers brand-loyal in their choice of restaurants, photo finishing, book, video rental, hardware, and shoe stores. Business-to-business marketers, such as courier services and office supply houses, offer similar incentives to their corporate customers.

Many of these programs don't maintain a database or track points, yet meet all the criteria to be a genuine loyalty program; some mail periodic communications to a house list. They rely on the customer to keep track of the paperwork needed to redeem the reward.

Some programs offer evergreen dollars-off or percent-off coupons. In these programs, each purchase generates a new coupon to use on the next purchase. Others have built-in discounts on sales above a certain amount. At The Athlete's Foot athletic footware stores, 10 percent of the amount of one's sales receipt can be used as a cash discount on the next purchase. Other companies use a punch card that's redeemable for a free meal/book/movie/messenger delivery when complete.

There are almost no costs to establish these programs beyond printing the cards or coupons, some promotional posters, and the cost of the awards. (And there's always slippage—people forgetting to bring their coupons with them, giving the store the sale without having to award the discount.)

As inspiration for how creative loyalty programs can be, we'll close by describing one of a famous diet doctor, who saw his revenue stream fluctuate as patients capriciously canceled their weekly appointments. He structured a price-based incentive: the cost of the office visit was reduced $5 after every 5 visits; "loyal" patients could soon pay a full $20 less per visit. But if they skipped a week, they started all over again at the full price. Too promotional for a doctor? With today's stiff competition and high cost of running a business, it makes sense.

PLANNING YOUR PROGRAM

Once you introduce a loyalty program, you can't take it away without generating adverse customer sentiment. Once live, your operations have to be flawless: your back office can't misfunction and alienate these most valuable customers you've worked so hard to attract. If you develop a database that can't supply all the information you need, you'll face costly revisions. Your challenge can be summed up in two words: careful planning.

It's true that some companies jump right into the fray—usually egged on by the spirit (or fear) of competition. However, they do so at the expense of their credibility with customers, who sign up for benefits that cannot yet be reported or delivered. And such companies also incur added expense and aggravation for themselves, as they race to patch and mend their programs every step of the way.

So give yourself the time not only to refine your marketing plan but to track through every operation and process involved. Imagine every scenario and think through every problem that could arise—not just in marketing but in systems and operations (tracking and reporting points, responding to customer inquiries and complaints). Think through *everything*...then think it through again.

Here are some "starters" for your thinking:

Your Objectives

What do you want your program to achieve: increased market share, greater revenue per customer, reduced attrition? Objectives will vary depending on your industry and your position in it. But whatever they are, your goals should be quantified so that everyone agrees on what is expected, and results can be measured against it. (One reason for requiring customers to sign up for the loyalty program is that it gives you an automatic control group.)

Insight: *If you're a latecomer "me-too" program, you especially need to think through your objective. If it's just to keep up with the Joneses, your program may not be as insightfully conceived and energetically pursued as it must be to justify the effort. If you think the program is "more trouble than it's worth," it will invariably prove to be so.*

Automatic Versus Required Enrollment

Usually, mass marketers can't identify their customers by name and address, so must require individuals to sign up for loyalty program membership. Direct marketers can easily offer automatic enrollment to their house files. If you have the option, should you choose automatic or required enrollment? It depends on your objective.

Citibank, whose Free Gifts Program was intended to increase spending, tested both options and found that when customers make a conscious decision to enroll, they are more motivated to modify their purchase behavior. Diners Club, on the other hand, began with required enrollment and progressed to automatic enrollment. Because their loyalty program is a key reason to use their product over others which target the business traveler (especially the airline and hotel affinity credit cards), they wanted to eliminate all obstacles to participation.

Participation figures vary by industry, but those with a required enrollment usually attract 30 to 50 percent of the customer base.

Insight: *If you're using an enrollment form, remember the principles of direct mail. Keep it short, like any response device. Collect only the data you'll truly use. An enrollment form is not a quantitative research study.*

Fee Versus Free

Most programs soliciting loyalty do not ask for a fee; but you still should think through your options. Obviously, more people will sign up for free, but ask if quantity is what you are striving for. Free programs attract a large number of unqualified members, resulting in a high percentage of inactives who engender database, fulfillment, and ongoing communications costs. With as many as 30 to 60 percent of the base inactive, a large national program can find itself carrying the cost of three to four million nonrevenue producers.

Membership fees have a multiple function. Sheraton Club International's $25 fee is intended as a qualifier to weed out nonfrequent travelers; it also helps to cover program costs. The annual renewal process enables them to cull out the dead weight (people who joined for the wrong reason, or who no longer travel frequently). Their member benefits are excellent so they have a high renewal rate. Holiday Inn has been similarly successful with a $10 annual fee. And the special added services that members of both of these programs receive, even before points are earned, more than justify the fee.

On the other hand, two major airlines that initially began with fee-based programs ultimately discontinued the fees. Their programs were no better than the nonfee ones. Any extra services that might have been included were not viewed by consumers as justification for the fee.

Future Vision

How will you respond if your competitors jump in and up the ante? Are there potential marketplace dynamics in your industry that may impact your program? Think through the blue-sky scenarios. The airlines never dreamed they would be told to count the billions of dollars of unclaimed awards as liabilities on their balance sheets. Nor did anyone imagine that the IRS would consider taxing mileage awards as "something of value an individual receives in conjunction with business activity."

Pilot Program

There simply is no substitute for learning from a pilot test. It will get the different support groups operating in tandem, enable you to pinpoint unforeseen problems, and help you make improvements before rollout. Equally important, it will quantify how much *incremental* business the programs generate (or determine if your program can stimulate enough demand to justify the cost and effort).

BUDGETING YOUR PROGRAM

When constructing the financials, be sure to include these items in your budget:

Costs

- *Database:* development, hardware, software, tracking, plus reporting

- *Awards:* purchase price, plus fulfillment (shipping, handling, warehousing)
- *Customer service:* staff, training, telephone lines, terminals, overhead
- *Member acquisition:* advertising (point-of-sale and direct-response)
- *Promotion:* special promotions plus activation programs; incentive programs for employees to meet enrollment and service goals
- *Member communications:* monthly or quarterly direct-mail (newsletters, statements)
- *Market research:* to monitor member satisfaction
- *Administration:* marketing, finance and accounting staff and overhead; internal communications

Revenues

- *Incremental sales*
- *Income from partnerships*

For large national companies, a loyalty program is a multi-million-dollar undertaking. Costs correspond to the number of customers served. Depending on objectives, programs may be cost centers, break even, or turn a profit. (Of course there is an initial liability before you realize your pay-out.)

In some cases, profits on the incremental sales alone more than pay for program costs. The most profitable programs generate income from other sources. The main opportunity is to set up partnerships with other companies (e.g., as the airlines did with hotels and car rental agencies) and earn income from advertising partners' services to their members. They also earn income from affinity bank cards. (American Airlines alone has almost two million holders of its American AAdvantage VISA card, issued through Citibank.) Annual membership fees and list rental revenues are also a possibility.

Loyalty programs offer other opportunities for creative financing. One company with a very large enrollment leverages the fact that the brand-name award merchandise will be advertised to millions of people, and buys their gifts virtually at manufacturers' cost. Recognizing that most business executives invest in the stock market, American Airlines developed a partnership with a brokerage firm. AAdvantage members get points for trading; the airline gets fee income from the brokerage house.

Partners allow you to buy awards from them at a deep discount. In a major coup, MGM Grand Air has managed to get an impressive selection of merchandise *donated.* A niche marketer that operates luxury planes for an extremely affluent customer base, the airline has attracted partners like Porsche, who in exchange for the advertising exposure provides one year's free use of the sports car to customers achieving the program's top level.

Insight: *Innovative marketers will examine the lifestyles and needs of their customers and determine which potential partners want to reach their members. With the right partnership deals, your program can be totally paid for.*

How much do companies spend on their programs? Depending on the business, budgets can be viewed as a percentage of sales or as a cost-per-participant. A major airline with $7 billion in revenues spends $30 million on its frequent-flyer program: $8.5 million in hard program costs, plus $20 to $25 million in travel awards. Says the manager of another program, "When you bottom line it out and factor in the millions of dollars of free publicity, it's not as expensive as most people think."

WHAT TO OFFER

As we've seen, loyalty rewards focus on four areas: free (or upgraded) services, merchandise, cash rebates or discounts, and status/recognition features. How can you decide what to offer your customers?

Make It What Members Want

This may seem obvious, but what the marketing department thinks are the customer's needs and wants can be very different from what the customer actually wants. Loyalty has to be bought on the customer's terms, not the marketer's. Conduct market research to find out what will really motivate them.

If your competitors already have a successful program, can't you simply adapt what they've done? Only at your own risk! Even though your customers may seem identical, you need only look at the direct mail control packages for competitors in the same industry to realize that different consumers respond to different offers. You also have to look at where you are in the life cycle of your industry's loyalty programs. If you're a latecomer and your target is already getting something for nothing, your offer has to be that much more attractive to get attention.

You don't have to begin with an elaborate award structure. As your program evolves, you will see what your customers actually select and identify additional reward opportunities. You'll also be able to identify segments within your member base and develop special opportunities for your most valuable customers.

Insight: *The customer's reward does not have to be of high dollar value. Special recognition and preferential treatment can be excellent loyalty-developers. A number of companies report that the special recognition features and small service perks are more important to their best customers than the freebies. And, service perks are a way to maintain loyalty that transcends awards programs.*

Develop a Structure That Isn't Easily Copied

A great idea is quickly imitated. If you're the first in your industry with a loyalty program, expect that the "me-too's" will mushroom, and design your program preemptively to keep a leg up on your competitors. As happened with frequent-flyer programs, newcomers raised the stakes, by allowing awards to be transferable, for example, or by lowering the number of points needed for redemption. These were not only costly for the newcomers, but for the established competitors who felt pressured to match them.

To protect yourself from costly skirmishes, consider how you can structure an offer that will remain unique. Ideally your program will stand out not just in your industry, but among all frequent-user programs. An exclusive arrangement for the most desired awards or partnership offers can differentiate your program. In multiproduct companies, look for opportunities to leverage your program across the organization (and cross-sell in the process).

Because of large accrued point balances, some airlines have sought unique rewards for their best customers. These include auctions in major cities where members can bid their points for golf trips with a top pro or a trip around the world with a famous astronaut, a pair of golden retrievers, and sponsored evenings at often-sold-out cultural and sporting events. Solutions like these also have been helpful in imparting the cachet of a private club, not just a giveaway.

Make Rewards Accessible

Don't give away the store, but structure awards that will be reasonably attainable within 12–18 months and will stretch the typical customer's usage behavior. While most participants will select baseline awards, high-level "aspirational" rewards are equally important to generate excitement. If your product is used by business executives and professionals, consider a corporate membership in which everyone in the firm can work toward the car, gymnasium equipment, computers, or other items that benefit the group as a whole.

Be sure there is absolutely no problem acquiring and delivering the items you select. You may wish to avoid merchandise that is more likely to create customer service problems, like stemware and clothing.

Keep It Simple

What you're offering should be crystal clear, and how to obtain it, foolproof. Formulas that are too complex will suppress participation or create misunderstandings that irritate your customers. The simplicity principle extends to every part of your program. After it was introduced, one frequent-user program actually changed its name from a slightly obscure but exclusive, trademarked name to two generic words that were explicitly understood by consumers.

Segment the Benefits

The 80/20 rule applies even within the frequent-user base. In service businesses like airlines and hotels, where rewards are usually free services, it's possible for the very best customers to earn more free flights and hotel rooms than they'll ever be able to use. This elite group ceases to be motivated by the accumulation of points. Since no company can afford to lose the 100,000 air miles or 50 hotel rooms purchased by these individuals each year, special service perks are lavished on these "gold" tier members.

The objective of these segmented perks is to spoil the most profitable customers so they won't even *think* of going to the competition. And it works, thanks to exclusive benefits like unlimited first-class upgrades on a standby basis or the opportunity to fly first class while paying the lowest available seat price on the plane. Gold-tier hotel guests are guaranteed rooms even when the hotel is sold out, and are automatically upgraded to the concierge floor. Let your members tell you what they want. Marriott's research pinpointed two other perks desired by its Honored Guest Award$® members: check-cashing privileges at any location, regardless of whether the member is registered there, and the opportunity to bring spouses free.

Establish a Point Structure

Not all programs use points to measure levels of rewards; some programs work on the basis of units purchased. In a point structure scenario, the most common formula is one point per dollar spent (or mile flown). Redemption *values* vary, based on margins in different industries; Sheraton's is a penny a point (or $1,000 in gifts per 100,000 points). Lower margin businesses generally require a higher number of points to get to the top. You'll want to structure yours so that awards at a cost per revenue dollar increase with the levels. This gives the customer a reason to work harder and hold out longer.

Depending on your objectives, you may choose to award points along other lines. U.S. Sprint structures its points to achieve long-term loyalty foremost: *increased* usage isn't even an objective. Thus, for each year of membership, a dollar is worth a larger number of points (10 points per dollar in year one, 11 points in year two).

Determine the Life Span of Points

A key strategic decision in structuring points is their life span, and this ties back into the awards themselves. Should you allow accumulation of points with no end date, encouraging members to aspire to the high-ticket awards and engendering longer-range loyalty? Or should your points expire and a gift be redeemed at the end of each year?

Diners Club started with the latter and moved to the former. Neiman-Marcus's In-Circle points expire in a year, and have had an expiration date since the program's inception in 1984. U.S. Sprint's points expire on a 24-month rolling period. With only 30 percent of airline miles redeemed (the high-balance members don't have *time* to use them; and as many as 60 percent of outstanding miles are spread among the inactive and infrequent travelers who are not likely to reach redemption levels), several airlines have converted to a system in which points expire in 24–36 months. This "use it or lose it" aspect may frustrate some members, but expiration dates encourage more intense use of the product, and certainly limit the company's liability.

Insight: *If you find yourself in a mega-accumulation situation vis-a-vis service awards, don't abruptly announce a termination date by which all points must be redeemed. A major airline gave its members a final redemption date, hoping to put an end to its obligation, but an unanticipated avalanche of members decided to redeem their points. Paying passengers couldn't get seats, and the airline wrote off a $40-million loss that quarter.*

Use Points to Achieve Specific Goals

Awarding points can get customers to modify their behavior to achieve very specific marketing goals, such as activating new and inactive members; getting current members to refer new members; getting marginal customers to purchase more often; promoting a new or slow-moving product or service; encouraging higher-ticket sales; or getting people to consume at off-peak times.

Bonus points, including double- and triple-point promotions, are popular with members, and they support program objectives too, as long as they don't create unmanageable liabilities. But as programs mature and customers have accrued a considerable points investment with you, you'll learn how to control liability, finding ways beyond "over-awarding" to motivate your members.

Insight: *In these and all promotions, be very careful about how offers are worded. What you think is crystal clear will be interpreted by your customers in ways you never could have imagined. One airline offered triple points for "tickets purchased" during a certain time period. The copy didn't explicitly state that members had to fly, and a surprising number purchased tickets assuming they could return them unused, and still collect the points! (Of course, they collected!)*

OPERATIONS

The largest problem faced by start-up loyalty programs is engendered by underestimating the amount of back-end administrative and database support a large-scale program requires. No one anticipates the range of full-time operational requirements; few people realize the enormity of systems development and maintenance (200 full-time people now work on Marriott Honored Guest Award$®: 20 of them on systems development and enhancement, 4 just in customer service training).

Avoid the temptation to focus the majority of your efforts on developing the more glamorous front-end: the program name and logo, reward structure, fulfillment kit, membership card, newsletter. It's critical to recognize that as soon as the program goes live, many thousands of people will enroll and expect something to happen — and happen flawlessly.

Database

Many companies use outside firms to build and maintain their databases. Since getting timely systems-support is critical, this makes sense for a labor-intensive project like a loyalty program. If you elect to undertake database development internally for cost reasons, be sure your company has a systems capability that can *consistently* support your need for timely and accurate tracking and reporting.

You will want to update totals at least monthly: even if you don't communicate them to members frequently, customer service will need the information to respond to direct inquiries. If your points tracking isn't automatic, be sure to make collection and tabulation foolproof.

Insight: *When reviewing the budget for your program, don't even think about skimping on technology and customer service. It will create problems that will drag your program down and cost you many times what you tried to save.*

Customer Service

Customer service is of paramount importance to loyalty-program members who have invested time and effort to earn their rewards. There is an inherent promise that frequent users will be treated better, and it is incumbent upon programs to deliver it. In all situations, frequent users have to be handled exceedingly well. Each of these top customers is worth so much more to you incrementally that there's a real liability if you let them down.

Insight: *Being recognized as a program member is important to the customer. In travel programs, for example, the membership status of the customer is recognized in the greeting of the check-in clerks and others who state how much the hotel appreciates his business. Research has shown that this small amount of recognition and appreciation have a large and lasting impact.*

If part of your program's benefit is extra special service, your company must have a service culture capable of delivering it. Sometimes this subtle differential is difficult to communicate to line employees who have been trained to provide excellent service to every customer. You'll need to communicate the economics of the 80/20 rule so they'll understand why some customers are more equal than others.

Program managers never cease to be amazed at the kinds of questions and levels of detail members want answered, from minute descriptions of the merchandise awards ("Is the knob on the drawer brass or brass-plated?"), to elaborate gift-wrap and delivery requests, to policy questions no one could anticipate ("Can I will my points to my heirs?"). Citibank created a special customer service unit to respond to the plethora of requests for information and special handling, and finds it has been instrumental in terms of back-office deliverability.

And program managers confirm that the key to the success of a loyalty program is to underpromise and overdeliver. You go through an enormous amount of effort and expense to acquire members. It is incumbent upon you to deliver the service in a way that is better than you promised. That's how you'll keep them in your franchise and make them disciples who refer other customers to you.

Insight: *Conduct quarterly focus groups or surveys to monitor satisfaction and ensure your programs keep on the pulse of what members want. They'll also make you aware of problems and potential problems that you can head off. Being able to identify and contact your best customers provides a great opportunity for all of your company's consumer research.*

Member Communications

The most successful loyalty programs sustain momentum by maintaining top-of-mind awareness. This means regularly communicating to the customer the points he has accumulated, along with reminders of the rewards he's working towards. Most large programs have newsletters which elaborate on product or service enhancements, include related feature stores, and promote the general "club" spirit.

Some programs achieve this through monthly communications. Many of these are companies that communicate monthly anyway (through credit card statements or book club mailings); all of them communicate at least quarterly.

Insight: *Monthly communications are preferable to quarterly. But if you aren't already paying for a regular monthly customer communication that your loyalty program can ride along on, consider more frequent mailings to your most active member tier.*

Smaller-scope loyalty programs without a reporting capability require the customer to keep track of coupons or proofs of purchase. While this technique certainly works, the level of participation (and therefore of both loyalty and incremental sales) isn't anywhere near as great. For nondirect marketers, the ability to use direct mail to further deepen relationships and sell products is the key to incremental revenues. So even a small program should maintain customer addresses and invest in a quarterly communication.

Dealing with Inactives

With as much as half of a member-base inactive in any 2-year period, it's important to try aggressively to activate or reactivate these potentially profitable customers. In some businesses (like travel) that can have cyclical use, there can be a good reason for 6 or 9 months of inactivity. Regular communications continue, so that when the member does return to your product category, *your* product is top-of-mind. But in most industries inactivity denotes a larger problem, so you'll want to start your loyalty program with activation programs already on the drawing board.

Monitor your program members closely. If usage ceases after 6 months of regular use, for example, you may want to contact the customer to see if there has been a problem with the product or service. Use promotions offering special incentives to activate at 6 and at 12 months in the cycle. A sizable number of inactives are still using the product—just not yours—and a good percentage of them can be restimulated.

If after two significant activation efforts (and regular ongoing member communications) you can't revive the customer, it may make sense to archive the account and save the substantial database and direct-mail expenses. Some companies won't retire inactive files for 18–24 months; some cruise lines will keep customer files active for 3 or more years. Your own industry's usage patterns will be your guide.

Insight: *Be sure to create a control group for your activation program. You'll need to measure the difference in behavior and understand how to modify your program to maximize success.*

Insight: *Archive, but never erase, inactive names. You never know when the customers will return; you'll need their records intact. And the names are still valuable for list rental.*

CONCLUSION

Critics have called loyalty programs "bribes" in exchange for business; but in fact loyalty programs are simply an extension of sales promotions which began long ago, in the days of the baker's dozen. What smart business *doesn't* take extra special care of its best customers?

Some loyalty programs have even shown that they can save the custome relationship (and the company from financial disaster) when the product itself fails. During a long stretch of unreliable and often deplorable service, one major airline might have gone out of business had it not been for the hundreds of thousands of program members with a vested interest in their generous rewards structure. When ongoing delays lost another carrier its positioning as the "on-time" airline, they retained their market share thanks to their large base of frequent fliers. In a more moderate vein, Diners Club has found it effective to award points as a palliative to customers with service complaints.

Marketing managers considering a loyalty program may ask, "If everyone starts one, what's the advantage—aren't we all spending money to get the same people?" The difference is how you execute and manage your program. If you understand your market better, know how to give your customer what he wants, apply the principles of direct response to target messages, maintain frequent communications, and build the relationship, then you'll achieve the ultimate goal: incremental revenues. Of course, the product has to come first. Frequent-user rewards won't convince a buyer to select a product or service that isn't good to begin with. But in a parity situation, if there's a perk behind your product, you've got a powerful marketing aid.

Consumers have wearied of other promotional devices; but after a decade, loyalty programs are more important than ever. They still are a huge idea. And until the next breakthrough marketing idea comes down the pike, they're food for thought for any aggressive marketer.

Index

700 pay-per-call telephone service, 340
Shareforce, 146, 149, 152, 176–177
Sheet-feed press, 389
Sheraton Corporation, 331–332, 785, 791
Shipping, 455
  bulk, 72, 436, 505, 506, 508, 528–529
  catalog, 480
  negative option program, 515–516
  (*See also* Mail distribution)
Shopping center intercepts, 564, 716
Shumer, Charles, 129
SICs (Standard Industrial Classification) (*see* Standard Industrial Classification)
Silhouettes, catalog, 731–732
Simmons Market Research Bureau, 144
Singer Corporation, 730–731
Single items, accounting for sale of, 608
Single-step promotions:
  back-end performance, 540, 542
  calculating cost of, 531–533
  club and continuity, 660
  cost per response (CPR), 537
  financial services marketing, 686
  response measurement, 536–537
Situation statement, preplanning:
  comprehensive, 27
  information needed for, 13–27
  preliminary, 12–13
Skil Corporation, 173
Skin care products, 165
Smart homes, 275
Smartfood, 164–165
SmartNames, 152
Smith, Rodney A., 699–700
Soft offers, 675–676, 680
Soft space, 73
Sooner Federal, Tulsa, 161
Source codes (key codes), 207, 208, 252, 276, 719
  co-op mailing and package insert, 315, 316
  internal database, 142
  lead management system, 468–469
  response list, 189
Sourcing, list, 244–245, 247
Space advertising (*see* Magazine advertising; Newspaper advertising)
Special graphics, 21, 24
Special issues, magazine, 280, 281, 705
Special mail-order rates, 280
Special-interest publications, 662
  (*See also* Magazine advertising; Magazine marketing)
Specifications, catalog, 725–726
Spectra, 762, 768–769
Split-run testing, 60–63, 286
  A-B, 60–63, 497, 500
  with bound-in reply cards, 65
  defined, 60

Split-run testing (*cont.*):
  magazines offering, 60–61
  multiple, 62–63
  significance factors in, 61–62
Spokesperson, selection of, 332, 371–372
Sports Illustrated magazine, 676
Sports Illustrated for Kids magazine, 159
Spreads, catalog, 725, 729, 730
SPRINT, 334, 340, 775, 788, 795
SRDS (*see* Standard Rates and Data Services)
Staged media testing, 568–569
Standard Industrial Classification (SIC) codes, 20, 184, 185, 209–210, 212–213, 652
Standard Rates and Data Services, 60–61, 268, 751, 766
Standards, fulfillment, 463, 477
Stanford Research International (SRI), 144–145
Stard, Daniel, 359
State name, 251–252, 255
Statement inserts, 666
Statistical Analysis System (SAS), 633–634
Stein, Gertrude, 220
Stepwise regression, 629–631
Stevenson, John, 141, 161
Still life shots, 735, 736
Stone, Robert, 751
Strategic marketing planning (SMP), 3–41
  benefits of, 5
  coregroup members, 7–9
  defined, 3
  importance of, 40–41
  list segmentation in, 237–238
  long-range planning (LRP) vs., 3–4
  managing process of, 5–9
  nature of, 4–5
  phase 1 (data into information), 11–27
  phase 2 (strategic objectives), 27–29
  phase 3 (obstacles and advantages), 29–30
  phase 4 (strategy), 30–31
  phase 5 (tactics), 31–35
  phase 6 (freezing the design), 35–40
  planning specialists in, 5–6
  tools of, 9–11
Strategy:
  defined, 30
  tactics vs., 30
Street address, 251, 255
Stride-Rite Shoes, 758, 779–780
Strome, Howard, 379
Subscriber lists, 179–180, 209, 234, 490, 491, 493–494
  club and continuity use, 661
  controlled-circulation, 180, 210, 212
  paid-circulation, 180, 210
  updating, 494–496